selves in question

Writing Past Colonialism is the signature book series of the Institute of Postcolonial Studies, based in Melbourne, Australia. By postcolonialism we mean modes of writing and artistic production that critically engage with and contest the legacy and continuing mindset and practices of colonialism, and inform debate about the processes of globalization. This perspective manifests itself in a concern with difference from the Euro-American, the global, and the norm. The series is also committed to publishing works that seek to make a difference, both within the academy and outside it.

OUR HOPE IS THAT BOOKS IN THE SERIES WILL

- engage with contemporary issues and problems relating to colonialism and postcolonialism
- attempt to reach a broad constituency of readers
- address the relation between theory and practice
- be interdisciplinary in approach as well as subject matter
- experiment with new modes of writing and methodology

ipcs

INSTITUTE OF POSTCOLONIAL STUDIES | WRITING PAST COLONIALISM

Selves in Question: Interviews on Southern African Auto/biography
Edited by Judith Lütge Coullie, Stephan Meyer, Thengani Ngwenya, and Thomas Olver

Boundary Writing: An Exploration of Race, Culture, and Gender Binaries in Contemporary Australia
Edited by Lynette Russell

Postcolonizing the International: Working to Change the Way We Are
Edited by Phillip Darby

selves in question

INTERVIEWS ON SOUTHERN AFRICAN AUTO/BIOGRAPHY

Edited by Judith Lütge Coullie, Stephan Meyer, Thengani Ngwenya, and Thomas Olver

University of Hawai'i Press   Honolulu

© 2006 University of Hawai'i Press
All rights reserved

Printed in the United States of America

11 10 09 08 07 06   6 5 4 3 2 1

Library of Congress Cataloging-in-Publication Data

Selves in question : interviews on Southern African auto/biography /
edited by Judith Lütge Coullie . . . [et al.].

    p. cm.—(Writing past colonialism)
    Includes bibliographical references and index.
    ISBN-13: 978-0-8248-3004-5 (hardcover : alk. paper)
    ISBN-10: 0-8248-3004-0 (hardcover : alk. paper)
    ISBN-13: 978-0-8248-3047-2 (pbk. : alk. paper)
    ISBN-10: 0-8248-3047-4 (pbk. : alk. paper)
    1. South Africa—Biography. 2. Interviews—
South Africa. 3. Autobiography. 4. Biography as a
literary form. I. Coullie, Judith Lütge. II. Writing past
colonialism series
    CT25.S465 2006
    920.00968—dc22

                        2005028943

University of Hawai'i Press books are printed
on acid-free paper and meet the guidelines
for permanence and durability of the Council
on Library Resources

Designed by Leslie Fitch
Printed by The Maple-Vail Book Manufacturing Group

CONTENTS

I Introduction

Auto/biographical Identities: Placing Selves in Question   1

Auto/biographical Accounts in South Africa in Three Parts   10

Thematic and Theoretical Issues in Southern African Auto/biography: An Overview   38

Scope of the Collection   62

Bibliography   83

II Singing the Praises, Performing the Persona

Versions of a Life in Poetry
D. L. P. Yali-Manisi interviewed by Jeff Opland   117

People Feel No Event Is Complete without a Poet
Zolani Mkiva interviewed by Duncan Brown and Susan Kiguli   132

Folk Music as Popular Culture: A Life-history Approach
Alex J. Thembela interviewed by Thengani Ngwenya   148

III Representing Silence

I Speak Their Wordless Woe
Dennis Brutus interviewed by Simon Lewis   153

Making History's Silences Speak
N. Chabani Manganyi interviewed by Thengani Ngwenya   160

IV Relating the Self

Creating a Climate for Change
Elsa Joubert interviewed by Stephan Meyer   173

This Miracle of a Book . . . It's Just Like the Bible to Me
*Mpho Nthunya and K. Limakatso Kendall interviewed
by Vanessa Farr* 186

Collaborators
Wilfred Cibane and Robert Scott interviewed by Thengani Ngwenya 200

The Making of Katie Makanya
Margaret McCord interviewed by Thengani Ngwenya 205

V Fact or Fiction

All Autobiography Is *Autre*-biography
J. M. Coetzee interviewed by David Attwell 213

We Would Write Very Dull Books If We Just Wrote about Ourselves
Sindiwe Magona interviewed by Stephan Meyer 219

Writing Autobiography and Writing Fiction
Doris Lessing interviewed by M. J. Daymond 231

VI Subject to Metaphor

Metaphors of Self
Es'kia Mphahlele interviewed by N. Chabani Manganyi 243

Aquifers and Auto/biography in Namibia
Dorian Haarhoff interviewed by Terence Zeeman 254

Reflections on Identity
Breyten Breytenbach interviewed by Marilet Sienaert 269

Rhythmic Redoublings
Rob Nixon interviewed by Sarah Nuttall and Cheryl-Ann Michael 277

VII From Daughters to Mothers

"Mummy, the Coolie Doctor Is at the Door"
Vanitha Chetty interviewed by Judith Lütge Coullie 291

Why Do You Abandon Me? I Am Your Daughter. Re-presenting Dona Ermelinda
Ester Lee interviewed by Duncan Cartwright 303

Every Secret Thing as Family Memoir
Gillian Slovo interviewed by Margaretta Jolly 315

VIII Disarming White Men

White Men with Weapons: Performing Autobiography
Greig Coetzee interviewed by Debbie Lütge   329

Reflections in a Cracked Mirror
Pieter-Dirk Uys interviewed by Mervyn McMurty   345

IX Commemoration, Confession, Conversion

These Two Autobiographical Books Are My Identity Document
David Wolpe interviewed by Astrid Starck   357

Philosophical Reflections on Chronicles of Conversion
Wilhelm Verwoerd interviewed by Stephan Meyer   366

X Confessing Sexualities

Speaking about Writing about Living a Life
Stephen Gray interviewed by Judith Lütge Coullie   379

Man-bitch: Poetry, Prose, and Prostitution
Johan van Wyk interviewed by Judith Lütge Coullie   395

XI Re-collecting the New Nation

Group Portrait: Self, Family, and Nation on Exhibit
Paul Faber, Rayda Jacobs, and David Goldblatt interviewed
   by Stephan Meyer   409

Resituating Ourselves: Homelessness and Collective Testimony
   as Narrative Therapy
Valentine Cascarino and Jonathan Morgan interviewed
   by Sam Raditlhalo   436

Glossary   451

Contributors   457

Index   469

I INTRODUCTION

THE AUTOBIOGRAPHY OF AN AFRICAN IS THE AUTOBIOGRAPHY OF A PLACE.
—Niyi Osundare

Auto/biographical Identities: Placing Selves in Question

THE DESIRE TO grapple with the riddles of existence through auto/biographical accounts permeates human symbolic expression.[1] Using self-representation to question and define our notions of self, we relate earlier to later selves, thereby constituting personal identity; we also relate ourselves to others, thereby constituting collective identities. Moreover, in addressing others through our auto/biographical accounts we enter the public sphere and situate ourselves in relation to an audience. *Selves in Question: Interviews on Southern African Auto/biography* pursues, by diverse means, the role of narrative in general and auto/biography in particular in the constitution of identities in a contemporary southern African context.[2]

The personal identity we create through auto/biographical accounts is connected to issues of time, meaning, and action. Pursuing the question *How did I become who I am?* we plot our stories along a timeline, tying together our past and present, our earlier and later selves. Notwithstanding the narrative identity we create over time, there are significant ways in which *auto*biography (an account of the self) is also, in the words of J. M. Coetzee (on p. 216), *autre*biography (an account of another self). In relating earlier and later selves to each other we seek to make sense of our experiences, with greater or lesser success. But we also relate earlier to current selves in order to place ourselves in the present. Guided by the question *Who am I?* we interpret ourselves in the hope of gaining some clarity about what our present identities and needs may be. To the extent that our lives are still in the process of unfolding, the specific connections and interpretations we establish are always open to revision. The accounts we produce of the past and the understanding this gives us of ourselves in the present also place us in a specific relationship to action and the future. Depending on the different stories we tell about our past and present selves, we open up different identities from which we can imagine different potential futures for ourselves in answer to the question *Who do I want to become?* In this sense, auto/biographical accounts can play a considerable role in the scaffolding of agency.[3]

The collective identities we create through weaving our auto/biographical accounts into those of others are tied to issues of association and disassociation, power, and social action. In situating ourselves in relation to others, we associate ourselves with them or distance ourselves from them. Through auto/biographical accounts we establish and cement relations to significant others, friends, colleagues, citizens, and comrades and disassociate ourselves from strangers, adversaries, opponents, and enemies. In this manner we construct social realities that open up or close off certain forms of collective existence. Placing ourselves in relation to others also means ranking ourselves in existing status hierarchies. By implication our auto/biographical accounts either entrench or challenge these hierarchies, sometimes also offering alternative ones. Through the collective identities they constitute and the status hierarchies they affirm or question, our auto/biographical accounts mobilize collective action. Citing colonialism, racism, fascism, sexism, homophobia, and religious intolerance as its consequences, critics of identity thinking have warned against the violent suppression of difference in individual and collective identities. This raises the pertinent question whether nonrepressive forms of identity constitution are possible and the role auto/biography could play in this.[4]

When we address an audience—testifying about our personal and collective identities through auto/biography—we enter into communicative relations in public spheres and engage ourselves in struggles for justice. Through publicly oriented self-reflection we cross the boundaries between the private and the public. Intentionally or not, and whether positively affirmed or contested by our audience, our auto/biographical accounts become entwined in struggles about justice. We use these accounts to hold up to public scrutiny the values informing our lives and those of other protagonists. In doing so, we appeal for recognition of individual and collective identities. Implicitly or explicitly, we also use these stories in struggles over distribution and redistribution and in demands to participate in the life of society. However, the communicative relations we enter into with our auto/biographies are shot through with power. As a result, the media of communication—language, media technologies, and institutions—through which they are conveyed mold the accounts we give of ourselves. These social settings of identity reverberate globally, within nations, families, and individuals, and affect notions of the self and the nature of auto/biographical accounts. Accordingly, auto/biographical accounts can function as sites of governmentality that produce normalized subjectivities as well as practices that hold the promise of emancipation and autonomy.[5]

Shifting our attention to the public spheres in which our auto/biographical accounts circulate along with auto/biographical accounts of others, it soon becomes evident that our identities are not only constituted by the accounts we offer about ourselves. Our notion of self is also constituted through the accounts others give of us. The coexistence of these two forces leads to a particularly interesting further way in which the self is constituted, namely, in the contestations associated with aligning the autobiographical accounts we give of ourselves and the biographical accounts others offer about us. The contestation involved in seeking to attain such alignment has implications for both the individuals and collectives involved.

Seyla Benhabib puts it as follows: "From the time of our birth we are immersed in a 'web of narratives,' of which we are both the author and the object. The self is both the teller of tales and that about whom tales are told. The individual with a coherent sense of self-identity is the one who succeeds in integrating these tales and perspectives into a meaningful life story" (1992:198. See also Benhabib 2002:15–16). Drawing attention to the larger social and political effects of aligning different auto/biographical accounts, Benhabib continues, "When the story of a life can only be told from the perspective of others, then the self is a victim and sufferer who has lost control over her existence. When the story of a life can only be told from the standpoint of the individual, then such a self is a narcissist and a loner who may have attained autonomy without solidarity. A coherent sense of self is attained with the successful integration of autonomy and solidarity" (1992:198; cf. also Bruner 2001:34 and Frisch 2004).[6]

This dialogical approach to auto/biographical accounts of the self, the contestation it may entail, and the effects of such contestation can be illustrated with a few southern African cases. Relatively harmless examples consist of the subtle addition of extra information or alternative interpretations of existing facts which are largely in harmony with a person's overall representation of him- or herself. This is common with sympathetic reviews, such as Lewis Nkosi's reviews of Es'kia Mphahlele's autobiography *Down Second Avenue* (Nkosi 1990a) and Bloke Modisane's autobiography *Blame Me on History*

(Nkosi 1990b). As Doris Lessing's altercation with Carole Klein (see p. 234) shows, matters can become less amicable, though, as struggles erupt for control over the narrative of a life.

The divergences in these two examples take place, so to speak, outside the autobiographical text. But they can also be made internal to it. This is the case with the divergence between her own account of a childhood journey, and the official family version that Doris Lessing offers us in the opening pages of the first volume of her autobiography *Under My Skin* (1994:40–43). There is also a genre that is common, but by no means unique to southern Africa, in which such alignment of self-representation and representation by others is internal to the production of the text. In collaborative auto/biographies—also known as "mediated testimony," and sometimes classified under oral history, such as Marjorie Shostak's *Nisa: The Life and Words of a !Kung Woman* (1981); Wulf Sachs's *Black Hamlet* (1996), and Raymond Mhlaba and Thembeka Mufamadi's *Raymond Mhlaba's Personal Memoirs* (2001)—an oral narrator tells her or his life to a writing author, who prepares it for publication. In most of these cases the amiable relations between collaborators smooth out contestation.[7]

The effects of contestation can be more severe and wide-ranging than mere personal squabbles. Contestations about the validity of an auto/biographical account can lead to the public shaming of individuals and to publishing scandals. They can also shatter existing assumptions about the nature of scholarship. All these consequences can be found in the debates surrounding Binjamin Wilkomirski's *Bruchstücke: Aus einer Kindheit 1939–1948* (1995) (Fragments: Memories of a Childhood, 1939–1948 [1997]). As the example of the contestations around Nobel laureate Rigoberta Menchú's *I, Rigoberta Menchú* show, cultural and political battles can be unleashed with repercussions for social movements.[8] In southern Africa too, there is a whole field of auto/biographical contestations with socially relevant and far-reaching consequences. This has been particularly evident in testimonies emerging from and around South Africa's Truth and Reconciliation Commission (TRC), in which there have been disagreements between perpetrators of injustice and their accusers. One prominent case is the account by the last apartheid president, F. W. de Klerk, *The Last Trek* (1998), and death squad operative Eugene de Kock's *A Long Night's Damage* (1998), in which de Kock contests de Klerk's protestations of innocence.

As these examples illustrate, while subjects may use auto/biographical accounts to situate themselves, these accounts themselves are also placed in relation to other accounts and in relation to larger narratives, which are in turn embedded in social relations and struggles. Pumla Gobodo-Madikizela's auto/biographical account of her meetings with de Kock, *A Human Being Died That Night* (2003), raises pertinent questions in this regard: to what extent does the project of social and political reconciliation between perpetrators and victims—which is necessary for future coexistence—hinge on the reconcilability of divergent auto/biographical accounts? How much divergence in our auto/biographical accounts can be borne by our social solidarity with each other? And when do divergences in the content of auto/biographical accounts also rupture the social fabric?

As noted, weaving our auto/biographical accounts into larger accounts about collectives—such as gender-specific groups, survivors, or citizens of a state—is crucial to our identities. Writing about the nature of the relationship between individual and collective identities, Kwame Anthony Appiah suggests that we think of the latter in terms of scripts. These scripts constitute "narratives that people can use in shaping their life plans and telling their life stories," either through copying or deviating from them (Appiah and Gutmann 1996:97; also Appiah 2001:243). Similarly, Benhabib asserts, "We are born into webs of interlocution or narrative, from familial and gender narratives to linguistic ones and to the macronarratives of collective identity. We become aware of who we are by learning to become conversation partners in these narratives" (2002:15. See also Kureishi 2004:7).

The idea that our identities are constituted in the relations we establish with other individuals or with collectives is a central tenet of symbolic interactionism and certain forms of feminism that theorists like Benhabib adhere to. It is also the essence of African humanism or *ubuntu*, elaborated on by Es'kia Mphahlele (2004:241–304), and which Ellen Kuzwayo (1990:122) sees encapsulated in the Tshivenda saying *"Muthu ndi muthu nga munwe"* (a person is a person through other persons).[9] It is such dialogical notions of the self that echo in Breyten Breytenbach's assertion that the "sense of I (identity, the I-ing of self, id-entity) is dependent on interaction with some thing or some body 'out there.' Community is usually the mirror. 'I am a human through people.' We identify/situate ourselves in our interaction with and relation to cultural constructs such as language, religion, ideology, a shared narrative of history or destiny, adherence or resistance to specific values. In this sense, the shaping of identity and the resultant (self)identification is very much the product of a given society" (see p. 274).

Exactly how individuals draw on collective identities in constituting their individual narrative identities, which collective narratives they relate their own lives to, and how they deal with the impact of shifts in these collective narratives on their narratives of self raise a multitude of questions to which an exploration of auto/biographical practices such as the one offered in this book may offer tentative answers. Regarding the relationships that are established with specific collectives, Botlhale Tema (2003 and 2005) prioritizes relations to the family, Ato Quayson (1995:87) foregrounds the relationship to the state, Carol Fleisher Feldman (2001) focuses on the nation, while Philip Holden (2005) elaborates on the continuities between the nation and global society.[10] Relations to the state and the nation are particularly interesting because they reveal some of the discrepancies common in southern Africa between the formation of identity through actual experiences on the one hand and the selves that are constituted in auto/biographical accounts on the other. While the actual experiences of many individuals in southern Africa are regionalist rather than national (in the sense that they either cross state borders or do not share in the real or imagined community of the nation-state in a meaningful way), most auto/biographical accounts lean towards a narrative alliance with national identities, a phenomenon which requires further scrutiny.[11]

The view that our identities are constituted in the contestation between accounts we offer of ourselves and accounts others give about us is informed by the arguable assumption that auto/biographical accounts are comparable. While this assumption is relevant to all auto/biography, it is particularly evident when a self intimately connects her or his auto/biographical account to that of other individuals or collectives. This applies to family memoirs like Athol Fugard's *Cousins* (1994) and Elinor Sisulu's *Walter and Albertina Sisulu* (2002).[12] It applies equally to memoirs of political movements such as Albert Luthuli's *Let My People Go* (1962) and Helen Joseph's *Side by Side* (1986). The extent and nature of such disjunctions is illustrated by Gillian Slovo's *Every Secret Thing* (1997)—her memoir of a family deeply steeped in the anti-apartheid struggle—which is constructed along the lines of personal memory rather than public history (pp. 319–320).

As the example of *Every Secret Thing* shows, we need to consider not only the strain on collective existence and solidarity when different selves tell the same type of story but disagree with each other about its content. We also have to consider the consequences of the possible incommensurability of different types of auto/biographical accounts—such as testimony, psychobiography, *izibongo*, confession, and oral history—and the notions of self they imply.[13] What are the consequences, we must ask, of the fact that selves are also constituted in webs of different types of auto/biographical accounts that resist comparison, in the same way as some theorists believe different scientific paradigms or natural languages are incommensurable? This may raise problems for scholars of auto/biography who pursue integrative approaches that seek to establish conversations among different auto/biographical accounts. For scholars, but also for the selves and societies concerned, interpretation may break down if there is disagreement about the nature of divergences, i.e., when there is disagreement whether they are divergences in content or whether they are disjunctions between different types of auto/biographical accounts and the notions of self these different accounts imply. Problems for the constitution of identities may arise when what appears to be a conversation among selves is at best a chorus of incommensurable soliloquies, of selves talking past each other. Finally, problems of integration can arise for societies if the various auto/biographical paradigms and the notions of self they are tied to are indeed so incommensurable that the communicative preconditions for the flourishing of solidarity are not fulfilled and what has the outer trappings of a community is in fact not—yet—one.

The interviews gathered in *Selves in Question* allow readers to explore these theoretical views regarding the role of auto/biographical accounts in the constitution of individual and collective identities from a southern African perspective in more concrete detail. To begin with, when read individually the interviews offer us insider views of the ways in which different individuals have reflected upon or constructed themselves in telling their own life stories. Read together, the interviews display the heteroglossic nature of individual and collective identities shaped by the intersection of a web of narratives.[14] Following from this, the interviews also reflect the ways in which various practitioners negotiate the discrepancies between self-representation and representation of self by others. Finally, the collection offers views of how auto/biographical accounts are positioned in relation to narrative accounts of collective identities and the consequences of this relationship for individuals and society at large. By implication, the interviews open the road to an exploration of the ways in which auto/biographical accounts in southern Africa foster the autonomy and solidarity crucial to the self and society.

Focusing on the constitution of selves through auto/biography need not necessarily imply a commitment to identity politics.[15] Therefore, while some readers may take the opportunity to fit these interviews into a larger project of state-guided identity construction through nation-building and the African Renaissance (Mante Mphahlele 2002, Faber pp. 418–420), others may find in them ample evidence of the extent to which identities are elusive, ruptured, and recalcitrant (see Spivak 1995; Butler 1995; Gilroy 2000 and 2004; and Cascarino, Morgan, and Raditlhalo p. 439).[16] In contrast to the coincidence—in Europe—of life narrative, the emergence of bourgeois subjectivity, the development of the bourgeois public sphere, and the nation state, the effects of hybridization, trauma, and large-scale social transformation may well mean that, through placing selves in question, auto/biographical practices in southern Africa point the way towards alternatives to identity politics.

The interviews in this collection are informed by the need to question both the ontological status and the representation of the self in autobiographical accounts.[17] They remind us that the self is constantly under construction and that its status and representation are always in question. The contributors explore ways in which auto/biographical acts contribute to the understanding of the self and selves. They deal with topics such as the contexts that are conducive to the flourishing of a rich variety of auto/biographical practices, the nature of the different production processes, the contents and the forms of auto/biographical accounts, and, finally, their impact on the producers and audience. In doing so they probe a multitude of variables—including the specific historical juncture, cultures, languages, geopolitical locations, ages, genders, social positions—in their relations to auto/biographical practices. The interviews bear witness to some of the specific southern African modalities of subjectivization. Looking back, they offer insight into the crises of agency and identity construction unleashed by colonization. Looking towards the future, they explore the new alternatives, dilemmas, and possibilities opened by decolonization and democratization in the postcolonial era.

Staking out a generic field is usually achieved through entrenching definitions. The spectrum of auto/biographical expression in the region, along with the specificity of some of its forms, prompts an ongoing search for appropriate terminology. Although it is only an approximation, we have settled on the term *auto/biographical account*.[18] We use auto/biographical account to signify a wide assortment of symbolic expressions in which the life or part of the life of a material person or persons is represented.[19] We find terms such as *life narrative* and *life writing* wanting because they are biased against nonnarrative, oral, and nonverbal accounts.[20] Within the parameters of the written word, local auto/biographical accounts take the form of narrative prose, which includes the conventional autobiography, biography, and memoir, as well as diaries, journals, and letters, but also extends to such nonnarrative forms as poetry.[21] Although this collection of interviews focuses largely on narrative verbal expression, this is not meant to imply that representation of the self is confined to the written or the spoken word. Many pertinent issues are also raised by the representation of lives and selves through nonnarrative forms such as *izibongo*, oral accounts such as dramatic performance of the self, and nonverbal representation such as music, painting, photography, cinema, television, and the exhibition of material objects from everyday life.[22]

The distinction signaled by the concepts *autobiography* and *biography* also does not capture the ways in which these forms actually flow into each other, which is why we use the term *auto/biography*. The use of two distinct concepts obscures the ways in which the differences between autobiography and biography are eroded by auto/biographical practices such as *izibongo* and collaborative auto/biography. *Izibongo*, for example, often fudge the distinction between the self-representation of a single individual (as in autobiography) and the representation of another person (as in biography). Collaborative auto/biography likewise questions the soundness of the distinction between autobiography, in which the self produces his autobiographical account about himself out of himself, and biography, in which an author produces a biographical representation of another person.[23] In other words, both *izibongo* and collaborative auto/biography reflect the ways in which the construction of selves happens at the interface between autobiography and biography, between the intrasubjective and the intersubjective.

The arrangement of the interviews is predominantly thematic rather than chronological. *Singing the Praises, Performing the Persona* deals with *izibongo* and popular culture. In *Representing Silence* the contributors discuss ways in which auto/biographers speak on behalf of others. *Relating the Self* focuses on relational notions of the self as constituted in collaborative auto/biographies. *Fact or Fiction* treats the constitution and representation of self in fictional and auto/biographical writing. In *Subject to Metaphor* the role of the imaginative in the constitution of auto/biographical identity is explored. *From Daughters to Mothers* probes the auto/biographically mediated relationship between daughters and their mothers, while *Disarming White Men* investigates the auto/biographical performance of masculinities on stage. In *Commemoration, Confession, Conversion* the use of auto/biography in coming to terms with the past is discussed. *Confessing Sexualities* looks at the politics of intimacy in auto/biography. The last section, *Re-collecting the New Nation*, explores contemporary notions of self-representation and the self in relation to collective identities.

The rest of this introduction provides background to auto/biographical practices in southern Africa and to the interviews. In "Auto/biographical Accounts in South Africa in Three Parts" we sketch some of the key features affecting the historical evolution of auto/biographical practices in South Africa (pp. 10–38). "Thematic and Theoretical Issues in Southern African Auto/biography: An Overview" groups some topics that contributors to this collection raise and fleshes out the theoretical issues at stake regarding the nature of auto/biography and the self (pp. 38–62). The introduction concludes with some comments on the scope of this anthology, its objectives, and limitations (pp. 62–68).

AUTO/BIOGRAPHICAL ACCOUNTS IN SOUTH AFRICA IN THREE PARTS

This survey of auto/biographical accounts in South Africa begins with a broad survey from precolonial times to the present and sketches a few of the theoretical issues related to the politics and epistemology of auto/biographical practices where indigenous, colonial, settler, and postcolonial traditions overlap.[24] The second part focuses on apartheid auto/biography in greater detail. It outlines the effects of brutal racial discrimination on auto/biographical practices and stakes out trends in the resistance or indifference to injustice as reflected in auto/biographical accounts. Part three explores the continuities and discontinuities in auto/biographical practices following the watershed years of the Mandela Republic and outlines emerging developments in the ways in which auto/biographical accounts contribute to the construction of alternative identities.

South African Auto/biography: *Izibongo*, Travel Writing, the Sciences of Man, Resistance, and Reconciliation

For hundreds of years indigenous peoples in southern Africa have formulated and performed self-representational compositions, the most notable of which are rather misleadingly referred to in English as "praise poems" (termed *izibongo* in isiZulu and isiXhosa, and *lithoko* in seSotho). Although neither static nor standardized—and ongoing transformations and differences in the practices are important—the custom of "praising" can be found in the distant histories and present-day practices of diverse southern African cultural groups such as the Sotho, Tswana, Swazi, Ndebele, Xhosa, and Zulu.[25] Referring to the custom among the Zulu—and we can generalize this to many other ethnic and linguistic groups in the region—Noverino N. Canonici describes the composition of *izibongo* in this way:

> [They] are developed from initial "praise names," that an individual is given or gives himself, which briefly describe or epitomize an event in his life, his achievements or failures, or a physical characteristic. When a praise name is explained or expanded, it becomes a "praise phrase" or a "praise sentence":

this may constitute the nucleus of a praise poem, which will then grow with episodic and occasional additions as demanded by events. (1996:226–227)

Izibongo are not now, and perhaps never were, uniform in style or length. They range in length, complexity, and theme from the praises of chiefs and other important people (past and present), which run into hundreds of lines, with intricate poetic patterns, to the short and simple praises of children and ordinary individuals. The praises of important persons are usually composed by professional bards; while retaining fundamental features in each performance, variations occur from one performance to the next. *Izibongo* are nonnarrative; furthermore, they may be performed by the subject of the poem or someone else. Since composition is not usually confined to any one author, *izibongo* generally blur the distinction between the autobiographical and the biographical.

Many *izibongo* of long-deceased individuals constitute scripts that continue to be performed and serve to communicate important aspects of the community's history and value system and thus to shape both individual and collective identities.[26] They constitute what Nancy Fraser (1989:144–160) terms the sociocultural means of interpretation and communication, which allow people to interpret themselves and their needs; they are a source of pride, and they can strengthen the community's sense of belonging. Moreover, if certain lines from a famous person's *izibongo* are incorporated into those of a living individual, then something of the status of the original subject will be conferred on that individual. With regard to the much shorter praises of ordinary individuals, there are the praises of childhood, composed by mothers and performed in the confines of the close family. Although *izibongo* are less common nowadays than they used to be, praising among common folk nevertheless continues. Noleen Turner has recorded and analyzed contemporary auto/biographical practices among the Zulu in both urban and rural locations: *izihasho* is the term given to these short, often scatological and frequently derisive "praises" (see Turner 1995). Comparatively recent adaptations of the genre include praises of trade unions, football teams, and religious movements.[27]

Izibongo are performed in social circumstances that warrant the "naming, identifying and therefore giving significance and substance to the named person or object" (Gunner and Gwala 1994:2). They are performed at community rituals, in intimate family circles, at clan gatherings, and recently on popular records and at mass political assemblies.[28] The genre has evolved in terms of form, function, and popularity. Writing about Zulu *izibongo*, Liz Gunner and Mafika Gwala point out that in the latter days of apartheid, *izibongo* were "used both within an 'authoritarian populism' and an emergent 'popular democratic' culture. They are thus at the center of contested terrain and are a key art form in the political discourse of the day" (1994:12).

So although indigenous oral auto/biographical practices tended to be overshadowed by the practices of writing in the colonial and apartheid eras, they were never eclipsed by them.[29] Many scholars have examined the relationship between orality and literacy. Jeff Guy, for instance, argues that "[o]rality and literacy are not isolated phenomena, they are relational, interacting with one another, coexisting, the nature and relative significance and strengths of each changing with context and with history. But the point is that their coexistence and interaction does not make them the same" (1994:8), thus reminding us of the complexities surrounding the in/commensurability of the oral and the written. Recent studies in oral history and oral performance that go beyond the barriers posed by focusing on hegemonic or official languages have extended the range of academic perception about what is going on in the field of lifetext (Lawrence 2001), and a cursory glance at the history of auto/biographical composition in southern Africa reveals layers of imported and indigenous influences equally evident in other parts of Africa.

Coullie, focussing more specifically on the relationship between orally performed auto/biographical texts and prose narrative, also argues for acknowledgment of the distinctions between the two approaches in essays on Ellen Kuzwayo (1996) and on the relationship between *izibongo* and narrative autobiography in South Africa (1999a). In the latter she investigates the sociopolitical implications of the different traditions.[30] Westernized self-representational practices, the published prose narrative auto/biographies including those of famous people, operate in terms of

> Modern capitalism [which] requires individuals to act in accordance with the ethos of bourgeois individualism: the self is, in this conception, largely private property.... It entails a distinction between the private and the public domains, so that there are parts of the self which can only be known to the self which—when revealed in personal testimony—enormously increase the value of that account. There is, in such a world, an individualisation of artistic production which is manifest in commodification, consumerism, reification of artistic process, and in increasing specialisation of practice which contributes to class and interest stratifications and a process of social fragmentation. (1999a:81)

She notes that the decline in vernacular oral auto/biographical practice and the increase in prose narrative auto/biographical publications (usually in

English) by Africans involves, for the practitioner, a shift to westernized interpretations of a range of fundamentally important features of experience and representations thereof: namely, time, creative productivity, responsibility and reward, notions of knowledge and belief, and—perhaps most important—conceptions of self (ibid.:81). She concludes, however, with the view that although western conceptions of authorship and authority seem to be gaining currency among indigenous sectors of the southern African population, "The continuing tradition of praising shows that African societies have . . . been able to accommodate literacy without entirely capitulating to it. . . . African beliefs, practices, ways of being are likely to survive (in ever-changing forms) the globalization of capitalism and the onslaught of American-European hegemony, at least in the short-term" (ibid.:82–83).

Auto/biographical compositions, both performed and published, by indigenous peoples were and are both vital and significant. Nevertheless, one should not underestimate the impact of European settlement in southern Africa. Many factors contributed to the domination of white writing in the output of printed auto/biographical texts. One key factor was the hegemony of Christian conceptions of self. Another was the dominance of the European languages (English, Dutch, Portuguese, and German)[31] and of that European-African hybrid, Afrikaans, in the official public spheres. Also important were the education systems designed by the settler leaders to prepare settlers for roles in the professions and in business and to curb the range of expression of the indigenous peoples so as to fit them exclusively for serfdom and proletarian labor. Moreover, the sealing-off of the technological means of production (first the print media and later the electronic media) from a wider populace (Hofmeyr and Nuttall 2001:6), and the insulation of various groups from each other on the basis of race and language served to skew auto/biographical production in favor of whites.

As elsewhere in sub-Saharan Africa, much colonial auto/biography has survived in the form of travel accounts written by Europeans.[32] These early travel writings by Europeans in Portuguese, Dutch, English, and French often portray a self who functions as the central narrating, focalizing, and ideological point from which the landscape and local peoples are interpreted.[33] This is especially evident in the seventeenth-century writings of administrators such as the first Dutch governor of the Cape, Jan van Riebeeck, whose 1652 journal (1952), kept for the benefit of his employers, the Dutch East India Company, seeks to convince them that he is in control of the land and people of the new colony. Slightly different angles are offered in accounts by European women who accompanied administrators, such as Lady Anne Barnard, by British settlers such as Thomas Pringle, who found themselves at loggerheads with the representatives of the colonial government, and by Catherine Barter's unique 1866 account of a settler woman traveling on her own with native helpers (*Alone Among the Zulus*, 1995).[34] Travel accounts written in the course of the eighteenth and nineteenth centuries by missionaries such as David Livingstone sometimes convey a philanthropic engagement in their representations of indigenous individuals and themselves (Pratt 1992:38–68).[35] Although these colonial travel narratives address a European audience, their attempts at centering authorial identity in the southern African landscape and among local people means that they inevitably contain kernels of auto/biographical accounts of the people in the contact zone between the indigenous inhabitants and arriving Europeans. This invites readings of, for example, the vignettes of Krotoa-Eva in Van Riebeeck's journal, as well as Pringle's journalism and poems, as constituting early forms of biographical writing about indigenous subjects.[36]

These early travel accounts provided the ground for auto/biographical accounts within the framework of the budding "sciences of man."[37] Often the amateur ethnology that emerged from travel writings contributed to the perception of indigenous individuals as ethnic types, paving the way for the display of persons like Saartjie Baartman as spectacularized bodies in the freak and ethnological shows of Europe.[38] In the course of the nineteenth century, Wilhelm von Humboldt's theories, according to which each language reflects a particular view of the world that needs to be taken note of, along with missionary policies to preach in the language of the audience, inspired a turn to greater communicative interaction between Europeans and indigenous peoples in the vernacular. Accordingly, philologists such as Lucy Lloyd and Wilhelm Bleek in the Cape (see Deacon 1996 and Szalay 2002) and missionaries such as the Ellenbergers in Lesotho (see Ricard 2003) initiated increasing scientific interest in the narratives of indigenous people, thereby paving the way for recordings of their lives in the vernacular. Around the turn of the twentieth century, as ethnology and the other sciences of man gained greater academic institutionalization in Europe and the United States, fieldwork became a sine qua non, and it supported a steady growth in interest in the lives of indigenous peoples as objects of inquiry in their own right rather than merely as a foil for the author's own inquiry into his or her personal identity.

Nevertheless, new problems arose regarding biographies of indigenous people generated within the framework of the sciences of man. To begin with, as Patrick Harries (2002) has argued with regards to the missionary anthropologist Henri Alexandre Junod's *The Life of a South African Tribe* (1912–1913), dubious interpretative schemas, such as those indebted to Darwin, were mapped onto local life with the effect that individual lives were eclipsed by social and cultural generalizations premised on built-in hierarchies. This tension between the generalizing requirements of ethnology, anthropology, and psychoanalysis as scientific disciplines seeking to make universal claims and the concern with the life of a particular southern African individual, remains evident well into the twentieth century in the collection *Ten Africans* edited by Margery Perham (1936), in Westermann's *Afrikaner Erzählen Ihr Leben* (1938), in Wulf Sachs's *Black Hamlet* (1996, first published in 1937), and in Hourwich Reyher's *Zulu Woman: The Life of Christina Sibiya* (1999, originally published in 1948). This trend is evident as late as the end of the twentieth century in American anthropologist Marjorie Shostak's *Nisa: The Life and Words of a !Kung Woman* (1981), a book that seeks to break with the model by alternating generalizing anthropological and ethnological theses on the !Kung-San with the individual life of her informant "Nisa." All in all, by defining large sectors of the population as colonial subjects who needed to be managed, as exotic subalterns whose cases had to be advocated, or as curiosities and cultural emblems that needed to be understood as scientific objects, autobiographical travel writing by Europeans and biographical narratives produced in the paradigm of the sciences of man usually meant that the accounts of indigenous southern Africans' lives were appropriated, reified, or instrumentalized for the author's own purposes.

As will be shown in the more detailed discussion of apartheid and post-apartheid life writing, this paradigm changed around the middle of the twentieth century as indigenous South Africans themselves, admittedly in small numbers and generally representing an educated élite, became authors and the subjects of their own life stories. The autobiographies of Peter Abrahams (1954), Ezekiel Mphahlele (1959),[39] Noni Jabavu (1960 and 1963), and Bloke Modisane (1963) were important not only because they wrested control of their own narratives from the hegemonic settler class, but also because their life stories, detailing—inevitably—the realities of racial oppression, served to support the liberation movement.[40] These autobiographies and others of that generation increasingly evince a kind of double consciousness, addressing both an international and local readership.[41] They can thus be contrasted with the travel narratives produced for a European home audience and the sciences of man texts written mainly for an academic readership in Europe and the United States. Because many of these texts have a different agenda from the sciences of man—namely, to inform and raise consciousness—they engage in a different rhetoric and provide contrary insights into colonialism and its consequences. From the 1950s to the 1980s the imperatives of the regional liberation struggles, followed by an era of political caution in the last decade and a half, often accorded these auto/biographies an untouchable status beyond the reach of criticism.[42] According to Breyten Breytenbach, the desire for a "'strong man'—as leader, prophet, saviour . . . who can give meaning and show the way forward" led to the construction of icons, "obliterating a critical reading" (see pp. 272–273). As discussions in this collection suggest, this may be changing, allowing more "rereadings now happily relieved of any need for solidarity" (Nkosi 1990a:3).

Since the 1970s there has been a phenomenal mushrooming of interest in auto/biographical accounts. The number of published accounts has boomed, and the genre has undergone significant transformations. These developments can be explained by real changes in auto/biographical output as well as by changed perceptions of the practice. Transformed political environments, contributing to the rise in literacy and greater access to the means of literary production, have resulted in increased numbers of potential local producers and consumers of written auto/biography. In the wake of democratization, local people have also shown a greater interest in the lives of their fellow citizens (see Nixon, pp. 279–280). On the one hand, the stature of public heroes such as Nelson Mandela (1994) and Walter and Albertina Sisulu (2002) has been reinforced by their auto/biographies. On the other hand, a reconsideration of the value of everyday life for history and the social sciences (Eckert and Jones 2002) and a return to the ordinary (Taylor 1992:211ff; and Ndebele 1991) has meant that the scope of what is perceived as a life worth telling has expanded from the narrow confines of the (white male) hero to the everyday lives of ordinary people. There is hardly a more striking barometer of these changes than the shift from the apartheid-inspired *Dictionary of South African Biography* (1968–1987) to the *New Dictionary of South African Biography* (launched in 1995). Endorsed with a foreword by Nelson Mandela (vol. I), with the sentiments echoed in a foreword by Kader Asmal (vol. II), the *New Dictionary of South African Biography* seeks to "record for posterity the role of many unacclaimed people" by extending the scope beyond the "lives of the illustrious minority who achieve greatness" to "those who are less famous" yet "also give us much inspiration . . . in a racial and cultural mosaic that is truly nation-building" (Asmal 1999; see also Mohlamme 1999). In addition, oral performance and popular culture in African languages have attained a new visibility previously denied by Euro-focused state apparatuses, publishers and academic institutions fixated on the valorized "high culture" of print (Brown 1998, Brown, ed., 1999; Coullie 1999a and 2002).

Contemporary auto/biographical accounts in the region have to a large extent liberated themselves from their precursors in travel writing and the sciences of man and gained a status of their own. The demise of the privileging of fiction, the deaestheticization of literary studies since the 1980s, and new trends in auto/biographical practices have meant that auto/biography, as genre and area of inquiry, has acquired respectability. Of course travel writing and texts informed by the sciences of man are still produced, they are still evolving, and they find ready markets even beyond the academy. And there is an ongoing production of texts inspired by a desire for emancipation, although the terms in which this is understood are increasingly broadening.

Travel by southern Africans of all races continues to be a theme. As may be expected, travels in other parts of the world feature heavily in the writings of those southern Africans who have studied abroad, or have lived (or continue to live) in exile.[43] Todd Matshikiza's *Chocolates for My Wife* (1961) offers an incisive look at British society; Ezekiel Mphahlele's *Afrika My Music* (1984a) explores his wanderings in Africa, Europe, and the United States and his return to South Africa in 1977, and Peter Abraham's *The Black Experience in the Twentieth Century* (2000) traverses the broad canvas of the Black Atlantic. With *Drawn in Colour: African Contrasts* (1960) and *The Ochre People* (1963), Jabavu offered the first books of travel in southern Africa written in English by a black woman, while Peter Abrahams's *Return to Goli* (1953) offers a view by another black South African who writes about his return to the country of his birth. Increasingly, white South Africans such as Breyten Breytenbach (1976, 1994, 1998), Sarah Penny (1997), and Antjie Krog (2003) are also using travel writing to inscribe their individual narratives into the collective sheaf of (southern) African narratives, thereby reinterpreting their white African identity. The transition to a democratic South Africa has initiated new ways in which black South Africans relate their individual narratives to the collective narratives of the country. Gobodo-Madikizela, for example, remarks on that change as follows:

> When I returned to South Africa in June of that year [1994] . . . I became aware for the first time that in my past travels I could not have described myself as a South African. I could only say that I was from South Africa. I remember thinking as my plane landed that day in Cape Town, This is *my* country, *my* home (2003:6–7).[44]

It is possible that, as travel narratives become more common and gain greater visibility, there may be a shift from the discrepancy between regionalist experiences and nationalist narrative identities still so widespread in auto/

biographical accounts from southern Africa to alternative individual narrative identities, emerging as auto/biographers increasingly construct their personal identities in relation to larger regionalist rather than national collectives.

More recent texts produced within academic institutions and written in the paradigm of the human sciences have been less hasty in their extrapolation of universalist conclusions from the narratives of individuals.[45] Instead, the life-history method is now often seen as a way of supplementing or even countering the tendencies in quantitative methods that construct aggregates from many samples, and historical accounts where the emphasis on categories such as class and modernization force the details of everyday existence into the background. Poised as they are between "the subject's worlds of knowledge and experience" and "a social construct which constitutes social reality," auto/biographical accounts within the human sciences are also perceived as a way of integrating the analysis of subject and society, agency and structure, private and public (Eckert and Jones 2002:9 and Van Onselen 1993).

In *The Women of Phokeng*, Belinda Bozzoli pursues such an equilibrium between the factual details drawn from auto/biographical accounts and sociological analysis. Drawing on oral life histories recounted in the vernacular in interviews with seventeen women, she strives for a qualitative, detailed, and varied picture of the connections between their consciousness, life strategies, and migrancy. In an attempt not to "impose upon qualitative and subjective material such as this the heavy artillery of the sociological armory, weighing down modest life stories with an interpretative framework" (1991:12), Bozzoli reproduces large extracts from the transcriptions of the life narratives that she hopes the reader will interpret "much as [she] would a work of literature" (ibid.). However, she displays no naiveté about the ability of "'raw' oral histories," which are "often opaque or merely anecdotal," to provide sociologically interesting information on their own to readers who lack knowledge of the context. Therefore she sees it as a task incumbent on the social scientist to embed these life narratives in a framework that will permit a richer understanding and hence the basis for more adequate sociological interpretations (ibid.). While resisting the historical tendency of the sciences of man to instrumentalize auto/biographical accounts in social engineering projects, Bozzoli's interest in social processes nonetheless smudges the distinctions between individuals. This raises the question, therefore, of the extent to which disciplines geared towards an understanding of social structures can, in fact, accord speaking subjects the degree of individuality that is a sine qua non of autobiography.

In addition to Manganyi's psychobiographies of the author Es'kia Mphahlele (1983; Mphahlele 1984b) and the artist Gerard Sekoto (1996 and 2004) (see pp. 162–170), one of the most striking recent auto/biographical accounts in the paradigm of the human sciences is Gobodo-Madikizela's psychobiography of one of apartheid's most notorious violators of human rights, Eugene de Kock. As the first black female South African psychologist to write extensively on a white South African male, Gobodo-Madikizela turns the tables on the tradition established by Wulf Sachs in *Black Hamlet,* in which white male psychologists take indigenous Africans as their subjects. On the basis of forty-six hours of interviews with de Kock, Gobodo-Madikizela draws a psychological and psychosociological profile of him driven by the question, "How does conscience get suppressed?" (2003:50) At the same time she keenly scrutinizes herself as well, assessing her compassion for both de Kock and his victims and the implications of this in terms of complicity. Thus she fulfils what Manganyi describes as one task of psychobiographers, namely, that "in seeking the truth of their subject, [they] must seek their own truth simultaneously" (1991:71). Interweaving her own memories of political violence in the 1980s and 1990s and her visceral revulsion to and yet sympathy for de Kock, Gobodo-Madikizela's account also probes the possibilities for individuals in southern Africa to use narrative as a forum for relating their individual identities to a collective narrative identity that includes the divergent life stories of those who perpetrated and benefited from violence, as well as the life narratives of their targets.

As could be expected, the first decade of democracy in South Africa has brought about several changes to auto/biography in the resistance tradition, which we will discuss in greater detail below. But resistance auto/biography did lay the important groundwork for the ongoing relevance of auto/biographical accounts in struggles for restitution, as, for example, in the joint action case brought by the Khulumani group against international businesses involved in upholding apartheid. Also, as has been the case in many other parts of the world that have seen an upsurge in identity politics, disputes or areas of protest and emancipation have multiplied. Auto/biographical accounts by individuals affected by HIV/AIDS serve both as testimony and protest against social disregard, and they feature prominently in struggles for justice related to health and gender equality.[46] A broadening of emancipation and resistance can be seen in accounts which have further diversified an area pioneered by feminist concerns with gender and reconceptualizations of masculinity.[47] Some of these explorations of sexual identity and sexual orientation include the contributions to the influential volume *Defiant Desire: Gay and Lesbian Lives in South Africa*, edited by Mark Gevisser and Edwin Cameron (1994) and Constitutional Court Judge Edwin Cameron's *Witness to AIDS* (2005).

As these examples suggest, auto/biographical accounts in the oral tradition, travel writing, the sciences of man, and resistance writing are still pursuing their own trajectories, while simultaneously leaving their traces in an ever-diversifying contemporary practice.

Apartheid Auto/biography, 1948-1994

Apartheid did not usher racism into southern Africa.[48] From the outset, many of the earliest European settlers on the southern tip of Africa in mid-seventeenth century held the indigenous peoples to be inferior and treated them accordingly. Over the next three centuries such prejudicial attitudes informed settler land-grabbing, legal, political, and economic policies, and fueled much bloody conflict. Conflict deepened the colonists' fear of the natives, and this fear, common to Briton and Boer alike, encouraged the effort to establish a pro-white union of the four European-controlled states after the South African (or Anglo-Boer) War (1899-1902). Inaugurated in 1910, the new "nation's" parliament promptly began to pass racist legislation, perhaps the most devastating of which was the 1913 Natives' Land Act which divided South Africa into "white" and "black" areas and prohibited Africans (67.3 percent of the total population, according to the 1911 census) from owning or renting land outside designated reserves (7.5 percent of the land).

Thus racism—institutionalized as well as informal—pervaded the South African landscape before the masterminds of apartheid, the predominantly Afrikaner National Party, won the election in 1948. Racism prior to apartheid is powerfully documented in the life writing of many, such as Clements Kadalie (*My Life and the ICU*, 1970), Naboth Mokgatle (*The Autobiography of an Unknown South African*, 1971), Dr. Goonam (*Coolie Doctor*, 1991), Pauline Podbrey (*White Girl in Search of the Party*, 1993), and Robert R. Edgar and Hilary Sapire's 1999 biography of Nonthetha Nkwenkwe, a woman prophet who was confined to a mental institution for thirteen years until her death in 1935. What distinguished apartheid from earlier racism (known as the color bar)—and life writing shows this too—was the slew of increasingly ruthless, as well as increasingly petty discriminatory laws and the brutal suppression of opposition. It was this intensification that prompted journalists Can Themba, Modisane, and Nkosi to leave South Africa on one-way exit permits.

Alan Paton's novel *Cry, the Beloved Country* (1948) put South African racism on the international agenda; texts like Peter Abrahams's *Return to Goli* and *Tell Freedom*, and Albie Sachs's *Jail Diary*, kept it there. Autobiographies—many of which were banned in South Africa—by Trevor Huddlestone (*Nought for Your Comfort*, 1956), by Nobel Peace Prize winner Albert Luthuli (*Let My People Go*, 1962), as well as biographies like Mary Benson's of Luthuli (1963) and of Nelson Mandela (1986) and Donald Woods's biography of Black Consciousness campaigner Steve Biko (1987), were effective in helping to ensure that apartheid was prominent in international debates.

Opposition voices, particularly in print, were to a large extent silenced in apartheid South Africa. Christopher Saunders and Nicholas Southey note that "in the early 1960s many of South Africa's black writers had their works proscribed, and by the later 1980s well over 30,000 works had been banned" (1998:40). On the one hand, this meant that oral vernacular performance "poetry" became extremely important at large political gatherings as reminders of the colonized/oppressed's once proud heritage and of their own heroes. Rousing performances of *izibongo* would reinforce group solidarity and strengthen the crowd's commitment to resist the apartheid state. On the other hand, the increasing output of published texts by black South Africans indicates that many had turned to narrative prose—in English—in order to give voice to their experiences of racism so that white South Africans and the international lobby would be alerted to circumstances in South Africa. English is the medium in which by far the largest number of auto/biographical texts are published, even by writers whose mother tongue is not English. This may be explained, in part, by writers' and publishers' awareness of the greater potential readership—within South Africa and abroad—for English texts rather than those written in isiZulu, seSotho, isiXhosa, Afrikaans, or other indigenous languages. But English may also have been the language of expression during the seventies and eighties because it was widely perceived as the language of liberation.

Once the Nationalist government came into power in 1948, laws prohibiting interaction between the races—even on such petty levels as standing at the same counter in a post office—were promulgated in rapid succession. As Modisane so powerfully narrates in *Blame Me on History*, normal social interaction between the races was outlawed. In this climate, it was possible for the state to control the movement of people—and to force people to move—to delimit economic prosperity in racial terms, to proscribe socializing and to disseminate only officially sanctioned versions of reality. From 1948 the white electorate had diminishing access to information and increasing exposure to state-controlled interpretations of events. It was to some extent because of massive white ignorance about the living conditions and daily humiliations of the voteless majority (who rarely appeared in "white" South Africa as anything other than laborers and servants) that life writing (especially prose narratives in English) during the apartheid period became an increasingly important weapon in the anti-apartheid struggle. Life writing—the openly anti-apartheid accounts by activists of all races (often illegally circulated), as well as the seemingly nonpolitical, and therefore uncensored, autobiographies and biographies with black subjects—strengthened and broadened the liberation struggle in part because life stories served to educate whites about the realities of life under apartheid and of the maltreatment of those who opposed it. Under apartheid, individual worth and a person's prospects for education, employment, decent living standards, and justice were all crudely determined solely by the hierarchical system of racial classification. Auto/biographies like Ezekiel Mphahlele's *Down Second Avenue,* which recounts in searing detail the degradation that ordinary and extraordinary "non-white/*nie blanke*" individuals were daily compelled to endure, contested apartheid's obsession with group identity and its concomitant erasure of individuals.

State repression under apartheid led to escalating violence and human rights violations. The experiences of being "banned"[49] and internal banishment (long-term house arrest) are recounted by many auto/biographers, such as Hilda Bernstein (*The World That Was Ours,* 1967); Winnie Mandela (*Part of My Soul Went with Him,* 1985, revised 1986); Helen Joseph (*Side by Side,* 1986); Frank Chikane (*No Life of My Own,* 1988). Over the forty-six years of apartheid, the greater proportion of life writing focused on the political, often correcting false official versions of history. Mokgatle's *The Autobiography of an Unknown South African,* Philip Kgosana's *Lest We Forget* (1988), Mosiuoa Lekota's *Prison Letters to a Daughter* (1991), and Maggie Resha's *'Mangoana Tsoara Thipa Ka Bohaleng: My Life in the Struggle* (1991) all seek to rectify patent lies in state-authorized accounts. Because of its potential political impact, much life writing was banned, including most of the aforementioned texts as well as everything written by banned or listed persons such as Ruth First's biography of Olive Schreiner and Mary Benson's biography of Luthuli (1963). Prison memoirs—that subgenre which responded precisely to the erosion of the rule of law and the concomitant emergence of the police state in apartheid South Africa—were also banned: Ruth First's *117 days* (1965), Albie Sachs's *Jail Diary,* Quentin Jacobsen's *Solitary in Johannesburg* (1974), Hugh Lewin's *Bandiet: Seven Years in a South African Prison* (1981), Molefe Pheto's *And Night Fell: Memoirs of a Political Prisoner in South Africa* (1983), Tim Jenkin's *Escape from Pretoria* (1987), Tshenuwani Simon Farisani's *Diary from a South African Prison* (1988) and Caesarina Kona Makoere's *No Child's Play: In Prison under Apartheid* (1988) are but a sample. Breyten Breytenbach's *The True Confessions of an Albino Terrorist* (1984) is a notable exception in that it escaped banning.

In the first half of the twentieth century, life writing accounts by whites heavily outnumbered those by all other race groups. However, as the apartheid machinery became increasingly sophisticated, growing numbers of South Africans across more representative class, gender, and race lines recorded and published their life stories. Documenting the early imbalance most startlingly is Rowse Ushpol's *A Select Bibliography of South African Autobiographies* (1958), which records 143 autobiographies published in English or Afrikaans over more than a century. Judging by the authors' names, out of this total of 143, 142 appear to have been written by white South Africans. In the 1950s only two black South Africans published autobiographies (Peter Abrahams and Ezekiel Mphahlele); by the 1980s, however, if one includes short pieces of testimony that were published in collections, black life writers had become more prolific than white.

In addition to the trend towards a more even racial spread of auto/biographical production, published life writing evinced greater gender diversity as apartheid progressed, even though throughout the period men continued to publish more than women, with white men usually predominating. Of the white women who published their memoirs in the fifties and sixties, most enjoyed some prominence. Sarah Gertrude Millin, the world-famous novelist, published two autobiographies (1941 and 1955); the singer Perla Siedle Gibson published her autobiography in 1964; Moira Lister, who made her name as an actress in London, published her autobiography in 1969. Sometimes the women autobiographers achieved prominence through their husbands or fathers: Marjorie Michael, whose husband was a game hunter and filmmaker, published the aptly titled *I Married a Hunter* (1956); Kathleen Mincher, the adopted daughter of the statesman Jan Smuts, published *I Lived in His Shadow* in 1965; and in 1969 Joyce Waring, whose husband was at the time the only English-speaking cabinet member in the Afrikaner Nationalist Government, published *Sticks and Stones* (a title that points to the hostility of English-speaking South Africans to the apartheid government). Also publishing during this period were those activists who had achieved fame/notoriety in South Africa. First's prison memoir was banned in South Africa, as were Joseph's works, the titles of which point to her embattled status and to intensifying state repression: *If This Be Treason* (1963) and *Tomorrow's Sun: A Smuggled Journal from South Africa* (1966).

Of course, famous personalities continued to publish memoirs throughout the apartheid period: Louwtjie Barnard (the former wife of Christiaan

Barnard, the surgeon responsible for the world's first heart transplant) published *Heartbreak* in 1971; Olympic athlete Zola Budd published *Zola* (with Hugh Eley) in 1989. However, toward the end they were joined by women who were relatively unknown outside their communities. Johannesburg councilor Janet Levine probably received more publicity in her adopted country America than she had done in South Africa. Her autobiography, *Inside Apartheid: One Woman's Struggle in South Africa* (1988), recounts her attempts, within a liberal framework, to undermine the apartheid state. Significantly, in the eighties it appeared that white women were more in evidence as scribes or editors of the stories of apartheid's underdogs than as autobiographers. Among these are Barbara Schreiner, who wrote Frances Baard's story (1986); Beata Lipman, who published interviews with women (*We Make Freedom: Women in South Africa*, 1984); Anne Benjamin and Mary Benson, who compiled Winnie Mandela's autobiographical text from tapes; Janet Hodgson, who attempted to reconstruct a Xhosa woman's story from three surviving letters (*Princess Emma*, 1987);[50] and Suzanne Gordon, who collected the life stories of South African servants (1985). Although the numbers of people concerned are admittedly small (though more than listed here), nevertheless this evidence does seem to indicate an important shift in the mindset of many white South Africans: a sense that the stories that needed to be heard were not their own, and that their most useful contribution would be to facilitate the dissemination of testimony by the oppressed. These mediated testimonial works were important not only as a means to inform the hugely complacent white public about the living conditions of the black majority, but also to assert the gravity of abuses heaped on the victims of apartheid. Black South Africans had for centuries been ignored or been the objects of others' study; now, in these texts, they were positioned as knowing subjects.

The first black South African woman autobiographer was Jabavu (*Drawn in Colour*, 1960, and *The Ochre People*, 1963). After fifteen years, the next autobiographical book with a black woman subject was the somewhat fictionalized life story of the Xhosa woman, "Poppie Nongena." This account, written on the basis of interviews by the white Afrikaans writer Elsa Joubert, was first published in Afrikaans as *Die Swerfjare van Poppie Nongena* (1978) and then translated into English (1980). Although it dramatizes in relentless detail the brutalities of apartheid (and thus a pseudonym was used to protect the identity of the informant, "Poppie"), the book escaped banning because it was hailed by most critics as a story of human tragedy, rather than as a black woman's personal tragedy arising out of the apartheid state's systematic racist assaults on her dignity and rights. After *Poppie*, more and more life stories of black women were published, some in full book-length conventional auto/biographies such as Kuzwayo's well-known *Call Me Woman* (1985); Emma Mashinini's *Strikes Have Followed Me All My Life: A South African Autobiography* (1989); and Phyllis Ntantala's *A Life's Mosaic* (1992) and some as collaborative autobiographies with black women subjects written by white writers. Examples of the latter include *The Diary of Maria Tholo,* written by Carol Hermer (1980) and Miriam Makeba's *Makeba: My Story* (1988), written by James Hall. Black women's memoirs also appeared as short pieces in anthologies like Lesley Lawson and Helene Perold's *Working Women* (1985); the collection edited by Jane Barrett, et al., *Vukani Makhosikazi: South African Women Speak* (1985); Hanlie Griesel's edited volume, *Sibambene: The Voices of Women at Mboza* (1987); and also in deindividuated accounts such as Bozzoli's *Women of Phokeng* (1991) and the quasi-autobiographical but anonymous *Thula Baba* (1987). Some collections did not confine themselves to the testimony of women of particular race groups: Diana Russel's *Lives of Courage* (1989) includes activists of all races, and Barbara Schreiner's anthology of women's prison writings, *A Snake with Ice Water* (1992), includes writings by prisoners of all race groups whose crimes were not solely related to political activism.

Early in the apartheid period the subjects of published autobiographies, whether black or white, usually enjoyed some eminence in their communities and belonged to the professional classes. Both Peter Abrahams and Ezekiel Mphahlele, poverty notwithstanding, belonged to the mission-educated class.[51] Jabavu's background was even more markedly élitist than that of Mphahlele and Peter Abrahams. She belonged to the small Xhosa, mission-educated, and Christian (thus westernized) intellectual class. (Her grandfather was founder and editor of the first black-owned newspaper in South Africa, and her father one of the first black South Africans to be awarded a professorship.) But gradually, notably in the 1980s, the stories of apartheid's most oppressed—the uneducated, unemployed, or blue-collar workers—were, for the first time, being published in significant numbers. There is, for example, the blue-collar worker and trade unionist, Alfred Temba Qabula's *A Working Life, Cruel Beyond Belief* (1989) and Caroline Kerfoot's collection of short testimonies by a diverse range of individuals entitled *We Came to Town* (1985). This trend towards inclusion of ordinary people in the archive could also be seen in printed collections of oral self-representational texts. For instance, where Trevor Cope's *Izibongo: Zulu Praise Poems* (1968) records versions of the *izibongo* (praises) of Zulu heroes, royalty, and chiefs (and a handful of prominent whites), Gunner and Gwala's *Musho: Zulu Popular Praises* (1994) includes those of ordinary Zulu men and women.

In addition to the widely performed vernacular oral poetry—in particular, those of trade unions and of national heroes like King Shaka and Nelson Mandela—there were also performances of western-style biographical and autobiographical dramas. Nat Nakasa's story of the black boxer King Kong Dlamini was reinterpreted in 1959 as the musical *King Kong* (Harry Bloom, 1961), the cast's adventures being recounted in Matshikiza's *Chocolates for My Wife* (1961). Other examples include Stephen Gray's biographical play about Olive Schreiner (1983), and Athol Fugard's autobiographical play, *"Master Harold" . . . and the Boys* (1983b).

As Chris Weedon has argued, the meaning of experience is perhaps the most crucial site of political struggle over meaning since it involves personal, psychic, and emotional investment on the part of the individual. It plays an important role in determining the individual's role as social agent (1987: 79–80). When experience is largely determined—and, for individuals under apartheid, this cannot be overemphasized—by racial classification, it is obvious that the experiences of one individual in a group will be similar in many respects to those of others in the same group (bearing in mind that racism, like most social systems, is not gender neutral). This is true of white South Africans to some extent, although there were important class and gender differences, but it is particularly true of apartheid's victims, whose lives were rigidly controlled by the state. What this means for life writing is that accounts of oppression tend to be remarkably paraphrastic. It also means that the experiences of one victimized individual can serve metonymically as commentary on the lives of millions. In turn, this means that readers who belong to the oppressed masses will readily find their experiences echoed in the testimony of others.

Thus, as the decades rolled on and as apartheid intensified, there was a corresponding increase in the value accorded to purportedly truthful personal narratives by an ever-broadening South African readership. Life writing more frequently addressed a wider black readership, sometimes including those who were themselves only semiliterate. *The Story of Mboma,* by Mboma Dladla and recorded by Kathy Bond (1979), is aimed at an unschooled black readership, as are the almost pamphlet-style account of a foundry worker's life, *The Sun Shall Rise for the Workers* (by Mandlenkosi Makhoba and an anonymous friend, 1984), and the aggregated story of a domestic worker entitled *Thula Baba.* Some of these testimonies, such as Kerfoot's *We Came to Town,* arose out of literacy classes and were designed to be used in such classes. Intending to validate the learners' sense that their lives and those of people whose circumstances were similar were important enough to record and disseminate, such testimonial texts were not overtly political, but they did undermine apartheid's goal to persuade all South Africans, black and white, that black people's lives were unimportant and to keep most black South Africans illiterate and thus part of the unskilled laboring class (and thus no threat to white jobs).

Conversely, the systematic and inexorable erosion of individual difference, the determination of people's lives in accordance with their racial classification, means that the life stories of victims who had all been subjected to the same indiscriminate legalized brutalities can begin to lose their shock value due to repetition.[52] The iterativeness of many of the life stories of the oppressed is also due in part to the fact that many writers chose not to focus on the *distinctiveness* of the subject's experiences, but rather on its *typicality*. This can be seen in a range of texts as divergent as Dugmore Boetie's purported "autobiography," the fanciful *Familiarity Is the Kingdom of the Lost* (1984), Kuzwayo's *Call Me Woman* (1985), Mark Mathabane's *Kaffir Boy* (1986).

By the 1980s and 1990s auto/biography was accorded greater prestige in the academy, and texts such as Breyten Breytenbach's *The True Confessions of an Albino Terrorist*, Christopher Hope's *White Boy Running* (1988), and Rian Malan's *My Traitor's Heart* (1990) won literary awards. Coinciding with a growing readership for life stories was greater ease of having such texts published, often because publishers were also motivated by their own opposition to apartheid. Examples include pioneering South African publishers such as Ravan Press, Skotaville, and Ad Donker; independent periodicals like *Staffrider*; and various publishers abroad, including The Feminist Press and Zed Books.

With greater inclusion of formerly silenced subjects, formal heterogeneity also occurred. Conventional, western-style prose narrative life stories by black South Africans appeared, such as Richard Rive's *Writing Black* (1981) and Frieda Matthews's *Remembrances* (1987); there were about thirty of these published in the eighties. And these were joined by researcher-authored or collaborative records, such as those already mentioned and Tim Keegan's *Facing the Storm: Portraits of Black Lives in Rural South Africa* (1988). Compilations of testimony usually comprise stories of illiterate or semiliterate victims of apartheid, many of whom, like Joanna Masilela in Barrett et al.'s *Vukani Makhosikazi* and *Sibambene*, edited by Griesel (1987), expressed their delight at being able to "make history." At the other end of the formal innovation scale are the self-reflexive—at times, almost deconstructive—experiments by Breyten Breytenbach *(The True Confessions of an Albino Terrorist)* and Lyndall Gordon *(Shared Lives,* 1992). Both Breytenbach and Gordon foreground generic convention in order to question it and to probe the limits of "the truth," a concept which would later gain considerable currency with the institution of the Truth and Reconciliation Commission (see pp. 56–57).

Interestingly, apart from biographies of Nationalist political leaders (usually in Afrikaans), texts supporting apartheid are scarce. Waring's *Sticks and Stones* is a rare example of explicit endorsement of apartheid. Roy Campbell's *Light on Dark Horse* (1951/1971) condemns apartheid but expresses startlingly crude racial prejudices. Marjorie Michael's *I Married a Hunter* is ostensibly apolitical, but expresses views—common among whites of the time—which now seem appallingly arrogant and racist. Some writers, like Meta Orton, reject apartheid but argue nevertheless for the retention of some racist policies. A sample of biographies on—and in support of—apartheid politicians includes John D'Oliviera's on B. J. Vorster (1977), and homages to H. F. Verwoerd (by Marie van Heerden, 1984, and Gert Scholtz, 1974) and P. W. Botha (by Dirk and Johanna de Villiers, c.1984). One little-known autobiographical account by a black South African—Nelson Mandela's nephew, in fact—supports the ultimate goal of the apartheid state to keep South Africa white by confining all black South Africans to ethnically delimited "self-governing" states. "Bantustan" leader Kaizer Matanzima's *Independence My Way* was published in 1976. The year of publication is noteworthy—Transkei having been the first "Bantu homeland" to gain "independence" from South Africa in 1976—as is the publisher: this text was published in Pretoria by the Foreign Affairs Association of the South African government. The extent to which the state influenced the shape of the text or motivated its writer to endorse the creation of unsustainable rural slums for disenfranchised black South Africans is unknown.

While not explicitly supporting apartheid, some South Africans continued to produce life stories that focus on the individual and pay scant attention to the profound impact of institutionalized racism on all lives, black and white. These include obscure texts like Ulf Boberg's *The Boberg Story* (1957), Gordon Forbes's *A Handful of Summers* (1978), E. G. Malherbe's *Never a Dull Moment* (1981), Ernie Duffield's *Through My Binoculars* (1982), and Ruth Gordon's self-published, *Alive, Alive-o!* (1984). All are by white South Africans for whom (it would appear in their memoirs) apartheid was unquestioned. What is signified by the failure of so many whites to address, in their life stories, the extreme political engineering that affected every aspect of their lives is open to interpretation. One can surmise that it was partly due to the effectiveness of apartheid: whites were so insulated from the realities of black people's lives—they were not permitted to enter black townships, and censorship created massive distortions in perceptions of political and social realities. But one must also consider that the apparent disregard of many white auto/biographers of the gross violations of human rights was due to conscious or unconscious racism: the horrors of apartheid for people of other race groups did not impinge on their day-to-day lives because those suffering were simply considered unimportant. Such an attitude was not, however, displayed by all whites or for any of those millions classified as "nonwhite." White South Africans who were compelled to address their peculiar political circumstances include Natie Ferreira, whose bilingual (English and Afrikaans) *The Story of an Afrikaner: Die revolusie van die kinders* (1980) agonizes over his Afrikaner identity, and Malan, whose multiple-award-winning *My Traitor's Heart* is, as the title implies, a guilt-stricken account of a privileged but confused individual. In his autobiographical works published during the apartheid era, Breyten Breytenbach questions all aspects of identity: his African-ness, his South African-ness, his ties to the Afrikaner *volk* and language, his whiteness, and his masculinity. During apartheid, Stephen Gray's *Accident of Birth* (1993) attempts to work through the personal implications of the trauma of the experience of violent crime. The experience, he tells his interviewer, is one which forces him to judge not only the thugs who robbed and assaulted him, but also himself, as a white South African.

Whereas autobiographical attempts by whites during the apartheid period to probe the meaning of race are few, those by blacks are more numerous: Modisane's *Blame Me on History* remains one of the most powerful works anywhere by a black man on the corrosive effects of racism on masculinity. Other texts depicting the erosion of self-esteem by systematic racism include Ezekiel Mphahlele's *Down Second Avenue,* Sindiwe Magona's two-part autobiography, *To My Children's Children* (1990) and *Forced to Grow* (1992), and Shula Marks's compilation, *Not Either an Experimental Doll* (1987), the collection of letters between a Xhosa schoolgirl (under the pseudonym Lily Moya) and a white academic, Mabel Palmer. Some South Africans indicated their refusal to be cowed by their racial classification through the mocking racial epithets in their titles: Breyten Breytenbach refers to himself as an albino; Hope, parodying the dismissive diminutive used for "nonwhite" men, calls himself a white boy; Goonam and Jay Naidoo (1990) call themselves coolies; Mathabane calls himself a kaffir boy.

Auto/biographical Accounts in the New South Africa

The desire for a clean slate is expressed—and perhaps even partly satisfied—in the rhetoric of the "new South Africa."[53] While this implies, incorrectly, that *everything* has changed—for most South Africans racially based disparities in living conditions remain—it does indicate, correctly, that political and legal transformation has been profound: South Africa's new constitution guarantees the protection of human rights and democratic freedoms, and there are growing black ruling and middle classes, as well as a widespread improvement in standards of living in terms of access to electricity, water, schooling, health care, and housing for the poorest of the previously disadvantaged sectors of the population. As a whole, current auto/biographical accounts reflect both the continuities and the changes. Astonishingly, given the fact there are about five times more black South Africans than white, auto/biographical writing with white subjects published in the first six years after the attainment of democracy in 1994 outnumbered that with black subjects by almost three to one (using these racial classifications much as the autobiographers themselves do). From 2000 to 2004 the output was less disproportionate, but still auto/biographical accounts with white subjects were slightly more than double those with black subjects. Overall, however, in the last ten years, the racial imbalance favoring whites reverses the trend manifested in the last decade of apartheid. If we focus on autobiography, the reasons may include the lack of desire or need, on the part of black South Africans, to recall oppression or adjust to political liberation. Those in power may be too busy running the country, while the majority are simply struggling to survive. In addition, oral testimony of victims of racism, published by white researchers, has dwindled, possibly because such work now seems patronizing or appropriative. Exceptions are Kendall's edition of the life of Nthunya, *Singing Away the Hunger* (1996) (see p. 186 ff.); Margaret McCord's *The Calling of Katie Makanya* (1995) (see p. 205 ff.); Wilfred Cibane's *Man of Two Worlds: An Autobiography* (written with the help of Robert Scott, 1998) (see p. 200 ff.); and *Madumo: A Man Bewitched* (Adam Ashforth, 2000): in each of these instances, but most notably in the first three, a significant prior personal relationship existed between the writer and autobiographical subject. There is also Charles van Onselen's award-winning biography, *The Seed Is Mine: The Life of Kas Maine, a South African Sharecropper* (1996). Most probably, however, the decline indicates that oral testimony was indeed perceived—as is stated in the title of Don Mattera's autobiography, *Memory Is the Weapon* (1987)—as a crucial weapon in the struggle; liberation having been achieved, this need no longer exists. It also points to a compulsion, arising out of the transformed political landscape experienced by many white South Africans—expatriates included—to review and question the past and their part in it as apartheid's beneficiaries.

Since 1994 three broad categories of auto/biographical production are discernible. The first group, comprising *personal memoirs,* includes texts by famous figures—sports personalities like Ian McIntosh (2000); media personalities like Felicia Mabuza-Suttle (1999) and Max du Preez (2003); performers like Antony Sher (2001), Patrick Mynhardt (2003), and Pieter-Dirk Uys (2002); writers like Nobel Prize winner J. M. Coetzee, with his autobiographical works *Boyhood* (1997) and *Youth* (2002) as well as those by individuals whose lives have changed dramatically. Some have been changed by illness, like Lin Zimbler (1997), or misfortune, like Victor Vermeulen (2000).[54] Some are the victims of crime, like Alison, who publishes under her first name only, who was raped and stabbed, or hostages of political extremists, like Monique and Kallie Strydom. Of these, a small number barely mention apartheid—Lin Zimbler's *Under the Dragon's Wing*, Mary Holroyd's *Weigh-less Forever* (1997), Gaynor Young's *My Plunge to Fame*—and the one-woman performances ("My Plunge to Fame" and "Gaynor Rising: The Celebration of a Life") which relate to this—and Kate Turkington's *There's More to Life Than Surface* (1998). Given that no black South Africans could be unaffected by racism, these (largely or wholly) apolitical accounts are all written by whites.

The second group, comprising *auto/biographical accounts which recover portions of history or experience suppressed by the apartheid regime,* remains important in post-apartheid South Africa as the full extent of the state's treachery and disinformation comes to light. The millions of black people who were grist to apartheid's mill—the workers who were the driving force of the economy—had to be dehumanized, their history excised, for apartheid to work. Indeed, de Klerk admits as much when he says that the planned forced removal of more than three million people failed to take into account "that human beings, not planning statistics, were involved" (1998:40).

Dramatic works like Fugard's *The Captain's Tiger: A Memoir for the Stage* (1997) look across generations. This quasi-autobiographical play has two plots: the external plot concerns the life of Betty le Roux, the protagonist's mother. Tiger, the protagonist-author, is writing a novel about her life. The internal plot concerns the particularity of Tiger's growth and maturity as a writer. Other post-apartheid autobiographical dramatic works are notable for dealing with the complexities of the protagonists' racialized identities: Lueen Conning's *A Coloured Place* (1998) probes the particularities of being a KwaZulu-Natal colored as opposed to a Cape colored; Rajesh Gopi's unpublished "Out of Bounds" explores the peculiarities of his South African Indian identity. Examples of texts that seek to revise historical records include new editions of previously banned prison accounts such as Lewin's *Bandiet: Out of Jail,* Jenkin's updated *Inside Out: Escape from Pretoria Prison* (2003), and Indres Naidoo's account, told to Albie Sachs, of his imprisonment on Robben Island (*Island in Chains*, 2000). There are also new releases such as Raymond Suttner's *Inside Apartheid's Prison: Notes and Letters of Struggle* (2001) and the biographies of six political prisoners (known as Mati, Mgabela, Mkunqwana, Ngxiki, Sitho, and Keke) collected in *Plain Tales from Robben Island* (ed. Jan K. Coetzee, 2000). Henk van Woerden's biography of Dimitri Tsafendas (2000)—the assassin of H. F. Verwoerd, apartheid's champion—seeks to probe beyond the official verdict of insanity (and a concomitant assurance that politics had nothing to do with the choice of victim) by examining Tsafendas's life, with its uncertainties of racial classification and national identity.

Included in this group of testimonies are the life stories of black South Africans written by whites, such as those of Makanya and Nthunya referred to above. There are also the recently published memoirs of residents of District Six, the Cape Town suburb that was razed to make way for white development: Linda Fortune's *The House in Tyne Street: Childhood Memories of District Six* (1996), Nomvuyo Ngcelwane's *Sala Kahle District Six: An African Woman's Perspective* (1998), and Noor Ebrahim's *Noor's Story* (1999). The extent to which the apartheid state threatened university autonomy at liberal, English-medium institutions is outlined by Stuart Saunders, former University of Cape Town vice-chancellor (*Vice-Chancellor on a Tightrope: A Personal Account of Climactic Years in South Africa*, 2000), and the curtailment of press freedom in liberal English newspapers is recounted by Benjamin Pogrund, a former *Rand Daily Mail* journalist (*War of Words: Memoir of a South African Journalist*, 2000). Max du Preez tells of the lesser-known anti-apartheid struggle carried on by a small group of Afrikaans journalists (*Pale Native: Memories of a Renegade Reporter*, 2003).

The life stories of many anti-apartheid activists have been published since 1994. Maskew Miller Longman published short biographies of political activists in a series called *They Fought for Freedom*. These include books on Chris Hani, David Webster, Dora Tamana, Helen Joseph, James la Guma, Lilian Ngoyi, Mohandas Gandhi, Oliver Tambo, Ruth First, Sol Plaatjie, Steve Biko, Yusuf Dadoo, and Z. K. Matthews. Autobiographies by both Sibongile Mkhabela (*Open Earth & Black Roses*, 2001) and Sifiso Mxolisi Ndlovu's *The Soweto Uprisings: Counter-memories of June 1976* (1998) recall the student uprisings in 1976. Ndlovu's personal recollections of, and collection of newspaper cuttings relating to, the events leading up to the massacre of black students by the police and the military contradicts not only accounts disseminated by the apartheid state but also more recent versions that privilege the new hegemony, the African National Congress (ANC), while suppressing the countermemories of the antiestablishment masses. Pan African Congress (PAC) activist and commander in the Azanian People's Liberation Army Letlapa Mphahlele tells about his life in the freedom struggle (*Child of This Soil*, 2002), as do Raymond Mhlaba (2001), Eddie Daniels (1998), Ronnie Kasrils (1998), Ismail Meer (2002), and Mmutlanyane Stanley Mogoba (2003). Most famous, of course, is Nelson Mandela's autobiography, *Long Walk to Freedom* (coauthored by Richard Stengel). Mandela's autobiography is one of many that tell about apartheid's obverse—the story of the liberation struggle that the apartheid state was able to suppress for so long. Another memoir that documents the subject's involvement with the liberation struggle and later with post-apartheid transformation is Mamphela Ramphele's *A Life* (1995). Dr. Ramphele, a Black Consciousness activist who worked with, and was in love with, Steve Biko, has now risen to a position of international eminence as a director of the World Bank. One feature that distinguishes most of the life stories referred to above from countless others produced during the apartheid era is the situating of the self in the new South Africa and the perceived need to account for one's position in the new dispensation. Ramphele, for instance, is defensive about what some have perceived to be her sell-out to the establishment, her betrayal of the political ideals of the radical left; Nelson Mandela acknowledges that the attainment of democracy, of "the right not to be oppressed," is not in itself sufficient for healing to begin.

Nelson Mandela's cachet cannot be overestimated. It has prompted some who have been associated with him to recount their experiences and the ways in which Mandela's graciousness and dignity forced them to reconsider the racism inherent in white thinking: *Goodbye Bafana,* (1995) by Mandela's jailer, James Gregory, and *One Step behind Mandela* (2000), by his bodyguard, Rory Steyn. The memoirs of his early life by Joe Slovo, Mandela's comrade in Mkhonto we Sizwe, were published posthumously by his widow (*Slovo: The Unfinished Autobiography,* 1995). Slovo's daughter, Gillian, tries to make sense of her parents' lives and her mother's death in *Every Secret Thing* (1997, see p. 315 ff.). Joe Slovo's widow, Helena Dolny, has contributed to what may be the start of a subgenre of reminiscences that are critical of the way the liberation movement has transformed itself into the governing official party. Her account of the scandal surrounding her brief tenure of the director's post with the Land Bank in post-apartheid South Africa (*Banking on Change,* 2001) alleges that some of those now in power are capable of treachery. More ambivalent about the struggle is Gavin Evans. His well-received—but now withdrawn due to a legal wrangle with one person implicated in the narrative—*Dancing Shoes is Dead: A Tale of Fighting Men in South Africa* (2002) recollects his youth inside the amateur boxing ring and as a young member of the ANC underground in the Eastern Cape. Described by one reviewer as a major addition to the literature of activist burnout, Evans expresses ambivalence towards both the heroic years of struggle against apartheid and the compromised realities of post-apartheid South Africa. Another autobiographer critical of the liberation movement is Richard Jürgens, whose *The Many Houses of Exile* (2000) censures both the apartheid state (he served in the apartheid-era South Africa Defense Force) as well as the ANC's treatment of those in exile.

Another English-speaking white male to depict his experiences of compulsory conscription into the apartheid government's military force is Greig Coetzee. His long-running play, *White Men with Weapons,* has won numerous awards (see p. 329ff.). Also involved in supporting the apartheid state by coercion—in the form of compulsory military service for young white men—was Rick Andrew. *Buried in the Sky* (2001) is a collection of anecdotes about the experiences of conscripts in the South African army in the seventies.

The "new South Africa" has also seen publication of the stories of those who were intimately, and by choice, connected with the apartheid state: Riaan Labuschagne's *On South Africa's Secret Service: An Undercover Agent's Story* (2002) describes his fifteen years as an undercover agent for the National Intelligence Service of the apartheid government. There is also the biography of and television documentary on Wouter Basson, head of the apartheid state's chemical and biological warfare program. In *Secrets and Lies: Wouter Basson and South Africa's Chemical and Biological Warfare Programme* (2002), journalist Marlene Burger and Chandre Gould, a researcher for South Africa's Truth and Reconciliation Commission, try to unravel the tangled web of events, people, and companies, stretching over many continents, implicated in South Africa's covert biological warfare program. Jan Breytenbach, a colonel in the permanent force of the apartheid army, was on the opposite side of the apartheid divide from his brother, writer/artist Breyten Breytenbach. Jan Breytenbach has published two autobiographical accounts: both *Eden's Exiles: One Soldier's Fight for Paradise* (1997) and *The Buffalo Soldiers: The Story of South Africa's 32 Battalion* (2002) are personal accounts of South Africa's military involvement in Angola and Namibia. Memoirs of paratroopers in the apartheid defense force have been collected in *Parabat* (ed. Mathew Paul, 2001).

On the fringes, observing the battles fought in defense of apartheid, were press photographers Kevin Carter, Greg Marinovich, Ken Oosterbroek, and Joao Silva. Their horrifying account of the bloodshed in the trouble-torn black townships of the early nineties, *The Bang-Bang Club: Snapshots from a Hidden*

War (2000), demonstrates that the devastations of apartheid affected not only black South Africans and activists but also those who witnessed the brutalities.

The third group of post-apartheid life writing includes auto/biographies in which *the auto/biographical subject attempts to adjust to a new political dispensation.* Some of these auto/biographies can be seen to be direct reactions to the collapse of the apartheid regime. Others are less obviously political; they explore the difficulties of achieving reconciliation between contradictory cultural and philosophical paradigms of African and settler worlds and grapple with the intersections of power, history, truth, and the insertion of the self within such networks.

Some texts represent attempts to reconcile the African and European worlds: whereas William Makgoba's *Mokoko; The Makgoba Affair* (1997) and Cibane's *Man of Two Worlds* are not primarily concerned with personal transmutation (unsurprisingly, since the colonized have always been obliged to adapt to the hegemony), Australian-born academic Ashforth's auto/biographical study of Madumo (2000) depicts the difficulties a young Soweto resident has in straddling the often irreconcilable realities of African tradition and globalizing modernity. Guy Butler's biography of three nuns (*The Prophetic Nun*, 2000) likewise explores the cross-fertilization between Euro-focused and indigenous traditions.

In the past decade it seems that an uncommonly large number of life stories evince uncertainty and questioning and also greater formal freedom. Political change has prompted many to seek to understand their role in apartheid and to reconcile their European heritage and white privilege with their identity as Africans. In his life story, conservationist Ian Player reverses the cliché of the white man bringing enlightenment to Africa; gradually overcoming his "civilized" European norms, he absorbs the wisdom of his illiterate Zulu mentor. And many South Africans are striving to measure up to the ideals of the new South Africa. The subjects in the autobiographies by Nicky Arden (1996), and Wilhelm Verwoerd (grandson of the architect of apartheid) (1996, also see p. 366ff.), Penny (1997), Peggy Norton (1997), Breyten Breytenbach (1998), and Krog (1998 and 2003) have each achieved a measure of transcendence in opening themselves up to new models of truth and negotiating new kinds of selves, without the defining and confining racial straightjackets of apartheid. It is not that they are wishing the racism of the past away, but they are now questioning their racialized identities, usually within the context of the effort to redefine national identity.

This outpouring of white auto/biographical accounts suggests that many whites are experiencing crises of identity as they reconceptualize the context in which their own narratives are embedded. The stories they might previously have told of themselves may now seem narrow or distorted. Life writing and self-representation in the new democratic nation often evince a compulsion to take into account the stories others have to tell about the subject and about whites in general, as well as broader narratives of a shared national destiny.

Much of the recent travel writing mentioned on p. 17 can be situated in this group of memoir-as-self-interrogation. Interestingly, the post-apartheid travel memoirs of South Africans are all written by whites, and most employ the genre to explore the land of their birth or the continent of Africa—closed to white South Africans during apartheid—but also the perceiving/narrating self. In *The Whiteness of Bones* Penny recounts her travels in Africa and problematizes her racialized identity and her liberal convictions. Breyten Breytenbach *(Dog Heart)* returns to his homeland to probe the elusiveness of personal and national identities. Leaning more towards adventure travel writing are Justin Fox *(With Both Hands Waving: A Journey through Mozambique, 2002)* and Kingsley Holgate *(Cape to Cairo: One Family's Adventures along the Waterways of Africa, 2002)*, whereas veteran news correspondent John Ryan *(One Man's Africa, 2002)* recounts his experiences in Africa over the last forty years, and expatriate Stephen Taylor (2000) follows in the footsteps of legendary missionary Livingstone to find out how whites have fared in post-independence Africa.

Another trend not previously evident in apartheid autobiography is that of the (usually only temporarily) returning expatriate. Expatriate South Africans who were to some extent prompted by political change to return to the land of their birth are Arden (1996), Justin Cartwright (1996), Nixon (1999), Prue Smith (2000), and Donald Woods (2000). In *The Spirits Speak* Arden recounts how, in training to become a *sangoma* (a traditional African healer and diviner), she resolves the conflict between contradictory value systems by yielding to African traditions.

While many whites seek accommodation in the new South Africa in their memoirs, not all engage in profound self-scrutiny. De Klerk exonerates Nationalists as "products of [their] time and circumstances" (1998:15). His narrative of the principled dismantling of apartheid is, however, undermined by Jacques Pauw *(Into the Heart of Darkness, 1997)* and de Kock, who reveal secret governmental involvement in torture, murder, gun-running, fraud, and theft.

De Kock's book apparently attempts to publicize his Truth and Reconciliation Commission (TRC) amnesty application. Many other narratives also arose in response to the Commission. There are the memoirs of commissioners Desmond Tutu (the chairperson) (1999), Alex Boraine (deputy chairperson) (2000), and Wendy Orr (2000), as well as the angry record of TRC investigator Zenzile Khoisan (with K. K. Rolfes, 2001), and the auto/biographical study of Eugene de Kock (and herself) by TRC psychologist Pumla Gobodo-Madikizela. George Bizos's call for understanding for perpetrators in *No One to Blame?* (1998) emerges from his position of difference from—and superiority to—Afrikaner Nationalists. On the other hand, similar calls by reporter on the Truth and Reconciliation Commission Krog (see *Country of My Skull*), and TRC researcher Verwoerd (see *My Winds of Change*) emerge from positions of conflicted identification with—and rejection of—Afrikaner nationalism. Krog and Verwoerd must negotiate shame and guilt to achieve self-reconciliation and the acceptance of their (reconstituted) Afrikaner identities. Verwoerd's is a typical conversion narrative, his conversion being spiritually motivated but political in content. His struggle is principally a clash between regimes of truth, since the truths of Afrikaner nationalism, built on mythical desire-driven versions of history and an eccentric Afrikaner Calvinist piety, had to be replaced by truths based on what he perceives to be a truly Christian humility and an acknowledgement of the evils of apartheid.

Focusing on the difficulties of the early years of democracy is poet and academic Stephen Watson. A *Writer's Diary* (1997) seeks an intensely personal, introspective mode, but the realities of contemporary South Africa intrude. Some South Africans resent what they see as the intrusion of other Africans into the new nation. Whereas South Africa's borders were fiercely policed during apartheid, since 1994 small numbers of Africans from the rest of the continent have been entering South Africa. *We Came for Mandela: The Cultural Life of the Refugee Community in South Africa* (ed. Keith Adams, 2001) is a collection of essays, poems, stories, and photographs written and taken by a diverse group of refugees in South Africa. *Finding Mr Madini* ("directed by" Morgan, 2000) gathers together the stories of South Africans and Africans who are homeless in Johannesburg. Exploring the seedy sides of life in post-apartheid South Africa are Van Wyk (1999, 2001; also see p. 395ff.), Zinhle Mdakane (2001), and Zazah Khuzwayo (2004) in their accounts of homelessness, drug and alcohol abuse, prostitution, and the AIDS pandemic. Mamphela Ramphela's *Steering by the Stars: Being Young in South Africa* (2002) explores the post-apartheid experiences of the youth of New Crossroads (an environment characterized by violence and alcoholism) near Cape Town. Ramphele finds that constitutional rights of the child are meaningless to the children of New Crossroads: corporal punishment, physical abuse, and rape are common, and she is scathing in her criticism of the ANC government's inaction.

Responding to changed conditions in the new South Africa (and often cutting in their criticism of the ANC government) are religious and other community workers who are contributing to a new form and function of auto/biographical practice: they work in poor communities and help dying AIDS sufferers to compile "memory boxes" aimed at filling the memory gap for children and others dear to them who will be left behind when they die. There are also those HIV-positive people—or those who fear having become infected like rape victim Charlene Smith (2001, 2002)—who have published their testimonies. Jane Fox's biography of young Nkosi Johnson, now deceased, as well as the autobiographical texts by Blaise Koch (2002) and the individuals who told their stories in *Living Positively* (eds. Susan Fox and Gisele Wulfson, 2000), by Charmayne Broadway (1998), and by activist Uys (2002) all point towards what is likely to become a new subgenre around HIV/AIDS in post-apartheid auto/biography. More HIV/AIDS-awareness-raising accounts, such as the online RedRibbon diary project endorsed by Metropolitan Life Insurance and the South African Business Coalition on HIV/AIDS,[55] will doubtless follow, since it is estimated that more than 20 percent of the South African population is HIV-positive.

THEMATIC AND THEORETICAL ISSUES IN SOUTHERN AFRICAN AUTO/BIOGRAPHY: AN OVERVIEW

The growing interest in auto/biographical accounts in southern Africa is manifested in a variety of approaches implicitly or explicitly associated with certain theoretical assumptions and emphasizing different aspects of the genre and phases in its production and reception. This section of the introduction systematizes some of the views explored in the interviews and links them to theoretical issues pertaining to auto/biographical practice. The focus is on the conditions conducive to the production of auto/biography, the actual production of it, the themes and textual characteristics of various auto/biographical accounts, and their dissemination and impact.

Conditions Conducive to Auto/biographical Practices

Several contributors to this collection discuss the conditions that allow auto/biographical practices to flourish and the extent to which these conditions actually exist in southern Africa. Among the enabling conditions are cultural, sociopolitical, and psychological factors, with specific topics including the relationship between a culture of individualism and auto/biographical practices; the impact of civil liberties, such as freedom of expression and movement; and the role of transparency of the self, self-awareness, and self-reflexivity in the production of auto/biographical accounts.

Cultural Preconditions: Individualism and Collectivism

Autobiography and biography are widely characterized as practices embedded in and reproducing the cultural values and practices of individualism and introspection. These values are often associated with modern European notions of the subject, for which Descartes' autobiographical *Discourses* and *Meditations* and Rousseau's *Confessions* are emblematic.[56] It is also the belief propagated by Georges Gusdorf (1980) in his influential essay "Conditions and Limits of Autobiography." This widely accepted view is represented in this collection by Gray, who agrees that "there is a link between autobiography and the western concept of the highly developed individual ego" (see p. 386). It also informs Coullie's question to Vanitha Chetty about the gender system in conservative Indian communities and its "potential for individualization called for by narrative autobiography" (see p. 300).[57] The focus on a discernable individual whose life is different from others' is indeed one of the features that customarily distinguishes auto/biography from history, and the assumption that there is a correlation between individualism and auto/biography may be confirmed by auto/biographical accounts that foreground uniqueness and individualism.[58] Rive, for example, opens his autobiography with the question "Is my life then unique that it warrants an historical account of its own—albeit selected?" which he answers as follows: "All lives are unique, and so many millions of others in South Africa and other countries have shared experiences as important or unimportant as mine. But these experiences which I describe are unique to me and to the way I respond to them and the way I articulate them" (1981:1). However, as several of the contributions to this collection suggest, perceptions of uniqueness and individualism as precondition to the flourishing of auto/biographical practices are only one side of the coin.

Many of the interviews also suggest the possibility that auto/biographical practice can thrive in collectivist cultures. This is reflected in the responses of authors who experience their identity in relational terms, those who have been persecuted as members of a collective, those who draw on collective identity as a source of support, and those who see their auto/biographical accounts as an extension of their engagement in collective struggle. To turn to Appiah's (1996:97) image of collective identity as a script, one could say that these authors closely write their own narrative identities into the narrative identities of the collectives with which they wish or are forced to associate. One prominent representative of this is Dennis Brutus, who asserts, "it is possible to be sufficiently in a community not to need to assert an individual identity and not to be particularly aware of oneself as a distinct individual." According to this view, collective identity need not contradict auto/biographical practice. On the contrary, as a politically engaged poet who advocates the case of a silenced collective, Brutus speaks in the representative voice. "Rather than asserting any kind of uniqueness," he says, regarding himself, that he is "a voice of a community" and concludes that "I speak their wordless woe" (see p. 154).[59] Similar attitudes are expressed by Es'kia Mphahlele (see p. 245) and by David Wolpe, who survived the extermination camp of Dachau before emigrating to South Africa.[60] Wolpe, for example, sees his autobiography as an affirmation of the value of his membership to a collective ethnic and cultural identity (see p. 360).[61] And the *imbongi* Zolani Mkiva even states, "In a sense I don't represent myself as Zolani, but I represent my forebears. It is my forebears who tell me what to say" (see p. 135). In contrast to these views on the indissoluble links between the auto/biographical account of an individual and the collective, Manganyi offers a psychobiographical one.[62] Citing his auto/biography of Es'kia Mphahlele as an example, Manganyi believes that even when the subject of a narrative is an individual life and even when a protagonist refrains from claims to represent a collective, "their personal troubles are a resplendent mirror of the public issues of our day" (see p. 162).

This contrast between the enabling conditions of individualism and collectivism creates the erroneous impression that we are dealing with two mutually exclusive possibilities. That this is not the case, but that these two apparently opposite positions are internally linked to each other, is evident from a range of considerations. To begin with, various aspects of individualism and collectivism can be distinguished. This makes it possible to be an individualist in certain respects but a collectivist in others. For example, living a distinct life that is different from other lives can be reconciled with at least two forms of collectivism, namely, collective action and the collective holding of property. Furthermore, if we grant that individual identity is informed by and expressed in—among other things—language and culture, then the uniqueness of a specific life can be sketched only by drawing on the reservoir of a shared symbolic order in which individual and collective experiences circulate. To the extent that we are individuated through our initiation into the shared medium of symbolic culture—what Brown and Kiguli refer to as "the cultural currency of the society" (see p. 132)—individual and collective identities are internally connected to each other. This shared symbolic order makes it both necessary and possible for authors to "tap into a tradition" (see Haarhoff, p. 258) in order to find a language to describe and interpret their personal experiences which can then be shared communicatively with others. Furthermore, as Dilthey (1970:242–251) suggested, and as mentioned on pp. 1–4, auto/biographical accounts commonly exist on a double axis. On the "vertical" intrasubjective axis, the subject seeks to create a narrative in which one aspect of her or his own life is integrated with other aspects of that life. On the "horizontal" intersubjective axis the subject seeks to create a narrative in which her or his life is integrated with the lives of others whom the narrator has encountered. This double axis is always present, but, as the interviews on *Group Portrait* (see p. 409) show, it is especially visible in accounts of collectives and significant others and can also become a structuring device, as Morgan explains (see p. 438).[63]

Finally, there is abundant evidence for the congeniality of individualist and collectivist aspects in southern African cultures and its conduciveness to auto/biographical accounts. One striking example is provided by Kuzwayo's autobiography *Call Me Woman*. In addition to providing ample evidence of an individual engaged in collective action, the structure of the book also takes the shape of a praise poem for other women (Coullie 1996). Her auto/biographical account also sits comfortably with her commitment to African humanism mentioned on p. 5. This is a view shared by Verwoerd, who describes *My Winds of Change* as "a reflection of my relational concept of self" (see p. 369) and perceptively embroidered upon by Lyndall Gordon (1992:88), who remarks, "Our pasts are laden with collaboration, the unrecorded action of shared lives."

Civil Liberties: Freedom of Expression

The civil liberty most closely associated with a thriving auto/biographical practice is freedom of expression. It seems to be such an obvious enabling condition of auto/biography that it hardly warrants scrutiny. Yet when looked at more closely, the unevenness of freedom of expression explains several features of southern African auto/biographical practice. Restrictions on freedom of expression—whether imposed by the state, patriarchy, or any other formal and informal systems of control—may serve as an explanation to those who believe that auto/biographical practice in southern Africa is rather meager. But these restrictions may also be used by those who believe that auto/biography in the region is flourishing to explain why this is the case. The monitoring and censoring of speech—so the second group of arguments would run—aims at silencing the outcry against human rights abuses. As was pointed out above, narratives about everyday life in southern Africa inevitably reflected these injustices of apartheid, thereby automatically making them a form of resistance writing. Such resistance was answered by greater curbs on freedom of speech, which in turn triggered a greater desire to publicize the injustices, followed by further restrictions (Mante Mphahlele 2002). The statistics mentioned earlier confirm to what extent restrictions on the freedom of speech in southern Africa prevented the publication of critical auto/biographies locally. At the same time the increased pressure that resulted from gagging was vented elsewhere. The links to liberation and independence movements in other parts of Africa and the world, along with the possibility of publication outside the region, explains both the boom in resistance auto/biographies and the fact that they were more often published and circulated outside southern Africa.

Freedom of Movement

One civil liberty whose impact on auto/biographical accounts is considered less often is freedom of movement. Given the connections between personal identity and the specific natural and social environments in which authors are situated (a point neglected by Benhabib [see pp. 3–4 above] and other social interactionists), it may be assumed that auto/biographical accounts thrive when authors can sustain their connection to these spaces.[64] This is certainly the view expressed by Mkiva when he asserts that "I draw my inspiration greatly and really from where I grew up . . . no fortnight . . . must end without me touching down at my home. I believe that's where my spear is, that's where my spear must be sharpened from time to time. I must go and sit in the manure, and grow for some time, so that I come out as a fresh tiger, biting like no other animal you have ever seen" (see p. 145). As Dorian Haarhoff's examples from Namibia also show, the different landscapes of the region offer specific symbolic resources for the interpretation of the self.[65] Furthermore, our location on the southern tip of Africa at the intersection of routes across the Atlantic and Indian Oceans accounts for a distinctive social landscape that has been shaped by the interactions of people from Africa, Asia, and Europe. The fact that this collection focuses on a specific region means that the contributors can be expected to grapple with questions regarding the extent to which the liberty to relate freely to these geographic and social spaces is a condition for the flourishing of auto/biographical accounts.

A consideration of the relationships between auto/biography and place must address the fact that freedom of movement has been curtailed in several ways in the southern African region. These restrictions range from incarceration to house arrest, banishment, forced removal, and exile.[66] Because they sever the narrator from the natural and social landscapes in which aspects of her or his identity may thrive, such dislocations unleash major crises in identity and have a decisive impact on auto/biographical practice. While condemning forced removals, incarceration, and exile in the strongest terms, it must nevertheless be acknowledged that several contributors suggest that the emergence of so many auto/biographical accounts from such extreme experiences of dislocation points to the conclusion that the severity of the rupture and the need to deal with absence may also serve as enabling conditions for a significant number of auto/biographical accounts. Several interviewees touch on the relationships between auto/biography and incarceration (Brutus, Slovo, Wolpe) and exile (Manganyi) and explore the nature of both inward-looking, self-reflective passages as well as calls for political action found in such narratives. A topic which they do not explore, but which may be of significance, is the effect of such dislocation on the representation of the distant spaces narrators have come from and the extent to which distance in space and in time may result in an "idealized concept of what one imagines the past to have been" (Rive 1981:74; Wicomb 2002:182–183).

While some authors, such as Es'kia Mphahlele and Mkiva, consider the southern African location and space essential to their identity, exile offers others, such as Peter Abrahams, Breyten Breytenbach, and Brutus a source for a cosmopolitan identity and internationalism.[67] Thus Brutus, who has experienced both imprisonment and exile, remarks, "The roots they were trying to sever were ones I had refused to develop" (see p. 155). These views on location and dislocation invite readers of the collection to compare and contrast colonial travel writing and the auto/biographical accounts of settlers, émigrés, and exiles who grapple with conundrums of identity through the question "Where do I belong?" (see Wolpe, p. 361). Increasingly, in dealing with the legacy of apartheid, there has also been a growing awareness that the significance some auto/biographical accounts give to place can be tied to issues of economic justice and land restitution (see Jacobs and Meyer, pp. 426–427) and to attempts to negotiate the borders of the new South African nation.

Psychological Preconditions: Transparency, Self-awareness, Self-reflexivity

Finally, popular opinion considers psychological preconditions such as transparency of the self, self-awareness, self-reflexivity, and the mental coherence to communicate these as essential preconditions for the production of auto/biographical accounts (Eakin:2001). Similar assumptions are also expounded in Enlightenment notions of the subject and knowledge, and to a certain extent seep into Manganyi's understanding of both biography and psychotherapy (see p. 167). One aspect disregarded by these approaches is mentioned by Benhabib (see p. 3), namely, that knowledge of the self is not produced simply through introspection, but also through encounters with others who sometimes correct our views of ourselves. Another aspect these approaches tend to disregard is the opaqueness and elusiveness of the self.

The validity of these assumptions about the psyche and the metaphysics of presence that inform them are problematized by psychoanalytical and poststructuralist approaches alike (Coullie 1991) and extensively probed in Breyten Breytenbach's *The True Confessions of an Albino Terrorist*. The problematization by psychoanalysis and the deconstruction of transparency and coherence under "normal" conditions is further compounded by the experience of trauma (Felman and Laub 1991; LaCapra 2001; Gobodo-Madikizela 2003:10). It is to be expected that the pervasiveness of trauma in southern Africa has significant implications for the existence and the nature of auto/biographical accounts from the region and that statements such as that by Van Wyk (see p. 397) that "apartheid has basically destroyed my ability to remember and to communicate" have far-reaching ramifications for auto/biography aimed at communicating events stored in memory.

Contrary to the assumption that the psychological ruptures caused by trauma disable auto/biographical practice, many contributors show how trauma and the need to come to terms with it serve as catalysts for auto/biography (Veit-Wild 1996). In a context of widespread trauma, auto/biographical accounts may offer an avenue through which individuals seek to exorcise the past as well as reconcile themselves with their tormentors and victims.[68] Thus Lütge's questions to Greig Coetzee—"Is autobiography for you an exorcism of the ghosts of the past? And was your intention to provide a release for your audience?"—are relevant to many other auto/biographers. Equally relevant is Coetzee's reply, "I suppose it was an exorcism of ghosts, although it wasn't conscious" (see p. 343). The significance of auto/biography for dealing with trauma is especially evident in the oral narratives presented to the Truth and

Reconciliation Commission.[69] Its effects are also palpable in, for example, Krog's *Country of My Skull*.[70] Rather than hinder auto/biography, these examples show that trauma can trigger it. Former Mozambican Ester Lee describes (as do other contributors) the writing of her auto/biographical account as a probing in order to understand personal and social trauma and loss (see Lee, pp. 303 ff.). According to Haarhoff (p. 256), "autobiography is a vital way of reconnecting to your identity especially in an authoritarian society where identity has been suppressed in favor of the powerful official version of who you are (a race, gender or religious classification)." And several contributors (Gray, pp. 389–393, and Magona, p. 229) attest to its therapeutic effect—either by working through trauma or staving off its aftereffects.[71]

While some minimal absolute preconditions for auto/biographical accounts may be identifiable—recourse to symbolic systems that enable interpretation and communication, for example—the foregoing discussion suggests that it is difficult to make categorical claims regarding enabling conditions in general. As the contributors' comments show, individualism, freedom of expression and movement, as well as the assumption of a self-transparent subject may be extrapolations from an idealized modern male European bourgeois notion of the subject and the nature of narratives of such a subject's life, rather than preconditions for the production of auto/biographical accounts as such. Rather, the comments on enabling conditions for auto/biography in southern Africa suggest that difficult conditions may even promote auto/biographical practice or give it a distinctive quality.

Production of Auto/biographies

The assumption that a general culture of individualism is a precondition for the flourishing of auto/biography is often coupled with the image of the introspective author who, like Descartes, locks himself in a room in order to produce the truth about himself out of himself (*Discourse:*116, *Meditations:*24). This view is probably more widely held than the actual practice of autobiography justifies. Whereas it cannot be denied that some autobiographies are produced in a Cartesian fashion, it is certainly not always the case. Instead, evidence from the interviews alerts us to the involvement of a host of people in the making of auto/biographical accounts, thus challenging monological notions of authorship and the subject that are associated with European Modernity.[72]

Several reasons for collaboration on auto/biographical accounts emerge in the interviews. Greig Coetzee (see p. 339) mentions the nature of the medium of self-representational theater as an explanation for the involvement of a director. In other cases the constraints flowing from illiteracy or semiliteracy mean that to publish, the person telling the story needs the mediation of an amanuensis. This is the case with a number of auto/biographies stemming from literacy classes (Kerfoot 1985), worker auto/biographies such as those included in Barrett, et al.'s *Vukani Makhosikazi,* and Joubert's *Die Swerfjare van Poppie Nongena.*[73] It is also part and parcel of the anthropological and ethnographic enterprise and oral history evident in Shostak's *Nisa,* in Hermer's *The Diary of Maria Tholo,* and in Van Onselen's *The Seed Is Mine.* However, as Chetty's remarks remind us (see pp. 292–294), the mediating presence of editors and publishers can be overbearing, causing some critics to question the authenticity of the life narrative rendered thus.[74] It may be in reaction to such perceived meddling, as well as a pursuit of cultural purity, that Mkiva felt the need to be both the producer and director of his own work "so that it does not lose the gist of its Africanness" (see p. 142).

There are also quite different cases, such as Margaret McCord's *The Calling of Katie Makanya,* Nthunya's *Singing Away the Hunger,* and Cibane's *Man of Two Worlds,* where textual collaboration mirrors an intimacy in personal relationships or in the last example, even possibly a symbiosis. Coullie (p. 30) and Farr (see pp. 186–189) refer to the increasing distaste for patronizing attitudes and skepticism about the possibility of speaking on behalf of others, as well as demands for transparency and accountability that have edged some ghostwriters out of the closet. And, as prefaces (McCord) and afterwords (Kendall in Nthunya) and the interviews with Cibane and Scott (see pp. 200–201) especially reveal, many white scribes are weary of accusations of appropriation. The emergence of a new generation of collaborative texts, where black southern Africans are the scribes (Mhlaba and Mufamadi 2001 and Gobodo-Madikizela 2003), not only reflects social changes that affect auto/biographical practice, but also promises new issues for theoretical consideration.[75]

Surprisingly, there is still little awareness of the ways in which a virtue can be made out of the necessity of collaboration by using the collaboration to explore the possibility of understanding across differences and perform relational notions of the person expounded by feminists, social interactionists, and the philosophy of *ubuntu.*[76] Furthermore, there is still no comprehensive study of collaborative auto/biography which explores the differences between advocatory texts, where the writing author speaks on behalf of the oral narrator (as in Pringle's "Makanna's Gathering" and "Bechuana Boy" [1911] and Joubert's *The Long Journey of Poppie Nongena*); texts in which the writing author plays a mediating role (as with Babenia Naidoo and Ian Edwards [1995] or Mhlaba and Mufamadi); and truly collaborative texts in which the participants are on a comparatively equal footing and also write about each other (as in *Finding Mr Madini,* directed by Morgan).

The Text

Various aspects of the auto/biographical text itself are discussed in the interviews. These include questions as to what constitutes an auto/biographical account and how an auto/biographical text is related to its paratext, that is, its marginalities and externalities. Discussions cover the themes broached in the different auto/biographical accounts; the participants explore the criteria employed to establish what should be included and what left out and speculate on the relationship between fact and fiction in auto/biographical accounts.

What Constitutes an Auto/biographical Text?

Several contributions touch on this unresolved—or maybe even irresolvable—question, and related issues regarding how far the category of the auto/biographical text can be stretched and how the auto/biographical text relates to its paratext.[77] It is now a commonplace in studies of the verbal arts—a view with which we have already expressed our agreement (see p. 8)—that the term *text* should embrace both written and oral form. Rather than thereby putting an end to the discussion, however, we have seen that this opens up various questions bearing on the relationship between the two. As both Magona (see p. 223) and Joubert (see p. 181) remark, this relationship raises issues such as the different discursive conventions regulating face-to-face communication as opposed to those regulating auto/biographies in print, and how these differences are negotiated in the transformation of the spoken into the written word in published auto/biographies based on oral evidence. Similar issues are raised by a practice whose tendencies run in the opposite direction, prioritizing the oral over the written, namely, *izibongo*. Although he draws on both oral and written sources for his praise poetry, Mkiva, for example, claims that "the oral tradition propels the modern" (see p. 141).

Generous use of the term "auto/biographical account" in this book has stretched the category *text* beyond the verbal to include actual *performances* of the persona by actors such as Greig Coetzee and Uys and *izimbongi* like Mkiva and Yali-Manisi. The significance of the visual in the performance of identity has moved Mkiva and Uys to supplement print matter and commercial sound recordings with video. It is open to debate how much these visuals, which form an integral part of these particular auto/biographical accounts, and their paratexts can be interpreted adequately in terms of textual analyses (cf. Ricoeur

1981:145–164, 197–221). As the interview (see pp. 409 ff.) with the curator Paul Faber, the author Rayda Jacobs, and the photographer David Goldblatt, all involved in the exhibition *Group Portrait*, show, this issue is particularly pertinent to multi-media approaches to auto/biography. In other words, many potential avenues of inquiry calling for closer interdisciplinary collaboration among scholars of text, performance, and the visual are opening up in southern Africa.

Themes

The auto/biographical themes treated here range from aspects of childhood and growing up, to relations to others, political repression and activism, gender, and work, to name but a few. As can be expected, the self is one of the central themes. This concern with a "heightened self rather than merely the presence of self" (see Lütge, p. 337), should not, however, be equated with self-conceit. Rather, as the discussions reveal, authors grapple with how to express their lives, whether they have led public and celebrity lives (see Thembela, p. 148 ff.), less conspicuous lives (see Magona, p. 226), or wish to convey delicate private issues (see Van Wyk, p. 395 ff. and Gray, p. 379–380, 390). Each category allows for different themes to be treated in distinctive ways.[78]

As elsewhere, the lives of celebrities and the relationship between official history, auto/biographical accounts of public figures, and the heroic is a common topic in southern African auto/biography.[79] While some autobiographies and biographies of public figures, such as Sam Nujoma's *Where Others Wavered* (2001)[80] and de Klerk's *The Last Trek,* seek to legitimate power, other biographies such as Stephen Chan's *Robert Mugabe: Life of Power and Violence* seek to delegitimate power.[81] In auto/biographical accounts of public figures, such as Nelson Mandela's *Long Walk to Freedom;* Paul Fauvet and Marcelo Mosse's *É proibido por algemas nas palavras: Carlos Cardoso e a Revolução Moçambicana* (2003), and Anne Marie du Preez Bezdrob's *Winnie Mandela: A Life* (2003), the heroic plays an important part.[82] By contrast, Gillian Slovo (pp. 318–321) seeks to disclose the ordinary in the public figures of her mother and father, Ruth First and Joe Slovo, which has the effect of signaling to the "ordinary" reader that acting heroically is within their reach too. At the same time Gillian Slovo wants to offer an alternative to the notion of the heroic that emerges when auto/biographical accounts use political events and traumas to chart out a life; she maps her narrative according to the very different trajectory of personal memory.[83] This is a new option that Nixon sees arising at the specific historical juncture after resistance. "Since South Africa's democratic turn," he notes, "a space has opened up for writing that probes the tensions between collective and personal commitments" (see p. 279), between the heroic and the quotidian.

Besides such unveiling of the everyday aspects of heroic lives, other contributors emphasize the need for publications about less conspicuous lives and the issues that engage them and for this to be done in a register different from the heroic. This is virtually a hallmark of collaborative auto/biography. It is particularly evident in Katie Makanya's request that Margaret McCord write her life story because "there are so many things he [Margaret McCord's father and Katie Makanya's former employer, Dr. James McCord] hasn't written about and now I want you to write my story and tell the things I remember."[84] According to Margaret McCord, "there was more to it than simply a desire for her own story to be told." Although Makanya was proud of the hospital, she was "more interested in people than in institutions and she wanted stories told about the patients" (see p. 206). Such accounts about less conspicuous persons are necessary for two reasons, one epistemological, the other political. According to Uys, who focuses on the former, there is no knowledge "without the texture of individual stories" (see p. 354). According to Nixon, who focuses on the latter, the need for "more angular memoirs, memoirs that deal with hidden histories, mobile geographies, familial peculiarities" (see p. 280) is tied to a notion of democratization, which means access to and participation in a public sphere open to all. Nuttall (1998) makes a similar point.

Since discrimination, resistance, and liberation affected the lives of less conspicuous individuals as much as public heroes, it comes as no surprise that the quotidian is a recurring theme in many of the interviews. Currently there seems to be an evolving awareness of injustices other than racism, including ethnic intolerance, sexism, homophobia, economic exploitation, and a host of other hurts that occurred independently and in combination with each other. This is evident in AIDS narratives (Fox and Wulfson 2000; and Smith 2001) and in narratives of gender abuse (as in Slaughter 2002; Broadway 1998; Alison 1998; Lottering 2002; Neville 1997) and prostitution (Khuzwayo 2001; and Mdakane 2001).

Besides the impact of public concerns as they have traditionally been understood on the lives of inconspicuous persons, the foregrounding of apartheid and anti-apartheid themes may be making way for topics previously considered too private and delicate for publication. This is evident in the praise the Noma Award jury bestowed on Elinor Sisulu's biography of Walter and Albertina Sisulu for "[b]ringing together the personal and political"[85] and even more so in texts such as Johnny Masilela's *Deliver Us from Evil* (1997; also see Meyer 1999), the opening of Rrekgetsi Chimeloane's *Whose Laetie Are You? My Sowetan Boyhood* (2001), and most of Joseph Marble's *Ek, Joseph Daniel Marble* (1999). These examples range from a subtle exploration of the emergence of sexual awareness in urban black boys to the flaunting of sexual violence. This break with the evasion of the delicate and sexually explicit are also hallmarks of Gray's *Accident of Birth* and Van Wyk's *Man-bitch*, which do not avoid confronting the politics of intimacy (see pp. 379 ff. and 395 ff.).

Criteria for Inclusion

What should be included in a specific auto/biographical account and what should not is a consideration that confronts all practitioners of the craft and on which critics conduct endless debates. Rousseau's (1953:65) claim that his *Confessions* are true because nothing is left out is thought by many to be a ruse, even an excuse to dish up those saucy details that some readers consider to be of little interest. Defying Rousseau's criterion, Rive begins his autobiography with an explanation of why he does not tell everything: "This is essentially a selective autobiography, since I have judiciously and purposefully selected the autobiographical material I am prepared to write about. I do not want to tell all, since I cannot tell all. Some incidents I have genuinely forgotten. Others I have glossed over. Still others are locked away in that private part of my world which belongs only to myself and perhaps one or two intimates. Many other incidents are too mundane and dreary to record" (1981:1). The practical impossibility of "captur[ing] everything that happened in your life" (see Mphahlele p. 244; see also Lessing p. 233) means that the aesthetic, ethical, and generic criteria of selection become important. Precisely because not everything can be told, what is actually told and what is not become crucial, with both the told and the untold becoming interesting precisely because they are disclosed or kept back.

Focusing on the aesthetic, Es'kia Mphahlele, Gray, and Greig Coetzee consider what Pratt calls the criterion of "tellability" (1977:132–151) to be most appropriate when deciding what to include. Because, in contrast to Magona (see p. 226), Greig Coetzee considers everyday life quite boring, he asserts the need for "editing the truth, not to cut out or distort it, but to get rid of all that stuff that's saying nothing about anything" (see p. 338). The criteria about what to include and exclude are obviously coupled to the type of account the author or editor considers it to be, whether a confession, commemoration, entertainment, or call to action, to name but a few. On this point interviewers and interviewees invite readers to speculate on the possible correlations between the type of auto/biographical account and the specific criteria for inclusion and exclusion.

Besides such aesthetic concerns—which apply to all narratives—there are at least two further reasons that make this question especially pertinent to auto/biographical accounts. The first is of an ethical nature. The second relates to the nature of the genre and its political implications. The ethical concern arises because auto/biographical accounts deal with real existing individuals whose lives can be affected by what is said about them (cf. Eakin 2001).[86] Gillian Slovo expresses this ethical concern as follows: "In a way one criterion for me, when I'm writing both fiction and nonfiction is, who's going to be hurt by this?" (see p. 317). As the interviews indicate, not all authors take the same stance as Slovo, and they deal differently with information that may cause harm. Some use publication to settle accounts (Makgoba using *Mokoko* as his rebuttal to senior academics at the University of Witwatersrand who questioned his integrity; also Wolpe, p. 359). Others conceal identities by altering names (Magona, p. 226), request permission to publish (Slovo, p. 317), or even let the individuals concerned approve the sections pertaining to them before publication (Gray, p. 386). Inevitably cases do crop up in which screening falters and published books are withdrawn, a recent example being Evans's *Dancing Shoes is Dead*, which was removed from circulation in October 2004 because of the threat of a libel suit. Magona, an author of both auto/biography and fiction, alludes to the difference between these genres as far as their impact on others is concerned with the advice: "I want to be circumspect, in that I do not want to embarrass anybody. If you want to be spiteful, write a novel, and then dare anybody to claim, 'That is my life'" (see p. 226).

Besides the limits on disclosure relating to others, there may also be limits on revelations about the autobiographer herself or himself. Here the problem is linked to the nature of the genre of autobiography itself and to the politics of the private and the public. On the one hand there is an imperative associated with the genre of autobiography inherited from the millennial yoke of confession (Foucault, 1976:17–35) to "tell it all."[87] But as Verwoerd admits, the demands associated with the confessional side of auto/biography to "reveal everything," especially the intimate, run up against the vulnerability of an individual who has disclosed weaknesses in public. "At a more theoretical level," he notes, "one may question the typical separation of the personal and the political spheres. But even from a feminist perspective, the right to privacy is vital" (see p. 368).

Grappling with the distinction between the private and the public has implications not only for individuals, but for the body politic at large. Seen in this light one can also read auto/biographical accounts as attempts to establish how much or how little obsession with the private lives of its citizens a community can be expected to endure and where the line between the private and the political should be drawn. In apartheid South Africa, the distinction between private and public was severely corroded by intrusive statutory discrimination and its enforcement. This corrosion is accompanied, according to Gray, by "a kind of prohibition, a sort of conspiracy of secrecy, about the very nature of privacy," which he sees himself digging away at (see p. 380). In this context auto/biographical accounts often strain under a tension: they may dwell on the private in order to illuminate the ways in which the state and the public infringe on the private sphere, but at the same time seek to shore up the distinction between the private and the public by resisting full disclosure on certain issues. Thus, even if authors adhere to the dictum that "the private is political, that what happens intimately in the household is directly connected to the outer political world," as Gray does (see p. 380), it does not mean that they indiscriminately disclose everything about their lives. On the contrary, private disclosures are made *up to a certain point* not only to make their content public, but more importantly, in order to mark the line between the private and the public beyond which they will not venture, a line which by extension they perhaps imply holds for society at large.

Fact and Fiction

The relationship between fact and fiction, truth and metaphor, and its particular inflection in auto/biographical accounts is another much debated feature of the genre. While Manganyi (see p. 168) insists on a watershed divide between biography and fiction—he categorically declares that "biography is not fiction"—others counter that this is a spurious distinction which can be questioned from both sides of the dividing line. Still others add that the dividing line itself constitutes the more interesting vast grey area whose importance resides in the fact that it flirts with the relationship between fact and fiction.[88]

The question from the fiction side concerns the extent to which fiction is autobiographical. This is a matter of particular interest to authors such as J. M. Coetzee, Lessing, Magona, and Es'kia Mphahlele, who write both fiction and autobiography. Many of the interviews confirm the Nietzschean assertion (which calls for some interpretation) endorsed by J. M. Coetzee (see Attwell in J. M. Coetzee 1992:3) that all writing is a form of autobiography. In this view, theoretical writing, fiction, or texts which are explicitly biographical and autobiographical all display a personal investment of the producer. It has even been suggested that a distinctive feature of the verbal arts in southern Africa is that fiction and nonfiction blur in ways in which the personal investment of the producer shines through even more strongly than elsewhere (Zander 1999:99).

While David Attwell (see p. 214) concurs with Coetzee that the boundaries between fiction and autobiography get fudged by the autobiographical nature of all writing, Magona is more ambivalent. She offers examples of how her personal experiences flow into her biographical writing of her parents and into her fiction writing. But she also asserts that, "writers write because they have imagination" and "we would write very dull books if we just wrote about ourselves" (see p. 222). The recognition of the assorted ways in which the auto/biographical informs other genres may easily lure readers into a simplistic equation of all fiction to autobiography. Here Wicomb's rebuttal (2002: 184–185) of the reduction of all writing by black women to autobiography—on the assumption that they are incapable of producing fiction—serves as a welcome warning. On the contrary, the contributions here require us to distinguish between legitimate and fanciful ways in which the connections between auto/biography and other genres may be made, without leveling the differences between them.

From the auto/biographical side, the question is to what extent auto/biographical accounts are fictional? Various contributors provide examples of fictional elements in life writing. Daymond and Lessing (see p. 238) discuss the use of dialogue as a technique typical of fiction that may also be employed in auto/biography. And Manganyi and Es'kia Mphahlele (see p. 245) examine the ways in which characterization informs autobiography. More specifically, they explore the ways in which autobiographical accounts require that one creates "metaphors of the self." This includes sifting the interesting bits from the less interesting ones, mixing several individuals into one, and creating symbols and objective correlatives (see p. 245). It also includes the use of narrative structures derived from the epic, the tragedy, and the comedy to shape the text, as Tim Couzens explains (2003b) regarding his *Murder at Morija* (2003a). What the contributors leave open, though, are the ambiguities of the distinction between novelization and fictionalization, and how this distinction can be used to differentiate between auto/biographical accounts which make truth claims and those which may cease to be auto/biography because they do not raise truth claims about the lives of people who actually live or lived.[89]

The extent to which auto/biographical accounts do indeed raise truth claims—as Joubert and Thembela believe when they assert that "people knew the story was true" (see Joubert, p. 179) and that "every statement in the book can be considered completely accurate and reliable" (see Thembela, p. 150)—is an issue which engages many scholars. Answering this question may require that we spell out which theory of truth we adhere to—semantic, pragmatic, verificationist, corroborationist, etc.—and how this relates to our views on auto/biography. Alternatively, these language-based notions of truth may be rejected in favor of existential ones. Verwoerd, for example, asserts that he has "become more cautious in using the word 'truth'" and "would be inclined to define truth as authenticity, as true humanity, as true humanness—instead of rational justification" (see p. 370). And Krog announces her mistrust of the word as such:

> "The word 'Truth' makes me uncomfortable," she writes. "The word 'truth' still strips the tongue."
>
> "Your voice tightens up when you approach the word 'truth,'" the technical assistant says, irritated. "Repeat it twenty times so that you become familiar with it. *Truth is mos jou job!*" (Truth is your job, after all!)
>
> I hesitate at the word, I am not used to using it. Even when I type it, it ends up as either *turth* or *trth*. I have never bedded that word in a poem. I prefer the word "lie." The moment the lie raises its head, I smell blood. Because it is there . . . where the truth is closest. (1998:36)

Whatever position one takes, this has decisive effects on our view of auto/biographical accounts as a genre informed by the distinction between fact and fiction.

Two very different approaches can be detected in the evaluation of and the explanation for the incursion of fiction into auto/biography. These two approaches go back to a debate which has its locus classicus in Aristotle's *Poetics*, namely, whether history or art is the most reliable bearer of truth. Often the answer to this question takes us on detours via discussions of memory and the nature of truth.[90] The first position, represented by Thembela and Joubert, is that the corrosion of memory (see pp. 149–150, 176) is a threat to the truth value of the auto/biographical record. This, they believe, can be remedied by drawing on other sources, such as the memories of others and/or written sources.[91] Quite a different approach is that of Haarhoff, who notes that "much of our memory is fiction" (see p. 260). Referring to Rabindranath Tagore's claim that "the one who paints his life imprinted on his memory is an artist not an historian" (see p. 266), Haarhoff calls on us to "trust the trickster 'memory' to fictionalize a more playful construction of a personal past" (see Zeeman, p. 255). It is this promise that fiction may be closer to a more deeply seated truth than the truth of a collection of facts "stored in memory," that prompts Uys not only to invent things about his own past, but to invent the biography of fictitious persons (such as Evita Bezuidenhout) "to create a 'virtual' truth" (see p. 351).

If "memory is an imaginative not a mechanical process" as Nixon (see p. 283) and Haarhoff would have it, scholars of auto/biography confront a whole set of issues. To what extent is the imagination structured? And to what extent is this structure determined by dominant attitudes about what counts as a narrative of a life? Thembela asserts that he "extracted, rearranged and systematized the main points in writing" (see p. 149), and Joubert comments that she "had to add structure to Poppie's story" (see p. 175). Both comments suggest that memory and the imagination may need the guidance of certain discursive conventions in order for an auto/biographical account to emerge.[92] It is this insight into the structuring of the auto/biography along popular conceptions and discursive conventions that informs Ngwenya's remark that "writers of life-stories, whether they are ethnographers or biographers, often have their own interpretative framework which they use to interpret and narrate their subject's oral narratives" (see p. 209) and his question to Thembela and Margaret McCord respectively about how they would describe the framework they chose in writing the lives of Joseph Shabalala and of Katie Makanya.[93] In response to a similar probe by Farr, Kendall (who collaborated with Nthunya on *Singing Away the Hunger*) replies, "I finally decided the way to *interfere the least* would be just to put them [Nthunya's narratives] in some order. And the *chronological order* was the simplest route to take" (see p. 196, emphasis added). Kendall's answer is telling because it offers an indication of the hegemonic power of chronology as a discursive convention whose structuring effect is less conspicuous only because it is so pervasive.

One way of looking at debates about structure in auto/biographical accounts is seeing these discussions as grappling with the relationship between discovery and creation and the connection of this relationship to truth. This debate can be summed up in two questions: to what extent do auto/biographical accounts lay bare the existing truths about a life? In other words, to what extent is auto/biography primarily a mimetic activity? And to what extent do such accounts create the truth about a life? In other words, to what extent is auto/biography primarily a poetic activity? According to critics like Gusdorf (1980), James Olney (1973, 1980a), and Jean Starobinski (1980), the giving of form adds to, rather than diminishes, the truth of autobiography.[94] Like Aristotle (*Poetics*, 1970:51b) they hold that giving form to the details of the historical narrative leads to the discovery of its deeper truth. According to this view, the imposition of a discursive design on memory is an epistemological necessity that reveals an already existing but concealed structure in the life itself. The imposition of form may tamper with the surface of events recalled, but such tampering is inconsequential, even necessary, in order to discover the truth about the life which emerges only in its deep structure and not in the multiplicity of its surface appearances. This is the position taken by Van Wyk when he notes, "I wanted to write a literary text that is subservient mainly to poetry in language. I was not concerned about facts—facts are lies as Aristotle already realized in his *Poetics* when he aligned poetry with philosophy rather than history. Other autobiographies are concerned with facts—facts which are blinding lies" (see p. 399). To some extent there is a similarity here with Mphahlele's assertion that "you have to modify a number of things because you are recreating, as in a work of art. In a work of art you don't try to reproduce concrete life and make a concrete representation of it. But rather you present it as a symbol of something else. You are also crafting it; you are giving it a meaning.... In that way you are striving to find that deeper meaning" (see p. 245). While Mphahlele shares the Aristotelian view that the meaning is below the surface and that finding it is a matter of making it, he differs from Aristotle in that he is skeptical about the possibility that this process can end in establishing a final truth or essence of being. "The meaning has no finality," he concludes, "because you are exploring" (see p. 244).

Regarding the implications of fictionalization in auto/biographical accounts, Greig Coetzee (see p. 332) comments on the tension between credibility and truth. Given the extremities of life in southern Africa, "if you present it unadulterated ... no one would believe it." In order to "make the truth more believable," it sometimes has to be watered down. In order to cope with criticisms that have been raised against empiricist notions of truth, the Truth and Reconciliation Commission made some suggestions that are as pertinent to the testimonies it heard as to auto/biographical practice in general. The Commission embraced a broad notion of truth, which it accompanied with some internal distinctions. This broader notion of truth covers so-called factual or referential truth, social truth, narrative truth, and restorative or healing truth (*Truth and Reconciliation Commission of South Africa Report*, vol. I:110–117).[95] As the examples of Mphahlele and Haarhoff show, such a broader notion of truth may create space for authors to bracket what is called "factual truth" in the interest of "metaphoric truth, emotional truth" (see Haarhoff, p. 266) and "narrative, social or healing truth." In similar vein, Verwoerd's experiences with this broadening of the notion of truth in the Commission and its implications for auto/biography, led him to note, "what seems to matter here is the crucial difference between knowledge and understanding, between analysis and awareness, between facts and truth. It was truth situated in relationships, as told by flesh and blood people, that brought insight. And what followed was a difficult process of reconciliation with myself" (see p. 371).

It may be with conundrums like these in mind that J. M. Coetzee asks whether it would not be more appropriate to distinguish between different notions of truth according to different genres (see p. 214). While broadening the notion of truth may encounter resistance from some quarters, many of our contributors clearly advocate it. It does raise the question, however, whether this extension simply shifts debates about truth per se to debates about what genre and which corresponding notion of truth are at stake. To what extent a broader understanding of truth solves more problems than it creates is therefore open to discussion. Furthermore, whether acceptance of a constructionist view of the self and auto/biographical accounts of the self necessarily means that we can no longer distinguish between auto/biography, fiction, and non-fiction is another question that readers of this collection need to ponder.

Postproduction

A thorough understanding of auto/biographical practices must also examine how postproduction affects the nature of auto/biographical texts and how representations of the self reflect back upon the self. Two broad areas are distinguished here: the nature and effect of the channels and scope of dissemination; and the impact of auto/biographical accounts on the producers, the protagonists, and the audience.

Dissemination

While some attention has been paid to the reception of life narratives in southern Africa, little has been said about its dissemination and the impact of dissemination on the form and content of the text.[96] From a southern African perspective, at least two issues relating to dissemination warrant attention. The one concern relates to the differences between oral and print dissemination. The other deals with the relationship between avenues of dissemination in the region, Europe and the United States, and globally.

Before the advent of reproducible sound recordings and video, oral and performed auto/biographical accounts such as those of Yali-Manisi could be disseminated only in live, face-to-face interaction as described by Opland (see p. 122 ff.; see also Opland's 2005 biography of Yali-Manisi, *The Dassie and the Hunter*). Because this meant that the presentation did not have to take into consideration a wider audience unfamiliar with some of the references, the content could be very specific and no glossing was needed to facilitate communication. By contrast, auto/biographical accounts that have a broad distribution that exceeds the initiated may increasingly be characterized by a double consciousness, a simultaneous awareness of the culture of an insider audience and the desire to go beyond it. This double consciousness may be detected in the added glosses, which take the form of notes or explanatory formulations in the text itself.

Such a broadening of the anticipated readership may indicate the spread of modernity. In traditional societies, notions of the good life are generally agreed upon. Modern societies, in contrast, are usually characterized by pluralistic and universalistic approaches to norms. As they cross the borders of traditional societies and inculcate other values, individuals can no longer count on automatic recognition from their "home" community for having lived a good life. In these situations one purpose of publishing an auto/biographical account may be to seek recognition from members of other communities. In their role as a potentially unlimited reading public, readers may then test the values for which auto/biographers seek recognition for their universalizability (see Habermas 1973:190–203 and 1988:192; and Freeman and Brockmeier 2001). This is especially evident in the case of persons who cross cultural borders, such as Katie Makanya (see p. 209) and Cibane (see p. 200). However, as Karin Barber points out (2001:16–17), this normative aspect of auto/biographical accounts may be equally driven by the logic of capital, which turns auto/biographical accounts into commodities and addressees into consumers.

The struggle of local publishers for survival and the hegemonic power of international publishers in the "North" (Nyamnjoh 2004) have strangely paradoxical effects on which auto/biographies get published at all and where. Publishers often blame the limited size of local markets for the failure of material to be published in southern Africa. One solution has been for authors such as Van Wyk (2001) and Khuzwayo (2001) to publish privately. Another solution is international copublishing, which can ensure a larger readership. Often, though, this second route is equally difficult. Both Margaret McCord (see p. 207) and Kendall (see p. 191) report failed attempts to get their manuscripts published in the United States. Only after they had proven themselves in the local market were they able to gain access to international publishing circuits. On a personal level, this can be a frustrating experience that delays or even destroys the possibility of publication for texts that do not promise financial success. As far as political theory is concerned, this also raises a question concerning the view held by McClintock (1991:198), Lara (1998:170), Iris Young

(2000:120–135), and Schaffer and Smith (2004a:3–6) that auto/biographical accounts offer an opportunity for formerly marginalized persons to enter the public sphere as a way of democratizing it.

When it comes to breaking into the public sphere, book awards are often crucial. Several contributors remark on how prizes facilitate publication and dissemination. The Alan Paton-Sunday Times Award for Non-fiction is one such a South African prize, for which auto/biographical accounts have often been short-listed. The very existence of the prize and the many life narratives that have won it indicates the growing significance of the genre in the region.[97] Other honors that have benefited auto/biographical accounts in the past are the now-defunct Central News Agency Award (won by Kuzwayo's *Call Me Woman*); the Africa's Hundred Best Books list (which includes Joubert's *Die Swerfjare van Poppie Nongena*, Nelson Mandela's *Long Walk to Freedom*, Mofolo's *Chaka* (1936), Ezekiel Mphahlele's *Down Second Avenue*, and Van Onselen's *The Seed is Mine*); the VITA Prize (which was awarded to Greig Coetzee); and the Noma Award (which went to Sisulu's *Walter and Albertina Sisulu: In Our Lifetime*).

Impact

When discussing the impact of auto/biography, contributors single out three areas: the impact on the producer or producers in the case of autobiography; the impact on the subject in the case of biography; and the impact on the audience. To begin with the first, an array of answers have been offered to the question J. M. Coetzee poses: "Has the enterprise of autobiographical writing changed my life?" Coetzee himself foregrounds the impact of the creative recreation of his past on the story of his life when he replies that "it has certainly changed the story of my life" by giving it shape (see p. 216). Nixon picks up on this notion when he suggests that what initially looks malleable before writing can be turned into a frozen image by publication (see p. 278). For this reason people like Lessing may seek to offer a definitive version of their lives by preempting other attempts at doing so. However, as Lütge (see p. 339) points out, this may have the effect that the performance of a former self entrenches that self and that authors find themselves tied to a self they have outgrown.

Besides the effect of publication on the authoritative story of one's life, Magona and Gillian Slovo also remark on its effect on their own memory. According to Magona (see p. 225), what has been consigned to writing no longer burdens her memory, while Slovo explains how her own memory was affected by release of her sister Shawn's film, *A World Apart*. As a result, the sisters' memories became "somehow injected into" each other's, so that Gillian has to "keep working out, 'Was that true? Was that how? Do I remember that? Or did I see it on celluloid?'" (see p. 324).

Some contributors report that writing has improved their understanding of their lives and themselves and add that this has had a therapeutic effect. Peter Godwin, for example, the Zimbabwean author of *Mukiwa: A White Boy in Africa* (1997), writes in the preface: "This book was both easy and traumatic to write. There are things here which I had very effectively buried under layers of emotional scar tissue. The process of tearing it away was in some cases pleasurable and in others deeply disturbing. But it was always liberating." Although they do not relate it to therapy, both Nthunya and Es'kia Mphahlele comment on the positive effect that publication of their auto/biographies had on their lives. Mphahlele soon overcame his feeling of vulnerability and "felt liberated" (see p. 246), and when Nthunya reads her *Singing Away the Hunger* she "feel[s] good. I feel like I am dreaming, as if this book told me stories that I know. And really I know that these are my stories. . . . I'm so happy. Very, very happy" (see p. 198). In similar vein Wolpe notes that "writing down the texts and the narratives of dread were to be the healing impulse that gives the individual person a shove back onto the tracks of a psychologically normal life . . . more than once, after such mental work, have I felt the pleasant rehabilitation and peace which I need—as urgently as air—to live. I am of the opinion that this formula of writing therapy is valid for all types of human creation" (see p. 362). Finally, Lee suggests that the therapeutic value of her autobiography may be an effect of its truth value. "I wrote the book," she remarks "because I am not afraid of the truth, I am afraid of the lie" (see pp. 311–312).

Other contributors, however, take a less optimistic view and do not see a necessary connection between the production of auto/biography and understanding or therapy. Joubert questions the assumption of transparency that informs certain modern notions of the subject and auto/biography. According to her, "we don't even understand ourselves all the time! The most outspoken autobiography still holds something back" (see p. 179). Similar experiences are recorded by Verwoerd and Slovo. According to Verwoerd, his type of confessional autobiography is propelled by "a quest for one's deepest self" (see p. 370). In the process of writing, however, he "came to a frightening conclusion that more was probably going on than I suspected." Although he has tried to "include these experiences in the text" he has grown increasingly "aware of the illusion of being really transparent about oneself" (see p. 375). Slovo similarly describes the writing process as a growing awareness of the

INTRODUCTION

limits of understanding. Although she finds that "writing the book was very good" for her because she could seek answers to all the questions she has never been able to ask, she discovered "something more important, which is that although there isn't *one* answer, there is an *understanding* that I could reach." Her family memoir, *Every Secret Thing,* "was about reaching an understanding that not everything can be explained" (see p. 323). These contributors seem to suggest that one of the effects on themselves of producing auto/biography is a disillusion with the search for comprehensive understanding of events, others, and themselves, but that giving up on this modern quest can have a soothing effect in itself.

Turning to the effect of biography on its subject, Mkiva quotes a telling common response from persons whose praises he sings. "In one way or another," they would say to Mkiva, *"undenza umuntu"* (you are making me a person) (see pp. 133–139). This strengthens Benhabib's view (dealt with on p. 3 above) that becoming a person is tied both to telling stories about oneself and having stories told about one. What it leaves open, though, is the nature of the recognition conferred on the subject of an auto/biographical account. Is what is being recognized the subject's membership in the human community or that person's distinctive achievements and identity? And how can the recognition of such a specific identity avoid reification and essentialism (Fraser 1997:23–31; and Fraser and Honneth 2003:72–78)?

Producers of auto/biographical accounts from various generations have put a premium on the ability of their narratives to influence their audience in some way. In the seventies, for example, Joubert "wanted to touch their feelings, their hearts" so that "people themselves would feel that the pass laws were wrong" (see p. 183). In the first decade of the twenty-first century Mkiva notes that "a praise singer or *imbongi* must be seen not only as someone who unleashes beautiful words, but as a practitioner who seeks to transform the society in terms of bettering the lives of the people" (see p. 135). As far as the actual extent and nature of the effect of their auto/biographical accounts is concerned, contributors offer various views. Greig Coetzee and Vanitha Chetty point to some of the negative effects. Coetzee suspects that his autobiographical performance is "more traumatic for the audience than it is for me" (see p. 335). And Chetty testifies to feelings of melancholy for the losses recorded when she reads her mother's autobiography. Turning to the social impact, Kendall (see p. 190) emphatically states that Nthunya's *Singing Away the Hunger* "made very little impact in Lesotho." Although Joubert is more positive than Kendall about the effect of her narrative, *Poppie,* she nevertheless endorses Rive's view that auto/biographical accounts do not themselves bring about social change, but that they create a climate for change (see p. 182). Mkiva is even more optimistic about the immediate effect of cultural artifacts such as auto/biographical accounts on society. According to him, it "is us as *imbongis*, the cultural activists, who have also led the processes of transformation in our country" (see p. 136). Whereas Mkiva focuses on the immediate impact of auto/biographical accounts on social transformation, Magona foregrounds the relationship between a past made present by auto/biographical recollection and the future. According to her, the truth told in auto/biography empowers not only the author but also the reader "about the fact that the truth cannot hurt" (see p. 226). Another possible larger effect of auto/biography, which reveals "the layers that we would not like to remember" is that "in that remembering . . . perhaps we will be forewarned; in that reminding of ourselves of who we are we might be more careful next time" to avoid both oppressing others as well as being oppressed by them (see p. 227).

SCOPE OF THE COLLECTION

Although auto/biographical accounts about oneself and about others is an age-old and thriving practice in southern Africa, it has only recently become a recognized area of inquiry, and scholarship about it is still dispersed.[98] Interest is often biased towards those texts that have acquired canonical status, such as Jabavu's *The Ochre People,* Mphahlele's *Down Second Avenue,* Kuzwayo's *Call Me Woman,* Mandela's *Long Walk to Freedom,* and Krog's *Country of My Skull.* As a result the actual extent of the practice and the various studies of it remain underreflected. One aim of this collection is to increase the body of research into auto/biographical practices by exceeding the boundaries set by some more prominent texts, by drawing in the popular and the obscure, and by bringing these various practices and a range of approaches and disciplines into greater focus.[99]

By rejecting restrictively narrow categories, this collection makes space for the marginalized alongside dominant auto/biographical forms in its approach to region, language, medium of communication, and genre. Although most of the interviews are with South Africans, the inclusion of others from neighboring countries allows readers to see both continuities and discontinuities across the subcontinent. This regionalist perspective is still the exception rather than the rule despite the regionalist approach suggested by titles such as the journal *Current Writing: Text and Reception in Southern Africa* and Michael Chapman's survey, *Southern African Literatures* (1996). There remain many hurdles to regional academic and cultural collaboration on projects such as these, as is evident in the predominance of contributions from South Africa. Where the influence of a common colonial power and common language (such as English) prevail, these borders are more easily crossed. But even where language facilitates crossings, interaction is often inhibited by an attitude of purported self-sufficiency on the part of academic institutions within South Africa, an attitude accompanied by a failure to question South Africa's economic, cultural, and political hegemony in the region. The constraints imposed by both local and international publishing and the position of English as the lingua franca in academic circles means that the interviews here appear in English. We have sought to curtail this dominance by means of interviews with authors who write and perform in other languages, or whose first language is not English. It is, however, regrettable that we were not able to correct this bias more.

Despite attempts to be embracing, a collection like this can never be comprehensive. There are various reasons for the absence of certain interviews, which does not reflect our estimation of the value of those texts. Sometimes an absence can be traced to the interview format, which requires at least two individuals willing and able to communicate with each other, either face-to-face or in writing. In spite of this limitation, the interview seemed to us a useful way to gather information, for it has in its favor the immediacy of a conversation. Those new to the field may find the interview format an accessible one through which they can garner information about authors of interest and then progress to a more solid understanding of specific texts and the various auto/biographical genres. In addition, interviews provide an insider perspective offered by practitioners of the craft. Besides eliciting empirical details pertaining to specific texts, which can only be had from the producers themselves, the interviewers also prompted the producers into theoretical reflection, thereby drawing into our understanding of the genre information and views previously unavailable. At the same time the issues raised by the interviewers introduce general readers and students to questions they may find useful with regard to other auto/biographical accounts they encounter. Often the interviewer is the reader's alter ego, asking what the reader would like to ask or that the reader wishes she or he had thought to ask. At best, and we think readers will find many such instances in this volume, the interviewers ask questions that emerge from an interpretative schema with which we are relatively unfamiliar, and which generates surprisingly rich yields. Throughout, the interviews encourage us all to guard against the arrogant assumption that "the researched merely experience, while the researcher theorizes that experience" (Stanley 1992:105). In many of these interviews with people who have grappled with the problems of representing a self (their own or another's), we find that any temptation to locate the researcher on a different theoretical or critical plane is rendered invalid.

The editors were keen to ensure that the interviews would reflect the divergence of the interviewers' disciplinary perspectives. In the guidelines we sent to all prospective interviewers, we wrote:

> We rely on your expertise regarding the specific contents, style, and structure of the interview. Consequently we would like you to follow the methods best suited to the material and interviewees you have chosen, exploring wide-ranging aspects of auto/biography in the broadest sense of the words. We encourage you to pursue specific disciplinary interests. Thus, if you are a scholar of, say anthropology or history, the issues that are pertinent to that field may open a fruitful line of inquiry that is not well represented elsewhere. ... At the same time we would like to remind you that the common theme of the collection is *reflection on representations of the self and/or other subjects* (rather than probing for first order auto/biographical information). ... (emphasis in original)

The interview required, in addition to discipline-specific knowledge, a prior knowledge of the text or texts under discussion, and was an application of that prior knowledge in order to extend understanding. These were qualitative interviews—some face-to-face, some conducted electronically—employing "a degree of structure" (for there is of course a structure, determined largely by the interviewer) "bound more by the implicit rules of conversation than any rules of research method" and which reflected a sense of knowledge which was, ideally, "co-constructed with interviewees" (Fielding 2003, vol. I:xii). Because of the interactive nature of the interview, the inquiry into certain aspects of the process of recall and representation of experience could be more fruitful than analysis by other research methods.

Perhaps unexpectedly, researchers into the interview as research tool have found that many respondents are able to divulge more sensitive and personal information via e-mail than in face-to-face interviews (Murray and Sixsmith 2003, vol. II:132). In both face-to-face and electronic exchanges, however, some degree of affinity between the interlocutors is a necessity, and this may result in a fruitful openness of exchange. The success of the interview can, paradoxically, be due either to the fact that the questions asked are ones that the interviewee wants to answer, or because of the opposite, that the interviewee has to answer questions which she or he does not expect.

Of course, the interview is no more neutral than are other methods of examination. Liz Stanley argues that the critical reader is likely "to embrace anti-realist principles but then also slip into quasi-realist readings of autobiographical writings" (1992:96). As J. M. Coetzee observes to Attwell, his interviewer, in *Doubling the Point,* the interviews form "part of a larger autobiographical text" (1992:vii). To the extent that all self-representation is marked by traces of role-playing and self-interest, interviews form—to an ineffable degree and for both parties—part of a larger self-representational text. The interview format, because of its affinity to other personal cooperative relationships, tends to reinforce a desire in each participant to take each other and the information given at face value. The interview is commonly characterized by degrees of politeness: in general, a strong element of wanting to please, which may affect either or both of the interlocutors, may facilitate communication, but it may also make the interview less effective. Furthermore, both parties are likely to have had some conscious or unconscious sense that they need the approval not only of their counterpart in the conversation but also of future readers. As readers we will be mindful of the fact that there is, ordinarily, a kind of naiveté in the interview, a sense that both speakers control the words and their meanings in ways that suspend the postmodern insistence on scare quotes for terms like "I," "you," "real," "true." But this naiveté, the very same naiveté that provides the glue of all social interactions, is qualified—profitably problematized—by discipline-specific critical analysis.

The interview as a form is, as Mark Benney and Everett C. Hughes (2003, vol. I:8–10) point out, conventionally governed by the principle of equality between the two participants, at least for the purposes and duration of the encounter.[100] Nevertheless, some have argued that it is more often than not a fundamentally unequal encounter. The interviewee may be someone of considerable standing (and there are many such in this volume), or may be older, or is of a gender or class or some other grouping which the interviewer's culture regards as demanding a measure of deference. Such circumstances may put the interviewer in a position of inferiority. But the interview is, Benney and Hughes argue, "designed to provide a bridge for communicating between the social strata precisely of the kind that sociability cannot provide" and in such situations, participants commonly minimize the inequalities by muting social inequalities "such as age, sex, wealth, erudition, and fame" (ibid.:9). Moreover, the interviewer will usually, they argue, consciously or unconsciously, work to establish rapport with the respondent by "encouraging as well as accepting the affect as well as the information the respondent offers" (ibid.).

Others have argued that the interview distributes power in just the opposite way, favoring not the interviewee but the interviewer, that it is an imbalanced, unidirectional conversation, with the interviewee under scrutiny and the interviewer determining the questions and the direction of the interview. J. M. Coetzee remarks upon the "inherently confrontational nature of the transaction" (1992:66):

> An interview is . . . , nine times out of ten . . . an exchange with a complete stranger, yet a stranger permitted by the conventions of the genre to cross the boundaries of what is proper in conversation between strangers. . . . There is also the question of . . . control over the interview. Writers are used to being in control of the text and don't resign it easily. . . . Writing is not free expression. There is a true sense in which writing is dialogic: a matter of awakening the countervoices in oneself and embarking upon speech with them. It is some measure of a writer's seriousness whether he does evoke/invoke those countervoices in himself, that is, step down from the position of what Lacan calls "the subject that is supposed to know." Whereas interviewers want speech, a flow of speech. . . . To me . . . truth is related to silence, to reflection, to the practice of *writing*. (ibid.:64–66)

Furthermore, J. M. Coetzee points to a possibility that the interview may distort rather than clarify: the interview may offer rational explanation when rational explanation per se would inevitably belie the irrationality of the creative process: "What I am doing when I am writing a novel either isn't me or is me in a deeper sense than the words I am now speaking are me" (ibid.:206). The author's position, Coetzee says, is weaker than the critic's, for he does not have the critic's distance, "nor can he pretend to be what he was when he wrote—that is, when he was not himself" (ibid.). The interviews may thus present questions which are, for the author, unanswerable; nevertheless, even these may help us to sharpen the ways in which we as readers or audience members approach these primary texts.

In some of the interviews collected here there may be evidence of the interviewee's resistance to the interviewer's interpretation. In such cases the balance of power tips in favor of the interviewee in the sense that the desire to know comes from the interviewer and the power to gratify that desire, to clarify or obscure, to reveal or evade, lies with the interviewee. But in many or even most instances, since interviewees were able to edit the transcription prior to submission—our guidelines to interviewers included the instruction that before submission the interview texts should be *"edited and authorised* by the interviewee"—the actual interview was not the only chance they had to exert some control over the dialogue.[101]

To some extent the interview duplicates the conditions under which self-representation occurs: every auto/biographical act, like every conversation, has its own peculiar balance of revelation and concealment of thoughts and intentions. The interview is not a confession and no absolution is sought or granted. In any case, interviews are not, of course, the final word. No interviewer can claim to have unearthed the whole truth, in part because the subject may not know the whole truth because she or he may have forgotten (as in Van Wyk, see p. 397), or because resistances and repressions may be too strong. Whatever the purpose of the interviewer's questions, what the reader gets is not the Truth, in the sense of an infallible claim about the self, but a further representation that exists in relation to preceding and perhaps contradictory representations.

Why the need to probe beyond the self-representational text? Is it not sufficiently self-revelatory? While auto/biographers by and large seek to reduce complexity to an interpretation, "rather than accepting that all these competing truths and selves may be true" (Stanley 1992:11), the interviews do go some way towards scrutinizing competing truths, to undermining realist versions of truth as something single and unseamed which emerges from the individual rather than as social product (ibid.:14–16). Nevertheless, the most successful interview will not strip the work "of its disturbing autonomy" (Coetzee 1992:237) or forestall the free play of interpretation; it will manifest what J. M. Coetzee refers to as "moments of analytic intensity," which are "also a matter of grace, inspiration," (ibid.:199) thus enriching interpretation.

The range of texts drawn into this collection allows readers to perceive something of the amazing variety of conceptions, cultural constructs of self and representational styles, and media in southern African auto/biographical output. It goes way beyond a dichotomous westernized individualism versus an African relational self. We believe that the heterogeneity of approaches taken by auto/biographers and their interlocutors will stimulate readers to question the suffusions of culture and history in the apparently self-evident genres of life writing. These interviews probe and provoke. Journalist Lynn Barber contends that "[t]he best interviews—like the best biographies—should sing the strangeness and variety of the human race" (quoted in Robert Andrews 2001: 26). We believe that the interviews gathered together here do just that; they remind us powerfully that the identity of each auto/biographical subject, as well as that which we perceive as our own, is a series of questions rather than answers.

A project like this is, of course, possible only with the valuable support of many individuals and institutions, not all of whom can be mentioned. We would like, however, to single out a few. Our first thanks go to the contributors, both the interviewers and the interviewees. We hope that they will see this publication and the scholarship that we believe will follow as a modest sign of appreciation for their enthusiasm and devotion to this project. Translations were professionally done by Anita Moore, for which we would like to thank her. Editing took place in various stages, and we would like to thank Hanneke Gagiano, Anita Moore, Vasanthie Padayachee, and André Haycock for their expert work. Margaret Black, our copy editor with University of Hawai'i Press, did a sterling job, ensuring precision and correctness in style. We are extremely grateful to her, to Keith Leber our managing editor, and Bill Hamilton, the director of University of Hawai'i Press for their professionalism in seeing the manuscript through publication. Infrastructure was provided by the University of KwaZulu-Natal and the Centre for Gender Studies of the University of Basel, for which we would like to thank Andrea Maihofer and Monika Schibig. The University of KwaZulu-Natal Research Fund, the South African National Research Foundation, and The Casa Zia Lina Foundation made funding available that allowed us to cover many of the expenses involved in this publication. The editorial board of the Writing Past Colonialism series, housed at the University of Melbourne, in particular David Bennett and Phillip Darby, facilitated the review and selection process, for which we are particularly grateful. The collection is dedicated to our loved ones, who sustain us and enrich our lives.

NOTES

Introduction

1. Both Judith Lütge Coullie and Stephan Meyer wrote the introduction. Coullie was responsible for pp. 10–13, 20–38, and 63–67; Meyer for pp. 1–10, 13–20, 38–63, and 67–68. Together they reviewed and edited the introduction as a whole. The other editors, Thengani Ngwenya and Thomas Olver, made valuable suggestions in discussions of earlier versions of the text.

In this introduction we use "auto/biographical accounts" to cover narrative and nonnarrative autobiography and biography as distinct genres, as well as mixtures of these. For more detail on terminology, see pp. 8–9 above.

2. On the pervasiveness of auto/biographical practice, see Schipper and Schmitz 1991; Appiah and Gutmann 1996:97; Jolly 2001:ix; Kearney 2002. For a dissenting view, see Gusdorf 1980. On narrative notions of the self, see Bruner 1987, 2001, and 2003; Dennett 1988; Taylor 1989; Kerby 1991; Ricoeur 1991a, 1991b, 1992:113–168; Schechtman 1996:93–135; Hinchman and Hinchman, eds., 1997; Brockmeier 1997; Brockmeier and Carbaugh, eds. 2001; Benhabib 1999; Burger 2000; McNay 2000:74–117; and Raditlhalo 2003. For a critique of narrative notions of the self, see Christman 2004; Strawson 2004; and Vollmer 2005. The view that understanding the significance of auto/biography in the constitution of identity is necessary is not meant to imply that auto/biography offers an exhaustive account of human identity. In southern Africa, as elsewhere, identities are constituted in a multitude of ways. Therefore, any conclusions about the nature of the self deduced from this book demand supplementation by investigations into the many other forces that work together in shaping identity. For social identities in South Africa, see the publications belonging to an ongoing National Research Foundation project: Zegeye 2001; Zegeye and Kriger 2001; Ebr-Vally 2001; Erasmus 2001; Badsha 2001; Sienaert 2001.

3. For the original formulation of the problem raised by the Enlightenment philosopher, namely, *What constitutes the identity of an earlier self with a later self?*, see Hume 2001. On the double axis (diachronic and synchronic) in auto/biography, see Dilthey 1970:242–251; and Habermas 1973:178–203. On creating different

identities and possibilities for future action through auto/biography, see Bruner 2001; and Eakin 2005.

4. On the intersubjective narrative constitution of identity, Charles Taylor writes: "One cannot be a self on one's own. I am a self only in relation to certain interlocutors: in one way in relation to those conversation partners who were essential to my achieving self-definition; in another in relation to those who are now crucial to my continuing grasp of languages of self-understanding—and, of course, these classes may overlap. A self exists only within what I call 'webs of interlocution'" (1992:36). For other relational notions of the self and the construction of collective identity through auto/biographical narrative see Dilthey 1970:242–251; Habermas 1973:178–203; Somers 1994; Kling 1995; Eakin 1999: 43–98; and Fleisher Feldman 2001. On collective identities in general, see Hall 1992; Gates and Appiah, eds. 1995; Appiah and Gutmann 1996; and Appiah 2001. For critiques of identity thinking, see Adorno 1973; Horkheimer and Adorno 1986; and Butler 1995.

5. On auto/biography in the public sphere, see Habermas 1989:27–56; and Lara 1998. On the public sphere in general, see Calhoun, ed. 1992; and Crossley and Roberts, eds. 2004. On the black public sphere, see The Black Public Sphere Collective 1995. On the transnational public sphere, see Fraser 2005. On women's writing and the public sphere in Africa, see Andrade 2002. On international communications media, see Castells 1999. On publishing in South Africa, see Evans and Seeber, eds. 2001; and Galloway 2002. On the global literary public sphere as a site of struggle and inequality, see Casanova 2004. On auto/biography in struggles for recognition and justice, see Habermas 1988:206–209; Benhabib 1999; Young 2000:52–80; and Schaffer and Smith 2004a and 2004b. On recognition, redistribution, and parity of participation, see Fraser and Honneth 2003. On language as an enabling condition as well as obstacle to the interpretation and representation of self, see Fraser 1989:181–187; and Bourdieu 1992. On governmentality in general, see Foucault 1988 and 1991. On colonial governmentality, see Scott 1995. On auto/biographical accounts and governmentality, see Dittmar-Dahnke and Pühl 2004.

6. For objections to Benhabib's views on narrative identity, see McNay 2002 and 2003.

7. Well-known examples from various parts of the world include Alex Haley's *The Autobiography of Malcolm X* (1965); slave narratives such as *The History of Mary Prince* (1997); *I, Phoolan Devi*, in which the Indian oral narrator Phoolan Devi cooperated with Marie-Therese Cuny and Paul Rambali (1996); and several accounts from the Australian stolen generation, such as *Rabbit-Proof Fence*, in

INTRODUCTION

which Doris Pilkington/[Nugi Garimara] recorded the auto/biographical accounts of her mother and aunt (2002).

8. For Wilkomirski, see Mächler 2000, Maechler [English spelling of Mächler] (2001); and Gross and Hoffman 2004. For Rigoberta Menchú, see Stoll 1999; and Arias 2001.

9. On African humanism, see Mphahlele 2004:241–304.

10. On national identity and auto/biography, see also Hunsaker 1999; Fay 2000; and Pouchet Paquet 2002. On auto/biography and other collective identity constructions, see also Hazlett 1998; and Mostern 1999.

11. This may echo similar discrepancies between the aspirations of regional organizations such as the Southern African Development Community (SADC). In July 2005, South African Reserve Bank Governor Tito Mboweni expressed his support for a common currency for SADC countries, which would have to converge around the South African rand and Botswana's pula. In general, economically and culturally, South Africa's dealings with its neighbors are informed by a sense of superiority.

12. Especially incisive in this regard is Nelson Mandela's foreword to the Sisulu volume (2003:7)

13. Commonly, if erroneously, known as praise poetry, *izibongo* are poems performed orally that can either praise or chastise an individual, whether she or he be prominent or less well known. See also pp. 10–12.

14. On heteroglossia, see Bakhtin 1981.

15. The term "identity politics" is usually associated with political movements that rally around ethnic and sexual identities and lobby for recognition as a collective bearing a distinct identity that deserves recognition as such. See Gutmann, ed. 1994; Hobsbawm 1996; Fraser 1997:11–40. On identity politics in South Africa, see Singh 1997; and Alexander 2002:81–110.

16. For an example of the use of auto/biographical accounts in nation-building, see the inclusion of prison and struggle biographies as well as current auto/biography on the official South African gateway: gatewayhttp://www.southafrica.info/ess_info/sa_glance/history/strugglebiography.htm

17. Compare Ngwenya 1989.

18. At times stylistic considerations necessitate the use of less precise expressions, such as the shorthand auto/biography. When this is the case, the reader is asked to take a generous interpretation of the term, keeping in mind the suggestions offered in the following two paragraphs.

19. For reference to a real person as a definitive characteristic of autobiography, see Lejeune 1989a:3–30, 1989b:119–137; and Eakin 1992:29–53.

20. For this reason Margaretta Jolly remarks in her introduction to the authoritative *Encyclopedia of Life Writing* that "it is also appropriate to shelter under life writing's umbrella several entries on life story originating outside the written form" (2001:ix).

21. Although this collection contains no interview focusing solely on diaries and letters, a considerable number of these have been published. These range from the historical *Dagboek van Adam Tas* (Fouché, ed. 1970); and Lady Anne Barnard's journals (1993, 1998–1999); to diaries from the Anglo-Boer war, such as Sol Plaatje's *Mafeking Diary* (1973); Deneys Reitz's *Commando: A Boer Journal of the Boer War* (1929); diaries of Afrikaner women in the concentration camps (see Ena Jansen 1999; and Liz Stanley 2002); and *Secret Fire: The 1913–1914 South African Journal of Pauline Smith* (1997). It also includes contemporary journals and diaries such as Albie Sachs's *The Jail Diary of Albie Sachs* (1990a); Athol Fugard's *Notebooks* (1983); Jan Rabie's *Paryse dagboek* (1998); Fatima Meer's *Prison Diary* (2001); Cathy Park's *Inside Outside: A Journey of the Spirit through the Gates of a Prison* (2001); Blaise Koch's *In, Around, Through and Out: An Actor's Life* (2002); Rayda Jacobs's *The Mecca Diaries* (2005); and Adam Levin's *Aidsafari* (2005). For commentaries on African diaries in general, see Oliver Lovesey 1996; Jane Wilkinson 1984; and John Cooke 1987. For published letters, see Lady Anne Barnard (1973) and Olive Schreiner (1988); and the more contemporary Es'kia Mphahlele (1984b); Shula Marks (1987); and Bessie Head (1991). For examples of excerpts of diaries published within auto/biography, see Lyndall Gordon (1992); and Wilhelm Verwoerd (1996).

22. For music, see Philip Glass's *Satyagraha* (1983); for painting, portraits by Gerard Sekoto can be seen at http://www.art.co.za/gerardsekoto/ as well as in the revised edition of his biography by Chabani Manganyi retitled *Gerard Sekoto: "I Am an African"* (2004). Portraits by Breyten Breytenbach are in Breytenbach 1976, 1983, 1994, 1998. For photography, see Omar Badsha's *Imperial Ghetto* (2001); David Goldblatt's *Some Afrikaners Photographed* (1975); and Jürgen Schadeberg's *The Fifties People of South Africa* (1987); for cinema, see Shawn Slovo's *A World Apart* (1988); and Richard Attenborough's *Cry Freedom* (1987); for material objects from everyday life, see the exhibition *Group Portrait: Nine South African Families* (pp. 409 ff. below).

23. For critiques of the quintessentially modern view of the self as an autonomous individual who is the master of himself and his narrative, see Woodmansee 1994a and 1994b; and Meyers's entry "Feminist Perspectives on the Self" in the *The Stanford Encyclopedia of Philosophy* http://plato.stanford.edu.

24. Although the collection as a whole seeks to open the way to a southern African treatment of auto/biography, this section focuses on South Africa. As

mentioned (pp. 62–63), there are still many obstacles to a more comprehensive, regionalist approach, one of them being the authors' field of specialization.

25. Scholars' claims that there are large areas of convergence in praising among different indigenous ethnic cultures in southern Africa, and indeed even further north on the continent, are borne out in the literature.

26. For a useful treatment of the notion of script in relation to identity, see Appiah (1996:97; 2001:243).

27. Regarding religious praises, Brown (1995) has analyzed the significance of oral forms, including *izibongo,* for the hymns of Isaiah Shembe, charismatic founder of a massively popular South African religious movement.

28. Muller discusses the role of personal praises in contemporary *maskanda* music (1995:123–125).

29. Brown argues that "the oral tradition has largely been written out of literary history" (1996:124). This is unfortunately true, but progressively less so. However, even when it is attended to, there may be a distorted view of the oral as a function of a past long gone. Chapman's recent comprehensive history of southern African literatures (1996:15) is to be commended for its inclusion of praise poetry, however, the oral tradition is described as "a usable past." Thus, although contemporary uses are mentioned, the section on praise poetry focuses discussion on the genre's history. The rubric's question, "The praise poem: a usable past? Shaka's court to trade union rally," implies that the genre is primarily of historical interest; its contemporary relevance inconclusive (1996:53).

30. Much of this part is drawn from Coullie's "(Dis)Locating Selves." Permission to use this material was granted by the publishers, James Currey.

31. See Gérard, ed., 1986.

32. See Trotter 2000; Ebron 2001; Hickey 2001; Sandomirsky 2001; and Vogel 2001.

33. For Portuguese travel writing, see Hart 1967; Camoens's *Lusiads* (1980); and Stephen Gray on Camoens (1979:15–37). For Dutch travel writing dealing with South Africa—such as Jan van Riebeeck's *Daghregister* (1652–1662)—see Kannemeyer 1978, vol. I:17–21; and Ampie Coetzee 1998. For English travel writing, see Cohen 2003; Mills 1991; and Romero, ed., 1992. For French travel writing, see Ricard 2000.

34. Cf. Anne Barnard 1993, 1998, 1999; and Pringle's 1834 *Narrative of a Residence in South Africa* (1966).

35. Autobiographies of early white settlers that constitute attempts to define new identities for themselves in the colonial context include Kingsley Fairbridge's *Autobiography of Kingsley Fairbridge* (1927) and Francis Carey Slater's *Settler's Heritage* (1954).

36. For a rewriting of Krotoa-Eva's narrative, drawing on Dutch travel accounts, see the historical novel by Bloem (1999). See Pringle's articles on South Africa (1826); and his poems "Afar in the Desert," "Makanna's Gathering," and "Bechuana Boy" (1912).

37. Thornton 1983; Kommers 1996; Stagl and Pinney 1996.

38. See Yvette Abrahams 1998; Lindfors, ed., 1999; Magubane 2001; F. J. G. van der Merwe 2002; and Shephard 2003.

39. Mphahlele published under Ezekiel Mphahlele until about 1984. With *Afrika My Music*, published on his return to South Africa, he started using the name Es'kia.

40. Likewise coauthored accounts, Luthuli's *Let My People Go* (with Charles and Sheila Hooper) and Winnie Mandela's *Part of My Soul Went with Him* (with Benjamin and Benson) also contributed greatly to publicizing the iniquities of apartheid (especially overseas, since both were banned in South Africa). Such coauthorship often counted as a sign of existing solidarity and at the same time served to promote international solidarity.

41. For the locus classicus of the notion of double consciousness, see du Bois 1999:11. On contemporary uses of the concept, see Gilroy 1993:111–145; and Bruce 1992:229–307.

42. See Dorothy Driver on Kuzwayo (1991).

43. For African travel writing in general, see *The Journal of African Travel Writing*. For Black Atlanticism, see Gilroy 1993; Pettinger, ed., 1998; Walvin 2000; and Rice 2003. For black South African travel in the twentieth century, see Higgs 2000. For the first black South African life and travel writing, written in Dutch, see Vos 1824; and Huigen 1997.

44. Cf. also Noni Jabavu's preface to the second edition of *The Ochre People*.

45. The impact of feminist studies has meant a greater sensitivity towards gender, with a concomitant shift from the sciences of man to a more inclusive practice of human sciences.

46. These include Morgan and the Bambanani Women's Group's *Long Life: Positive HIV Stories* (2003) and the RedRibbon diary project on http://www.redribbon.co.za.

47. For feminism, see especially the journal *Agenda;* and Daymond, ed., 1996. For masculinity, see Morrell's, *Changing Men in Southern Africa* (2001). See also Ratele 2003 and Ratele "Contradictions in Constructions of African Masculinities" on the website of the African Regional Sexuality Resource Centre: http://www.arsrc.org/features/issue005.htm

48. Much of the material in this section and in the section on auto/biography after apartheid first appeared in Coullie 2001.

49. Typically, "banning" restricted a person to a magisterial district or even house arrest; the individual was required to report regularly to the police and was usually under police surveillance, could not be quoted, and could not meet with more than one person at a time. See Saunders and Southey 1998:17–18.

50. See Daymond and Lenta 1994:1018–1019.

51. Most schools for black South Africans in the first half of the twentieth century were run by churches and missions. Although insufficient in number to cope with education for black youth in general, those youngsters lucky enough to get into mission schools formed a small educated minority and had the mobility to rise out of the massive unskilled labor class.

52. The anonymity of racism is reflected in the title of Mokgatle's autobiography, *The Autobiography of an Unknown South African*, and in the name "Bloke" which Modisane chose to replace his given name, William.

53. For a longer version of auto/biographical accounts in the new South Africa, see Coullie 1999b.

54. Vermeulen tells of his paralysis due to a dive into a too-shallow pool.

55. http://www.redribbon.co.za/kufe/default.asp

56. For the autobiographical character of these founding texts of European modernity, see Pavel 1996:354; Rorty Oksenberg 1986; and Kosman 1986.

57. For Gandhi's reflection on this, see Gandhi 1982:13–14.

58. On the relationship between auto/biographical accounts and individualism in Africa, see also Grohs 1996a:3 and 1996b:190–193; and Quayson 1995:81.

59. On representative voice in African autobiographical poetry, see Niyi Osundare in Arnold 1996:158. On the problems involved in speaking on behalf of others, see Alcoff 1992; and Bourdieu 1992:163–228.

60. On the relationship between concentration and refugee camps, racism, and identity in the twentieth century, see Gilroy 2000.

61. On working-class autobiographies as the forging of identities counter to those enforced by a hegemonic power such as the state and employers, see Thale 1995.

62. On psychobiography, see McAdams and Ochberg 1988; Manganyi 1991; and Schulz 2001.

63. See, for example, Lyndall Gordon 1992; Mathabane 1994; Gillian Slovo 1997; Morgan 1999; Brink, et al., eds., 2001; Sisulu 2002; Faber and van der Merwe 2003.

64. Nkosi (1990b), for example, makes out a convincing case that Bloke Modisane's autobiography, *Blame Me on History*, is premised on the social space of Sophiatown. On the tyranny of place, see Es'kia Mphahlele 1987.

65. On the relationship between subjectivity and landscape, see J. M. Coetzee

(1988:36–63); and the 2000 issue of *Transformation* (no. 44), which is devoted to landscape in southern Africa.

66. For incarceration, see the autobiographical accounts by First 1965/1988; Indres Naidoo 1982; Makhoere 1988; Fatima Meer 2001; Mhlaba as told to Mufamadi 2001; and the commentaries by Jacobs 1986, 1991a, 1991b; Gitti 1991; and Schalkwyk 2000. For house arrest, see Naudé 1995; and Joseph 1986. For banishment, see Joseph 1966; and Winnie Mandela 1985. For forced removals, see Modisane 1963; Fortune 1996; and Ngcelwane 1998. For exile, see Hutchinson 1960; Peter Abrahams 2000; and commentaries by Nkosi 1965; and Watts 1989:107–131.

67. For both these strands, see Pettinger 1998.

68. Cf. Head 1973; Fuller 2002; Keitetsi 2002; Letlapa Mphahlele 2002; Slaughter 2002; and Wylie 2002.

69. The literature on the Truth and Reconciliation Commission is extensive. Besides the official report, which contains transcripts of several hearings, there have been numerous publications. One of the more recent is Posel and Simpson, eds., 2002. See also Graham 2003; and Coullie forthcoming.

70. On Krog, see Snyman 1999; Sanders 2000; Jacobs 2000.

71. Likewise Osundare remarks: "Whenever I wasn't writing, all the trauma would come back to my mind and I was very close to a psychological defeat. But whenever I held my pen and started working on the poems the burden would lift" (quoted in Arnold 1996:154).

72. For critiques of monological notions of authorship and for collaborative authorship, see Ede and Lunsford 1994, 2001; Stillinger 1991; Woodmansee 1994a, 1994b; Laird and Ede 2001.

73. On working-class auto/biographies, see Thale 1995; and Coullie 1997.

74. The poem "Stories retold," by the Malawian poet Susan Nalugwa Kiguli, one of the interviewers in this book, is worth quoting in full because of the elegance with which it formulates this view:

> Someone will rewrite our life
> And interpret the bare huts
> We built to shelter our bones.
> Someone will pin together
> Our suffering telling
> Clever narratives about
> Why we bore and brought up
> These children giving them
> The stories of our survival.

Someone will chant about
Why our homesteads were
Round like craters,
Why we were knit
Together like the blankets
Which keep our blood from
Congealing.

This life we have lived in earnest
Will be twisted into gothic tales.
These children we share
Will be numbered and separated.
Strangers will strive to understand
These souls melted into each other,
And my sister,
Our life will stop meaning
What it has meant to us
Who have fought for sanity
Who have combed for roots
To charm hunger
Who have hidden in jungles
To evade the crash of boots.

Our breath will become
Someone else's story
And it will never be restored to us,
It will scamper away
To create other lives
In distant places.

For some of the epistemological and ethical problems associated with collaborative auto/biography, see Couser 1988, 1998, 2003; and Rios and Mullen Sands 2000.

75. Related issues are raised by intergenerational auto/biographies, such as Agnes Lottering's *Winnefred & Agnes,* a "joint" auto/biography in which the daughter, Agnes, tells the deceased mother's story as well as her own in the first person.

76. For feminist relational notions of the self, see Benhabib 1992, 2002; Benjamin 1990, 1995, 1998; and Gilligan 1982. For social interactionism, see Mead 1967:144–152, 245–260. See also Eakin 1998; and Meyer 1999.

77. On the paratext in general, see Genette 1997. Examples of paratexts include the photographs reproduced in the auto/biographical book as in Johnny Masilela's *Deliver Us from Evil;* the cover design of an auto/biography (see Coullie and Gray on p. 384); or the self-portraits exhibited in a separate venue (see Sienaert on Breyten Breytenbach 2001).

78. See also Boyce Davies 1991.

79. Auto/biographical accounts of public figures constitute a considerable chunk of southern African life writing and the list that follows is but a sample. For political figures and intellectuals, see Kuper's biography (1978) of King Sobhuza II of Swaziland; Z. K. Matthews's autobiography 1981; Mamphela Ramphele's autobiography 1995; Clingman's biography (1998) of Bram Fischer; Frieda Matthews's autobiography (1995); Higg's biography (2002) of D. D. T. Jabavu; Harlan's biography (2000) of Mamphela Ramphele; Ismail Meer's autobiography (2002); Charlene Smith's biography (2002) of Patricia de Lille; Nxumalo, Msimang, and Cooke's biography (2003) of King Goodwill Zwelinthini; and Rall's biography (2003) of Sol Plaatjie. For the clergy, see Huddlestone's autobiography (1956/1985); Guy's biography (1983) of John William Colenso; and Hudson-Reed's biography of Clement Doke (1998). For artists, see Makeba and Hall (1988); Jaap C. Steyn's biography (1998) of N. P. Van Wyk Louw; Gray on literary freelancers (1999); Kannemeyer's biographies of C. Louis Leipoldt (1999) and of Uys Krige (2002); Willemse, et al.'s book (2000) on Peter Clarke and James Matthews; books on Ingrid Jonker by Van Wyk (1999) and Mettlerkamp (2003); Karel Schoeman's autobiography (2002); Manganyi's revised biography of Sekoto, (2004); Masekela and Cheers's auto/biography of Hugh Masekela (2004); and Gray's biography of Herman Charles Bosman (2005).

80. For a critical appraisal of Nujoma's book, see Christopher Saunders 2003.

81. For Mugabe, see also Mugabe 1983. For public life writing in Zimbabwe, see also Samkange 1975; Ranger 1995; and Veit-Wild 1996.

82. For commentaries on Nelson Mandela, see Cheryl-Ann Michael 1995; and Chapman 1995. For a critical review of Du Preez Bezdrob's *Winnie Mandela,* see Van der Spuy 2004.

83. Connecting this to questions of memory and agency, Sarah Nuttall asks, "If political events set a framework for memory, do we still see memory and agency as proceeding from the inside out, as structured by an internal set of needs and desires? What about memory that is structured from the outside in? And if memory is structured in this way, does this mean that a private self is ignored, or seen as 'unpolitical'?" (1996:64). For the discussion of the ways in which Dr. Goonam's *Coolie Doctor* shapes the narrative of her personal life according to the narrative of the political struggle and the gender associations of this, see Govinden 2001.

84. For the writing Makanya refers to, see James McCord's ghostwritten autobiography, *My Patients Were Zulus*, 1946.

85. Although the jury for the Noma Award said that *Walter and Albertina Sisulu: In Our Lifetime* "is a powerful and searing book, told with honesty and authority, of the lives of two heroic figures in South Africa's history" and prized it for "[b]ringing together the personal and political," the emphasis on Walter Sisulu's life and the coincidence of his life with the history of the political struggle means that the public draws much more attention than the private in the sense of an insider view on a family (http://allafrica.com/stories/200311030276.html).

86. This also applies to cases where the subject has passed away and the memory others have of her or him is tarnished by what is said.

87. This imperative also carried through to the Truth and Reconciliation Commission, where it was one of the requirements for those seeking amnesty (see Promotion of National Unity and Reconciliation Act of 1995). See also Heyns 2000; Graham 2003; and Schaffer and Smith 2004b:53–84.

88. In Richard Rive's words, "autobiography is structurally the marriage between personal history and the novel" (1981:1). See also Flannigan 1982; Schipper 1985; Ibrahim 1989. In June 2005, a symposium at Stellenbosch University entitled "Fact Bordering Fiction" focused on precisely this issue.

89. Novelization is defined by the Oxford English Dictionary as the use of novelistic techniques to convey facts about the world. Fictionalization is variously defined by the Oxford English Dictionary as the distortion of the truth and as the suspension of truth claims. See also Wolfe 1980; and Barnet 1981. For Barnet's own application of novelization and fictionalization, see Barnet 1991, 1994.

90. Two recent autobiographies, written by people whose memories are damaged by drug abuse and physical injury (Steve Hamilton and Gaynor Young, respectively), provide interesting extremes on the problems of memory fallibility.

91. For written and oral corroboration of oral sources, see Van Onselen 1993.

92. Despite Ezekiel Mphahlele's assertion, "No use to put the pieces together. Pieces of my life. They are a jumble" (1959:74–75), it is of course not the case that there is no discursive arrangement of the events. Declarations such as these may be used to lure the reader into the belief that she or he is getting the raw material, unfalsified even by authorial intention.

93. In this regard, see also Ngwenya 2000.

94. According to Gusdorf, autobiography is the product of reflection, which he equates to the giving of structure. This is a precondition for but also the "original sin" (1980:41) of autobiography. Likewise, Olney holds that the autobiographer "half discovers, half creates a deeper design and truth than adherence to historical

and factual truth could ever make claim to" (1980a:11). Starobinski (1980) argues that style is itself a truthful indicator of identity.

95. See also Riffaterre 1991 and Spence 1992.

96. The special issue of *Current Writing* on *The Book in Africa* that deals with such matters, for example, has no contribution dealing specifically with the dissemination of auto/biography. Similarly, Jolly's comprehensive *Encyclopedia of Life Writing* does not contain any entries on this topic either.

97. Arguably, the Paton Award has a similar effect as the Prize for Testimonio awarded by the Cuban Casa de las Américas, which certainly contributed to the proliferation and the visibility of the genre in Latin America (see Beverley 1996:39, fn 3). Some of the Paton Award past winners and short-listed authors include Albie Sachs for *Soft Vengeance of a Freedom Fighter;* Tim Couzens for *Tramp Royal;* Nelson Mandela for *Long Walk to Freedom;* Mathabane for *Miriam's Song;* Van Onselen for *The Seed is Mine;* Margaret McCord for *The Calling of Katie Makanya;* Mpho Nthunya for *Singing Away the Hunger;* and Henk van Woerden for *A Mouthful of Glass*.

98. The only freely available (on the internet) book-length work is Sam Raditlhalo's PhD dissertation (2003). Other dissertations include Choonoo 1982; Makhathini 1987; Tsiga 1987; Ngwenya 1991, 1997; Pillay 1992; Coullie 1994; Hlongwane 1995; Gilfillan 1996; Nattrass 1996; Pridmore 1996; Koyana 1999; Mokgoatsana 1999; Graham 2001; Sicweba 2000; Thale 2000; Pelser 2001; Meyer 2003. There have, however, been significant publications in journals and as chapters of books reflecting the variety of theoretical approaches to auto/biography (see *Current Writing* 3, 1(1991); and *Alter*Nation 7, 1(2000). For an earlier bibliography of South African autobiography, see Westley 1994.

99. Even though this collection focuses on the southern African region, there are some obvious relations to auto/biography in other regions. Jolly's comprehensive *Encyclopedia of Life Writing* (2001) offers a good entry into the field. The most pertinent connections are to other colonial, postcolonial, and Commonwealth settings. The list is extensive, but some relevant studies could include MacDermott's *Autobiographical and Biographical Writing in the Commonwealth* (1985); *Genres autobiographiques en Afrique/Autobiographical genres in Africa* edited by Riesz and Schild (1996); the special issue on autobiography and African literature of *Research in African literatures* (1997); Whitlock's *The Intimate Empire: Reading Women's Autobiography* (2000); the special issue of *Commonwealth* devoted to biography, autobiography and fiction (2001); Chinsole's *African Diaspora and Autobiographies: Skeins of Self and Skin* (2001); and Pouchet Paquet's *Caribbean Autobiography: Cultural Identity and Self-representation* (2002). Latin-American discussions can be found in Lara 1998; Gugelberger, ed., 1996; and Hunsaker 1999. Schaffer

and Smith (2004) give a valuable up-to-date overview of life narrative in connection to human rights in South Africa, Australia, Japan, the United States, and China. The leading journals in the English-speaking world are *Biography* (published by the Center for Biographical Research at the University of Hawai'i at Manoa, whose website—http://www.hawaii.edu/biograph/—offers a good starting point); *A/B: Auto/Biography Studies* (published at the University of Wisconsin); and *Auto/biography: An Interdisciplinary Journal* (published by the Auto/Biography group of the British Sociological Association). There is also a new Australian journal, *Life Writing*, published by Curtin University. The International Auto/biography Association, founded at the first International Auto/biography Conference organized by Zhao Baisheng at Peking University in 1999, organizes regular conferences and runs an active listmail at http://www.hawaii.edu/biograph/cbriaba-1.html through which publications and calls for papers are announced.

100. According to Benney and Hughes (2003, vol. I:11), a relationship governed by the conventions of equality and comparability can occur "only in a particular cultural climate; and such a climate is a fairly new thing in the history of the human race," dating back respectively to John Locke and Jeremy Bentham.

101. It may be argued that interviewee control was enhanced in the case of electronic interviews, as the respondent could edit answers before initial submission.

BIBLIOGRAPHY

A/B: Auto/Biography Studies. Madison: University of Wisconsin 1985–.
ABRAHAMS, PETER. *Return to Goli.* London: Faber and Faber, 1953.
———. *Tell Freedom: Memories of Africa.* London: Knopf, 1954.
———. *The Black Experience in the 20th Century: Autobiography and Meditation.* Bloomington: Indiana University Press, 2000.
ABRAHAMS, YVETTE. "Images of Sara Bartman: Sexuality, Race and Gender in Early 19th Century Britain." In *Nation, Empire, Colony: Historicising Gender and Race,* edited by R. Roach Pierson and N. Chaudhuri, pp. 220–236. Bloomington: Indiana University Press, 1998.
ADAMS, KEITH, ed. *We Came for Mandela: The Cultural Life of the Refugee Community in South Africa.* Rondebosch: Footprints Publishers, 2001.
ADORNO, THEODORE. *Negative Dialectics.* Trans. E. B. Ashton. London: Routledge and Kegan Paul, 1973.
ALCOFF, LINDA. "The Problem of Speaking for Others." *Cultural Critique* 71 (Winter 1991): 5–32.
ALEXANDER, NEVILLE. *An Ordinary Country: Issues in the Transition from Apartheid to Democracy in South Africa.* Pietermaritzburg: University of Natal Press, 2002.
ALISON, (No surname given). As told to Marianne Thamm. *I Have Life: Alison's Journey.* Sandton: Penguin, 1998.
ANDRADE, SUSAN. "Gender and 'the Public Sphere' in Africa: Writing Women and Rioting Women." *Agenda* 54 (2002): 45–59.
ANDREW, RICK. *Buried in the Sky.* Sandton: Penguin, 2001.
ANDREWS, ROBERT. *The New Penguin Dictionary of Modern Quotations.* London: Penguin, 2001.
APPIAH, KWAME. "The State and the Shaping of Identity." Tanner lectures. Cambridge, Apr. 30 and May 1, 2001. http://www.tannerlectures.utah.edu/abcd.html
APPIAH, KWAME ANTHONY, and AMY GUTMANN. *Color Conscious: The Political Morality of Race.* Princeton: Princeton University Press, 1996.

ARDEN, NICKY. *The Spirits Speak: One Woman's Mystical Journey into the African Spirit World.* New York: Henry Holt, 1996.

ARIAS, A. ed. *The Rigoberta Menchú Controversy.* Minneapolis: University of Minnesota Press, 2001.

ARISTOTLE. *Poetics.* Ann Arbor: University of Michigan Press, 1970.

ARNOLD, STEPHEN, H. "A Peopled Persona: Autobiography, Post-modernism and the Poetry of Niyi Osundare." In *Genres autobiographiques en Afrique/Autobiographical genres in Africa,* edited by János Riesz and Ulle Schild, pp. 143–165. Berlin: Dietrich Reimer Verlag, 1996.

ASHFORTH, ADAM. *Madumo: A Man Bewitched.* Claremont: David Philip, 2000.

ASMAL, KADER. Foreword. *New Dictionary of South African Biography.* Vol. II. Pretoria: Human Sciences Research Council, 1999.

ATTENBOROUGH, RICHARD. *Cry Freedom.* Universal Studios, 1987.

BAARD, FRANCES, and BARBIE SCHREINER. *My Spirit Is Not Banned.* Harare: Zimbabwe Publishing House, 1986.

BADSHA, OMAR. *Imperial Ghetto, South African Images.* Cape Town: Kwela, 2001.

BAKHTIN, MIKHAIL. *The Dialogic Imagination.* Ed. Michael Holquist. Austin: University of Texas Press, 1981.

BARBER, KARIN. "Audiences and the Book in Africa." *Current Writing* 13, 2 (2001): 9–19.

BARNARD, ANNE. *The Letters of Lady Anne Barnard to Henry Dundas 1793–1803 from the Cape and Elsewhere, Together with Her Journal into the Interior and Certain Other Letters.* Ed. A. M. Lewin Robinson. Cape Town: Van Riebeeck Society, 1973.

———. *The Cape Journals of Lady Anne Barnard 1797–1798.* Ed. A. M. Lewin Robinson, with Margaret Lenta and Dorothy Driver. Cape Town: Van Riebeeck Society, 1993.

———. *The Cape Diaries of Lady Anne Barnard 1799–1800.* Vols. I & II. Ed. Margaret Lenta and Basil le Cordeur. Cape Town: Van Riebeeck Society, 1998–1999.

BARNARD, LOUWTJIE. *Heartbreak.* Cape Town: Howard Timmins, 1971.

BARNET, MIGUEL. "The Documentary Novel." *Cuban Studies* 1, 1 (1981): 19–32.

———. *Rachel's Song.* Willimantic: Curbstone, 1991.

———. *Biography of a Runaway Slave.* Willimantic: Curbstone, 1994.

BARRETT, JANE, et al. *Vukani Makhosikazi: South African Women Speak.* London: CIIR, 1985.

BARTER, CATHERINE. *Alone among the Zulus.* Pietermaritzburg: University of Natal Press, 1995.

BENHABIB, SEYLA. *Situating the Self.* Cambridge: Polity, 1992.

———. "Sexual Difference and Collective Identities: The New Global Constellation," *Signs* 24, 2 (Winter, 1999): 335–361.

———. *The Claims of Culture.* Princeton: Princeton University Press, 2002.

BENJAMIN, JESSICA. *The Bonds of Love.* London: Virago, 1990.

———. *Like Subjects, Love Objects.* New Haven: Yale University Press, 1995.

———. *Shadow of the Other: Intersubjectivity and Gender in Psychoanalysis.* New York: Routledge, 1998.

BENNEY, MARK, and EVERETT C. HUGHES. "Of Sociology and the Interview." In *Interviewing*, Vol. I., edited by Nigel Fielding, pp. 5–12. London: Sage Publications, 2003.

BENSON, MARY. *Chief Albert Lutuli of South Africa.* London: Oxford University Press, 1963.

———. *Nelson Mandela.* Middlesex: Penguin, 1986.

BERNSTEIN, HILDA. *The World That Was Ours: The Story of the Rivonia Trial.* London: SA Writers, 1989.

BEVERLEY, JOHN. "The Margin at the Center: On *Testimonio*." In *The Real Thing*, edited by G. Gugelberger, pp. 23–41. Durham: Duke University Press, 1996.

Biography. Center for Biographical Research. Manoa: University of Hawai'i, 1975–.

BIZOS, GEORGE. *No One to Blame? In Pursuit of Justice in South Africa.* Claremont: David Philip, 1999.

THE BLACK PUBLIC SPHERE COLLECTIVE. *The Black Public Sphere.* Chicago: University of Chicago Press, 1995.

BLOEM, TRUDIE. *Krotoa-Eva: The Woman from Robben Island.* Cape Town: Kwela, 1999.

BLOOM, HARRY. *King Kong: An African Jazz Opera.* London: Collins, 1961.

BOBERG, ULF. *The Boberg Story.* Cape Town: Howard Timmins, 1957.

BOETIE, DUGMORE, with BARNEY SIMON. *Familiarity Is the Kingdom of the Lost.* London: Arena, 1984.

BORAINE, ALEX. *A Country Unmasked: Inside South Africa's Truth and Reconciliation Commission.* Cape Town: Oxford University Press, 2000.

———. *The People of Welgeval.* Cape Town: Struik, 2005.

BOURDIEU, PIERRE. *Language and Symbolic Power.* Cambridge: Polity, 1992.

BOYCE DAVIES, CAROLE. "Private Selves and Public Spaces: Autobiography and the African Woman Writer." *College Language Association Journal* 34, 3 (1991): 267–289.

BOZZOLI, BELINDA, with the assistance of Mmantho Nkotsoe. *Women of Phokeng: Consciousness, Life Strategy, and Migrancy in South Africa, 1900–1983.* New Haven: Heinemann, 1991.

BREYTENBACH, BREYTEN. 'n Seisoen in die paradys. Cape Town: Human & Rousseau, 1976.
———. The True Confessions of an Albino Terrorist. London: Faber and Faber, 1984.
———. Return to Paradise. London: Faber and Faber, 1994.
———. Dog Heart: A Travel Memoir. Cape Town: Human & Rousseau, 1998.
BREYTENBACH, JAN. Eden's Exiles: One Soldier's Fight for Paradise. Cape Town: Queillerie, 1997.
———. The Buffalo Soldiers: The Story of South Africa's 32 Battalion. Alberton: Galago, 2002.
BRINK, ELSABE, DUMESANI NTSHANGASE, GANDHI MALUNGANE, and STEVE LEBELO, eds. Soweto 16 June 1976: It All Started with a Dog. Cape Town: Kwela, 2001.
BROADWAY, CHARMAYNE, as told to SHELLEY DAVIDOW. My Life with AIDS: Charmayne Broadway's Story. Johannesburg: Southern Book Publishers, 1998.
BROCKMEIER, JENS. "Autobiography, Narrative, and the Freudian Concept of Life Story." Philosophy, Psychiatry and Psychology 4, 3 (1977): 175–199.
BROCKMEIER, JENS, and DONAL CARBAUGH, eds. Narrative and Identity: Studies in Autobiography, Self and Culture. Amsterdam: John Benjamins, 2001.
BROWN, DUNCAN. "Orality and Christianity: The Hymns of Isaiah Shembe and the Church of the Nazarites." Current Writing: Text and Reception in Southern Africa 7, 2 (1995): 69–95.
———. "South African Oral Performance Poetry of the 1980s." In New Writing from Southern Africa: Authors Who Have Become Prominent since 1980, edited by Emmanuel Ngara, pp. 120–148. London: James Currey, 1996.
———. Voicing the Text: South African Oral Poetry and Performance. Oxford: Oxford University Press, 1998.
———, ed. Oral Literature and Performance in Southern Africa. London: James Currey, 1999.
BRUCE, DICKSON. "W. E. B. du Bois and the Idea of Double Consciousness." American Literature 64, 2 (1992): 299–307.
BRUNER, JEROME. "Life as Narrative." Social Research 54, 1 (1987): 11–32.
———. "Self-making and World-making." In Narrative and Identity: Studies in Autobiography, Self and Culture, edited by Jens Brockmeier and Donal Carbaugh, pp. 25–37. Amsterdam: John Benjamins, 2001.
———. Making Stories: Law, Literature, Life. Cambridge, MA: Harvard University Press, 2003.
BUDD, ZOLA, and HUGH ELEY. Zola: The Autobiography of Zola Budd. London: Transworld Publishers, 1989.
BURGER, MARLENE, and CHANDRE GOULD. Secrets and Lies: Wouter Basson and South

Africa's Chemical and Biological Warfare Programme. Cape Town: Zebra Press, 2002.

BURGER, WILLIE. "Die storie van identiteit." *Aambeeld* 28, 2 (November, 2000): n.p. http://general.rau.ac.za/aambeeld/november2000/storie.htm

BUTLER, GUY. *The Prophetic Nun.* Johannesburg: Random House, 2000.

BUTLER, JUDITH. "Collected and Fractured: Response to *Identities*." In *Identities*, edited by Kwame Anthony Appiah and Henry Louis Gates, pp. 439–448. Chicago: University of Chicago Press, 1995.

CALHOUN, CRAIG, ed. *Habermas and the Public Sphere.* Cambridge, MA: MIT Press, 1992.

CAMERON, EDWIN. *Witness to AIDS.* Cape Town: Tafelberg, 2005.

DE CAMÕES, LUÍS. *Lusiads.* New York: Penguin Books, 1980.

CAMPBELL, ROY. *Light on a Dark Horse.* Harmondsworth: Penguin, 1971.

CANONICI, NOVERINO N. *Zulu Oral Traditions.* Durban: University of Natal, 1996.

CARTER, KEVIN, GREG MARINOVICH, KEN OOSTERBROEK, and JOAO SILVA. *The Bang-Bang Club: Snapshots from a Hidden War.* London: Heinemann, 2000.

CARTWRIGHT, JUSTIN. *Not Yet Home.* London: Fourth Estate, 1996.

CASANOVA, PASCALE. *The World Republic of Letters.* Cambridge MA: Harvard University Press, 2004.

CASTELLS, MANUEL. "Information Technology, Globalization and Social Development." United Nations Research Institute for Social Development. Discussion Paper No. 114, September 1999.

Center for Biographical Research at the University of Hawai'i at Mānoa. http://www.hawaii.edu/biograph/

CHAN, STEPHEN. *Robert Mugabe: A Life of Power and Violence.* Ann Arbor: University of Michigan Press, 2002.

CHAPMAN, MICHAEL. "Mandela, Africanism and Modernity: A Consideration of *Long Walk to Freedom*." *Current Writing* 7, 2 (1995): 49–54.

———. *Southern African Literatures.* London: Longman, 1996.

CHIKANE, FRANK. *No Life of My Own.* Braamfontein: Skotaville Press, 1988.

CHIMELOANE, RREKGETSI. *Whose Laetie Are You? My Sowetan Boyhood.* Cape Town: Kwela, 2001.

CHINSOLE, N. *African Diaspora and Autobiographies: Skeins of Self and Skin.* New York: Peter Lang, 2001.

CHOONOO, R. NEVILLE. "Parallel Lives: Black Autobiography in South Africa and the United States." PhD diss., Columbia University, 1982.

CHRISTMAN, JOHN. "Narrative Unity as a Condition of Personhood." *Metaphilosophy* 35, 5 (October 2004): 695–713.

CIBANE, WILFRED. *Man of Two Worlds: An Autobiography.* Cape Town: Kwela, 1998.
CLINGMAN, STEPHEN. *Bram Fischer: Afrikaner Revolutionary.* Cape Town: David Philip, 1998.
COETZEE, AMPIE. "Duytsman Altyd Kallom: Icke Hottentots Doot Makom." Alter*nation* 5, 2 (1998): 36–42.
COETZEE, GREIG. "White Men with Weapons." *South African Theatre Journal* 15 (2001): 206–228.
COETZEE, J. M. *White Writing: On the Culture of Letters in South Africa.* New Haven: Yale University Press, 1988.
———. *Doubling the Point: Essays and Interviews.* Ed. David Attwell. Cambridge, MA: Harvard University Press, 1992.
———. *Boyhood: Scenes from Provincial Life.* London: Secker and Warburg, 1997.
———. *Youth.* London: Secker and Warburg, 2002.
COETZEE, JAN K. *Plain Tales from Robben Island.* Pretoria: Van Schaik, 2000.
COHEN, WILLIAM B. *White Response to Blacks, 1530–1880.* Bloomington: Indiana University Press, 2003.
Commonwealth. Special issue on Biography, Autobiography and Fiction. 24, 1 (Autumn 2001).
CONNING, LUEEN. "A Coloured Place." In *Black South African Women: An Anthology of Plays,* edited by Kathy A. Perkins, pp. 9–22. London: Routledge, 1998.
COOKE, JOHN. "African Diaries." *World Literature Today* 61, 2 (1987): 211–213.
COPE, TREVOR, ed. *Izibongo: Zulu Praise-poems.* Oxford: Clarendon Press, 1968.
COULLIE, JUDITH LÜTGE. "Not Quite Fiction: The Challenge of Poststructuralism to the Reading of Contemporary South African Autobiography." *Current Writing* 3, 1 (1991): 1–24.
———. "Self, Life and Writing in Selected South African Autobiographical Texts." PhD diss., University of Natal, 1994.
———. "(In)continent I-lands: Blurring the Boundaries between the Self and Other in South African Women's Autobiographies." *Ariel* 27, 1 (1996): 133–148.
———. "The Power to Name the Real: The Politics of the Worker Testimony." *Research in African Literatures* 28, 2 (1997): 132–144.
———. "(Dis)Locating Selves: *Izibongo* and Narrative Autobiography in South Africa." In *Oral Literature & Performance in Southern Africa,* edited by Duncan Brown, pp. 61–89. Athens, OH: Ohio University Press, 1999a.
———. "New Life Stories in the New South Africa." Paper delivered at *Approaching the Auto/Biographical Turn.* First International Conference on Auto/Biography Studies, Peking University, 1999b.
———. "Apartheid and Post-apartheid Life-Writing." In *Encyclopedia of Life-Writing,* edited by Margaretta Jolly, pp. 42–44. London: Fitzroy Dearborn, 2001.

———. "A Proper Conversation: Some Reflections on the Role of Psychoanalysis in Literary Study in South Africa." *Journal of Literary Studies* 18, 1 (2002): 24–60.

———. "Testimony, Truth and Reconciliation and the Genesis of the New South African Nation." Forthcoming.

COUSER, G. THOMAS. "Black Elk Speaks with Forked Tongue." In *Studies in Autobiography*, edited by James Olney, pp. 73–88. New York: Oxford University Press, 1988.

———. "Making, Taking, and Faking Lives: The Ethics of Collaborative Life Writing." *Style* 32, 2 (Summer 1998): 334–350.

———. *Vulnerable Subjects: Ethics and Life Writing*. Ithaca: Cornell University Press, 2003.

COUZENS, TIM. *Tramp Royal: The True Story of Trader Horn*. Johannesburg: Ravan Press, 1992.

———. *Murder at Morija*. Johannesburg: Random House, 2003a.

———. "A Swiss Role in Lesotho." Paper read at Imperial Culture in Countries without Colonies: Africa and Switzerland Conference at the University of Basel, October 23–25, 2003b. http://www.unibas.ch/afrika/nocolonies/couzens.paper.rtf

CROSSLEY, NICK, and ROBERTS, JOHN MICHAEL, eds. *After Habermas: New Perspectives on the Public Sphere*. Oxford: Blackwell, 2004.

Current Writing. Special Issue on life writing. 3, 1 (1991).

Current Writing. Special Issue on the Book in Africa. Edited by Isabel Hofmeyr, Sarah Nuttall and Cheryl-Anne Michael. 13, 2 (2001).

DANIELS, EDDIE. *There and Back: Robben Island 1964–1979*. Bellville: Mayibuye Books, 1998.

DAYMOND, M. J., ed. *South African Feminisms: Writing, Theory, and Criticism 1990–1994*. New York: Garland, 1996.

DAYMOND, M. J., and MARGARET LENTA. "Memoirs." In *The Encyclopedia of Postcolonial Literatures in English*, edited by Eugene Benson and L. W. Conolly. London: Routledge, 1994.

DEACON, JANETTE. "A Tale of Two Families: Wilhelm Bleek, Lucy Lloyd and the /Xam San of the Northern Cape." In *Miscast: Negotiating the Presence of the Bushmen*, edited by Pippa Skotnes, pp. 93–113. Cape Town: University of Cape Town Press, 1996.

DE KLERK, F. WILLEM. (Ghost writer: David Steward). *The Last Trek—A New Beginning: The Autobiography*. Basingstoke: Macmillan, 1998.

DE KOCK, EUGENE (as told to JEREMY GORDIN). *Long Night's Damage: Working for the Apartheid State*. Johannesburg: Contra Press, 1998.

DEJONG, CONSTANCE, and PHILIP GLASS. *Satyagraha: M. K. Gandhi in South Africa 1883–1914*. New York: Tanam Press, 1983.

DENNETT, DANIEL. "Why Everyone Is a Novelist." *Times Literary Supplement*, Sept. 16–22, 1988, pp. 1028–1029.

DESCARTES, RENÉ, *The Philosophical Writings of Descartes*. Trans. John Cottingham, et al. Cambridge: Cambridge University Press. *The Meditations*. Vol. II., 1984; *Discourse*. Vol. I., 1985.

DEVI, PHOOLAN, with MARIE-THERESE CUNY and PAUL RAMBALI. *I Phoolan Devi*. London: Little, Brown and Company, 1996.

DE VILLIERS, DIRK, and JOHANNA DE VILLIERS. *P. W*. Cape Town: Tafelberg, 1984.

Dictionary of South African Biography. 5 vols. Cape Town: Human Sciences Research Council, 1968–1987.

Dictionary of South African English on Historical Principles. New York: Oxford University Press in association with The Dictionary Unity for South African English, 1996.

DILTHEY, WILHELM. *Der Aufbau der Geschichtlichen Welt in den Geisteswissenschaften*. Frankfurt am Main: Suhrkamp, 1970.

DITTMAR-DAHNKE, COSMO, and KATHARINA PÜHL. "Narrate Yourself! Governmentality and Transgender Self-representation." Paper delivered at Heteronormativity workshop with Judith Halberstam. University of Basel, July 10, 2004.

DLADLA, MBOMA, as told to Kathy Bond. *The Story of Mboma*. Johannesburg: Ravan Press, 1979.

D'OLIVIERA, JOHN. *Vorster: The Man*. Johannesburg: E. Stanton, 1977.

DOLNY, HELENA. *Banking on Change*. London: Viking, 2001.

DRIVER, DOROTHY. "*M'a-ngoana o tšoare thipa ka bohaleng*—The Child's Mother Grabs the Sharp End of the Knife: Women as Mothers, Women as Writers." In *Rendering Things Visible: Essays on South African Literary Culture*, edited by Martin Trump, pp. 225–255. Athens: Ohio University Press, 1991.

DU BOIS, W. E. B. *The Souls of Black Folk*. Eds. Terri Hume Oliver and Henry Louis Gates. New York: Norton, 1998.

DU PREEZ, MAX. *Pale Native: Memories of a Renegade Reporter*. Cape Town: Zebra Press, 2003.

DU PREEZ BEZDROB, ANNE MARIE. *Winnie Mandela: A Life*. Cape Town: Zebra, 2003.

DUFFIELD, ERNIE. *Through My Binoculars*. Pietermaritzburg: Shuter and Shooter, 1982.

EAKIN, PAUL JOHN. *Touching the World: Reference in Autobiography*. Princeton, NJ: Princeton University Press, 1992.

———. "The Unseemly Profession: Privacy, Inviolate Personality, and the Ethics of Life Writing." In *Renegotiating Ethics in Literature, Philosophy, and Theory*, edited by J. Adamson, R. Freadman, and D. Parker, pp. 161–180. Cambridge: Cambridge University Press, 1998.

———. "Relational Selves, Relational Lives: Autobiography and the Myth of Autonomy." In *How Our Lives Becomes Stories: Making Selves*, pp. 43–98. Ithaca: Cornell University Press, 1999.

———. "Breaking Rules: The Consequences of Self-narration." *Biography* 24, 1 (Winter 2001): 113–127.

———. "Living Autobiographically." *Biography* 28, 1 (Winter 2005): 1–14.

EBRAHIM, NOOR. *Noor's Story: My Life in District Six*. Cape Town: The District Six Museum, 1999.

EBR-VALLY, REHANA. *Kala Pani: Caste and Colour in South Africa*. Cape Town: Kwela, 2001.

EBRON, GRACE. "Africa East." In *Encyclopaedia of Life Writing*, edited by Margaretta Jolly, pp. 11–13. London: Fitzroy Dearborn, 2001.

ECKERT, ANDREAS, and ADAM JONES. "Introduction: Historical Writing about Everyday Life." *Journal of African Cultural Studies* 15, 1 (2002): 5–16.

EDE, LISA, and ANDREA LUNSFORD. "Collaborative Authorship and the Teaching of Writing." In *The Construction of Authorship: Textual Appropriation in Law and Literature*, edited by M. Woodmansee and P. Jaszi, pp. 417–438. Durham: Duke University Press, 1994.

———. "Collaboration and Concepts of Authorship." *PMLA* 116, 2 (2001): 354–369.

EDGAR, ROBERT R., and HILARY SAPIRE. *African Apocalypse: The Story of Nonthetha Nkwenkwe, a Twentieth Century South African Prophet*. Johannesburg: Witwatersrand University Press, 1999.

ERASMUS, ZIMITRI, ed. *Coloured by History, Shaped by Place: New Perspectives on Coloured Identities in the City*. Cape Town: Kwela, 2001.

EVANS, GAVIN. *Dancing Shoes Is Dead: A Tale of Fighting Men in South Africa*. London: Doubleday, 2002.

EVANS, NICHOLAS, and MONICA SEEBER, eds. *The Politics of Publishing in South Africa*. Frankfurt am Main: Holger Ehling, 2001.

FABER, PAUL, comp. and ed., and ANNARI VAN DER MERWE, ed. *Group Portrait South Africa: Nine Family Histories*. Cape Town: Kwela, 2003.

FAIRBRIDGE, KINGSLEY OGILVIE. *The Autobiography of Kingsley Fairbridge*. Preface by L. S. Amery, epilogue by Arthur Lawley. Ed. V. F. Boyson. London: Oxford University Press, 1928.

FARISANI, TSHENUWANI SIMON. *Diary from a South African Prison*. Ed. John A. Evenson. Philadelphia: Fortress Press, 1987.

FAUVET, PAUL, and MARCELO MOSSE. *É proibido por algemas nas palavras: Carlos Car-*

doso e a Revolução Moçambicana. Maputo: Ndjira, 2003. (English translation: *Telling the Truth in Mozambique*. Cape Town: Double Storey, 2003.)

FAY, MARY ANN. *Autobiography and the Construction of Identity and Community in the Middle East*. Basingstoke: Macmillan, 2000.

FELMAN, SHOSHANA, and DORI LAUB. *Testimony: Crises of Witnessing in Literature, Psychoanalysis, and History*. London: Routledge, 1991.

FERREIRA, NATIE. *The Story of an Afrikaner: Die revolusie van die kinders*. Johannesburg: Ravan Press, 1980.

FIELDING, NIGEL, ed. *Interviewing*. Vols. 1–4. London: Sage Publications, 2003.

———, ed. "Editor's Introduction: Hearing the Social." In *Interviewing*, Vol. 1. pp. ix–xxii. London: Sage Publications, 2003.

FIRST, RUTH. *117 Days*. London: Bloomsbury, 1965.

FIRST, RUTH, and ANN SCOTT. *Olive Schreiner*. New York: Schocken Books, 1980.

FLANNIGAN, ARTHUR. "African Discourse and the Autobiographical Novel: Mongo Beti's *Mission Terminée*." *French Review* 55, 6 (1982): 835–845.

FLEISHER FELDMAN, CAROL. "Narratives of National Identity as Group Narratives: Patterns of Interpretive Cognition." In *Narrative and Identity Studies in Autobiography, Self and Culture*, edited by Jens Brockmeier and Donal Carbaugh, pp. 129–144. Amsterdam: John Benjamins, 2001.

FORBES, GORDON. *A Handful of Summers*. Johannesburg: Jonathan Ball, 1978.

FORTUNE, LINDA. *The House in Tyne Street: Childhood Memories of District Six*. Cape Town: Kwela, 1996.

FOUCAULT, MICHEL. *The History of Sexuality*. Vol. 1. London: Penguin, 1976.

———. "Technologies of the Self." In *Technologies of the Self: A Seminar with Michel Foucault*, edited by Luther H. Martin et al., pp. 16–49. Amherst: University of Massachusetts Press, 1988.

———. "Governmentality." In *The Foucault Effect: Studies in Governmentality, with Two Lectures by and an Interview with Michel Foucault*, edited by Graham Burchell, Colin Gordon, and Peter Miller, pp. 87–104. London: Harvester Wheatsheaf, 1991.

FOX, JANE. *Nkosi's Story*. Parkview: Spearhead, 2002.

FOX, JUSTIN. *With Both Hands Waving: A Journey through Mozambique*. Cape Town: Kwela, 2002.

FOX, SUSAN (interviews), and GISÈLE WULFSON (photographs). *Living Openly: HIV Positive South Africans Tell Their Stories*. Pretoria: Department of Health, 2000.

FRASER, NANCY. *Unruly Practices: Power, Discourse and Gender in Contemporary Social Theory*. Cambridge: Polity, 1989.

———. *Justice Interruptus: Critical Reflection on the "Postsocialist" Condition*. New York: Routledge, 1997.

———. "Transnationalizing the Public Sphere." In *Globalizing Critical Theory*, edited by Max Pensky, pp. 37–47. Lanham: Rowman & Littlefield Publishers, 2005.

FRASER, NANCY, and ALEX HONNETH. *Redistribution or Recognition? A Politico-philosophical Exchange.* London: Verso, 2003.

FREEMAN, MARK, and JENS BROCKMEIER. "Narrative Integrity: Autobiographical Identity and the Meaning of the 'good life.'" In *Narrative and Identity: Studies in Autobiography, Self and Culture*, edited by Jens Brockmeier and Donal Carbaugh, pp. 75–102. Amsterdam: John Benjamins, 2001.

FRISCH, ANDREA. "The Ethics of Testimony: A Genealogical Perspective." *Discourse* 25, nos.1 & 2 (Winter and Spring 2004): 36–54.

FUGARD, ATHOL. *Notebooks: 1960–1977.* Johannesburg: Ad. Donker, 1983a.

———. *"Master Harold" . . . and the Boys.* Oxford: Oxford University Press, 1983b.

———. *Cousins: A Memoir.* Johannesburg: Witwatersrand University Press, 1994.

———. *The Captain's Tiger: A Memoir for the Stage.* New York: Theatre Communications Group, 1999.

FULLER, ALEXANDRA. *Don't Let's Go to the Dogs Tonight.* London: Picador, 2002.

FYNN, HENRY FRANCIS. *The Diary of Henry Francis Fynn.* Comp. and ed. James Stuart and D. M. Malcolm. Pietermaritzburg: Shuter and Shooter, 1950.

GALLOWAY, FRANCIS. "Notes on South African Book Production during the 1990s." Paper delivered at the Time of the Writer Festival (Durban, March 2002). http://www.litnet.co.za/indaba/galloway.asp

GANDHI, M. K. *An Autobiography: Or the Story of My Experiments with Truth.* London: Penguin, 1982.

GATES, HENRY LOUIS, and KWAME ANTHONY APPIAH, eds. *Identities.* Chicago: University of Chicago Press, 1995.

GENETTE, G. *Paratexts: Thresholds of Interpretation.* Trans. Jane E. Lewin. New York: Cambridge University Press, 1997.

GÉRARD, ALBERT. ed. *European-language Writings in Sub-Saharan Africa.* Vols. I and II. Budapest: Akadémikai Kaidó, 1986.

GEVISSER, MARK, and EDWIN CAMERON. *Defiant Desire: Gay and Lesbian Lives in South Africa.* Johannesburg: Ravan Press, 1994.

GIBSON, PERLA SIEDLE. *The Lady in White.* Cape Town: Purnell, 1964.

GILFILLAN, LYNDA. "Theorising the Counterhegemonic: A Critical Study of Black South African Autobiography from 1954–1963." PhD diss., University of South Africa, 1996.

GILLIGAN, CAROL. *In a Different Voice: Psychological Theory and Women's Development.* Cambridge, MA: Harvard University Press, 1982.

GILROY, PAUL. *The Black Atlantic: Modernity and Double Consciousness.* London: Verso, 1993.
———. *Between Camps: Nations, Cultures and the Allure of Race.* London: Penguin, 2000.
———. *After Empire: Melancholia or Convivial Culture?* London: Routledge, 2004.
GITTI, GITAHI. "Self and Society in Testimonial Literature: Caesarina Kona Makhoere's *No Child's Play in Prison under Apartheid.*" *Current Writing* 3, 1 (1991): 193–199.
GOBODO-MADIKIZELA, PUMLA. *A Human Being Died That Night.* Johannesburg: New Africa Books, 2003.
GODWIN, PETER. *Mukiwa: A White Boy in Africa.* London: Harper Collins, 1997.
GOLDBLATT, DAVID. *Some Afrikaners Photographed.* Sandhurst: Struik, 1975.
GOONAM, DR., with FATIMA MEER. *Coolie Doctor: An Autobiography by Dr. Goonam.* Durban: Madiba Publishers, 1991.
GORDON, LYNDALL. *Shared Lives: A Memoir.* Cape Town: David Philip, 1992.
GORDON, RUTH. *Alive, Alive-o!* Pietermaritzburg: Privately published, 1984.
GORDON, SUZANNE. *A Talent for Tomorrow: Life Stories of South African Servants.* Johannesburg: Ravan Press, 1985.
GOVINDEN, DEVARAKSHANAM. "*Coolie Doctor:* Woman in a Man's World." *Current Writing* 13, 1 (2001): 22–48.
GRAHAM, SHANE DWIGHT. "Trauma Representation and Public Memory in South Africa: Apartheid Prison Narratives and the Truth Commission." PhD diss., Indiana University, 2001.
———. "The Truth Commission and Post-apartheid Literature in South Africa." *Research in African Literatures* 34, 1 (Spring 2003): 11–30.
GRAY, STEPHEN. *Southern African Literature: An Introduction.* Cape Town: David Philip, 1979.
———. *Schreiner: A One-woman Play.* Cape Town: David Philip, 1983.
———. *Accident of Birth: An Autobiography.* Johannesburg: Congress of South African Writers, 1993.
———. *Free-lancers and Literary Biography in South Africa.* Amsterdam: Rodopi, 1999.
———. *Beatrice Hastings: A Literary Life.* London: Viking Penguin, 2004.
———. *Life Sentence: A Biography of Herman Charles Bosman.* Cape Town: Human & Rousseau, 2005.
GREGORY, JAMES, with BOB GRAHAM. *Goodbye Bafana: Nelson Mandela, My Prisoner, My Friend.* London: Headline, 1995.
GRIESEL, HANLIE. *Sibambene: The Voices of Women at Mboza.* Johannesburg: Ravan Press, 1987.

GROHS, GERHARD. Preface. In *Genres autobiographiques en Afrique/Autobiographical genres in Africa*, edited by János Riesz and Ulla Schild, pp. 3–5. Berlin: Dietrich Reimer Verlag, 1996a.

———. "Changing Social Functions of African Autobiographies with Special Reference to Political Autobiographies." *Genres autobiographiques en Afrique/Autobiographical genres in Africa*, edited by János Riesz and Ulla Schild, pp. 191–204. Berlin: Dietrich Reimer Verlag, 1996b.

GROSS, ANDREW S., and HOFFMAN, MICHAEL J. "Memory, Authority, and Identity: Holocaust Studies in Light of the Wilkomirski Debate." *Biography* 27, 1 (2004): 25–47.

GUNNER, LIZ, and MAFIKA GWALA, trans. and eds. *Musho: Zulu Popular Praises*. Johannesburg: Witwatersrand University Press, 1994.

GUGELBERGER, GEORG, ed. *The Real Thing*. Durham: Duke University Press, 1996.

GUSDORF, GEORGES. "Conditions and Limits of Autobiography." In *Autobiography: Essays Theoretical and Critical*, edited by James Olney, pp. 28–48. Princeton, N.J.: Princeton University Press, 1980.

GUTMANN, AMY, ed. *Multiculturalism: Examining the Politics of Recognition*. Princeton, NJ: Princeton University Press, 1994.

GUY, JEFF. *The Heretic: A Study on the Life of John William Colenso 1814–1883*. Johannesburg: Ravan Press, 1983.

———. "Making Words Visible: Aspects of Orality, Literacy, Illiteracy and History in Southern Africa." *South African Historical Journal* 31 (1994): 3–27.

HABERMAS, JÜRGEN. *Erkenntnis und Interesse*. Frankfurt am Main: Suhrkamp, 1973.

———. *Nachmetaphysisches denken*. Frankfurt am Main: Suhrkamp, 1988.

———. *The Structural Transformation of the Public Sphere*. Cambridge, MA: MIT Press, 1989.

HALEY, ALEX. *The Autobiography of Malcolm X*. London: Penguin, 1965.

HALL, JAMES, see Makeba.

HALL, STUART. "The Question of Cultural identity." In *Modernity and Its Futures*, edited by Stuart Hall, David Held, and Tony McGrew, pp. 273–325. Cambridge: Polity Press, 1992.

HAMILTON, STEVE. *I Want My Life Back*. Johannesburg: Penguin, 2002.

HARLAN, JUDITH. *Mamphela Ramphele: Challenging Apartheid in South Africa*. New York: Feminist Press, 2000.

HARRIES, PATRICK. "From Site to Sight: Some Origins of African Studies in Switzerland." Inaugural lecture. University of Basel, May 2002.

HART, ROWLAND. *Before van Riebeeck: Callers at South Africa from 1488 to 1652*. Cape Town: Struik, 1967.

HAZLETT, JOHN DOWNTON. *My Generation: Collective Autobiography and Identity Politics*. Madison: University of Wisconsin Press, 1998.

HEAD, BESSIE. *A Question of Power*. Portsmouth: Heinemann, 1973.

———. *A Gesture of Belonging: Letters from Bessie Head, 1965–1979*. Ed. Randolph Vigne. Portsmouth: Heinemann, 1991.

HERMER, CAROL. *The Diary of Maria Tholo*. Johannesburg: Ravan Press, 1980.

HEYNS, MICHIEL. "The Whole Country's Truth: Confession and Narrative in Recent White South African Writing." *Modern Fiction Studies* 46, 1 (2000): 42–66.

HICKEY, A. "Africa: European Exploration and Travel Writing." In *Encyclopedia of Life Writing: Autobiographical and Biographical Forms*, edited by Margaretta Jolly, pp. 17–19. London: Fitzroy Dearborn, 2001.

HIGGS, CATHERINE. "Travel with a Purpose: A South African at Tuskegee, 1913." *Journal of African Travel Writing* (2000): n.p. http://www.unc.edu/~ottotwo/eightandninecontents.html

———. *The Ghost of Equality: The Public Lives of D. D. T. Jabavu of South Africa, 1885–1959*. Johannesburg: New Africa Books, 2002.

HINCHMAN, LEWIS. P., and SANDA. K. HINCHMAN. *Memory, Identity, Community: The Idea of Narrative in the Human Sciences*. New York: SUNY Press, 1997.

HLONGWANE, GUGU DAWN. "Autobiographies of Three Transitional Women: Ellen Kuzwayo, Emma Mashinini and Sindiwe Magona." PhD diss., University of Guelph (Canada), 1995.

HOBSBAWM, ERIC. "Identity Politics and the Left." *New Left Review* (May/June 1996): 38–47.

HODGSON, JANET. *Princess Emma*. Craighall: Ad. Donker, 1987.

HOFMEYR, I., and S. NUTTALL. "Introduction." Special Issue on the Book in Africa. *Current Writing* 13, 2 (2001): 1–10.

HOLGATE, KINGSLEY. *Cape to Cairo: One Family's Adventures along the Waterways of Africa*. Cape Town: Struik, 2002.

HOLROYD, MARY. *Weigh-less Forever*. Durban: Weigh-Less Publications, 1997.

HOPE, CHRISTOPHER. *White Boy Running*. Harmondsworth: Abacus, 1988.

HORKHEIMER, MAX, and THEODOR ADORNO. *Dialektik der Aufklärung*. Frankfurt am Main: Fischer, 1986.

HOURWICH REYHER, REBECCA. *Zulu Woman: The Life of Christina Sibiya*. Pietermaritzburg: University of Natal Press, 1999.

HUDDLESTONE, TREVOR. *Nought for Your Comfort*. Glasgow: Fount Paperbacks, 1956.

HUDSON-REED, S. *Clement M. Doke: Man of Two Missions*. Cape Town: South African Baptist Historical Society, 1998.

HUIGEN, SIEGFRIED. "Michiel Christiaan Vos: De eerste Swarte schrijver in Zuid-

Afrika." *Tydskrif vir Nederlands & Afrikaans* 4, 2 (December 1997). n.p. http://academic.sun.ac.za/afrndl/tna/972/index.html

HUME, DAVID. *Enquiry Concerning Human Understanding*. Oxford: Clarendon Press, 2001.

HUNSAKER, STEVEN V. *Autobiography and National Identity in the Americas*. Charlottesville: University Press of Virginia, 1999.

HUTCHINSON, ALFRED. *Road to Ghana*. London: Victor Gollancz, 1960.

IBRAHIM, HUMAS. "The Autobiographical Content in the Works of South African Women Writers: The Personal and the Political." In *Biography East and West: Selected Conference Papers,* edited by Carol Ramelb. Honolulu: University of Hawai'i Press, 1989.

JABAVU, NONI. *Drawn in Colour: African Contrasts*. London: John Murray, 1960.

———. *The Ochre People: Scenes from a South African Life*. London: John Murray, 1963.

JACOBS, JOHAN. "Breyten Breytenbach and the South African Prison Book. *Theoria* 68 (1986): 95–105.

———. "Confession, Interrogation and Self-interrogation in the new South African Prison Writing." *Kunapipi* 13, nos.1–2 (1991a): 115–127.

———. "The Discourses of Detention." *Current Writing* 3 (1991b): 193–199.

———. "Reconciling Languages in Antjie Krog's *Country of My Skull*." *Current Writing* 12, 2 (2000): 38–51.

JACOBS, RAYDA. *The Mecca Diaries*. Cape Town: Double Storey, 2005.

JACOBSEN, QUENTIN. *Solitary in Johannesburg*. London: Michael Joseph, 1973.

JANSEN, ENA. "'Ek ook het besluit om van my bittere lydingskelk te vertel.' Het meervoudige (post) koloniale vertoog in outobiografische vrouwenteksten over de Zuid-Afrikaanse oorlog (1899–1902)." *Tydskrif vir Nederlands en Afrikaans* (Dec. 1999): n.p. http://www.sun.ac.za/afrndl/tna/623.htm

JENKIN, TIM. *Escape from Pretoria*. London: Kliptown Books, 1987. (Republished as *Inside Out: Escape from Pretoria Prison*. Johannesburg: Jacana, 2003.)

JOLLY, MARGARETTA, ed. *Encyclopedia of Life Writing: Autobiographical and Biographical Forms*. London: Fitzroy Dearborn, 2001.

JOSEPH, HELEN. *Tomorrow's Sun: A Smuggled Journal from South Africa*. London: Hutchinson, 1966.

———. *Side by Side*. London: Zed, 1986.

———. *If This Be Treason*. Johannesburg: Contra Press, 1988.

JOUBERT, ELSA. *Die swerfjare van Poppie Nongena*. Kaapstad: Tafelberg, 1978.

———. *The Long Journey of Poppie Nongena*. Johannesburg: Jonathan Ball, 1980.

Journal of Southern African Studies. Special Issue on Masculinities in Southern Africa. 24, 4 (December): 1998.

JUNOD, HENRI ALEXANDRE. *The Life of a South African Tribe*. Neuchâtel: Attinger, 1912–1913.

JÜRGENS, RICHARD. *The Many Houses of Exile*. Weltevreden Park: Covos Day, 2000.

KADALIE, CLEMENTS. *My Life and the ICU: The Autobiography of a Black Trade Unionist in South Africa*. Ed. Stanley Trapido. London: Frank Cass and Co., 1970.

KANNEMEYER, JOHN. *Geskiedenis van die Afrikaanse literatuur*. Vol. 1 and 2. Kaapstad: Academica. 1978.

———. *Leipoldt: 'n Lewensverhaal*. Kaapstad: Tafelberg, 1999.

———. *Die lewe en werk van Uys Krige, die goue seun*. Kaapstad: Tafelberg, 2002.

KASRILS, RONNIE. *Armed and Dangerous: From Undercover Struggle to Freedom*. Revised edition. Johannesburg: Mayibuye Books, 1998. (Original: *Armed and Dangerous: My Undercover Struggle against Apartheid*. Oxford: Heinemann, 1993.)

KEARNEY, RICHARD. *On Stories*. London: Routledge, 2002.

KEEGAN, TIM. *Facing the Storm: Portraits of Black Lives in Rural South Africa*. Cape Town: David Philip, 1988.

KEITETSIE, CHINA. *Child Soldier: Fighting for My Life*. Bellevue: Jacana, 2002.

KERBY, ANTHONY. *Narrative and the Self*. Bloomington: Indiana University Press, 1991.

KERFOOT, CAROLINE. *We Came to Town*. Johannesburg: Ravan Press, 1985.

KGOSANA, PHILIP ATA. *Lest We Forget: An Autobiography*. Johannesburg: Skotaville Press, 1988.

KHOISAN, ZENZILE, and K. I. ROLFES. *Jakaranda Time: An Investigator's View of South Africa's Truth and Reconciliation Commission*. Observatory: Garib Communications, 2001.

KHUZWAYO, ZAZAH P. *Never Been at Home*. Claremont: David Philip, 2004.

KLEIN, CAROLE. *Doris Lessing: A Biography*. London: Duckworth, 2000.

KLING, JOSEPH. "Narratives of Possibility: Social Movements, Collective Stories, and the Dilemmas of Practice." Paper delivered at the New Social Movement and Community Organizing Conference, University of Washington School of Social Work, November 1–3, 1995. http://www.interweb-tech.com/nsmnet/docs/kling.htm

KOCH, BLAISE. *In, Around, Through and Out: An Actor's Life*. Spearhead: Kenilworth, 2002.

KOMMERS, JEAN. "Koloniale etnografie en antropologie." *Tydskrif vir Nederlands en Afrikaans* 3, 2 (December 1996): n.p. http://www.sun.ac.za/afrndl/tna/962/Kommers.html

KOSMAN, ARYEH. "The Naïve Narrator: Meditation on Descartes." In *Essays on Descartes' Meditations*, edited by Amélie Rorty Oksenberg, pp. 21–45. Berkeley: University of California Press, 1986.

KOYANA, SIPHOKAZI Z. "The Heart of a Woman: Black Women's Lives in the United States and South Africa as Portrayed in the Autobiographies of Maya Angelou and Sindiwe Magona." PhD diss., Temple University, 1999.

KROG, ANTJIE. *Country of My Skull*. London: Jonathan Cape, 1998.

———. *A Change of Tongue*. Johannesburg: Random House, 2003.

KUPER, HILDA. *Sobhuza II Ngwenyama and King of Swaziland: The Story of an Hereditary Ruler and His Country*. New York: Africana Publishing Company, 1978.

KUREISHI, HANIF. *My Ear at His Heart: Reading My Father*. London: Faber and Faber, 2004.

KUZWAYO, ELLEN. *Call Me Woman*. London: Women's Press, 1985.

———. *Sit Down and Listen*. London: The Feminist Press, 1990.

LABUSCHAGNE, RIAAN. *On South Africa's Secret Service: An Undercover Agent's Story*. Alberton: Galago, 2002.

LACAPRA, DOMINICK. *Writing History, Writing Trauma*. Baltimore: Johns Hopkins University Press, 2001.

LAIRD, HOLLY, and LISA EDE. "'A Hand Spills from the Book's Threshold': Co-authorship's Readers." *PMLA* 116, 2 (2001): 344–353.

LARA, MARIA PIA. *Moral Textures: Feminist Narratives in the Public Sphere*. Cambridge: Polity Press, 1998.

LAWRENCE, MARTIN. "Africa: Oral Life Histories." In *Encyclopedia of Life Writing: Autobiographical and Biographical Forms*, edited by Margaretta Jolly, pp. 15–17. London: Fitzroy Dearborn, 2001.

LAWSON, LESLEY, and HELENE PEROLD, eds. *Working Women: A Portrait of South Africa's Black Women Workers*. Johannesburg: Ravan Press, 1985.

LEE, ESTER. *I Was Born in Africa*. London: Minerva Press, 1999.

LEJEUNE, PHILIPPE. "The Autobiographical Pact." In *On Autobiography*, edited by Paul John Eakin, trans. Katherine Leary, pp. 3–30. Minneapolis: University of Minnesota Press, 1989a.

———. "The Autobiographical Pact (bis)." In *On Autobiography*, edited by Paul John Eakin, trans. Katherine Leary, pp. 119–137. Minneapolis: University of Minnesota Press, 1989b.

LEKOTA, MOSIUOA PATRICK. *Prison Letters to a Daughter*. Bramley: Taurus, 1991.

LESSING, DORIS. *Under My Skin: Volume I of My Autobiography to 1949*. London: Flamingo, 1994.

LEVIN, ADAM. *Aidsafari*. Cape Town: Zebra, 2005.
LEVINE, JANET. *Inside Apartheid: One Woman's Struggle in South Africa*. Chicago: Contemporary Books, 1988.
LEWIN, HUGH. *Bandiet: Seven Years in a South African Prison*. Cape Town: David Philip, 1981. (Republished as *Bandiet: Out of Jail*. Johannesburg: Random House, 2002.)
Life Writing. The Life Writing Research Unit at Curtin University of Technology, Western Australia 2004. http://www.lifewriting.humanities.curtin.edu.au.
LINDFORS, BERNTH, ed. *Africans on Stage: Studies in Ethnological Show Business*. Bloomington: Indiana University Press, 1999.
LIPMAN, BEATA. *We Make Freedom: Women in South Africa*. London: Pandora, 1984.
LISTER, MOIRA. *The Very Merry Moira*. London: Hodder and Stoughton, 1969.
LOTTERING, AGNES. *Winnefred & Agnes: The True Story of Two Women*. Cape Town: Kwela, 2002.
LOVESEY, OLIVER. "The African Prison Diary as 'National Allegory.'" In *Nationalism vs. Internationalism: (Inter)national Dimensions of Literatures in English*, edited by Wolfgang Zach and Ken Goodwin, pp. 209–218. Tübingen: Stauffenburg Verlag, 1996.
LUTHULI, ALBERT. *Let My People Go: An Autobiography*. London: Collins, 1962.
MABUZA-SUTTLE, FELICIA, with THEBE IKALAFENG. *Felicia: Dare to Dream*. Johannesburg: Zebra, 1999.
MACDERMOTT, DOIREANN. *Autobiographical and Biographical Writing in the Commonwealth*. Barcelona: Editorial AUSA, 1985.
MÄCHLER, STEFAN. *Der Fall Wilkomirski: Über die Wahrheit einer Biographie* (The Wilkomirski affair: A study in biographical truth). Zürich: Pendo, 2000.
——— (English spelling Maechler, Stefan). "Wilkomirski the Victim: Individual Remembering as Social Interaction and Public Event." *History & Memory* 13, 2 (2001): 59–95.
MAGONA, SINDIWE. *To My Children's Children*. Cape Town: David Philip, 1990.
———. *Forced to Grow*. Cape Town: David Philip, 1992.
MAGUBANE, ZINE. "Which Bodies Matter: Feminism, Poststructuralism, Race, and the Curious Theoretical Odyssey of the 'Hottentot Venus.'" *Gender & Society* 15, 6 (2001): 816–834.
MAKEBA, MIRIAM, with JAMES HALL. *Makeba: My Story*. Johannesburg: Skotaville Press, 1988.
MAKGOBA, M. W. *Mokoko: The Makgoba Affair: A Reflection on Transformation*. Florida Hills: Vivlia, 1997.
MAKHATHINI, BHEKA. "Crossing Borders: A Critical Study of Michael Dingake's

My Fight against Apartheid and Helao Shityuwete's *Never Follow the Wolf: The Autobiography of a Namibian Freedom Fighter.*" PhD diss., University of Natal, 1987.

MAKHOBA, MANDLENKOSI. *The Sun Shall Rise for the Workers.* Johannesburg: Ravan Press, 1984.

MAKHOERE, CAESARINA KONA. *No Child's Play: In Prison under Apartheid.* London: Women's Press, 1988.

MALAN, RIAN. *My Traitor's Heart.* London: Bodley Head, 1990.

MALHERBE, E. G. *Never a Dull Moment.* Cape Town: Howard Timmins, 1981.

MANDELA, NELSON. *Long Walk to Freedom.* Randburg: Macdonald Purnell, 1994.

MANDELA, WINNIE. *Part of My Soul Went with Him.* Ed. Anne Benjamin. Adapted by Mary Benson. New York: Norton, 1985.

MANGANYI, CHABANI. *Exiles and Homecomings: A Biography of Es'kia Mphahlele.* Johannesburg: Ravan Press. 1983.

———. "Psychobiography and the Truth of the Subject." In *Treachery and Innocence: Psychology and Racial Difference in South Africa*, pp. 68–91. Johannesburg: Ravan Press, 1991.

———. *A Black Man Called Sekoto.* Johannesburg: Witwatersrand University Press, 1996.

———. *Gerard Sekoto: "I Am an African": A Biography.* Johannesburg: Witwatersrand University Press, 2004.

MARBLE, JOSEPH. *Ek, Joseph Daniel Marble.* Cape Town: Kwela, 1999.

MARKS, SHULA, comp. *Not Either an Experimental Doll: The Separate Worlds of Three South African Women.* Pietermaritzburg: University of Natal Press, 1987. See also http://www.bbc.co.uk/radio4/discover/archive_column/12.shtml for a BBC program on *Not Either an Experimental Doll.*

———. "The Context of Personal Narrative: Reflections on *Not Either an Experimental Doll*—The Separate Worlds of Three South African Women." In *Interpreting Women's Lives: Feminist Theory and Personal Narratives*, pp. 39–58. Bloomington, Indiana University Press, 1989.

MASEKELA, HUGH, and MICHAEL CHEERS. *Still Grazing: The Musical Journey of Hugh Masekela.* New York: Crown Publishers, 2004.

MASHININI, EMMA. *Strikes Have Followed Me All My Life: A South African Autobiography.* London: Women's Press, 1989.

MASILELA, JOHNNY. *Deliver Us from Evil: Scenes from a Rural Transvaal Upbringing.* Cape Town: Kwela, 1997.

MATANZIMA, KAIZER. *Independence My Way.* Pretoria: Foreign Affairs Association, 1976.

MATHABANE, MARK. *Kaffir Boy: The True Story of a Black Youth's Coming of Age in Apartheid South Africa*. New York: Macmillan, 1986.

———. *African Women: Three Generations*. New York: Harper Collins, 1994.

———, as told by Miriam Mathabane. *Miriam's Song: A Memoir*. New York: Touchstone, 2001.

MATSHIKIZA, TODD. *Chocolates for My Wife: Slices of My Life*. Cape Town: David Philip, 1961.

MATTERA, DON. *Memory Is the Weapon*. Johannesburg: Ravan Press, 1987.

MATTHEWS, FRIEDA. *Remembrances*. Bellville: Mayibuye Books, 1995.

MATTHEWS, Z. K. *Freedom for My People: The Autobiography of Z. K. Matthews*. London: Collins, 1981.

MCADAMS, DAN, and RICHARD OCHBERG. *Psychobiography and Life Narratives*. Durham: Duke University Press, 1988.

MCCLINTOCK, ANNE. "'The Very House of Difference': Race, Gender, and the Politics of South African Women's Narrative in *Poppie Nongena*." In *The Bounds of Race*, edited by D. LaCapra, pp. 184–201. Ithaca: Cornell University Press, 1991.

MCCORD, JAMES. *My Patients Were Zulus*. London: Frederick Muller, 1946.

MCCORD, MARGARET. *The Calling of Katie Makanya: A Memoir of South Africa*. New York: John Wiley, 1995.

MCINTOSH, IAN, with JOHN BISHOP. *Mac: The Face of Rugby*. Cape Town: Don Nelson, 2000.

MCNAY, LOIS. *Gender and Agency: Reconfiguring the Subject in Feminist Social Theory*. Cambridge: Polity, 2000.

———. "Communitarians and Feminists: The Case of Narrative Identity." *Literature and Theology* 16 (2002): 81–95.

———. "Having It Both Ways: The Incompatibility of Narrative Identity and Communicative Ethics in Feminist Thought." *Theory, Culture & Society* 20, 6 (2003): 1–20.

MDAKANE, ZINHLE CAROL. *No Way Out: Story of an X-street Kid*. Durban: University of Durban-Westville, 2001.

MEAD, G. H. *Mind, Self, and Society*. Chicago: University of Chicago Press, 1967.

MEER, FATIMA. *Prison Diary: One Hundred and Thirteen Days*. Cape Town: Kwela, 2001.

MEER, ISMAIL. *A Fortunate Man*. Cape Town: Zebra, 2002.

MENCHÚ, RIGOBERTA. *I, Rigoberta Menchú, an Indian woman in Guatemala*. London: Verso, 1984.

METELERKAMP, PETROVNA. *Ingrid Jonker: Beeld van 'n digterslewe*. Hermanus: Hemel en See, 2003.

MEYER, STEPHAN. "Intersubjectivity and Autobiography: Feminist Critical Theory and Johnny Masilela's *Deliver Us from Evil: Scenes from a Rural Transvaal Upbringing.*" Alter*nation* 7, 1 (2000): 97–124.

———. "The Intersubjective Generation of Truth and Identity in Two South African Collaborative Auto/biographies" MA thesis, University of South Africa, 2003.

MEYERS, DIANA. "Feminist Perspectives on the Self." *The Stanford Encyclopedia of Philosophy,* edited by Edward N. Salta. Spring 2004 Edition. URL = <http://plato.stanford.edu/archives/spr2004/entries/feminism-self/>

MHLABA, RAYMOND, as told to Thembeka Mufamadi. *Raymond Mhlaba's Personal Memoirs: Reminiscing from Rwanda and Uganda.* Pretoria: HSRC Publishers, 2001.

MICHAEL, CHERYL-ANN. "Gender and Iconography in Auto/biographies of Nelson and Winnie Mandela." In *The Uses of Autobiography,* edited by Julia Swindells, pp. 73–80. London: Taylor and Francis, 1995.

MICHAEL, MARJORIE. *I Married a Hunter.* London: Odhams Press, 1956.

MILLIN, SARAH GERTRUDE. *The Night Is Long.* London: Faber and Faber, 1941.

———. *The Measure of My Days.* Cape Town: CNA, 1955.

MILLS, SARA. *Discourses of Difference: An Analysis of Women's Travel Writing and Colonialism.* London: Routledge, 1991.

MINCHER, KATHLEEN. *I Lived in His Shadow: My Life with General Smuts.* Cape Town: Howard Timmins, 1965.

MKHABELA, SIBONGILE. *Open Earth & Black Roses.* Braamfontein: Skotaville Press, 2001.

MODISANE, BLOKE. *Blame Me on History.* Craighall: Ad. Donker, 1963.

MOFOLO, THOMAS. *Chaka.* Morija, Basutoland: Sesuto Book Depot, 1936.

MOGOBA, MMUTLANYANE STANLEY. *Stone, Steel, Sjambok: Faith Born on Robben Island.* Johannesburg: Ziningweni Communications, 2003.

MOHLAMME, J. S. Introduction to *New Dictionary of South African Biography,* Vol. II, pp. viii–ix. Pretoria: Human Sciences Research Council, 1999.

MOKGATLE, NABOTH. *The Autobiography of an Unknown South African.* Parklands: Ad. Donker, 1971.

MOKGOATSANA, SEKGOTHE NGWATO CEDRIC. "Identity: From Autobiography to Postcoloniality: A Study of Representation in Puleng's Works." PhD diss., University of South Africa, 1999.

MORGAN, JONATHAN, director, and the Great African Spider Writers. *Finding Mr Madini.* Claremont: Ink, 1999.

———, and the Bambanani Women's Group. *Long Life: Positive HIV Stories.* Cape Town: Double Storey Press, 2003.

MORRELL, ROBERT, ed. *Changing Men in Southern Africa*. Pietermaritzburg: Natal University Press, 2001.
MOSTERN, KENNETH. *Autobiography and Black Identity Politics: Racialisation in 20th Century America*. Cambridge: Cambridge University Press, 1999.
MPHAHLELE, ES'KIA. *Es'kia: Continued*. Cape Town: Kwela, 2004.
MPHAHLELE, EZEKIEL. *Down Second Avenue*. London: Faber and Faber, 1959.
———. *Afrika My Music: An Autobiography, 1957–1983*. Johannesburg: Ravan Press, 1984a.
———. *Bury Me at the Marketplace: Selected Letters of Es'kia Mphahlele*. Ed. Chabani Manganyi. Braamfontein: Skotaville Press, 1984b.
———. "The Tyranny of Place and Aesthetics: The South African Case." In *Race and Literature*, edited by Charles Malan, pp. 48–59. Pinetown: Owen Burgess, 1987.
MPHAHLELE, LETLAPA. *Child of This Soil: The Life of a Freedom Fighter*. Cape Town: Kwela, 2002.
MPHAHLELE, MANTE. "A Gesture of Defiance: Selected Texts by Black South African Women Writers." *Journal of Literary Studies* 18, 1 (2002): 168–181.
MUFAMADI, THEMBEKA. See Mhlaba, Raymond
MUGABE, ROBERT. *Our War of Liberation: Speeches, Articles, Interviews 1976–1979*. Gwero: Mambo, 1983.
MULLER, CAROL. 1995. "*Chakide*—The Teller of Secrets: Space, Song and Story in Zulu *Maskanda* Performance." *Current Writing: Text and Reception in Southern Africa* 7, 2: 117–131.
MURRAY, CRAIG D., and JUDITH SIXSMITH. 'E-mail: A Qualitative Research Medium for Interviewing?" In *Interviewing*, Vol. II, edited by Nigel Fielding, pp. 128–148. London: Thousand Oaks, 2003.
MYNHARDT, PATRICK. *Boy from Bethulie*. Johannesburg: Witwatersrand University Press, 2003.
NAIDOO, BABENIA, and IAN EDWARDS. *Memoirs of a Saboteur*. Belville: Mayibuye Books, 1995.
NAIDOO, INDRES, as told to Albie Sachs. *Island in Chains: Ten Years on Robben Island*. Harmondsworth: Penguin, 1982.
NAIDOO, JAY. *Coolie Location*. Johannesburg: Taurus, 1990.
NATTRASS, A. J. "Degrees of Transgression: The Writing of South African Black Women Writers Miriam Tlali, Ellen Kuzwayo, Sindiwe Magona and Zoë Wicomb." PhD diss., 1996.
NAUDÉ, BEYERS. *My land van hoop: Die lewe van Beyers Naudé*. Cape Town: Human & Rousseau, 1995.

NDEBELE, NJABULO. *Rediscovery of the Ordinary: Essays on South African Literature and Culture.* Johannesburg: Congress of South African Writers, 1991.

NDLOVU, SIFISO MXOLISI. *The Soweto Uprisings: Counter-memories of June 1976.* Randburg: Ravan Press, 1998.

NEVILLE, DEBBIE, as told to Jenny Harrison. *Debbie's Story: A Journey to Healing.* Halfway House: Southern Book Publishers, 1997.

New Dictionary of South African Biography. Pretoria: Human Sciences Research Council, Vol. I. 1995, Vol. II. 1999.

NGCELWANE, NOMVUYO. *Sala kahle, District Six.* Cape Town: Kwela, 1998.

NGWENYA, THENGAMEHLO HAROLD. "The Ontological Status of Self in Autobiography: The Case of Bloke Modisane's *Blame Me on History*." *Current Writing* vol. 10 no. 1 (1989): 67–76.

———. "Autobiography as 'Life' and 'Art': A Critical Study of Bloke Modisane's *Blame Me on History* and Es'kia Mphahlele's *Down Second Avenue*." MA thesis, University of Natal, 1991.

———. "Ideology and Form in South African Autobiographical Writing: A Study of the Autobiographies of Five South African Authors." PhD diss., University of South Africa, 1997.

———. "Ideology and Self-representation in *The Calling of Katie Makanya*." *Alternation* 7, 1 (2000): 145–162.

NIXON, ROB. *Dreambirds: The Natural History of a Fantasy.* London: Doubleday, 1999.

NKOSI, LEWIS. *Home and Exile and Other Selections.* London: Longman, 1965.

———. "Es'kia Mphahlele at 70." *Southern African Review of Books* 13/14 (Feb./May 1990a). http://www.uni-ulm.de/~rturrell/antho4html/Nkosi1.html

———. "Bloke, Modisane. *Blame Me on History*." *Southern African Review of Books.* 13/14 (Feb./May 1990b). http://www.uni-ulm.de/~rturrell/antho4html/Nkosi2.html

NORTON, PEGGY. *Found in My Mouth: The Journal of Peggy Norton.* Somerset West: Options, 1997.

NTANTALA, PHYLLIS. *A Life's Mosaic.* Cape Town: David Philip, 1992.

NTHUNYA, MPHO 'M'ATSEPO. *Singing Away the Hunger.* Pietermaritzburg: University of Natal Press, 1996.

NUJOMA, SAM. *Where Others Wavered: Autobiography of Sam Nujoma.* Lontoo: Panaf Books, 2001.

NUTTALL, SARAH. "Reading and Recognition in Three South African Women's Autobiographies." *Current Writing* 8, 1 (1996): 1–18.

———. "Telling 'Free' Stories? Memory and Democracy in South African Autobiography since 1998." In *Negotiating the Past: The Making of Memory in South Africa*, edited by Sarah Nuttall and Carli Coetzee, pp. 75–88. Cape Town: Oxford University Press, 1998.

NUTTALL, S., and C.-A. MICHAEL. "Autobiographical Acts." In *Senses of Culture: South African Cultural Studies*, edited by S. Nuttall and C.-A. Michael, pp. 298–317. Cape Town: Oxford University Press, 2000.

NXUMALO, O. E. H. M., C. T. MSIMANG, and I. S. COOKE. *King of Goodwill: The Authorised Biography of King Goodwill Zwelinthini kaBhekuzulu*. Cape Town: Via Afrika, 2003.

NYAMNJOH, FRANCIS B. "From Publish or Perish to Publish and Perish: What the 'Africa's 100 Best Books' Tells Us about Publishing in Africa." Paper prepared for the African Studies Association Conference *Debating Africa?* Goldsmith College, University of London, September 13, 2004.

OLNEY, JAMES. *Tell Me Africa: An Approach to African Literature*. Princeton, NJ: Princeton University Press, 1973.

———. 'Autobiography and the Cultural Moment: A Thematic, Historical, and Bibliographical Introduction." In *Autobiography: Essays Theoretical and Critical*, edited by James Olney, pp. 3–27. Princeton, NJ: Princeton University Press, 1980a.

———, ed. *Autobiography: Essays Theoretical and Critical*. Princeton, NJ: Princeton University Press, 1980b.

OPLAND, JEFF. *The Dassie and the Hunter: A South African Meeting*. Pietermaritzburg: University of KwaZulu-Natal Press, 2005.

ORR, WENDY. *From Biko to Basson: Wendy Orr's Search for the Soul of South Africa as a Commissioner of the TRC*. Saxonwold: Contra Press, 2000.

ORTON, META. *The World and Umhlanga Rocks*. Durban: Privately published, 1983.

PARK, CATHY. *Inside Outside: A Journey of the Spirit through the Gates of a Prison*. Senderwood: BEntrepeneurING, 2001.

PATON, ALAN. *Cry, the Beloved Country: A Story of Comfort in Desolation*. London: Jonathan Cape, 1948.

PAUL, MATHEW, ed. *Parabat*. Johannesburg: Covos Day, 2001.

PAUW, JACQUES. *Into the Heart of Darkness: Confessions of Apartheid's Assassins*. Johannesburg: Jonathan Ball, 1997.

PAVEL, THOMAS. "Literature and the Arts." In *Descartes: Discourse on Method and Meditations on First Philosophy*, edited by D. Weissman, pp. 349–370. New Haven: Yale University Press, 1996.

PELSER, A. C. "Die literêre biografie: 'n tereinverkenning" (The literary biography: An exploration of the field). PhD diss., University of Pretoria, 2001.

http://upetd.up.ac.za/thesis/available/etd-08272002-142815/unrestricted/dissertation.pdf

PENNY, SARAH. *The Whiteness of Bones*. London: Penguin, 1997.

PERHAM, MARGERY, ed. *Ten Africans*. London: Faber & Faber, 1936.

PETTINGER, ALASDAIR. *Always Elsewhere: Travels of the Black Atlantic*. London: Cassell, 1998.

PHETO, MOLEFE. *And Night Fell: Memoirs of a Political Prisoner in South Africa*. London: Heinemann, 1983.

PILKINGTON, DORIS. *Rabbit-proof Fence*. New York: Miramax Books, 2002.

PILLAY, ALMA LAVINIA. "Breyten Breytenbach se outobiografiese werke." PhD diss., University of Natal, 1992.

PLAATJE, SOL T. *Mafeking Diary: A Black Man's View of a White Man's War*. Ed. John Comoroff. Athens: Ohio University Press, 1973.

PLAYER, IAN. *Zululand Wilderness: Shadow and Soul*. Claremont: David Philip, 1997

PODBREY, PAULINE. *White Girl in Search of the Party*. Pietermaritzburg: University of Natal Press, 1993.

POGRUND, BENJAMIN. *War of Words: Memoir of a South African Journalist*. New York: Seven Stories Press, 2000.

POSEL, DEBORAH, and GRAEME SIMPSON, eds. *Commissioning the Past: Understanding South Africa's Truth and Reconciliation Commission*. Johannesburg: Witwatersrand University Press, 2002.

POUCHET PAQUET, SANDRA. *Caribbean Autobiography: Cultural Identity and Self-representation*. Madison: University of Wisconsin Press, 2002.

PRATT, MARY LOUISE. *Toward a Speech Act Theory of Literary Discourse*. Bloomington: Indiana University Press, 1977.

———. *Imperial Eyes: Travel Writing and Transculturation*. London: Routledge, 1992.

PRIDMORE, J. "Henry Francis Fynn: An Assessment of His Career and an Analysis of the Written and Visual Portrayals of His Role in the History of the Natal Region." PhD diss., University of South Africa, 1996.

PRINCE, MARY. *The History of Mary Prince, a West Indian Slave: Related by Herself*. Ed. Thomas Pringle. Rev. ed. Moira Ferguson. Ann Arbor: University of Michigan Press, 1997.

PRINGLE, THOMAS. "Letters from South Africa No. II. Caffer Campaigns: The Prophet Makanna." *New Monthly Magazine and Literary Journal* (Nov. 1826): 69–76.

———. *Thomas Pringle: His Life, Times, and Poems*. Ed. W. Hay. Cape Town: Juta, 1912.

———. *Narrative of a Residence in South Africa*. Cape Town: Struik, 1966.

Promotion of National Unity and Reconciliation Act of 1995. http://www.polity.org
.za/html/govdocs/legislation/1995/act95-034.html?rebookmark=1
QABULA, ALFRED TEMBA. *A Working Life: Cruel beyond Belief.* Durban: NUMSA, 1989.
QUAYSON, ATO. "Memory, History and 'Faction' in Wole Soyinka's *Aké* and *Isara.*" In *The Uses of Autobiography,* edited by Julia Swindells, pp. 73–81. London: Taylor and Francis, 1995.
RABIE, JAN. *Paryse dagboek.* Versorg deur André P. Brink: Kaapstad: Human & Rousseau, 1998.
RADITLHALO, SAMUEL ISHMAEL. "Who Am I?": The Construction of Identity in Twentieth-century South African Autobiographical Writings in English." Groningen: University Library Groningen, 2003. http://www.ub.rug.nl/eldoc/dis/ arts/s.i.raditlhalo/
RALL, MAUREEN. *Peaceable Warrior: The Life and Times of Sol T. Plaatje.* Kimberley: Sol Plaatje Foundation, 2003.
RAMPHELE, MAMPHELA. *A Life.* Cape Town: David Philip, 1995.
———. *Steering by the Stars: Being Young in South Africa.* Cape Town: Tafelberg, 2002.
RANGER, TERENCE. *Are We Not Also Men? The Samkange Family & African Politics in Zimbabwe, 1920–1964.* Oxford: Heinemann, 1995.
RATELE, KOPANO. "We Black Men." *International Journal of Intercultural Relations* 27, 2 (March, 2003): 237–249.
———. "Contradictions in Constructions of African Masculinities." African Regional Sexuality Resource Centre. http://www.arsrc.org/features/issue005.htm
REITZ, DENEYS. *Commando: A Boer Journal of the Boer War.* London: Faber and Faber, 1929.
Research in African Literatures. Special issue on autobiography and African literature. 28, 2 (Summer 1997).
RESHA, MAGGIE. *'Mangoana Tsoara Thipa Ka Bohaleng': My Life in the Struggle.* Johannesburg : Congress of South African Writers, 1991.
RICARD, ALAIN, ed. *Voyages de découvertes en Afrique.* Paris: Robert Laffont, 2000.
———. "The Ellenbergers (D. Frédéric, Victor, Paul): Interpreting seSotho." Paper read at Imperial Culture in Countries without Colonies: Africa and Switzerland Conference at the University of Basel, October 23–25, 2003. http://pages.unibas.ch/afrika/nocolonies/ricard.paper.rtf
RICE, ALAN. *Radical Narratives of the Black Atlantic.* London: Continuum, 2003.
RICOEUR, PAUL. *Hermeneutics and the Human Sciences.* Cambridge: Cambridge University Press, 1981.

———. "Life in Quest of Narrative." In *On Paul Ricoeur: Narrative and Interpretation*, edited by David Wood, pp. 20–33. London: Routledge, 1991a.

———. "Narrative Identity." In *On Paul Ricoeur: Narrative and Interpretation*, edited by David Wood, pp. 188–199. London: Routledge, 1991b.

———. *Oneself as Another*. Chicago: University of Chicago Press, 1992.

RIESZ, JÁNOS, and ULLA SCHILD, eds. *Genres autobiographiques en Afrique/Autobiographical genres in Africa*. Berlin: Dietrich Reimer Verlag, 1996.

RIFFATERRE, MICHAEL. *Fictional Truth*. Baltimore: Johns Hopkins University Press, 1991.

RIOS, TED, and KATHLEEN MULLEN SANDS. *Telling a Good One*. Lincoln: University of Nebraska Press, 2000.

RIVE, RICHARD. *Writing Black*. Cape Town: David Philip, 1981.

ROMERO, PATRICIA W., ed. *Women's Voices on Africa: A Century of Travel Writings*. Princeton, NJ: Markus Wiener Publishing, 1992.

RORTY OKSENBERG, AMÉLIE. "The Structure of Descartes' *Meditations*." In *Essays on Descartes' Meditations*, edited by Amélie Rorty Oksenberg, pp. 1–20. Berkeley: University of California Press, 1986.

ROUSSEAU, JEAN-JACQUES. *The Confessions*. London: Penguin, 1953.

RUSSEL, DIANA E. H. *Lives of Courage: Women for a New South Africa*. New York: Basic Books, 1989.

RYAN, JOHN. *One Man's Africa*. Jeppestown: Jonathan Ball, 2002.

RYAN, PAMELA. "Singing in Prison: Women Writers and the Discourse of Resistance." *Journal of Literary Studies* 9, 1 (April 1993): 57–68.

SACHS, ALBIE. *The Jail Diary of Albie Sachs*. London: Grafton, 1990a.

———. *Soft Vengeance of a Freedom Fighter*. London: Grafton, 1990b.

SACHS, WULF. *Black Hamlet*. Baltimore: Johns Hopkins University Press, 1996.

SAMKANGE, STANLAKE. *The Mourned One*. London: Heinemann, 1975.

SANDERS, MARK. "Truth, Telling, Questioning: The Truth and Reconciliation Commission, Antjie Krog's *Country of My Skull*, and Literature after Apartheid." *Modern Fiction Studies* 46, 1 (2000): 13–41.

SANDOMIRSKY, NATALIE. "Africa: West and Central (Francophone)." In *Encyclopedia of Life Writing: Autobiographical and Biographical Forms*, edited by Margaretta Jolly, pp. 1–14. London: Fitzroy Dearborn, 2001.

SAUNDERS, CHRISTOPHER. "Liberation and Democracy: A Critical Reading of Sam Nujoma's *Autobiography*." In *Re-examining Liberation in Namibia: Political Culture since Independence*, edited by Henning Melber, pp. 87–98. Uppsala: Nordic Africa Institute, 2003.

SAUNDERS, CHRISTOPHER, and NICHOLAS SOUTHEY. *A Dictionary of South African History*. Cape Town: David Philip, 1998.

SAUNDERS, STUART. *Vice-chancellor on a Tightrope: A Personal Account of Climactic Years in South Africa*. Cape Town: David Philip, 2000.

SCHADEBERG, JÜRGEN. *The Fifties People of South Africa*. Lanseria: Bailey's African Photo Archives, 1987.

SCHAFFER, KAY, and SIDONIE SMITH. "Conjunctions: Life Narratives in the Field of Human Rights Biography." *Biography* 27, 1 (Winter 2004a): 1–24.

———. *Human Rights and Narrated Lives: The Ethics of Recognition*. New York: Palgrave Macmillan, 2004b.

SCHALKWYK, DAVID. "Writing from Prison." In *Senses of Culture: South African Cultural Studies*, edited by S. Nuttall and C.-A. Michael, pp. 278–297. Cape Town: Oxford University Press, 2000.

SCHECHTMAN, MARYA. *The Constitution of Selves*. Ithaca: Cornell University Press, 1996.

SCHIPPER, MINEKE. "'Who Am I?' Fact and Fiction in African First Person Narrative." *Research in African Literatures* 16, 1 (1985): 53–79.

SCHIPPER, MINEKE, and PETER SCHMITZ. *Ik is anders: Autobiografie in verschillende culturen*. Baarn: Ambo, 1991.

SCHOEMAN, KAREL. *Die laaste Afrikaanse boek: Outobiografiese aantekeninge*. Kaapstad: Human & Rousseau, 2002.

SCHOLTZ, GERT. *Dr. Hendrik Frensch Verwoerd*. Johannesburg: Perskor, 1974.

SCHREINER, BARBARA, ed. *A Snake with Ice Water: Prison Writings by South African Women*. Johannesburg: Congress of South African Writers, 1992.

SCHREINER, OLIVE. *Olive Schreiner Letters*. Vol. 1. *1871–1899*. Ed. Richard Rive, with historical research by Russell Martin. Oxford: Clarendon Press, 1988.

SCHULZ, WILLIAM. "Psychology and Life Writing." In *Encyclopedia of Life Writing: Autobiographical and Biographical Forms*, edited by Margaretta Jolly, pp. 73–74. London: Fitzroy Dearborn, 2001.

SCOTT, DAVID. "Colonial Governmentality." *Social Text* 43 (Autumn 1995): 191–220.

SHEPHARD, BEN. *Kitty and the Prince*. Johannesburg: Jonathan Ball, 2003.

SHER, ANTONY. *Beside Myself*. London: Century Hutchinson, 2001.

SHOSTAK, MARJORIE. *Nisa: The Life and Words of a !Kung Woman*. Cambridge, MA: Harvard University Press, 1981.

SICWEBA, N. Z. "The Representation of Character in Es'kia Mphahlele's Writings: A Comparison of the autobiography of *Down Second Avenue* (1959) and the novel *The Wanderers* (1971) with his philosophy in *The African Image* (1974)." PhD diss., University of South Africa, 2000.

SIENAERT, MARILET. *The I of the Beholder: Identity Formation in the Art and Writing of Breyten Breytenbach*. Cape Town: Kwela, 2001.

SINGH, MALA. "Identity in the Making." *South African Journal of Philosophy* 14, 3 (1997): 120–123.

SISULU, ELINOR. *Walter and Albertina Sisulu: In Our Lifetime.* Cape Town: David Philip, 2002.

SLATER, FRANCIS CAREY. *Settler's Heritage.* Lovedale: Lovedale Press, 1954.

SLAUGHTER, CAROLYN. *Before the Knife: Memories of an African Childhood.* London: Doubleday, 2002.

SLOVO, GILLIAN. *Every Secret Thing: My Family, My Country.* London: Little, Brown, 1997.

SLOVO, JOE. *Slovo: The Unfinished Autobiography.* Randburg: Ravan Press, 1995.

SLOVO, SHAWN. *A World Apart.* London: Faber and Faber, 1988.

SMITH, CHARLENE. *Proud of Me: Speaking Out against Sexual Violence and HIV.* Sandton: Penguin, 2001.

———. *Patricia de Lille.* Kenilworth: New Africa Books, 2002.

SMITH, PAULINE. *Secret Fire: The 1913–1914 South African Journal of Pauline Smith.* Ed. Harold Scheub. Pietermaritzburg: University of Natal Press, 1997.

SMITH, PRUE. *The Morning Light: A South African Childhood Revalued.* Claremont: David Philip, 2000.

SNYMAN, JOHAN. "To Reinscribe Remorse on a Landscape." *Literature and Theology* 13, 4 (1999): 284–298.

SOMERS, MARGARET. "The Narrative Constitution of Identity: A Relational and Network Approach." *Theory and Society* 23, 5 (October 1994): 605–649.

South Africa Gateway website. http://www.southafrica.info/ess_info/sa_glance/history/strugglebiography.htm

SPENCE, D. P. *Historical Truth and Narrative Truth.* New York: Basic Books, 1992.

SPIVAK, GAYATRI CHAKRAVORTY. "Acting Bits/Identity Talk." In *Identities,* edited by Henry Louis Gates and Kwame Anthony Appiah, pp. 147–180. Chicago: University of Chicago Press, 1995.

STAGL, J., and C. PINNEY. "Introduction: From Travel Writing to Ethnography." *History and Anthropology* 9, nos. 2/3 (1996): 121–124.

STANLEY, LIZ. *The Auto/biographical I: The Theory and Practice of Feminist Auto/biography.* Manchester: Manchester University Press, 1992.

———. "Women's South African War Testimonies: Remembering, Forgetting and Forgiving in *Should We Forget?*" *Tydskrif vir Nederlands en Afrikaans* 9 (2002): 93–118.

STAROBINSKI, JEAN. "The Style of Autobiography." In *Autobiography: Essays Theoretical and Critical,* edited by James Olney, pp. 73–84. Princeton, NJ: Princeton University Press, 1980.

STEPHEN, ARNOLD. "A Peopled Persona: Autobiography, Post-modernism and the Poetry of Niyi Osundare." In *Genres autobiographiques en Afrique/Autobiographical genres in Africa*, edited by János Riesz and Ulla Schild, pp. 143–166. Berlin: Dietrich Reimer Verlag, 1996.

STEYN, JAAP C. *Van Wyk Louw: 'n Lewensverhaal*. Kaapstad: Tafelberg, 1998.

STEYN, RORY, and DEBRA PATTA. *One Step behind Mandela*. Rivonia: Zebra (New Holland Struik), 2000.

STILLINGER, JACK. *Multiple Authorship and the Myth of Solitary Genius*. Oxford: Oxford University Press, 1991.

STOLL, DAVID. *Rigoberta Menchú and the Story of All Poor Guatemalans*. Boulder, CO: Westview Press, 1999.

STRAWSON, GALEN. "Against Narrativity." *Ratio* 17, 4 (December 2004): 428–452.

STRYDOM, MONIQUE, and KALLIE, as told to Marianne Thamm. *Shooting the Moon: A Hostage Story*. Claremont: Spearhead, 2001.

SUTTNER, RAYMOND. *Inside Apartheid's Prison: Notes and Letters of Struggle*. Pietermaritzburg: University of Natal Press, 2001.

SZALAY, MIKLÓS, ed. *The Moon as Shoe: Drawings of the San*. Zurich: Scheidegger and Spies, 2002.

TAS, ADAM. *Dagboek van Adam Tas*. Ed. L. Fouché. Cape Town: Van Riebeeck-Vereniging, 1970.

TAYLOR, CHARLES. *Sources of the Self*. Cambridge: Cambridge University Press, 1992.

TAYLOR, STEPHEN. *Livingstone's Tribe: A Journey from Zanzibar to the Cape*. London: Flamingo, 2000.

TEMA, BOTLHALE. "Henri Gonin and Wegeval Farm: From Servitude to Salvation." Paper read at Imperial Culture in Countries without Colonies: Africa and Switzerland Conference at the University of Basel, October 23–25, 2003. http://pages.unibas.ch/afrika/nocolonies/tema.paper.rtf

THALE, THOMAS. "Paradigms Lost? Paradigms Regained: Working-class Autobiography in South Africa." *Journal of Southern African Studies* 21, 4 (Dec. 1995): 613–622.

———. "Activism and Narration: Construction of Self in Working-class Autobiography." PhD diss., University of Witwatersrand, 2000.

THORNTON, R. "Narrative Ethnography in Africa, 1850–1920: The Creation and Capture of an Appropriate Domain for Anthropology." *Man* 18 (1983): 502–520.

Thula Baba. Johannesburg: Ravan Press, 1987.

Transformation: Critical Perspectives on Southern Africa. Special issue on land and landscape. (No. 44) 2000.

TROTTER, HENRY M. "Sailors as Scribes: Travel Discourse and the (Con)textualisation of the Khoikhoi at the Cape of Good Hope, 1649–1690." *Journal of African Travel Writing* 8/9 (2000): n.p. http://www.unc.edu/~ottotwo/eightandninecontents.html

Truth and Reconciliation Commission of South Africa Report, vols. 1–5, ed. Susan DeVillievs. Cape Town, 1998 http://www.info.gov.za/reports/2003/trc/

TSIGA, ISMAIL ABUBAKAR. "To Tell Freedom: A Study of Black South African Autobiography." PhD diss., University of Essex, 1987.

TURKINGTON, KATE. *There's More to Life than Surface*. Sandton: Penguin, 1998.

TURNER, NOLEEN. "Censure and Social Comment in the *Izihasho* of Urban Zulu Women." *Alternation* 2, 2 (1995): 55–73.

TUTU, DESMOND MPILO. *No Future without Forgiveness*. London: Rider, 1999.

USHPOL, ROWSE. *A Select Bibliography of South African Autobiographies*. Cape Town: University of Cape Town School of Librarianship, 1958.

UYS, PIETER-DIRK. *Elections and Erections: A Memoir of Fear and Fun*. Cape Town: Zebra, 2002.

VAN DER MERWE, F. J. G. *Frank Fillis: Die verhaal van 'n sirkuslegende*. Stellenbosch: FJG Publikasies, 2002.

VAN DER SPUY, PATRICIA. "Winnie Mandela is Not a Shakespearean Creation." *Chimurenga* (November, 2004). http://www.chimurenga.co.za/modules.php?name=news&file=article&sid=71

VAN HEERDEN, MARIE. *Stokkiesdraai: Die Verwoerdversameling in beeld en dokument*. Pretoria: Folio, 1984.

VAN ONSELEN, CHARLES. "The Reconstruction of a Rural Life from Oral Testimony: Critical Notes on the Methodology Employed in the Study of a Black South African Sharecropper." *The Journal of Peasant Studies* 20, 3 (April 1993): 494–514.

———. *The Seed is Mine: The Life of Kas Maine, a South African Sharecropper*. New York: Hill and Wang, 1996.

VAN RIEBEECK, JAN. *Daghregister*. Historisch Genootschap Utrecht, Nieuwe Serie No. 39, 1884.

———. *Journal of Jan Van Riebeeck (1652–1662)*. Vols. I–III. Ed. H. B. Thom. Cape Town: Balkema, 1952.

VAN WOERDEN, HENK. *Een mond vol glas*. Amsterdam: Podium, 1998. (English translation: *A Mouthful of Glass*. Trans. and ed. Dan Jacobson. London: Granta, 2000.)

VAN WYK, JOHAN. *Gesig van die liefde: Ingrid Jonker*. Durban: Self-published, 1999.

———. *Man-bitch*. Durban: Self-published, 2001.

VEIT-WILD, FLORA. "'An Outsider in My Own Biography': From Public Voice to

Fragmented Self in Zimbabwean Autobiographical Fiction." In *Genres autobiographiques en Afrique/Autobiographical genres in Africa*, edited by János Riesz and Ulla Schild, pp. 131–142. Berlin: Dietrich Reimer Verlag, 1996.

VERMEULEN, VICTOR, and JONATHAN ANCER. *The Victor Within*. Norwood: Tenacity Publications, 2000.

VERWOERD, WILHELM. *Viva Verwoerd? Kronieke van 'n keuse*. Cape Town: Human & Rousseau, 1996. (English translation: *My Winds of Change*. Johannesburg: Ravan Press, 1997.)

VOGEL, AMBER. "Africa East," In *Encyclopedia of Life Writing: Autobiographical and Biographical Forms*, edited by Margaretta Jolly, pp. 9–11. London: Fitzroy Dearborn, 2001.

VOLLMER, FRED. "The Narrative Self." *Journal for the Theory of Social Behaviour* 35, 2 (June 2005): 189–205.

VON HUMBOLDT, WILHELM. *Schriften zur Sprachphilosophie*. Werke Bd. 3. Stuttgart: Cotta, 1963.

VOS, MICHIEL CHRISTIAAN. *Merkwaardig verhaal aangaande het leven en lotgevallen van Michiel Christiaan Vos, Als predikant der Hervormde Christelijke gemeente op onderscheidene plaatsen in Nederland, Afrika en Azië; Van zijne Jeugd af tot den tijd van zijn Emeritusschap: Door hem zelven in den jare 1819 briefsgewijze aan eenen vriend medegedeeld*. Amsterdam: A B. Saakes, 1824.

WALVIN, JAMES. *Making the Black Atlantic: Britain and the African Diaspora*. London: Cassell, 2000.

WARING, JOYCE. *Sticks and Stones*. Johannesburg: Voortrekkerpers, 1969.

WATSON, STEPHEN. *A Writer's Diary*. Cape Town: Queillerie, 1997.

WATTS, JANE. *Black Writers from South Africa*. London: Macmillan, 1989.

WEEDON, CHRIS. *Feminist Practice and Poststructuralist Theory*. Oxford: Blackwell, 1987.

WESTERMANN, DIEDRICH. *Afrikaner erzählen ihr Leben*. Essen: Essener Verlagsanstalt, 1938.

WESTLEY, DAVID. "A Select Bibliography of South African Autobiography." *Biography* 17, 3 (1994): 268–280.

WHITLOCK, GILLIAN. *The Intimate Empire: Reading Women's Autobiography*. London: Cassell, 2000.

WICOMB, ZOË. Interviewed by Stephan Meyer and Thomas Olver. *Journal of Literary Studies* 18, 1 (2002): 182–198.

WILKINSON, JANE. "African Diaries." In *Autobiographical and Biographical Writing in the Commonwealth*, pp. 245–253. Barcelona: Editorial AUSA, 1984.

WILKOMIRSKI, BINJAMIN. *Bruchstücke. Aus einer kindheit 1939–1948*. Frankfurt am

Main: Suhrkamp, 1995. Translated from the German by Carol Brown Janeway as *Fragments: Memories of a Childhood, 1939–1948*. London: Picador 1997.

WILLEMSE, HEIN, CRAIN SOUDIEN, ELZA MILES, and KAYZURAN JAFFER. *More than Brothers*. Cape Town: Kwela, 2000.

WOLFE, TOM. *The New Journalism*. London: Picador, 1980.

WOODMANSEE, MARGARET. "On the Author Effect: Recovering Collectivity." In *The Construction of Authorship: Textual Appropriation in Law and Literature*, edited by M. Woodmansee and P. Jazi, pp. 15–28. Durham: Duke University Press, 1994a.

———. *The Author, Art, and the Market: Rereading the History of Aesthetics*. New York: Columbia University Press, 1994b.

WOODS, DONALD. *Biko*. London: Penguin, 1987.

———. *Rainbow Nation Revisited: South Africa's Decade of Democracy*. London: Andre Deutsch, 2000.

WYLIE, DAN. *Dead Leaves: Two Years in the Rhodesian War*. Pietermaritzburg: University of Natal Press, 2002.

YOUNG, GAYNOR. *My Plunge to Fame*. Ed. Shirley Johnston. Claremont: Spearhead Press, 2000.

YOUNG, IRIS. *Inclusion and Democracy*. Oxford: Oxford University Press, 2000.

ZANDER, HORST. *Fact—Fiction—"Faction": A Study of Black South African Literature in English*. Tübingen: Gunter Narr, 1999.

ZEGEYE, ABEBE, ed. *After Apartheid*. Vol. I: *Social Identities in the New South Africa*. Cape Town: Kwela, 2001.

ZEGEYE, ABEBE, and ROBERT KRIGER, eds. *After Apartheid*. Vol. II: *Culture in the New South Africa*. Cape Town: Kwela, 2001.

ZIMBLER, LIN. *Under the Dragon's Wing: The Story of Lin Zimbler*. Somerset West: Options, 1997.

II SINGING THE PRAISES, PERFORMING THE PERSONA

Versions of a Life in Poetry

D. L. P. Yali-Manisi interviewed by Jeff Opland

BIOGRAPHICAL INTERVIEWS OFFER testimony of widely varying value, and this was especially so in apartheid South Africa. I was privileged to know and work with the great Xhosa praise poet *(imbongi)* D. L. P. Yali-Manisi (1926–1999) for nearly thirty years, an oral poet whose public career was almost exactly coterminous with the apartheid regime. The following texts are selected to show the different ways Manisi presented himself in varying contexts.

As a brash young PhD student, I first met the poet on December 19, 1970, and, having briefly introduced myself, returned to his rural home in the Khundulu valley north of Queenstown the following day for an extended interview. We sat in my car outside his mud hut; he started by producing an oral poem about his chief, K. D. Matanzima. In the conversation that followed, Manisi was guarded and not especially forthcoming. I was a white stranger, I had a tape recorder running, and he could not but have been suspicious of my intentions. I was ill prepared for the interview, as became apparent when he mentioned the circumcision rites of the initiates *(abakwetha)*, and I revealed myself as ignorant of his customs. I was also besotted on academic theory, seeking to test the ideas of Milman Parry and Albert Lord. I was more interested in aspects of his craft relevant to current scholarly debate than I was in the man himself. Though it produced two magnificent poems for my collection and was helpful in advancing my theoretical inquiries, this interview (here slightly edited) revealed little to me about Manisi personally, though it left me wishing to see him again.

After producing his first poem, Manisi lit a cigarette and I started my questions.

JEFF OPLAND: That was wonderful. Thank you. Can you sing other praises as well? You can sing praises of just about all the chiefs, can't you?

DAVID YALI-MANISI: You want me to proceed now?

JO: If you wish.

YM: I just puff a little.

JO: Shall we talk a bit then while you're puffing?

YM: Right. That's what I thought.

JO: Where did you learn to sing?

YM: Actually, I didn't learn it. I grew up as a young boy in this location looking after my father's cattle and sheep. Then I used to hear old men singing praises when you bring in cows for milking. From that I got such little experience. Then from it I see myself now being called—a poet.

JO: So you got ambitious, to be a poet?

YM: Well, I believe so.

JO: How old are you, Mr. Yali-Manisi?

YM: I'm forty-four.

JO: Have you been an *imbongi* for a long time?

YM: As from 1943.

JO: Why that particular date?

YM: I know it because there were *abakwetha* in this location. Then when the *bakwetha* hut, the *bakwetha* place up in the mountain, was burnt, they were brought to their homes. It was a great day. Then I started singing praises, and I praised them and their fathers.

JO: Was that the first time you started praising?

YM: That was the first time then.

JO: What made you start then?

YM: I felt myself happy because I saw it was a nice time then, I could say. But I cannot express myself well. But I felt it was a very good time for me to praise these fellows because they were looking nice and their fathers were happy because they were coming from the mountain all well.

JO: Safe from the fire? You were pleased that they were safe from the fire?

YM: No, no, not that they were from the fire. It's the custom that when they leave their *bakwetha* place, the place in which they were living is supposed to be burnt, of course.

JO: Oh, I see.

YM: Yes, it is the custom.

JO: You of course are well educated. How much schooling have you had?

YM: It's only—I'm only Standard 7.

JO: Standard 7?

YM: Yes, I passed my Form 2 at the Mathanzima Secondary School at Cala. I was at Lovedale in 1945, then I left Lovedale in 1948 to complete my Form 2 at Mathanzima Secondary School.

JO: So you can read and write quite easily?

YM: Oh yes.

JO: Are you a Christian?

YM: Yes.

JO: You belong to a church?

YM: Yes.

JO: Right. I hope you don't mind: these are just—

YM: I understand.

JO: —some personal facts that I want to know. What is your full name and your clan?

YM: My full name is David Livingstone Phakamile Yali-Manisi.

JO: And your clan? You are a Thembu?

YM: I am a Hala.

JO: A Hala.

YM: I'm a Hala.

JO: Yes. Most of the Xhosas, when they're young boys, when they're *abakwetha*, they can then—or they do—learn to praise themselves and praise their clans?

YM: They do sometimes, but nowadays that is not usually happening.

JO: Not any more?

YM: No.

JO: It used to be so, though?

YM: Yes.

JO: So you would find that most of the older people can still praise themselves and praise their clans.

YM: They do so even now.

JO: Yes. Is this the same kind of praising as what you were doing now?

YM: Oh no, that's something different.

JO: But you would use the same word to describe it, *ukubonga* (to chant poetry)? Both *ukubonga*?

YM: Yes, we have the same, *ukubonga*.

JO: Why is it different?

YM: It is different because now I'm praising a particular chief. I'm not concerned about clans or anything, but I am praising the chief of the country.

JO: But many people could make up a poem about Mathanzima and sing it?

YM: Certainly, it is, of course.

JO: Would their poems, the ordinary tribesman, would they be different from the poems of the *imbongi*?

YM: Well, sometimes others could quote from the *imbongi*, but they cannot do it, all of them. And others cannot even sing a word from their own meditations.

JO: What do you mean "quote from an *imbongi*"? Do they listen to the words you say and then use them, use the same words?

YM: They do sometimes listen to the *imbongi* praising the chief and then they would repeat it.

JO: The same words?

YM: Not actually the same word, but the theme.

JO: The same theme?

YM: Yes.

JO: When you sing, do you make up what you're singing while you're singing it, every time?

YM: How do you mean by making it up?

JO: I mean that you're not memorizing: this song that you've just sung now to Daliwonga [K.D. Mathanzima]—

YM: No, it's from my mentalities.

JO: Yes, but if I asked you to sing the same song, you wouldn't—

YM: I wouldn't do it.

JO: —use the same words.

YM: I wouldn't do it now.

JO: No, but you wouldn't—

YM: I would do something else now.

JO: —use the same words. But you wouldn't use the same words that you used. This is not a song that you hold in your mind?

YM: The theme is the same, but I wouldn't use the same words—

JO: The theme?

YM: —in the same way I was doing.

JO: That's right: the theme is the same, but the words differ.

YM: Yes.

JO: So each time you sing, each time you praise your chief, you will make up different words while you're singing?

YM: Yes.

JO: You haven't got it memorized and kept in your mind?

YM: No.

JO: You don't sing the same words every time you sing?

YM: No, I don't do it.

JO: Tell me something about your book.

YM: Which book is it, by the way?

JO: *Izibongo zeenkosi zama-Xhosa* (Praise poems of Xhosa chiefs).

YM: Well, I started writing that book in 1947 and I completed it, it was late in 1947, I completed it early 1948.

JO: Did you just sit down with the purpose in mind of writing all the *izibongo* of the Xhosa chiefs?

YM: Yes. When I started writing it, I was at Lovedale. Then I thought of writing a poem. Then I went towards the river called Tyhume. Then I got among the trees there. I slept on my stomach. Then I started writing. The first poem I wrote there.

JO: While you were sleeping?

YM: I slept on my stomach. What do you say: I lay or I lied? Which is it?

JO: You lay.

YM: I lay on my stomach. Then I started writing.

JO: Where did you get the knowledge about all the chiefs? I mean, you've praised here chiefs of the Rharhabes, of the Gcalekas, all the country. Where did you get all that knowledge?

YM: I got it, I got the knowledge from my grandfather, Jim Mcinziba, and my father's older brother, Mdubane Manisi, and other old men. Then I visited many places after that and I met old people, including chiefs and old counselors, and I got stories about chiefs and they related to me histories of our nation. Then I started collecting the names of the old chiefs with their generations.

JO: So you didn't get all your information from books?

YM: No, not at all. There's a little I got from the books, but most of the information I got is from the old people.

JO: The old people?

YM: Yes.

JO: In your book you set out different sections: you spoke for example of the *izibongo* of the chiefs and then you have a section of *izibongo mbaliso,* you have a section of this other one, *izimbonono.* Are they different kinds of—

YM: When I talk of *mbaliso,* my poems there relate: I would say they are based on history.

JO: They're narratives?

YM: Yes. Then when I talk of *izimbonono,* they are particularly concerned for mourning for the dead.

JO: Would you call these different kinds of praise poems?

YM: On my own, I call them different kinds of poems.

JO: Tell me about the *mbaliso*. Does the *imbongi* often sing narrative poems, *mbaliso*, or is it only you?

YM: Well, I couldn't say we are all doing the same thing, but I myself, I feel I can do it.

JO: Do you think this is a traditional kind of praise poem, *mbaliso*?

YM: It is, of course, because our history was never written before the white man came to the country, and then we got the story of our people from the history related to us by our old people.

JO: Yes, but they would relate the history as you are talking to me now.

YM: Yes.

JO: Did the *iimbongi* ever sing the history?

YM: Well, I have no idea of the old people concerning the *iimbongi* (poets) of their time, but I myself, I feel I can do it.

JO: What kind of stories do you tell? Have you ever sung of Nongqawuse, for example, or of the Battle of the Axe, history like this?

YM: No, there is no Nongqawuse among my *mbaliso izibongo*.

JO: Yes, but you could do this if you wanted to?

YM: I can do it even now.

And after a few more minutes' conversation, and a pause of just twenty-three seconds, he did.

The two poems Manisi gave me on this occasion, and the proof he afforded through word and deed that, as a Xhosa *imbongi*, he could compose poetry with no premeditation (a central tenet of the theory of oral poetry propounded by Parry and Lord), left me well satisfied with the interview. But compare the quality of the information I elicited about Manisi, his life, and his art, with what he offered in response to the questions of two groups of Xhosa schoolchildren in Grahamstown.

On June 11, 1979 Manisi and I addressed seventy-four boys and girls from Standards 7 and 8 of the Samuel Ntsika Junior Secondary School who had assembled for their weekly lecture at the Albany Museum. Only three of the children claimed ever to have witnessed a performance by a Xhosa *imbongi*, although they were all familiar with the idea of an *imbongi* from literature they studied at school. After Manisi's performance of a poem, I answered a few questions in English and then Manisi answered questions in Xhosa. (The Xhosa exchanges were transcribed and translated by Vuyani Mqingwana and subsequently checked and corrected by Manisi.) Less conscious of the presence of a microphone, more comfortable speaking in Xhosa, Manisi offers much richer, more poetic testimony than he did in response to my fumbling questions in 1970.

STUDENT: How do you become an *imbongi?*

YM: You cannot be an *imbongi* if you do not know your nation. To be a national *imbongi* you have to know the nation's history, its origins and the main events; you should know how its leaders—like chiefs—are related to one another. You must be familiar with the battles that your great-grandfathers and their chiefs waged, fighting for their land and the nation of which you are a member. If you do not have that history, what would be the basis of your *izibongo* (poetry)?

Of course, you can be an *imbongi* even if you do not know the history of your people. But then you won't praise your nation: you will praise the *toktokkie* (a beetle); you will praise the gait of the rock lizard and talk about the crab's dancing in the river. We praise chiefs and honorable men. If you don't have knowledge of their family trees and history in general you wouldn't know what to say about them. But if you are going to praise a nation, you must know its origins, the course of its history, where and when it experienced setbacks and difficulties until there was you—its member of today.

STUDENT: Is it possible to be an educated *imbongi,* or an *imbongi* who has learnt his art at school, or is *bongaing* (singing praises) something you have to suck during early childhood?

YM: Yes, I understand your question. *Bonga*ing is of different kinds. First, you don't suck it: it is not something people can leave for each other in the breast. As you grow old, if in your blood by birth you have excitement and passion about domestic affairs, long before you participate as a member of the nation, it will be clear from your habits that you are likely to be a certain thing. You will grow up then. When you are involved in national affairs, and if you have a keen mind, you will learn the practices of your nation, and you'll like them. You will hate what is bad among your people. You will like what is an incentive and progress among your people. You will find yourself gradually appreciating what is good until you become what you are destined to be by the Almighty.

Well, if you have a love of your people, you could start by learning. You can derive inspiration from the poems that have been written for us. For example, if you can read Mqhayi's *Ityala lamawele, Inzuzo,* and *Imihobe nemibongo,* and come across two or three words, and four or five lines, these could inspire you.

And then you use these as a springboard, in order to be an *imbongi*. But it's not something that is acquired through education. No, you don't go to school for it. If it's not inborn, it's just not there, son of the nation. You must have it in your veins. If you bear it in your veins, and if I suddenly appear, when you had been thinking of me, and if you know me, you will exclaim, saying "I recognize you!" and then go on *bonga*ing. If you have learned it, then it's not inborn. And if you prepare it in advance when you are attending rites and ceremonies, you'll get there having made your preparations and find that the feast has taken a different direction, and you will praise on the way to Ndenxa while the nation is going to Hala.

STUDENT: Would you regard Mqhayi as an educated poet or as a poet who acquired his skill during his early childhood?

YM: He comes up with it. He grew up with it when he was still a boy. He also confirms this in his autobiography. He used to listen when he was at Centane before he came to Alice.

STUDENT: What about Jolobe?

YM: He went to school. He cannot speak; he cannot *bonga;* his way is to use the pen, that's all.

STUDENT: But is he an *imbongi*?

YM: Yes, an educated one.

And there we had to call a halt to the proceedings. Manisi and I presented ourselves again at the lecture theatre in the Albany Museum on 13 June. Our audience this time consisted of sixty-four Standard 8 boys and girls and their teacher from Nathaniel Nyaluza High School. Of the children, only three had heard an *imbongi* before. Once again I spoke briefly in English about the Xhosa traditions of oral poetry, and once again Manisi produced a poem.

The children's teacher asked a series of questions in English, ending with this one:

TEACHER: One more thing is that I've just listened to Manisi right now. He seems to know all the chiefs and kings, everything: does he have to memorize all the kings or is it something that can come in your brain? He calls all the chiefs and kings correct as they are. Or does he perhaps study, go to school, learn how this chief or that chief was there and there? I'd like to know from you or from him.

Manisi offered his response in Xhosa, and further questions came from a series of students in Xhosa.

SINGING THE PRAISES

YM: No, sir, I am a child of this country. I am a son of this land. Right here in Grahamstown. I am a son of Grahamstown because I am a Xhosa in the land of the Xhosa people, an African in Africa. In this way: the first chief I saw was Ndabamfene Maqoma of the Jingqi at Ntselamanzi in Alice. I used to be with him in Alice, and during weekends I visited his place at Ntselamanzi. We used to tell each other stories about how this land was settled in the past. I also spent some time here in Grahamstown at Vukile Fobe's place in 1949. When I was here I stayed at Vukile's place and we used to talk about this fatherland of ours.

I know chiefs because I am a frequent visitor at great places; and I stay with chiefs and I travel with chiefs there in my own country and I go about with chiefs. I say then that my knowledge of chiefs emanated from staying with them, being a counselor, and being one of the headmen at the great place. I don't mix with women, I mix with men.

STUDENT: Did your inspiration start at Lovedale or did it start elsewhere?

YM: I was inspired as a small boy, younger than you are. I was herding cattle above those fields that are situated below the small ridges of the location where I live. We used to hunt grass warblers. Do you know the grass warbler? We were hunting those birds, and chasing the widowbirds, riding and racing with donkeys. We would compete, and the donkeys would toss us off and we would graze our backsides. I started at that time. By the time I came to Alice, I had already started to learn my craft.

STUDENT: Were you not influenced by the poems taught at school, such as those of Mqhayi and Jolobe?

YM: You see, the poems that interested me were Mqhayi's. Jolobe makes me drowsy when I read him because he speaks slowly, he's not lively. I still enjoy reading Mqhayi, even now, because his style inspires you, it gives you vigor. It impels you to move forward; it doesn't make you walk around in circles.

STUDENT: All in all, you had the inspiration, but you received the encouragement from reading Mqhayi, or is it something deep in you that you should want to rise like Mqhayi?

YM: It is something in me. But I've enjoyed Mqhayi's Xhosa and the eloquent style in which he has conveyed his ideas in Xhosa. I followed my own path. But Mqhayi has taught me one thing, that if you are going to speak about a nation you must have the feeling and the spirit of the nation.

STUDENT: Is it possible for an *imbongi* to start praising just on the spur of the moment? For example, as you are looking at me, would it be possible for you to start *bonga*ing me?

YM: As I was talking to you here just now, referring to all of you, taking aim at you, I became joyful and moved to see the beautiful cream of Rharhabe. I realized that I had to speak about you, and send you on a mission on behalf of the nation whose future leaders I hope you will be.

STUDENT: When you are *bonga*ing, let's say you are *bonga*ing Daliwonga, do you have a picture of him or is it just blankness and you do not know who you are talking about?

YM: No, sir, we do not close our eyes, we see. But then if you say I must *bonga* Daliwonga: he is a chief of our nation with whom I live. Even when I'm asleep you can prod me awake and say "Please speak so that I can hear what you say about him." When we *bonga*, perhaps if the chief arrives here, if I arrive here and it's reported that a Ngqika chief is here, whether I'm in the location or not—I mean to say, that's how it is—and it's reported that he's the son of So-and-so, that is enough: when I come face to face with him I start blazing away. It's just like that.

STUDENT: Did you ever keep company with *iimbongi*, say Mqhayi, and observe the way they *bonga*'d?

YM: I never saw Mqhayi. He died in 1945 and I never saw his face. I have seen his books. There are other *iimbongi* I've seen, and with whom I *bonga*. There are some I had seen before, the old men who were in my location during my youth.

STUDENT: Just on that point: I'm sorry to say it appears that there are very few poets who can do what Mqhayi did, and I was about to include you, sir. For the poets we have today depend on writing alone. Is this due to the fact that poets like Mqhayi and you are born with this talent or they take after their parents?

YM: No. Let me say that it is God's gift to the particular person. It's not hereditary. You do not become an *imbongi* simply because your father was an *imbongi*. Mqhayi has a son, but he is not an *imbongi*. Mqhayi's father and grandfathers were not *iimbongi*. He alone was born with that talent. I too am not the son of *iimbongi*, and I haven't heard that any of my ancestors were *iimbongi*. This ability is a specific talent. There are quite a number of *iimbongi*: don't think that it's only Mqhayi and me. But I haven't seen them all.

STUDENT: Some poets, before they assume the craft, usually have visions which are not seen by other people. Did you just start *bonga*ing, or did you have a vision?

YM: No. When we were looking after cattle as boys, or when we were driving them home, or to the veld, or taking them out before the morning milking, or driving them home towards sunset, the bulls bellow and the cows low. Every boy *bonga*s his father's cattle, whether or not they're in a team: "You watch that bull So-and-so: it will act like this and like that." Perhaps they're drawing a wagon. "That bull's stronger than yours." "Do you see that bull of ours of such-and-such a color? Its name is So-and-so, its name is So-and-so." That's how it develops. We don't see visions which come to us and announce, "Here's something new." To us it's an inspiration, the mind starts working.

STUDENT: How can you say fine things about a chief or anybody you meet for the first time? And when you *bonga* him, how do you speak so eloquently?

YM: This is caused by the fact that the history of the nation, its paths and its pains, its way of life when it comes into contact with whites, its way of life before that contact, has been narrated to me when I became a member of the chief's court. I mixed with chiefs and old men. We know what happened to each chief, how he lost his chieftainship, how Chief So-and-so regained his chieftainship. And in that way I know the history of my nation.

And there we ended.

In the course of time, my relationship with Manisi grew in intimacy: he became a valued research officer in the Institute I served as director; we worked and traveled together and shared joy and heartbreak. I was well aware of Manisi's past involvement with the African National Congress (ANC), but this was not something we could freely discuss under apartheid, certainly not with a tape recorder running. Two months before I emigrated from South Africa, I called on Manisi at his new home in the Matyhantya location for what might well have been my final visit and our last farewell. With my eighteen-year-old son, Daniel, in attentive attendance at my side, I sat at the small table in Manisi's house, concerned about his condition—suffering from tuberculosis of the spine, he could walk only with difficulty, aided by a cane—and taxed by the emotion of the occasion; we probed areas we had only touched upon in previous conversations. I scribbled a transcript of our exchange in longhand, declining to use a tape recorder by tacit common consent. Manisi huddled opposite me, indistinct in the unlit gloom, a crumpled sack of a man in stark physical contrast to the intense and vital *imbongi* whose poetry I had been recording since December 1970. Fifteen years had passed: it was November 26, 1985, and the afternoon shadows were lengthening on the crags behind his home. We talked first of his books, those already published and those awaiting publication, before we turned to more sensitive matters. The quality of his responses is a measure of the mutual trust and respect that had grown between us.

JO: David, tell me about your involvement in politics.

YM: As a youth I had the feeling that we as a people had lost all of our rights. So, as I was at school at Lovedale, I learnt that though we were at a missionary institution we were not treated well as human beings. From there I learnt from historical books, and I got the knowledge that all we had was grabbed by the white man. So that remained in my mind till I grew up to be a young man who could make his own decisions. So there was an ANC organization fighting for the rights of our people. In 1952 I joined the ANC to take part in the struggle for our freedom. In 1953 I was at the great place Qamata as a praise singer. It so happened that one day my paramount chief, K. D. Mathanzima, brought the *Daily Dispatch,* and he read to us a portion saying that the Nationalist government was going to give power to the chiefs, and he was pleased with that and he wanted to know our opinion. Well, I questioned him: if at all we are freed by the Nationalist government, why do they choose to give freedom to the chiefs instead of to the people who are fighting for their freedom—the ANC and other organizations? Even in the past, it was not the chiefs who fought for the country, it was the people who were the warriors. So I was out with him, telling him that I don't take it as freedom that is given to the chiefs because there were organizations fighting for the freedom of the people and the leaders of those organizations were the very people who should be consulted by the government. Well, my chief was not pleased with my question and my explanation. He took me to be abnormal.

JO: Did he ask you to leave then?

YM: In actual fact, he didn't say I must leave the great place, but I saw myself that we weren't friends as we used to be after that discussion. So I decided to leave, as I was in fact not paid as a praise singer, and look for some work elsewhere and carry on the ideas of the ANC.

Manisi became secretary of the ANC branch in Queenstown. In 1960 he was imprisoned in East London; no charges were laid, and he was released after five months. He continued to work for the ANC until he was hounded from Queenstown by the authorities. He moved back to Khundulu, spending nights on the open mountains hiding from the security police. He left home to attend a conference in Paarl in the Western Cape, but he was arrested in Paarl before he could attend the meeting and spent three days in prison. He was released when he paid a fine for entering Queenstown.

JO: Did you ever *bonga* at ANC meetings?

YM: Oh yes. At one time I was threatened by Major Heidelberg of Port Elizabeth, saying I was going to be arrested if I *bonga*'d again, saying I was encouraging people to be rude against them as they were taking notes at a conference in Queenstown.

JO: David, tell me something more about your political beliefs in general.

YM: Well, Prof, as I see it, black and white have come to stay in South Africa, so each and every racial group has the right to participate in the making of the laws of the country irrespective of color or creed, but as long as the white man keeps the rule of law with him in his own hands alone, there shall be no peace or happiness in South Africa. My own idea is that if blacks and whites and every racial group in South Africa are given the right to participate in the affairs of the country, everything would be calm and cool. We would live happily and be prosperous as one South African race. Homelands mean nothing to us blacks because we are there divided according to our languages, whereas in the urban areas of this country we mix together, we intermarry. So homelands are the other way around, to keep the black man a slave in the land of his birth.

JO: You often mention the missionaries in your poetry. What do the missionaries mean to you?

YM: The missionaries who brought the Bible to South Africa were not all good ambassadors of Jesus Christ, for some of them helped to conquer the black man instead of preaching the word of God which they said they brought. Their sons became soldiers to kill the black man to whom their fathers were preaching the word of God. Some of these missionaries took off their collars and became magistrates to victimize the black man to whom they said they brought the word.

JO: Obviously tradition is important to you: you are proud to be an *imbongi*, and you always assert in your poetry the value of tradition and a knowledge of history. You always criticize the missionaries for inviting you to lay aside your traditions and accept the Bible.

YM: To my mind, our tradition is something which could have left us free from oppression were we not told by the missionaries that our traditions were paganism. So because of the missionaries we neglected our traditions. As a result we are scattered, divided apart. Those who kept their traditions were told they were nonbelievers, and those who neglected their traditions were good servants of the white man.

JO: And in your poetry?

YM: Mentioning tradition in poetry is to remind our generation of the past, when tradition formed unity among our forefathers, to show how our forefathers stood together because of their traditions. But now that we have neglected more or less of our traditions we don't trust one another, and that exposes us to our enemies, for we lack the backbone of our nationality.

A pause before a final question, for Danny and I had to be on our way.

JO: Why do you write poetry?
    YM: Why don't you ask me why do I sing praises?
    JO: Why do you sing praises, David?
    YM: Well, I sing praises because it's one of the ways to make our people feel what one is telling them. So I write poetry to keep that form of language for generations and generations to come, which we think is a right form of putting right what is wrong, of elaborating to make people understand what is right.

We would prolong the conversation indefinitely if we could, in order to stay my departure, but we rise. Manisi hobbles out with us to our car, with dignity—ever with dignity—and we exchange last words.

JO: If I can get money in America—I don't know if I can—but if I can get money to bring you out, would you come for a visit?
    YM: Wherever you are, Prof, send for me and I will come.
    JO: Stay well, David.
    YM: Go well, Prof.

Further Reading

OPLAND, JEFF. *Xhosa Oral Poetry: Aspects of a Black South African Tradition.* Cambridge: Cambridge University Press, 1983.

———. *Words That Circle Words: A Choice of South African Oral Poetry.* Johannesburg: Ad. Donker, 1992.

———. *Xhosa Poets and Poetry.* Cape Town: David Philip, 1998.

———. "What's in a Poem?" The Philip Balkwil Memorial Lecture. Charterhouse, Goldaming, Apr. 28, 2000. *Current Writing* 12, 2 (2000): 1–20.

———. "The Early Career of D. L. P. Yali-Manisi, Thembu *imbongi.*" *Research in African Literatures* 33, 1 (Spring 2002): 1–26.

———. "First Meeting with Manisi." *Research in African Literatures* 35, 3 (2004): 26–45.

———. *The Dassie and the Hunter: A South African Meeting.* Pietermaritzburg: University of KwaZulu-Natal Press, 2005.

YALI-MANISI, D. L. P. *Izibongi zeenkosi zama-Xhosa.* Lovedale: Lovedale Press, 1952.

———. *Inguqu*. Bolotwa: Self-published, 1954.

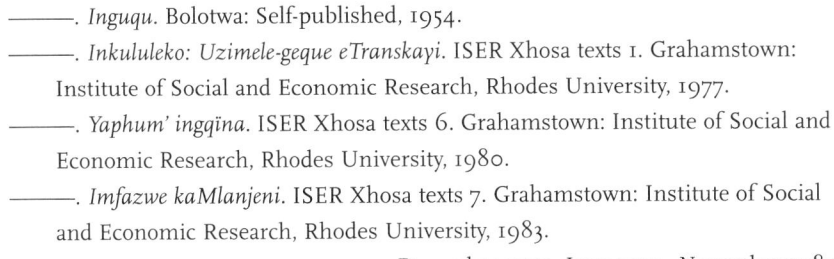

———. *Inkululeko: Uzimele-geque eTranskayi*. ISER Xhosa texts 1. Grahamstown: Institute of Social and Economic Research, Rhodes University, 1977.

———. *Yaphum' ingqīna*. ISER Xhosa texts 6. Grahamstown: Institute of Social and Economic Research, Rhodes University, 1980.

———. *Imfazwe kaMlanjeni*. ISER Xhosa texts 7. Grahamstown: Institute of Social and Economic Research, Rhodes University, 1983.

December 1970, June 1979, November 1985

People Feel No Event Is Complete without a Poet

Zolani Mkiva interviewed by Duncan Brown and Susan Kiguli

MOST AFRICAN SOCIETIES on the subcontinent, historically and in many cases in the present, are characterized by the different forms of praises that people perform, including praises to animals, personal praises, praises to the clan, praises to the ancestors, and the praise poems of the king or ruler (including recently political organizations and activists). The larger function of praising is to establish cognitive maps within society—of relations between humans and animals, individuals and other individuals, personal identity and communal life, and ruler and ruled. Personal praising—as a form of life telling or life naming—is associated initially with the personal praise name given to a child, which may be self-composed, or granted by peers or parents. Over a period of time the praise name is elaborated into the individual's personal *izibongo* (praises), which may reflect in a flattering way or otherwise on the person's physical appearance or moral character. Such personal *izibongo* are highly intertextual, since they often comprise elements that are self-composed, others that are drawn from the praises of friends, relatives, or ancestors, praises that are given by others, or that are simply part of the cultural currency of the society.

Izibongo for leaders are in many ways an extension, development, and formalization of personal *izibongo*. Instead of the ruler collecting or creating his own praise names or accounts of his military/political prowess, however, this would be done by someone else—an *imbongi* (plural *iimbongi*) or praise poet. *Izibongo* for leaders are regarded with greater seriousness by members of the society than are personal *izibongo*, and they function in more complex and far-reaching ways. The *imbongi* is not paid by the king or ruler, does not come from a separate caste or class, and is not designated as a poet through heredity. He (the office is reserved for men) has to earn the acclaim of the people (Opland 1983:64–65). There is no formal apprenticeship for *iimbongi:* an aspiring poet learns the craft of oral composition and performance by hearing other *iimbongi* perform and then memorizing their poems and adapting or extending them. The office of *imbongi* is signified by the poet's dressing in skins and carrying two sticks, or a *knobkierie* or shield and spear, though modern poets, including Zolani Mkiva, are often more eclectically attired. Mkiva praises mainly in English and Xhosa; the interview was conducted in English.

DUNCAN BROWN AND SUSAN KIGULI: Could you tell us a little about your early life?

ZOLANI MKIVA: I was born in Bolotwa, which is a location in Idutywa, right in the middle of the Transkei. That's where I grew up, that's where I was raised, where I went to my grandmother's school, higher primary, junior secondary, and high school.

DB AND SK: You come from a family of poets?

ZM: I come from a family that has got a rich history in terms of personality: we have played a pivotal role as cultural activists as well as community activists. In my family, and especially my forebears, we have always had praise singers, *iimbongi*. We have had historians, that is, oral historians, who were recognized in their community and beyond. They played a role both in my immediate community and also in the royal family. We have also had orators. So it's a combination of those elements in terms of the personality that has been produced by my family—I come from that particular lineage of historians, cultural activists, orators, and *iimbongi*.

DB AND SK: Your great-grandfather, Pauzen Mkiva, was an important *imbongi*.

ZM: He was one of the founding members of the liberation movement. And he was a mine worker. He played a very important role as an *imbongi* in motivating workers at work, and that gave him a theater that is almost closer to the one that I enjoy right now. He was a combination of two things: a very dynamic poet, a praise poet, and a historian. He had a flair for these things. And I thought maybe an *imbongi* should know these two. At a personal level, I was grateful and honored to have had an opportunity to live with him. In a sense, therefore, I have understudied him, I have lived with my ancestor. That I take as a blessing on its own. And I think he's the main person who really polished and honed my skill as a poet.

DB AND SK: How did your interest in performance begin?

ZM: There are three dynamics that make one a true *imbongi*. One is that generally you must have a love of the culture. When I was growing up, I had to look after the livestock of my father. And in that process, like any other boy who comes from that kind of family, I used to sing the praises of the cows that belonged to my father. In doing so, I would also sing my family names, my clan names, combining with the praises that I would chant for the cows that belonged to my father. Number two, there is a traditional game that is called stick fighting. The one who has the skill of singing the praises to motivate—because you actually form teams—will praise your team as it plays against the other, to motivate it. So in that way you also generate and regenerate the skill of praising. The third one, which is very important, is what I normally refer to as the University of Traditions—when you go to the mountain for circumcision, the school of initiation. The school of initiation is not just an exercise of cutting the foreskin of the boy. It goes beyond that, and what's beyond is the main issue. It gives you the courses and the modules for how best you should conduct yourself, how you are being prepared to take over the leadership, to lead your family, and all that. So you are really taught to become a true leader, a true gentleman, a true man, a true African guy. So it is those three dynamics that make one an *imbongi*. At a personal level, and coming from a heritage where in the family unit I have heard praising, I have actually inherited what belonged to my forebears, and taken it from there and developed it according to modern times. It's a God-given talent or a talent that has been given by your ancestors, combined with the wealth of experience, the wealth of cattle, the wealth of everything else that I've told you of where I come from.

DB AND SK: What inspires you as a modern *imbongi,* and what do you see as your role in society, specifically in South Africa?

ZM: Well, what inspires me—if I speak of contemporary society—is development, issues around the revival of my own heritage, which was on the brink of extinction before we took over the reins of power. The African Renaissance, African history—those are the issues that inspire me in terms of the current situation in the country. And sometimes you don't necessarily stand up to sing the praises because you have been inspired by something. Sometimes you take up the cloak because you have been angered, you understand? So in the majority of cases, of course, on a positive note, you get inspired, and you get this kind of feeling that you want to say something that isn't bad, to actually congratulate, or to motivate, and so on. But in the olden days it was mainly anger, protest and everything else, that really made you stand and raise a finger against the draconian laws.

A praise singer or *imbongi* must be seen not only as someone who unleashes beautiful words, but as a practitioner who seeks to transform the society in terms of bettering the lives of the people. This is deeply centered around the fact that where we come from as a community we honestly believe that at the center of life is human investment. And other forms of investment —capital investment, infrastructural investment—come in as a convenience to enunciate and consolidate human investment. So my personal philosophy is that if you want prosperity for a period of a year, you grow maize. If you want prosperity for a period of ten years, you grow trees. But if you want prosperity for a lifelong term, you grow people. And *izibongo* are about the growth of people, in one way.

DB AND SK: In interviews you've talked quite extensively of the role of ancestors in your career. You held a ceremony in January 2000 to thank them for their support and direction in your career, and you have said, "There is no training to become an *imbongi*. It is a gift from the ancestors that is transferred to you through a long line of inheritance" (Gerardy 2000). Could you explain the influence of the ancestors, not only in your role as an *imbongi*, but in your role as a cultural leader, as someone who has a heart for the traditions of society?

ZM: It's quite a complex question, but it comes to the critical role that is played by an *imbongi* in any given society. The first thing that I would like to say is that really it is true that my career is what it is because of the ancestors— I have the approval of the ancestors in what I am doing. In a sense I don't represent myself as Zolani, but I represent my forebears. It is my forebears who tell me what to say. It is my forebears who gave me the knowledge about my oral tradition. And therefore I am convinced that you combine emotion and knowledge when you recite poetry. But that emotion is what drives you to sift, to actually have a way of putting the words, the way they have to be put. There's an element of spontaneity in African poetry, and it is amazing how one creates a logic out of spontaneity—that you move from one stanza, having marshaled your facts perfectly, to the next one. That connection, that incredible connection, comes through that divinity that is inside you, and is a gift from your ancestors.

There's no training. It's a transfer of the skill from your forebears to the youngsters. Talent gets transferred from one generation to the other via the genes. *Poetry is in the bloodline of my family,* and I want you to underline that line. It is in the bloodline of my family. It's something that I picked up from my father. My father got it from his forefather. His forefather got it from his great-grandfather. His great-grandfather got it from his great-great-grandfather. So it comes through that pipeline, you see. It's an inherited trait. But it is therefore imperative that if you live in a society like ours, you must grasp as much knowledge as possible in order to complement the talent that you have been given. Otherwise the talent will be extinct before you can actually rise to the occasion and reach the majestic heights. So, the systematization of my thinking through the knowledge that I got from the institutions of higher learning has actually helped consolidate so that I have incisive teeth to cut the real, immediate poetry of our times.

But there's one thing that I would like to tell you, that the role of an *imbongi* has been a very, very important one to date. It is us as *imbongi*s, the cultural activists, who have also led the processes of transformation in our country. The *imbongi* is naturally a seal of approval, not to be used—an independent thinker, an independent mind, an independent institution. The institution of *imbongi* in African society is there to give recommendation for legislation to be passed, it is there during the time of conflict to act as a go-between between leadership and the rank-and-file people. So an *imbongi* has always played the role of mediator, an *imbongi* has always played the role of being a traditional historian, in the sense that he calls upon the nation to introspect as well as retrospect. For instance, if I may take an example, a great poet by the name of S. E. K. Mqhayi wrote a book (1914), based on a true story, showing how an *imbongi* played the role of adjudicator—he acted as a judge to resolve the issue. An *imbongi* is also a cultural and a community commentator, someone who articulates the feeling of the people on the ground into concise poetic phrases when the leadership is going astray. He's the only one, the only one, who has an incredible license to criticize anyone, anywhere, but not anyhow. The criticism from time to time has to be a constructive one. That's what a true *imbongi* has to do.

DB AND SK: So the *imbongi* both praises and criticizes at the same time.

ZM: Actually the name "praise poet" is not a true translation of *imbongi*. There's no true translation. The true translation is an *imbongi* in itself, and an *imbongi* for itself. People, understandably, take the positive side and make it the translation; and leave an important element out that is not necessarily negative, but you will understand that we come from a history where critique is regarded as destructive, whereas critique in Africa is a constructive thing. So you are a critique singer and a praise singer.

But you also actually profess as to what will happen in the future, informed by what is happening in the present. It's not just imagination, or maybe you would say it's a combination of imagination and what is actually.

DB AND SK: How would you compare *izibongo*—as a kind of life telling—with biography?

ZM: Well, to some extent, yes, *izibongo* are a biography. But that's not necessarily always the case. Sometimes *izibongo* can come in the form of a critique. Hence I always stress that we don't necessarily have to say *izibongo* are songs of praise. They can at the same time be songs of critique. They are biographies when they are necessarily focused on the particular life of an individual, but sometimes *izibongo* are a collection of ideas that come from the grassroots level, and then they are packaged to be *izibongo*. On another level, *izibongo* can also be a myriad of questions, questions of clarity from leadership, and they also suggest to leadership that answers are then required to these questions that have been asked of them. They can also be words of caution. Equally they can be words of wisdom that actually conscientize and massage the thinking process of that given community. And they can be words of conciliation during the times of conflict. A biographical account of *izibongo* is just one dimension of the bigger picture of what *izibongo* are.

DB AND SK: What about the religious or spiritual aspect of *izibongo*? We're thinking about the fact that in *izibongo*, the belief is that in the performance the person's presence or power is actually evoked, even if it's someone who is dead, which is a rather different conception from that of biography.

ZM: *Iimbongi* form part and parcel of traditional leadership, and spiritual leaders, traditional healers, are part and parcel of traditional leadership. There's always a connectivity to spiritualism, African spiritualism in particular. Some people are healed by the mere fact of listening to these words—this lyrical beauty can actually change lives.

DB AND SK: What sources do you draw on—other praises or oral sources, personal interviews, books, television, print media—composing *izibongo* for a specific person?

ZM: It's a culmination of a number of things. But the most fundamental source of inspiration is where I come from. The valleys and the hills where I come from, the rivers and the streams, those are the things that are the inspiration to me. But most importantly, on a personal level, as I have said, I had the honor to live with my great-grandfather, and he is a direct kind of inspiration to me, in the sense that he was a combination of all these things that I have told you about. But what actually sharpened my thinking tools was to read, to watch television, to be current about things that are happening around me—to read newspapers because that solidifies your particular knowledge. Information is an incredible ingredient for any particular praise singer or *imbongi*.

DB AND SK: How does the transformation of each of these different types of sources into *izibongo* take place?

ZM: As an *imbongi* you wouldn't look only at one means of communication. You deal with the collective, of all these sources, and then you transform it as a package, not as singles or jingles.

DB AND SK: This book is called *Telling Lives,* and you have most famously told, or performed, the life of Mandela, on many occasions—in fact, many people regard you as his *imbongi*. How do you go about composing for him?

ZM: Mandela is a walking book, he's a readable book. It's very easy to recite about him because he's an open book in the sense that you can't run short of facts as to what to say about him if you know his history, if you know him, if you have spoken to him, if you have listened to him. I've had the honor of listening to him, at close range, at a personal level, and I've heard people talking about him. So it's a combination of issues, events, and so many things. It's a very, very difficult and a very, very emotional question for me to enter. But it's a very easy thing to deal with. So I can't tell you specifically that this is how I go about it. With Madiba [the honorary title adopted by older male members of the Mandela clan], I don't know how many poems I've done for him—myriads of different ones, because I don't repeat myself. But I say the same thing basically, maybe in a different way.

DB AND SK: If you are praising someone who has already got an autobiography or biographies—like Mandela—do you use those as well?

ZM: No, you see with someone like Mandela, you listen as you live in a community to the people—how do they see this particular guy?—because you are in a sense a mouthpiece of the broader community as a praise singer, you are a social commentator, you take the feelings of the toiling masses and polish them into concise and precise poetic phrases. The book is just a recent thing. Before there was the book there were also praises to Mandela. So the book you can actually use now to extend on the knowledge that you already have.

DB AND SK: How have specific individuals responded to what you have said about them and to them in public performances?

ZM: It differs from one person to the other really, from one context to the other, and from one content to the other. Mandela will always stand up, even if he was sitting when you finished your praises, and say, "Thank you very much for those words. I am humbled, I am overwhelmed." But another person, like Bantu Holomisa, says, "I am too young Zolani, for you to talk to me like that, and I feel you are like overrating me"—something of that sort.

DB AND SK: Does he always say that? Is it a kind of formulaic refrain?

ZM: Not always, but in one way or another he will say, *"Yini Gcwanini,"* that's my clan name, *"undenza umuntu"* (you are making me a person). It depends on what he wants to say at that particular point in time. Two days ago I was introducing the mayor of eThekwini [Durban], Obed Mlaba, and he said before he spoke, "What a true African welcome. Thank you ever so much Mr. Mkiva." Kofi Annan maybe would be a bit shocked for the first time and actually laugh when he understands some of the things that you said. President Thabo Mbeki would say, "*Siyabulela* poet, keep up the good work."

DB AND SK: Has anyone responded negatively?

ZM: I have never heard that, and I don't know whether it's because often people know me or about me. James D. Wolfensohn, the president of the World Bank, said something that I thought was really funny. I was introducing him in the Africa Business Day Forum in Washington and he said, "You know, ladies and gentlemen, I would like this kind of thing to be done for me as I wake up, as I come back home to meet my wife—I would like to *hear* this resonant voice." But I guess he was joking. Mahathir bin Mohamad, the current prime minister of Malaysia, said to Thabo Mbeki about me before he spoke, "You see this young man, he will definitely make a very good politician!"

DB AND SK: Russell Kaschula and Samba Diop have suggested that your poetry is comparable to that of Bongani Sithole, in that it is evaluative and draws less on genealogical reference than that produced by many traditional *iimbongi*. Yet they note that in later performances for Mandela, you do include genealogical references (Kaschula and Diop 2000). Could you comment on this? When do you feel the need for genealogical references?

ZM: It is my view that genealogy is a very important feature in Africa, that you can't talk about genealogy out of context, out of proportion. You've got to proportion it in the sense that when you talk of genealogy, you've got to give a message to the people as well that is going to educate them, that is going to conscientize people. There's no point just reciting it for the sake of reciting it. You've got to give a message to the people that must ring a bell and that must tell them something—what has to be done. So that's the main logic. I use genealogy. I *do* include it, but it is not *the* big issue. You bring in genealogy to talk about the roots of the particular person you are talking about in the sense that genealogy is heartically and rootically the source of lineage. If Phalo, for instance, was a great hero, you would say, "Phalo the son of Chiwo." Phalo became great because he did these specific things, and Phalo gave birth to Gcaleka. Gcaleka was notorious, you understand, but he gave birth to a very constructive king, who was to reconcile all that was messed up by his father. So it depends—sometimes you pass through those references without mentioning the discrepancies or irregularities, and you go in with the positives because it depends on the end point.

DB AND SK: Are there ever times when you actually withhold genealogy, even if you know it?

ZM: It's not uniform that when you sing praises of a particular individual, you focus on genealogy. Genealogy mainly applies in *izibongo* when you are talking about traditional leadership, about kings. If I'm talking about you, I could say your success can not be seen in you as a person, but we can see your success through your kids. So I would say "Duncan Brown gave birth to a glass, a glass that was going to be filled with the water of sanitation, gave birth to a stone, a stone that was going to be a protection to this family that you gave birth to." And so I am mentioning your lineage: your first kid is glass, your second kid is stone, and so you go on. There's no one way of doing this thing.

DB AND SK: In your poetry you often allude to the tenets of Black Consciousness or the African Renaissance without actually using the terms. An example is the lines in your poem "Son of the Soil": "I do not have a soft hair texture / But I do have the so-called kaffir hair / And I can carry the crown."

ZM: Certainly, we have been stripped of our dignity by the powers that be. And you are correct that I don't really have to use sloganeering or tags, but it is the content of what I am saying that must educate the people, without putting on a tag and saying, "Let's uphold Black Consciousness." The content of what I'm saying must work deep into the hearts and minds of my fellow Africans to say that we are people, we are fully fledged human beings and therefore we have got to have pride, we have got to have a sense of dignity in ourselves. These are the issues that I'm talking about, that we can never forget our past, because it is our past that conscientizes us about what we do in the present and how to project for the future. Black Consciousness is a cornerstone because at one stage we looked down upon ourselves and we also undermined ourselves in our own selves. I'm saying, these are the things that must be monitored, and we must speak through art and art forms to change the mind of the government.

DB AND SK: You're a graduate of the University of the Western Cape, someone who has studied oral literature, who has read Fanon, Senghor, Finnegan, Opland, and the like. To what extent is your performance, and your sense of yourself as performer, shaped by critical discourse or an awareness of theoretical debates, including those about oral literature, biography, postcolonialism?

ZM: I have always told myself that I want to be as original as I can. And

SINGING THE PRAISES

that if I acquired anything from academics, it should not dictate terms to my oral tradition. My oral tradition must remain the umbrella of what I do all the time. It gives the guidelines, it gives me norms, it remains the framework within which I operate. When I draw some lessons from academic issues, those things must be customized primarily and really within the context of my tradition.

DB AND SK: You appear on the cover of the book *Voicing the Text* (Brown 1998), which engages with critical debates.

ZM: The book talks about what I think has to be said. It talks about my tradition. I think it was the right thing for me to appear on the cover because the subject matter of the book engages with and dissects the internal logic of African poetry, and it makes a comparison between poets who operate in the cities vis-à-vis poets who operate in the countryside.

DB AND SK: So you are uniquely placed as a performer who can negotiate critical debates?

ZM: It is very important to be able to negotiate change, to be able to negotiate everything that happens around you. It is critically important that you also negotiate the contradictions and the challenges that face you as an oral poet or as a performer generally. And that particular process is what makes you develop in your career and broadens your scope and your thinking.

DB AND SK: You use both oral and written modes in your poetry. Do you see any contradictions or disjunctures between the two?

ZM: No, I don't see any disjuncture. The important thing about me is that I like what I recite, and I recite what I like. Having said that, the starting point of my poetry is the performance. The writing point of my poetry is the end result of the performance. If you understand my English correctly, what I'm trying to say is that after having made a performance, that particular performance gets written. I don't first go to the desk and write what I'm going to perform tomorrow. That's the difference with me, that the oral tradition propels the modern tradition. It gives birth to the modern one. As to how that happens, I think it's scientific. You see if I'm going to make an appearance tomorrow at the opening of parliament, I give myself the framework of the issues at stake for the people of South Africa—it's HIV/AIDS, it's poverty, it's unemployment, it's crime—therefore the skeleton that I'm going to build in my mind is around these issues. But once I'm in the function itself, having listened to the various speakers and various issues, I then begin to use what I have heard at that particular occasion as flesh and veins to put on that skeleton. And I produce a rendition. Having done that I go home and I rewind and I listen to myself, that's the time I start typing.

DB AND SK: How do you come up with the images and symbols in your poetic performances?

ZM: That's the divinity I'm talking about. I don't know. It comes through that particular calling, from the connection between the living and the dead. There's a saying that goes, "The dead open the eyes of the living. But it is the living that close the eyes of the dead."

DB AND SK: So your affinity for molding words, playing about with them, making them communicate what you want—it comes from your ancestors?

ZM: They have done it so. They have done it so. But I also have an incredible romance with words.

DB AND SK: Oral poetry and performance are fast being absorbed into the technological arena. For example, your poetry and music are recorded on CD now. What do you make of this development?

ZM: It is an incredible development, a milestone that makes me want to beat my chest and believe that I have actually jumped some barriers, for I have successfully put my words on a compact disc, which is something historical that has never been done by any other traditional poet in this part of the region of Africa. That in itself is a development. The good thing is that you dictate terms of how it must happen. I have produced and directed the recording because no one in the technological world understands what I am doing. I had to be a producer and director of my work, so that it does not lose the gist of its Africanness. It's good to be recorded so that generations to follow will have a point of reference. I don't have recorded oral material from my forebears. It would have been incredible if I'd had it. You can imagine, you would have been able to reproduce that stuff, relate it, and master it. But my recording happens under the umbrella, as I indicated, of my oral tradition. Recording, of course, also allows you to reach broader audiences before you are actually there physically.

DB AND SK: Are you concerned that CD recording detracts from the visual-performative aspect that is so evident when you are on stage?

ZM: Whenever I make a CD, I make as many videos as possible—about 90 percent of the songs are actually recorded also as videos—so that they can give a clear picture of the gestures and the style of the praise singer. So most of the songs and poems on CD are complemented by a video.

DB AND SK: Are there any specific techniques that guide you as a composer and performer of oral poetry?

ZM: No, there's no specific technique. The only thing that happens is that when words come, you stand up and save them into your hard disk. In the middle of the night, when they come, whatever comes, you repeat it, the praise you are given in your sleep, you repeat it, until it's saved in your disk. You keep it for something that will come in the future. So there's no specific technique.

DB AND SK: You have been referred to as "the S. E. K. Mqhayi of our time," and also as "National Praise Poet" and "Royal Poet to the Republic"—obvious echoes of Mqhayi's title *"imbongi yesizwe jikelel"* (praise poet of the whole nation). What does this comparison mean to you?

ZM: It's an honor for me to be called the S. E. K. Mqhayi of our time. The comparison would be unfair in the sense that we lived in different times, and Mqhayi was not known as I am known, for instance, and he couldn't address people from other areas, who spoke different languages from him. He was only a Xhosa-known poet. But I'm a poet who is recognized by English people, Venda people, and everybody else in South Africa. That's the difference. But he's a great poet. If he had lived at this time, he would obviously be the main man. It's an honor for me to be called after him.

DB AND SK: You have also been referred to as "Poet of Africa" several times, especially outside Africa. What do you see as your role in this respect?

ZM: As "Poet of Africa," I think that my inspiration is to make sure I am part and parcel of the leadership that brings about the birth of the United States of Africa. That's the only thing that I want to dedicate my life to, in terms of the continental politics, because I see business leadership is busy, the political leadership is busy, talking about the African Renaissance and a USA for Africa. They have always talked about these things. But my concern is that we need to engage the youth, we need to engage the cultural organizations, so that when we talk about this, we touch the lives of the people. The people must decide as to how this unity of Africa must actually be brought about.

DB AND SK: As "Poet of Africa," are you making the effort to learn more of what happens in other parts of Africa?

ZM: That's what I'm doing. I want to learn about the diversity. I want to take the diversity that we have here and say "diversity in unity" for the whole continent. I think it is important for me to draw as much knowledge as possible so that I know more of Africa. So my view is that we must establish a movement to help mass mobilization, to consolidate and enunciate the idea of African unity, truly, beyond the legislative powers.

DB AND SK: You've performed at poetry and musical festivals, at fashion shows, even at boxing matches. What do you see as your role at these particular functions?

ZM: It's "edu-tainment"—educational entertainment. I educate people, and I also entertain people.

DB AND SK: Even at boxing matches?

ZM: Motivation. It's motivation. It goes back to the stick fighting I mentioned earlier, when you used to praise the teams at stick fighting in order to motivate them to win the matches.

DB AND SK: Performance poets literally have their audiences before them, or around them, but—like writers—they often also have an imagined audience in mind; and this is obviously the case when, as you have done, you release your performances on CD. Who do you see as your audience?

ZM: The people.

DB AND SK: Could you elaborate on that?

ZM: The people of all sorts. I cannot as a poet begin to identify a target audience. I am not a brand. I am not a brand that is for sale. I am a human, I speak with human beings, and I believe that my message is universal. It's a message that is born and bred in Africa, but it's for a universal consumption. So my audience are people all over the world, and truly the invitations that I am receiving all over the world are as a result of that. I never said I must be invited by anybody, but because of my message, which runs through the technology of our time, people got the message that they need to hear me speaking to them. So everybody is the target audience.

DB AND SK: You perform both in English and in other languages. How important is this code-switching in recreating the world you are trying to depict?

ZM: It is very important. It's like you lead by example. We talk of a global village, not under the auspices of imperialism—I'm not talking about that crap—I'm talking about the global village, that if we live along the banks of the same river, eating the same food planted in the same soil, and drinking from the same water, that there is somewhere where we must meet. Basically humans have a common denominator—wherever you are, wherever you were from, wherever you live, we are made of blood, we are made of flesh, we have eyes. A human in Russia and a human here are the same. These languages are our own creation, culture is our own creation, it is a true design of life. And if we need redesign of life, it's going to be done by us. If we talk of the global village, it will be created by us. If we talk of a united Africa, it will be done by us and nobody else. And it is through using these languages, you see.

DB AND SK: You have worked at Spoornet as a communications specialist, and you have performed at corporate functions; you have been in parliament; you have been across the country at different forums, and you represent the country and the continent internationally. But you are also deeply committed to the revival of Xhosa tradition in the Eastern Cape and throughout South

Africa, serving, among others, as the chief executive officer of the newly formed Xhosa Royal Council and as spokesperson for the Xhosa royal family. How do you negotiate these very different roles or allegiances?

ZM: In order for you to have a balanced view, you must have a balanced mind. You must live what you talk. You must put your words into action from time to time. For me there is no conflict of interest because the common feature here is transition and transformation. We're talking about the transformation of our society at all levels. Therefore we are part of the struggles for transformation, whether they are taking place in our own little town of Idutywa, or whether they are taking place in Angola. I will not be overstepping my mark if I participate in the struggles for transformation overseas. The world must be transformed, starting from a little location to a bigger location. So I am not overstepping the mark. Fortunately I'm young, energetic, and I have the mind, I have the perspective. So I have told myself that if I have that, then my soul will work until I die.

DB AND SK: You constantly stress the connection with your home at Idutywa.

ZM: Yes, in fact I draw my inspiration greatly and really from where I grew up. For me that's very important, that no fortnight must end without me touching down at my home. I believe that's where my spear is, that's where my spear must be sharpened from time to time. I must go and sit in the manure, and grow for some time, so that I come out as a fresh tiger, biting like no other animal you have ever seen.

DB AND SK: As part of your work at Spoornet, and your own engagement as a poet, you compiled a collection of poetry by railway workers, published by the University of Natal Press (Mkiva, ed., 2000). Could you say a little more about the project—how it came about, and what it seeks to achieve?

ZM: The reason why I decided to do *Railway Poetry* is that I wanted to combine different expressions of people who worked in the railways, because the poetry that you are talking of was mostly written by people anonymously. Some people were writing from the premise of pain that they have undergone having worked in the railways, some people were writing out of happiness at seeing this amazing environment. So I combined the experience, the hardships, the celebration, within the same framework.

The clear thing, which we are not saying and which we must be vocal and audible enough about, is that we encourage the nation to *read,* but are not encouraging the nation to *write.* For me, that's an imbalance. I'm saying, let's encourage the kids to write, and let's also encourage them to read. Our history must be rewritten, yet how do you begin to prepare the rewriters of history when you don't encourage this kind of culture of writing? So the point is, let's celebrate these workers who wrote under a position of anonymity and produced poems through the railway magazine. For me as the poet of the nation, I felt the need to use the resources within the corporate world to actually produce the thing in style, and this also adds value to the whole notion of rewriting our history—our history has been rewritten. For the first time we've produced a railway poetry book, which is a compilation—a step towards the direction we are seeking. So we aim and seek to achieve exactly the rewriting of our history—telling our own story.

DB AND SK: In the wake of the political transformations within South African society, we've seen praise poets at important public gatherings: the opening of parliament, the presidential inauguration, sports events, and so on. In one way spaces seem to be opening up for praise poets, but in another way, with the vexed question of the powers of traditional leaders under the new constitution, spaces may be closing down. What is your sense of the place of *izibongo*, both public and personal, at present?

ZM: I think South Africa has known very quickly the role of the *imbongi* and his *izibongo*. Today it is not the productivity of the poets themselves that makes them appear. Sometimes they are invited. People feel no event is complete without a poet. So for me that's an achievement that I think I personally have helped make possible.

DB AND SK: What are you busy with at the moment?

ZM: I no longer work at Spoornet. Basically I'm writing—genealogies in the *Daily Dispatch* every week, notes on a number of issues, that sort of thing I do. I also perform and produce CDs. My latest CD is entitled *Mazenethole*, which is a deep idiomatic expression to say thanks in the highest way you can ever think of. It's like saying you do not have the right words to say thank you. It's thank you to Mandela for the wonderful opportunity he has given us as a nation, as a people, as a continent. He is indeed an icon—I explain in the album exactly what I mean by that. I'm also thanking the ancestors as well, for giving me the opportunity to live with my great-grandfather, who passed away in 2000, to give me eyesight, insight, and hindsight. It's not a hard-hitting album like *Qadaffi*, but in terms of the language it works with isiXhosa at a very deep level.

Acknowledgment

Thanks to Ashlee Lenta for her assistance in collecting material for this interview.

References Cited

BROWN, DUNCAN. *Voicing the Text: South African Oral Poetry and Performance.* Cape Town: Oxford University Press, 1998.

GERARDY, JUSTINE. "From 'Bundu Boy' to Premier Poet: It's Written in the Blood Says Mkiva." *Dispatch Online.* Dec. 20, 2000. http://www.dispatch.co.za/2001/12/20/easterncape/mblood.htm

KASCHULA, RUSSELL H., and SAMBA DIOP. "Political Processes and the Role of the *Imbongi* in Africa." *South African Journal of African Languages.* May 2000. http://www.mweb.co.za/litnet/seminarroom/imbongi,asp

MKIVA, ZOLANI, ed. *Railway poetry.* Pietermaritzburg: University of Natal Press, 2000.

MQHAYI, S. E. K. *Ityala lamawele.* Alice: Lovedale Press, 1914.

February and September 2002

Folk Music as Popular Culture: A Life-history Approach

Alex J. Thembela interviewed by Thengani Ngwenya

AT THE TIME of the interview, Alex J. Thembela was a retired professor of education with a long-standing interest in traditional music. He studied music at the Trinity College of Music in London. In his long and distinguished career as an educationist, Thembela taught in schools, teacher-training colleges, and at the University of Zululand. At the time of his retirement in 1993 he occupied the position of vice-director in charge of academic affairs and research. Professor Thembela has published books and journal articles on a variety of educational topics. He is coauthor of Joseph Shabalala's biography, *The Life and Works of Joseph Shabalala and the Ladysmith Black Mambazo* (1993), along with E. P. M. Radebe, an attorney who is a legal advisor and manager of Ladysmith Black Mambazo.

THENGANI NGWENYA: How were you chosen to write Shabalala's biography?

A. J. THEMBELA: During one of his tours to the United States of America, Joseph was approached by a certain professor who requested his permission and cooperation to write his biography. Joseph thought this task should be performed by a local person or persons who would understand the language and the cultural background of the artists and their songs. He subsequently approached me to write the biography. The biography was produced in isiZulu, which captured the nuances and idiom of the Zulu culture, for example, *ubusoka beculo* (the aesthetic appeal of the song). The English version was written for non-isiZulu speakers in general and the international community.

TN: Could you briefly tell us about your own interests and values as an academic and whether these had any bearing on your decision to conduct a study of Shabalala's life and art?

AJT: I have always had a strong interest in traditional music. I grew up listening to *isicathamiya* and other forms of folk music, and as I was gradually initiated into Western culture through education, I developed an interest in choral and classical music as well. When I was studying the theory and practice of music in Britain, I was amazed by the extent to which Western or European music in its various forms or genres was based on a particular identifiable cultural ethos. This confirmed my belief that there is a symbiotic and very complex relationship between music and culture. Thus when Shabalala approached me to write the story of his life as a musician, I consciously chose to look at art as a product of the culture that nurtured and sustained it in various ways. It could be argued that I approached the task of writing the biography from the perspective of ethnomusicology.

TN: Did you see your research into Shabalala's life as an ethnographic study relying on life history methodology?

AJT: Yes, you could say that. But when I was working on the book, I did not consciously think of the theoretical and conceptual underpinnings of life history methodology. I'm convinced that anthropologists and other social scientists may see this short biography as having a strong ethnographic dimension as it examines a relatively unique form of Zulu cultural expression.

TN: Could you briefly describe the research process that culminated in the publication of the book?

AJT: The research process consisted of oral interviews with Joseph himself at his place of birth to facilitate his recollection of events. This was not a question-and-answer encounter. This was recorded on tape with his permission. The researcher listened to the tapes and extracted, rearranged, and systematized the main points in writing. The written narration was read to him so that he could feel free to amend or confirm the written form. The interviews with Joseph's mother, sister, and friends were conducted on a question-and-answer basis merely to check the authenticity of Joseph's narration. The documents consulted consisted mainly of newspaper commentaries in various cities and countries of the world. Concert programs and advertisements provided evidence of their performances. Tape records and compact discs provided the list of songs they (the Black Mambazo) composed and performed over the twenty-year period (1960–1980) covered by the biography.

TN: To what extent is the book based on oral evidence provided by Shabalala himself? Would you describe his recollection of events and incidents in his life as fairly accurate and reliable?

AJT: To a very large extent the book is based on oral evidence provided by Shabalala himself. Lapses of memory on matters of dates or places were easily checked in the documents mentioned above. Events in his life were checked with his mother, sister, and friends. Every statement in the book can be considered completely accurate and reliable.

TN: Would you briefly describe the writing process? As collaborators how did you divide the tasks of research, writing up, editing, negotiating with publishers, and marketing the book?

AJT: I was almost exclusively responsible for recording, listening to the tapes, and going through all the documentation consulted. I was also responsible for writing the drafts and proofreading the typed copies and negotiated with the publishers. Radebe provided all the logistical support, such as obtaining a sponsor to cover the expenses incurred and providing the actual means of transport. He also proofread the final product and discovered a major error of fact that would have embarrassed the authors immensely had it gone undetected. The marketing of the book was undertaken by the publishers.

TN: Is the book (both the isiZulu and English versions) aimed at a particular readership?

AJT: The isiZulu version is aimed particularly at the followers and admirers of the group called Ladysmith Black Mambazo who can read isiZulu. Music students at colleges and universities are also targeted. The English version is aimed at all non-isiZulu speakers who like traditional African music. If properly marketed, it is also aimed at the international community where the Black Mambazo has performed.

TN: The structure of the biography: did you choose a sequential or developmental structure or a thematic one? Why?

AJT: The structure is developmental. The aim was to present the life and works as they unfolded chronologically over a period of two decades (1960–1980). Since then another two decades have elapsed. The Black Mambazo have made their mark worldwide, and some author may like to consider writing the second edition with a thematic structure. Good luck to her or him.

TN: Briefly describe Shabalala's involvement in the writing of this book.

AJT: Shabalala's involvement in the writing of this book is limited to supplying information verbally and providing documents.

TN: There is an important sense in which this is a collective biography and not just the story of one person—your comments on this point.

AJT: This is true only insofar as there would be no Joseph Shabalala without the group called the Ladysmith Black Mambazo. But it is more significant to note that there would be no Black Mambazo without Joseph Shabalala. Individuals came and went, but Joseph was the constant pillar throughout this period.

TN: *Isicathamiya* music has been described by Veit Erlmann as "one of the most complex statements of expressive culture isiZulu-speaking migrants have developed since World War I." Do you think Shabalala's biography would be useful to researchers interested in the development of *isicathamiya* as a distinctive musical genre?

AJT: We agree with Veit Erlmann's description of *isicathamiya*. We submit that no future researcher would be successful in developing *isicathamiya* as a distinctive musical genre without referring to the biography of Ladysmith Black Mambazo.

TN: Do you regard the music of Ladysmith Black Mambazo as part of contemporary popular culture?

AJT: We are not aware of a precise scientific definition of "contemporary popular culture." But if popular culture means or embraces *kwaito* music, we would definitely *not* include the Mambazo music in the category.

TN: Don't you think we need to broaden our understanding of popular culture to include forms of cultural expression that would be frowned upon by elitist critics?

AJT: The word elitist implies class distinctions—yes, I have no problem with a broad and all-inclusive understanding of the concept of culture. But we need to acknowledge the fact that *kwaito* and *isicathamiya* are different musical forms that could be categorized as "popular forms" depending on the criteria used to assess them.

TN: Are you aware of any current research on the music of Ladysmith Black Mambazo?

AJT: Before he passed away recently, I was aware that Masonto Buthelezi (may he rest in peace) was engaged in research on *isicathamiya* as a genre, and not on the Mambazo version in particular. Professor Muxa Xulu was also very interested in Zulu traditional music. You may find more information in this regard from Mr. Elliot Pewa, senior lecturer in the Department of Music at the University of Zululand.

TN: Do you have any additional comments or views on the role of Ladysmith Black Mambazo in promoting contemporary popular culture?

AJT: We would like to dispute the assertion that the music of Ladysmith Black Mambazo had a role in promoting "contemporary popular culture." We would have to agree first on the definition of this concept. As things stand now, I would submit that the music of the Ladysmith Black Mambazo is an authentic expression of Zulu culture in a unique combination of melody, harmony, dance, and rhythm. Our suggestion for further research is an analysis and description of the Mambazo melody, harmonics, and rhythm which produce this unique product that has captured the imagination of millions of admirers right round the world.

References Cited

ERLMANN, VEIT. "The Past is Far, and the Future is Far: Power and Performance among Zulu Migrant Workers." *American Ethnologist* 19, 4 (1992): 45–66.

THEMBELA, ALEX. J., and E. P. M. RADEBE. *The Life and Works of Joseph Shabalala and the Ladysmith Black Mambazo.* Pietermaritzburg: Reach Out Publishers, 1993.

Further Reading

BALLATINE, C. "Joseph Shabalala: African Composer." In *Senses of Culture: South African Culture Studies,* edited by Sarah Nuttall and Cheryl-Ann Michael. Cape Town: Oxford University Press, 2000.

———. "Joseph Shabalala: Portrait of an African Composer." *British Journal of Ethnomusicology* 5 (1996): n.p.

CAWELTI, JOHN G. "Notes toward an Aesthetic of Popular Culture." *Journal of Popular Culture* 5 (1971): 255–268.

ERLMANN, VEIT. "A Conversation with Joseph Shabalala of Ladysmith Black Mambazo: Aspects of African Performers' Life Stories." *Journal of the International Institute for Comparative Music Studies and Documentation* 31, no.1 Berlin (1989): 31–58.

———. *Nightsong: Performance, Power, and Practice in South Africa.* Chicago: University of Chicago Press, 1996.

———. *African Stars: Studies in Black South African Performance.* Chicago: University of Chicago Press, 1991.

THEMBELA, A. J. "A Socio-cultural Basis of Ethnic Music with Special Reference to the Music of Ladysmith Black Mambazo." *Symposium on Ethnomusicology* Number 13, 1995: 35–36.

October 2001

III REPRESENTING SILENCE

I Speak Their Wordless Woe

Dennis Brutus interviewed by Simon Lewis

BEING BLACK AND a writer in South Africa in the apartheid years was necessarily a political matter. The authorities in the late fifties and early sixties, when Dennis Brutus first came to prominence, did their very best to silence him as they silenced many others through censorship, imprisonment, enforced exile, and murder. Neither repeated banning, however, nor imprisonment on Robben Island, nor being shot in the back, nor separation from the land he loved, could silence Brutus. For more than thirty years he has lived in exile, mainly in the United States, writing and speaking out against the evils of racism generally and the evils of what he sees as the violence of a new world order more determined to create and perpetuate an underclass than to work for freedom and justice, including economic justice, for all. The interview, conducted by phone, fax, and e-mail between March and May 2000, addresses the impact that leading such a public political life has had on Brutus's practice of a craft—poetry—generally regarded in the west as private and personal.

SIMON LEWIS: In teaching your poems from the Heinemann edition of *A Simple Lust*, I was struck by the coherence of the book; my students and I found that one could read the book whole, as an autobiography, rather than as a collection of autobiographical fragments. We found ourselves following what Donald Herdeck, in reference to *Stubborn Hope*, calls the "quiet voyage of the soul of the poet with the slow transformations over time" (McLuckic 1995:158). As a politically engaged poet, what position does the self occupy in your work?

DENNIS BRUTUS: It cannot, of course, be excluded or ignored, but I think it is not ego-centered; that is, I tend to see myself as one in a community experiencing a communal or community experience. I think the politically engaged poet probably functions best when his voice, and his experience, is that of his community, his "polis," if you like.

SL: How would you suggest we read your work against the prose autobiographies and memoirs of political figures of your generation, in contrast with? Or as confirmation of?

DB: Both, but largely confirmatory; we cover much the same ground.

SL: Again, reading your poems in and as collections, I'm struck by the consistency and the way that they suggest an unusually high degree of integration between your art, your life, and your politics. Laypersons probably think of autobiography as writing about oneself, but the autobiographical nature of your work seems more performative in nature; it's part of your activism. Is that an accurate observation, and, if so, how might you account for it?

DB: I like that comment; it seems true to what I perceive myself. I know that the emphasis of the volume seems to be, or seeks to be on "identity," but I may be unhelpful in this respect: I believe I define myself by my activity. Certainly I am impatient of categories, especially "racial" ones, with which people in South Africa, and the United States, are often obsessed! I think I am very aware of the value inherent in the team concept. And much of my work has been in "teams," in sport, the divestment campaign, forming the African Literature Association, etc.

SL: To frame that question in terms of English-language Literature, with a capital L, autobiographical poetry has a long and distinguished history, but it's usually concerned with self-analysis, identity formation, family relations, and so on, which is not exactly what you do. In fact, those kinds of concern are largely absent; there's very little sense, for instance, of the child who was father of the man.

DB: There are, of course, autobiographical poems—of childhood, for instance, "Bury the Great Duke" or "My Father, That Distant Man"; or of identity questions like "What Am I in Her Eyes" and others from Algiers. But you are right in saying there are not many. I like your narrowing the focus to the individual, but it is not really the strength of my work. What I was experiencing was being experienced by many others. I write: "I speak their wordless woe" in the poem that closes *A Simple Lust* and that is an attempt to sum up the substance of the whole collection. I am more a voice of a community, rather than asserting any kind of uniqueness.

SL: Why is that? Was—is?—the Wordsworthian self an impossible luxury for black South Africans of your generation?

DB: When apartheid South Africa affirmed that I was less than human, only humans could vote, I had to assert I was not part of that society; I became a citizen of the world. I think it is possible to be sufficiently in a community not to need to assert an individual identity and not to be particularly aware of oneself as a distinct individual.

SL: Even in *Letters to Martha,* where your language seems pared down to the bone, and where you're often talking to yourself alone, where you explore the "labyrinth of self," the poems are never exclusively introspective. Instead they report on what was happening to and around you as if from the outside. You use pronouns such as "you" and "one" and generalizing statements such as "there are times/when the mind is bright and restful/though alive." And in the same sequence you talk about "resolv[ing] to embrace the status of prisoner." How did your sense of that "status," both personal situation and social identity, affect you in jail and as a writer afterwards?

DB: I'm glad you note my use of "one," etc. as a way of downplaying the ego and choosing to be "one" of many. Some critics have missed this. What was happening to me in prison was happening to, and could have happened to, any other. The acceptance of status as a prisoner was a way of dealing with the frustrations that could have led to a futile raging against the situation, "getting ulcers." It was not submission to imprisonment by an unjust system, as some critics seem to have thought!

SL: Actually, I've read that line as a very positive statement, even proud in some ways: I presumed you were again using your experience as a kind of demonstration; in other words, that the "status" of prisoner is something that you can manipulate; you're not a prisoner because of a crime committed but because apartheid had criminalized black South Africans.

DB: Your reading is correct, but in addition I am referring to the very common impulse of prisoners to plot escapes (after all, I had done it twice!) and to rage against the confinement and restraints, not to speak of the indignities and humiliations of prison, and so to have a destructive anger fester inside themselves. In a very real sense, one has to come to terms with one's sense of being a prisoner; of one's status as a prisoner, in order not to have it as a destructive force within oneself. (Perhaps it helps, too, to recall that there was at least one other Brutus who found strength in adopting Stoicism as a philosophy!)

SL: Reading your poems written in exile, one gets the sense that the apartheid regime knew what they were about in forcing their enemies into exile. In breaking your ties with your comrades, they were attempting to destroy you psychologically no less unequivocally than when you were physically shot.

DB: I think my lack of roots began when I refused to accept being a South African on the terms dictated. The roots they were trying to sever were ones I had refused to develop.

sl: The rootlessness of your poems in exile comes across particularly strongly in the poem "I am alien in Africa and everywhere," where you end "only in myself, occasionally, am I familiar." Can you describe the effects of exile on your psyche and on your writing?

db: I think this recognition of alienness is rare: I tend not to emphasize this sense of alienation. It cuts one off from the community (which I try to avoid).

sl: Exile, censorship, and banning did destroy some wonderful writers of your generation: in their various ways, for instance, we can surely consider Nat Nakasa, Can Themba, Arthur Nortje, and Bessie Head all as victims of apartheid. How do you see yourself in relation to those writers? And to those writers (say, Fugard and Gordimer) whose whiteness apparently protected them?

db: Can Themba, Alfred Hutchinson, Bessie Head were among those who had self-destructive tendencies. Perhaps apartheid had a hand. Suicide: Nat Nakasa, yes; other South African exiles, George Peake, my prison mate on Robben Island, hanged himself in Britain; Robin Farquharson died, unexplained in a fire in a barn in the UK. Nortje's death has been questioned. There may be a pattern; I'm reluctant to suggest one. But I have contrasted my reaction to those who claimed that their inspiration was cut off when their roots were severed (Zeke Mphahlele, perhaps), by saying my continued involvement in the struggle from outside was what sustained my energy or "inspiration"—for example, the Olympic and other campaigns, the STST [Stop the Seventy (rugby) Tour] in the United Kingdom, and divestment campaigns in the United States, which made a significant contribution: these have, I think, received less acknowledgment than is due to them. But to recognize my role might be also to recognize, possibly, the justness of some of my subsequent criticisms of the betrayal of the struggle, for example, the ANC retreat from the principles of the Freedom Charter and the capitulation to corporate interests in the face of labor protests. On my visit to South Africa in May, I was part of the labor protests *toyi-toying* through the streets of Johannesburg.

sl: Living in exile in the United States has obviously not been comfortable for you. In 1980–1983, for instance, you faced deportation proceedings. Such legal and practical considerations aside, how awkward has it been for you living in the belly of the capitalist beast, "Amerika the beautiful/cesspool," as you call it in one poem?

db: My test has only been "Where can I function?" And the United States is obviously a center of power where one can focus on the nature of oppression. At first hand! Particularly since the United States government (and corporations) were major supporters of the apartheid regime. Students react strongly to that line. It startles them. They demand explanation, and it may help them to recognize how they are seen by others.

SL: Of the nineteenth century, Nancy Stepan has written that while the battle against slavery was being won, the war against racism was being lost. A couple of years ago the Zairean economic historian Jacques Depelchin pointed out a similar, contemporary paradox, that just as formal apartheid was being dismantled, apartheid was "going global." How do such considerations affect the poetry you've been writing in recent years?

DB: It is good to recognize that just when we emerged from apartheid, we entered the new "globalizing" oppressive phase, and thus entered a new phase of the struggle, which has global implications.

SL: Cardinal Newman famously declared, "To live is to change, and to have changed often is to be perfect!" Your stubborn hope and simple lust seem unchanging. Have you changed?

DB: There is constancy in my struggle, but it is also protean, that is, it changes as the nature of oppression changes. Currently I am engaged in the struggle against 1) the WTO (I participated in pre-Seattle planning), and 2) the Superior Court in Washington, DC on April 18 for obstructing traffic at the Supreme Court on February 28 as part of the protest demanding a new trial for Mumia Abu-Jamal (a black writer on death row for a murder he did not commit), and the abolition of the death penalty. (On June 2, 2000, Dennis Brutus added that it was declared a mistrial after a hung jury. A new trial was possible by August 14.)

SL: What is your stubborn hope for South Africa in the twenty-first century?

DB: South Africa must and will change, that is the "stubborn hope" of human nature; but there is always resistance to change that we must challenge.

References Cited

BRUTUS, DENNIS. *Letters to Martha, and Other Poems from a South African Prison.* London: Heinemann, 1968.

———. *Poems from Algiers.* Austin: African and Afro-American Research Center at the University of Texas Press, 1970.

———. *A Simple Lust.* London: Heinemann, 1973.

———. *Stubborn Hope.* London: Heinemann, 1978.

DEPELCHIN, JACQUES. *Silences in African History: Between the Syndromes of Abolition and Discovery.* Dar es Salaam: Mkuki na Nyota, 2005.

HERDECK, DONALD. "Thoughts on Dennis Brutus's *Stubborn Hope.*" In *Critical Perspectives on Denis Brutus*, edited by Craig W. McLuckie and Patrick J. Colbert, pp. 157–161. Colorado Springs, CO: Three Continents Press, 1995.

STEPAN, NANCY. *The Idea of Race in Science: Great Britain, 1800–1960.* Hamden, CT.: Archon, 1982.

Further Reading

ABDUL, YESUFU. "Smeared Magnificence: Nature and Denaturalisation in the Poetry of Gerald Manley Hopkins and Dennis Brutus." *Acta Academica* 34, 3 (2003): 33–52.

BURNESS, DON, ed. Introduction. "Constellations of Exile." In *Echoes of the Sunbird: An Anthology of Contemporary African Poetry*, edited by Dennis Brutus, pp. 24–34. Athens: Ohio University Center for International Studies, 1993.

BRUTUS, DENNIS. *Sirens, Knuckles, Boots.* Ibadan: Mbari, 1963.

———. *Thoughts Abroad.* [John Bruin]. Del Valle, TX: Troubadour Press, 1975a.

———. *China Poems.* Austin: African and Afro-American Research Center at the University of Texas Press, 1975b.

———. *Salutes and Censures.* Enugu: Fourth Dimension, 1984.

———. *Airs and Tributes.* Camden, NJ: Whirlwind, 1989.

———. *Leafdrift.* Camden, NJ: Whirlwind, 2005.

CHIPASULA, FRANK M. "A Terrible Trajectory: The Impact of Apartheid, Prison, and Exile on Dennis Brutus' Poetry." In *Essays on African Writing: A Re-evaluation*, edited by Abdulrazak Gurnah, pp. 8–55. London: Heinemann, 1993.

EGUDU, R. N. "Pictures of Pain: The Poetry of Dennis Brutus." In *Aspects of South African Literature*, edited by Christopher Heywood, pp. 131–144. London: Heinemann, 1976.

EZENWA-OHAETO. "Shriek of Nerves: The Rational Voice of Dennis Brutus and the Poetry of Exile in *Salutes and Censures.*" In *Exile and African Literature*, edited by Eldred Durosimi Jones. Trenton: Africa World Press, 2000.

GOODWIN, KEN. *Understanding African Poetry: A Study of Ten Poets.* London: Heinemann, 1982.

HARLOW, BARBARA. *Resistance Literature.* London: Methuen, 1987.

JANMOHAMED, ABDUL. "Dennis Brutus." In *Dictionary of Literary Biography*, Vol. 117, pp. 98–106.

LEWIS, SIMON, ed. *Illuminations: An International Magazine of Contemporary Writing.* Special Issue on Dennis Brutus. 20 (August 2004).

LINDFORS, BERNTH. "Somehow Tenderness Survives: Dennis Brutus Talks about His Life and Poetry." *Benin Review* 1 (June 1974): 44–55.

———. "Dennis Brutus and the Lay of the Land." In *Routes of the Roots: Geography and Literature in the English-speaking Countries,* edited by Isabella Maria Zoppi. Rome: Bulzoni, 1998.

MCLUCKIE, CRAIG W. *Critical Perspectives on Dennis Brutus.* Boulder, CO: Three Continents, 1995.

NKOSI, LEWIS. *Tasks and Masks: Themes and Styles of African Literature.* Harlow: Longman, 1981.

OGUNYEMI, CHIKWENYE OKONJO. "The Song of the Caged Bird: Contemporary African Prison Poetry." *Ariel* 13, 4 (Fall 1982): 65–84.

OJAIDE, TANURE. "The Troubadour: The Poet's Persona in the Poetry of Dennis Brutus." *Ariel* 17, 1 (Spring 1986): 55–69.

TEJANI, BAHADUR. "Can the Prisoner Make a Poet? A Critical Discussion of *Letters to Martha* by Dennis Brutus." *African Literature Today* 6 (1973): 130–144.

WYLIE, HAL. "Creative Exile: Dennis Brutus and René Depestre." In *When the Drumbeat Changes,* edited by Stephen Arnold, Hal Wylie, and Carolyn Parker. Washington, D.C.: Three Continents, 1981.

March, May 2000

Making History's Silences Speak

N. Chabani Manganyi interviewed by Thengani Ngwenya

THE FOLLOWING INTERVIEW with N. Chabani Manganyi, conducted at the University of Pretoria where he is a vice principal, explores his roles as a writer, theorist, and critic of biography. Besides theoretical works on psychology, society, and auto/biography (1981, 1990, 1991), Manganyi has published three biographies of eminent South African artists, *Exiles and Homecomings: A Biography of Es'kia Mphahlele* (1984) and *A Black Man Called Sekoto* (1996) and *Gerard Sekoto: 'I Am an African'* (2004). The interview seeks to elicit responses to probing questions regarding the theoretical underpinnings in the psychology of Manganyi's practice as a biographer and theorist of life writing.

THENGANI NGWENYA: You have written three biographies and theoretical essays on auto/biography, but your formal training is in clinical psychology. Would you like to comment on how your background in clinical psychology influences the way you conceive of the process of the biographical reconstruction of people's lives?

CHABANI MANGANYI: Well, I think in my case the interest in life writing was in important respects related to the fact that I am a clinical psychologist by training, but, in addition to that, a socially aware clinical psychologist who had been struggling intellectually with understanding the conditions under which we lived in South Africa before 1994 and wanting to use my academic and professional training to deepen that understanding and use that academic and professional training to find ways of answering certain important questions of the time. It's also the case that I happened in the 1970s to be in an environment in which both the professional discourse and academic discussions that were going on had a strong social bias. You must remember that the early seventies in the United States, which is where I was at that time, came after a period of considerable social upheaval.

TN: The civil rights movement?

CM: Yes, the civil rights movement and attempts to redefine everything that was being done even by psychologists and so on. For example, there was a great deal of talk about community psychology at the time. But at Yale University at the time we were also interested in what is called social systems theory, which is a way of trying to understand behavior within organizations and large social movements. So it was a multifaceted impulse, if I may put it that way.

TN: You also write very well; do you have a background in English literature as well?

CM: As it turns out, I majored in English when I did my first degree and had hoped to pursue a career in English studies and perhaps even to write fiction; but that didn't happen.

But I just want to add one other thing—the interest in life history among psychologists is actually not spurious. You might know that there are quite a number of important contributions in this area. You can take the psychoanalyst Erik Erikson, formerly of Harvard University, who wrote two landmark studies, one on Martin Luther, *Young Man Luther,* and another on Gandhi, called *Gandhi's Truth.* So there is such a tradition. The fact of the matter is that as a clinical psychologist one is always working with people, and in trying to help them understand their dilemmas one undertakes quite an in-depth and detailed reconstruction of their lives.

TN: In one of your essays on psychobiography entitled "Psychobiography and the Truth of the Subject," you mention that biographers must seek their own truth while simultaneously seeking the truth about their subjects. I take this to mean that as a biographer, while writing about somebody else's life, you are at the same time writing about yourself.

CM: Well, I'm certain that the intention and the meaning of that statement is not that one writes about oneself. The psychological meaning of that statement—I think it comes from a kind of practice that is demonstrated in the work of Erik Erikson, which is to say that you have to, as Jean-Paul Sartre once put it, overcome your own prejudices, you must write against yourself—is trying to understand and overcome your own prejudices. What I was trying to say is that it's important to understand yourself, your own curiosity about the life you are writing about, what prejudices you might hold and so on, so that you do not contaminate the narrative of the other person's life with your own burdens.

TN: Is there any aspect of your personal philosophy and values that made you choose Es'kia Mphahlele and Gerard Sekoto as your subjects for biographical study?

CM: I think that there are two statements that I'll always remember as having been very formative in my experience and work in the area of biography. The one statement, and I don't recall who made it, reads something like "to make history's silences speak." That is a very profound statement in my view. And then, of course, you would have come across perhaps more than one reference in my work to C. Wright Mills's classic: *The Sociological Imagination,* in which the dominant idea has to do with the private and public spheres.

TN: And an attempt to link the two through biography?

CM: Yes, Mills argues that there is a private sphere that can tell us a great deal about the public sphere and vice versa. Those two ideas had a very profound impact on my thinking so that I wouldn't say that the choice of the two protagonists, if you wish, was just a matter of accident—they happen to be very significant South Africans in their own right. In a profound way they are the kind of individuals in whose case it can be said that their personal troubles are a resplendent mirror of the public issues of our day.

TN: Yes, that's true.

CM: I was concerned with "making history's silences speak" by saying to my compatriots that there are many black South Africans like these two who are unknown to large segments of our society but who deserve to be heard. However, there was a certain degree of tentativeness in my work at the time because I did not see myself as someone who was going to become a professional biographer. I wanted to start a movement so that other people could write about our people. They could do some more work on these individuals, but I would have cut some of the trees of the forest.

TN: It's interesting that you mention your reservations about being a professional biographer because with two biographies behind you most people would regard you as an established biographer. However, your tentativeness is understandable because when these biographies were being researched and written, you were busy with other professional commitments.

CM: Yes, I was doing other things. I must say that tentativeness must not be mistaken for limited intellectual seriousness or even rigor. Both Sekoto and Mphahlele were engaging subjects who left little room for a lighthearted touch. Most biographical writing is tentative since in theory, and in practice at least, there should be no such a thing as a definitive biography. Interestingly enough, during the decade of the eighties, there were several auto/biographical studies, such as Z. K. Matthews's *Freedom for My People* and Brian Willan's *Sol Plaatje:*

A Biography (1984), that I subsequently reviewed in *Research in African Literatures* (1986).

TN: The titles of both your books are very suggestive; would you care to explain how and why they were chosen?

CM: It's difficult to go back to original impulses after so many years. But in the case of *Exiles and Homecomings,* the title summarized for me the kind of journey or life journey that Mphahlele embarked on. You might remember that he lived in many countries. So he had many experiences of exile, initially in Nigeria, as well as Zambia, Kenya, France, and finally the United States. Homecomings are not only acts of actual return from exile. There are many homecomings in the lives of exiles, since memories of home are inevitable.

TN: The title of Sekoto's biography is even more interesting—why the almost platitudinous *A Black Man Called Sekoto?*

CM: That comes from a heartfelt tribute that was written by one Parisian critic on one of Sekoto's exhibitions in which he praised Sekoto's work and went on to say that the painter "is a black man called Sekoto." The title originated from that description.

TN: Did you at any stage during your research into the lives of your subjects assume the role of a psychotherapist who could empower his subjects with appropriate skills to cope with the psychologically debilitating condition of exile? Did you think of them as "patients" requiring psychological intervention?

CM: No, not at all. In the worst of circumstances it would be difficult to make Zeke, or Es'kia as he later became known, or someone as life-loving as Gerard a "patient."

TN: So while interviewing your subjects you never consciously thought of your role as a psychotherapist?

CM: No—I saw myself as someone who was engaged in an interesting journey with them. Look at the extended interview with Mphahlele that appeared in *Looking Through the Keyhole* (1981)—it's a very long interview that I did in Grahamstown at Rhodes University, in one sitting as I recall—probably one of the most exciting things I ever did. It was an intellectual or maybe an emotional tangle. We were dealing with a wide range of things covering different kinds of situations and so on. The Sekoto interviews, which are in my personal possession, were never published. I interviewed him similarly in Paris and in some suburbs of Paris over a number of years. It was the same kind of engagement. I was getting to know the person but not thinking in any way that they were in need of help.

TN: Yes, I see.

CM: I wanted to understand what I was dealing with. The pain of exile happens to be an important issue in its own right and as such it was unavoidable. The circumstances of those two individuals, as it was for hundreds and hundreds of South Africans including myself at one stage, was an important subject.

TN: My question arose out of a comment you made in your Introduction to *Exiles and Homecomings:* "Method in the study and writing of lives is not a matter of research strategy. The situation here is, for a psychologist at least, very much like the work of a therapist whose very method, his intervention, is that which is intended to effect the reconstruction of the individual's life history." (1984:4).

CM: Yes, that is precisely because biography is a written narrative. Psychotherapy is a verbal narrative reconstruction. Both are enriched by and brought to life by the interpretations of the biographer and the psychotherapist. Interpretation is a search for meaning requiring confirmation.

TN: Your comment is simply a reference to an analogy.

CM: Yes, that's what it is—and much more.

TN: Would you say that your training in psychological research methodology has made you inclined to be empiricist in your approach to the study of lives?

CM: I'm sure that both books do not move in the empiricist or positivist direction to the extent that one might have thought would happen because of my social science training. Remember, I'm a therapist as well. Therapy is not about calculations or abstract logical connections. Well, it's about logical connections of a different order from what you deal with in a laboratory or anywhere else. So being a therapist and a very avid reader . . . I was someone who had studied literature seriously. I was not an average sort of disinterested undergraduate. I read all manner of things. For instance, I read Russian literature, *The Brothers Karamazov,* when I finished matric. And that is part of what colors my perspective. So it couldn't have been empiricist. The Sekoto book may be closer to some kind of framing developmental theory, but that is just a holding utensil, if you wish. The affinity to psychotherapy is at two levels, namely, the sustained use of empathy and the construction of a meaning creating historical narrative.

TN: The biographies of your subjects are different in many respects; as the titles suggest. Mphahlele's is a story of a writer's "exiles and homecomings," and Sekoto's is a biography of an exiled artist. Significantly, the two books also display marked structural differences. While Mphahlele's biography reads very much like an autobiography because it has a protagonist who is also a first-person narrator, Sekoto's life story assumes the form of a conventional biographical narrative in which the biographer presents carefully researched facts alongside his own interpretations and analysis. Can you briefly account for these different approaches?

CM: You're quite correct. The approach in the Ezekiel Mphahlele undertaking was very experimental. You must remember also that *Exiles and Homecomings* was accompanied by *Bury Me at the Marketplace,* a collection of letters that is quite substantial, and it is meant to be part of that story. So it was not just an isolated publication.

TN: The two books had to go together.

CM: Yes, that's right. So I was really trying out something there in recognition of the fact that I wasn't writing a critical biography but writing about a writer. Therefore I needed to search for a particular kind of voice, because biography is about voice. Autobiography and biography are about voices and from time to time you have to ask yourself which voice is speaking and so on. I was struggling with those kinds of issues with regard to the voice that would be appropriate. At the time when I worked on the two volumes on Mphahlele, I was intuitively struggling with a complex problem in auto/biographical accounts that I later recognized as the problem of the voices within the text—the "figure under the carpet" if you wish—that assume the authority of speech. A section (see p. 246 of this collection) in which Es'kia speaks about childhood and adult voices in *Down Second Avenue* illustrates the problem to some degree.

TN: I'm sure you were aware that you were going against orthodox practice in presenting what is essentially an autobiographical text as a biography.

CM: Indeed I was very conscious of that. Yet again, if you consider the matter from the perspective of a therapist, the approach that you described as autobiographical makes a lot of sense. I was letting the subject, that is Mphahlele, speak for both of us. Although it is the therapist who makes interpretations in treatment, it is ultimately the voice of the patient (his or her interpretation) that counts.

TN: In the Preface to the Sekoto biography you refer to your collaboration with Daniel Levinson in turning your interviews with Sekoto into a structured and coherent narrative. What was the nature and extent of this collaboration?

CM: In 1985 I spent a year as a visiting scholar at Yale University. I was a guest of Professor Daniel Levinson, an internationally renowned Yale psychologist who had been my friend for many years and had been my supervisor at one time in the seventies. As you know there are many theoretical approaches to biography that have come from psychologists. Levinson was using a biographical approach (the biographical interview) to study adult development. He used biography (life history) to investigate and understand adult development. Other people would use the available psychological theory in order to write biography, which is like going the other way round.

TN: I'm not sure I follow you there. He would begin with the life itself? He wouldn't start with theoretical assumptions?

CM: He didn't start with the theory of development. I mean one can use psychology to write a biography and start with Freud's theory of personality or mental structure, using concepts such as the ego, the superego, and the id. One may use that theory in order to write a story or to understand a biographical subject. Now Levinson was going the other way in the sense that he was using the "biographical interview method," which he and his team developed in order to get an understanding of how adults change and develop. That's why I say it's like going the other way round from conventional practice.

TN: I see—and he called his method the "biographical interview"?

CM: He used the biographical interview in order to study the lives of men and subsequently women in mid-life and beyond.

TN: His theory, as outlined in his seminal book, *The Seasons of a Man's Life* (1985), seems to be based on untenable assumptions about human development. One such assumption is that human development follows a predictable and predetermined pattern or structure.

CM: When that book came out, it broke new ground because the assumptions in psychology for many years were that human beings develop predictably until a certain stage in early adulthood. What Levinson's work established is that we develop further and that there are many significant changes throughout our lives. Developmental periods are characterized by different types of opportunities and challenges. I don't think there is a suggestion that life is predetermined. The theory just says that there is a structure and a sequence. There is a predictable sequence of development throughout the life cycle that can be empirically validated.

TN: Did you find Levinson's theory useful, particularly in your work on the Sekoto biography?

CM: Well, what we did with Levinson at Yale was to have what I described as "two-person seminars" in the preface to the Sekoto biography. I would construct a chronological account based on biographical data for a certain period in Sekoto's life. We would then take this apart and try to understand what it meant in terms of his life history and consider the life structure issues that were coming into play and so on. So we did a lot of that. That was a fascinating engagement with a very senior and astute observer of people. That's how we worked with the material. I always had the responsibility not only of getting the raw data in terms of the interview material and so on, but also constructing the chronology.

TN: Did you not see that what you were doing could be seen as imposing theoretical principles on your subject's life story or attempting to adapt the life history to fit Levinson's theory of adult development?

CM: I don't know why there would be a temptation to do that because in the first instance we were not trying to prove a theory. The theoretical work that underpinned his work had already been done as you'll recall from the book, through very extensive investigations of the so-called Yale Research Group on Adult Development. The theory was extremely well based, so that could not have been the intention. I think Sekoto's life was far more interesting in its own right. In any event, the writing of biography is based on either explicit or less explicit assumptions about the "psychology" of individuals.

TN: In your introduction to *Exiles and Homecomings* you cite C. Wright Mills's comment about the relationship between biography and history. How do you reconcile Levinson's idea of a "an integrating life structure," which seems to imply that each individual life has its own unique "structure," with Mills's views about the construction of an identity within a historical, social, and cultural context?

CM: I'm not sure about the extent to which you are interpreting Mills correctly. I think that central to Mills's thinking—the idea of the sociological imagination—is the connection between what he calls, if I remember correctly, private troubles and public issues. This is one way of saying that if you look closely enough at the private troubles of an individual in a particular society, you have a very good chance of understanding public troubles, that is, the social fabric of that society. In other words, the nature of the society in which that person lives or the burning sociological issues of that particular society—that is the connection. But this does not in any way disprove the notion that there is a developmental order or sequence to adult development. The fact that a society may be organized differently does not necessarily mean that the biosocial trajectory in which people develop from childhood to, say, adolescence and so on is in any way undermined. In some ways, with variations, because things are relative in the mental sphere, I would assume that the central notion that there is an organizing life structure for everyone's life is a helpful concept for understanding why we make certain choices and why we make them at particular times.

TN: Do you have any comments on what seems to be an unbridgeable gap between the humanist conception of identity, according to which the self is unified and coherent, and the postmodernist view of the self as decentered and fractured and discursively constructed? Contemporary postmodernist critics of life writing who see themselves as the disciples of French theorists such as Michel Foucault, Roland Barthes, Jacques Derrida, and Jacques Lacan, would sneer at such concepts, which seem to be central to your work, as "the truth of a subject's life," "an integrating life structure," "turning points," "evolution," etc. They would argue that all these are discursively constructed and do not inhere in the lives being represented. Where would you place your own practice as a biographer in this complex scenario?

CM: It's very interesting stuff. I think that the semiotics people in literature and the neopsychoanalysts who were teaching literature in New England and elsewhere picked up Lacan, Derrida, and people like that. It became so self-absorbed, in my view, that sometimes they didn't understand what they were saying to each other. It was a play on language in some cases. So I think it's intellectually interesting, but somewhere along the way I think it loses its sheen, as it were. I would say that Levinson, in the categories that you are using, would be a humanist. He could not have thought of identity as decentered or fractured in the senses in which we are using the language of the postmodernists. Coherence, a sense of self or personal identity, as well as predictability within some known limits, are the stuff of life of ordinary men and women. Psychotherapists know that there is an interpretive coherence to be achieved even in work with the most mentally disturbed amongst us. For psychotherapists at least, it is the presumed potential centerlines of the self and its relative predictability that justify years of narrative and interpretive reconstruction. Biography is not fiction. In a way, biographical subjects are closer to the characters one meets in the consulting room than in *The Brothers Karamazov*!

TN: Do you think Levinson would have been aware of the capacity of language to half-create the reality it describes or represents?

CM: But surely once you start talking about representation, you are saying there is something else as well. The representation achieved through language in biography and psychotherapy is what I have described on another occasion as a truth supposed possible, an interpretation. In psychotherapy, interpretations can achieve relative closure. In biography, they remain open to future reinterpretation. Doubtless language does "create" reality. It does so in fiction, in poetry, and in theater. It is less successful in psychotherapy and biographical writing. In both these instances, reality in the form of real-life protagonists places a limit on what language on its own can "create."

TN: In the Sekoto biography, was it a conscious strategy on your part to separate your interpretations of the data you had collected through "biographical interviews" from your own analysis of the information ?.

CM: Well, I think that was a by-product of the seminar approach that we used: the interrogation of the chronology of Sekoto's life from the biographical interviews and determining what it all meant in the end. So it was a partly conscious strategy that had a lot to do with how one worked with the material. On yet another level, the sequence from chronology (life events) to interpretation is the way of the psychologist in psychotherapeutic mode who is an active listener and depends for interpretations on the story of the subject.

TN: Did you not think of a technique that would integrate the "story" with the "analysis"? In other words, analyze as you narrate?

CM: Well no, that didn't occur to me. I'm not sure how well it would have worked for me. That's not the approach that seemed to be most suited to the kind of *understanding* that one was trying to arrive at.

TN: How does your book differ from Barbara Lindop's biographical book on the life and work of Sekoto?

CM: I don't think Barbara Lindop set out to write a biography in the strict sense of the word. Her aim was to write a professional art book.

TN: So it's not a conventional biography at all.

CM: It's a work on an artist written by an art historian (with an autobiographical piece) on the work of Gerard Sekoto.

TN: In your essay "Psychobiography and the Truth of the Subject" you caution potential biographers against heroization—approaching their subjects with a sense of veneration. To what extent were you successful in avoiding this trap in your two biographies?

CM: I was even more self-conscious when I wrote the book on Sekoto. My voice is even more present there than it is in the other book. *Exiles and Homecomings* is in the voice of the writer, Mphahlele, himself. So if there is any heroization, he was doing it himself and not the biographer. In the case of the Sekoto book—if you read it carefully, you'll see that what you see is what you get. He was a difficult bugger when he wanted to be difficult, in ways that are quite intriguing. There can be no heroization when both the grandeur and the lows in a man's life are placed side by side as they are in the Sekoto book.

TN: You conclude your story of Sekoto with the observation that "many questions about his life and work still need to be answered" (1996:174). Did you have any specific issues in mind when you made this statement? Do you think there is a need for a more comprehensive biography of Sekoto?

CM: Let's put it this way, the Sekoto biography was conceived as a biographical starter pack, if you want. I put it aside for a number of years when I came back here and the country was burning, and I went to the courts to defend freedom fighters. So I didn't have time to continue with the research. But I had thought about it at the beginning not as a very big tome on Sekoto. I knew that because of my other commitments I wouldn't be able to do that. I wanted to generate sufficient curiosity about Sekoto so that other people who had more talent and time could follow this up. People who deserve biographical studies often have more than one attempt. So that's what I was talking about. The genius of Gerard Sekoto remains wide open. There is still much about the man that we still need to know. In this regard, his intriguing relationship with his family is a case in point. But more important is the work in Europe and America, which has yet to be rediscovered.

TN: In your Introduction to *Exiles and Homecomings* you rightly point out that it is not a critical biography. One might add that it is also an incomplete biography as it was published while its subject, who is still alive and active, was still in full-time employment. Are you considering writing a wide-ranging critical biography of Mphahlele?

CM: I think that biographies of people such as Mphahlele and Sekoto are extremely important for South Africa. Overcoming adversity is a challenge to humanity. It reassures us about what is potentially good about people. Pioneers such as myself must now leave the field to the professionals because we have other responsibilities to take care of.

The interview was conducted for this collection. It has also been published in *Biography* 26, 3 (Summer 2003): 428–437. We thank the editors of *Biography* for permission to reprint.

References Cited

ERIKSON, ERIK. *Young Man Luther: A Study in Psychoanalysis and History.* New York: Norton, 1958.

———. *Gandhi's Truth: On the Origins of Militant Nonviolence.* New York: Norton, 1969.

LEVINSON, DANIEL J., et al. *The Seasons of a Man's Life.* New York: Alfred A. Knopf, 1985.

LINDOP, BARBARA. *Gerard Sekoto.* Johannesburg: Dictum Publishing, 1988.

MANGANYI, N. CHABANI. *Looking through the Keyhole: Dissenting Essays on the Black Experience.* Johannesburg: Ravan Press, 1981.

———. *Exiles and Homecomings: A Biography of Es'kia Mphahlele.* Johannesburg: Ravan Press, 1983.

———. Review of *Sol Plaatje: A Biography*. *Research in African Literatures* 17, 3 (1986): 393–395.
———. "Psychobiography and the Truth of the Subject." In *Treachery and Innocence: Psychology and racial difference in South Africa*. Johannesburg: Ravan Press, 1991.
———. *A Black Man Called Sekoto*. Johannesburg: Witwatersrand University Press, 1996.
MANGANYI, N. CHABANI, AND ANDRÉ DU TOIT, eds. *Political Violence and the Struggle in South Africa*. New York: St. Martin's Press, 1990.
MATTHEWS, Z. K. *Freedom for My People*. Cape Town: David Philip, 1981.
MILLS, C. W. *The Sociological Imagination*. London: Oxford University Press, 1959.
MPHAHLELE, ES'KIA. *Bury Me at the Marketplace: Selected Letters of Es'kia Mphahlele*. Ed. Chabani N. Manganyi. Braamfontein: Skotaville, 1984.
SEKOTO, GERARD. "A South African artist." *Presence Africaine* 14, 5 (1957): 281–289.
———. "Autobiography." *Presence Africaine* 69, 1 (1969): n.p.
WILLAN, BRIAN. *Sol Plaatje: A Biography*. Johannesburg: Ravan Press, 1984.

Further Reading

BERNSTEIN, J. M. "Self-knowledge as Praxis: Narrative and Narration in Psychoanalysis." In *Narrative in Culture: The Uses of Storytelling in the Sciences, Philosophy, and Literature*, edited by Christopher Nash, pp. 51–77. London: Routledge, 1990.
RADITLHALO, SAM. "Forgotten Son." Review of *A Black Man Called Sekoto*. *South African Review of Books* 46 (Nov/Dec 1996) http://www.uni-ulm,de/~rturrell/antho3html/Radit.html
SARBIN, THEODORE R. "The Narrative as a Root Metaphor for Psychology." In *Narrative Psychology: The Storied Nature of Human Conduct*, edited by Theodore R. Sarbin, pp. 3–21. New York: Praeger, 1986.
SCHAFER, ROY. "Narration in the Psychoanalytic Dialogue." *Critical Inquiry* 8 (1980): 29–53.
SPIRO, LESLEY. *Sekoto: Unsevered Ties*. Johannesburg: Johannesburg Art Gallery, 1989.
THUYNSMA, PETER N. *Footprints Along the Way: A Tribute to Es'kia Mphahlele*. Braamfontein: Skotaville, 1989.
WORSFOLD, BRIAN. Review of *Bury Me at the Marketplace: Selected Letters of Es'kia Mphahlele*. *Research in African Literatures* 17, 3 (1986): 395–398.

March 2002

IV RELATING THE SELF

Creating a Climate for Change

Elsa Joubert interviewed by Stephan Meyer

PUBLISHED IN 1978, two years after the outbreak of the Soweto uprising, *Die swerfjare van Poppie Nongena* became a bestseller overnight and won several literary prizes. It was soon translated into English *(The Long Journey of Poppie Nongena)* by its author, Elsa Joubert, and into thirteen other languages. The stage production drew large audiences in South Africa and abroad, where it tapped into various anti-apartheid movements. The narrative, which retains the colloquial Afrikaans of the oral interviews on which it is based, is a novelized collaborative auto/biography covering the rural childhood of the narrator, "Poppie Nongena" (the pseudonym chosen by the oral narrator), her family life and various displacements by the apartheid economy and state, as well as her first-hand experiences of the uprising in the Cape townships of Nyanga and Guguletu. At the time of publication the book triggered a debate about structural violence in South Africa. Responses varied from critical acclaim by Jakes Gerwel (1978) to a recent attack by Allan Boesak (2001). Although it was initially hailed as a feminist milestone crossing the racial divide (Lenta 1984; Schalkwyk 1989), more recent criticisms have emphasized aspects of appropriation in the collaborative process (Boyce Davies 1992; Gardner 1991; McClintock 1991). The skepticism of the latter can be questioned in the light of the continued value contemporary audiences and the post-apartheid state attach to this auto/biography. *Poppie: Die drama* (Joubert and Kotzé 1984), the Afrikaans stage script, is in its twelfth run, and the play was performed at the Suidooster Arts Festival in 2004 and the Oudtshoorn Festival in 2005. Elsa Joubert received two important awards from the state, both related to *Poppie*: the Order of Ikhamanga (see http://www.info.gov.za/aboutgovt/orders/2004/joubert.htm) and the Department of Arts and Culture award for the best Afrikaans prose in May 2005. This interview with Elsa Joubert, in which she hints at the identity of the now-deceased "Poppie," (since disclosed by Smith 2005) looks back on the relations of production, aspects of the text itself, and the history of the book's reception. The interview was conducted orally in January 2000 and in August 2001 at Elsa Joubert's home in Oranjezicht, Cape Town. Since then, she has written the first volume of her own autobiography, *'n Wonderlike geweld* (Magnificent violence) (2005). The interview was translated by Anita Moore.

STEPHAN MEYER: Could you tell us how "Poppie" [Eunice Msutwana] came to you, and how it happened that you decided to tell her story?

ELSA JOUBERT: Poppie worked for me, and we often chatted. We got on well; we always conversed in Afrikaans. When she started telling me about her Aunt Lenie, Aunt Hetta, and Aunt Hanna, I became extremely interested: where did these traditional Afrikaans family names come from in a Xhosa family? And that was how it occurred to me to write something about her life. To find out more. Perhaps, I thought, it would give me an answer to all the other questions I had about our country. She found me a sympathetic listener. She started sharing more and more of her life.

Then, on Boxing Day 1976 we were packing, preparing to go down to Onrus for our annual holiday, when Poppie arrived at our home, looking utterly bewildered. I told her to sit down and made tea for us. I asked my children to carry on with the packing and we started talking. Then she told me about a fight that had started in Nyanga between the so-called "City-borners" and the people from the rural areas, and about the violence and killings and all the horrific things that had taken place between these two groups, even though all of them were Xhosas and they were all black. She told me everything that had happened in those two days.

After that I went on holiday; she also went away for the holidays, to Herschel. While on holiday, I thought about everything Poppie had told me and discussed it with my husband [Klaas Steytler], also a writer. I decided to put aside all my other work and try to put her life story into words, to make known the restrictions of the passbook system and everything else black South Africans had to contend with. She desperately needed money; she could purchase a house in Mdantsane, and I wanted to help her. Then I told her, "If you tell me everything and answer all my questions, and I write a book, we will share the money." At the time I was already an experienced writer. I felt quite certain that I'd be able to cope with the story. So every morning, she sat down and told me the story of her life.

We worked as follows: I asked her questions and she answered. I recorded everything on a tape recorder and afterwards had it typed out. Later I would lay out the transcriptions on two beds and try to make a whole from her memories told at random. Because, as you know, if you had to tell your life story, or I had to tell mine, it would be merely small slices of humanity. There would be no order in or structure to it. I had to add structure to Poppie's story to hold the reader's interest. And that was my whole aim: to relate her story and get people to read it. It would be futile to write her life story as esoteric speculation, or as blatant criticism of the government. I had to tell her story in such a way that it would touch the hearts of people and that the woman and her plight would be experienced as something universal: her problems were those of many other women and mothers.

Her story became a wide canvass on which I could paint, involving all her brothers, family, and friends. Well, as I continued the story, a beginning, progression, climax, and conclusion gradually unfolded. Obviously the climax comprised an account of the 1976 unrest. Afterwards I still had to fill in bits of information. Just organizing her account of the events was a huge task in itself, although that was not the most difficult. The hardest part was working out the details of every scene because she would say something like: "My husband and I went to the Ciskei, and we enjoyed staying there, and then we came home again." Well, that certainly didn't make a story yet. At this point I found my previous research very helpful. I knew Upington; I knew Lambert's Bay; and I knew the Transkei. When Stone—Poppie's husband—went to a *sangoma,* I was able to describe the scene because I myself had visited a tribal doctor before. In many ways I felt prepared to tell her story. At times I felt it was not pure coincidence that she came to me.

And another thing that simplified matters—which actually made it possible—was that she spoke Afrikaans so well. In fact, Afrikaans was her mother tongue, and we communicated extremely well on a human level. I've often found that when I speak English to a black woman (it's her second language, it's my second language), we can never reach each other on quite the same deep level as with an Afrikaans-speaking black woman. Quite obviously, it would have been preferable if I knew how to speak her language. However, Poppie was far more comfortable speaking Afrikaans than isiXhosa. So that smoothed the path considerably.

SM: How would you describe the relationship of trust that existed before you started writing her story that enabled her to take you into her confidence to such a degree that it was possible for you to work together?

EJ: It was a relationship based purely on friendship. She was in my employ, of course. But I knew everything about her children, and she knew everything about mine. The contrast was immensely painful: when the phone rang, we both wanted to answer it. I wanted to answer it because it could be my child, studying at Stellenbosch University, who might have a problem and was phoning. And she wanted to answer it because it could be her child phoning with worse problems than a child at university. She was like one of my friends.

SM: May I ask you for how long you had known each other before you began recording her testimony?

EJ: I can't remember exactly, probably about four or five years.

SM: Did the fact that you worked together on the book in any way influence your relationship?

EJ: No, it didn't; no, not in the least! She and I always said that we were doing it for our children's sakes. Because our children had to go on living in this country, and our children could not continue living in the same ignorance as we had done for such a long time. In fact, it was our motto: "We are doing it for our children." Then she was very willing to speak to me. And she had an excellent memory. I'll tell you this, though, I didn't take anything she said for granted because anyone can forget things. I checked everything she told me because I realized that I could not afford to be caught out on any detail since that could affect the book's credibility. And credibility was my primary focus.

SM: Before you started the whole process, did you come to any agreement on how you planned to write Poppie's story and what you wished to accomplish?

EJ: No, she trusted me, especially because I had already written and published two books in the time she had known me. I simply used to tell her, "Both of us must sit down comfortably, and then I will ask you a question, and you just tell me for instance: 'What can you remember of your life as a young girl?' or 'Who was your granny and who was your mother?'" These were the type of questions I asked her. And then, when something interesting cropped up, I would ask her to elaborate, or at a later stage I would ask her to tell me more. However, neither she nor I knew what form the book would take. She left everything to me.

The only thing I had to promise her was that I would not reveal her real identity. In the first place she was scared that her family might be upset because she had spoken frankly about them; secondly, she was scared that her pass, allowing her to stay in the Cape, would be revoked; thirdly, she was worried that she would be inundated with requests by her entire family and by other people for financial support and assistance. So that was the only agreement between us—that we would share the money and that her real name would not be revealed. She helped me to choose all the names. All the names in the book are fictitious. She thought them out herself.

SM: With whom did you conduct interviews for the book?

EJ: With everyone! Her brothers Hoedjie, Plank, and Mosie, and their wives sat around my dining room table with the tape recorder in the center of them and then they would start talking. These group interviews were enjoyable and sociable, friendly occasions and the atmosphere was warm. But it was pretty difficult to type these interviews out afterwards because everybody talked at once, and they laughed more than anything else. It used to be great fun when the whole group came together. And her mother visited me—and then I visited her. In that way I became acquainted with everyone about whom I wrote. And my relationship with them continued for much longer afterwards. However, I would like to draw your attention to this: everything in the book cannot be attributed entirely to Poppie. I have said this before in an interview that the book is a conglomeration of the experiences of various women, a point I would like to reiterate.

SM: How would you describe your own presence during the interviews?

EJ: Well, I made myself available to her, that's all. I closed the door behind us. I simply devoted myself to what she was sharing with me from her life. Sometimes we laughed, sometimes we cried together—I simply made myself part of her life. And—I can hardly stress this enough—because we were chatting in Afrikaans, we felt comfortable with each other.

SM: May I generalize the question: under what conditions do you think one person is able to understand another's life? What do you think made it possible and what complicated matters to understand Poppie's life and relate her life to readers?

EJ: Besides language, I should think that you need to understand her background and her circumstances. I knew Poppie's world almost as well as my own, but from a different perspective. Then she shared her perspective on her world with me. And that enabled me to write about her world. I tried to write from her point of view all the time. I tried to view society in its entirety from other people's perspectives, especially since I had always had only a one-sided white person's view. And that restricted view always bothered me. That is why I spent so much time and energy on the book. Because I wanted all the readers of my book, especially Afrikaans-speaking people, to take note of this world we had composed and created—but from a black person's point of view.

SM: Besides language, do you think there were other important similarities that contributed to your collaboration?

EJ: Yes, the fact that we were both mothers. That was extremely important.

It was actually vital. And that her whole life, especially after Stone's death, was focused only on her children, to help them cope in life. At the time, my children were away at university—they had just left home—and we had the same concerns about the injustices in our society. I felt that we had to do our utmost to put things right so that our children—white and black—could have a future together.

SM: Did you have the same religion?

EJ: This is an important point. She was a Christian believer, and so am I. In this respect we were similar. Although to a certain extent I had turned my back on the church because the church didn't take a sufficient stand against apartheid and I did not attend church services as regularly as she did.

SM: Those were the similarities. Could you tell me something about the differences between you?

EJ: Well, there were outward differences: the more affluent, professional class versus the working class. When I went to my seaside cottage, she went to the location. It is easy for people to say that everything has to do with race and color, but then they forget that you get more privileged people and lowly skilled and poorer people almost everywhere. This difference was blatant and very real. I was born into a professional family. Poppie came from the working class, a fact that you cannot disregard. But this fact did not keep me from trying to understand the unnecessary hardship of her life. I was acutely aware of her circumstances at a time when many white people were not even vaguely aware of the circumstances of anyone in her position.

SM: How do you view the claim that representation and understanding across differences are impossible?

EJ: I know it is being said that white people are in no position to write about the lives of black people, that they may not dare to do it. I feel that any novelist must be able to enter the lives of his or her characters if they feel deeply enough about them. And remember, *Die Swerfjare van Poppie Nongena* was published in 1978. At that stage it was essential for someone to write about the daily life of a black person under apartheid laws. I think her story carried weight—mainly for the Afrikaans-speaking public responsible for those laws— because it was written by an established Afrikaans writer.

SM: There are significant similarities and differences between how you deal with the relations between yourself and Poppie and the relations you describe in your biographical novel, *Missionaris* (Missionary) [this novel has been translated into English but has not yet found a publisher] and the short story "Agterplaas" (Backyard), from the volume *Melk* (Milk) published subsequent to *The Long Journey of Poppie Nongena*. One of the differences is that *Mis-*

sionaris starts by emphasizing the separation between the narrator-researcher and the person whose life is being reconstructed. And the narrator of "Agterplaas" comments on her relationship to her servant: "My life moves on the periphery of a level of existence that I do not know." How did you cope with these problems of understanding across differences when you were writing *Poppie*?

EJ: While conducting the interviews I was never aware of any distancing gaps separating us; it was such a positive experience. She came eagerly to the sessions and there was never any hesitation on her part. Whatever she disclosed simply came out naturally. I never asked her about any intimate details because I didn't want to embarrass her. One may understand people only to the extent they allow one to understand them. Perhaps one may be able to understand basic feelings and/or motives—but never someone's innermost feelings. The most outspoken autobiography does not reveal all, it still holds something back, even the autobiographer to himself. The same went for "Poppie"—I respected her inner privacy.

SM: How do you see the relationship between power and truth? How did you view the influence of power, equality/inequality and dependency (in both directions) when you were writing *Poppie*?

EJ: That is quite difficult to answer. Do you mean power in the sense that I could hand her over to the authorities? Or power in the sense that the passbook authorities might become aware of her? That is why it was vital for the real narrator to remain anonymous so that the issue of power would not affect her. Through that, she had the freedom to say anything.

SM: You mentioned that there might be certain things on which she didn't elaborate. What do you think were the types of things she didn't share with you?

EJ: Do you mean intimate details? In writing the book I was never interested to know whether she had other lovers. I would never ask her about that. She didn't divulge anything either. I only wrote what she wanted and allowed me to write.

SM: Was censorship ever an issue relating to *Poppie*?

EJ: No, and that was the weirdest thing. As my husband said, the fact that I never received a single piece of hate mail was one of the greatest surprises to him. As far as I know, there was never any question of censorship. I'll tell you why. People knew the story was true. It had an effect on all and sundry because they knew it to be true. One cannot ban something that is true. I had no desire to write a political pamphlet. I wanted the events in the story to speak for themselves, for it not to convey *my* opinion of what was right or what was wrong. I had to write the story in such a way that people themselves would feel that the pass laws were wrong. The old adage for writers—"to show, not to tell."

SM: In your article on how the book originated, you say that you had read some of it to Poppie, who would then say, "No, it didn't happen that way" or "It wasn't that bad!" (Joubert 1987:253). How exactly did you present the text to Poppie?

EJ: She did not see her way clear to reading the text herself. She only read her Bible. That's what she said—that she only read her Bible. When I wasn't too sure about some of the scenes, I would read parts of them aloud to her. For example, the scene when she gave birth. She would then tell me that Africans were not that weak and sickly *(pieperig)*. Or, for instance, when I wrote about the time they had had a house built for Poppie, and her Mom came visiting, I wrote, "She walked through to the bedroom and sat on Poppie and Stone's bed, and then told her to rethink the Mdantsane story." Poppie corrected me and cried, "No, no, no! A mother-in-law never sits on the bed of a married child." A very strong image!

SM: And then you would change that and consult with her again?

EJ: No, I just changed it the way she asked me to.

SM: And did some of the other people with whom you conducted interviews comment on the text?

EJ: No, no one—except after the play. When they produced a play of *Poppie*, I let her know and asked her, "Would you like to see the play?" She phoned me back and said she didn't feel like seeing all those events again. She had been through it once. She didn't want to go through it again, but her family would like to come. I reserved a whole row of seats for them for the opening of the play. We sat at the back and, you know, it was a great occasion. The group sitting in the front recognized all the people and the sayings. They started singing along and they laughed a great deal. It was a joyous occasion indeed. The next day Poppie phoned me. She said that her family who had been to the play had told her how they had enjoyed it and that she also wanted to go. The following evening I got seats for her and a few of her friends. She told me later, "Yes, it was very good; it was exactly the way it had been."

When the book was published, she didn't really read it, but her brother who is Mosie in the book did. She was given the first copy, and she took it home with her over the weekend. On Monday she told me, "I looked through the window and I saw the old car wreck in the front garden and the whole time it was rocking." And she kept on looking at this car and couldn't understand why it was moving to and fro all the time. Then she saw that Mosie was sitting in it; he was reading the book and he was convulsed with laughter—which accounted for the rocking movement of the car. You know, they are a joyful people. The tragedies of her life didn't overcome her. But when it came to her reading the book, she herself reiterated that she only read her Bible: "The Bible is my mainstay."

SM: Generally speaking, how do you see the difference between oral narration by a person himself or herself (as in an interview) and written rendition, as in a classic autobiography?

EJ: Anything that is written down should obviously be more structured and more controlled. For instance, when writing an autobiography, one needs to give structure to one's own life. That is something I didn't ask her to do. I let the facts and the memories speak for themselves. Gradually a pattern emerged. But I think in this kind of book one goes much further with an initial oral narration. One finds certain depths that would not be possible in a written narrative.

SM: Although you were present at the interviews and in writing the book, you are not really part of the story yourself, and you explain it in this way: "It was my heart's desire to write down the truth as it existed and not my own interpretation. As a human being and an author I had to stay out of the book completely" (Joubert 1987:256). Why did you want to stay out?

EJ: Because it wasn't my story. But quite obviously, what I said above is wrong. To stay out of the book completely was impossible; I as the writer had to make certain choices, to decide which scenes to include, which dialogue to choose. In fact, what I should have said was that I simply wanted to be a channel. As a person, I stayed out of the book, but the book was created by me. It flowed through me. That's why I placed specific emphasis on the children—perhaps because I myself am a mother—and on faith—because I too believe. A writer is always present in what he or she is writing. Even in what he or she omits or includes.

SM: Some people felt that you should have used a long prologue or some other reflective strategy to show your relation to the text, as Margaret McCord has done in *The Calling of Katie Makanya,* or the narrator does in Zoë Wicomb's novel, *David's Story,* and that in this way you might have eliminated much of the criticism leveled at you.

EJ: Believe me, I did try—but it created a hindrance in the text. My role was not important. It was her story that had to make an impact.

SM: Malcolm X said to Alex Haley, "A writer is what I want, not an interpreter" (Haley 1965:7). Is that how you saw your own position?

EJ: Yes, I think that's right. Although, as I said earlier, purely and simply by virtue of what one omits and includes, one is undoubtedly an interpreter.

Although my whole purpose in writing the book cannot be denied. I wouldn't have been interested in her story if it weren't for the injustices she had suffered. The circumstances in which the writer finds himself or herself are equally important in such a project. I'm not sure whether I would write the same things in the same way today in view of all the new concepts and everything else. It was written with a sense of urgency. I wanted it to be a breaking story. So something like this also depends on one's time and circumstances, one's temperament, one's own past. Here I refer to my own past as a conservative, privileged Afrikaans woman. Still, although it was a book of its time, people are still coming to me to say: "*Poppie* was a 'mindchanger.'"

I was extremely upset by a production in the Market Theatre. A woman with glasses like mine sat on stage. She sat there typing away while the whole story unfolded before her. Then she walked to and fro and stood watching the actors from the side. I was extremely irritated by her action. I told them to stop the production immediately. I kept an extremely watchful eye on all the productions because I didn't want to sacrifice the immediacy of the story. I didn't want it to fall into a cliché of madams and maids. And I didn't want anyone to use it as an overt political weapon because then it wouldn't have had any effect on the Afrikaans audiences whom I actually targeted when writing the story. Then, you know, my whole attempt at touching people's hearts would be spoilt.

I agree with Eudora Welty, who once wrote: "The ordinary novelist does not argue; he hopes to show, to disclose. His persuasions are all toward allowing his reader to see and hear something for himself. He knows another bad thing about arguments: they carry the menace of neatness into fiction." (Welty 1965) A great friend of ours, the author Richard Rive—he was tragically murdered—always said to me, "Elsa, writers cannot change the world, but they can create a climate in which the world can be changed." That was my aim—to create a climate for things to be changed. But then you had to touch the hearts of the people. Those were wise words indeed!

SM: How do you feel about the accusations that you took advantage of someone in order to become famous and make a lot of money, repeated most recently by Alan Boesak?

EJ: It's never been said to me personally, but I think that it is absolute nonsense. I didn't know that the story would become famous or that it would be translated, because I wrote it primarily for the Afrikaans-speaking public. I felt that the Afrikaans people were the ones in power—and they were the ones supposed to read the book. The rest just happened. Regarding the money I received, I shared the proceeds from the book as well as any prize money fifty-fifty with Poppie. My conscience is clear there. In that area I did not take advantage of her. If I had not written her story, she would have been much poorer. And afterwards I assisted her children with tertiary education, etc. In that respect I feel the book was only to her benefit, as it was meant to be.

sm: In the critical literature it is sometimes hinted that you used *Poppie* to legitimate your position as white writer, in the same way as you describe the missionary Kicherer, influenced by the explorer James Cook, searching for his Omai in your book *Missionaris*.

ej: That is totally wrong! I reject the idea that Poppie served as my Omai, someone to show off and thereby legitimate my own position. On the contrary, she was my guide. I didn't fabricate her to show people what I was able to do for her. The opposite is true: she taught me and showed me what a true Christian is.

sm: The reaction to *Poppie* is typified by two diverse views: Audrey Blignaut, among others, stresses that the book is about the universally human and not at all political. But Johan Degenaar values the book precisely because it addresses politics in South Africa in a very direct manner (Schalkwyk 1986). I detect similar diverse trends in your work. You said, on the one hand, that you didn't want *Poppie* to be a political pamphlet, and that it has a universal theme of womanhood and motherhood. But, on the other hand, it has been described as a beacon in the antidiscrimination struggle, aimed at the Afrikaans reader, to bring home to him or her the devastation caused by apartheid. I suspect that this tension between the transcendent, ideal, ahistorical, and universal on the one hand, and the immanent, material, historical, and particular on the other, typifies all of your work.

ej: Johan Degenaar thought that the power of *Poppie* lay precisely in the fact that it exposed the structural violence without becoming a pamphlet. With regard to the relationship between the immanent-particular and the transcendental-universal, one needs the immanent, the particular, and the historical to reach the universal and transcendent. A person cannot write a novel about an idea or a feeling; he or she has to use people. One moves through the immanent to get to the transcendent. I didn't want people to say after they had read *Poppie*, "Oh shame, the laws are so unfair," and then simply go on with their lives. I wanted to touch their feelings, their hearts; I wanted them to cry, "Oh no, she suffered the most atrocious injustices! This must be stopped!" If I simply proclaimed that apartheid was bad, it would have had no impact—but when you reach someone's heart . . . The main thing is that the one is essential to the other. One needs characters and real situations to get to the conclusion or to the ideal. To write is to embody an emotion.

sm: What lies behind my question is the criticism that the transcendent and universal are an escape from the unbearable present and material existence and a denial of the real differences between black and white women and mothers.

EJ: No, it's not an escape, it's almost like a revelation. One is allowed a new perspective or insight. One can never escape. It is a transformation, and one moves a step closer to the universality of the Deity in the world. All of us are on the verge of touching it, but we can only do so through a fellow human being.

References Cited

BOESAK, ALAN. "Die rol van die Afrikaanse skrywer in die postapartheid-tyd." Opening Address at the Afrikaanse Skrywersvereniging. Pinelands, September 14, 2001. http://www.mweb.co.za/litnet/seminaar/09boesak.asp.

BOYCE DAVIES, CAROLE. "Collaboration and the Ordering Imperative in Life Story Production." In *De/colonising the Subject: The Politics of Gender in Women's Autobiography*, edited by Sidonie Smith and Julia Watson. Minneapolis: University of Minnesota Press, 1992.

GARDNER, JUDY H. *Impaired Vision: Portraits of Black Women in the Afrikaans Novel*. Amsterdam: VU Press, 1991.

GERWEL, JAKES. "Elsa Joubert is een van ons belangrikste outeurs." *Oggendblad* (Feb. 28, 1979): 1–2.

HALEY, ALEX. *The Autobiography of Malcolm X*. London: Penguin, 1965.

JOUBERT, ELSA. *Die swerfjare van Poppie Nongena*. Kaapstad: Tafelberg, 1978.

———. *Melk*. Kaapstad: Tafelberg, 1980a.

———. *The Long Journey of Poppie Nongena*. Johannesburg: Jonathan Ball; 1980b.

———. "Die ontstaan van *die swerfjare van Poppie Nongena*." In *Race and Literature*, edited by Charles Malan, pp. 253–257. Pinetown: Censal and Owen Burgess, 1987.

———. *Missionaris*. Kaapstad: Tafelberg, 1988.

———. *'n Wonderlike geweld* (Magnificent violence). Kaapstad: Tafelberg, 2005.

JOUBERT, ELSA, and KOTZÉ, SANDRA. *Poppie: Die Drama*. Kaapstad: Tafelberg, 1984.

LENTA, MARGARET. "A Break in the Silence: *The Long Journey of Poppie Nongena*." In *Momentum: On Recent South African Writing*, edited by M. J. Daymond, J. U. Jacobs, and Margaret Lenta. Pietermaritzburg: University of Natal Press, 1984.

MCCLINTOCK, ANNE. "The Very House of Difference: Race, Gender, and the Politics of South African Women's Narrative in *Poppie Nongena*." In *The Bounds of Race*, edited by Dominick LaCapra. Ithaca: Cornell University Press, 1991.

SCHALKWYK, DAVID. "The Flight from Politics: Analysis of the Reception of *Poppie Nongena*." *Journal of Southern African Studies* 12 (Apr. 1986): 183–195.

———. "Women and Domestic Struggle in *Poppie Nongena*." In *Women and Writing in South Africa,* edited by Cherry Clayton, pp. 253–274. Marshalltown: Heinemann, 1989.

SMITH, FRANÇOIS. "Die swerfjare van Eunice Msutwana." *Insig* (March 2005). http://www.insig.com/blad_vorige/maart_2005/05_03_04.html

WELTY, EUDORA. "Must the Novelist Crusade?" *The Atlantic* (Oct. 1965).

WICOMB, ZOË. *David's Story.* Cape Town: Kwela, 2001.

Further Reading

HERMER, CAROL. *The Diary of Maria Tholo.* Johannesburg: Ravan Press, 1980.

HOURWICH REYHER, REBECCA. *Zulu Woman: The Life of Christina Sibiya.* Pietermaritzburg: University of Natal Press, 1999.

MILES, JOHN. *Deafening Silence.* Cape Town: Human and Rousseau, 1997.

NAIDOO, BABENIA, and IAN EDWARDS. *Memoirs of a Saboteur.* Belville: Mayibuyo Books, 1995.

January 2000, August 2001

This Miracle of a Book ... It's Just Like the Bible to Me

Mpho Nthunya and K. Limakatso Kendall interviewed by Vanessa Farr

SINCE THE BEGINNING of the twentieth century, life writing has been one of the preeminent literary forms in South Africa. Promoted and supported by the resistance movement and the alternative press, it played a vital part in countering the hegemony of the apartheid state. Its significance has not waned in the period of reconstruction and recovery in which the country finds itself today. However, the life writings that are most famous, both in South Africa and abroad, recount the stories of men. As a result, it is all too easy to assume that there has only been one story of opposition worth hearing in South Africa, and to have heard that story being told by those who are known worldwide as heroes of the struggle—Nelson Mandela, Walter Sisulu, Govan Mbeki, Steve Biko, Chris Hani, Desmond Tutu, even F. W. de Klerk. The life stories of these men have been written and rewritten, determining and underpinning popular views of what constituted resistance, and from that basis, deciding and supporting the concept of the nation that has been brought into being since the first democratic elections in 1994. The life stories of famous men have helped produce a new myth of foundation for the new nation. Capitalizing on the impression that these are the only stories which need to be told and heard, however, heroic life writing implicitly supports a perspective of nation-building that runs the risk of creating a new form of hegemony in which the perspectives of women, their heroic acts of defiance to apartheid, and their contributions in this period of healing and reconstruction, are lost.

By contrast, many women's stories have been told in collaboration: their collective life writing has come about in a diversity of ways, attesting to the multiplicity of situations in which women have found spaces to work together and the ingenious ways in which they have negotiated their relationships. The range of strategies that have been employed to make women's voices heard proves that women's life writing is a resource which can help lead us away from the re-creation of hegemonic power in the post-apartheid era. It allows more inclusive forms of democracy because it tells a much more complex story of what apartheid was and how it tried to achieve its goals in South Africa and the region, than can be found in mainstream accounts. It recounts a story of resistance to a supremacy that was not only racialized and determined by the maintenance of asymmetrical class relations, but designed to uphold and benefit from "indigenous as well as colonial" traditions of gender inequality (Cock 1991:29). It serves as a reminder that although resistance within South Africa grew from a heightened awareness of the forms of tyranny imposed by the racist and classist colonial and apartheid regimes, patriarchal values that were common to all ethnicities and social orders obscured awareness of the subjugation of women. This situation did not change until women themselves developed a language to address gender oppression and made gender awareness central to the liberation movement both within South Africa and without.

Feminist theorists of life writing, in South Africa and elsewhere, have commented that the collection and preservation of women's stories, and the political activism that has led to such stories becoming increasingly valued, "has its impetus in the recent feminist movement, which provides the space and the need to hear women's voices" (Boyce Davies 1992:5–7; Gunner 1999; Heilbrun 1989; Kadar 1992; Reyher 1999). Yet in the women's movement itself, there have been numerous debates about the problems of power in work collectively undertaken by privileged and less-privileged women. As a result, finding increasingly effective methods for recording women's voices in a manner that is empowering for the most marginalized has been a central goal of antiracist activists (Fester 1988; Gluck and Patai 1991; Personal Narratives Group 1989).

Since their work is informed by a political imperative to make the lives of all women visible, critical or antiracist feminists (Mbilinyi 1992) have worked hard to avoid perpetuating the kinds of power imbalances that lead to the "victimisation of the storyteller/subject" that some critics have viewed as an unavoidable feature of collective life writing (Boyce Davies 1992:10; Goldman 1996). To establish how collective life writing can move away from old patterns of "unvoicing" less powerful women, feminists focus on agency, paying careful attention to the ways in which women with different strengths negotiate to bring a life story to light. To make empowering collective work possible, feminists have struggled to develop a variety of strategies by means of which to effectively challenge the negative impacts of hierarchies of race, class, age, geographical location, and the dominant discourse of heterosexuality. Identifying the specific challenges that face women writers, beginning with a lack of money, time, and quiet space to work (Woolf 1977), feminists have found innovative ways to overcome these problems. They have also pushed the boundaries of traditional assumptions about who is regarded as a knower, and whose knowledge counts (Code 1995; Maqagi 1990).

In the process of recording the life stories of those who cannot write with ease, critical feminists have challenged the view that the "author" of the text is the same as the "writer" (Boyce Davies 1992:8). Instead, they regard the storyteller as a powerful agent, one who understands "stories as existing in multiple forms" that do not always conform to western academia's finite view of what counts as valid knowledge production. The editor is seen as a "facilitator" who is committed "to ensur[ing] that the woman's story is not obliterated," and who promotes this process through a careful "re-creat[ion] of the words and voice of the subject" (ibid.: 4–9). The "contract" between narrator and writer, argues Boyce Davies, "turns on the concept of 'trust,'" which is a "critical ingredient in having the stories told at all" (ibid.: 12). To refuse to understand this, she argues, is to refuse to acknowledge the struggles and negotiations which accompany collective work, and it is when this indifference marks the relationship of the speaker and editor that the "victimization" of the narrator occurs.

Coalition-building, as antiracist feminists are careful to observe, is never very easy (Johnson Reagon 2000), and when difference has been reified, as it has in southern Africa, it is particularly important to discover how women are working to overcome the divisions between us. It is also useful to observe how women have found ways to move their work into the public eye when the publishing industry has been largely indifferent to the writing of marginal women (Farr 2000a).

Thinking about these questions, I went in search of feminist collective life writing that has been produced in South Africa since the end of apartheid. My quest soon brought me to *Singing Away the Hunger*, the life story of 'M'e Mpho Nthunya ('M'e is a term of respect for a mature Basotho woman), written with American feminist activist and academic K. L. Kendall. I first interviewed the two women in Pietermaritzburg, South Africa, when their book was newly published and sales were quite sluggish. In the years since then, the book has gone on to become one of the University of Natal Press's most successful volumes. I have continued to maintain contact with 'M'e Mpho and Kendall as they embark on their new collective project "When Spirits Call Me Home: Spiritualities in Southern Africa." What follows is the story of how they first came to work together, and how their work is bound by friendship, pleasure, trust, and a strong commitment to sharing their diverse strengths.

VANESSA FARR: Why did you begin to tell Kendall stories?

MPHO NTHUNYA: We went up to talk to a lady in the mountain there, because Kendall said she wanted stories.

LIMAKATSO KENDALL: 'M'e Mpho was my translator.

MN: So when we arrived there, the lady kept on talking about the same thing, same thing. When Kendall asked, "Do you know anything about your life or your mother's life?" she said only, "We were poor, and we were always poor," so we didn't stay a long time. And on the way home I asked Kendall, "What kind of story do you want?" She said, "Any kind of story 'M'e Mpho, about your life."

I started telling her the story of my mother, and from that day Kendall said, "No 'M'e Mpho, we must make a story and we are going to make a book." I said, "*Hau*, sure!" [she shrugs]. I know that books are written by people who are educated, the people who go to university and I don't know where. So how am I going to make a book *hona joale* (right now)? Kendall says, "We will do it."

From that day, we used to be waiting to write on Saturdays, on Saturdays or Sundays we wrote this book. With my little English, sometimes it was hard. My English would go away, I would forget everything, everything. We won't do anything that day. Then I'd say I will come back next week: next week I'll have lots of stories and I will tell them to Kendall and it will be all right.

LK: You thought about the stories during the week and between our times.

VF: So in this time that you were making the stories, 'M'e Mpho, you were working full time?

MN: Yes, I was working full time.

VF: And you, Kendall, you were working full time?

LK: Yes.

VF: But where did the time come from, where did you find the time on Saturdays, was it time that you took from work? What would you usually do on a Saturday before the book?

MN: Saturdays in Lesotho we wash the laundry, clean the house.

VF: So when you started to make the book, you had to . . .

MN: . . . leave everything.

VF: And when did you do that housework?

MN: Maybe on Sundays if I didn't go to Kendall's house.

LK: And 'M'anthunya showed up, tell her about 'M'anthunya.

MN: My brother's daughter came to me and she was living with me, so I know how to do this book because she was helping me do everything.

LK: She was a wonderful woman. We have a picture of her; she helped 'M'e Mpho do everything. She died just this year, basically from hunger.

VF: So she believed in stories. She wanted you to get the stories written?

MN: I don't think she thought about the book, she just thought I was playing, playing.

LK: And she wanted you to be able to play, because she loved you. She did everything she could to make your life easy.

VF: So if it wasn't for her helping and coming to do the domestic work for you at your house, you probably couldn't have made the stories. It would have been very much more difficult.

MN: Yes, I think so.

VF: So to make stories, women need support in the house. Do you think, 'M'e Mpho, that this book will not be important in Lesotho, or do you think it will be?

MN: I don't think so, I don't know. I saw it in Maseru, and in Roma.

LK: Times are so bad in Lesotho now that I don't think anybody will be reading books. The book made very little impact in Lesotho.

VF: Have you met anybody who has read the book?

LK: In Lesotho?

VF: Just around, generally.

LK: Well, all of our white visitors have, and many people in America. We went on a tour in America; Indiana University Press brought us there last year. And we met hundreds of people who had read the book and were very excited about it. But in South Africa, no.

VF: And black women?

MN: No.

VF: They haven't got access to it?

MN: Black women like me can't read the books.

LK: Some can!

MN: Like who?

LK: Like you.

MN: I went to school.

LK: And you always loved books, even in the guest house you loved them.

MN: Yes, I always take everything that I see to read. If it has got photos I'll read and sit down, forget about work.

LK: I think you are not the only one. There are other women who do the same. Maybe. But it is true we don't know them. It's not a reading culture. Oh but, Sephefu's children. Tell about Sephefu's children, her brother's children. They have read it.

MN: The husband is a teacher, and the wife is a teacher. They enjoyed it, and they are very, very proud.

LK: And they learned about their father.

MN: Yes, they didn't know how their father died.

LK: They were passionately interested to hear the story of their father's death. And also Mathankiso, her son's wife, is an educated woman, and she read the book. Did her mother read it? She never said.

MN: I know that Mathankiso's brother took the book with him to Johannesburg. They came back to Lesotho. Their children are very big; they took it and read and read. They just told the older people, "This book is so nice of 'M'e Mpho! 'M'e Mpho will get a lot of charity, money." They don't know the truth!

LK: They imagine she's getting a lot. And this is another problem because now that they think she's rich, they think she's holding out on them, and that she should be giving them more of this money that she gets from the book. It's very sad. They won't believe her that it wasn't until last week that she got one penny. They think she's lying.

VF: So writing a book makes you different from other people. Now they see you in a different way; they see you as a rich woman. A woman who's traveled.

MN: They think I'm rich.

VF: I would like you to tell me, I think this may be more your story Kendall, the story of how you got the book to a publisher?

LK: Yes, well in America I have a friend who is a reader for Alfred Knopf, so I sent it immediately to her and she loved the book; and she said, yes she would give it to Knopf, and she wrote a very positive review. And they decided that they needed a famous person to write an introduction to make it saleable. So they sent it to Toni Morrison, three weeks before she won a Nobel Prize. So she then didn't answer, and months went by and they nudged her, and she didn't answer. So at that point they turned it down . . . . So all of this took a whole year, and, maybe a little more than a year, and my heart was in my throat the whole time. It was such a beautiful book, and I so wanted it to be published.

And I began to be discouraged, and in that time I got a job at the University of Natal in Pietermaritzburg, so it ended up that I was in South Africa, and the publishers were in America. I had also collected a book of short stories called *Basali*, which the University of Natal Press published. When I was talking to them about that, I told them I had one that's much better, but I've offered it to an American publisher. So after the second rejection, I gave it to the University of Natal Press, and they just gobbled it up. They really wanted it very badly, and they got it out in one year. Now they had a prior connection with Indiana University Press, so the editor of the press, Mobbs Moberly, wrote to Indiana and said, "I have another book you may be interested in." So finally they agreed and they published it. And John Galman, who is the head of Indiana, asked me, when they brought us to Indiana last year, if there had ever been any other book like this. And I said, "The only one I know is *Child of the Dark* by Carolina Maria de Jesus from Brazil, who told her story with the help of a male journalist." And he said, "Souvenir published that book, I'm going to write to them," so he did, and Souvenir indeed was delighted that it was something like *Child of the Dark*, and they grabbed it up.

VF: How's your relationship with these editors? Was there any further editing from the publishers, because you had done the editing between you before you submitted it.

LK: No. I had spelled things in the American way, so the South African publisher changed those spellings, but otherwise nothing. They wanted me to write an introduction, and I refused because I said I would write after and not before. They actually twisted my arm on that for quite some time, but I was adamant. Given the Toni Morrison experience, I knew that it would help to have a name on the cover. So I suggested Miriam Makeba. But we couldn't find her. Then I suggested Ellen Kuzwayo, and I think it was Mobbs Moberly at the University of Natal Press who actually found Ellen Kuzwayo, made the contact, and Ellen and I talked on the phone and sent faxes back and forth. She wrote about three different versions of this introduction, and then . . . well, to tell you the truth she was very critical in the first one. She said, "Why didn't 'M'e Mpho fight back more? And why was she so placid?" and so on. So then I had a long correspondence with Ellen Kuzwayo explaining to her in what way this book is seditious, and in what ways 'M'e Mpho had resisted, and what her choices were. And Ellen gradually came round. Finally she wrote the introduction that you see there, which was really the product of a dialogue between Ellen and me, in which she gradually came to the point of changing her opinion about the book.

VF: That's interesting, so she didn't actually get the book at first.

LK: She didn't. But then 'M'e Mpho was nominated for the Alan Paton Award. We were invited to Johannesburg for the big Alan Paton dinner. She was one of the top five for the award. And Ellen sat at the table with 'M'e Mpho, so they finally met and talked, and it was a wonderful evening.

VF: So the book was almost given a prize? Wow, that must have been very exciting. Did you ever think this would happen to your book?

MN: No! I didn't even think about it.

VF: Has anybody asked you to come and speak to them about the book?

MN: Where?

VF: Public speeches.

MN: Yes.

VF: Where have you spoken?

MN: Indiana.

LK: And Purdue University, and Smith College, and just recently at the Alan Paton Center.

MN: Oh yes.

LK: The Alan Paton center had a celebration called "Our Elders are our Heritage." It was a Heritage Day and Elder Day celebration, and they asked 'M'e Mpho to come and talk about the book. She spoke so beautifully. People in the audience wept, they were so moved. I think that was the best speech you ever did. You were brilliant. Did you feel you were really good on that day?

MN: Yes.

VF: What did you say?

MN: I prayed.

LK: You always pray.

VF: What did you pray for?

MN: I prayed that day to talk nicely and slowly so that I can be heard.

LK: You were beautiful. Do you remember what you talked about? How we made the book.

MN: Yes, I started to tell them about how we made this book, and how I met you in the guest house, then we started to make this book. And when you started to tell me about doing this book, I said, "Maybe this white lady is crazy. How can a person like me write a book? *Oa Hlanya!*" (she's crazy). But we did it. So I am so happy to make this book. It's just like the Bible to me. I read it every day. When I am lonely, I just go to my room and take it and read it where I like, I just open it like a Bible, like this. I find what I want to read.

VF: How do you feel when you read it?

MN: I feel good. I feel like I am dreaming, as if this book told me stories that I know. And really I know that these are my stories, but I didn't think that one day I could save these stories in a book.

LK: One time you said, "I take this book in my hands and it's like holding my whole life in my hands."

MN: Yes.

LK: And I think it must be wonderful to hold your whole life in your hands.

MN: Yes.

LK: And now you have had a lot of time to be alone in the house. To read your stories.

MN: To read and think about my stories, how they come.

VF: Have you got more stories to tell?

MN: Yes.

LK: She tells stories every day. Every day she tells me more stories I never heard before.

VF: Can you make another book?

MN: I can't make it alone. Kendall is very busy, every day busy.

VF: Can I ask you about the language that the book is in, because you talk about it. You say that this is an English that is spoken by people living in Lesotho and living in South Africa. Did you ever think about writing a book in seSotho?

MN: No, never. I didn't think to write a book. I always thought that a book is written by the people who are educated.

VF: And if somebody came now and said I'd like to keep Kendall's work, but I'd also like to make a book with you in seSotho, would you make a book in seSotho?

MN: Yes, I think I can. It will be hard because nobody can be like Kendall.

VF: No, I know. I realize that.

LK: It's also a problem. Who would read it? Very few people in Lesotho read seSotho. They speak, but they don't read, and those who read, read English. So where would be the market for the book? There are some, few books, but maybe they sell twenty-five copies. So they can only be printed, sort of like photocopies, otherwise you will lose a great deal of money, and nobody reads them. The school children in Lesotho, they read baby books in seSotho, but once they get to high school, they are reading English because their country is dual language.

VF: And the books are in English?

LK: And they don't want to read seSotho because they don't want to read in the first place. I taught at the university there, I know. Students hate reading; they think it's painful. And if they have to read, then they would rather read English because they think it will get them advantages in the world. So it's interesting this question about doing this book in seSotho. Only people who are not Basotho have suggested and asked about that. No Mosotho person has ever suggested that that was a good idea. I tried to interest some people in Lesotho in translating this book into seSotho, and they said, "Who will read it?

I'm going to do all this work translating this book for what? Where am I going to get money for that?" It would be a lot of labor.

VF: So, 'M'e Mpho, when you were making the book, you were thinking out the stories in seSotho, they were in your head in seSotho.

MN: Yes.

VF: And then they had to come into your mouth in English. Wow.

MN: It was hard. Sometimes I'd get a headache because I'd forget even the word "and."

LK: It was hard. Those times when we didn't get any stories, I think they were times when you were very tired. You had had a hard week and you came on Saturday, and you were just too tired. And after we would work—normally we would work four hours—'M'e Mpho was so tired. Oh, you would sleep those nights wouldn't you? It was work to you.

MN: Hard.

LK: But the magic that you have told me is that you had thought about it all week long. So all week you were thinking about it and trying to find English words, so by the weekend, when we worked together, it was in your head, and if you weren't too tired you could pull it out.

VF: And then you picked and chose, and then you took the stories and you read them and you spoke them out loud? To hear that they sounded right?

LK: Then sometimes she would change them. Sometimes she would say, "Oh I have said that twice."

VF: I think it is so incredible that you can do that. Because it must be so hard, it must be so difficult to speak your story in another language and to hear what sounds right, to say, "It is not right now, it must go like this." Amazing.

LK: The kinds of things that you would say to me while we were editing would be, "I have said that thing twice," or sometimes you would say, "We haven't explained who that person was." Then we would go back and add something to explain.

MN: That's why I say there is no person who can write a book like you, because you know how to go forward. When I say to her, next time when I say, "no, we are supposed to say this," you take that part again, put it there. It was a lot of work *hona joale* (and so it is); it was a lot of work!

LK: The thing about her stories—you know it from reading them—is that they were so powerful and clear. 'M'e Mpho's voice is so strong that I could hold them all in my head, and that's what she's talking about. If she would remember something that we worked on three weeks ago, and she would say "I think I'm going to have to change that," I knew right where it was because the stories just carved themselves on my bones as they came into my head, and they are there until now. I can quote from this book so easily, it's just something that I couldn't forget. Once you had spoken the story [looking at 'M'e Mpho], it stayed in me.

VF: So you helped each other by asking questions, talking, "Does that sound right," "Is that what you mean?"—those kinds of questions. 'M'e Mpho, I also was interested in this: Kendall talks about how the stories came out, just they came out as they came. And then Kendall decided to put the stories of your youth in the beginning, the stories of your middle age in the middle, and then the stories of your later age at the end. And it didn't matter to you how the stories went? It wasn't an interesting question for you?

MN: To me, it was not interesting because Kendall fixed them in order.

LK: But you said it didn't matter to you. Like sometimes I would say to you, "This story is sort of out of order," and I would say, "'M'e Mpho, where should we put this story?" And 'M'e Mpho said, "I don't care. Put it anywhere you like."

MN: I didn't care what was going on. But Ellen Kuzwayo, she told me that day when we were sitting together at the awards, "You know how to put this in order." The reader doesn't say, "So where am I going now, what is that?" No they are reading like this, very straight like this.

LK: So she thought that was a good thing?

MN: Yes.

LK: You see I felt insecure about it, because I thought it's corny to start a book when you are born, and it's more interesting if it could be a more nonlinear narrative and all that. But if I tried to arrange it into a nonlinear narrative, then I would be interfering more, you see. So, I finally decided—'M'e Mpho wouldn't discuss it with me, she just wouldn't have any part of it—I finally decided the way to interfere the least would be just to put them in some order. And the chronological order was the simplest route to take. But I don't admire that particularly. One of my favorite books in the world is Tsitsi Dangarembga's *Nervous Conditions,* and it starts, "I was not sad when my brother died." Oh, it's a beautiful way to start a novel or a life story or whatever. So I would have liked if we did not start at the beginning. But I couldn't find a way to do that without interfering with the stories, and I wanted to stay out of the way.

VF: You've spoken to me quite a lot about how much hard work this writing was, how much time it took and how tired it made you. And it must have been very hard for you, because Kendall had the picture of books like this that came before in her mind to keep her going. But for you, you thought she was just crazy?

MN: Uh-huh.

LK: Talk a little bit about the first time you saw it typed. I think that moved you very much. You remember the first time you came to my house, and I had the story typed, and I gave it to you?

MN: Yes. And I asked you, "*Hona joale* (right now), is it me who is talking here?" and you say, "Yes, I don't know anything about that story, you told me." I say "Hey, it's amazing!"

VF: Does it feel like a different story?

MN: Yes, it feels like a different story. But that day I remembered many stories because I was reading it, so lots of stories came.

LK: I think there was magic that day. I felt that when you looked at the page and you saw your words typed, that's when you saw that maybe it could be a book.

MN: Yes.

LK: And I was watching you, and I was thinking with my heart, the way I do with you, and I was thinking, "'M'e Mpho is feeling larger than herself." You were looking at the paper and knowing other people can look at these words, if they are typed, if they are in a book. It is not just me and the person who is listening to me now. I'm in the world! And I saw you thinking that, and from that day there was a change in how we worked. You worked harder, and it wasn't playing, you could see something was happening.

VF: Did you think that money would come?

MN: No, I didn't think about the money.

LK: So what inspired you was just making the words go into the world.

MN: Yes. It was just making this *mohlolo* (miracle) of a book. Because to me it was a miracle, so I wanted to do this miracle. I didn't think of money, anything, I didn't even know that when you write a book you can get money.

LK: And it's good because you almost didn't get the money!

VF: If Kendall hadn't come to you, your stories wouldn't have been told?

MN: No.

VF: And you are much happier that your stories have been told?

MN: I'm so happy. Very, very happy.

References Cited

BOYCE DAVIES, CAROLE. "Collaboration and the Ordering Imperative in Life Story Production." In *De/colonising the Subject,* edited by Julie Watson and Sidonie Smith. Minneapolis: University of Minneapolis Press, 1992.

COCK, JACKLYN. *Colonels and Cadres: War and Gender in South Africa.* Cape Town: Oxford University Press, 1991.

CODE, LORRAINE. "How Do We Know? Questions of Method in Feminist Practice."

In *Changing Methods: Feminists Transforming Practice*, edited by Sandra Burt and Lorraine Code, pp. 13–44. Peterborough: Broadview Press, 1995.

DANGAREMBGA, TSITSI. *Nervous Conditions*. London: Women's Press, 1988.

DE JESUS, CAROLINA MARIA. *Child of the Dark: The Diary of Carolina de Jesus*. Trans. David St. Clair. NY: E. P. Dutton & Co., Inc., 1962.

FARR, VANESSA. "Making This Book Is a Strange Thing to Me: *Singing Away the Hunger* and the Politics of Publishing in Collaborative Autobiography." *Alternation* 7, 1 (2000a): 125–144.

FESTER, GERTRUDE. "Closing the Gap—Activism and Academia in South Africa: Towards a Women's Movement." In *Sisterhood, Feminisms and Power: From Africa to the Diaspora*, edited by Obioma Nnaemeka, pp. 215–237. Trenton, NJ: Africa World Press, Inc., 1998.

GLUCK, SHERNA BERGER, and DAPHNE PATAI, eds. *Women's Words: The Feminist Practice of Oral History*. London: Routledge, 1991.

GOLDMAN, ANNE E. *Take My Word: Autobiographical Innovations of Ethnic American Working Women*. Berkeley: University of California Press, 1996.

GUNNER, ELIZABETH. "Afterword: 'Let All the Stories Be Told': Zulu Woman, Words and Silence." In *Zulu Woman: The Life Story of Christina Sibiya*, edited by Rebecca Hourwich Reyher, pp. 199–213. Pietermaritzburg: University of Natal Press, 1999.

HEILBRUN, CAROLYN G. *Writing a Woman's Life*. London: Women's Press, 1997.

JOHNSON REAGON, BERNICE. "Coalition Politics: Turning the Century." In *Home Girls: A Black Feminist Anthology*, edited by Barbara Smith, pp. 343–355. New Brunswick, NJ: Rutgers University Press, 2000.

KADAR, MARLENE. "Coming to Terms: Life Writing—from Genre to Critical Practice." In *Essays on Life Writing: From Genre to Critical Practice*, edited by Marlene Kadar, pp. 3–16. Toronto: University of Toronto Press, 1992.

KENDALL, K. LIMAKATSO, ed. *Basali! Stories by and about Women in Lesotho*. Pietermaritzburg: University of Natal Press, 1995.

MAQAGI, SISI. "Who Theorises?" *Current Writing* 2 (1990): 22–25.

MBILINYI, MARJORIE. "Research Methodologies in Gender Issues." In *Gender in Southern Africa: Conceptual and Theoretical Issues*, edited by Ruth Meena, pp. 31–70. Harare: SAPES Books, 1992.

NTHUNYA, MPHO 'M'ATSEPO. *Singing Away the Hunger: The Autobiography of an African Woman*. Edited by K. Limakatso Kendall. Bloomington: Indiana University Press, 1997.

PERSONAL NARRATIVES GROUP. *Interpreting Women's Lives: Feminist Theory and Personal Narratives*. Bloomington: Indiana University Press, 1989.

REYHER, REBECCA HOURWICH. *Zulu Woman: The Life Story of Christina Sibiya*. Foreword by Marcia Wright. Afterword by Liz Gunner. Pietermaritzburg: University of Natal Press, 1999.
WOOLF, VIRGINIA. *A Room of One's Own*. London: Grafton, 1977.

Further Reading

BEHAR, RUTH, and DEBORAH A. GORDON, eds. *Women Writing Culture*. Berkeley: University of California Press, 1995.
BOZZOLI, BELINDA, and PETER DELIUS, eds. *History from South Africa: Alternative Visions and Practices*. Philadelphia: Temple University Press, 1991.
FARR, VANESSA. "The Pain of Violence is a Powerful Silencer: African Women Writing about Conflict." *Canadian Women Studies*. Special Issue on Women in Conflict. 19, 4 (Winter 2000a): 102–109.
———. "To Write a Story Can Change a Life: Women's Life History in the New South Africa." *Agenda* 41 (1999b): 100—103.
GORDON, SUE. *A Talent for Tomorrow: Life Stories of South African Servants*. Johannesburg: Ravan Press, 1985.
KENDALL, K. LIMAKATSO. "When a Woman Loves a Woman in Lesotho: Love, Sex and the (Western) Construction of Homophobia." In *Boywives and Female Husbands: Studies in African Homosexualities*, edited by Stephan O. Murray and Will Rose, pp. 223–241. New York: Palgrave, 1998.
———. *A Passionate Guest: Two Years in Southern Africa*. New Orleans: Graeae Press, 2005.
NUTTALL, SARAH, and CHERYL-ANN MICHAEL, eds. "Autobiographical Acts." In *Senses of Culture: South African Cultural Studies*, edited by S. Nuttall and C.-A. Michael, pp. 298–317. Oxford: Oxford University Press, 2000.
SOMMER, DORIS, "'Not Just a Personal Story': Women's Testimonies and the Plural Self." In *Life/lines: Theorising Women's Autobiography*, edited by Bella Brodzki and Celeste Schenck, pp. 107–130. Ithaca: Cornell University Press, 1988.
STANLEY, LIZ. *The Auto/biographical I: The Theory and Practice of Feminist Auto/biography*. Manchester: Manchester University Press, 1992.

October 1998

Collaborators

Wilfred Cibane and Robert Scott interviewed by Thengani Ngwenya

WILFRED CIBANE AND Robert Scott have a long-standing relationship as business partners and close friends. They started doing business together, with restrictive apartheid laws and conventions at times forcing Cibane to pass as Scott's assistant. Unwilling to suffer further harassment, they relocated to Britain, where they established themselves as successful entrepreneurs. They returned to South Africa in the 1990s, where Cibane's wife and children had remained all the intervening years—to retire to a common home in Kloof outside Durban. Although the interview was conducted mainly with Cibane as the author, Scott also contributed additional information and explained some unclear points. Like the book *Man of Two Worlds*, the interview could be seen as a collaborative venture.

THENGANI NGWENYA: Do you have a Zulu name?

WILFRED CIBANE: Yes. Kadengayi.

TN: Before publishing your autobiography in 1998, had you written any other publishable material?

WC: *Man of Two Worlds* was my first book to be published not because in the past I had nothing to say but because I had to learn how to say it. My life has been a long rough journey, and only when I could see the end of the road did I feel qualified to write about the challenge. But let me hasten to add, I did not write the book to tell you about myself. I wrote the book because we have a new South Africa, a black Renaissance offering opportunities to 40 million of my people. That has been the first miracle. Now, I hope *Man of Two Worlds* will be an inspiration to my own people how to succeed. Let us face it. There are two worlds with a large gap between. I was born in the rural world of the

African, in the country, going to the river to get water, to the forest for wood to light a fire . . . That was the life I was born into—the twenty-seventh child of my father, the fifth child of his fourth wife. At twelve years of age, I left my father's farm to work for a white lady in Durban and saw for the first time you could get water, light, heat at the flick of a switch. No schooling, speaking Zulu only, then and there I decided I was going to have the goodies of the white man.

TN: In the blurb of your book you are described as follows: "From rural goat-herd to cosmopolitan man of means, Wilfred Cibane's life carries him between the two worlds of tradition and commerce." What would you describe as the main theme of your life story?

WC: The main theme would be how I succeeded in embracing the white commercial world without turning my back on the rural African tradition.

TN: Autobiography is as much about the past as it is about the present. Is there anything in your present circumstances that you think influenced you to want to tell your story?

WC: My friends thought that I had a story to tell. I had to set about educating myself, but later I discovered overseas when I had to sit with the capitalist world, education was not enough, I had to be "civilized!" I could not take with me into this new world old Zulu traditions of *sangoma, muti* medicines, *umutsha, ibeshu, assagay,* and shield.

TN: In your book you seem to be rather dismissive of traditional cultural practices, including traditional healers and religion. To what extent, if at all, are you still attached to the traditional value system?

WC: Democracy means respect all people and their beliefs.

TN: Your relationship with Robert Scott as a business partner and close friend is central to your life story. After the death of his mother, with whom you were also very close, Robert seems to have become very dependent on you. In your book he is quoted as saying, "Don't ever leave me, Wilfred. I can't face the world alone" (1998:72). This is a deeply emotional plea; would you like to elaborate on this relationship?

WC: Robert Scott had survived the war of 1939–1945; his wife had died. He was a lonely man.

TN: Could you briefly describe how the book was written?

WC: I told my story my way, and Robert Scott put it on computer, showing my feelings. It took a long time but chapter by chapter I recounted my story and Robert Scott put it on computer. We gave it to a literary agent in Durban who edited it and submitted it to Kwela Publishers in Cape Town who were enthusiastic and published it. It became a best seller and received great acclaim.

TN: The meaning of the title of your book?

WC: The African world is essentially rural and the western world essentially competitive capitalism. Changing from one to the other is not easy.

TN: Did you ever regret leaving your wife and three children alone in South Africa in order to pursue business interests overseas?

WC: Of course. But it was a question of priorities. My life in exile was not easy. We worked hard, but I was treated with respect. It was difficult, but each and every year, we tried to find the money for me to come home to my wife and family. Before leaving, we had built for them a Swiss chalet brick house in Clermont. We had to find finance for the children's education, electricity, water, telephone, rates, and housekeeping. It was not easy. We had to pay taxes and save for our retirement. Regardless of the excellent schooling my three children were receiving, each time I came home to visit my wife and family, in one way or another they managed to disappoint and annoy. The children refused to accept responsibility, and my wife clung to her Zulu customs and refused to learn or speak English. When we retired, Robert and I went to live in Spain. Now my children were all qualified and had obtained responsible teaching jobs, but each time I returned home, I found the house needed painting, the inside was neglected, the rates not paid.

TN: How would you describe your current relationship with your wife and children?

WC: Possibly I have changed. Maybe I think like an overseas person—have a wider vista. Because since I returned to the new South Africa, I find communication with many Africans extremely difficult.

TN: During your early years in Britain you speak of having reached "a point of no return." To quote your exact words:

> I had time to think about the new world into which I had been thrust and looked back on the world I had left. It had seemed normal when my father told me to marry and raise a family. Now, thinking back on my wife and family in Clermont, I was wondering whether I, now emancipated, living in London, would ever be happy to return. . . . I began to ask myself if I had reached a point of no return. (ibid.: 109)

Would you like to elaborate on what you saw as the options available to you at this stage in your life?

WC: When one is engrossed in high-pressure business, it is difficult to be patient with the slow rural peasant mentality. My responsibility was to find the money to educate three children and to pay the expenses of a wife and a house in Clermont. I could not make this sort of money in South Africa under apartheid conditions and therefore I was at a point of no return.

TN: In what ways has the new political dispensation in South Africa affected your life as an individual?

WC: In the new South Africa I am glad to say we are all recognized as individuals. I hope in time we become more multiracial and work together as South Africans for the good of the country. We are both amazed at the miraculous peaceful transition to democratic black rule. We are saddened by bewildered unemployable Africans looking for a handout. My dream is a United States of Africa from Cairo to Cape Town, richer and greater than the United States of America. It will come, but I won't live to see it. It will be my grandchildren who will start this second miracle, the children now in multiracial schools, who do their homework together and don't see color.

TN: Have you ever been suspected of being a gay couple? If so, how have you responded to such suspicions?

WC: Often. We have many, many friends, straight and gay. We couldn't care less. Their personal life is their own affair. We respect people as people and are not in the least dependent on what they think about us.

TN: There is an episode in your book in which you describe the attitude of the black community towards gay men. In the post-apartheid South Africa where the right to sexual orientation is enshrined in the constitution, have you observed any significant changes in the attitude of black people to gays?

WC: African people are slow to respond to change. I think I should reword that statement. *MOST* people are slow to respond to change—black or white.

TN: Autobiography is a means of confession, of self-analysis, and of revealing your normally hidden or unknown self for public scrutiny. Do you think writing *Man of Two Worlds* has afforded you the opportunity to do this, that is, to make yourself known to the reading public?

WC: Not particularly. If the book is a help and encouragement to my people, then writing it was worthwhile.

References Cited

CIBANE, WILFRED. *Man of Two Worlds*. Cape Town: Kwela, 1998.

Further Reading

DAVIS, ROĆIO. "Dialogic Selves: Discursive Strategies in Transcultural Collaborative Autobiographies by Rity and Jackie Higgins and Mark and Gail Mathabane." *Biography* 28, 2 (Spring 2005): 276–295.

FILTER, H., comp. *Paulina Dlamini: Servant of Two Kings*. Pietermaritzburg: University of Natal Press, 1986.

LESTER, JAMES D. *Diverse Identities: Classic Multicultural Essays*. Lincolnwood, IL: NTC, 1996.

MCBRIDE, JAMES. *The Color of Water: A Black Man's Tribute to His White Mother*. New York: Riverhead Books, 1996.

February and April 2000

The Making of Katie Makanya

Margaret McCord interviewed by Thengani Ngwenya

MARGARET MCCORD WAS the daughter of the American missionary doctor James McCord, who founded the McCord Zulu hospital in Durban in 1909 (cf. James McCord 1946). Besides Katie Makanya's life story, McCord has written short stories and articles for women's magazines in the United States. In *The Calling of Katie Makanya* (1995), which is based on Katie's oral history recorded in 1954, McCord chronicles Makanya's life as Dr. McCord's first general assistant and one of the leading black feminist activists of her time. Notwithstanding her experiences as a member of the African Native Choir, which toured the United Kingdom from 1891–1893 (Erlmann 1999), and her relationship to her prominent sister, Charlotte Maxeke, founder of the Bantu Women's League, Katie led an unassuming life devoted to her local community. *The Calling of Katie Makanya* won the 1996 Alan Paton–Sunday Times Award, which is bestowed on publications that illuminate "truthfulness, especially those forms of it which are new, delicate, unfashionable, and fly in the face of power." While one commentator praises the book because it "gives voice" to Katie's "experiences as an African woman marginalised by racist settler society and subjugated in complex ways by the patriarchal attitudes of white and black men including the medical missionaries for whom she worked" (Mager 1996:300), others have problematized Margaret McCord's mediating interventions, especially the ways in which testimony and autobiographical anecdotes are turned into a text that "departs from the etiquette of biography in order to satisfy novelistic conventions" (Merrington 1995:156).

THENGANI NGWENYA: Perhaps the best way to begin this interview is to ask you to comment on the reception of *The Calling of Katie Makanya* when it was published four years ago.

MARGARET MCCORD: The reviews I've seen have been generally positive. So far the only negative review I've had was in *The London Economist*, and that was really negative. They reviewed it with that very long biography of a sharecropper up in the Transvaal. It was sort of an academic review. This reviewer gave a long review of Charles van Onselen's book, *The Seed Is Mine*, and commented on the importance of the book and then went on to point out that, by comparison, my book was rather lightweight. When I wrote this book I was thinking of the American public and I wanted to get the story out to the American public. So I wrote it for the general public; I didn't mean it to be an academic treatise. Anyway, the reviewer in *The London Economist* didn't actually say anything negative about it, but by comparing it to this very long, 700-page academic book, he implied that my book was rather lightweight. I haven't had any other negative reviews. In the States it has been reviewed in *The New York Times*, *The Washington Post*, and *The San Francisco Chronicle*. Those are the three major papers, and it has been reviewed in other papers too. The book was widely reviewed in the book sections of the Sunday newspapers here in the States, but I am not aware of its having been reviewed in magazines, though I was interviewed several times by various radio commentators in 1998. And I am still being asked to speak to book clubs here on the West Coast.

TN: What was the main rationale for writing the book?

MM: Katie wanted me to, and she wasn't somebody you said no to. I think that before her death, Katie's sister Charlotte had tried to write her autobiography, but it never got published. Also, Katie had seen the book that my father wrote called *My Patients Were Zulus*. This essentially is the story of how the medical work got started. It wasn't a story about his patients really, and Katie wanted the story of the patients told. As my father had died by then, she brought the book to me and said, "There are so many things he hasn't written about and now I want you to write my story and tell the things I remember." As I have already said, you couldn't say no to Katie.

TN: In your father's book I think there is only a paragraph or two on Katie; there isn't much said about her. Do you think this could have been another reason why she would want her own personal story told?

MM: I think so. Besides, there was always a certain amount of competition with Charlotte. At least that was my impression. She herself would never have admitted to that competition, and I doubt that she recognized it as such. She wanted her story told and rightly so. But I think there was more to it than simply a desire for her own story to be told. She was proud of the hospital but actually was more interested in people than in institutions and she wanted stories told about the patients.

TN: You referred to your projected readership as the American public; did you also have South African readers in mind when you wrote Katie's story?

MM: While I was writing the book, I had the American public in mind. Back in 1954 the popular view of South Africa and of the continent as a whole was still dominated by *Tarzan of the Apes* and Kipling's *The Jungle Books*. I wanted people here to appreciate the fact that barely seventy years after the first Europeans landed in Natal, there were Zulus (only a few to be sure) coming here and to England for a university education. I also wanted it published in South Africa first because it is a South African story. I got in touch with David Philip because my agent was not getting a very favorable response from publishers in the United States, who felt that the American public wasn't sufficiently interested in South Africa yet. So my agent was trying academic presses and sent it to the University of Indiana Press and their senior editor, who actually came from Natal, suggested that we send it to David Philip. So we sent the manuscript off to David Philip and got an immediate and positive answer back. After it was published over here and won the Alan Paton–Sunday Times Prize, John Wiley & Sons in New York decided to publish it in the United States.

TN: Could you briefly describe the research process that went into the writing of the book? For example, the people you interviewed, history books you read, etc.

MM: We were here in Durban in 1954, and I checked the facts and dates Katie spoke of as far as I could. I interviewed George Champion, Sibusisiwe Makanya, Bertha Mkhize, Mrs. Sililo—a long-time friend of Katie's with whom she had worked in the Bantu Women's Society. I also spoke to the nephew of Mr. Marwick and to a number of the American Board for Foreign Missions missionaries who had known Dr. Goodenough and Mr. Kilborn during Katie's stay in Johannesburg. And to tell the truth I found that in many instances Katie's memory was clearer than theirs. This was a subjective impression, of course, but I had to go with my instincts. However, there were certain things Katie told me in confidence, like the story of her falling in love in Kimberley; she called the man involved by the name his European employer used, but what she didn't mention was that he was a cousin of hers. She didn't want his real name given because she was afraid that his children or grandchildren would be upset at her comments about alcoholism in the family.

TN: So in the book Katie's cousin is Gershom?

MM: Yes. So there were certain details like that that I just simply omitted out of respect for Katie's own wishes. I have them in my notes at home. The other thing is that when we were over here in 1954, we were poor academics and we didn't have the money to buy tapes for my projects. I borrowed my husband's tapes, transcribed the interviews, erased them, and then used them over and over again. The paper I used for the interviews was very cheap and the ink has now faded and the paper is very fragile.

TN: In writing Katie's story what position did you adopt? Did you consciously adopt the role of a writer, researcher, or simply friend?

MM: Well, it's a little hard to explain. I suppose it would be correct to say as a family friend except that my relationship with Katie was much closer than that. It's not quite right to say that she was a surrogate mother, but she certainly played that role when my mother was out of town. When I was a little girl, if my mother was busy, my father would take me down to the dispensary and I would play with Katie's youngest son, John, at the dispensary, and she and my father sort of watched us from the window. My mother had very strong opinions about many things and one thing she did not approve of was having white women employ nannies for their children. She felt that children should be brought up by their mothers. Of course, what she didn't realize was that Katie was in a sense my nanny too, as I was put in her charge. Except that she was much more than a nanny. Looking back, it amuses me because my mother was a little smug about the fact that I didn't have a nanny. So, yes, I wrote the book as a family friend, but a very intimate family friend.

TN: Do you think Katie belonged to the educated black middle class of her time?

MM: Charlotte did, but Katie didn't because she had only completed Standard 6 because of her eyes. She had a tremendous respect for education. She had this one son [Livingstone] who was apparently very brilliant but who was also psychotic, and she had wanted very much for him to study medicine. From the time he started school and showed superior intelligence, she had saved every penny she could for him to go to America and stay with her brother John; of course, that didn't work out. I think the other children all belong to that middle class.

TN: How would you describe the impact of Christianity on Katie's moral and cultural outlook?

MM: Well to begin with, she was a very devout Christian and I think, rather fundamentalist in her beliefs. On the other hand, I think her father had not become a Christian until his marriage; he had grown up without any contact with Europeans. She was very fond of her father. So she and Charlotte as children had talked about going back and converting her father's people to Christianity. When she did go back and really got to know her grandfather, she loved him very much and also began to appreciate the ethical and moral character of her traditional group of relatives. So I think that although she never wavered in her own Christian beliefs and would never permit any criticism of her Christian faith, she understood those who had not been converted and seldom criticized them. There was an *inyanga* out at Adams—I don't know what his name was but he was quite famous in the area. Katie tried to reach him with the hope that he could help her psychotic son. She felt guilty about that. But when you're desperate, you try anything. Generally speaking, she was very much opposed to African medicine; she was very antagonistic towards *izinyanga* and *izangoma* (traditional healers and diviners).

TN: Would you know why she was turned away from the *inyanga*'s home? Do you think the *inyanga* knew that she was a Christian or that she worked for a white Christian doctor?

MM: I don't know and she didn't know either. She wondered about that. But you know there are many instances in life where things like that happen that you can't explain; who knows whether there is something about ESP—I don't know. He could have sent somebody out who actually realized that Livingstone was psychotic and didn't want anything to do with him.

TN: Writers of life stories, whether they are ethnographers or biographers, often have their own interpretive framework which they use to interpret and narrate their subject's oral narratives. How would you describe your own analytical framework in your narrative reconstruction of Katie's life?

MM: To some extent I think I used an analytical framework. Her whole relationship with Charlotte was pretty clear to me, I think clearer to me than it was to her. There was this competition from an early age, the fact that Charlotte had been to the Edwin School at Port Elizabeth and Katie had been to the same school and she could never compete with Charlotte intellectually and Charlotte was quite a dominant personality. I think she tended to overshadow Katie.

TN: Yes, Charlotte's achievements were nothing short of phenomenal.

MM: So this whole question of competition was something that to some extent I looked at from an analytical point of view, but Katie herself was not aware of it. She was not, but every now and then, she would make a comment, and you would realize that she was actually envious of her sister.

TN: In your view, did Katie's lifestyle and beliefs reflect the conflict between African traditionalism and European modernity?

MM: No, I was always impressed with the way Katie seemed to combine two very different points of view, but in her mind they were parallel in many ways . . . I try to bring that out with the story of her grandfather. I don't think that for Katie it was a conflict. She saw God as a personal influence, but in traditional religion he was more distant and one didn't have a direct relationship with him, you reached him through the ancestors, not directly. There wasn't really a conflict because they both [she and her grandfather] believed in one God.

TN: Would she openly approve of the role of the ancestors?

MM: No, I don't think she would; but she was lucky she had a personal relationship with God.

TN: Would you describe Katie as a feminist?

MM: I think in a very loose way I would say yes because nothing really deterred her from doing what she thought she should do. On the other hand, she was always very careful to follow certain conventional patterns, and she always managed to get Ndeya Makanya [her husband] to tell her what she wanted to do; she was very respectful of her husband. There were two things about writing the story that were problems for me: first of all, I have since learned that Ndeya was quite active politically, though I didn't know that at the time; Katie didn't talk too much about his political activities. On the other hand, my father and the missionaries who respected Katie very highly felt that Ndeya was a loser, that he wasn't worth much. I can understand that in one sense because Katie was so outstanding. Ndeya didn't have any money; Katie was the one who supported the family. From a European point of view, Ndeya wasn't worth very much, but I've since gleaned from some of my Zulu friends of the older generation that Ndeya was quite astute and active politically. So I think I would call Katie a feminist although she would not have called herself a feminist because she had to get her husband to tell her what to do. In a sense she manipulated him.

TN: How would you characterize her political awareness?

MM: She was very active in terms of protesting passes for women and she felt very strongly about all the time that she was in Natal. Yes, when it came to political issues that affected women she was aware of them. I think she followed John Dube's lead. Rather than being politically active herself, apart from issues regarding women, I think she tended to follow the example of John Dube, the first president of the African National Congress (ANC) who, like other early leaders of the ANC, was a very politically moderate person.

TN: Do you have any comments on your father's relationship with Katie?

MM: I wish I had brought the copy of the transcript to show you because Katie's feeling about her own work was that the major contribution she made to her community, to her people, was working for my father. She felt very much involved with his medical practice and the medical work, and it's true I don't think my father would have accomplished as much as he did without her support. I think my father was a little afraid of her.

TN: Really, why?

MM: Because she was a very dynamic person.

TN: She must have had a very strong personality.

MM: Oh, she did, there's no question about that, and of course she was an inspiration to Bertha Mkhize and Sibusisiwe Makanya. They may have disagreed, but in their hostel days, Katie influenced a great many of the young women of that time.

TN: To what extent is Katie Makanya the story of your family, the story about the writing of the life story, and your own personal story?

MM: To some extent I think Katie's story was entwined with my parents' story; they were different but there were common factors. My own relationship with Katie I think I've already covered.

TN: Would you like to comment on the authorial interventions in the narrative of Katie's life in which you, in your role as author, comment on the process of putting together Katie's story?

MM: That started because I knew from my experience in the United States that the American blacks would say, "A white woman wrote that story, it doesn't mean anything." I was not just any white woman growing up in Africa who felt she could "explain" the African problem, and I didn't want to write about the "African problem." So I tried first of all to get across the fact that Katie did indeed insist that I write the story, secondly, that my relationship with her was different from that of most young white women growing up in this country, and finally, by inserting my own recollections now and then, I hoped to keep in the reader's mind that this was a true story and not fiction.

References Cited

The Economist. April, 19, 1997: 6.

ERLMANN, VEIT. "'Spectatorial Lust': The African Choir in England, 1891–1893." In *Africans on Stage: Studies in Ethnological Show Business*, edited by Bernth Lindfors, pp. 107–134. Bloomington: Indiana University Press, 1999.

MAGER, ANNE. Review of *The Calling of Katie Makanya*. *South African Historical Journal* 34 (1996): 299–301.

MCCORD, JAMES. *My Patients Were Zulus*. New York: Reinhart and Co., 1946.

MCCORD, MARGARET. *The Calling of Katie Makanya*. Cape Town: David Philip, 1995.

MERRINGTON, PETER. Review of *The Calling of Katie Makanya*. *Kronos: Journal of Cape History* 22 (1995): 155–157.

The New York Times. April 6, 1997: 20.

The San Francisco Chronicle. Sun. April 20, 1997: n.p.

VAN ONSELEN, CHARLES. *The Seed Is Mine: The Life of Kas Maine, a South African Sharecropper.* New York: Hill and Wang, 1996.

The Washington Post. July 6, 1997: X8.

Further Reading

KOSSICK, SHIRLEY. "A Moving Act of Feminist Retrieval." Review of *The Calling of Katie Makanya. Mail and Guardian.* Oct. 6–12, 1995: 34.

MEYER, STEPHAN. "Collaborative Auto/biography: Notes on an Interview with Margaret McCord on *The Calling of Katie Makanya: A Memoir of South Africa.*" *Oral Tradition* 15, 2 (2000): 230–254.

NGWENYA, THENGANI H. Review of *The Calling of Katie Makanya. Southern African Review of Books* (Sept. & Oct. 1995): 39–40; (Nov. & Dec. 1995): 6–7.

———. "Ideology and Self-representation in *The Calling of Katie Makanya.*" *Alternation* 7, 1 (2000): 145–162.

———. "Ideology and Self-representation in Autobiography: The Case of Katie Makanya." In *Missions of Interdependence,* edited by Gerhard Stilz. Amsterdam: Rodopi, 2002.

SHEPHARD, BEN. *Kitty and the Prince.* Johannesburg: Jonathan Ball, 2003.

September 2002

V FACT OR FICTION

All Autobiography Is *Autre*-biography

J. M. Coetzee interviewed by David Attwell

J. M. COETZEE is the author of ten novels including *Waiting for the Barbarians* (1980), *Life and Times of Michael K* (1983), *Foe* (1987), and *Disgrace* (1999). He has written numerous critical essays, collected in *White Writing* (1988), *Doubling the Point* (1992), *Giving Offense* (1996), and *Stranger Shores* (2001). He has been honored with, among others, the Nobel Prize, and the Booker Prize (twice). Before his retirement from academic life Coetzee held professorships at the University of Cape Town and the University of Chicago. He lives in Australia.

Boyhood: Scenes from Provincial Life and *Youth* are the memoirs of his childhood in South Africa and his *émigré* years in metropolitan London, respectively. While the "relentless fixation on the humiliations and failures of life" places *Youth* in the confessional genre of Rousseau and St. Augustine (Jaidka 2002), Coetzee also uses these memoirs to reject the millennial compulsion to confess in its gaudy heroic mode. Both books employ the sparse prose used to evoke the anguish typical of Coetzee's fiction. Their harrowing self-portraiture, the linguistic craftsmanship, along with the technique of writing about himself in the third person, has led commentators to describe them as novels (Van Zyl 2002; de Kock 2002; and Cowley 2002). Besides "raising large questions about his relationship with himself," Deresiewicz (2002) concludes that Coetzee's use of the third person means that he "has turned his back on the entire autobiographical tradition, which has always grappled with the tension between the 'then' of event and the 'now' of recollection as a way of drawing out the complexity of individual experience over time." The interview was conducted in July–August 2002.

DAVID ATTWELL: When we last discussed this question in *Doubling the Point,* you spoke of the "massive autobiographical writing-enterprise that fills a life" and remarked that "all writing is autobiography." You also pointed out, however, that "all autobiography is storytelling." Between these elements—the life and the story—there is obviously a great deal of ground to be covered.

Theories of autobiography since the 1970s (since Paul de Man's "Autobiography as De-facement," for example) have done away with hard distinctions between autobiography and fiction: generally speaking, we have come to accept that despite autobiography's supposedly greater reliance on memory, all life writing invents its object, whether or not it declares its fictionality.

But let me pause there and pose this question in the light of authorial practice. Surely, at some level, any genre implies a certain narrative pact in which one works with readers' expectations. One may break the pact, of course, but in order to do so, not only must one know what one is doing, but one must also assume that the reader knows what one is doing.

J. M. COETZEE: If we accept, for the moment, that all writing is autobiography, then the statement that all writing is autobiography is itself autobiography, a moment in the autobiographical enterprise. Which is a roundabout way of saying that the remarks you refer to, published in *Doubling the Point,* do not exist outside of time and outside of my life story.

I would still say that all writing is autobiography; but whether, when I say so today I mean quite the same as what I meant when I said so ten or twelve years ago is a matter of memory, fallible and unverifiable memory. What I do know for a fact is that between then and now I have published two books, *Boyhood* and *Youth,* which are in some sense autobiographical. I have also, at the University of Chicago, run seminars on Wordsworth's *Prelude,* Roland Barthes' *Roland Barthes,* and other texts that lead one to think hard about what autobiography is. I cannot believe that my thinking about autobiography has not been deepened to an extent by these reading and writing experiences. So perhaps we should distinguish: I cannot *intend* quite the same as I originally intended, though the two statements, then and now, may *mean* the same.

You ask about genres and about the, to some extent, legitimate demand of readers that they be told what genre territory they are being asked to enter. But genre is not, to my mind, a refined concept. Genre definitions—at least those definitions employed by ordinary readers—are quite crude. What if the writer wants to trouble the boundaries of the genre? Does the autobiographical pact between writer and reader—the pact that says that, at the very least, the reader will be told no outright, deliberate lies—trump the disquiet one may feel about the quite crude definition of lying that many readers may hold? What if young William Wordsworth never *in fact* stole a boat and went rowing on Ullswater? There are two things to say in response to this question. One is that, barring the discovery of fresh historical evidence, we will never *know for a fact* whether Wordsworth actually stole the boat. The other is that, while it does not matter, with respect to our response to *The Prelude*, that we *know for a fact* whether he actually stole the boat, *knowing for a fact* that he did *not* steal the boat, and therefore facing the fact that a pact we assumed to be in operation has been violated, might very well alter that response.

These two observations stand somewhat athwart each other. They do not lead to any neat conclusion that I can see.

DA: In *Doubling the Point* you also argued that since being true to the facts entails a crude conception of truth, a more serious conception would accept the narrativity of autobiography but insist on certain kinds of rigor. In other words, even if the truth about the self or the past is never wholly available— contrary to the ways in which religious confession, and to some degree even psychoanalysis, are often conceived—certain ways of committing oneself to its pursuit have more integrity than others. Being open to the countervoices released by writing, for example, is one measure of that integrity.

You also argued that the will to truth can be obscure: it could come from a source outside the rational self, or at least from a source that contradicts one's self-interest. In retrospect, these meditations would have been part-preparation for your own, later work in autobiography. How do they strike you now, looking back over the last decade?

JMC: If I were to be presented with the opinions you quote, and were not told their source, and were asked what I thought of them, I would say, frankly, that they seem congenial, that I have no quarrel with them, that I could live with them.

You ask further how they strike me now, looking back, and here I must say that my gaze right now is not backward, or not only backward. Principally it is forward: after *Youth,* is there anything more that can be made with my life, or is that life for practical purposes now exhausted? Secondarily it is backward: what *has* my mature life, the life of my mature or more mature years, consisted in? Has the enterprise of autobiographical writing changed my life, if at all?

DA: Perhaps I could treat this as an invitation to ask the obvious questions. The first arises from *Youth*. It is partly (though also deeply) the story of a man treading water, being in a state of paralysis. To anyone who has read your early fiction, it begs the question, what precipitated the breaking of the impasse: presumably (though here I speculate), the somewhat unplanned return to South Africa (after a further period in the United States, not covered in the text)? This leads on to whether readers, like myself, who are eager to hear your version of the next phase of the story, can expect a third memoir?

The second question is, well, *has* the enterprise of autobiographical writing changed your life?

JMC: Not a man treading water but, precisely, a *youth* treading water. If his problem is how to launch himself into a stroke, who knows, maybe that will turn out to be the same as the problem of getting beyond youth.

How does one get beyond youth? If I could answer that question in a couple of quick sentences, the labors of autobiography would have no point. Has the enterprise of autobiographical writing changed my life? It has certainly changed the story of my life, or rather, since the story before I wrote these two books was rather inchoate and fragmentary, given it a shape it did not have before.

Will there be a third volume? My feeling at present is, no. Enough is enough.

DA: Your own autobiographical practice would seem to confirm an aspect of De Man's argument, in which he points out that when one tries to put the historical self into writing, what emerges, inevitably, is a substitute for that self. Would you agree that at a basic representational level, all autobiography is, in fact, *autre*-biography? If so, is your decision to write autobiography in the third person a case of making this process explicit?

JMC: Yes, all autobiography is *autre*-biography, but what is more important is where one goes from there. With regard to my own practice, I can only say that to rewrite *Boyhood* or *Youth* with *I* substituted for *he* throughout would leave you with two books only remotely related to their originals. This is an astonishing fact, yet any reader can confirm it within a few pages.

DA: What is the relationship between autobiography and confession? Presumably, in autobiography as *autre*-biography, the third-person mode of address enables one to achieve greater leverage, possibly extending to the writing subject diagnosing the written subject or protagonist as belonging to a certain historical condition. If I may say so, in *Boyhood* and *Youth*, this kind of self-detachment is very much in evidence, for example, in the irony directed at the protagonist's provincialism. Autobiography that is closer to confession, on the other hand, would have the potential, at least, to be more anguished. One thinks, for example, of Derrida and Barthes writing about their departed mothers (and in doing so, incidentally, following in the tracks of Augustine).

JMC: I think your observations are, in that curious English colloquialism, or perhaps it is only South African, dead on target.

DA: If I could end with a question about autobiographical writing and cultural politics. One finds mixed agendas in the uses made of autobiography—for example, certain readings of Rousseau treat him as engaging in an elaborate self-deception. But it doesn't take much imagination to read his opening gambit—"I have entered on a performance which is without example, whose accomplishment will have no imitator"—as suggesting exactly the kind of creative self-invention that contemporary identity politics might admire. In postcolonial or feminist autobiography, how does one acknowledge the process of self-invention, the inescapable fictionalizing of the self, without undermining the historical sensitivities that insist on using the genre as a form of historical self-reclamation?

JMC: On the subject of Rousseau, let me merely say that I have not got to the bottom of Jean-Jacques yet, and, given the lack of nuance in my knowledge of French, probably never will. As for postcolonial or feminist autobiography, as long the agenda that drives it remains political, I don't see it being allowed to venture far into the realms of invention. I look forward to being proved wrong.

References Cited

BARTHES, ROLAND. *Roland Barthes by Roland Barthes.* Trans. Richard Howard. London: Macmillan, 1977.

COETZEE, J. M. *Doubling the Point: Essays and Interviews.* Ed. David Attwell. Cambridge, MA: Harvard University Press, 1992.

———. *Boyhood: Scenes from Provincial Life.* London: Secker & Warburg, 1997.

———. *Youth.* London: Secker & Warburg, 2002.

COWLEY, JASON. "Asking for Trouble. *The Observer.* Sunday, Apr. 21, 2002. http://www.observer.co.uk/review/story/0,6903,687695,00.html

DE KOCK, LEON. "A Painful Youth." *Sunday Times* [Johannesburg]. July 21, 2002. http://www.suntimes.co.za/2002/07/21/lifestyle/life04.asp

DE MAN, PAUL. "Autobiography as De-facement." In *The Rhetoric of Romanticism,* pp. 67–81. New York: Columbia University Press, 1984.

DERESIEWICZ, WILLIAM. "Third-person Singular." *The New York Times.* July 7, 2002. http://www.nytimes.com/2002/07/07/books/review/07DERESIT .html?ex=104943200&en=f0191 efc411176e6&ei=5070

JAIDKA, MANJU. "An Unflinching Look at the Man behind the Author." *The Sunday Tribune* [India]. Oct. 6, 2002. http://www.tribuneindia.com/2002/ 20021006/spectrum/book7.html

ROUSSEAU, JEAN-JACQUES. *The Confessions*. London: Penguin, 1953.
VAN ZYL, JOHAN. "Ons het hom lief." *Insig* July 2002. http://www.boekwurm.co.za/blad_boeke_abcd/coetzee_j_m_3.html
WORDSWORTH, WILLIAM. *The Prelude*. Books I and II. Ed. Helen Wheeler. Basingstoke: Macmillan, 1988.

Further Reading

COETZEE, J. M. "Truth in Autobiography." Inaugural lecture. University of Cape Town. 1985.
———. "He and His Man." Nobel Lecture at the Swedish Academy, Dec. 7, 2003. http://www.nobel.se/literature/laureates/2003/coetzee-lecture-e.html
COLLINGWOOD-WHITTICK, SHEILA. "Autobiography as *Autre*biography: The Fictionalisation of the Self in J. M. Coetzee's *Boyhood: Scenes from Provincial Life*." *Commonwealth: Biography, Autobiography and Fiction* 24, 1 (Autumn 2001): 13–24.
HEYNS, MICHIEL. "The Whole Country's Truth: Confession and Narrative in Recent White South African Writing." *Modern Fiction Studies* 46, 1 (2000): 42–66.
LENTA, MARGARET. "*Autre*biography: J. M. Coetzee's *Boyhood* and *Youth*." *English in Africa* 30, 1 (May 2003): 157–169.
LEJEUNE, PHILIPPE. "Autobiography in the Third Person." *New Literary History* 9, 1 (1977): 27–50.
———. *On Autobiography*. Ed. John Paul Eakin. Minneapolis: University of Minnesota Press, 1989.
MARAIS, MICHAEL. "J. M. Coetzee and the Protocols of Writing the Self." *English Academy Review* 14 (1997): 223–225.
PHILLIPS, CARYL. "*Boyhood: Scenes from Provincial Life* by J. M. Coetzee." *English in Africa* 25, 1 (May 1998): 61–70.
SÉVRY, JEAN. "Coetzee the Writer and the Writer of an Autobiography." *Commonwealth: Crossing Borders* 22, 2 (Spring 2000): 13–24.
VIOLA, ANDRÉ. "Two Mothers and No Father: J. M. Coetzee's *Boyhood*." *Commonwealth* 20, 1 (1997): 96–99.

July–August 2002

We Would Write Very Dull Books If We Just Wrote about Ourselves

Sindiwe Magona interviewed by Stephan Meyer

HER AUTOBIOGRAPHY, *To My Children's Children* (1990), immediately put Sindiwe Magona on South Africa's literary map. It was soon followed by a collection of short stories, *Living, Loving, and Lying Awake at Night* (1991), the second volume of her autobiography, *Forced to Grow* (1992), a second collection of short stories, *Push-push* (1996), and a biographical novel, *Mother to Mother* (1998), which was nominated for the M-Net Prize and is now being turned into a film. The isiXhosa version of the first volume of her autobiography, titled *Kubantwana babantwana bam*, appeared in 1995. She has completed a manuscript of essays, "Imida," in Xhosa, and her play *Vukani!* (Wake up!) was performed on World AIDS Day in New York in 2003. *Anatomy of Infidelity*, a forthcoming book, is her first publication set mostly outside South Africa. Among other things, she has been employed as a teacher and domestic. Shortly after receiving an MA in social work from Columbia, she started working at the United Nations in New York, where she remained until her retirement and return to South Africa in 2003. Magona has been awarded an honorary doctorate in Humane Letters from Hartwick College, New York, and appears regularly at literary events such as the Time of the Writer festival in South Africa and abroad. In her autobiographies Sindiwe Magona relates her childhood life in the Transkei and her struggle as a single mother raising three children in Guguletu while at the same time pursuing her studies. Her short stories, for example, the cycle "Women at Work," tap into her personal experience. She also draws on her personal knowledge of the circumstances and the people when she reconstructs, from the perspective of the mother of one of the young men involved, the events leading to the killing in Guguletu of the American

Fulbright student Amy Biehl. The interview was conducted orally in Switzerland, when Sindiwe Magona gave lectures at the Universities of Zurich and Basel.

STEPHAN MEYER (STME): Your first two volumes of autobiography, *To My Children's Children* and *Forced to Grow*, are fairly linear narratives. This contrasts with your short stories "Two Little Girls and a City," where you use montage, and "Now that the Pass is Gone," where you use the flashback, and your biographical novel *Mother to Mother* which combines these two techniques, so that (quoting from *Mother to Mother*), "slowly, haltingly, out came the story." How do you see this double complication, montage and flashback, in the development of your view of the writing of lives?

SINDIWE MAGONA (SIMA): I think the double complication comes out of the complication I find myself in when I am structuring a work such as *Mother to Mother*. At one and the same time I am in the present as the storyteller and the character that comes out of me and becomes part of me. I am here with full awareness of where I have come from. So sometimes that place from whence I have come illumines what is happening today, and the other way round. Sometimes I am back at that place in the past, and I have fears or am completely blind as to where it is leading me to. And then as I go on, I find, "Voilà, here I am!" It is like when you cross a street; you do a simple thing of trying to stay alive. In that moment of crossing the street, all the fear of death is in you, all the stories you have heard or witnessed of car accidents and suicides. There is the hope of your surviving this moment of extreme danger intact so that you may have a tomorrow. You are an embodiment of your past and your future at this present moment. In life there is this now, and in this now, there is yesterday and there is tomorrow. So sometimes it is very hard to just stick to now, without remembering tomorrow and yesterday.

Sometimes I feel it is awkward, but I have not learnt how to extricate myself so that I can stay linear. But even with the novel I have just finished, *Anatomy of Infidelity*, I can see the same kind of complications you are talking about. I know I can no longer hide behind labeling myself as a new writer, but relatively speaking, I am a new writer—I have only been writing for one decade. I set out to tell a single story, but in the telling I find myself with the complication that I know the things I want to say, but not when and where. It is in solving these problems that I end up with these structures. I do not cleverly say, "Oh I am going to use montage or flashback."

STME: Looking for an explanation for this shift, would you thus say that it is the craft of a no-longer-new-writer that developed out of finding your feet with these techniques in short stories, or is it because *Mother to Mother,* for example, is more imagined biography rather than autobiography?

SIMA: It is both. When I started writing I never thought that I would write short stories. It is a surprising shock to me. I think that in a way I am more comfortable writing short stories. And yet I had a fear of writing short stories when Marie Philip [the partner and wife of the publisher David Philip] first suggested that. I wrote what has since become two volumes of autobiography as one. It was divided into two parts by the publisher. *To My Children's Children* came out in 1990. I thought *Forced to Grow* would come out the next year. But Marie said, "No, I want *To My Children's Children* to have a full life." I wanted a book out the next year, so she said, "Write short stories, and I'll tell you if I like it." That is how I got to write the short stories in *Living, Loving, and Lying Awake at Night.*

In writing *Mother to Mother* I needed to explain the problems that confronted this boy and our history as a people. It is not just the boy, it is the society. It goes much further back; it is the stories with which we grow up. It is the hatred that we are taught when we are children. It is the suspicion with which we regarded white people. It is all these things and the irresponsibility of learned grown people who teach children slogans like "One settler, one bullet!" that they themselves know they will never translate to reality—but the children, being children, perhaps do. Some psychologists believe that when someone cracks in a family, the schism is not necessarily the problem. This is the manifestation of what is not right in the family, and the child who has a breakdown may just happen to be the more sensitive, not necessarily the most troubled. People like these four boys who killed Amy Biehl may have been the most sensitive and susceptible among us, not necessarily the most cruel or the most evil.

STME: Not the faultline but the alarm.

SIMA: Yes. And that was what I was trying to say. In the new novel *Anatomy of Infidelity,* the question is how grown people forget the pain that they have gone through that makes them think they can go through this thing called marriage again. When the flaws begin, they are reminded of what happened before. And the question arises, how do they then negotiate the present in view of that past?

STME: How would you interpret the claim that all writing is autobiographical, also in the light of your latest book?

SIMA: I would take a middle-of-the-line view. Coetzee says that all writing is autobiographical, and he is right. But Doris Lessing once said, "Every time I hear that question posed to a writer, I could weep." Writers write because they have imagination! For me it is a fusion of the two. If I were not who I am, if I had not lived through the experiences I have lived through, I do not think I would write. So yes, he is right, all writing is autobiographical. But if I were only to write autobiography, I think I would have stopped at those two autobiographies. There is imagination too. With "Two Little Girls and a City," I was touched by what I had read in the newspaper. It did not happen to me. I was sorry for the white family in Sea Point who lost their child. But I was also sorry for the black family who I never got to know. And that incensed me, that something was so near me. So that is the autobiography, how I *felt* about it. All writing is autobiographical because it comes out of the self. It comes out of one's experiences and one's orientation. If I did not feel like that about the discrepancy in the way that Cape Town responded to these two tragedies, I would not have written it. But I had to use my imagination to dig out these stories, especially the black one. So it is really a fusion of the two.

With the novel *Anatomy of Infidelity*, too. I married the second time as an older woman. I married someone who was also coming into a second marriage. Some of the experiences I depict in the novel of course are my experiences—*some*. But some are experiences of other people that I have heard about or read about or imagine purely. The way things happen in the book is an interesting interplay between autobiography and imagination. That is why I do not call it a memoir. It is a novel. But I would be lying if I said there was not anything of me in there. The feelings, for example. So when you imagine how another woman will feel if this happened, you come back and draw on your own feelings in similar situations or your imaginings of those situations. So it is a delicate balance; I think writers are acrobats. We would write very dull books if we just wrote about ourselves.

Also "Lillian and Penrose," the biography of my parents which I am working on at the moment, is not a strict biography. It really depicts major themes in their lives. I just was not there with some of the things. I may know the facts, but then to flesh them out I have to use my imagination. For instance, I know their marriage was an arranged marriage. I know, for example, how my father tricked my mother into eating fish when she first came to Cape Town and she would not touch fish. And I weave this story into how they fell in love three children later. Because my mother never comes up with an answer if I ask, "Did you ever fall in love and when did you fall in love?" This is a question to my mother that is stupid. She respected my father and I am sure she loves my father, but when exactly they fell in love I have not been able to figure out. So the fish-*frikkadel* story becomes their falling in love.

STME: In any of your autobiographical writing and your biographical writing about your parents as well as your novelized biography of Mxolisi, Mandisa, and Amy Biehl, did you do any research, for example, oral research, print (like newspapers), or did you dig up your own letters or photographs?

SIMA: The reason I do not write nonfiction is that I have a handicap as far as research is concerned. I try to shy away from it. But in works such as *Mother to Mother* obviously one had access to the newspapers and TV. I relied very much on these to depict the reality around the story, like the day it happened, where it happened, how it happened. I collected that material. With the book on my parents I do some oral research too; I talk a lot to my mother, I write to her, send tapes to her. I have encouraged one of my nieces to sit down with the questions I send and tape the responses because I want the authenticity. I want the feelings. When I write something, even if it is not factual, even if I change places and names, as in *Anatomy of Infidelity*, I want some of the things to be really true. I had to go to Oxford because that is where this husband is when they meet. She is in London promoting a new book, he is a student at Oxford. I had to go there because I did not know Oxford. I had to see things and take pictures so that I can have them stand there and look at the river gliding by, so that there can be some degree of authenticity around the imagined work. In my own autobiography I did very little research for that because it was all things that were in my head for as long as I remember. But once I wrote them down, some of those things left me. I am happy that some of the hurts were reduced to things that are laughable now. I hope I can say the same about some of the hurt I feel around my parents and their lives. For me, writing about myself was a healing experience.

STME: Could you tell me more about your interviews with your mother?

SIMA: They are a type of letter writing, in which I ask, "How are you? Are you taking your tablets?" and then I would ask, for example, about her wedding day. That is how I got to know that she went to her wedding on horseback. Sometimes I would have to go back and she will just give me an overall thing, and I would say, "Who was with you? Who were your bridesmaids? Are they still alive? Do you know where they are?"

STME: And is this all done in isiXhosa?

SIMA: Yes.

STME: And then you translate?

SIMA: It would be an easy book to write in Xhosa, wouldn't it? But then who is going to publish it?

STME: What problems do you see in making a biography out of interviews?

SIMA: Well, the first thing that I have to do is to make the knowledge mine. I grew up with some of the stories and have always known them. For example,

I knew my father had grown up without a father, and he was very intense about being a father because he had grown up without a father. I knew those feelings from way back. When I come to the stories of my mother, there are things I knew, but there were things that I didn't know, and she still being alive, I can ask her. But first I listen to the interviews. I do not write them down, I just listen.

STME: So they are never transcribed?

SIMA: No. I just listen, and then I just know it. It becomes something I know. Another color to this painting that is my mother that I know. And when I come to write about that part I will weave it in. Out of a whole tape I might just get one morsel that I am going to use because I am not writing a novel. I want to show that in our traditional ways there was a lot of wisdom. I am not doing it to make my parents grand people. It is because in the traditional, non-school way of being, there was a lot that we should have and that we might still keep preserved. We were very wise in our natural state.

STME: Can you compare the writing of autobiography and biography? In your autobiography you said you had it all in your head and that you relied on your memory. How is it different with your parents' biography and with *Mother to Mother*?

SIMA: With my parents' biography it is very different. First of all, it is coming out in poetry form. So because it is coming out in that form, I suspect that it is very sparse. It is not as detailed as a prose biography because poetry does not allow for that. Rather than a detailed story, it is episodic. But I still put in my feelings about it. So it is biography in that it depicts their lives. But it is also *my* autobiography; I do not altogether escape my feelings about it. I think one can detect when I am happy and when I am sad because the choice of words will tell you. Also when it is autobiography it is things I have really known intimately. With the biography it is mostly secondhand. It is things that I heard when I was growing up, and things I am digging up from my mother, and things I imagine. If I take the scene, for instance, where my father is being stripped naked with a group of other men—I was never there. And I never talked to him about it. In fact, I did not imagine that he was there until recently when I had him working in the mines and it came to the induction ceremony. And I realized from the Peter Magubane pictures what it must have been like for him. So there are a lot of things that I have to synthesize. Whereas, writing about myself it was really just telling of something that I always knew; sometimes having to remind myself of things I have forgotten because the more you tell of your own story the more you remember. There were things that I have slightly forgotten that, as I was telling the story, came up again.

STME: You have mentioned that writing these things down allowed you to deal with the pain and forgetting some of the pain. Can you remember which things you were able to forget?

SIMA: A lot, both happy and sad. Sometimes I realize that having written about something it has stopped being a burning issue. For example, at school the girls used to call me ugly and spelled it backwards thinking I did not know. The way I look has been a source of endless pain and embarrassment to me for the longest while. It is only recently that I suddenly realized it no longer matters to me. It has stopped being a way of how I define myself. There was a time for more than a decade that I would never leave the house without endless layers of paint on my face. Because I had terrible blotches, I would use concealers. It was just terrible.

And the story of the informer is a story I have not forgotten, but it does not hurt me as much. I dare say this is something I still have to deal with in my writing to completely rid myself of. As with the stories of the man in my life. That is no longer important; it really is not. In a way writing really helped me deal better with the disintegration of my second marriage. I am not saying it did not hurt, but the hurt was just so swiftly gone. In fact, my husband even said before we married that the writing matters more to me than he did, and I said, "You can walk away, but the writing will not walk away. This is the one thing I can be sure of." In writing about the scars of love and life, I have come to a situation in which, in my own life, I clearly have not come out as warped as I might have been. I am not bitter or even angry at anyone. This is such a relief, that I carry no anger against the men who have wronged me (and I dare say they might feel that I have wronged them). So there are things that no longer bother me and there are things that I just no longer remember. Take poverty—I am not saying I needed it to grow as a human being . . . I am just grateful it came when it did and not later in my life when it might have been more difficult to deal with it or to overcome it.

STME: I would like to pursue that last remark. How does writing affect your memory of your own life?

SIMA: It somehow relieves me of the burden of carrying all those things. Some things were apparently not important enough for me to carry to my grave. Those things have gone, and I am not sorry. Other things, for whatever reason, are still with me. I just feel it is a natural selection: the things that remain must be important. The things that have gone are not that important.

STME: So you do not see writing autobiography as something that eats up your memory?

SIMA: It does. But I do not begrudge it because I derive so much joy from writing. If *this is* the price, then this is the price I am quite happy to pay. It might even be physiological for all we know. But certainly emotionally and spiritually some memories can be burdensome. And if I am relieved of this, I really am happy.

STME: That is the effect of the writing on *you*. But what happens to a life when it comes under the public eye, when the story is out there?

SIMA: Well, you know when the story is out there, there can no longer be any secrets. Writing about it sheds light on a life. Also it empowers both the writer and the reader about the fact that the truth cannot hurt you. When I wrote my autobiographies, I was naïve. I really wanted to write plays. But each time I wanted to write, I would see my life before me. And I thought, "When you write, you are not supposed to write about yourself unless you are writing autobiography." So I thought, "Let me write this and get this stupid thing out of the way." But then I had the problem of who will read me? Who wants to read about a common life like mine? Then I thought, in 200 or 300 years to come, things will have so changed in South Africa, people will want to know what an ordinary life was like. That is how I started writing. Once I overcame the handicap of an uninteresting life, I realized in 200 years it will be an interesting life to someone who, in the manner of the archaeologist, will be digging facts up about the past. I wrote it with a lot of detail, with no sense of embarrassment, because stupidly I did not really believe anybody would read this today. I was writing for the future. Now I do not trust myself to be quite as explicit. If I wrote the third part of my autobiography, it would demand courage. I no longer have the innocence and straightforwardness with which I came to the first two books.

STME: What do you mean when you say the truth does not hurt? Has no one ever come to you and said, "What you said about us hurts?"

SIMA: Only my children. They were very happy at first, but now as they grow older they feel they would like to change their birth dates, especially the girls. So when I write now, I have to realize that I have decided to go public with my life, but nobody else has agreed to this. When I write my memoirs I definitely will not write about other people unless it is something favorable. And if it is not favorable, but it is important to my story, I will change their names. But if it is not important, then I will abbreviate. Like when talking about my second marriage. I would not want to embarrass my second husband by writing about him. I could write about the good times. I want to be circumspect in that I do not want to embarrass anybody. If you want to be spiteful, write a novel, and then dare anybody to claim, "That is my life."

STME: To what extent do you see it as your task as a writer to use language to show how language is abused to cover up injustice?

SIMA: Part of why I write is to share with people what I have seen, what I feel, what I have gone through or have heard from others. Some of the stories I want to tell go back to my parents' childhood. The beauty of South Africa will be in the quilt of all those stories and colors. The more stories that are told the better because more perspectives will come out that way. And part of my writing is really that this is our story, this is who we are, this is what we have done, this is where we have failed, and this is where we have been perhaps singularly triumphant. But I have no intention of writing for convenience or courting popularity. That is not the point of writing.

The point of writing is reminding me perhaps of who I am, and in that revelation perhaps others may see themselves too: what has made me feel ashamed of the people of who I am a part, I cannot divorce myself. I am South African, I am African, I'm all those people—white, colored, Indian—because we all live in the same geographical confine. We share experiences. It does not matter who killed who. It does not matter who is raping who. That is part of *my* pain and part of my shame. Because somewhere, if there is a flaw in that design I am part of that flaw, as much as I am part of any triumph. So when there is disgrace in my country, I feel ashamed. You cannot select how you can be a South African. You are a South African in the totality of that experience.

So sometimes we have to dig to reveal the layers that we would not like to remember. Because it is in that remembering that perhaps we will be forewarned; in that reminding of ourselves of who we are that we might be more careful next time. If black people can see themselves as no less, but also no more than white people, they might be more careful and remember that they can make the same mistakes when they are in power that the white people made. They are not saints. We are not saints. It is not as if we were created black or white so that one can be more cruel than the other. And because we have suffered under oppression, I do not believe that necessarily makes us stronger in the sense that we will never oppress. I am not convinced that just because I am oppressed, this makes me a candidate for sainthood.

STME: How do you see the influence and the role of the addressee in autobiography? For example in *Mother to Mother* Mandisa addresses the other mother, God, and her community.

SIMA: In *Mother to Mother* I became Nontuthuzelo, the real life mother on whose experience the life of the narrator of *Mother to Mother* is based. Magona had known her personally in Cape Town. Those two years I had heard that she was implicated, I thought, "How is this poor woman dealing with this?" I was pregnant with what was to become this book, I carried her pain. You have no idea what happened after I wrote that first chapter; I felt so much lighter after that. For two years I felt her anguish and her agony; her need to rid herself of this pain by talking to the other mother. But in that sense of bewilderment, God is also present as she addresses him, "Why has this happened? Why *my* child?" The community is present because you feel, I felt, that people were not sympathetic, people were laughing at me, people were laughing at her. Sometimes when you begin to empathize with someone very strongly—as I did with Nontuthuzelo—you invite those emotions into your body physically. And that is what happened to me without me knowing. I became possessed of the pain she was in because I refused to do what I was being asked to do, which was to sit down with Mrs. Biehl and talk to her. And the only way I freed myself from that pain was writing that book.

And the confusion that Mandisa/Nontuthuzelo was in, the sense of bewilderment, that is all that that book is. So when you are in that place of exceeding pain in one and the same moment you talk to this woman, you are also angry at the community, angry at the dead girl, angry at God. It is all one emotion. That is what bewilderment is. Mandisa wants to say to Amy Biehl's mother, in humbleness, and if she will allow it, "I am sorry that you are suffering." But she also wants to say, "I am suffering too. My suffering does not belittle your suffering. It is part of your suffering. I am suffering because you are suffering. I want to say, 'I feel your pain because you have lost a child.' But do you know, I too have lost a child, because I will never look at this child again and not see your dead child, and not wonder, where did I fail?" I am also angry at the community who are blaming me now. What did we think we were doing when we said, "One settler, one bullet?" *Mother to Mother* is a peculiar book in that really the addressee was Mrs. Biehl and then by extension all of us, all the mothers and the fathers in the South African community saying, "Let's be a little more mindful of how we raise the next generation." The collectivity of the responsibility of raising the next generation is ours together.

And in writing about my own life it was really a way of affirming my life as having meaning. For a long time I really didn't believe I was important. I didn't believe my life had any meaning. Also at one and the same time I thought it was such a plain life that everybody had a perfect understanding of what that life was about. It's only once I got out of the ghetto of the township, when I was teaching at Herschel High School (1977–1981) and met other people, that it dawned on me with a sense of shock—and really I am not apologizing for white South Africans—and that I began to understand and see and gradually began to accept that a lot of white people really didn't know what the life of black people in South Africa was like. They didn't know that we in Guguletu didn't have electricity in the houses, or hot water. Experiences such as those began to say to me, if South Africans who are alive today don't know how we live, how can I hope that my story will be understood after apartheid is gone? If I had not worked at Herschel, if I had not been in the Women's Peace Movement, if I had not been in Churchwomen Concerned, I doubt I would have written that autobiography. But the more I went around talking in South Africa, the more I realized that really South African whites did not understand. We were so successfully divided in South Africa that it became apparent that we owe it to ourselves and to the people who will people that country long after we had gone to paint a picture of our reality.

But more and more now, I write for myself. I write to remind myself of what my life has been like and hopefully I learn something from that life. With *Anatomy of Infidelity* I am examining second marriages and disappointments for me as a woman, and the way you seldom escape contributing to your own abuse. Since I have examined it, it is clear to me now that I will never again be part of my oppression by a man.

STME: So it is not only the experience itself, but the reflection through the writing about it that forms your views.

SIMA: Yes, it's within the writing that you are forced to unlock doors you have closed, to unveil yourself to yourself, to examine things you skim through and gloss over because, as you put them down, they ring a false note. You suddenly know you can't have done such a stupid thing because of what you say you did it for. Therefore you have to be more truthful to yourself and say, "What exactly was I doing here?" Which, on a daily basis, you don't ask yourself. The emotion of the moment carries you and then you don't go back and examine. But when you're writing, you have the scope and the time and the obligation to go back and look and say, "Okay, when I was saying this, what exactly was I saying?" That's your next line: I said *this*, but of course, what I meant was *that*, which you didn't examine at the moment and as it popped up, you squashed it and never went back. Knowing what I know about who I am now, I can never again lie to myself the way I did, because I know I am lying.

STME: So if you hadn't been a writer, you would not have been as consciously aware of the ways in which you deceive yourself?

SIMA: I might have been lucky enough that I might have talked it through with someone, which is another form of therapy. But sometimes when we talk to friends, we still hide. In writing I find I can be more foolish in this regard because you fictionalize something and you can afford to reveal yourself in your stupidity, because it is not really you, but you know it's you. The writing does not help me to be wiser, but it helps me definitely to see myself clearer, and perhaps that's another way of wisdom.

References Cited

MAGONA, SINDIWE. *To My Children's Children*. Cape Town: David Philip, 1990.

———. *Living, Loving, and Lying Awake at Night*. Cape Town: David Philip, 1991.

———. *Forced to Grow*. Cape Town: David Philip, 1992.

———. *Kubantwana babantwana bam*. Cape Town: David Philip, 1995.

———. *Push-push*. Cape Town: David Philip, 1996.

———. *Mother to Mother*. Cape Town: David Philip, 1998.

———. *Vukani!* Unpublished, 2002.

Further reading

DAYMOND, M. J. "Class in the Discourses of Sindiwe Magona's Autobiography and Fiction." *Journal of Southern African Studies* 21, 4 (1995): 561–572.

———. "Complementary Oral and Written Narrative Conventions: Sindiwe Magona's Autobiography and Short Story Sequence, 'Women at Work'" *Journal of Southern African Studies* 28, 2 (June 2002): 331–346.

JACOBS, J. U. "Cross-cultural Translation in South African Autobiographical Writing: The Case of Sindiwe Magona." *Alternation* 7, 1 (2000): 41–61.

KOYANA, SIPHOKAZI (Ed.) *Sindiwe Magona: The First Decade*. Pietermaritzburg: University of Kwazulu-Natal Press. 2004.

MAGONA, SINDIWE. "South Africa's Curse." *The New York Times*. Aug. 4, 998: A13.

———. *Life Is a Hard but Beautiful Thing!* Cape Town: Juta, 2005.

———. *Bunzima nje buhle ubomi!* Cape Town: Juta, 2005.

———. *The Best Meal Ever*. Cape Town: Tafelberg, 2005.

———. *16 Children's Stories: In isiXhosa*. Cape Town: Oxford University Press, 2005.

ROYEPPEN, LORELLE. "*Mother to Mother*'s Moral Ambivalence." *Alternation* 7, 1 (2000): 233–235.

June 2002

Writing Autobiography and Writing Fiction

Doris Lessing interviewed by M. J. Daymond

AFTER RESISTING PRESSURE to write an autobiography and dismissing autobiographical interpretations of her novels for many years, Doris Lessing "invaded her own privacy" (Gottlieb 1994) and published two volumes of autobiography in what can be described as a "pre-emptive strike against the various biographers . . . working on her" (Bridgman 2000). Volume I, *Under My Skin* (1994a), which recounts her sensuous memories of a childhood in Persia (now Iran) and Southern Rhodesia (now Zimbabwe), her youth and her maturing as a writer first on the fringes of Empire and then in London, won the James Tait Black Prize for autobiography and a Los Angeles Times Book Prize. Volume II, *Walking in the Shade* (1997), has been described by one reviewer as a book of "statesmanlike [!] length" that is "justified by the extraordinary variety of her achievements, her exceptional memory and her facility as a writer" (Kermode 1997). According to Lessing herself, writing her autobiography has changed her view of the genre. She no longer sees autobiographies as "something fixed" but as "interim reports." Paradoxically, after having written two volumes of autobiography herself, she questions the necessity of memory to identity and personal well-being and challenges the view contained in the assertion that "I am my memory, my identity is my memory" (1994b).

The interview was conducted for this collection. It has also been published in *Current Writing* 13, 1 (April 2001): 7–21. We thank the editors of *Current Writing* for permission to reprint.

M. J. DAYMOND: You have recently published two volumes of autobiography, *Under My Skin: Volume I of My Autobiography, to 1949* and *Walking in the Shade: Volume II of My Autobiography, 1949–1962*. What are the processes of writing autobiography? For example, you have said that writing fiction involves what you call a wool-gathering process in which things have to settle gradually. Did the autobiography involve the same kind of process?

DORIS LESSING: No, that was different because I started up with trying to remember. And I was amazed at the big gaps in my memory. I did have a good memory for short, intense periods, but I hadn't realized that you make a kind of picture of the past, like scenes of emotions and what you've seen, but in between there are long dark spaces. I hadn't realized that when I first started thinking about it. And then the question arises, why do you remember one weekend of total unimportance and a great deal else, when you've forgotten very important events that you know happened. In fact I spent a lot of time thinking about all this, which caused me to . . . instead of just sitting down and starting off, I spent literally weeks and perhaps months thinking. It's very different from writing a novel where you sort of let things float around and coalesce. So there's the whole business of memory. I started thinking about it because the question is what of what you remember is true because you know a lot of it could only have come from your parents. They say, "Do you remember darling how you used to . . . ," and then you dutifully remember. So I came to the conclusion that there were only two kinds of memory you could rely on. One was when you were so small, you know, the door handle is up there by your head and the cat is vast and the dog is like a cow. All of these, when you're very small, can be relied on. And then the ones that happen again and again—let's say every Friday you did something. Those I think you can more or less rely on. What you can't rely on is the family history because a family makes its own history and, you see, it's *your* memories you want, and they are not your memories. There is an example in Volume I where I described a journey across Russia from Teheran to the Caspian and the family had a memory of that journey. It was a vivid chronicle of that journey, but when I actually sat down to compare what they said happened—I'm not saying it didn't happen—with what I remember, it was two completely different things. So I made a great point of that in the book.

MJD: You have also said that from quite an early age you practiced holding certain things in your memory as you wanted to remember them, to protect them, I imagine, against anyone else's account of that event.

DL: Yes, I did. And probably, I should imagine almost from my earliest memories. That is, I obviously had very great pressure on me to concur with other people's version of events. And I remember saying, "Now remember this, remember it, this is what happened, not that." And I kept it. And I used to work on these memories as a child to see if they were still there. And I did that for years. So these little scenes are very bright.

MJD: Was it any particular kind of event for which you did that?

DL: Not necessarily. I had a very forceful mother who really wanted us to see the world as she saw it, and I can only deduce that it was a defense against her. But I don't actually remember her forcing memories on me, except for family memories, which were another thing altogether.

MJD: And do you keep a diary of any kind?

DL: I have done for about twenty years, before that I didn't.

MJD: When you came to write the autobiography, did you write from the beginning straight through?

DL: I wrote straight through. I've never been happy with what I know some novelists do, write the last scene and then go back. I've never been able to do that because it seems to me there's some kind of an invisible line through, pattern through, which you're not always conscious of.

MJD: I can see that in fiction everything has to be chosen and held together by a guiding idea. Did you find that in writing autobiography as well?

DL: The similarity between novels and autobiographies is that you're always throwing things out when you're writing. You cannot conceivably write all your memories because there'd be millions of words and readers would be asleep within the first chapter. So then you have to choose and this is what, after all, you sometimes do with a novel—cutting, cutting. So I found myself shaping it in a way, and life isn't terribly shapely! So this bothered me a good deal, because life is actually full of people you meet once, or groups of people you meet once, things you never do again, all kinds of false starts. You can't put that in an autobiography. And so I was asking myself, "Look, I have left out whole groups of people, never mentioned them. How then can this be called an autobiography?" Well, it's a good question. I think that all the important things are there. I did change the names of some people—particularly in *Volume II.* Because when I did *Volume I,* I was fascinated by the children and grandchildren who wrote to me and came to see me, and they had no idea about a lot of their parents' lives. It was very interesting. So I thought, "Well, I don't want to tell on my old comrades, I shall shut up because it's very upsetting for grandchildren." Some of them, you know, they don't know about close friends their parents had, all kinds of adventures their parents had, let alone lovers. So I've left a lot out about other people.

MJD: At what stage did you decide it would be a two-volume autobiography?

DL: Well, actually it should be three or four, but I can't write number three because of too many people . . . I simply thought, well it's a natural end to all this, *Volume I*, when I leave Africa. So I wrote that, and then I thought a lot about doing *Volume II* because the problem was people might suffer from it. But I thought that, on the whole, I didn't really involve anybody that much.

MJD: Your reasons for writing. You said in the autobiography that you wanted to claim your understanding of your life and prevent other people from getting in. But I gather that at least one person has already written a biography, and it's full of untruths.

DL: Yes, I couldn't understand it. This woman respects so little the things that I put in the autobiography and which I thought would prevent all of this [see Lessing (2000b); the reference is probably to Klein (2000)]. She didn't bother to check, so facts are all wrong, all the way through. So I just give up. You can't do anything about it, obviously.

MJD: You spoke, in *Volume II* I think it is, of a kind of energy that is generated by something else that is then transmuted into the fiction. You mentioned that *The Fifth Child* (1988), for example, was energized by your feelings about the Russian invasion of Afghanistan and the fact that no one was taking any notice. And you spoke of how the fiction has to have a set of ideas that can absorb that energy. Was there anything like that going on in the writing of your autobiography?

DL: No, I don't think so. Not that kind of energy at all. *The Fifth Child* was . . . I think every writer will understand this . . . this kind of driving energy which fills a book. I didn't have that for the autobiography. It was very slow and I was thinking a lot and trying to, you know, I was trying to get back things, and I did get back things, utterly unimportant things—like the design on a tablecloth.

MJD: That's quite amazing, especially when you say you didn't keep a diary.

DL: Well I didn't. But I do have a very good memory, as I say, for some things. But then you see, I don't understand it, I don't understand why you can remember something absolutely unimportant in such detail. Why, it just doesn't make sense. And this is another thing, when you are living a life, it never occurs to you that there is anything odd about it. It's only later that you realize that you've had quite an extraordinary life. So then I thought it was disappearing, and when I spoke to my children, John and Jean, about my early years, they didn't know things. And yet theirs is only a generation later. They had no idea, and perhaps didn't want to know, of the roughness of the early settlers' lives. You know it wasn't at all cozy, and *Homes and Gardens*. Then I thought all this is going to disappear if I don't write it.

MJD: And a point you have made is that the quality of the life lived then is almost inexplicable now.

DL: The Cold War is the most difficult because practically anything you say sounds like lunacy. Anything political you say sounds like lunacy—but that is the nature of politics I think.

MJD: Did you find it very difficult to move back to the emotions of those days?

DL: Very difficult. Partly because you think, "I couldn't possibly have believed that. I couldn't possibly have done that." But we did. For example, my French publisher came over here and I said to him, because he is quite young, I said, "You're not going to understand some of the things I've put in the book I've just finished because you won't know anything at all about the Comrades." He said, "Don't be silly, my grandfather was a Red, my father was one, and I understand it all'. And he told me this story. He told me that when *Darkness at Noon* came out—Koestler's book—the Communists went round to all the bookshops and took out the copies of *Darkness at Noon,* hid them, or burnt them. So then what happened was that queues formed outside publishing houses to get the book and the queues were lined on either side, on orders of the Communist Party, by Communists shouting abuse at the people buying the book. Now, you tell this story now and people just don't understand it. Yet it was absolutely normal then. It was this kind of crazy, angry bitterness, and antagonism—all perfectly normal, and part of everything.

MJD: At the beginning of *Volume I* you talk quite a lot about the problem of truth in autobiography—what is truth. And then you talk about truths, about seeing things in different ways in different times. Given that today's way of seeing things is going to change as well, how do you imagine people will read the autobiography in the next decade, or when the climate has changed?

DL: Well it's true of all novels as well. Some novels become documents, just historical documents. I wonder, for example, how that "After the War" period will seem. You know Eric Hobsbawm, the Marxist historian, did say something quite fascinating, which was that Europe was practically flat after the Second World War and yet fifteen years later it was rebuilt and prosperous. And he said this was an astonishing achievement. At any time in history it has never been matched. Rebuilt completely from nothing. It made me think— what living through that was like. Coming out of . . . like coming out of dark water really, things steadily got better and better and better all the time, so that by the end of the fifties everything was quite jolly, you know, and no one talked about the war. Whereas in the first part of that decade no one talked about anything else. They were obsessed by it. Well naturally, of course, they were. They'd just come out of the battlefields or just seen Belsen or something like that. And so people talked about nothing else, but then, at the end of it, the new generation—they didn't want to know. That took me back to my father. He used to complain that the Great War had become "the Great Unmentionable"—apparently that was in some cartoon or another—the Great Unmentionable. And I think the old soldiers were quite bitter. But I saw it again in Zimbabwe. I went there in 1982 and everybody was talking about the Liberation War, day and night. I went again in 1986, and there was already a young generation who didn't want to hear about it, and once again you have bitter old soldiers. It's very interesting.

MJD: In the *Children of Violence* sequence of novels, especially in *Martha Quest* and *A Proper Marriage*, you're dealing a lot with personal struggles, difficult relationships with parents, and so on. And then you had to come back to that in writing the autobiography. Was it more difficult in writing the autobiography to deal with those matters?

DL: Well I suppose I really had to give more to a memory. It was very difficult for me to go back and remember certain things like the nightmares I used to have, and then I had to do a lot of thinking because . . . you see this is not all a question of a family story or even . . . It's just that I remember things that can only have an explanation back before I can remember. I knew theoretically . . . you know the fact was that my mother had me long before she had her baby boy. She was apparently an old-fashioned woman, and she didn't really like me, which I don't blame her for. You know, we can't govern this kind of thing. And the nanny in Teheran didn't like me—I remember this distinctly. And I was a very difficult little girl. And then my father was always just . . . You knew he could always be relied upon for justice. But you know what really went on was my mother—this great, powerful, insensitive woman—none of this was her fault. So I actually had to really force myself to remember it all and I didn't want to. So I was very pleased when I got out of the first part.

MJD: It seemed to me that you were able to be more generous towards your mother when you were writing your autobiography than *Martha Quest*.

DL: But when you are fighting for survival, you really fight. I was terrible. So what I had was this combination, even when I was a tiny girl, of being desperately sorry for her and hating her at the same time. I really knew I had to be sorry for her. But when you are adolescent and you've got all this focused on you . . . Incidentally, it's very interesting this—they've gone, at least in our culture, those women who should have had careers and haven't got them. All my women friends in my twenties, every one had *A Mother*, and we knew what was wrong with them. They should have had jobs. We knew that. But that didn't prevent us from having to fight every inch of the way. Now women have jobs, and they don't have to focus everything on their kids. When I hear this business about women should be back in the home, I think, "You don't know what you're talking about. You just don't know what you're saying." It's just to introduce more middle-aged women with nowhere to go.

MJD: May I ask you a similar question about your recording your views of your brother's politics as they come across in *African Laughter: Four Visits to Zimbabwe* (1992), because you make it very clear that he seems benighted to you.

DL: Well he is. You couldn't even call him reactionary, he was beyond any normal classification for a brother. He was so reactionary—I mean words just fail me. There was nothing bad he didn't believe, but that didn't stop him being a very kindly man in his ordinary relationships with people. You know, this is a common combination. But I heard more sickening racism from my brother than I'd ever heard from anyone, and he'd sit there—he was usually a bit tight—and there was no point in saying anything, but you'd listen to him. It was disgusting racism. There was this decent, kindly man, pillar of the church no doubt and all that, talking this poison, and I don't think that was uncommon.

MJD: How do you understand the way you've diverged?

DL: It was most extraordinary. But children are born different, that's all. He remained all his life intensely conventional, intensely respectful of all authority. It never occurred to him . . . whatever authority it was, it was good. This is how he was all his life. He never criticized anything, he never thought it was possible, it never occurred to him to criticize anything. And there I was. So how do you account for that?

MJD: Your father's influence was the strong one there, as I understand it. He was the questioner.

DL: Yes, he was. My mother was an intensely conventional woman and she liked authority. She was by nature an authoritarian, but my father was a natural skeptic about everything. He questioned everything, but it had no effect on my brother. My brother never read anything, whereas I was reading everything in the bookshelves. He was essentially an outdoor child; he was brilliant in anything outdoors. You know, anyone who's had more than one child just marvels at how different they can be. Look at my two kids, John and Jean. John is dead —you probably know. He was a coffee farmer. He was born a fighter. He was unspeakably energetic, tough, physical, fighting. When he was born, I remember the nurse saying, "This one's a little tiger." And that is how he was all his life. My daughter, Jean, is a very quiet, thoughtful, sensitive woman. You couldn't imagine two more different people.

MJD: One of the other comments you have made is about being able, in fiction, to invent a character in order to embody a process. For example, in *Martha Quest,* you put the Cohen brothers in to explain her reading and the opening of her mind and so on. That can't be done in autobiography. What takes its place?

DL: Well, were I to write about the question now, I wouldn't put the Cohen boys in; but the fact was that I was predating something. When I went to Salisbury and joined the Communists, the Jews—most of them local—and not the air force, were enormously interesting. A lively lot and I owed them a great deal. They were always saying, "Well, you haven't read that book? Well you mean, you haven't read that?" So I just put them earlier, the Cohen boys. There were actually two people, two men I knew, one the romantic, noisy, flamboyant type and the one the serious, solid type. And I simply put them into Banket [then a village at the center of a farming area about a hundred kilometers northwest of Harare], which is impossible because in actual fact there was no Jewish storekeeper in Banket. They were all Greeks. And a Welsh garage man.

MJD: In autobiography, when you have to handle something that is unusual or slightly mysterious, is it that you just have to say, "Well that's how it was, strange as it may seem"?

DL: Yes, there are some things that are so odd. But then life is all the time full of the impossible, so many incidents, and we often tend not to notice. I mean how often do you hear someone say, "My God, no novelist could put that into a novel." You hear it all the time.

MJD: And yet at some points you do use novelistic techniques. There's a scene, a very sympathetic scene, where your mother is writing a letter home, and you move into her mind and bring it to life from her point of view.

DL: That's a novelist's technique all right. The thing is also that when you use dialogue it's a novelist's technique because you don't remember the exact words, or very seldom, but you do remember more or less what was said, so you invent the dialogue. But, I mean, I think all autobiographers do that.

MJD: May I ask you about the kind of context that you need for writing? You came away from Rhodesia partly because it was an impossible place in which to write, and you came here. What is it about London—do you ever write anywhere other than in London?

DL: Well, I need to have . . . I need to be rather bored with the same things happening every day. I don't want to be stimulated and don't want things to be happening. I think that's true of most writers, really. But I have to say, I know writers who thrive on stimulation and can dance on all night. I just couldn't, I don't understand it. Like Salman Rushdie, for example. Perfectly happy to go to parties all night and write the next day.

MJD: And is London the kind of city where you can control things to the extent that you need?

DL: Listen, here, now, there's no sound. At night, too, there's not a sound. August is always pleasant, because London empties, there's peace, it's lovely. But I didn't only come here because it's a good place to write. It's because at that time everybody was coming to London. You know, you think you're doing something you need to, then you discover you're part of the trend. I would say that half of the writers, a third of the writers around came from outside England. Because it seemed the obvious place to be, just as the Americans went to Paris. So I was just part of an influx.

MJD: Do you feel yourself to be a rooted writer? Is that a concept that is important to you?

DL: I am. I mean, my parents were so very British I couldn't be anything else but. But then when I grew up, it was not Zimbabwean towns that I liked. I never liked the towns, while I'm very happy in the bush. But then how could I be rooted there? It's disappearing. When you go out into the bush and the animals are gone and the birds a fraction of what they used to be, it's quite sad.

MJD: I had at the back of my mind the character in *Landlocked* (1965) who talks about the time when his grandfather and great-grandfather had grown up, living always under one tree. Do you feel at all awkward about still being associated, as a writer, with southern Africa?

DL: No, because it seems to me I belong to both places really. I certainly think I am returning to southern Africa when I write. And now the novel that I've just finished owes everything to a country I call "Zimlia" at the end of *The Sweetest Dream*.

MJD: It seems that what you are doing in many different ways in your fiction is questioning received assumptions. All that complacency, all those comfortable ideas. In writing autobiography did you feel anything like the same process going on? Was there anything like the same motivation?

DL: Well yes, I was definitely interested in questioning the hold of Communism. I wrote this whole thing about why possibly it happened, or one of the reasons why. So yes, I was questioning all the time because a great deal of the things that seemed perfectly normal then now seem so bizarre. I'm amazed we didn't question them earlier. But then I don't have to write an autobiography just to question what is going on.

MJD: I was wondering whether the difference in genre was telling for you because it seems to me that fiction is a much more free mode of writing and could be much more exploratory and therefore more questioning.

DL: I don't think it is so much different. All the time in writing the autobiography I was saying, "Why did I do that; did I have to do that? Could I have done it differently?" Whereas when you're writing fiction, the characters are there. When you think about your characters, your fictional characters, they become so real to you. They suggest their own behavior. Just as you can't change your behavior no matter how much you want to; your own behavior is there, with you, engraved in stone, unfortunately.

MJD: And does it mean that the range of possible things that your characters do is also a limited one?

DL: They can't do more than . . . they can't do things outside their nature, you know, they can't suddenly take off into another character. But if they're strong characters, if you set them out as strong characters at the start, then after that they really do take over in what they are going to do. And that's quite surprising. For example, out of my unconscious came this old German woman who was born at the same time of the century as the grandmother of the protagonist in the novel that I have just finished, *The Sweetest Dream*. And I'm quite amazed at this woman because I don't remember ever having met her. But she's obviously there somewhere. And she's such a strong character I'm amazed at what she does, but it's right for her to do these things.

MJD: And that's an equivalent kind of discipline? Autobiography is disciplined by what actually happened. Or, the best recovery you can make of it. And the characters are disciplined by . . .

DL: . . . by what's possible.

MJD: You mentioned a couple of times that you are the kind of writer who writes to find out what you think.

DL: It's true.

MJD: The South African writer J. M. Coetzee has suggested that autobiography is an exploratory process and one that does give insight, but that the autobiographer is also playing a kind of game, one of giving and withholding. And yet it would seem that if you are writing to find out what you think, then the two processes can't go on side by side; the one will exclude the other.

DL: I don't think so. Because as you go along, either as an autobiographer or as a novelist, you are thinking thoughts that you haven't thought before. But that's only laziness, there's nothing to stop you thinking. You don't really need a typewriter to have new insights. But it seems to be the way that *I* find out about things. Like this whole business of my coming to the conclusion that the reason why so many Communists stayed in the Party or, for that matter, joined it, is because of masochism bred into us by war. I hadn't thought of that before I started. It was only as I was writing that I kept thinking, "Yes, it could be possible."

MJD: Did writing the autobiography make you relive a lot? For example, did it make you rethink the position of women in society and their difficulties of getting recognition and the conditions under which they had to work?

DL: But that's not writing that does that, because don't forget that when I go back to Zimbabwe, and I see the women battling out there, it's reinforced all the time. It's the battle women have in most parts of the world.

MJD: Can I ask you a question about being interviewed? You have to submit to it quite a lot I should imagine. And at the same time interviews are becoming in literary, scholarly circles quite important. Do you find it an unnecessary chore or do you . . . ?

DL: On the whole, yes, I do. I mean there was a time when I didn't do any interviews at all on principle. I never went to any publicity things because it got utterly intolerable. Then it suddenly occurred to me that this is how books are being sold now. It's no good finding it awful, and, you know, it's not always a chore. Sometimes it's extremely interesting.

MJD: You often speak about a mistaken desire readers have to find that something is autobiographical. Do you worry that giving interviews might encourage that kind of reading?

DL: Well it does, I mean there's no question of worrying, it does. What happens is that we have a whole persona created by interviews and television, all this kind of thing, which actually need not have very much to do with the personality that writes. Not really.

MJD: A public self, not the writer's self.

DL: Yes. I'm not saying it's untrue or anything, but when I talk in that autobiography about the way a writer sort of stooges around in a room for hours or days wool-gathering, that's not thinking what to write. That's really the reality, and not clever remarks such as I am making now. What is amazing is there's always this moment, which all writers know. You have spent months or years on this mass of paper and all that has gone into it, ups and downs and problems, and then you deliver this wodge. Next thing what turns up is this artifact, all neat and clean and rounded. It is such a shock, always, it's such a shock.

References Cited

BRIDGMAN, JOAN. "Doris Lessing and Her Unwanted Biography, Review." *Contemporary Review*. Aug. 2000. http://www.findarticles.com

GOTTLIEB, ROBERT. Introduction to *On Life and Autobiography: Doris Lessing at The 92nd St. Y, New York City*. Oct. 24, 1994. http://www.nytimes.com/books/97/09/14/reviews/970914.14kermodt.html#hear

KERMODE, FRANK. "'The Bliss of the Big City." Review of *Walking in the Shade*." *The New York Times*. Sept. 14, 1997. http://www.nytimes.com/books/97/09/14/reviews/970914.14kermodt.html

KOESTLER, ARTHUR. *Darkness at Noon*. New York: Bantam, 1966.

LESSING, DORIS. *Martha Quest*. London: Joseph, 1952.

———. *A Proper Marriage*. London: Joseph, 1954.

———. *Landlocked*. London: MacGibbon & Kees, 1965.

———. *The Fifth Child*. London: Cape, 1988.

———. *African Laughter: Four Visits to Zimbabwe*. London: Harper Collins, 1992.

———. *Under My Skin: Volume I of My Autobiography, to 1949*. London: Flamingo, 1994a.

———. "Doris Lessing Talks about Writing Autobiography" in *On Life and Autobiography: Doris Lessing at The 92nd St. Y, New York City*. Oct. 24, 1994b. http://www.nytimes.com/books/97/09/14/reviews/970914.14kermodt.html#hear

———. *Love, Again: A Novel*. London: Flamingo, 1996.

———. *Walking in the Shade: Volume II of My Autobiography, 1949–1962*. Flamingo: London, 1997.

———. "I Know What It Is To Be a Subject." *The Spectator*. Apr. 15, 2000.

———. *The Sweetest Dream*. London: Flamingo, 2001.

Further Reading

KLEIN, CAROLE. *Doris Lessing: A Biography*. London: Duckworth, 2000.

LOWRY, ELIZABETH. "Yeti." *London Review of Books* 23, 6 (March 2001). http://www.lrb.co.uk/v23/n06/print/lowro1_.html

DORIS LESSING can be heard reading from *Under My Skin* and talking about autobiography at: http://www.nytimes.com/books/97/09/14/reviews/970914.14kermodt.html#hear

July 2000

VI SUBJECT TO METAPHOR

Metaphors of Self

Es'kia Mphahlele interviewed by N. Chabani Manganyi

ES'KIA (EZEKIEL) MPHAHLELE is an internationally renowned writer and academic who has lectured in various African countries, Europe, and the United States of America and has several titles on African, Caribbean, and African-American literature to his name. He is a leading figure of what came to be known as the *Drum* generation (Chapman 1989), and his first volume of autobiography, *Down Second Avenue* (1959), a classic of African literature, is listed as one of Africa's hundred best books. According to Lewis Nkosi (1990), part of the power of *Down Second Avenue* is the "enthralling picture it provides of an African childhood and its intransigent will to truth." Nkosi suggests that this will to truth is the effect of the "spare uncluttered prose" and the virtually "transparent" text, which at times "gives the impression of having written itself, making the reader forget that there is an author behind all these recollections busily shaping the narrative for us." Mphahlele's second volume of autobiography, *Afrika My Music,* which Nkosi describes as "a long apologia for a sad nostalgic retreat from the inhospitability of exile" relates his exile in Paris, Ibadan, Nairobi, Denver, Lusaka, and at the University of Pennsylvania in Philadelphia and his return to South Africa in 1977, where he later became professor of African literature at the University of the Witwatersrand.

N. CHABANI MANGANYI: Well, Zeke, as I talk to you about biography today, many years after the publication of *Exiles and Homecomings* and *Bury Me at the Marketplace*, my curiosity takes me in numerous directions. First, I remind myself of the singular fact that as an intellectual and literary scholar the corpus of your work has covered a very wide canvass indeed, to say the least: autobiography, one thinks here of *Down Second Avenue;* short story anthologies such as *In Corner B; essays, The African Image, Voices in the Whirlwind;* extended fiction, *Chirundu* and many other contributions too numerous to list. A writer, literary critic, and activist all in one is a difficult act to follow. Complexity is the word that comes to mind. I could not help thinking, once confronted with this complexity, of the classic study of autobiography by James Olney, published several years ago, entitled *Metaphors of Self: The Meaning of Autobiography.* I found, and I find up to this day, Olney's idea of metaphors of self exceedingly interesting. What is more, it is even more interesting in the context of writers such as you who write autobiography and what would normally qualify as fiction. To stretch Olney's ideas a little further, how do metaphors of self or what Hopkins once described as "a taste of myself" play themselves out in *Down Second Avenue* when compared, say, to *The Wanderers, Chirundu,* and your other less autobiographical fiction?

ES'KIA MPHAHLELE: The "metaphors of self" is an interesting concept. Considering that one is telling one's own story and you are trying to follow the line of your life to the present maybe, which is autobiography, you are remembering a number of events. You place yourself as the narrator. It is in the first person, narrating your own life. There is no way that you are going to capture everything that happened in your life. There is no way that you can even approximate the sequence of those events in your autobiography. So, what you indeed do is to recreate yourself. It is in a sense a monument of self. In its becoming, it's a monument and in its composition it is a metaphor. You are saying here is my life story and yet at the same time it's a metaphor rather than absolute fact.

NCM: Yes.

EM: You are [aware], [that] you have to modify a number of things because you are recreating, as in a work of art. In a work of art, you don't try to reproduce concrete life and make a concrete representation of it. But rather you present it as a symbol of something else. You are also crafting it; you are giving it a meaning that will be understood by the rest of the world who come and view it. In a way, you try to say more than one thing at a time. Because that makes your work a form of art. You are also embellishing it in many ways. In writing, you embellish it with images, symbol upon symbol upon symbol. In that way, you are striving to find that deeper meaning, and that inner meaning makes poetry. In poetry, you try to go beneath the surface appearance of things. The meaning has no finality because you are exploring. So there is the poetry and there is the telling of the story and there is the metaphor of self. The monument is in the sense that you are saying: here is my life and I am reconstructing it as closely as I possibly can. It is not a monument in the sense of "here I am! I have qualities of a hero and here is my monument." But rather that here is something built on memory. You compose it, you craft it and produce it as a work of art. Now, that is how I understood my mission in autobiography.

NCM: Yes.

EM: In *Down Second Avenue,* as a concrete example, I had just finished my masters with UNISA in 1956. When I was with *Drum,* Jenny, the wife of Sylvester Stein, the editor of the magazine, said to me: "Zeke why don't you write something about your life? I have been reading what you have been writing in *Drum.* Why don't you say something about your life story." I did not think much of it at the time. I had never thought of it before. I had always just thought that I was a fiction writer.

NCM: Yes.

EM: And so I mulled over it until it grew on me. I started it the beginning of 1957, and things came rolling out, memories came rolling out, often in their starkness. I went to Nigeria and worked on the second half and repolished it. I thought I was saying to the reader, the reading public: here is the story of my life and it is not unique. It is shared by so many people, those at Maupaneng and in Marabastad. Those are the people who shared my life. This is a typical story of an African in South Africa.

NCM: Yes.

EM: I was saying that this is me but it is not singularly me. To that extent, again it is a metaphor, a metaphor of self, a metaphor of the way our people lived and the way they struggled. I try to bring out in *Down Second Avenue* the toughness of our people, my grandmother, my aunt, my mother, and the women in the street in Second Avenue. The heroism in a sense and also the grit they had to survive.

NCM: Yes

EM: So it is metaphor upon metaphor upon metaphor.

NCM: That is an interesting way of thinking about it. It is interesting to me that you made the connection with poetry. I think T. S. Eliot recognized the proximity between poetry and autobiography. As you were speaking, I was thinking about the role of the imagination in the writing of autobiography, and I was also thinking about character in fiction. Characters have a very important role to play in the power of the narrative. That led me to wonder what your views are on the role of character in autobiography. You have already referred to some of the people who populate the pages of *Down Second Avenue.* How do you think about character if you move away from the central character, namely, the monument to the self and its surroundings or social context?

EM: You know as I was working from that memory, the memory of those people under whom I grew up, I remembered very distinctly their most outstanding traits. I told myself that I want to bring these out. I wanted to paint a clear picture of each one of them according to their individual characteristics. As I was not inventing as I would do with fiction, I wanted to represent them as I understood them. I could not write it as a fiction writer tries to do. He or she tries to use a superior voice when he or she writes fiction. The one that says I know what the character is going to think, I'm in control.

NCM: The one that pronounces.

EM: The one that pronounces. I know what he is going to think and I know what he is leading to. With autobiography, I take them as they come. Yes, I add a few things in order to liven it up. To liven up the picture.

NCM: To spice it up.

EM: To spice it up. And I throw in a little ginger here and a little ginger there in order to fill the picture up instead of a stark character of a person. And I do it as clearly as I can and as clearly as I understand it. I also wanted to be careful not to imagine things that an adult would be expected to imagine.

NCM: Oh, yes.

EM: I had to write as a boy growing up. And I think you see the division there between me the adult and the boy growing up. The little things that go on in my mind, the prejudices. How I interpreted the cruelty of my teachers sometimes. When I am grown up and I am talking as a person who is politically conscious of what has happened to him and what is still happening to him and other people, I take on an adult pose, I talk ideas. Not so, in the latter part of the book. I talk ideas as a grown up, as a family man. Let me say after I finished it I felt I had stripped myself almost naked. I was vulnerable. It never occurred to me that this was something that could happen. But in a short time I ceased to feel vulnerable, I felt liberated.

NCM: Yes, yes.

EM: I was determined to write this thing as I wanted to write it and embellish it the way I wanted to. It was much later after that when I said, "My! I am vulnerable." Everything that people will say about the book, they will be saying about me. Yet at the same time one could not have done it otherwise.

NCM: Zeke, I think you made a very important point about the different voices. I came across this issue while I was still engaged in the serious study of biography and autobiography—the problem of an adult writing about childhood. You recognize that there are different voices that need to be used. One has to recognize this almost in a self-conscious way to avoid a cluttering of the narrative voices—the person who speaks, the person who recollects, and the person who makes interpretations. What about literary criticism of autobiography in the light of the sense of vulnerability that you were talking about?

EM: Often one felt that when critics were writing about it, I would say to myself they got a point wrong here. That is not what I was feeling.

NCM: Some years ago at an international symposium which was billed as "new directions in biography" in Honolulu, I read a paper and made the point that there was a notable surge in the publication of autobiographies, largely by exiled black South African writers such as yourself, Peter Abrahams, Bloke Modisane, and Todd Matshikiza during the late 1950s and early 1960s. I remember saying at the time that this coincidence between exile and the flowering of autobiography was something intriguing. I advanced my own pet theories at the time. I wonder what your own thinking is.

EM: That is a very interesting question and very much to the point of autobiography, the way I see it, Chabani. And I seem to feel this in a way that some people don't. They thought I was overplaying the theme of exile at one point, especially South Africans and those who were against my coming back. One feels as an exile that one is out there away from any social support systems of your native land. You are out there exposed to the elements of a new terrain. And you want to let people at home know what it is to be an exile. Being in that condition of exile you want to tell the world what South Africa is like. What it means to grow up in South Africa right from day one. As a native of South Africa, you really have a strange kind of childhood. A childhood in which perhaps the only love there is, is between you and your mother, your father, and within the family and ends there. As a child, I always felt that this was a world for adults because of adult bullying. As I grew away from it and became independent, I wondered what was it all about? Adults seemed to gang up against children, and they seemed to feel that they display their own concerns about your growing up. But it got so oppressive. It always struck me how one had to survive that adult siege. Everyone wanted to show you that they were grown up and you had to do their bidding. It's strange that way. In time, you grow up and reconcile things and begin to understand your culture. I feel that in exile one wants to do this. When I started *Down Second Avenue* I wasn't in physical exile. But in a sense I was already an exile, spiritually and intellectually being constantly in conflict with a vindictive administration. I felt I had already begun my exile and moving out was the physical exile. You hope your story will resonate in people's minds and become a meaningful text, be a stimulus for more voices. I think that is why exile brings about autobiography. You feel you have lived that extraordinary experience.

NCM: We have dealt with the question of autobiography in your work. What I have been thinking about are the implications, if any, for your other work, say, *The Wanderers,* other fiction, and so on.

EM: Now, *The Wanderers* is fictionalized. Let me say it is mostly fiction, but it follows a mainly autobiographical line, mostly in the travels from one place to another. It has that sequence which is autobiographical. The people are fictionalized, even the ones that are in the autobiography: Ribs, my eldest son. And also my experiences in those places. And yet again there are events that took place. I fictionalize them, place them in a fictionalized context.

NCM: Yes.

EM: So it is largely fictional. Where it becomes autobiographical is when it comes to the intimate parts where I talk closely about my family and so on and the helpers who were working for us in Nigeria. Now that is a work of the imagination in a larger frame. And also again it was to show the reader what the other worlds were like to me and to show those worlds and the experiences that shaped me, that helped to shape me in later life. They are stamped in my memory. They have been there a long time. They are still alive in my memory. Once you have written a book like that, an outline of autobiography and fictional detail, you seldom want to go back and read it as a published work. For one thing, I don't know why I can go back and read *Down Second Avenue.* When it comes to *The Wanderers,* I hesitate, even only to reread snatches.

NCM: Yes.

EM: Again that is something I can never explain. Chirundu, the narrator in *Chirundu,* is himself an exile. Other South African exiles in Zambia feature, those in prison and those who were not. Their concerns are about exile. Someone would come up with a story about pre-exile life often with such painful nostalgia. And yet the central theme of the book is this Chirundu and his wife Tirenje. They are estranged, and I go into the details of their lives. All of it is fiction. I did read in the newspaper about a man who had been arrested for bigamy. I thought to myself: here is something I want to explore. Why would a man of his standing, of his enlightenment, go and do something that is illegal like bigamy. Not the ethics involved at all. That is another matter. Who knows what the ethics of bigamy should be and should not be?

NCM: Yes.

EM: Even the exiles. It's all made up. The conversation is not anything that I ever recorded in real life. Now, a man whose judgment I always had a tremendous respect for was the late Martin Jarrett Kerr, the Anglican priest—himself a notable critic—who was always writing to me about my writing. He was very fond of this novel. For the first time it moves away from the mainly autobiographical. It is a change since *Down Second Avenue* and *The Wanderers*. It comes after them. Then again, he wrote to me after *Father Come Home,* which he said he enjoyed immensely, saying also it was strangely beautiful.

NCM: Yes.

EM: It is this whole thing about the imagination. I wrote an article at one time that is published in an American journal called *Kenyon Review* entitled "Educating the Imagination." I am here pleading for a place in the curriculum for teaching oral poetry and moving into modern poetry; showing how the very use of metaphor is intensely traditional. We have metaphors in our languages and a teacher can bring these metaphors out and have them translated from one language to another. They show how people in their daily speech use metaphor in serious situations. Whenever they are assembled to talk seriously about a matter. It's the older people I am talking about. They start using metaphor because they feel that it goes deeper into the meaning of what they are saying. And also, metaphor is memorable. People will constantly repeat it. What the English poet Auden (1935), writing about poetry, calls "memorable speech."

NCM: Yes.

EM: From there it's an easy movement into written poetry. There you are using images, contemporary images that make up your world. Then I give an example of my own upbringing at Maupaneng, being a child of nature, moving freely in the wilds and so on as a herd boy. I began to learn a lot about natural phenomena without being taught by any teacher. Given that kind of educative imagination I bring it into the whole idea of how to teach poetry. You notice that very few of our teachers know what poetry is. They shy away from teaching poetry in class. It is a formidable handicap for them. And yet it is so closely related to the use of the imagination; so closely related to the traditional use of the imagination and the formation of metaphors and other figures of speech.

NCM: Right.

EM: I am giving this example in order to move into the connection between autobiography and the fiction that I write and the poetry. I was always intrigued by folk tales. I was always intrigued by the world of mystery and the wonder they encompassed when I was a boy. That imagination grew bigger as I was growing up and getting more education. So it never left me. My imagination will move when I am writing from one genre to another, even when I am writing a factual paper.

NCM: Yes.

EM: When I am writing exposition, the imagination keeps working and I find myself creating images in my mind. So this is how it worked with *The Wanderers* and with *Chirundu*, with *Father Come Home*, and the short stories, of course.

NCM: Yes.

EM: It never was a problem. In fact, I always had to rein it in. Reining it in is always an act of art. To create art you need to put your imagination together so that it does not run wild when shaping your work of art.

NCM: Right, what about *Afrika My Music*?

EM: In *Afrika My Music* I go deeper into my thinking and come up with ideas. I begin with that interview, that weird interview at the University of the North for the job of head of English. What education, what university education means to me. Along the way, in certain chapters I discuss music. I pick up a number of things outside my own normal activities that engage the intellect in a way that does not occur in the other books.

NCM: Again, there often are statements, allusions when people are talking or writing about what are sometimes described as the *Drum* writers of the 1950s to resonances with the Harlem Renaissance. Would you like to comment on this with regard to your own development as a writer and the genres you took up as you went along?

EM: Yes. The fifties were a fascinating time. We actually did experience a revival quite a distance away from the Dhlomos, the Plaatjes—that is stylistically.

NCM: Yes.

EM: The fifties, because *Drum Magazine* was patterned after the two American magazines *Life* and *Look*, because it was a picture magazine like them although it was bound to have articles of investigative reporting and political articles about ANC activities, generally political personalities. We read a lot of African-American literature, which we found in good supply at a bookshop in Joubert Street—Vanguard, now defunct.

NCM: Oh yes.

EM: We found a lot of literature there by African-Americans. That was one stage. Before that there was Peter Abrahams. We were not yet tuned in to Peter Abrahams's writing. He had been long in exile. But we were able to get his books in the country. *Dark Testament,* his first collection of sketches and short stories, and later *Mine Boy* and others. One could see that his style had been influenced by African-Americans. We only learnt later that he came into contact with African-American literature at the Bantu Men's Social Centre in Eloff

Street. There was a library set up by an American missionary called Ray Phillips.

NCM: A famous personality of the time.

EM: Quite a famous personality of the time. People like Dhlomo and other African personalities also had access to it. Peter Abrahams plunged into it and read everything that was African-American. We first heard from him about Marcus Garvey in the mid-thirties when we were in high school together. He was greatly influenced by them. His style was clearly influenced by the Harlem Renaissance: short sentences, vivid images. We took off from there in *Drum* each on his own. We created quite a noise that had not been heard before. The strangest thing is that the white people did not bother to read that literature, the *Drum* literature. Our famous writers were largely unknown to them. It appealed to the proletariat, to the black townships. And went abroad too, to East and West Africa. So it was an institution and does deserve the term renaissance. It was certainly a revival. We realized for the first time, at least I did, that, hey, there is something more in African-American writing than we had ever created. I got hold of Richard Wright's *Uncle Tom's Children,* a collection of short stories. My! It really shook me up! I realized the style I was using in *Man Must Live* was way out. It was so unrealistic, so postured. It was just sterile. I jumped on to Richard Wright's style and Langston Hughes's in the Harlem Renaissance. So it really intrigued us. Even Todd Matshikiza, who was inventive stylistically. It was largely the Harlem Renaissance that influenced us and others like Bloke Modisane, Arthur Maimane, and Can Themba, and later, Bessie Head. The Cape Town three—Alex la Guma, Richard Rive, and James Matthews—simultaneously came under African-American influence. As a literary renaissance, it was also a rediscovery of a new kind of consciousness among us. An urban consciousness that used language in a way that is felt, that is heard, and that immediately strikes on the emotions, that is not highly intellectual. You could also see then that the imagination was at work then because so many of us who were writing for *Drum* were writing from personal experience of the life we were living. You felt the environment impacting on you all the time. You went to bed angry with what happened to you with white folks in the city. Those things that you experienced at work and the struggle to survive. You felt life physically and emotionally all the time. And the writing was bound to change in a way you would not have imagined in the days of Dhlomo and Sol Plaatje. A number of people say the *Drum* writers were not politically minded, except for a few. This comes mostly from those who don't read critically or at all. The fiction by *Drum* writers reflected the turbulence, the pain, the police terror, generally the cruelty of the times. Alongside this is the other human drama that reveals a life of escapist activities, entertainment. People found ways to relieve the tensions.

References Cited

ABRAHAMS, PETER. *Dark Testament*. London: George Allen & Unwin, 1942.

———. *Mine Boy*. London: Dorothy Crisp & Co., 1946.

AUDEN, W. H., and JOHN GARRET. Introduction. *The Poet's Tongue*. London: G. Bell and Sons, 1935.

CHAPMAN, MICHAEL. *The Drum Decade: Stories from the 1950s*. Pietermaritzburg: University of Natal Press, 1989.

KELLER-COHEN, D., and C. GORDON. "On Trial: Metaphor in Telling the Life Story." *Narrative Inquiry* 13, 1 (June 2003): 1–40.

MANGANYI, CHABANI. "Biography: The Black South African Connection." In *New Directions in Biography*, edited by Antony M. Friedson. Honolulu: University of Hawai'i Press, 1981.

———. *Exiles and Homecomings: A Biography of Es'kia Mphahlele*. Johannesburg: Ravan Press, 1983.

MPHAHLELE, ES'KIA. *Man Must Live, and Other Stories*. Cape Town: African Bookman, 1946.

———. *Down Second Avenue*. London: Faber and Faber, 1959.

———. *The African Image*. Nairobi: East African Publishing House, 1962.

———. *In Corner B*. Nairobi: East African Publishing House, 1967.

———. *The Wanderers*. London: Macmillan, 1972.

———. *Voices in the Whirlwind and Other Essays*. London: Macmillan, 1973.

———. *Chirundu*. Johannesburg: Ravan Press, 1979.

———. *Afrika My Music: An Autobiography*. Johannesburg: Ravan Press, 1984a.

———. *Bury Me at the Marketplace: Selected Letters of Es'kia Mphahlele 1943–1980*. Ed. Chabani Manganyi. Johannesburg: Skotaville, 1984b.

———. *Father Come Home*. Johannesburg: Ravan Press, 1984c.

NKOSI, LEWIS. "Es'kia Mphahlele at 70." *Southern African Review of Books*. (Feb./May 1990). http://www.uni-ulm.de/~rturrell/antho4html/Nkosi1.html

OLNEY, JAMES. *Metaphors of Self: The Meaning of Autobiography*. Princeton: Princeton University Press, 1972.

WRIGHT, RICHARD. *Uncle Tom's Children*. New York: Harper & Brothers, 1938.

Further Reading

ATTWELL, DAVID. *Rewriting Modernity: Studies in Black South African Literary History*. Pietermaritzburg: University of KwaZulu-Natal Press, 2005.

MPHAHLELE, ES'KIA. *Es'kia.* Cape Town: Kwela, 2002.
———. *Es'kia Continued.* Cape Town: Kwela, 2004.
OBEE, RUTH. *Es'kia Mphahlele: Themes of Alienation and African Humanism.* Athens: Ohio University Press, 1998.
STEIN, SYLVESTER. *Who Killed Mr. Drum?* Bellville: Mayibuye Books-UWC, 1999.
THUYSMA, PETER. *Footprints along the Way: A Tribute to Es'kia Mphahlele.* Braamfontein: Skotaville, 1989.
WILLEMSE, HEIN, "Es'kia Mphahlele–A Doyen of African Literature." *Tydskrif vir letterkunde* 41, 2 (2004): 157–162.
WOEBER, CATHERINE. "The Influence of Western Education on South Africa's First Black Autobiographers." *English Studies in Africa* 44, 2 (2001): 57–74.
WOEBER, CATHERINE, and JOHN READ. *Es'kia Mphahlele: A Bibliography.* Grahamstown: National English Literary Museum, 1989.

May 2002

Aquifers and Auto/biography in Namibia

Dorian Haarhoff interviewed by Terence Zeeman

THE NEED TO recount, or at least "to account for" the past is perhaps most pressing in those communities where expression, both personal and public, has been savagely stifled. Namibia's communities are examples. This last colony in Africa has only recently been able freely to begin to commit to text those testimonies once censored by apartheid. Some deal with the "biography" of a body politic; some invite controversy by challenging the liberator's record and exposing "reconciliation" as a ploy to hide uncomfortable truths. Others deal more directly with a personal account of a life lived within the context of the struggle. Haarhoff's work, however, excavates stories that are less concerned with an engagement in collective, political acts and the project of setting the record straight. His efforts are more attentive to deeply personal and perhaps more mythically resonant articulations. For Haarhoff, politics is about the personal. His preoccupation is not "to tell"—to coin the root of the word in the sense of "to count"—or to provide an accurate, albeit contextualized, sequence of facts. Truth and "fact" for Haarhoff are not necessarily comrades. Instead, Haarhoff would more readily enlist fiction as a friendly aid to personal disclosure and discovery. I am reminded of the old woman in Harold Pinter's *Mountain Language,* who, after years of being forbidden to use her language, forgets it when finally released to speak it. So it can be in "postcolonial" communities, where the erstwhile need to channel all personal energies to the cause of the struggle has sometimes atrophied the exercising of a personal, subjective, voice. When deeply traumatized peoples have lived so long with lies and propaganda, the need to set the record straight (to commission a mass confession of the truth as a precursor to reconciliation) can deny attention to more urgent, more personal creative crises in the individual. It is at the site of these blockages to tentative, deeply rooted personal articulations that Haarhoff seeks to intervene: to heal, to restore the flow. And to share the capacity to trust that trickster "memory" to fictionalize a more playful construction of a personal past—one that entertains the possibility of constructing a version of the self that seeks to be truly autobiographical. Terence Zeeman interviewed Dorian Haarhoff in April 2002 via email.

TERENCE ZEEMAN: Was there a spring or font from which your own writing experience flowed?

DORIAN HAARHOFF: I wrote my first poem at age eleven when my father died. Words to hold grief. A simple ballad. Since then writing and healing have been close cousins. Then in my twenties working with words. At first sounding like the poets I admired. Hopkins. Dylan Thomas. Echoing them. Then striving so hard to find my own voice that I became contrived. Then relaxing and coming home. And out of my struggles and passion understanding emerged that anybody can write, can engage the discipline. So I began to think about the theory of the craft. How to breathe life into writing—my own and the pieces I mentor.

TZ: Is that eleven-year-old still writing? Or reading your work?

DH: Your question reminds me of Garcia Lorca's "Give me back the soul I had as a boy matured in fairy tales." We are many voices. We are in conversation with a community or chorus of past and future selves. So, yes, the eleven-year-old and the fifty-eight-year-old talk of keeping the heart and intelligence central to the work.

TZ: Work for children has been a productive part of your career. *Desert December* (1991b), *Water from the Rock* (1992), *Legs, Bones and Eyes* (1994a), *Guano Girl* (1994b), *Big Red and Dangerous* (1996, and as *Space Racer* in 2001), *Grandfather Enoch's Pipe,* (2002a). Dare one ask if you have a favorite?

DH: *Desert December.* A boy, Seth, undertakes a mythical journey through the Namib desert at Christmas time. He finds gifts from the desert to give to his newborn sister. In a sense it's about making the place where you are holy. Mythologizing the landscape. I'm thinking too how one develops a personal mythology. The book is partly about that. It's also about me setting out on a writer's journey. And on a journey into workshops to encourage others to write. As we travel we find writing gifts in the desert.

TZ: While acknowledging that every workshop will have its own character and dimension, what are some of the more common activities that mark your workshops?

DH: Activities to get people into relationship—with themselves, their words, their readers. Activities to connect people to their creativity and imagination. Building confidence. These activities involve nondominant hand drawings, symbolic work with natural objects, responding to music, walking, creating collages. In these activities the unconscious arrives as an unexpected guest and connects us to energy. Writing is a form of energy.

TZ: Briefly sketch the background to the workshops in Namibia.

DH: They began as an extension to my university teaching. So many students wanted to write creatively. Then I met Carl Schlettwein, director of Basler Afrika Bibliographien. He encouraged me to seek the support through the Carl Schlettwein Foundation that enabled me to work in communities. We ran many workshops and produced two BAB publications—one on personal memories and the other a poetry volume. We focus on autobiography, the mother of the other genres. Anyone with a desire to write attends. Those who have a personal story to tell.

TZ: Why autobiography as a focus?

DH: Autobiography is a vital way of reconnecting to your identity especially in an authoritarian society where identity has been suppressed in favor of the powerful official version of who you are (a race, gender, or religious classification).

TZ: You speak of autobiography as "the mother of the other genres"—a generative act rather than a summary or account or report of a life lived, of actions the individual has already taken before and is now recalling.

DH: Our experience and imagination form the basement of the house of writing. We draw up the material and shape the other genres—the rooms in the house. And not so much a summary but the focus on a formative incident. A life change. A paradigm shift. Some incident that reverberates through the length of a lifetime. Set against the political. This kind of memory differs from conventional Namibian autobiography in that it foregrounds the politics of the personal rather than the party political. Participants instead begin to write their own stories that grow out of a personal, interior landscape.

TZ: I see you mark a difference between "conventional" autobiography and the work you undertake in your workshops. Does this difference lie in exercising an internal, personal memory/voice as opposed to a struggle-sanctioned collective-fashioned account? Is this then the emerging project of the self—the "auto" in autobiography—and an acknowledgement that the individual, so long harnessed to the political collective struggle, is now encouraged to find interior collective psyches that comprise protagonists and antagonists within the person as opposed to merely without. Perhaps I refer to the expectation that an autobiography is expected to set the record straight or to record the contexts of the public and private life as it has been lived. But can the act of engaging with the writing self "wright" another, alternative self?

DH: The inner life is often neglected in conventional autobiography. This makes for an exterior text. The drama of identity is an internal one, played out in the unconscious. So this approach brings the interior and exterior into balance.

TZ: Samuel Johnson said: "The use of travelling is to regulate imagination by reality, and instead of thinking how things may be, to see them as they are." I imagine you could respond to the use of travel in a very different way.

DH: An interesting juxtaposition—imagination and reality. Poet Wallace Stevens says, "We entertain the fantastic in order to understand the actual." Let's take that further. We entertain the fantastic in order to *transform* the actual. Imagination is not an unreality but a heightened reality leading to possible changes, shifts in perception—another form of knowing . . . a visual intuition. I think of Elie Wiesel, who asks, "When does imagination become knowledge?" and of Einstein, who asserts, "Imagination is more important than knowledge." Imagination and travel are twin companions. I think when we travel, we travel outside and inside—a mirror trip. We take in experiences that can open us and alter the shape of our belief bubble. Travel offers us parallel ways of being and suggests that we are in conversation with our reality more than we think we are. Travel as opposed to touring can involve risking. It places me in the unfamiliar. Disorientates me . . . I lose my geography and sense of where home is. But what I discover is that "there are hundreds of ways to kneel and kiss the ground" (Rumi). And travel projects the imagination beyond the next horizon as I come to understand Rumi's truth.

TZ: Images and metaphors of travel/journey feature prominently in your own work. These quests, personal and communal, map a topography or geography marked by juxtapositions such as desert/aquifer, fluidity/fixity, and fiction/"fact." In "The Editor's Note" to *The Inner Eye: Namibian Poetry in Process* (1997), you write of the difficulty of defining "this elusive country of the image and the spirit."

DH: I think we are travelers. We come from a long line of travelers. On the move. The word "motion" huddles inside the word "emotion" waiting to stretch its legs. Migrants in time and space. Namibian history has created much traveling—desert exploration, prospecting, migrant workers, exiles fleeing, and returnees coming home. The autobiographies of those who went into exile are marked by the imagery and topography of home. So many Namibians have lived a tortoise existence. As I look down on Namibia from the air I see, as I wrote in the poem "Tortoise Land," "The back of this land is tortoise shell."

Namibia loves tortoise stories. In one, the eagle takes the tortoise for a ride and the tortoise returns with an enlarged understanding of life beyond the water hole. Perhaps that is why I'm fascinated by the tortoise—a recurring motif in my work. Rich in myths, its home is on its back.

My play, *The Missing Namibian* (not yet published, performed in Sweden and Namibia 1996), features an unusual Namibian—a tortoise traveler. It is based on the travels of Saul Shepherd, a Herero herd boy, in the 1830s. The travel writer Capt. James Alexander took Shepherd to England to school him. Shepherd returned to work for missionaries, teach, and eventually become interpreter for a powerful chief. Shepherd must have known five languages. Then his trail disappears into the desert sand.

When I seek a language for what is happening to my body or for inner states of consciousness, I tap into a tradition that invokes the journey as an inner landscape. This features in *Desert December* in the life of Seth, the boy, who travels by donkey cart across the desert. And we are creatures of climate, of longitude and latitude. Turn up the heat a few degrees and we sizzle. Turn it down and we freeze to death. We live in that narrow band. So we wander through contrasting landscapes, between extremities, put down our tent for a while, and travel on. Namibia is a land of such extremes. These are some of the inscapes I inhale and exhale when I put a word onto paper. In French the words "journey" and "journal" share the same root.

TZ: One of the recurrent metaphors in *The Writer's Voice* (Haarhoff 1998) is that of an aquifer—an underground water—that rests in the deep psyche of the person setting out to write. From this aquifer, if tapped and allowed to flow, springs the faculty and facility to "green with text the land we live in."

DH: Deserts are holy extremities. Places of aloneness and solitude. Yet of community. Namibia has struck me as a Jungian country, if there is such a thing. A biblical "dry and thirsty land" where like Moses you try to take water from the rock—the underground porous rock that holds the pocket of water. Dry on the surface but with deep underground lakes beneath. All that inaccessible water is like the unconscious. You know of its existence because of the steam that rises up from a place such as Dragon's Breath in the north of Namibia. Much of Namibian travel writing involves a search for a mysterious source of water. A lake with no bottom. Other writings feature the Herero in the war of 1907 fleeing the Germans, dying in the Thirstland crossing, while inaccessible, far underneath were the deep waters.

In a country where history has involved water-hole politics, the land breeds those mythical figures—water diviners. I once scripted a TV documentary on a man who combined skills—ancient rods and seismic soundings—to locate the aquifer. The program featured a traditional diviner in Damaraland and his connection to the earth, and a German hydrologist who believed in dowsing. First he used the rod, then the sounding machine. As wells were for the Celts, so windmills are for Namibians—icons. They are scattered individually throughout the land, but if you dig enough, you find connection to communal streams.

So aquifers become a powerful metaphor for the writing life. Seamus Heaney, the Irish poet, likens poetry to divining underground water—an attractive image for people writing in an arid Namibia: "The diviner resembles the poet in his function of making contact with what lies hidden and in his ability to make palpable what was sensed or raised." I noticed this process emerging in student writing as workshop participants connected their inner journey to the outer Namibian world. Namibians seem keen on documentaries that feature an individual up against the mysteries of the land and its lack of surface water.

TZ: You move between many genres. Any thoughts on the way words work in different forms of writing?

DH: In TV, of course, unlike the written text, the word is often in competition with the visual stimulus which you are framing as a writer. The medium encourages a diet of words, whereas in the text the word is the conjurer of the visible. Radio—a widely popular medium in Namibia, where the wind-up radio is taking waves to remote areas—also depends on the word as a visual stimulant, as in my children's radio drama for the Namibian Broadcasting Corporation *The Colour of Water,* aimed at raising awareness about water issues.

TZ: In *Skeletons,* your Windhoek play presented on the eve of Namibia's independence, the characters Dorsa (Thirsty) and Sonderwater (Without water) journey into the earth in search of "skeleton kin" and for the purer, life-giving waters of the past. There they reticulate the aquifers, directing the springs to the orchids of the workers' communes on the surface. The Chorus explains: "Long ago we were water. Strong water. Then the colonials came and we dried up. Now we can break this drought and we can flow again like a strong stream." Then, the puzzle and its answer: "We are thirsty for freedom. We don't have water, but we are water" (*Goats, Oranges and Skeletons* 2000a), *The Writer's Voice* reminds us that all too often, teaching methods in southern Africa have eroded "our belief in our creative abilities and in the possibilities of our imaginations . . . the message many of us have received has left us feeling like a barren land. Few teachers have affirmed that we each contain deep communal wells inside us." To use the question in *The Writer's Voice:* "How do we divine story water hidden in deep aquifers and raise it to the surface?"

DH: As a young aspirant writer I looked with envy on those who grew green patches of words and fed themselves and fed their readers. It was called talent: writers born, not made. And many "successful" writers have cultivated that idea to protect their territory. Through my own struggles I have come to understand that anyone who has the gift of literacy can write. It's a question of connecting to the stories inside, to the dreaming brain and engaging the discipline. Practicing this applied art.

In a workshop I'd tell stories, for stories don't impose meaning but allow the listener to determine their own meanings. For example, the story about the gods hiding the secret of life so no humans could find it. And one god coming up with the idea "let's hide the secret inside the human being, for that is the last place they'll look." I try to build confidence, getting (sometimes tricking) workshop participants into their own creativity and imagination and convincing them that if they have enough words (and they don't need to know the whole dictionary), then they can teach themselves to write, and so tap the aquifer to green the land.

Then there is much schooling to unlearn. Learning how to express, not impress. Learning that you grow a text from humble beginnings. It does not arrive instantly perfect from an inspired pen. Mark Twain suggested if we were taught to speak the way we are taught to write we would all stutter.

TZ: When you work with others, how does this work begin?

DH: We begin by recollecting and recreating the drama and detail of that formative incident I mentioned. I also encourage imaginative reconstruction, for much of our memory is fiction. Then we look at how to structure a story. We begin to craft the piece through several drafts. Teasing out the drama, the detail, the description, the dialogue. Beginnings and endings. Then I involve the group in editing each other's stories. I act as a mentor, a writer's guide.

TZ: Do you find that encouraging personal, individual stories creates a resonance elsewhere?

DH: I move in a circle between the uniqueness of my thumb print and a place of belonging to the universe (all is one). Paradoxically when I honor the drama, details, and dialogue of my unique story that is when readers say, "That is my story too." In this way stories constitute a common language beneath our different languages. A few years back I was working with street teenagers in Kampala. They were illiterate so we worked orally. One teenager told his story. "I was abused. I ran away from home. I ended up on the streets." The other teenagers were disinterested because this was everybody's story. So I asked the teenager, "Where did you sleep on your first night?" (a veranda), "What did you sleep on?" (a cardboard box), "What was on the box?" (a picture of soap),

"Where did you find it?" (a trash can). And so on. The response to these questions elicited the interest and involvement of the street audience.

TZ: Apartheid's "dominant narrative" prescribes zones of exclusion and is obsessed with the demarcation of others by producing what you call the "group lie," or the "minor myths" that "depend on defensive strategies and on guarding cultural boundaries." (*The Writer's Voice*, 12). Apartheid's legacy bulldozed not only the physical habitat but the soul-soil as well—engineering, engraming, and etching into the consciousness of all within its reach the prohibitors and inhibitors of creative expression. Instead of the prescriptive, do you find a use for the pre-script-ive?

DH: I love the word play. And I go for your pre-script-ive. It is not only schooling but a society that has denied many their creative expression. Many have had the word "No" said to them. I believe there is a place of "Yes" to go back to. Before the limiting script was imposed. That we are alive and have work to do in the world is a "Yes." Often in childhood there is something we can reconnect to—a way of being and seeing. Or a story of how a grandfather or grandmother coped—an ancestral memory of an alternative story that we can reactivate in our own lives. Through writing we can recreate and reclaim our creativity, imagination—our birthright.

For example, in the collection of autobiographical texts arising from the workshop supported by the Basler Afrika Bibliographien: Namibia Resource Centre–Southern Africa Library, *Personal Memories: Namibian Texts in Process,* Dolores Soloman remembers her grandparents having to leave their land in terms of group area relocation. Instead of portraying them as victims, the focus is on the vibrant life and sense of community that such an imposition engenders.

TZ: The preparedness of the writer to posit "as if" fictions resonates with childhood's necessity to play. The capacity to (re)move boundaries and borders, to explore the ambivalent (the right and left brain interplay), through an ambidextrous duality if you will, avoids, as you cite in *The Writer's Voice,* what Achebe has called "malignant fictions"—those fictions that "never say let's pretend." Strangely, this playing with fiction (the "fluids of fiction") produces truth, but not necessarily fact. How reliable a healing is this? How does the scribe avoid the coagulation of literalness or literalism—of becoming fixed or penned in by his or her own words?

DH: "As if" or "let's pretend." Fine words. They open us to the imaginative life that affects and changes our reality. These words can shape-shift our belief bubbles and bring healing. Because through imagination we connect one memory to another. We re-member as opposed to dismember. In *Personal Memories* Gerhard Narimab describes his Grade One nightmare—the sadistic teacher. "When Mr. Beukes asked a question, I was new and excited. I jumped up and answered. The next thing I knew was that something painful and hot was cutting through my skin." This experience prompted Narimab, who used his imagination, to create a positive outcome, to take up a teaching career. I think we love fiction because we are fiction—fiction overlaying the facts of our lives.

TZ: Could you expand on the connection between fiction and autobiography? Are the stories we tell about ourselves fiction/autobiography? Where does the one merge into the other?

DH: My understanding of story is that what happens to me and how I choose to tell it is not bound in a cause-effect relationship. So in an autobiography, for instance, the personal version of what happened is one of the truths among many. It is relative, a postmodern perspective, a way of seeing that sits alongside other versions. Victor Frankl, who goes through the worst that humans can do to humans, asserts that the greatest freedom we have is the freedom to choose how we will respond to a given set of circumstances.

For example, in Kavevangua Kahengua's story "The Grey Overcoat" *(Personal Memories)*, the boy Rinongee's great passion is to move from "herdsboy to schoolboy." He falls asleep near the fire in his older brother's precious overcoat earned from hard labor in the mines. The coat catches fire. His brother beats him and prevents him from going to school for a few weeks and makes him look after the donkey. Rinongee chooses to dismiss the incident as a hurdle, and it intensifies his aim to get an education.

When you literalize a metaphor, you then end up with a malignant fiction that passes itself off as fact: apartheid, gender superiority, religious fundamentalism, national egotism. In these instances I assert my space, my version of the story at the expense of somebody else or another group. That is why it is important to develop a national literature comprising a people's own stories to counter the official versions about them. The book on black South African women's poetry, *Breaking the Silence,* is one example of this.

The danger is that someone—a writer—can get stuck on a story, a particular way of seeing reality. That's when we get trapped. Perhaps the answer is to keep on reinventing ourselves. As the ninety-five-year-old poet Stanley Kunitz suggests at the end of one of his poems, "I am not done with my changes." So a writer also needs to find new metaphors for saying, "living on the edge of language."

TZ: The edge of language?

DH: I'm thinking here of the interrelationship between words and experience. We experience something and find language for it. Then the experience moves on and sometimes the language gets stuck. Our words grow old. Clichéd. Worn down from overuse. Blunted. We no longer have the words. The map no longer depicts the territory. So we have to coin, recreate. Find a new metaphor that in turn shifts the experience. Our language helps create our reality so we also need new language to shift that reality. Southern African jargon such as "shifting the goalposts" or "leveling the playing fields" or even "struggle literature" needs new definition.

TZ: I recall that you have acknowledged that at this edge a surprising yet familiar guest seems to start to take up habitation in your own work—and that this only takes place after the house of the work is scrubbed and cleaned. Authoring, then, as a collaboration with resonances of the self that cannot be circum"scribed" or a"scribed" by an act of conscious crafting?

DH: I think that we draw the writing from deep within us. The unconscious seeking voice. When this raw rock surfaces from the mine, only then can we sift, cut, and polish it and give ourselves the joy of crafting a piece of work. First right-brain discovery, then left-brain attention to technique. There is a story of a nobleman who compliments a roadside potter on his pot. The potter responds: "What interests me is the shape inside the pot. What interests me is what is left after the pieces have been broken."

TZ: Are these the silences that surround the text?

DH: The shape inside the pot is possibly the silence. We are in the presence of mystery. What we leave out of a text is still present, ghosting in the tone, allowing the reader to cohabit the house of text. Share the space. As writers, we need to allow the reader to co-create. If you look at any national literature, there are overt texts that attempt to dictate to the reader as to how they should respond. Other texts invoke a conversation by allowing the imagination of the reader to fill in the spaces.

TZ: Is it possible, then, that the project of working towards defining a national identity stultifies a more resonant autobiography?

DH: When you travel, you reflect on who you are. V. S. Naipaul said that the British traveling in India reflected not on India but on their Britishness. Namibia has a travelogue history that reflects this same inward gaze. There is a tendency to constitute what you see as fact.

TZ: Tell us more about "re-membering" and "re-story-ing." What are the tools you use in workshops that assist in this healing process?

DH: Re-membering is putting together what belongs together. In a workshop we look at alternative versions of the same event. Salman Rushdie says, "Every story is an act of censorship." If I'm telling it one way, I am excluding other ways of telling. When I was teacher training in Namibia, I noticed that despite my intervention, students in the classroom reverted to the way they had been taught. They had not processed that formative story. I got them to write out how they had been taught. Then they wrote the hidden story that the dominant version was masking. Then they had a third go at the story—writing it out in the third person—beginning to fictionalize it. Once they had processed the story to the power of three, they were free to choose how they wanted to teach.

TZ: So, the difference between "writing" and "wright-ing"?

DH: Writing for me is the first outpouring of text—a kind of chaos, as in the creation myths of the world. "Wright-ing" is allowing the order hidden in all that jumble of words to arrive—setting that world to order.

TZ: In the theater we encourage actors not to develop a "third eye"—that imagined critical audience that causes an actor to stifle engagement in the moment and to replace action with indicative, self-censured performance tailored for a/effect. Is this problem perhaps similar to the right-brain-creator and the left-brain-editor tension?

DH: I respond to this distinction. In the Upanishads there is a text: "Two birds—inseparable friends—sit in the same tree. The one eats the sweet fruit. The other watches without eating." A writer is both birds. But perhaps passionately in the beginning, the first bird. Then the watcher bird. In an autobiography this could take the form of the writer witnessing her or his own story. The kind of text where you feel the writer is also writing for their own understanding. But watching with compassion not judgment.

TZ: And if we call being caught between two brains "writer's block," how do you work through this?

DH: One definition of writer's block is that I am not meeting my standards (a left-brain imposition from outside or within). So perhaps the way around this is to give myself permission to write anything. Whatever I write is acceptable. To play in the right brain. Tomorrow I'll recover standards. I.e., holding off the critical left-brain judgment that says that the writing must come out perfect or it is no good at all. We grow a piece of writing. I also think we need to get away from the notion of writing as "good" or "bad." Rather talk of aliveness or a draft still needing the breath of life to be blown into it.

TZ: How has your relationship with this lack of flow changed as you have grown?

DH: I have become kinder to myself. Letting a piece of writing be. Holding back prejudgment. Giving it time to find its way. The Spanish poet Garcia Lorca spoke of the goblin wind of creativity—*el duende*. In Spanish *el duende* is similar to a muse—the quixotic force behind a person's creative life. Lorca writes "*El duende* can even overcome inexperience and poor material." He tells the story of a flamenco contest where an eighty-year-old woman, competing against young women with "waists like water," won the dance event. Such stories have grown me.

TZ: The trickster figure is common to much African theater—a necessary inverter and subverter of predictability. The trickster features in your own thoughts about writing, as memory personified.

DH: Ah the trickster . . . the joker . . . the god . . . reminding me of lightness, of standing on my head and looking at the world upside down. A child does this naturally before the education system hypnotizes him or her to construe the world in a particular way. The trickster welcomes and hosts the ghosts in my life. Invites them in. The monster who threatens is befriended and given a task to do. It becomes guardian of the forest. Joseph Campbell, that great mythologist, argues that devils are unacknowledged gods. And Carl Jung suggests that there is another me (who ghosts around my version of me) that I need to get to know. A twin possibility. The trickster plays with these alternatives.

In Namibian folklore there is the Heitsi Eibeb of the wounded knee or the praying mantis. These figures are ambivalent in that they are both gods and tricksters. They work against seriousness in a text, against one-dimensional readings. Tricksters also perform a prophetic function. In my play *Guerrilla Goatherd* (in *Goats, Oranges and Skeletons* 2000a), Maljan, the mad one, observes with a mythic eye the 1922 Bondelswartz rebellion against the South African forces.

TZ: It seems that even the fleshing of a fiction (a false or generated memory) as text harnesses possible maverick and malicious psychological forces in a more positive way. This auto/biography (the trickster "memory" generating fictions of past and present) may lead a writer to reinvent or to "re-member" our lives. Is this the joy of metaphor?

DH: This is one of the tentacles of the giant octopus, metaphor. Another is that metaphor elevates the writing into mystery. Into the unknown. Metaphor moves us from the expectation that truth is literal. And then we stumble on the hidden connections.

TZ: What do our personal life stories have to do with our writing? Our life fictions?

DH: I think our fictions draw on our lives. Stanley Kunitz suggests, "First I must create the person who will write these poems." Often the energy point or resonance in a story is where the incident or character touches on the life of the writer even if the writer is not aware of it.

TZ: Myth, as you remind us, is story. But "a myth," casually used, is a description of something nonfactual, or nonscientific. What is it, in the act of writing, that secures a resonance with fidelity?

DH: Joseph Campbell's definition of myth is a lie on the outside and a truth on the inside. I don't think we can ever get to literal truth. Only metaphoric truth, emotional truth. Rabindranath Tagore, the Indian writer, says the one who paints his life imprinted on his memory is an artist, not an historian. He retains or omits, makes big things small or small things big, and exchanges foreground for background. Fidelity to a deeper "who" rather than the presented surface "who."

TZ: One last question, if I may. We talked earlier of travel, and you used a tortoise metaphor: "The word 'motion' huddles inside the word 'emotion' waiting to stretch its legs." Share more of your tortoise(s) with us.

DH: The tortoise is both African and universal. A mythical creature whose shell was used for divination. A story-rich creature, the tortoise symbolizes the waters, the moon, the Earth Mother; the beginning of creation, time, immortality, fecundity, regeneration . . . In China it is possessed with oracular powers. The Cosmic Tree grows out of the back of the tortoise. William Carlos Williams writes about it:

> In the beginning
> there was a great tortoise
> who supported the world.
> Upon him
> all ultimately rests . . . .
> He is all wise
> and can outrun the hare.
> In the night his eyes carry him
> to unknown places.

Apart from content, poems are also about the poetic process. We rest on language just as the Native Americans lived on the back of the mythical Turtle Island (one of the original names for America). Friend and poet Bob Commin's cover design for my recent poetry volume, *Tortoise Voices* (2002b), depicts a tortoise in a blue sea, the world (with Africa prominent) mapped on its back. So we writers travel with the tortoise. When we write, we gather tortoise wisdom at a more intuitive level than the rational mind can comprehend. We see with night eyes. I trust that this ancient creature will keep carrying me in words.

References Cited

HAARHOFF, DORIAN. *Bordering*. Johannesburg: Justified Press, 1991a.
——. *Desert December*. Cape Town: Songololo, 1991b.
——. *The Wild South West: Frontier Myths and Metaphors in Literature Set in Namibia*. Johannesburg: Witwatersrand University Press, 1991c.
——. *Water from the Rock*. Windhoek: New Namibia Books, 1992
——. *Legs, Bones and Eyes*. Windhoek: New Namibia Books, 1994a
——. *Guano Girl*. Johannesburg: Justified Press, 1994b.
——. *Aquifers and Dust*. Johannesburg: Justified Press, 1994c.
——, ed. *Personal Memories: Namibian Texts in Process*. Basel: Basler Afrika Bibliographien, 1996.
——. *Big Red and Dangerous*. Cape Town: Kagiso, 1996. (Title changed to *Space Rider* 2001.)
——, ed. *The Inner Eye: Namibian Poetry in Process*. Basel: Basler Afrika Bibliographien, 1997.
——. *The Writer's Voice: A Workbook for Writers in Africa*. Johannesburg: Zebra/Struik Press, 1998.
——. *Goats, Oranges and Skeletons: A Trilogy of Namibian Independence Plays*. Ed. Terence Zeeman. Windhoek: New Namibia Books, 2000a.
——. *Tortoise Stories: Stories from Africa and the Great Elsewhere*. Vol. 1. Johannesburg: Goblin Studios, 2000b. (compact disc)
——. *Space Racer*. Cape Town: Miller, 2001.
——. *Grandfather Enoch's Pipe*. Windhoek: Gamsberg Macmillan, 2002a.
——. *Tortoise Voices*. Cape Town: Mercer Books, 2002b.
——, ed. *Once Upon a Life: Stories from a Creative Writing Workshop*. Cape Town: Mercer Books, 2002c.

Further reading

DOBELL, L. *Swapo's Struggle for Namibia, 1960–1991: War by Other Means*. Basel: Basler Afrika Bibliographien, 1998.
GROTH, S. *Namibia—The Wall of Silence: The Dark Days of the Liberation Struggle*. Cape Town: David Philip, 1995.
LEYS, C., and J. SAUL, eds. *Namibia's Liberation Struggle: The Two-edged Sword*. Athens: Ohio University Press, 1998.

LOCKET, CECILY, ed. *Breaking the Silence: A Century of South African Women's Poetry*. Johannesburg: Ad. Donker, 1990.

NUJOMA, SAM. *Where Others Wavered: The Autobiography of Sam Nujoma*. Loontoo: Panaf Books, 2001.

SAUNDERS, CHRISTOPHER. "Liberation and Democracy: A Critical Reading of Sam Nujoma's *Autobiography*." In *Re-examining Liberation in Namibia: Political Culture since Independence 2003*, pp. 87–98. Uppsala: Nordic Africa Institute, 2003.

SHITYUWETE, H. *Never Follow the Wolf: The Autobiography of a Namibian Freedom Fighter*. London: Kliptown Books, 1990.

SWAPO. *To Be Born a Nation*. London: Zed, 1981.

ZEEMAN, TERENCE. "Confronting the Mask: Some Contemporary Namibian Contexts of Protest." In *African Theatre: Southern Africa*, pp. 23–38. Oxford: James Currey Publishers, 2004.

April 2002

Reflections on Identity

Breyten Breytenbach interviewed by Marilet Sienaert

THROUGH HIS FORMAL and stylistic innovations—such as the erosion of the generic distinctions between poetry and prose and the use of surrealist techniques—along with thematic innovations brought about by his interest in Buddhist thought, Breyten Breytenbach has made an invaluable contribution to the transformation of South African writing in general and Afrikaans literature in particular. At the same time, his stance as human rights activist, his imprisonment on a charge of terrorism during the apartheid era, and his role as cofounder of the Gorée Institute in Senegal made him a public figure (Galloway 1990) whose provocative views are both contested and acclaimed. His *oeuvre* covers a wide range, with the travel memoir *'n Seisoen in die paradys* (A season in paradise) (1976), an account of his imprisonment *The True Confessions of an Albino Terrorist* (1984), and *Return to Paradise* (1994) forming an autobiographical triptych. *Dog Heart: A Travel Memoir* (1999), in which he explores his relationship to the area of his birth, has been described as a "loose, almost miscellaneous" memoir "[p]art journal, part essay on autobiography" and containing "searching meditations on the elusiveness of memory" (Coetzee 1999). In addition, Breytenbach is an accomplished painter, who has produced several self-portraits that interlace with his autobiographical texts in an exploration of the vicissitudes of the I.

This interview first appeared in Marilet Sienaert, *The I of the Beholder: The Art and Writing of Breyten Breytenbach* (Cape Town: Kwela, 2002). We would like to thank Marilet Sienaert for permission to reprint it here.

MARILET SIENAERT: Exile and associated identities of the drifter, the nomad, and the outsider feature prominently in your writing. It is often used positively to evoke a state you describe as inhabiting the "Middle World." Could you elaborate on this notion of identity, and what exactly it implies?

BREYTEN BREYTENBACH: In my essay "Notes from the Middle World," I tried to suggest that the Middle World is an emerging archipelago somewhere beyond exile. Exile is a state of waiting for the changes that would permit you to return to the place of origin; it is also a way of life defined by your relationship to that lost paradise. The Middle World, inhabited by the bums of the Global Village, is the position of being neither here nor there: you can neither return to where you came from, nor will you ever be integrated in the place you fled to. (To accede to the Middle World it is not necessary to be geographically displaced: Kafka lived there although he never really left Prague.) Middle World "uncitizens," as I call them, share a number of traits, notably in their attitude to the state, power, patriotism, morality, food, aesthetics, property, language, hybridity, identity itself. Of itself it implies the acceptance and practice of multiple identities.

MS: The mirror as powerful metaphor of identity can be traced throughout your art and writing. Similarly, in your recent play *(Die Toneelstuk)* the many selves mirror our multiple identities but also confront the viewer with a real mirror-as-prop to include him or her in the transmutations of the characters on stage.[1] The play offers a provocative social commentary on a futile collective attempt at self-retribution for past wrongs, but the mirrored identities paradoxically imply a *one for all* and *all for one* sense of shared responsibility, not only in South Africa, but for all the wrongs ever committed in the whole world. Your alter-ego Baba Halfjan parodies this as follows: *"As swart man is ek skaam dat ek nie meer gedoen het om die wit varke uit die bome te verwilder nie. En ek is jammer oor die Tutsi's wat so in hulle honderdduisende met knuppel en skoffelpik deur die Hutus uit die lewe gehelp is. En ek is jammer vir die Palestyne wat so onderdruk word deur die rassistiese en terroristiese staat van Israel . . . ek belowe om dit nooit weer te doen nie . . ."* (As a black man I am ashamed that I did not do more to expulse the white pigs from the trees. And I am sorry about the Tutsis who in their hundreds and thousands helped the Hutus out of life with *knuppel* and *skoffelpik* (club or bludgeon and pickaxe). And I am sorry for the Palestinians who are so oppressed by the racist and terrorist state of Israel . . . I

---

1. *Buraq, the Unemployed Donkey* is Breytenbach's most recent play. It was published as a "workbook" for the production of the play and was published in-house by the Danish Centre for Culture and Development, in collaboration with the Gorée Institute, Senegal. The production workshop was held in South Africa in 2003 to consolidate the artistic contents of the work and to seek cultural exchange and collaboration with South African artists and cultural organizations.

promise never to do it again . . .). Am I correct to assume that this shared responsibility springs from our shared identity as human beings (hence the futility of self-flagellation), and could you please elaborate on this? And also, specifically in this context of social responsibility, whether you experience the creative act as a social act?

BB: The creative act, as displacement or extension of consciousness, always has social resonances. It is an intervention provoking an interaction with the environment in which we all live—social, political, cultural, or physical—even when that act is confined to its page or space of inception. It furthermore relates to the rhythm, the flow, and the breaks of the primordial movements and spaces, the need to placate and exorcise and escape and imitate, underlying all shared human consciousness. The mirror can be seen as the physical location where transformation becomes visible.

It is a pity the South African authorities do not understand how vitally important it is to promote free and vigorous, even conflicting, cultural spaces. South Africa is historically, politically, and culturally a construct. The only way it can progress is to keep on inventing itself—and it must progress, because stagnation will allow the unhealed wounds to fester; things will fall apart. It is in the cultural terrain, by means of creative acts, that the *deep questions* can be identified, enunciated, shaped, and transformed: identity, memory, responsibility, hybridity, diversity, inclusive tolerance, the function of imagination, the progressive dialectic between shared national goals forged in a painful struggle for dignity, and emancipation (maybe even "nationhood"), and the specificities of mother tongues and religions and cultures linked to localities and own histories.

The creative act, ideally, is ethical: naked, as close as possible to "truth" in experience and observation, carrying its recognition and acceptance of responsibility. However, it does not necessarily conform to the constructs and discourses of public morality; in fact, in order to be effective (heightening the awareness of textures) it will probably challenge those comforts.

We obviously share responsibility for our story on earth and even for that invention or interpretation called History—for the shaping of communal perception through the ordering of past time in categories and ages and epochs such as the Classical Period and the Middle Ages and the Renaissance . . . is always a retrospective definition. "Collective guilt," however, is an ahistorical and apolitical enterprise (one may even suggest that it is amoral) to retroactively impose a morality on the past in the light of present-day convictions and hypocrisies. Not only is it a self-indulgent effort to simplify complex processes, but this accusation of group guilt (a flimsily camouflaged power play), preferably addressed to those of another tribe (and thus it becomes racist), is also intended to paint those of us on "the right side" a paler shade of snow. "Collective guilt" promotes amnesia; it obfuscates the understanding of how and why oppressive systems and régimes came about; it obliterates the demarcations between "good" and "evil" because the criminally responsible actors can now be seen as products of group characteristics; it takes away personal responsibility. Consciousness is also "free will" since it leads to an understanding of the implications of thought and action, at least potentially. As a conscious human being making my own decisions, I reject the notion of shared guilt and thus the need to confess and restitute, defined and confined solely by a shared color and culture.

Of course this does not mean that the creative act ("the sweetest form of lying") can save your skin from contamination. Are there not compromises when we attempt to transform "life" into words and images? The mirror of speaking can be obscure. It is said that poetry and the practice of Zen are faced with a similar conundrum: they try to directly convey the essence of reality (or experience), knowing full well that the conveyance can only be an allusion. Or is it an illusion? Worse, the means of trying to trap reality constitute its own realness, subject to specific laws. In poetry, as in Zen, we doubt metaphor, possibly because it so often is only an approximation. In Zen philosophy the inadequacy of language is emphasized, and yet Zen endlessly produces "verses of truth." It attests to the fact that we have to employ words and letters (as also images and sounds) if we wish to move beyond the ordinary conditions of being human. The task of realism in pursuing reality beyond metaphor will always have to be accompanied by endless battles against metaphor fought through metaphors.

MS: I am interested in the scapegoat identity which you persistently emphasize in your recent work such as the plays, and also in "pathological victimhood" (*Die Toneelstuk:* 72) as its underbelly. . . . It is again exemplified in your painting on the cover of this book, by the central hand reminiscent of the pierced hands of Christ. Traditionally, of course, the scapegoat had a deceptively salutary role in society as it acted as receptacle for all our projected fears and hatred that could then seemingly be destroyed. Can you elaborate on the way in which you use the contemporary scapegoat to drive your point?

BB: In South Africa, maybe more than elsewhere, we glorify victimhood. Blame us on history, we say. We are fashioned (buffeted, maimed, oppressed) by dark forces beyond our control and understanding. We mistake slothful ignorance for pragmatic realism. Do we not live on a harsh continent, and is it not true that Africa is not for sissies? So we embellish the cult of "the strong man"—as leader, prophet, savior, he who can give *meaning* and show the way forward. There *must* be *meaning*. And meaning, of course, will be simple. We believe we are entitled to simple and meaningful "truths." The dissident, he or she who brings doubt, must be ignored, ridiculed, or chased away. The effect of this macho mumbo-jumbo is a brutalization of public awareness, a dumbing down of shared intelligence, a reinforcement of our traditional patriarchal and hierarchical social structures, a confirmation of religious orthodoxies and political barbarism and cultural hegemonies, a renunciation of personal responsibility, an impediment to the development of vigorous civil societies, a repression of the creative power of hybridization, a flourishing of hypocrisy.

Somebody—I don't remember who—made the perceptive point that Russians since all time and right through communism to their present liberal democracy, depended and still do on a patron-protegé relationship. The patron might have been the boyar or the abbot or the tsar or the commissar. . . . This meant, and still means (as also in our South African case) that democratic and civil institutions are not granted the possibility to develop real power. Since things cannot work in that way, it also means that only a strong and undemocratic leadership can try to ram through the necessary transformations of society (this, again, is true also of South Africa), but they always fail because they think they can do so *without being transformed themselves.*

The other side of the "scapegoat" coin is the "icon." If I may add a personal note: finding myself in the scapegoat/icon configuration, I notice that the possible area of perception of my work is putrid and poisoned, obliterating a critical reading and focusing in a pathological way on the person behind the work. This is why I have decided never to exhibit in South Africa again and have to consider very carefully before ever again publishing.

MS: How would you comment on the boundedness of identities on the one hand (for example, the broad sense of belonging to a group of people who share the same language, the same history, and the same place) and, on the other hand, the evolving yet perfectly complete self-in-metamorphosis evoked in your work? I understand this latter self, this "I" in the poem or painting which is premised on transformation, to always reinvent itself as a matter of principle. In this lies the potential for renewal and change, for relating to the familiar in new and creative ways. Is it possible to marry this state of being to a sense of belonging and of social community, so often ring-fenced by specific traditions or limiting ways of thinking?

BB: Identity is the result of a process of awareness. "It" comes into being through consciousness. I don't believe its existence predates the process, even though there are aspects of identity—inherited cultural traits—which you have or may be given without knowing so, and these you may discover only later in life. In other words, what we call "identity" is the reflection of a process to which all our senses and attributes, such as memory and imagination, contribute. By the way, if you know this, you can trace how the various components of "self" interact to generate consciousness. That is why I say, *the I is a mirror to the self.* Or the other way around: *the self is mirror to the I.* The apparent dichotomy is between "the moment of taking note," using a (temporarily) fixed take on the self to serve as orientation and situation, in order to recognize the "process" which is change and motion. (That, too, is why I claim, thing is process, i.e., our apprehension of its "thingness" is never static, quite beside the fact that the object [and the subject!] will be going through modifications, however slow, due to aging and positioning.)

This sense of I (identity, the I-ing of self, id-entity) is dependent on interaction with some thing or some body "out there." Community is usually the mirror. "I am a human through people." We identify/situate ourselves in our interaction with and relation to cultural constructs such as language, religion, ideology, a shared narrative of history or destiny, adherence or resistance to specific values. In this sense, the shaping of identity and the resultant (self)identification is very much the product of a given society.

For the person involved in the transformation and expansion of awareness, it is *consciousness* that matters, the flow with its rhythms and breaks—not the successive stops and crutches and snatches of I. I is but the focal and transit point (and transition) of perception. The awareness of awareness grows from the constant dialectic between self and nonself. Self is mirrored in nonself, and the other way around. Self is ever-expanding emptiness—which doesn't mean that it isn't cluttered and clamorous; more precisely, the *awareness* of the changing, making, and unmaking of "self" is the dilation of emptiness. One is always becoming nothing. Put differently, one is always becoming death. And that's as physical a fact as a black cat!

Paradox: no awareness of perception except through I/growing perception brings the rubbing out of I. This is what's known as *using the I to destroy it.*

From what I've tried to say now flow a number of observations referring to your questions. Mirror, in a manner of speaking, is the tool and the manifestation of self. This is self-evident! Mirror is "soul." Mirror is the other. Ego is the departing echo of being. Measuring the time of remembering will allow you to establish the distance between the small bang of inception and the fetus of definition. And further: it goes without saying that one is never just one fixed identity—except maybe in the arbitrariness of some administrative grid: one is always many selves, shoals and shelves and elves of self, depending on the need or the circumstances and environment—private/public, child/woman/ mother/lover, Afrikaner/South African/African/human ... What we know as memory may well be the dwelling-place of all the salvaged ghostly selves, the "ancestors," the "ghosts of saved and unsaved versions of history competing for attention."

To "itself," self is a compass, not a map. Sometimes a grace of forgetting. To society, self is a way of being and of behaving. Descartes, it would seem, had as motto, *Larvatus prodeo*, "I set out behind an actor's mask." This allows for an interesting link between the larva, waiting to become the butterfly of death, and mask! As well that I move for and towards "God"! Martin Versveld wrote: "... the ego is the mask of the person."[2] In this sense then, identity is a mask imagined by communal traditions, conventions, and expectations: a larva in the process of becoming the butterfly which will fly away.

References Cited

BREYTENBACH, BREYTEN. *'n Seisoen in die paradys*. Cape Town: Human & Rousseau, 1976.

———. *The True Confessions of an Albino Terrorist*. London: Faber and Faber, 1984.

———. *Return to Paradise*. London: Faber and Faber, 1994.

———. *Dog Heart: A Travel Memoir*. London: Faber and Faber, 1999.

———. *Die toneelstuk ('n belydenis in twee bedrywe)*. Cape Town: Human & Rousseau, 2001.

COETZEE, J. M. "Against the South African Grain." *New York Review of Books* 46, 14 (Sept. 1999). http://www.nybooks.com/articles/article-preview?article id=373

VERSVELD, MARTIN. *Food for Thought: A Philosopher's Cookbook*. Cape Town: The Carrefour Press, 1991.

Further Reading

COETZEE, AMPIE. "Breyten Breytenbach." In *Encyclopaedia of Life Writing*, edited by Margaretta Jolly. London: Fitzroy Dearborn, 2001.

COULLIE, JUDITH LÜTGE, and J. U., JACOBS eds. *a.k.a. Breyten Breytenbach: Critical Approaches to His Writings and Paintings*. Amsterdam: Rodopi Press, 2004.

GALLOWAY, FRANCIS. *Breyten Breytenbach as Openbare Figuur*. Pretoria: HAUM-Literêr, 1990.

---

2. Versveld is an Afrikaans philosopher at the University of Cape Town and author of, among other things, *Food for Thought*.

GOLZ, HANS-GEORG. *Staring at Variations: The Concept of "Self" in Breyten Breytenbach's Mouroir: Mirror Notes of a Novel*. Frankfurt: Peter Lang, 1995.
JACOBS, J. U. "Breyten Breytenbach and the South African Prison Book." *Theoria* 68 (1986): 95–105.
PEDRI, NANCY. "The Verbal and Visual Mirrors of Postcolonial Identity in Breyten Breytenbach's *All One Horse*." *Journal of Literary Studies* 2 (2002): 295–312.
SCHALKWYK, DAVID. "Confession and Solidarity in the Prison Writing of Breyten Breytenbach and Jeremy Cronin." *Research in African Literatures* 25, 1 (1994): 23–45.
SIENAERT, MARILET. *The I of the Beholder: Identity Formation in the Art and Writing of Breyten Breytenbach*. Cape Town: Kwela, 2002.
WILKINSON, JANE. "A Lexicon of Exile: Migrations of Meaning in Breyten Breytenbach's *Return to Paradise*." *Textus*. Special issue on Narratives of Exile, 10, 1 (1997): 167–180.

June 2001

Rhythmic Redoublings

Rob Nixon interviewed by Sarah Nuttall and Cheryl-Ann Michael

THIS INTERVIEW TOOK place in the air, in cyberspace, and across the ocean floor between Cape Town and New York City, where Rob Nixon was living at the time. Almost certainly this kind of fluid location breathes new meaning into what it is we say to one another. In any case it seems a suggestive form of dislocation, feeding well into the concerns of Nixon's writing. Nixon grew up in South Africa and has lived for long periods in England and the United States. He has been fascinated in his work by themes of exile, migrancy, and displacement and the effects of these on writing and the making of identities. What it is to be here and what it is to be there, what it is to be both here and there, are personal and intellectual preoccupations that shape his work. His first book, *London Calling: V. S. Naipaul, Postcolonial Mandarin* (1992) tackles the controversial reputation of the West Indian novelist and essayist Naipaul, who shares with Salman Rushdie, as Peter Hughes has remarked, "a power to strike outside the text—and to provoke its targets to strike back." In his next book, a collection of academic essays called *Homelands, Harlem and Hollywood: South African Culture and the World Beyond* (1994), Nixon turns his attention to the diverse ties between South Africa and the United States, from 1948 to South Africa's first democratic elections in 1994. He is interested in what he sees as a vexed sense of half-shared histories and a sometimes illusory sense of mutual intelligibility, as well as idioms of cosmopolitanism, transculturation, hybridity, and internationalism. *Dreambirds* (1999), a memoir based on his childhood in South Africa and his life in America as an émigré adult, is perhaps Nixon's best work yet. It returns to the themes explored in his academic writing in a new register and with a particularly powerful use of language. Nixon, in all his work, draws on the trope of mobility to breathe air and space into the words and worlds he sees and creates.

This interview originally appeared as "An Interview with Rob Nixon" conducted by Sarah Nuttall and Cheryl-Ann Michael, in *Contemporary Literature* 43, 3 (Fall 2002), pp. 423–440. We would like to thank the editors of *Contemporary Literature* (Thomas Schaub and Mary Mekemson), the University of Wisconsin Press (Margaret Walsh), Cheryl-Ann Michael, Sarah Nuttall, and Rob Nixon for kindly agreeing to this reprint and for waiving fees.

SARAH NUTTALL/CHERYL-ANN MICHAEL: Can we begin by talking about your book *Dreambirds: The Natural History of a Fantasy* as memoir—which is how you have described it? Why this choice of form? What for you are the distinctions between memoir and autobiography?

ROB NIXON: The book is a more-or-less memoir. In bookshops I have seen it shelved under biology, biography, history, memoir, and travel. I view it as an experimental hybrid. But clearly there is a strong memoir component. The distinction between memoir and autobiography is mainly one of degree: the latter ordinarily attempts to be comprehensive, whereas a memoir tends to focus on a shorter period, a single strand of one's life, or a particular trauma. It's the difference between writing My Life and writing Me and Ostriches.

One consequence of the memoir boom has been a major shift in the generational distribution of nonfictional writing about the self. Autobiographies have tended to be (although there are exceptions) end-of-life affairs. Often, like Doris Lessing's recent autobiographies, they are written by an aging author expressly to exert control over her life story, as a kind of preemptive strike against future biographers. But the recent spate of memoirs has largely been written by younger people in their thirties and forties, even in their twenties.

I'd add a further distinction. Conventionally, autobiographies provided overviews of a life of distinction; they were preceded by fame, or at least public visibility. While there have been some celebrity memoirs, the memoirs that have received the most attention—at least in America and Britain—have been written by people who were previously obscure. I'm thinking of writers like Mary Karr, Kathryn Harrison, and James McBride.

SN/CA: Presumably the histories and meanings attached to "memoir" differ considerably in the North American and South African contexts out of which you write. How, if at all, did you see yourself responding in the context of these different traditions?

RN: Yes, there are definite differences. In the United States the nineties memoir boom derived much of its buzz from the extraordinary rise of confessional talk shows: Geraldo Rivera, Ricki Lake, Jerry Springer, Jenny Jones, etc. More scandal-oriented versions of Oprah. I know South Africa has its own versions of this phenomenon. However, in the United States this TV culture of self-exposure, self-aggrandizement, and self-abasement helped fuel a literary boom in memoir and unduly influenced (in my view) what kinds of stories got told. If your agent or editor said, on reading your manuscript, that the memoir was "quiet," you knew she meant it would be hard to sell. Not enough serial killings, not enough interspecies sex.

In South Africa I suspect the situation is rather different. Not least because book culture itself is so precarious. For all sorts of reasons: poverty, the outrageous cost of imported books relative to the cost of living, the challenge of publishing in a ten-language society, and the declining status of liberal arts degrees, nonprofessional degrees, and nonprofessional knowledge in general. And, of course, the primacy of a visual/oral, TV/video/cell phone/talk radio culture. That primacy is manifest in the United States as well. But compared to the South African context, American book culture looks relatively sturdy.

Recent South African memoirs have emerged in a very different context from their U.S. counterparts, in a situation closer to the situation described by the Croatian writer, Slavenka Drakulic, in her essay collection, *Cafe Europa*. Drakulic talks about the challenge and novelty for many East European and Balkan writers of giving voice to "I." Of writing from a more personal space, rather than through the collective conventions of "us" and "we." Of course, parallels between Eastern Europe and South Africa are always very approximate, yet I think there is some genuine overlap. Especially in comparison to the United States, where "I" can seem genetically implanted as the only admissible pronoun.

I have heard that when the American publishers of Mandela's autobiography saw an early draft they were panicked by his insistent use of "we" (we in the struggle, we in the ANC) and hired an American ghostwriter both to speed up the writing and to Americanize the pronouns. To nudge him out of his collective mindset and into an American-style "I." Disturbing, that, the power of the dollar to dictate the voice of history.

On the other hand, I do think that since South Africa's democratic turn, a space has opened up for writing that probes the tensions between collective and personal commitments. The kind of tensions that Gordimer's *My Son's Story* anticipated in fictional form. During the apex of the struggle, understandably, a more Manichean vision tended to prevail. Politically and imaginatively, one saw (to adapt Gayatri Spivak's phrase) a kind of "strategic essentialism" in operation.

You asked to what extent I was responding to these different traditions. Subliminally, I was aware of potential South African, American, and British audiences. I felt the tug of these audiences, as if I were living somewhere in the middle—in St. Helena, say. But that's really less a question of audience pressure than of who I am. I have lived for long periods in all three societies, and they've all left their mark on me.

Mostly one tries not to write too deliberately. That's where writing this book felt very different from my academic ones. I had to lose my academic habit of laying down an analytical floor plan, trusting to the nerve ends of image and memory instead.

I came to understand more viscerally a comment Nadine Gordimer once made, that she tried to write posthumously, as if she were already dead. Especially in writing something as personal as a memoir, it's imperative to write from a creative space where none of the people you care about (or loathe) exist. Parents, siblings, colleagues, friends, enemies, tenure committees, imaginary American, British, South African readers . . . you have to forget them, spirit them away.

Where the issue of audience came up most directly was in diction. My diction is pretty hybrid, pretty mid-Atlantic. I use some American words (such as "roadkill") that I like and are inimitable. On the other hand, I wanted to stick to South African diction in the childhood sections. For instance, Americans don't know what a "wonky" watch is. Sometimes I would try to cut it both ways, using both "bonnet" and "hood" with reference to our car. One editor wanted me to explain who Verwoerd was. But I declined: the South African in me balked at that, it would simply have been too estranging, too much of a capitulation to an overseas vantage point.

SN/CA: A particularly interesting feature of the book is that although it is presented as memoir or autobiography, it includes a number of biographical profiles, in which people tell their stories in the first person. Why have you chosen to include these stories within a genre which conventionally explores selfhood? Would the metaphor of "ghostwriting" (a phrase you yourself use at one point in the text) be useful here? Do you see one part of what you are doing as writing lost stories, forgotten stories, untold stories?

RN: That's a good question. I believe there is a continuing need in South African writing for more angular memoirs, memoirs that deal with hidden histories, mobile geographies, familial peculiarities. Perhaps *Dreambirds* can be read in this context. South Africa is such a diverse society. A town like Oudtshoorn, with its historic colored majority, its *verkrampte* history, its possession of South Africa's largest rural Jewish population, its obsession with ostriches

... then turning into a town with a black mayor. A place like that is so specific, as different from Soweto and Johannesburg as Straight Fork, West Virginia, is from Seattle. Yet if you look at South Africa from the United States, it's like looking through the wrong end of a telescope. A place like Oudtshoorn, with all its fascinating peculiarities, is utterly invisible, vanishes beneath the generalities.

Yes, the book does involve ghostwriting. At the most intimate level, I came to feel that my father (as a journalist and an amateur botanist) had ghostwritten me. Or at least the version of me who loves to write and is moved by natural history—above all, the natural history of the desert. This indebtedness was a fairly recent revelation for me. For most of my long period abroad, I shut down that side of me; I looked back at places like Port Elizabeth and Oudtshoorn and shuddered. Those places were my father's worlds. In writing them off, I didn't recognize some crucial ways in which, through my father's example, he and they had shaped me. So although our relationship was complex, sometimes painful, I hope the book serves as something of a homage to my father.

While the emotional heart of *Dreambirds* is my painful, grateful, ostrich-mediated relationship to my father, I was adamant that I didn't want to write a conventional memoir circumscribed by family. In retrospect, I recognize that this probably had to do with my own reading tastes. I am a gluttonous reader of both newspapers and nonfictions: I simply can't get enough. What I'm drawn to in both are stories about the unexpected (courage, humor, inventiveness, despair) hidden amidst the everyday. The marginal or forgotten stories that you refer to in your question.

Especially in America, but even in South Africa, celebrity takes up more and more of the storytelling space that's available. Maybe I wasn't born with the part of the brain that is supposed to be in thrall to celebrity. My mind fuzzes over when I come to those stories: airbrushed and endlessly recycled. I feel quite strongly that our *zeitgeist* narrows our responsiveness to the full spectrum of the extraordinary in the ordinary that colors all our lives. There are remarkable, remarkable stories that just never get told.

There is another context in which to read my decision to embed minibiographies and miniautobiographies in *Dreambirds*. Some time during the nineties memoir boom, I began, as a reader, to suffer from narcissism fatigue. I found myself recoiling from memoirs whose sole premise seemed to be "if-it's-me-it's-interesting." Too many of these books were fuelled by little more than the broader cultural boom in self-absorption.

Of course, suffering-recovery memoirs (on, say, incest, alcoholism, or bulimia) can play a genuine therapeutic role, creating community through stories that ease shame, rage, and the solitude of trauma. However, I felt in America, at any rate, the lucrative market for melodramatic self-revelation was creating waves of literary soap opera in a culture already drowning in shock schlock.

What about the improbable stories, the untold, offbeat ones, that don't center on an addiction or a violation? I can see now that in writing *Dreambirds* my approach (whether successful or not) was consistent with the stories I seek out as a reader. I feel magnetized by the personal energy of memoirs. Yet the ones that move me most tend to transport me to other times and other worlds. They leave me with unpredictable, even unimaginable stories and take me beyond the narrow, formulaic cast of parents, siblings, and a personal trauma.

SN/CA: The potential of people and places to generate stories—old, new, and hybrid—appears compelling to you. J. M. Coetzee's *Boyhood*, by contrast, is heavy with a sense of the possibility of stories being futile—of a proliferation of stories for which there is no room, of the stifling atmosphere of stories unread or untold. What does the idea of story mean to you?

RN: Children are imaginative. They dream. And in their dreaming they remake the stories they find around them, even the dreary ones. Some adults, especially artists, writers, filmmakers, nurture that childhood capacity. That's part of what I was trying to communicate in the Owl House chapter. I have always had great faith in the transforming power of the right story told at the right time. It can take root and you never know what may come from it.

Stories do hybridize. Some of the stories that have affected me most powerfully are stories I've misremembered, have remade emotionally. I think this a common experience.

I'm fascinated by the way children, through stories, develop a historical capacity. What are the stories that first allow a child to imagine, to dream historically? To put on the clothing of the past? Ostrich stories did that for me. Obviously not just ostrich stories, but they were the kind of stories that allowed me to cross-dress across history.

I feel almost sentimentally attached to the value of historical imaginings. And the value of seeding them in children early on. We live in an age in which the market value of history has fallen. In part, because we live in an American age. America has become the superpower of memory, and America has always tended to side with amnesia. This impatience with the past isn't all bad: I think some good things have emerged from Americans' restless optimism, their faith in the future, in the remake, the chance to start again. Yet I simply cannot identify with the tendency to write off the past in the dismissive sense of the phrase "that's history."

Here I would circle back to your previous question. The small stories, the lost stories, the ones that have been written out and written off... those are the ones that continue to charm me. I'm convinced of their value.

SN/CA: The book is subtitled *The Natural History of a Fantasy*. This is intriguing in the light of its evasion and questioning of generic categories like autobiography, biography, and memoir. Could you comment on the choice of subtitle in relation to questions of genre?

RN: Clearly, memory is an imaginative, not a mechanical process. *Dreambirds* spirits together a congregation of people from three continents and two centuries, people who are imaginatively bonded to the ostrich as their obscure object of desire. The ostrich is both a natural historical and a fantastical creature. Not much more probable than the unicorn.

I would add that although I see *Dreambirds* as essentially nonfictional, the borderlines between nonfiction and fiction are always permeable. Some of the recent books I most admire—like Amitav Ghosh's *In an Antique Land* and W. G. Sebald's *The Emigrants* and *The Rings of Saturn*—are works of historical redress, works of alternative memory, that explore this fictional-nonfictional borderland.

Interestingly, for the U.S. edition, the subtitle was changed to *The Strange History of the Ostrich in Fashion, Food, and Fortune*, a more deliberate title than the one I had chosen for the South African/British edition. The American marketing people wanted ostrich in the title. And they wanted something concrete to signal that the book wasn't, say, a novel. There are probably good practical grounds for the switch, but I still feel attached to the elusive mix of the original. It feels closer to how the book developed generically and emotionally.

SN/CA: In *Dreambirds*, you luxuriate in the evocativeness of words. You speak of "bookwords" and indulge in word play and make reference, too, to the size of words in relation to the worlds they conjure. What makes words special to you, as distinct from stories?

RN: Your point is well taken. I do believe the distinction is important. I'm drawn to writers whose turns of phrase surprise me, who keep the language lively. We live in an age so dominated by TV, video, film, and computer graphics that visual plot tends to be given primacy. With much contemporary writing I feel that a lot of what is written is seen (and, in the mind, sold) as story before it's felt as words. I can only write as I read. Narrative is important, but a book wilts in my hands if there's nothing special going on linguistically, if there's nothing to it but narrative drive. I'm not one to derogate visual creativity, but I do think there are some things books will continue to do differently. I can't just see them as dummy runs for films.

My attitude, I'm sure, has something to do with growing up in South Africa without TV and with very little film. Books did most of my imaginative work for me. Compared to my American students, who are third generation TV-viewers, I'm a visual illiterate.

My attachment to words probably also has something to do with growing up in a South Africa that felt very cut off. Books came from far away, and most of what they described was equally distant. There was a gap between the world I inhabited and the things that books evoked. That gap was alienating, yet it also opened up a space for fantasy.

SN/CA: A great deal of the pleasure of reading *Dreambirds* lies in your reveling in fantasy—in the giddy world of haute couture and in tempting flights of fancy, in the sensuality of things and in sexual memory. You have spoken of fantasy as redemptive. South African prose fiction has tended to be dominated all too often by a dour realism. How would you relate your work as a writer to this tradition?

RN: I'm not sure how I would position it except to say that fantasy can be redemptive. I'm not, of course, some transcendentalist nutter who believes that fantasy can substitute for bread, shelter, and water. But fantasy can make a difference in some unbearable situations. I was talking to David Schalkwyk recently about his fascinating recent research into how often, in South African prison writing, the authors mention the indispensable role books played during incarceration. Books served as places to disappear, as temporary respites from intolerable realities.

In the shut-down, censorious world that was sixties and seventies South Africa, ostrich feathers served me as a strange, but emotionally important entrée into the possibility of other worlds. They were an odd, illicit, but suggestive starting point for fantasy. Fantasy is deviant. And I'm all for deviation.

SN/CA: *Dreambirds* is a book seamed through with other books and writing—classics, adventure and travel narratives, poetry, natural history. There are also references to unwritten books, burnt books. You have spoken of the value of books in turning "the ordinary things in life" into something "wild and strange," It is interesting that in Lessing's writing, say, or Gordimer's autobiographical essays, European literature is often seen as obscuring the African context. In your book, though, books are not confined to distinct cultures and locations: Albert Jackson's book—a book about Africa—offers you a different take on African reality, and in Ozymandias you "recognize" the Karoo. Would you like to comment in any way on your relationship as reader and as writer to books of all kinds?

RN: Your comments would seem to pick up on your earlier question about my attachment to words. I think here of a poignant V. S. Naipaul essay called "Jasmine." In it Naipaul recalls standing as a young man on a verandah in Guyana and being overwhelmed by the fragrance pouring off a vine. He asks the woman who lives in the house what the flower is. "Jasmine," she replies. Naipaul knows the word; he has read it in books that come from England. But he can't integrate the foreign word and the local fragrance—they have spent too long apart. I think many South Africans, and others who live far from the media powerhouses like Hollywood, New York, and London, can identify with that kind of disconnection.

I am fascinated by misrecognitions. I remember reading Kafka for the first time and being certain he was writing in code about South Africa. When I first arrived in America, in Iowa, I was so mistrustful of everybody's niceness that, to redress the Iowa paranoia deficit, I hid beneath the blankets and reimmersed myself in Kafka. That for me was an act of nostalgia, a way of returning, imaginatively, to South Africa in the face of my inability to decode Iowa.

My interest in cross-readings probably also relates to the fact that I come from a family of immigrants. For three generations, each generation has moved to a new continent and started afresh. There's very little by way of continuity. You're constantly living across codes, remaking what you read or see into what you need.

Of course, this cross-reading doesn't only apply to books. My trips across the Arizona desert were emotionally and imaginatively transforming because they allowed me to return and face certain passions, certain fears, that had suffused my early life in South Africa. I don't think I could have done that in the same way head-on in the Karoo. The powerful echoes I encountered in the Arizona landscape, ecology, and ostrich world, enabled me to open myself to places in my Karoo past that I'd shut down, sealed off. At the same time, that wasn't enough. I had to go back and reread my childhood world politically as well. The epochal elections of 1994 gave me the perfect opportunity for that. They let me integrate the collective euphoria I felt with the more personal emotional momentum I had gathered through my Arizona travels.

SN/CA: Your book draws much inspiration for ways of living, for considering the complexities of identity, from the natural world. Your finding fellowship with migratory birds whose "loyalties are not so much divided as rhythmically redoubled," and your sense of being able to begin to mourn your father's death through finding "common ground" in contemplating convergent evolution, is striking in this regard. You appear to hold up the natural world as a space of irreproachable authority—or at least your invocation of it seems to be at times an attempt to "naturalize" your own sense of "strangeness"?

RN: That's a legitimate question. "Irreproachable authority"? Definitely not. This is, after all, the natural history of a fantasy. One of the things that so enthralled me about the display of Karoo and Arizona plants I encountered in the Sonoran Desert was the imperfection of convergent evolution. The resemblances were genuine, but that was all they were, resemblances. There is no mirror world. That moment of recognition—indeed, the whole journey that the book inscribes—involved reopening myself to the natural world which was indissociable for me from childhood and my father. It was a way of acknowledging him in me, a route to love through grief. It took some emotional and imaginative work for me to reconnect with the natural world, having mistrusted it for most of my adulthood. For so long I'd cast nature, rather crudely, as a betrayal of politics.

Clearly, I wasn't attempting to set up nature in the book as a blueprint for human behavior or as a way of simplifying the complexities of immigrant life. There is no prior, no higher order. Nor was I trying to vindicate the immigrant's hybrid existence: it doesn't need vindication. What I was reaching for was an imaginative node that made emotional sense. Something to ease the pain, something to express my experiential embrace of both the Karoo and Arizona, of childhood and adulthood.

This imaginative need is deeply felt and pervasive in creative works of any kind. One thinks, for instance, of the symbolic role that music plays in Nick Hornby's *High Fidelity*, Sartre's *Nausea*, or the closing scene of Isaac Julian's film *Young Soul Rebels*. In all of them, there is a reaching through music for some still point, for some temporary, imperfect closure. That doesn't make music a blueprint for anything. Even a theoretical work like Paul Gilroy's *The Black Atlantic* has been taken to task for its reliance on images of music and ships to evoke fluid, transnational identities. From a purely analytical perspective, such imaginative evocations are inherently limited. But perhaps those limits are outweighed by the emotional charge they release, the felt sense of possibility.

SN/CA: Is there a mistrust of the image in *Dreambirds*? You refer to the deceptive appearance of things, of camouflage as a metaphor for life in South Africa. Sometimes, reading the text, it is as if the force of images lies beyond reach. Were you aware of working a lot in registers outside of the visual—in sound, smell, and the tactile? Might such explorations have been a part of your search for "a deeper word than memory"—where memory is so often tied to the visual?

RN: That's perceptive. I wasn't aware of doing anything like that deliberately. But then there was a lot that was, that had to be, written unawares. There is something to that mistrust of the image, though. From having been partly deaf as a child, sound has always seemed for me some kind of recovery. It's as deep as the senses get.

I think my mistrust of the surface image goes back to my early discovery of natural camouflage in the Karoo: that appearances deceived. Even more radical, though, was the disjunction I experienced between growing up in South Africa with almost no understanding of what apartheid was and plunging into what Nadine Gordimer has described as "falling, falling through the South African way of life," that one could live so self-deceived.

My experience as an immigrant was then superimposed on that earlier mistrust of surfaces. Eva Hoffman has a poignant description of her Polish immigrant father shouting at everyone in Vancouver. Whether he is trying to sell a vacuum cleaner or embracing a friend, he has only one tone because he lives outside the local repertoire of cultural registers. Often what (in the airbrushed account of American history) is depicted as immigrant energy is little more than immigrant fear. I experienced some of that myself. Of having my codes, my sense of normality, scrambled, and of struggling to decode the surfaces around me.

SN/CA: The genres of memoir and autobiography apparently focus on the past, yet are also explorations of the writer's present. In many ways the writing of the book itself seems a way of "finding the present." You describe your childhood as a state of being locked into the past and projecting onto the future. "It was the present that seemed remote," you say of your life in South Africa. Perhaps this suspension between the past and the future is also the state in which the migrant often finds himself? By the end of the book you find a way of existing in the "deep present." Is it the present that is the site of the traumatic as well as the place that can offer rejuvenation in this story?

RN: It's always useful to ask what occasions a memoir. Very often, as in my case, that catalyst is the death of a parent. Inevitably, the loss leaves you feeling exposed, unless you've already been totally estranged. A parent's death changes the shape of your future and your relationships to the past. The present that you're stranded in begins to feel like a much more mortal space. What ritual forms of grief and acknowledgement are there to help you give meaning to that derelict present? We don't have many such rituals left, at least in a secular middle-class culture. Writing was the ritual that helped ease me from one present into the other, from abandonment to embrace.

Perhaps there is an immigrant component to this too. If you move a lot, the past is always elsewhere. And, as an outsider, your claim on the future seems precarious. You're driven back into the present and have to find ways of turning into something expansive rather than confining.

SN/CA: Yet, on another reading, you seem to refuse boundaries of past, present, and future. You describe your return to South Africa to vote as a "trip suspended as if in a tense yet undescribed by grammarians." Why is time and tense of such importance in *Dreambirds*? Moreover, there is also a sense, isn't there, that the autobiographical act itself is or can be about retrospective consolation—the making of connections one never could have at the time—and the relationship to time that this implies?

RN: My biggest challenge in writing *Dreambirds* was how to find a voice that was personal yet historically encompassing. This challenge was intimately related to the question of tense. I kept casting and recasting different sections in the present and in the past. In childhood, the present is such an enveloping tense. Later we lose that: we fret about the future, regret past acts. (But that shift is not all loss, for we gain historical perspective.) I wanted *Dreambirds* to draw energy from the huge, present-tense passions of childhood. The child's angle of vision can open up memoir to so many possibilities: for humor, fantasy, innocent honesty, and the kind of incomprehension that unwittingly penetrates.

However, the child's perspective is also limiting. It cannot reach easily into history, politics, biology, or foreign lands—all places I wished the book to go. So I had to experiment with splicing personal and impersonal story lines in a way that would allow me to move between a boyhood memory of an ostrich eating my watch and the Russian pogroms, *belle époque* fashion, nineteenth-century racial politics, and Aristotle's crackpot theories of bird migration. This challenge of voice, of point of view, was intimately connected to the question of tense that you raise.

SN/CA: Finding the present, and "knowing how to be known" also seems to relate to writing your way out of certain versions of masculinity. If the desert, which so captured your childhood (and adult) imagination, was full of "hidden, deceptive" things, then the metaphor of keeping things hidden is also one you use to characterize the men in your family, and in the story generally: you refer to the way men "hide." You describe your father as having "gone public to stay hidden." Some men—in this case you and your father—are characterized as having no words, as inhabiting a "dead-silent turbulence." How explicitly is your own story written in relation to these registers of masculinity you articulate? Is [your] memoir or autobiography in general a way of "going public to stay hidden"?

RN: Yes, *Dreambirds* involves an exploration of masculinity. Growing up in South Africa, I never felt comfortable with the codes available to me. Not just racially, but sexually as well. I think the butch-femme thing about ostriches subliminally appealed to me. These can-can dancers of the veld that, with a single kick, could eviscerate a man. That cross-over thing, that element of ambiguity, is something I'm drawn to in women and men. It's less brittle, makes for better company.

From adolescence onwards, I recoiled from what I saw around me of what it meant to be a man. My father had a capacity for happiness. But he was in many ways emotionally inarticulate. His response to fear was to work harder. I could sense in him some of the loneliness of that unvoiced, pent-up fear. I craved some version of manliness that could embrace emotional vulnerability and give voice to it.

I don't say this accusingly. By South African standards we could scarcely call ourselves underprivileged. But my father was, on a very modest salary, the sole breadwinner for nine mouths. From where I stood, his over-the-top work ethic, his emotional unavailability, was intimately connected to that daunting responsibility.

In *Dreambirds* I tried to be self-revealing, self-exploratory. But because the book doesn't attempt to be a comprehensive personal memoir, there are obviously some personal things that I don't address directly. Let me mention one. Between the lines the book was my effort to understand my decision—something I've felt since an early age—not to have children. I have always recoiled from the thought of being a father, far less a patriarch. I wanted to get to the root of that and could only do so by working back through my father's fears, my Karoo childhood, and my immigrant uncertainties.

SN/CA: *Dreambirds* tracks diasporic identities and histories and this is an important departure in relation to South African writing at least. It is interesting that the local "one-mistake" towns of your childhood, as you characterize them, are nevertheless seamed through with connectivity. Places, including South African places, are diasporic spaces where diverse stories are always imminent, even though they may be silenced. You also begin to unpack the many strands—partly through the complex ethnicities of your own family—

which exist within the blanket term "white South African." Did you explicitly see yourself as exploring the official silence surrounding whitenesses that are at odds with the everyday inventions and amplifications of these ethnicities?

RN: Yes, breaking down the uniformity of whiteness is essential. Following the fractures and seeing where they lead. Historically, politically. I do think these are potentially interesting times for South African writers, not least memoir writers. I'd love to see more writing about these fractures, these cover-ups, and obviously not just in the so-called white communities.

References Cited

COETZEE, J. M. *Boyhood*. New York: Viking, 1997.

GILROY, PAUL. *The Black Atlantic: Modernity and Double Consciousness*. London: Verso, 1993.

GORDIMER, NADINE. *My Son's Story*. London: Bloomsbury, 1990.

NIXON, ROB. *London Calling: V. S. Naipaul, Postcolonial Mandarin*. Oxford: Oxford University Press, 1992.

———. *Homelands, Harlem and Hollywood: South African Culture and the World Beyond*. London: Routledge, 1994.

———. *Dreambirds*. London: Doubleday, 1999.

SCHALKWYK, DAVID. "Writing from Prison." In *Senses of Culture: South African Culture Studies*, edited by S. Nuttall and C.-A. Michaels. Cape Town: Oxford, 2000.

Further Reading

JABAVU, NONI. *The Ochre People: Scenes from a South African Life*. Johannesburg: Ravan Press, 1995.

LESSING, DORIS. *African Laughter: Four Visits to Zimbabwe*. London: Harper Collins, 1992.

SOYINKA, WOLE. *Ake: The Years of Childhood*. London: Collins, 1983.

May 2002

VII FROM DAUGHTERS TO MOTHERS

"Mummy, the Coolie Doctor Is at the Door"

Vanitha Chetty interviewed by Judith Lütge Coullie

DR. GOONAM WAS born in 1906 in Durban, in what was then the British colony of Natal. Her autobiography, *Coolie Doctor*, was the first to be published by a South African woman of Indian extraction. In it she recounts her experiences of a rapidly changing South Africa. The prejudice and restrictions that she faced as a young professional woman and an Indian in a society that was divided by the "color bar" were later to be supplanted by the more ruthless racism of the apartheid regime. Dr. Goonam overcame seemingly insurmountable obstacles. Never one to avoid a fight in a just cause, she was active in the struggles against segregation and racism. She was imprisoned eighteen times for her passive resistance activities and was eventually forced into exile. In 1990, as the negotiations with the ANC and other banned organizations commenced, she returned to Durban. She passed away in 1998. This interview with her daughter, Vanitha Chetty, was conducted in Durban in 2000.

JUDITH LÜTGE COULLIE: Your mother was a high-profile figure in the South African Indian community. Was your mother the first Indian woman doctor in South Africa?

VANITHA CHETTY: I don't know because her very good friend Dr. Beryl Peters also qualified around about the same time, or perhaps even a little earlier. But it was only those two at that stage. However, she was certainly the first in Durban, as Dr. Peters was from Pietermaritzburg.

JC: Did you know that your mother was writing an autobiography?

VC: I did, but my memories of the process are vague because she started writing her memoirs when she was in England, between 1977 and 1981, and

I was in South Africa at that time. A lot of the work was done there and then in Harare, and when she came back to South Africa in 1990 it was almost complete. All that was needed was the editing and the finalizing of the draft.

JC: Your mother also wrote some short stories. Were they ever published?

VC: No, because she didn't have the time really.

JC: In the preface your mother said that she started writing her memoirs but then gave up and only took it up much later. Do you know why she gave up for a time?

VC: Well, initially, she wanted to begin the process of publishing in England. There was a friend of hers who promised to publish it, but I think in the meantime she had made plans to go to Australia; between 1981 and 1983 she was in Australia. In 1983, in Harare, I think, she took it up again. It was only finalized when she came to South Africa.

JC: The last part of the narrative is rather perfunctory. What I mean is that it seems that there she took much less pleasure in the writing process. Was this part written much later, in haste to get the book finished?

VC: I don't recall the last part, but I think what also may explain that is the fact that the book was badly edited. One of my mother's major complaints with the book was that chunks were left out and hence there was no flow. So that may account a lot for the way it ended.

JC: Do you have the full manuscript?

VC: No, I don't. She enlisted the help of so many people, and even in the last few months prior to her death I know she enlisted someone's help, but these people were in and out, in and out, on a daily basis. I have some of her writing, but I have not looked through those boxes and I don't know whether the contents are the original because she was busy rewriting it when she died because, as I said, she felt a lot had been left out that should have been included.

JC: Who has the original draft?

VC: I really can't tell you that. There are so many people who were so interested in it and who had promised her that they would help her. I think one had to know her to know the number of people who were constantly in and out of her house.

JC: The published version was written in collaboration with Professor Fatima Meer. How did this collaboration come about?

VC: Well, she and Fatima Meer were old friends. She knew Fatima from the time Fatima was a teenager. In fact, she was there at Fatima's wedding. And in those days the Indian community was so small that she knew most of the people in the community. The arrangement came about when my mother came back to South Africa from Zimbabwe and obviously Fatima was a visitor in her home, a friend of long standing as well as a political ally. Naturally, the book was discussed, and Fatima offered to take it over because she was with the Institute for Black Research, and my mother readily agreed, because this is something she had been wanting for a long time. And once she had come back to South Africa she knew that she would end her life here, and she thought she would have the book published.

JC: Did Professor Meer have quite an active role in shaping the final manuscript?

VC: Yes. She would sit with my mother, and they would sort through the old photographs together and select the ones they wanted to include and so on.

JC: So regarding the final shape: who determined what was omitted?

VC: Fatima, obviously, because she was the publisher then. I don't think, during the editing phase, that my mother had much input. I think once she handed it over, she felt it was in capable hands and that her job had been done. I think she was just satisfied that it was going to see the light of day. But subsequent to that, once the euphoria had died down, once the book had come into print, she realized that there was a lot more that should have been included, such as her terms of imprisonment and especially the time when she was locked up with her friend . . . I think it was Amina Cachalia, and Nelson Mandela came to visit them while they were in prison. This was in the 1940s. She was very, very upset that that was left out of the book. But there were other incidents too.

JC: There are quite a few spelling errors and typos in the texts. Was your mother aware of them or disturbed by them? For example, the name of Dr. Abdurahman appears in a variety of forms. If you didn't know that you were reading about the same person, you would think . . .

VC: . . . they were different people. As I said she was unhappy about the book.

JC: And the caption to the photograph of you and your sister: is it accurate?

VC: The names are reversed.

JC: Also describing her practice in Durban during the Second World War, she says, "My life began to fill once more with patients and social and political interests. While I still did find Indian women with whom I could share my interests, I had Indian men friends and white women friends." Surely this should read: "While I still did not find Indian women with whom I could be friends, I had more Indian men friends and white women friends"?

VC: Yes. That was also a typo, I think.

JC: You mentioned that she would have wanted to publish the revised version.

VC: Oh, yes, definitely. She was writing furiously before she died. And she would have definitely wanted to publish a revised version.

JC: I just wish that she could have fulfilled this wish! Why are the Institute for Black Research joint copyright holders?

VC: I don't know. My mother wasn't very good with these sorts of details. I don't think she read the fine print very carefully. That's why she very often became the victim of con-people in her life, simply because I think she trusted that people would not shortchange her. But it did not always work that way.

JC: Would her friendship with Fatima Meer have made the collaboration easier or more difficult? Sometimes a friendship makes it harder for one to be honest and business-like.

VC: The friendship would have made it easier because my mother was straightforward anyway.

JC: Can you comment on the title of the text?

VC: Lots of people have asked me why she called it *Coolie Doctor*. She always told the story that when she first came back to South Africa after qualifying, a lot of the Indian community were very wary of having her as a doctor because she defied a lot of the conventions and taboos; here she was smoking, driving, and wearing short dresses, stockings, and lipstick, short hair, and what have you. So they didn't become her patients initially, but the lower class of white people, especially from the Greyville area, were her patients. On one occasion when she was doing a house call, she knocked on the door and a child came to the door and said, "Mummy, the coolie doctor is at the door." It's something that stuck in her mind so she thought she would call her book *Coolie Doctor* [laughs].

JC: Your mother changed her name from Naidoo to Goonam because of the caste connotations. Can you explain?

VC: Her first name was Goonam, and her surname is Naidoo. In India it is common practice to drop the surname or caste name. You find most Indians are referred to as doctor so-and-so, using the first name. It wasn't unusual. So she was known as Dr. Goonam, or, to her friends, as just Goonam.

JC: So does the surname not carry the same kind of legal connotations as it does in western societies?

VC: It does, but it's also acceptable just to use the first name.

JC: Your mother mentions the name Gonarathnam. Is that just a version of Goonam?

VC: Goonam is short for Gonarathnam.

JC: But in the diary of imprisonment she gives her name as K. Goonam. What was the K?

VC: She went as Dr. K. Goonam. K. was her father's name—Kasavel—his first name, because he was R. K. Naidoo. So she called herself Kasavel Goonam.

JC: And when she changed her name to Goonam, how did her family respond?

VC: The family accepted it as Goonam is the shortened form of Gonarathnam. And in any case the family would not have challenged her. I mean, she was a law unto herself, so they would not dare question her. Apart from that, the person that was paramount in her life was her mother, and her mother accepted it. It was perfectly natural.

JC: In spite of her refusal to endorse the caste system in her own life, she seemed unconcerned about the caste system in India. When she describes her experiences in India, she refers a few times to caste relationships without any accompanying comment. Could it be that these comments were cut out by the editor?

VC: Could be, but it could also be because perhaps it wasn't really her priority at that time. I know one of her foremost concerns was the dowry system. She was totally against it. That she would elaborate on at great length. But maybe it could also be that caste never featured in her upbringing. It didn't really matter. But you know she never really discussed caste systems with us.

JC: Can you say a bit more about the dowry system your mother opposed? Has it been imported into South Africa?

VC: It did come to this country, but only amongst certain sectors of the Indian community. It was very prominent among the Gujarati community and, I think, to a lesser extent amongst the Muslims. The dowry shows the in-laws how much you've got so that they know that this girl comes from an important family and they can't just treat her anyhow. But with the Southerners, with the Tamil-speakers, which is what we are, it has never been an issue.

JC: How does it work?

VC: It is similar to *lobola,* a bride price, but it works the other way round: for a dowry, the bride's family pays the price. The dowry system was outlawed in India because of the bride burnings. When families of brides didn't pay the stipulated amount, it was common practice to abuse and burn those women. And it's still happening now, although it's outlawed. But as I said, here, dowry isn't a big thing.

JC: In your mother's book, her parents sound like wonderful people.

VC: I never met them because they died in the 1940s before I was born. From what my mother tells me, when my grandfather first came to South Africa, he worked for a merchant or something in Johannesburg or Pretoria. And then he got a bride from Mauritius. They settled in Durban, and he became a businessman. He ran a flourishing import and export business. But then he lost that . . . , I think because he wasn't a good businessman. I think he was a bit of a philanthropist. He lost his business, and he decided that he was going back home to India. My grandmother followed him. He was there for a while before he died. Grandmother came back to South Africa.

JC: From your mother's descriptions, your grandmother sounds as if she was a very strong woman, without being confrontational.

VC: My mother adored her father, and apparently she had her father's temper. People used to dread his temper—even my mother. But my grandmother managed to sort of temper his temper. And she was the driving force in the family because, according to my mother, she had a brain. She had a valid driver's license in the early 1900s. She was the first Indian woman driver—maybe even the first woman driver, who knows? Both of her parents were high-spirited, and my mother had the same feistiness.

JC: Do you remember your mother being imprisoned?

VC: No. That was before I was born.

JC: Your mother's life was obviously very full with her work and with activism; who took care of you and your brother and sister?

VC: We had housekeepers, and I had a nanny, a white woman, Sister Margaret. She lived in the house. But there were always servants, gardeners, dogs, people, and family in and out. And then the older ones, my brother and sister, would look after me.

JC: Were you spoilt?

VC: No, no. My mother used to say I was very spoilt [laughter]. But you see I was very asthmatic as a child, so I think my brother and my sister were always protective, and I suppose I was given extra care. But I wasn't indulged.

JC: And your mother worked full time when you were all children?

VC: Yes. But we had some wonderful servants who were like members of the family. Like when we lived in England between 1955 and 1959, we had a housekeeper, a wonderful woman, Aunty Rani. She lived with us. She cooked for us when my mother went off to work in India for a year. And when we came back from England in 1959—I was nine years old—we had servants and I was at school and fairly independent. Then I went off to Pietermaritzburg for two years because of my chest, and I lived with friends.

JC: The narrative is remarkably silent about your father, your birth, and the raising of you and your sister and even more markedly your brother. Why is this?

VC: I was born when my mother was forty-three. Initially she used to tell me that I was adopted, but that wasn't true [laughter]. She had a liaison with this man who is still alive today. We all sort of knew that I was her child and he was the father. I remember he visited us in England. But after that there was some trouble. You see, she had invested some money in their family business when we went to England, and when we came back there were disputes and she took them to the Supreme Court. She won the case, and they had to repay £17,000, which was a lot of money. Because of all this bitterness, there was no contact between them at all after that. About my brother: when we left England in 1959, he didn't come back with us because he was doing his A-levels then, and he wanted to go into the RAF. Maybe that's why she is a bit silent about him. She absolutely adored him, but I think the relationship between them soured a bit when he married an Englishwoman my mother felt was cold and what have you. And he had become very much of an Englishman at that stage as well. So although initially they had a very good relationship, once he became independent I think, in a way, she resented the fact that he did not need her anymore. But he did come back to South Africa, with his wife, in 1995 for a brief visit.

JC: This reticence is true, too, of personal relationships. She mentions briefly a number of friends and companions and also her relief at not marrying a man she was in love with during her student days and says that the thought of marriage never entered her head again. This is a remarkably unconventional attitude, especially for her time.

VC: Well, there was the one man I know about, my father, and the one that she had as a student—an Egyptian, I think. But since then she never had a man in her life. Her friends were mainly men, but all they ever spoke about was politics. I don't know whether she just cut that part of her life completely or was too preoccupied with politics. When we were coming back to South Africa, there was a man that she had a little liaison with on the ship . . . Mr. Brown, if I remember correctly. But once we docked in Cape Town, that was it [laughter].

JC: She seems to have regarded the men she had been involved with as dangerous, in the sense that they would have been bad for her.

VC: Probably these two men had made her very vulnerable emotionally and having burnt her fingers with those two, she must have thought she would not let that happen again.

JC: One can imagine that she would have had to battle continually to establish her independence because so few women had professions or were independent—and that the thought of losing that must have been a deterrent.

VC: Yes, and then I think her focus changed. You know, she was so involved in the political arena and in her social activities and she used to be talking everywhere, not only about politics, but also persuading people to let their daughters go to school and get some type of higher education.

JC: She says in the Preface that: "My mentors, guides and friends have always been women—my Mother, Aunt Mary, Fatima Devi, Zubeida Seedat, Ramini, the list is endless." But you just said that most of her friends were actually men?

VC: The women were mentors; the men, friends. It's not entirely true that women were more important in her life. There were some other boys and men that she had a special place in her heart for. I mean, Monty Naicker was her bosom buddy. So was Yusuf Dadoo. And there was this South African Indian surfer that she took under her wing. Mangla Moonsamy. He was an orphan growing up in Asherville. He was a top swimmer, and through her efforts he was sent by the Surf Life Saving Association to Sydney, Australia. He used to pass himself off as her adopted son, and she would refer to him as her son. But then he tried to swindle her money so that fell off. So she has had these attachments, but she wasn't discerning. Although she was a very intelligent woman, she could sometimes be taken in by people.

JC: So perhaps what motivated her saying, "My mentors, guides and friends have always been women," was the fact that none of those women betrayed her?

VC: Yes.

JC: Has the publication of the text had any impact on your life?

VC: Not really. I don't publicize the fact that my mother wrote her autobiography. And younger generations don't know her as well. She ran her practice in Durban from 1936 until 1976. Forty years, virtually uninterrupted. And most of the kids at that time were delivered by her. I mean, how many functions did she go to over the years, where they would come and say: "Do you remember my son? You delivered him. This is my daughter; you delivered her."

JC: But as you say the Indian community has exploded in size. Nearly a million Indians in South Africa now, most in KwaZulu-Natal. Has the book lessened your sense of loss, now that your mother has passed away?

VC: No, if anything all the memories and things that are contained in the book increase my sense of loss as time goes by. Now, September [2000], it is two years since she died. I am missing her more now.

JC: How much like your mother, as you knew her, is the narrator/protagonist of the text? Is this is a fair representation of her?

VC: Yes. I felt it was her.

JC: What sort of mother was she? She doesn't describe her mothering skills at all.

VC: Well, she was a good mother in many ways. I also used to be very much in awe of her, and her temper I used to dread. But as I say, I was a very sickly child and she was always there, night and day. She would come back from meetings or parties or what have you, and I would require an intravenous injection at two or three in the morning, and she was always there. We were always well provided for physically, and she was loving and warm. She was an excellent role model. But she left us also very much to our own devices to form our own characters and personalities; although she was such a strong woman, she never tried to make us into her. But she did have expectations of us that we did not fulfill. She was very disappointed. But I was in awe of her, and my personality did take a back seat to hers. I was always in her shadow. I was Dr. Goonam's daughter. Then when I married, I was someone's wife. I was never myself. It's only in the last few years that I came into my own.

JC: Did she attend your graduation when you got your PhD?

VC: Yes, she did. She was sitting there in the audience in the front row. And the minute my degree was conferred and I came back to my seat, she toddled across and came and sat next to me for a while. She was very proud of me. You see she didn't want me to marry initially. She was totally against it because of my age and because of the person that I married. And as it turned out, she was right. But she was proud of my achievements and of my children. So I think she was quite satisfied when she died.

JC: The autobiography describes with much pleasure the Tamil feasts that your mother experienced as a child. Did she observe these festivities in later life?

VC: No, I think that, prior to her going away to Edinburgh, it was very much a part of the community spirit. But she changed while she was there. She was always an Indian at heart. She loved the language, the culture, the people, but she was totally against rituals when she got back. The only special day that she did observe was Diwali. It was a whole two days' celebration, and at my aunt's place there used to be big celebrations.

JC: Your grandfather is quoted as being afraid that your mother might marry a white man. What was the nature of that fear, as you understand it?

VC: I think the fact that she was going away to Scotland: it's only white people there, and what if his daughter happens to marry someone while she's there? It just wasn't the done thing in those days. And I suppose, knowing how rebellious she was, she may well have brought home a white man—which perhaps wouldn't have shocked the parents so much, but imagine the community! And in those days community meant everything.

JC: Your mother describes her first years as a woman doctor in Durban as unhappy and difficult because of her failure to conform to conservative norms for Indian women.

VC: I don't think that her early days were quite that bad because she was very well received on arrival in South Africa, in fact it was a big thing. They were at the docks to meet her, and they came with banners and what have you, and they had a big reception for her. Perhaps they were mildly disapproving of her ways or suspicious or she took them by surprise. I think also they were in awe of her. She wasn't saddled by social constraints. She led the way, and if they didn't like it they could go to hell as far as she was concerned. And her family supported her.

JC: There were no troubles concerning her style of dress and with her smoking?

VC: No, not with her family.

JC: To my knowledge, no other South African Indian women have published narrative autobiographies, at least not in English. Phyllis Naidoo published only a short piece in a collection of South African women's prison writings.

VC: Fatima [Meer] has written about social issues and community issues. [Fatima Meer's autobiographical account of her imprisonment, *Prison Diary*, was published in 2001 subsequent to this interview.] And Ansuyah Singh did write a book, what was that, *Summer Moonbeams on the Lake*?

JC: Do you think that the gender system in conservative Indian communities suppresses the potential for individualization called for by narrative autobiography?

VC: No, not any more. Over the last two or three generations, Indian women have become very liberated. There are no constraints on our behavior.

JC: So why are they not publishing life stories?

VC: Well, how many of them have led colorful lives? Perhaps they would go into writing short stories or poetry or other kinds of writing, because a lot of them are academics, professionals, writing in journals, but not writing life stories.

JC: Among your mother's friends, was there a clear link between the struggle against racism and the struggle against sexism?

VC: I think that in her case they were separate struggles. But for many other Indian women who were activists, the political struggle enabled them to shake off the shackles of conventionality.

JC: Was your mother involved in a separate women's movement?

VC: No. She was with the Black Sash and what have you. But there were no women's movements then.

JC: Your mother passed away in 1998. What were her impressions of the new South Africa?

VC: I think initially, prior to democracy, she was over the moon. She was so happy that in her lifetime she would witness democracy, equality, freedom for all. But, if one has to be honest, she became disenchanted with the ANC towards the end.

References Cited

GOONAM, K. *Coolie Doctor: An Autobiography.* Durban: Madiba Publishers, 1991.

Further Reading

BADSHA, OMAR, and ZEGEYE ABEBE. *Imperial Ghetto.* Cape Town: Kwela, 2001.

DHUPELIA-MESTHRIE, UMA. *From Canefields to Freedom.* Cape Town: Kwela, 2000.

GOVINDEN, BETTY (DEVARAKSHANAM). "Space and Identity in Jayapraga Reddy's Unpublished Autobiography, 'The Unbending Reed,' and her 'On the Fringe of Dreamtime and Other Stories.'" *Alternation* 7, 1 (2000): 178–200.

GOVINDEN, DEVARAKSHANAM. "'Sister Outsiders': The Representation of Identity and Difference in Selected Writings by South African Indian Women." PhD diss., University of Natal, 2000.

———. "*Coolie Doctor:* Woman in a Man's World." *Current Writing* 13, 1 (2001): 22–48.

MEER, FATIMA. *Prison Diary: 113 Days in 1976.* Cape Town: Kwela, 2001.

NAIDOO, JAY. *Coolie Location.* London: SA Writers, 1990.

NAIDOO, PHYLLIS. "Ten Days." In *Snake with Ice Water: Prison Writings by South African Women,* edited by Barbara Schreiner, pp. 85–121. Johannesburg: Congress of South African Writers, 1992.

NOBEL, VANESSA. "Ruffled Feathers: The Lives of Five Difficult Women in Durban in the 20th Century." PhD diss., University of Natal. 1997.

PODBREY, PAULINE. *White Girl in Search of the Party.* Pietermaritzburg: Hadeda Books, 1993.

SINGH, ANSUYAH. *Behold the Earth Mourns.* Cape Town: Privately published, n.d.
———. *Cobwebs in the Garden, and a Tomb for Thy Kingdom.* Durban: Purfleet Publications, 1966.
———. *Summer Moonbeams on the Lake: Poems, Short Stories and a Play.* Durban: Purfleet Publications, 1970.

August 2000

IT WAS NOT IN MY MOTHER'S CHARACTER TO MAKE SUCH SUDDEN CHANGES.
PART OF HER DOWNFALL WAS REMAINING FAITHFUL TO HER DECISIONS.
NOTHING SO FAR CONVINCED ME SHE HAD CHANGED.
SHE WAS STILL ERMELINDA.
    —Ester Lee

Why Do You Abandon Me? I Am Your Daughter. Re-presenting Dona Ermelinda

Ester Lee interviewed by Duncan Cartwright

IN *I WAS Born in Africa,* Ester Lee gives a biographical account of her mother's courage and pain in living through the chaotic revolutionary changes that swept through Mozambique in 1974. The book, however, is also about the author's own personal pain in having to endure her mother's decision to stay committed to Mozambique, whether under Portuguese or postcolonial rule. Her mother's will to stay drives a wedge of incomprehension between mother and daughter, leaving significant parts of Dona Ermelinda's life a mystery. Most significantly, her mother's relationship with a young black Mozambican man, Mucavele, whom she takes into her house, leaves Ester Lee having to challenge past preconceptions of their "old" life together, a life where nothing could come between them.

In my interview with Ester Lee in Durban in January 2002, she reflects on her relationship with her mother, her mother's own struggle to belong, the changes in Mozambique, and her need to write in order to understand the "truth" about her mother. A central theme that emerges in the interview relates to her own transformation through writing and understanding—a means of reconnecting with her dead mother. Here, changes in her thinking bear testimony to the reparative and healing qualities that might come from re-presenting, and in a sense "owning," what will always be lost to her. This, however, as Ester Lee reminds us, has less to do with the recounting of fixed "facts"—something we are often seduced into believing—and is more about staying true to one's own experience of the world, a narrative truth rather than a historical one (Spence 1982).

DUNCAN CARTWRIGHT: *I Was Born in Africa* seemed to me to tell a story of struggle and loss in a number of different ways: There is, of course, the loss of the old colonial Mozambique. There is your mother, who chooses to live through war and threatening and destructive postcolonial times. But it seems that it is also very much about the difficulty and loss experienced in your relationship with your mother as a result of her decisions. In terms of that, I was wondering about your thoughts regarding the need for writing this book and how you eventually came to do so?

ESTER LEE: I've changed a lot since I wrote the book. I was angry then. I didn't know what was happening. I needed to see the events in writing so as to better understand the loss of my country and my mother. My first attempt to put the story into book form was during the filming of my son's documentary (A. Lee 1995) about my relationship with my mother and her life in Mozambique. My short stories, published by Umsinzi Press at the time (Ester Lee 1995a, 1995b), and the positive response I received, also helped and encouraged me. At first I was going to publish three small volumes: "Mãe" (Mother), "Ermelinda: The Diaries," and "A Luta Continua" (The struggle continues). But that turned out to be too confusing so I put it together in one book, *I Was Born in Africa*, published by Minerva Press.

People were fascinated with the story of my mother and that's when I thought I would write the book. But in making the film, people wanted a different story. They wanted to hear about the affair between my mother and Mucavele, but that was not important. To me, that was simply something that was happening. In my book I was concerned with my mother and the disappointment and horror she must have gone through, the pain she must have gone through. Because at the time that she was experiencing this I didn't know; you had to be there to really know what was going on. When you see somebody suffering, you are sympathetic, you are not feeling the pain. Because we had disengaged, I could not understand my mother; why had she stayed there? Why didn't she come and live here in this paradise [Durban, South Africa]?

But I still love Mozambique today and have no antagonistic feelings towards those people. I love Mozambican people. They are still the same, the war has not changed that . . . and I think that gave my mother hope that she could live to see a great Mozambique for everybody—not in terms of material things, but in terms of its beauty and peace. She died without seeing that— which was sad. Peace in life is the most important thing. I only understand that now. I knew very little about what was really going on there. I used to sit glued to the radio trying to find out what was going on. But for us kids it was very difficult to imagine, as we had lived in Mozambique before the problems.

The space, the sea, we could run off on our own, no one was going to strangle you or shoot you, so it was very hard for me to realize what it had become. It was only once I started really growing up that I started to realize it. I didn't live through war, I lived in paradise, such a beautiful country . . . But today the country is doing very well again.

DC: You talked about a kind of gap in understanding your mother, what she was going through. Was writing, after her death, a way of trying to find out more, to understand?

EL: Yes, to find out what I didn't know.

DC: It seemed to be a way of reconnecting with your mother in a way that you couldn't when she was alive?

EL: Yes, yes. My mother was everything to me; it was me and my mother. As I grew up I was my mother's companion because she didn't go out on her own. She loved going out shopping and to the cinemas. She liked going everywhere, we were very close . . . and then suddenly there was a change and from then on I didn't understand. Particularly because she was Catholic, you know the word of God, you've got to do it the right way, you never see it but you believe it.

But somehow this man [Mucavele] was doing the best for her. I was saying, "This man you don't know and he's going to rule and control your life, but you trust that he knows what he is doing." And for us Europeans in Mozambique this was natural, because the Portuguese were colonialists and had done many unfair things to the local population, and I considered myself as one of them as I was born there.

The whole thing was a total disaster. Samora Machel[1] had been trained with this Marxist ideal and he came in to put his ideal on the people of Mozambique, but this was not what the people of Mozambique were. In the end it was a pity because I think when he died he had the real life of Mozambicans at heart and he really loved his country. He would have been a very changed Samora Machel, and it is very sad that he died. Me and my mother were distraught when he died because we thought this man is going to see that good happened. In the beginning he wanted to be the boss and didn't trust anybody, you know it was his work. But if you knew him face-to-face, there was a warmth. I was sad that he was killed in the plane accident and sad that he went when he did.

DC: Talking about this in terms of change, you say that you felt that Samora

---

1. Samora Machel became the first president of independent Mozambique on 25 June 1975 when his organization, FRELIMO, defeated the Portuguese colonialist government. Shortly after independence, war broke out between FRELIMO and RENAMO, the anti-Marxist opposition in the country.

Machel went through a number of changes, and you mentioned earlier that writing *I Was Born in Africa* had changed you. It sounds as though you were talking about a process that you have been through, a kind of mourning for what you missed. You say that things are quite different for you now as a result of writing the book. Can you say a bit more about that?

EL: My relationship with my mother was very, very good. But when she died there was all this, "You shouldn't have died because I want to know. I want you to tell me which is Mucavele and what is going on? Why do you abandon me, I am your daughter, you were everything in my life? Suddenly this Mucavele is the only thing that is important in your life." It was a kind of jealousy—rage and jealousy at my mother. But later in the book and actually being there, I understood what was happening and why she did it and the pain she went through. I was only able to find that out in this process of writing.

DC: In the process of writing, as you said, you began to understand the pain, struggle, and destruction she lived through. I found the parts of the book that depicted the struggle she went through very painful to read. What did you actually come to understand through writing about it?

EL: She went through a great deal of pain with me because I was quite against what she thought. But I admired her because she was strong enough to keep to what she believed. I began to understand why she was not coming with me to South Africa. She didn't want to come and live in comfort; it was not where she belonged. In Mozambique she had nothing, but she was free, free in her own decisions. Many times I criticized her decisions. I was influenced by the comfort of South Africa and having things and possessing things and showing the world that I am successful. I have a good car and house, those kinds of things. I was probably ashamed of my mother . . . because when she came to visit me in South Africa, she was dirty and badly dressed. She used to go to the supermarket, and she would look at the shelves and call my daughter and say, "These beautiful tins, do they have food inside?" She thought they were decorations. She hadn't seen anything like that. She was so disconnected from our world. And maybe she was an embarrassment to me when we would go out. My daughter did buy clothes for her, but she didn't wear them. She would touch them and look at them, "They're so pretty, they're so lovely." They were precious to her. I have changed a lot due to the writing of the book.

In my book, you see, there are no real evil people, because I don't believe in that. . . . When it got really bad, I came to South Africa. I felt I had the privilege of walking away . . . and I didn't feel bad about it because I was doing nothing there for me. I would have got myself into trouble and got arrested and tortured and killed. Post-revolution Mozambique had nothing to attract my return. Both during the period of Portuguese colonialism and subsequently with Samora's regime, to disagree or oppose government policies could and would lead to arrest, torture, and worse. Machel, just like the Portuguese before, imposed rule on the Mozambican people: they had no choice. There were no elections in Mozambique until after Machel's passing, so Mozambicans went from being forced to being Portuguese to being forced to being Marxists.

So I walked away and left the country, but I didn't walk away emotionally. And when I look back from what I was reading in the South African papers, I was imagining so many frightened people. But on my first return visit to Mozambique, there was this warmth—it was all there. As I left the plane I remember clutching my passport because I think if you are an immigrant, then your papers are all you have to prove that you are a part of your country, that's all you have to prove that you exist. And when I got there, all my old friends were waving and the passport officials were so nice, you know, they weren't rigid like in South Africa where I was quite frightened of those sorts of things. . . . People were having parties, I mean people were still partying. I found people there every day with such strength and happiness. "Hey, we made it, we are still alive" [laughs].

I still have this story to tell. I met this war child once . . . because children were trained to kill. I still remember this child. I was talking to this kid who was a murderer; he looked somewhere between nine and twelve, and he came and sat next to me; he must have felt "mother," you know. I said to him, "What would you like to do with your life? Be a soldier? Be the president?" He looked at me and said he wanted to go to school. So here is a child, you know; the troubles hadn't killed him yet. He was a murderer child, but he still had a soul. And I find those people in Mozambique every day . . . there is no such thing as hate, even after all they have been through—it is amazing.

We never had apartheid; it was a social thing. At the end of the day Machel was the same as those in Portugal, Portugal was in Mozambique. They were the *assimilados,* someone black who became like a Portuguese, spoke like a Portuguese, same education, dressed like a Portuguese. They received special treatment, a fake special treatment that local Mozambicans hated. But Machel was making the same mistakes. He went through a life of being told he was Portuguese and he was not. Then he imposed his own kind of oppression on the people, inspired by Soviet Marxist ideals. This was not something the people were ready for or wanted. So in that way he was repeating the mistakes of the Portuguese fascists.

With the Portuguese fascist regime you were not allowed to write, only now writing is coming out. Even if you wrote a poem you got arrested and were tortured unless you, along with your family, apologized. Spies were constantly on the lookout for people against the government; this is Portugal, not Mozambique. But both regimes imposed strict censorship. Portugal had the Policia Internacional e de Defesa do Estado (PIDE), the Portuguese secret police, and Machel founded Republica Popular de Moçambique, which was inspired by Soviet Marxism and enforced by the Grupo Dinamizador.

DC: You talked about precious, material things and how your mother became disconnected from that kind of life. That also seems to symbolize the fall of Lourenço Marques and the change to Maputo.

EL: Yes, it was a beautiful place. Even now with all the buildings and all the destruction, there is a beauty to that. I have been back. I have friends and family in Mozambique today, and they have a happiness that I don't have. When they come and visit me, they are all colors. My second-generation cousins now have such good Portuguese and black influences; they are the most beautiful people. Always happy, no inhibitions. They have a kind of happiness that we don't have. I don't know, I can't explain it.

DC: To go back to the way you describe your mother in *I Was Born in Africa* and what she went through, there is a kind of mystery to her story. You have her diaries up to a certain point and then there is a gap where she stops writing, particularly, it seems, when she met Mucavele. How do you understand what happened to her?

EL: Mucavele was just a lost drunk. He was not an evil nasty gigolo like I thought. I never saw him face-to-face. The first time I saw him was in my son's film about my mother, and I couldn't face this man. He was drunk and offensive, but now I understand, not in an evil way. Mucavele said once to my son when he was drunk, "I am your grandmother," and I think I understood that. He was saying if you ever want to come and be with your grandmother, here I am to be your friend . . . so there was a softness about him.

My mother would go to the Scala Cafe and drink black coffee; sometimes she would take sedatives because at the end she was losing it, she was losing her strength. That's where she met Mucavele. She fell down the steps. Just think about it, this young black man, very poor, my mother was very poor, she was quite disturbed, and then she fell down the stairs and immediately he helped her and they became friends. She was incredibly lonely. Loneliness for her got worse and worse. What do you do to a prisoner to torture them? Put them in isolation. Life isn't the same if you're alone; you are a sufferer; you are no longer a person. And that was what happened to my mother.

I am still living with the guilt about this. I was jealous of her, I was jealous of everything that she stood for. I was jealous of her strength, her ability to stick with what she believed in, and I was jealous of her being in love, her and Mucavele. She never took any notice of my kids, but Mucavele's daughter—my mother would have died for that child. I still today don't know whether Mucavele and my mother had a sexual relationship. But then you must understand that children never see the sexuality of their parents. Parents are pure, and it is always shocking when your mother or father sleeps with another, or each other [laughs]. I suppose I was living that dream: my mother was pure; how could she have an affair sexually, with a man, and a black man? That is important, not because I am racist, it was just that I was not used to it. But he gave her something, I don't know exactly what.

DC: So these were the difficulties you had to deal with . . .

EL: Yes, I still don't know today, because the whole world said they were sexually involved and she was crazy about him. They made a big thing about it. But I've been thinking about it as a daughter; I just was not able to accept this as a daughter . . . because she lived in the house with them—he, his children, and his wife.

When I went back to the house to get back what was mine, she [Mucavele's wife] would walk past the house and say, "Don't worry. I'm coming back. This house is mine." She went through a lot of suffering to get the house. We all suffered for the house. I suffered from the loss; I suppose it stood a lot for my mother and what she didn't leave me. When I went back to see the house, he was there with my mother and he was hiding because I was in the house. He didn't come and see me. This is the thing; I like fights, and people don't like fights. Very few people like confrontation; they talk about it, and then they run away or they change. . . . But she loved him like a son. It was love. People don't understand love. They try to make things out of it. And now I realize that I tried to put all these things into him: "You want the house. You want my mother's money which you spent and wasted." But maybe he also loved my mother; she was easy to love. Once, when she stayed with me, the next morning I was saying to her, "What's this Mucavele? What is he to you? Whose house is this?" [laughs]. I wanted the house. What for? . . . And my mother said, "I'm going to drown in your fish pond because I can't take you anymore," and I said, "Wait a minute, I will put more water, there is not enough water for you to drown."

When I wrote this book, and my mother was no longer here, I felt bad. The pain she must have felt with her own daughter saying, go and drown yourself, when she was in such pain and all she wanted was to get out of that pain.

DC: But in terms of her diary, it interested me that she stopped writing at a particular time when she began to see Mucavele, leaving a mystery about how she felt and about the whole affair....

EL: Yes. I understand that now. She stopped writing the diary. There were forty pages cut. My son says I cut them because she was saying bad things about how she didn't want me to have the house. Or my son says maybe it was my cousin because she found the diary. My cousin is a very wonderful person, a pure-hearted Mozambican [laughs], and perhaps she took the pages because my mother said, "Don't show anyone," and she loved my mother dearly. Those are their interpretations. My interpretation, because my mother promised she would tell me about Mucavele and what went on, is that she did write about it. But you know when you're really emotional about something, you can't write it correctly. I think she kept on taking out the pages because she couldn't bring herself to tell about Mucavele.

DC: You're saying that she remained conflicted about talking about Mucavele, about bringing her "old" and new life together?

EL: Yes, my son called the film *The Double Life of Dona Ermelinda* . . . because she did love us. My daughter adored her . . . It is very sad on this earth that we cannot go back and erase. If I could now go back again to the beginning and start again, I wouldn't have done things I did to my mother and said things I said to my mother. I would want to stay connected with her and admire her for what she did independently. Now I am aging myself; I am getting near to the age that if you can't survive financially, you're either going to be a hobo or you're going to be dependent on somebody. It is a very frightening thing about aging. I say to my kids, if I'm not independent and if I'm getting old, put me in an old age home and I'll drive everybody crazy, and I'll like that [laughs]. Don't come and visit if you're going to be embarrassed—and again I find myself being my mother. Because I'm not thinking I'll go to Paris and live there with my son, or I'll live with my daughter. I'm not thinking like that. I don't want that [laughs]. I'd much rather be in Cato Manor housing scheme [a low-cost housing development nearby] instead of having my children at the end of the month give me a check. So that's how I feel, and my mother was doing that.

As you get older it's very interesting because you start seeing your parents in yourself. You start catching mannerisms, like sometimes I'm combing my hair and I think, that's my mother, a little of my father, like ghosts. . . . She told me she would haunt me. I'm not into that, but I'm starting to think: is it the soul, or is it like a vibration with another world? Can somebody see us, like television or a radio transmission? There is something. What it is I don't know, but I feel very strongly my mother is back.

DC: In many ways you describe her commitment to Mozambique as unwavering. Do you still wonder why a person, your mother, would stay in such adversity?

EL: She stayed there because she felt she belonged and that was the one place she could love. Secondly, she believed and hoped it was going to get better. She was an optimist. She had this sense that everything would be okay, even if somebody was being nasty, she would see the light. She had this thing which I am only starting to get to know; I didn't have it. I was more like my father. My father was very mean and punishing; he wouldn't wait for God to punish you, he would like to punish you. He was revengeful, even though he could be kind. As you get older, there is an importance, an obsession, with belonging somewhere . . . especially immigrants, they need a place to belong. Should it be where they come from or the country they're in at the time? This interests me, and I'm writing about it in my next book. But maybe some are just lonely and they don't want to be lonely. I've discussed even my grave and where I want to be buried. It is in Freixeda Do Torrao, Portugal, where my grandparents are buried. This is a lovely thing in Portugal; people buy their own graves, their own stone, and they put their name and date of birth on it. I've been to the cemetery many times [laughs], you know it's quite fun.

DC: Talking about graves, "The Nightmare," one of the first chapters in your book, interested me. You write about your mother saying to Mucavele, "I want to be buried alive," and I wondered about the importance of you putting it that way?

EL: That was about her knowing that I wouldn't bury her where she wanted to be buried . . . and my guilt when I put her in the sarcophagus, which is where she didn't want to go. She wanted to be buried in a box in Mozambican soil. She didn't want to be with my father; she didn't want to be in a box above the ground, but at the time she was buried like that. She was my father's wife, and I had to keep up appearances. But she won in the end. [Ester Lee's mother was eventually buried "in the ground" after the sarcophagus was plundered by local Mozambicans living in the cemetery.]

DC: Reflecting on the book, after the book . . .

EL: . . . I can't remember what I wrote in the book. Because there is much more that isn't in the book but in my mind.

DC: . . . are there things that you would change or write differently?

EL: Yes. I would look more kindly towards Mucavele. He is not such a bad person . . . . Only now I'm understanding those things. That was my "vision" at the time when I wrote the book because I was wanting the truth. I'm sure what happened; why I wrote the book was because I am not afraid of the truth,

I am afraid of the lie. If I pretend I am what I am when I am not, then they will catch me. This is because I'm not certain of what I'm not, and that's more embarrassing than actually taking your clothes off and saying this is who I am and who I think I am. Pretending, that's more embarrassing . . . and at the time, with my mother, everyone was going around saying all sorts of things about the sexual relationship. People didn't understand, they thought it was witchcraft—he bewitched her and she became disturbed. That's not what happened. I think when I wrote the book they were kinder to her in their thoughts, and they realized that she was good to them, she was nice to them.

DC: Can we talk about your theory of the lie? You've spoken about how your ideas have changed regarding your relationship with your mother. Does that mean that truth changes?

EL: Yes, because you see it differently. With my mother, she was giving them everything and would not let me in the house. I was enraged. I had this rage. I can't say hate. Hate is a very extreme word. I wanted to shake her and get something out of her, "Tell me, tell me." But today, I know the pain she went through, the loneliness.

DC: Earlier you were talking about writing coming out of Portugal. What about Mozambique? Has there been much biography or autobiography?

EL: There is a brilliant writer who is now in Pretoria, Luis Bernado Honwana. He is a brilliant man, finding a new way of writing on his own. But he doesn't write biography, he never writes about himself. Mozambique is really a country of incredible writers and poets, Mia Couto is one of the famous ones. But few have written about their experiences of the war of independence and afterwards. There are some writings from outside but not from inside the country.

DC: Earlier, you were saying that the lack of writing in Portugal was because people were being silenced by the authorities. Do you think a similar reason explains why there is so little autobiography coming out of Mozambique?

EL: Yes, it is, or was, similar. I haven't come across anything about that. I have never seen anything coming out of Mozambique that is autobiographical saying, "I was there and this is what happened to me." You must realize, though, that writing about yourself is like taking clothes off in public. There I am: naked, look at me! Also, it is never quite exactly the same as you experienced it because something is forgotten, something is not clear, and other things, you wanted them to be that way. It is not like you are sitting down and writing at that moment. It feels like it was in your mind. When I write, I find that a week later I can't remember, but today, on the day, truth is very important.

DC: What interests me about what you're saying is that there is an inevitable loss that comes with writing about one's own experience; you can never absolutely represent your experience and it is, as you mentioned earlier, always changing. But that is as close to truth as you can get. Is that the way you see it?

EL: I write about what I know. If I write about you, I invent you. I have to invent you first. If I want to write about the garden outside, I have to invent it first, and so it comes to life, but that is still truth. Biography is about truth and the telling of experience. This will always change depending on what I experience or know. I could forget and in its place imagine other things, and so it changes. It also depends on what you read, or even the languages you read in. I think I write because I love reading . . . I read in many languages. I love language, different languages, because when you read, or speak, in different languages they open up different realities. A word in one language will show you something different from what can be touched on in another language.

References Cited

LEE, A. *The Double Life of Dona Ermelinda*. Dominant7, 1995. dominant7@free.fr

LEE, ESTER. "Rosa's Journey into the Land of Dark Sunshine." In *South African Short Stories*, Vol. 2 of *Cadences*, edited by F. Keats, p. 67. Durban: Umsinzi Press, 1995a.

———. "The Saints with a Werewolf or Two." In *South African Short Stories*. Vol. 1 of *Sundowners*, edited by F. Keats, p.39. Durban: Umsinzi Press, 1995b.

———. *Mãe*. Durban: Umsinzi Press, 1997

———. *I Was Born in Africa*. London: Minerva Press, 1999.

SPENCE, D. *Narrative Truth and Historical Truth: Meaning and Interpretation in Psychoanalysis*. New York: W. W. Norton & Co., 1982.

Further Reading

DONOSO, BENJAMIN PUERTAS. *Across the Footsteps of Africa: The Experiences of an Ecuadorian Doctor in Malawi and Mozambique*. Boulder, CO: Africa World Press, 1999.

HONWANA, RAÚL. Introduction. In *The Life History of Raúl Honwana: An Inside View of Mozambique from Colonialism to Independence, 1905–1975*, edited by Allen F. Isaacman. Boulder, CO: L. Rienner, 1988.

ISAACMAN, ALLEN. "Colonial Mozambique, an Inside View: The Life History of Raúl Honwana." *Cahiers d'études Africaines* 109 (1988): 59–89.
MAGAIA, L. *Dumba Nengue/Run for Your Life: Peasant Tales of Tragedy in Mozambique.* Lawrenceville, NJ: Africa World Press, 1988.
SACHS, ALBIE. *The Soft Vengeance of a Freedom Fighter.* London: Grafton, 1990.
SCHAFER, R. "Narratives of the Self." In *Psychoanalysis: Toward the Second Century,* edited by A. M. Cooper, O. F. Kernberg, and E. S. Person. New Haven: Yale University Press, 1990.

January 2002

Every Secret Thing as Family Memoir

Gillian Slovo interviewed by Margaretta Jolly

GILLIAN SLOVO WAS known for her elegant thrillers before her memoir of her parents, two of South Africa's most prominent white anti-apartheid activists, Ruth First (1925–1982) and Joe Slovo (1926–1995). A childhood of painful uncertainty had made detective writing come naturally, but it was much harder to confront the secrets of her own past. Starting with the murder of her mother in Maputo in 1982, Slovo uses flashbacks to recollect growing up in the leafy suburbs of Johannesburg in the early 1960s, experiencing years in exile, and ultimately, the triumph of the ANC, the new South Africa, and Joe's untimely death from cancer in 1995. While recalling the events that surrounded her family's persecution and exile, and reconstructing the truth of her parents' relationship and her own turbulent childhood, tracking down the men who ordered her mother's killing is only one of the intimate secrets uncovered. *Every Secret Thing* was widely praised for its unsentimental examination of the conflicting needs of children, parents, and activists in the struggle against apartheid, Nadine Gordimer viewing it as "an extraordinary expression of the very nature of loving." Slovo's portrait of her undeniably courageous parents also challenges South African hagiographic tradition by showing heroes to be ordinary human beings as well. Margaretta Jolly interviewed Gillian Slovo orally at her home in London.

MARGARETTA JOLLY: To start with the question of autobiographical cultures and traditions, were you consciously or unconsciously working within an autobiographical tradition, particularly, if you relate it to Englishness or South Africanness?

GILLIAN SLOVO: I didn't set out to do anything consciously in the sense of style. When I set out, I actually was going to write a book about my mother. While I was researching the book, my father died, and I got to the feeling that I could not write this book without having him in it. So the conception of what it was completely changed as I was writing it. And I'm not even sure I would call what I've done an autobiographical text. I would describe it as a family memoir. Partly because, although it is seen through my eyes, it's actually not my story. It's the story of my relationship with my parents, and my view of their relationship with each other. But I think, inevitably, because I live in England, I was affected by a trend in autobiographical writing which is more confessional, I think, than has been in South Africa. In a way I think I was influenced by relatively new books that have come up: Blake Morrison's *As If*, for example, that pushed the limits of what you were allowed to do in this kind of text.

MJ: I was also thinking of Blake Morrison, and even of Jenny Diski, as examples of a culture of writing autobiography through parental biography. But perhaps also the other way round, a kind of blurring the two.

GS: Yes, and I think the next step is the blurring of fiction and nonfiction. I think there were a lot of similarities in writing this book and fiction. In writing a novel, the structure of your book is very important. It was exactly the same with *Every Secret Thing*—how was I going to structure it? And also there was a similarity in the method of getting to write it. In the beginning I was aware that I was writing not only about myself, but my parents. Particularly in South Africa, my parents hold a place which is in effect the subject matter of the book, namely, the place that the heroes and the dead heroes and even the dead heroed martyrs have. When I started, I was rather scared of some of the things that I was trying to do. I found it quite difficult to ask some of the questions I needed to ask, and this made me realize how thoroughly I had censored myself all my life. It was at this point that Barney Simon [playwright and director, one of the founders of the Market Theatre] gave me a great piece of advice. In effect what he said was: "Don't first try and work out what you are going to say. First find out everything that you can and then shape the material. There's no point in directing your research at what you think is acceptable and isn't acceptable or what you think you want to include and what you don't think you want to include." It was very good advice that freed me up to think about this book in the way I was accustomed to freeing myself up in fiction. That is, I had learned *not* to decide where the limits were before I started but instead sometimes to stretch the limits to as far as they would go. Writing nonfiction in *Every Secret Thing* wasn't such a dissimilar process, although, obviously, there was a world out there that I was trying to reflect in a way you don't necessarily have to do in fiction. In fiction you can perhaps reflect your own feelings about that world much more strongly—it's perfectly permitted. But in autobiographical writing you are much more pinned down by the world that exists outside the pages of the book.

MJ: This raises the question of the ethics of writing auto/biography. It is a lot more fraught than fiction. You work within what Philippe Lejeune terms "the autobiographical pact." In the promise of truth there is some sort of mimesis so people hold biographers to their words in a certain way they don't do with fiction. This connects to the ethics about honoring people, especially if you are doing commemorative writing. How did you interview people and collect the material?

GS: Well, the way it worked in practical terms was that if I was interviewing anybody whom I thought might be adversely affected by what I was writing, I took a tape-recorder and said, "You don't mind if I put this on your desk," and then it was up to them what they told me. I told them that I was writing a book and that I didn't know exactly what would be included in it, but this was part of my research. It was up to them to decide what to tell or not to tell. But this was also a potent issue for me in writing this book, because of my father's reaction. He didn't particularly want me to delve into his past and my mother's past. The way he put it was that the subject matter of my book was his life and not mine. That was a very difficult situation for me, and I sometimes did feel as if maybe I was stepping over the line, that I shouldn't be doing it. I took his feelings very seriously, but, in the end, the way I selected the material has to do with the fact that actually it was also my life, it wasn't just his life (see Paul John Eakin [1998], Bonnie Friedman [1994], and Nancy K. Miller [2000]). And I am very clear in the book that this is a text that is seen entirely through my eyes, and that I'm talking of these people as my parents and from my viewpoint. In that way I wasn't writing biography. I wasn't trying to make a semi-objective assessment of what their lives were like. I suppose that's the only way that I could actually keep myself honest in the project and also know that I am writing a truth, not *the* truth, but *my* truth.

In a way one criterion for me, when I'm writing both fiction and nonfiction is, who's going to be hurt by this, and I applied this criterion when writing *Every Secret Thing*. So, for example, although I didn't give him the right of veto on what I've written, I did ask my father's son whether he wanted to be included in the book or not. And if he had said he didn't want to, I would have left him out, I think. I don't actually think that the written word is so precious that the absolute truth has to be said. And I don't say that I have put everything in the book that I've found out.

I was still criticized by several of my parents' friends for what I had done, for a slightly different reason actually. Part of what I was talking about was an examination of the nature of heroism in the twentieth century. I was trying to talk about the fact that heroes are real people as well, that they are not necessarily your ideal person, that in fact what makes a person heroic is that they are also an ordinary person. But some of my parents' friends and comrades disagreed with this. Because my parents had been so vilified in the old South Africa, these friends felt that I had given an opening to my parents' enemies to say the kind of vile things that they had always wanted to say about my parents but couldn't before, because of the laws of slander and libel. The accusation was therefore that I had broken ranks and that, in doing so, I had let the enemy in. To me, that's quite a difficult issue.

MJ: I'd love you to say a little bit more about heroism and ordinariness. I think that could be related to a more general shift in thinking of biography and the history of biography from Victorian heroic, where your subjects in autobiography always had to be spotless and stainless. Then you have a reaction of debunking. But I've often felt that in a way now it's a bit facile to simply debunk, especially as the genre itself depends on people's need for some kind of role model.

GS: I'm not so sure that people any longer want to look upon a hero as somebody who is untouchable, who is perfect, who one is unable to relate to. I do think that some of the failures of the twentieth century have to do with the idealization of the revolutionary hero, which is the model my father fitted into, as somebody who always put their private lives second. But if heroes do that, how can they understand the fact that most people put their private lives first? That what most people are concerned about is clothing and feeding their children and their families and being okay in their old ages. At moments of great change, ordinary people will sacrifice all that for an ideal, but in general, normality is what they want. And if your hero cannot understand this, then I think you are talking about a very different model of what a hero is, which actually no longer fits modern society. And I do think that that is something about writing about people: it is one thing to allow people the privacy of their lives (which I think everybody should be allowed); but I think it is another thing to present a picture of a person in their lives that really bears no relationship to who the person is, but more to do with the role they played in their life.

MJ: What about other auto/biographies of the modern heroes that have brought down apartheid, for example, Ellen Kuzwayo's *Call Me Woman*? They do tend to stress the public, the sacrifice to the struggle.

GS: Ellen Kuzwayo's book came out at a time when heroism was very important in the struggle. I think South Africa has changed. I wish there was, but I don't think that there is such a place for heroes. And I think it's much more complex now. If you're fighting for a justice that unites all people, heroism is much easier than when you're dealing with a complex society in the modern world and with no obvious enemy. In a way the hero is created by the opposition to the hero, by the devil.

In a recent paper Elaine Unterhalter (a South African historian working in London) made the very interesting point that many autobiographical texts written by South Africans always go over the same ground, the same political events, the Women's March on Pretoria for example, or the Freedom Charter, almost as if that litany of repetition and participation in those particular events has to be there to justify the personal life. But when you write autobiography, you don't actually have to put in every political event—and it is something that I decided not to do. I was going to do it through my memory, not through what actually happened.

MJ: I want to go back to your point about putting your father's private life alongside his public life and trying to make a whole person, about not abandoning heroism but showing the complexities of a human being. How did you find doing that with your mother's life?

GS: This is where what a person is in the world, and what their child writes about them, become separate. In a way, when I was growing up, my mother was the dominant member of the family. She, rather than my father, was the wage earner, the person who stood on platforms and spoke publicly about what was happening in South Africa. From the perspective of us, her three daughters, therefore, we had a very successful, very dominant, wage-earning mother. To write that wasn't a problem for me. What was a problem for the daughter of these two parents was to go to South Africa and experience the fact that *my father* had become the world figure, not my mother. Part of this is due to the fact that my mother was killed and therefore was not around to make her mark in the new South Africa. But this was also partly a personal obliteration brought about by death and the fading of memory and so, in writing about my mother, I felt I rediscovered her for myself. I had all these memories of who she was, and yet in writing about her I had to actually put them into a story that made sense, not only to me, but also to people who didn't know her. I did things that I hadn't done for very many years: I went and read her letters; I looked at photographs of her. So it was a very different process of rediscovering this woman. And what's more, when I wrote about her, I was really a grown woman, and I was looking at her, not from the vantage point of a child to her mother, but actually as a woman to this woman who had not aged, because she was dead. It was very different with my father, because he had just died, because his impact on the world was so much a part of his death, was so much a part of who he was in the last years of his life.

MJ: I am interested in female heroism, in women taking a very public role and sacrificing some of their private life for that public cause.

GS: It was a crucial struggle in my mother's life. It was much more difficult for her, because she was a woman, and because she bore the guilt of what the choices she made were doing to her children, and I think this made her a more abrasive character than my father. It was much more difficult for my mother because she had white women in South Africa as models, who, with only a few exceptions, not only did not take part in the struggle, but who didn't actually have working lives, and many of them didn't look after their children either because they had domestic workers. For my mother, her struggle was to try and be out in the world, and to be recognized out in the world. She had a very sharp mind and an equally sharp tongue; she did not censor what she said. It was a challenge to write about that person without making her unlikable, and of course it's the same kind of challenge that she faced in life. Everybody who knew my mother well knew that some of her unlikability came from the fact that she was terribly shy and that she really fought against this. So it was more difficult to write about her in a way that allowed her to be the full person that she was, without sacrificing the truth, but also without sacrificing the many-faceted parts of her.

MJ: You said that you had gone back to their writings as part of your research. How did you negotiate this; how did you find your own way to tell it?

GS: My mother had written quite a lot of books, most of which were not relevant to what I was writing because I wasn't doing biography. But there was one book that was very relevant, and that was her autobiographical account of her time in prison in 1963–1964, which was one of the most traumatic periods of my life. When I read this book, *117 days*, for my research, it was probably the third or fourth time that I had read it. The first time I read it was when it was first published. While she was in prison, my mother had attempted to kill herself, had taken sleeping pills. She writes about it quite honestly: about what drove her to it, and how she felt when she woke up. But when I was in my twenties, and a friend of hers made reference to this, I realized that I had read the book without taking in this part. I think it was too painful to know that my mother might have attempted to leave us. So as an adolescent, my mind just skipped over what was written there. Now when I came to write my book as an adult, I read hers anew. And I decided that because I was writing about her time, I should use her words to describe it. This wasn't difficult: it's such a beautiful book. It is such an act of courage from a really brave woman, whose one problem might have been that she found it difficult to expose herself.

My father's autobiography is a completely different thing: partly because it's unfinished, and partly because he wrote it after my mother was killed. I think as a way of keeping himself sane. Basically he was reliving the past with it. He wrote it during the early 1980s when the struggle was at its heights and so he couldn't really write very honestly about very many aspects of his political life. It doesn't have the honesty nor the scope of my mother's book, nor is it finished as a book. It has some lovely chapters about his childhood. I think the latter is interesting as a text, but not as an autobiographical text because he never really went into himself in that way. In a way his book makes my point about heroes, but from the other point of view, because although there is a paragraph or two about family life where he talks about his guilt at what his children experienced because of the choices that he and our mother made, this is limited to such few paragraphs and is buried in a larger chapter called "Politics, Mass Mobilisation and Family Life"—a combination that always makes me chuckle.

MJ: Something I want to ask you about is the Truth and Reconciliation Commission, and the writing that has come out of it, like Antjie Krog's *Country of My Skull*. You also talk about it at the end of your book—the call for reconciliation and forgiveness. I wondered about that as another context in which writing and repairing the past has taken place.

GS: You got me at a very bad time in my thinking on this because Ruth's killers were given amnesty two days ago. I'm not only furious, outraged, and upset, but I think it is a great injustice and unfair. I think that the problem is that the Truth Commission is more than one thing. It is the hearings that bore witness to what had happened in South Africa, and those are the things that Antjie Krog writes about. That seems to me to have been an absolutely wonderful and valuable exercise in understanding the past—not only understanding it, but taking a record of the past.

Then there's the amnesty process, which has effectively been a separate process. It has been run by the Truth Commission, but the people who have judged it are separate from the Truth Commission. They're not commissioners. They're not put into place because of their place in the Truth Commission or their feelings about it or their understanding of it. They're put there because of their legal expertise and because they're so-called balanced, that is, there are some judges from the left and some from the right, because they're hearing all these things. In a way, through the lens of our experience, I do feel that *this* commission has served as the opposite of what I would say the other part has done. I think it serves as a rewriting of history that bears no relationship to what happened. I certainly had the experience that some of the perpetrators' lawyers (and these are people who do not represent just one person, but they have applied for amnesty for a whole lot of people) actually have an agenda, which is about the rewriting of history through the verdicts and also through the kind of justifications that they give. At the moment, but I'm not sure that I will change my opinion on this, I do feel that this "wonderful" Truth and Reconciliation Commission that South Africa flaunts all over the world and makes people feel so "good," in some cases has been used as a justification for war crimes—which is what I believe Craig Williamson committed by killing my mother and another woman, Jeanette Schoon and her six-year-old daughter. I don't actually think there's a political motive for that. I think to give amnesty to that is to say: in a war, anything goes. That total war, which is what the apartheid state quite consciously said it was committing in order for them to keep on in power. And in fact the Truth Commission has validated that. It has actually said, yes, total warfare was justified, and those people who committed acts as part of this total war should not ever be held to account.

What is quite wonderful about the Truth Commission report is that in a sense this is the writing down, the collection of the stories of the past, combined with all the statistics and people's voices. What you have there is a different kind of autobiographical text. You have people talking directly about what happened to them, and some of it is stunning, and so upsetting and also so inspiring. There is heroism actually in the way that people have dealt with a grief that has been given to them, and sort of survived it, and are able to talk about it. In that there are all kinds of amazing things, amazing expressions of people's humanity and of a different kind of heroism. And I think Antjie Krog's is rather a good book, partly because she hasn't tried to join up the different accounts. That seems to me to reflect something very accurate about South Africa. It was certainly my experience when I first went back there that people live in the same country and yet they inhabit such completely different lives. Antjie Krog has used this reality as a way of giving you a flavor of what went on in that country, and she has done this very successfully. She gives the reader both the wonder and the horror of the past and present, and the wonder and the horror of the Truth Commission.

MJ: What you've just said reminded me of the end of your memoir. You make a similar point about coming to accept that the jigsaw puzzle won't be whole, and living with the kind of contradictions and lack of resolution you had initially hoped for. But it seems that that was still something you found livable with, or some sort of healing.

GS: I think that's why writing the book was very good for me, because I set out to ask all the questions I have never been able to ask and to find the answers. But in the process I think I discovered something more important, which is that although there isn't *one* answer, there is an *understanding* that I could reach. *Every Secret Thing* for me was about reaching an understanding that not everything can be explained.

On the other hand, the new novel *(Red Dust)* I have just completed on the Truth Commission is a piece of fiction and has little to do with my life or my mother. What interested me when I was writing this book is not the way people live their very different lives, but rather how people from such different lives are also so connected. One of the central themes of the book is the feelings and the ties that bind a torturer and his victim.

MJ: Going into a different genre altogether, I wondered if you could say something about your sister Shawn's film *(A World Apart)*. It doesn't seem so different from *Every Secret Thing* in also emphasizing a child's perspective.

GS: I think the great achievement of Shawn's film is that it is fiction combined with fact. The things that didn't happen that are in the film don't make the film any less realistic, because the emotional truth is still there. What interested me personally about the film was how it actually changed my memories. To give a very silly example: Barbara Hershey acted Ruth. Before she did, she met with us to talk to us about what Ruth was like. At that time I didn't want to assume that anybody could take my mother's place, but my experience of talking to Barbara was to think, "Phew, this woman is nothing like my mother. She isn't my mother—it's fine." And when eventually I watched the finished film, I thought that although she'd done a very good job, for me she wasn't my mother. For an audience she might be, but for me she wasn't. When Shawn was writing the film, I was very clear about which were the fictional elements and which were taken from our lives. Now I don't think that I am nearly as clear. In fact, many years after first seeing the film, I was on an escalator in the tube and I saw a picture of Barbara Hershey advertising some other film and before I could censor myself the thought that went through my mind was:

"There's my mother!" Perhaps that's why when people write South African political autobiography, they are continually reiterating the same parts of history—the same demonstration, the same political document—because of what has already been written about and this in turn affects what they remember, or now think of, as important. It certainly seems to have worked this way with me. I don't know whether my sisters' experience will prove to be the same thing, whether because I've now written about the family, my memory is somehow injected into theirs. I certainly do know that, especially over time, some of Shawn's memories have gone into my head in a way that I have to keep working out, "Was that true? Was that how? Do I remember that? Or did I see it on celluloid?" It's a very interesting process.

MJ: The other point that struck me about your book was the element of detective genre. It was very painful, but you had to do some detective work, and you made us as readers go through that suspense.

GS: That has to do partly with my history as a writer. When I started writing, I wrote detective stories. Now that has in turn got to do with my childhood. I had learnt to live with a lot of tension, and so when I started to write, creating tension was relatively easy for me. When I came to write *Every Secret Thing*, this thriller element wasn't a conscious attempt on my part. As a writer I have tried to train myself to give reign to my unconscious, to not try too hard to control what I'm doing, because that can lead to deadness. I find that if I try and exert too much conscious control over my writing, not only can I lose its drive, but I also can lose the feeling involved in it. So I'm not sure that I could actually say that I had a well-worked-out plan when I started *Every Secret Thing*. I had a start, that's all. For me the book is divided into thirds: the first is my mother; the second is my father; and the third is kind of both of them, but more to do with my father and a return to my grandmother.

The first third did not take a great effort on my part to structure. I often find it very difficult to start a book. In fact in every previous book—except for this one—I have speeded up towards the end. I rewrite less towards the end, and I always have to go back and reshape the beginning. But with this one, because it was so clear to me that the point of my wanting to write this book was the murder of my mother, it became obvious that I had to start on her last day; to not just talk about the end of her life, but how she began in Mozambique. The nature of my memories about South Africa is incredibly sporadic. Partly as a result of having a traumatized childhood, I tend to have very sharp memories of times of difficulty, and the rest, because it is less fraught, merges into the background. So instead of trying to regurgitate the whole twelve years in South Africa in its entirety, I chose to focus on what I remember as important. That also really structured the way the thing went.

The first third was really about my experiences, and my experiences with my mother. The second part required a lot more research because this is about my nonexperience of my father. There are memories, but they are also memories of not knowing. So that has a different kind of structure, and it has a different kind of pace. But again the very nature of what he was doing does give it a narrative drive because that is the nature of a military struggle. The last third is more reflective and in some ways less successful. Less successful in a way, because the Craig Williamson chapter had not reached the end of its process, and it shows. It had to be in there, but I hadn't gone far enough along the line of that. I was too close to the material to do it.

MJ: You leave me as a reader wanting more revenge and less reconciliation. It's quite painful to read.

GS: I think my account of my meeting with Craig Williamson is of an encounter without emotion. Which is precisely what I experienced at the time. It has taken me a long time to feel the rage. More recently I wrote a piece about being in the Truth Commission that was in *The Guardian,* and that is a furiously enraged piece. Three years after my first meeting with Craig Williamson I managed to not only write about it, but *feel* it. It was too surreal at that time. Maybe because it was too painful. The only way I could write it was in a kind of a deadpan way. But I think the experience was deadpan.

MJ: It also was like a panning back and seeing the bigger determinations and generations as opposed to the immediate. Could you say something more about writing about the politics of apartheid?

GS: I suppose I didn't write explicitly about the politics because I was definitely trying to avoid the landmark explanation of history. That isn't the way that I learnt politics in my life. And I was trying to give a flavor to a reader of what it was to inhabit this family where in fact I had two parents who, although politics was their life, never talked politics with us. My mother was indoctrinated by her own mother and felt very strongly that she was not going to indoctrinate her children. My father went along with it, although in later life he said that it was a mistake. So they never talked politics to each other in front of us, partly, of course, because what they were doing was so dangerous. I tried to give a reader a flavor of what it was like to understand a history of South Africa through what happened inside my family, that is, to give people a feeling of politics as dynamically as I experienced it. Not as something that happens out there by politicians, but as a kind of a political movement that one might be—as I was—inadvertently part of, and that completely affects one's life.

MJ: Maybe we could finish by you saying something about the reception here in England and in South Africa.

GS: One of the interesting aspects of its reception in South Africa was that it obviously spoke to people who came from very different backgrounds than mine. In particular, a lot of Afrikaner women would come up to me and say, "You think your life was difficult because of the choices your parents made. Imagine what it's like being me and asking my parents, 'Why did you do nothing?'" The book really did talk to a lot of people because I made my parents real to them. It is such a relief to know that your heroes could be like you, and it means that you also could be heroic. It also spoke to a lot of South Africans about the choices they didn't make, for example, in leaving the country and not being involved in politics. When people say, "I've read your book," they have a look on their faces that is pain. I guess it's my pain and their pain mixed together. But now I don't feel pain about the book. Once, at a reading in England, I was talking away, with all the anger you wanted me to have in the book. I looked into the audience, and they were weeping en bulk. But I certainly didn't experience that I wanted to cry. So I thought it was rather good—let them. I was clear that it was my and their pain, and this expression of grief was allowed by the book.

References Cited

DISKI, JENNY. *Skating to Antarctica*. London: Granta, 1997.
EAKIN, PAUL JOHN. "The Unseemly Profession: Privacy, Inviolate Personality and the Ethics of Life Writing." In *Renegotiating Ethics in Literature, Philosophy, and Theory*, edited by Jane Adamson, Richard Freadman, and David Parker, pp. 161–180. Cambridge: Cambridge University Press, 1998.
FIRST, RUTH. *117 days*. London: Bloomsbury, 1965.
FRIEDMAN, BONNIE. "Your Mother's Passions, Your Sister's Woes: Writing about the Living." In *The Best Writing on Writing*, edited by Jack Heffron, pp. 37–57. Cincinnati: Story Press, 1994.
KROG, ANTJIE. *Country of My Skull*. London: Jonathan Cape, 1998.
MILLER, NANCY K. *Bequest and Betrayal: Memoirs of a Parent's Death*. Bloomington: Indiana University Press, 2000.
MORRISON, BLAKE. *As If*. London: Granta, 1997.
SLOVO, GILLIAN. *Every Secret Thing: My Family, My Country*. London: Little, Brown, 1997.
———. *Red Dust*. London: Virago, 2000.

———. *Ice Road*. London: Little, Brown, 2004.
SLOVO, JOE. *The Unfinished Autobiography*. Randburg: Ravan Press, 1995.
SLOVO, SHAWN. *A World Apart*. London: Faber and Faber, 1988.

Further Reading

EAKIN, PAUL JOHN. *How Our Lives Become Stories: Making Selves*. Ithaca: Cornell University Press, 1999.
———. *The Ethics of Life Writing*. Ithaca: Cornell University Press, 2004.
EGAN, SUSANNA. "Changing Faces of Heroism: Some Questions Raised by Contemporary Autobiography." *Biography* 10, 1 (Winter 1994): 20–38.
KUZWAYO, ELLEN. *Call Me Woman*. Johannesburg: Ravan Press, 1996.

June 2000

VIII DISARMING WHITE MEN

White Men with Weapons: Performing Autobiography

Greig Coetzee interviewed by Debbie Lütge

FIVE YEARS AFTER being conscripted into the South African Defence Force in 1989, the memoirs of actor, director, and playwright Greig Coetzee evolved into an autobiographical collage entitled *White Men with Weapons*. In autobiographical drama, the gap between actor and playwright that generally characterizes theatrical performance is transformed. Instead of the interpretation being abstracted from the playwright's specific frame of reference, in self-representational theater the writer is also the performer; the performance thus reengages rather than reimagines the experience. Moreover, whereas in the written form of autobiography, the recollection is concrete, fixed, in performance, a living memory is re-presented in the momentary recollection and immediacy of the author-turned-performer.

Greig Coetzee's one-man show demands transformational acting skills, as a number of characters interface with their narrator. The irony of the work stems as much from the honest depiction of these characters as from the commentary delivered in the narration. The crafted characters, so plausibly drawn from differing social strata, portray a kaleidoscope of political, emotional, and psychological responses to conscription into the South African Defence Force during the apartheid era. It is in the bittersweet examination of their humanity, in their juxtaposition with the cynical narrator, that Coetzee's autobiographical treatment emerges. Together they form a record of the culmination of civil war in which South Africa was embroiled from 1958 to 1994. Each performance takes its toll: in warmth, in humor, in anger, in frustration, in justice, and in guilt.

Performing Autobiography: The Text

DEBBIE LÜTGE: *White Men with Weapons* has received much critical acclaim and public acknowledgment. What awards has the text won, and how, if at all, have these awards influenced the play's reception?

GREIG COETZEE: It's won six National Vita Awards, eleven Regional Vita Awards, and two Fleur du Cap Awards. Yes, these have definitely influenced the reception of the play. The first year it was financially disastrous, even though it was critically successful right from the beginning. I toured it for a year and averaged about twelve people a night for five weeks, in both Jo'burg and Durban, sometimes playing to four people. The two things that seemed to pull people in were the awards and performing overseas. South Africans, I think, have this sort of snobbery. When I advertised it as a local boy, no one was interested, but the moment I could say "direct from New York," then people wanted to come and see it. I must be fair, though; once I got a few decent audiences, word of mouth would always work well after that. So yes, the awards did help and also they helped me dig myself out of, what was then, a horrible financial hole. I mean, I owed thousands and thousands and in that first year and a half of doing *White Men* I probably took in about thirty thousand rands worth of award money. So, in fact, I was making more out of the award money than I was out of the play.

DL: Has the text received any awards that have not simultaneously been bestowed upon the performance or vice versa?

GC: No. For the Fleur du Cap Awards, it got Best Actor and Best New Play. I think my play just filled a vacuum at the time. It was just after a black government came into power and writers didn't know what to write about, and as a result there weren't many new exciting plays around. At the National Awards every award it was nominated for, it received. In fact, whenever it's been nominated for anything—the acting, writing, and often for directing as well—it's got the award. Once or twice it even won for lighting because I had a very innovative lighting designer in Cape Town. In fact I think it's got too many. I'm sure I will write other things that are better than *White Men with Weapons* that might not get any awards because they are the wrong play at the wrong time or there are other good plays on at the time. I'm very proud of it, but nineteen awards are ridiculous.

DL: Has the script been published?

GC: No. I'm hoping to get together three solo shows that I've written, and I'm thinking of compiling them as an anthology and trying to get them published.

DL: Is there any documentation of productions?

GC: Never a good one! I've sort of been jinxed with the video thing. I paid someone a lot of money to video a performance without an audience, but because there was no audience, the performance is flat, flat, flat. Then it was illegally recorded by someone from a television production company. When he came back to rerecord it properly, that night there was a block booking of seventy schoolboys, which was more than half the audience, and their laughter was so inappropriate that it upset the whole recording. When I do it in Edinburgh, in August, I'm going to video.[1] That's probably the last run—well, I've been saying it's going to be the last run for the last two years, so it probably won't be the last run—but I think it will be nice to have a record of it at the world's biggest festival.[2]

DL: In 1995 your play was a forty-minute script entitled *Men Only*. Six months later you added to the text. When did you decide to change the title to *White Men with Weapons* and why?

GC: Originally I called it *Men Only* because they were all male characters, I suppose. Then I took it to the Grahamstown Festival, and there was a lot of confusion about the title. I mean, some people thought women weren't allowed, and some people thought they were going to have some sort of tits-and-arse cabaret, and then instead they got this one skinny guy doing a whole lot of army sketches. So part of it was just me being facetious—acknowledging that you've got to get literal with South Africans, and then I also realized that for the show to get any profile, it had to be a little bit provocative. The subject matter was provocative, so it wasn't as if the title was out of keeping.

I'm still quite angry about the army experience so I suppose I gave it quite an angry title, and in many ways that title's worked to my advantage because overseas people have liked the title. Here it's gone through a stage of originally being alienating and now it's lodged in people's consciousness. But the thing is, the fact that I used "white men" in the title, in itself, is quite provocative in South Africa.

DL: The script, which evolved from a notebook, records your army experiences. How faithful is the text to the actual experience?

GC: Well, it's faithful in that there are no events in the script that didn't actually happen. This is true of little events like checking the light bulb for dust

---

1. At the Edinburgh Festival in 2000, Greig Coetzee received the Stage Award for Best Actor on the Edinburgh Fringe and the coveted Scotsman Fringe First Award.
2. In 2004, Coetzee performed both *White Men with Weapons* and *Johnny Boskak is Feeling Funny*, his fifth self-penned solo show, at the National Arts Festival in Grahamstown, South Africa.

or polishing the soles of your boots, and the major events like the rape or the story of the tracker having to stay with the injured staff sergeant while the rest of the platoon went for help. But I didn't experience all of them firsthand. Some of them were stories I heard from other people. It's also true in that the characters are all based on people I knew, with the exception of the rapist. The rape was recorded in a court case, and all three guys involved in the rape were hanged. It was in 1983. The only difference was it was a colored woman and her boyfriend. In fact, in many cases I had to take the truth and water it down because if you present it unadulterated on the stage, no one would believe it. So the rapist in the play tries to mitigate what has happened; but if you look at the cold facts, it was heartless murder and rape. In fact, they shot the boyfriend first, raped the woman, put her in the boot of the boyfriend's car, and set the car alight. The weird thing is when you put that on stage, it seems melodramatic. Another example of that is the staff sergeant who actually is based on two people.

In fact, a lot of characters, although they were real people I met or worked with, are combinations of two or three of those people because individually they're too stereotypical. Also, there are only so many characters you can fit into an hour and a half, so sometimes I fitted two or three stories into one character. The one was that staff sergeant, the other one was a major. I had studied isiZulu at university, and I had to give isiZulu courses in the army. It was weird, because up until then I was terrified of anyone with rank. When I taught the major, he behaved like a pupil and sort of opened up to me. He had these blue scars all over his face, shrapnel scars from a landmine explosion. What had actually happened—again, the truth was far more melodramatic for me to put on stage—is that he had been virtually disemboweled. Bits of him were hanging out, and this black guy had to hold him together until the helicopter came. And he would talk about how he hated black people, but he respected a good black soldier. He said he would never like a black person, but he has more respect for that black tracker than he had for virtually any white soldier. He just wouldn't admit that this guy was his friend—because he was his friend. He had to find another name for it. It was respect, not love.

And so for me that was the important thing that was coming through there, and I thought, well, make the truth more believable by watering it down.

DL: In writing about real-life situations, writers habitually distance themselves from the events before writing about them. How important was the five-year time lapse from the end of your army service to the commencement of writing your script?

GC: It was absolutely essential. Funnily enough, when I was in the army, I read *Slaughterhouse 5* by Kurt Vonnegut Jr., which is also an autobiographical piece. He writes about how, when he was in the army, he thought he was going to come out and write this wonderful army story and get rich. But the thing is, you come out of that military experience and you've got nothing to say about it. It was a very confusing experience. I mean, when I went in there, I was a very cut-and-dried self-righteous lefty student. By the end of it I despised most of those people as much as I did when I went in, except now I despised them in three dimensions as opposed to two dimensions. I knew I had legitimate reasons for despising them, but I also despised what I was when I went into that situation. I'm not saying the army made a man of me because it didn't. It taught me to lie and cheat and steal, but you come out of there with such a strange mixture of emotions because you meet some people who two years before you would have written off as artless racists, and you suddenly see a human side to them. Like this major, for example, as much of a killer as he was, there was also a very human side to him. I mean, he was a very damaged human being. So you come out of that not sure what to say.

The other reason I needed distance is that I was very angry when I came out. I was angry, angry with myself even. You come out of that situation angry with yourself because you went into it so self-righteously, and then you realize it isn't all so simple. I realized that I couldn't judge these characters. I was with them.

But, *ja*, that five-year cooling-off period was necessary also to learn to laugh at some of the things. When I first presented it as *Men Only*, it was a very serious piece of theater, and I got up there and after five minutes I did the corporal and people started laughing. Then I realized that it's probably good for South Africans to laugh at these things. So when I rewrote the script I tried to find that balance between finding the laughter, but avoiding flippancy, and also I found that the laughter acted as a foil and made the punches more effective.

DL: What catalyst prompted you to begin scripting the play after this five-year time lapse?

GC: There was a very specific reason: I was two weeks away from opening the play at the Grahamstown Festival and I had written two pages! Although, initially, I think it was teaching. I taught at a lovely school and I enjoyed teaching. Nevertheless it was always part of a five-year plan: teach for five years, pay back my loan, and be a writer. Since the age of thirteen I've known I'm going to be a writer. I didn't have a voice at the age of twenty-two, twenty-three. So to find a voice in those five years was very important. What prompted me to write a play was this frustration building up over the five years of wanting to be a writer. My school plays became increasingly elaborate, and in the final year of teaching, I decided to call my bluff. I'd always said that if I hadn't made inroads into the theater by the time I'm thirty, then I must forget it, and I was three months shy of my twenty-ninth birthday. Well, in the last year of my teaching, I thought I'm going to register for the Grahamstown Festival. So I came up with a title *Men Only*. I just entered a title and a description of what I thought the play would be about. Then the rest of the year descended into mayhem, and eventually I was left with two weeks and all I'd written was two monologues. Luckily it was exam time and I had about seven free afternoons. I managed to get off forty minutes of script in that time. Obviously, these characters had been building up in my head for a long time. I've actually developed this now as a way of writing in that I don't expect it to come at first. I'll just keep a file on my computer and write down key words. Then suddenly it's like waiting for a boil to come to a head before you lance it.

I think the Grahamstown Festival helped, because it's a place you can fly a kite at less than half the cost of setting up a five-week run in a city, and it focuses you. Also people know that in Grahamstown the edges are going to be a bit rough, so it's okay.

DL: Did teacher training and practice influence your approach to this text?

GC: Well, it was sort of a classroom joke: if you wanted to get Mr. Coetzee off the topic, you just had to get him talking about the army. In fact, I tried a lot of material out on schoolgirls—obviously without all the four letter words and without all the explicit detail—and that's when I realized that the piece had potential.

I'll never regret those five years. People have asked me whether, because I entered theater at the age of twenty-nine, I am sorry that I missed out on those eight years that I could have been in theater. I don't, because the lessons I learnt in teaching have enabled me to leapfrog over the backs of many other people who've been in theater since they were twenty. Some of the success was the quality of the piece, but a lot of it was the skill I picked up as a teacher—the ability to organize. I think I learnt more from doing school productions than I would have learnt directing professionals. Some people go to India to find themselves; I went to a girls' high school.

DL: Drama imposes stringent time constraints on the text. How did this influence the final product?

GC: That's a big lesson I've learnt because, in fact, I'm a very verbose writer. There's a novelist in me somewhere who wants to describe rolling hills and sunsets and ants crawling across the table. I probably will give the novel thing a bash one day, but I think I'll be a better writer for having written theater, because I think, like poetry forces writers to pare their writing down, theater does it at an even more complex level than poetry. In playwriting, to establish a character in such a short time, you've got to choose your words and deeds carefully.

Also what has helped me as a playwright is to be a performer. I honestly don't know how people write for the stage if they're not involved in the process as a director or as an actor. I would write these long flowing narrative interludes, and the actor in me would say, "Forget it chum, you're losing this audience," and I found myself literally editing my script in performance.

Performing Autobiography: The Performance

DL: The performance reflects moments of extreme trauma and anguish. How different was the act of scripting from the task of performance?

GC: All of it was cathartic. I must qualify that, because when I was in the army, I was twenty-one or twenty-two. I wasn't like the other seventeen-year-olds around me. The corporals were a little bit wary of me because I had a big mouth. I knew my rights. I was a qualified teacher, but for the seventeen-year-olds the pain and trauma are greater. So much arises out of empathy with what was happening to people around me, rather than what was happening to myself.

DL: So could performance not be described as reinscribing the trauma?

GC: No. I think the performance is more traumatic for the audience than it is for me. You get men in tears, and you see a gaggle of very morose-looking men sitting on one side. *Ja!* I just love performing the piece. I was angry at first, but in 400 of those 430 performances, I have just relished the performance.

DL: As the original script was written in 1995, and your first production of the revised script was later on your birthday, March 11, 1996, how much, if any, of the text was cut or adapted to meet performance requirements?

GC: When I opened *White Men with Weapons*, it was about one hour thirty-five minutes. Since then I've cut out a character called Milton van der Spuy; he became another play on his own.[3] I cut him out because he was the only character I had invented completely and because he was sugarcoating the pill, too nice a boy to be with those other guys. Now it's down to between eighty and eighty-five minutes. I got rid of the unnecessary narration, a lot of which was a bit cowardly in that I was consciously trying to distance myself from the

---

3. *The Blue Period of Milton van der Spuy* was performed in 1998 in Belgium.

characters so that the audience understood that I'm not like them. Suddenly I realized that if you're going to display these guys in public, warts and all, you've got to do it without judging them. If the audience don't know where you are coming from, so be it.

DL: Have there been any textual changes in the last few years?

GC: Not much! Although from night to night I do vary it slightly for my own sanity.

DL: Were any improvisational techniques used in scripting the play?

GC: No, it was just desperate scriptwriting, although yes, in performance it changed. For example, the bed-making scene was originally just a guy making a bed. That rifleless rifleman never raised a laugh when I first performed him because I didn't know how to time it, where to place the pauses. People respond to him like a stand-up comic now.

DL: Your performance requires great physical agility. Did you use any of Grotowski's exercises to enhance your performance?

GC: I didn't use Stanislavsky [who developed a scientific approach to naturalistic acting based on psychoanalysis] or Grotowski [who focused on the actor's body as a theatrical tool]. From about performance number thirty I realized that it needed incredible focus, and now I have a warm-up that's virtually a ritual. Whenever possible I do it to James Phillips's music from the eighties. All that sort of "Shot Down in the Street" and "Hou My Vas, Korporaal" (Hold me tight, corporal). I do a very physical warm-up. I mean, I actually get myself tired. I normally do a full thirty minutes physical warm-up because I've got to manufacture adrenaline to get on stage. When you've done the show this many times, it's easy to become blasé. I end with a headstand to get blood into my head. To get worked up about it, you've got to revisit the aggression because in the army you just wake up in a bad mood; I mean, the first thing I do is jump out of bed at the beginning of the play. You've got to be in that mixture of that rush, the fear of that corporal arriving, the fact that you're pissed off because it's another bloody day in Oudtshoorn, and all of that, and just take the play by the scruff of the neck and go for it. I find a different warm-up, a little ritual, for every piece that I do. I think that applies specifically to a solo performance.

DL: In portraying a part, the performer merges his or her self with the role in various ways. In the performance I didn't notice any difference in the portrayal of the "live models" as opposed to the characterization based on an imaginary character. Was the self-representation involved in an autobiographical performance different from that of the characterization of characters you had previously met?

GC: Yes! There's the confidence factor of knowing the person is real. Maybe in the actual performance there isn't much of a difference. I think what I do as well, even when I've invented a character, is to find a live model for them. In fact, even Milton is based upon real people—his voice, the sort of defeated physical quality about him—so, *ja*, I'd have to contradict myself there and say that I will always find a real model for the character.

DL: Method actors relate to characterization via the process of emotional recall. In what way does an autobiographical work like *White Men with Weapons* complicate or facilitate the actor's function?

GC: I was not just an observer, I was involved, so what I have to try to avoid is my emotions at the time conflicting with the characters' emotions. So, for example, when I'm the staff sergeant at the end with a beer can in his hand, I was actually in that scene, I was the guy he was shouting at. At the time I had no sympathy for the staff sergeant at all. So I've got to stop being the person I was, the guy standing at attention, and become the guy behind the desk. Being autobiographical, the one possible source of interference is your own emotion as opposed to the emotions of the other person you are portraying.

DL: The medium of dramatic communication implies a portrayal or imitation of the heightened self rather than merely the presence of self. How did your approach to characterization differ in regard to portraying a third party, as opposed to dramatizing your own persona?

GC: Initially, in the very first performance, I was self-conscious about playing myself in public, but I became very comfortable with that. The character who is closest to me would be the rifleless rifleman, but I've created a distance from him. I've given him this sort of sardonic Jo'burg accent and a slightly different turn of phrase to what I would use and so, in fact, he's become a third person as well. I think that's important; otherwise there's a terrible chance of self-indulgence creeping in.

DL: Performers constantly differentiate between "seeming" to be the character and "being" the character. Did playing yourself as a character offer any insight into Stanislavsky's theories?

GC: I think so, because there is a constant tension. I mean, there are times when I will feel what those characters are feeling. It's a strange duality. There's a sense of observing yourself, and a sense of feeling—*ja*, I mean, it's a sort of Pavlovian association, that when you say those words and use that tone of voice, you feel the emotion. Sometimes the staff sergeant cries and it's something I do out of technique, or he'll just cry because he's feeling those things. And other times I'm actually thinking about shopping lists while I'm performing and I've got to stop and think, did I actually say that?

DL: Would you comment on your sense of "truth" in autobiographical performance?

GC: Firstly, generally speaking, life is not a sort of truth in the sense of a life of an everyday reality. It's quite often boring, and it's often devoid of metaphor. The art is to choose the interesting bits. It's editing the truth, not to cut out or distort it, but to get rid of all that stuff that's saying nothing about anything. Autobiography is not self-indulgent. One mustn't assume that every minute of one's life is interesting enough to put on stage.

DL: A rehearsal process always begins with an in-depth examination and analysis of the character and usually ends with a discovery or uncovering of various elements. Was this fragmentation of the text into meaningful bites conceived from the onset in your scripting?

GC: Well, when I wrote it, I didn't come up with any sense of narrative at all because I didn't have a story about my army life, I had a collection of people that I'd met. And then when I took it to Garth Anderson, the director, he said, 'Why are you doing this first?' And I actually had to start thinking about that, and I thought, no, it can't just be a revue, it has to have an overarching narrative. So I just wrote about people who had the strongest effect on me. Then I lined them up, and I saw a structure emerge from that: the first third of the play deals with orientating the audience into a military culture, of reminding people who were there what it's like and of initiating people who weren't there. The middle section deals with the sort of dehumanization of the enemy, and that culminates in the rape scene. What happens when you dehumanize people completely? And then what happens when you take that enemy away? If you take the fox away, the hounds turn on each other sort of thing. That's implosion. Those are the three stages of the play. So I began with character because I think that's the strongest point of theater. People don't sit there thinking what a clever story, or what an interesting structure—they live in the moment of the character. That's the way I start with all my writing now; build the characters first and find their story afterwards.

DL: Have your characters, even though they are combinations, been given specific names?

GC: Yes, just for marking in my head. I don't know why, sometimes I had to give them rank.

DL: In performance you maintain a consistent level of excellence. Stanislavsky's insistence on "emotional recall" is a concept to aid actors not performing their own life history. How draining is this production for you, when forced by your close relationship to the text to reexperience rather than recall an analogous situation or emotion?

GC: I think it changes after the first hundred or so performances. So, in fact, what I now associate the performance with are other performances, rather than actual experience. For example, I've made that bed more times out of the army than I did in the army.

DL: To what extent is the contemporary performance experience that of performing a self that you have outgrown? Or does performance of a former self serve to entrench that self?

GC: No, I do not think performance of a former self inhibits growth. Not at all! I think it helps you realize how much you've changed.

DL: What shifts do you foresee in a reinterpretation of your work by another actor, considering the fact that the text, in another actor's performance, shifts from the field of autobiography to one of imparting biographical material?

GC: I suppose they'd have to do some sort of research. I assume that the actor would be younger as well, so they probably wouldn't have had a conscription experience to base it on. I'd say they were in for a tough time, and I'd have very little advice to give except be sure you pay me my royalties!

Performing Autobiography: Staging and Audience Reception

DL: A director operates as a collaborative artist, unifying the vision and creating a cohesive bond between the playwright, the performer, and the product. You have worked as a director on other one-man shows. What is the essential difference between directing oneself and directing someone else?

GC: It's the letting go, realizing that this other person is entitled to their own interpretation. I have a very clear vision of the way I want a piece to look. I think I'm probably difficult to direct because of that, because I have my own ideas, and you've got to persuade me why I should do it differently. And yet I expect other actors to be willing to do exactly what I tell them. It's a lot more difficult transferring your vision. Compromise is not an easy thing to do.

DL: How does Garth Anderson's direction affect the autobiographical nature of the work?

GC: In fact, Garth had a far more bitter army experience than I did. I was a pariah because I wouldn't carry a rifle. Garth was a pariah because he was gay. He was also in the army at a particularly heavy time. I mean, Garth is about thirteen years older than me, and he did many military camps. I remember when we went into Natal Command [an army base in Durban] together to ask for equipment—years after Garth had left the army—I could see he was scared and he was angry. He said suddenly he just got angry again being there, you know. So I think Garth added to the autobiographical nature of the piece because his reactions to my writing were based on his own experience, and I think, in fact, he was the perfect director. Apart from the fact that he's a very imaginative director. Unless you've actually done it, it sounds like it's part of this boys' own club. So many guys have come backstage and said: "You know, I'm so glad I brought my wife to this, because I've been trying to tell her for years what it was like, but you can't." I mean I even found it difficult to tell people. I had to show them. So, *ja,* I couldn't have chosen a better director.

DL: In the metalanguage of the play, conveyed via the visual spectacle, you have chosen a multifunctional set with minimalistic staging. The staging implies spartan conditions, an uncluttered discipline, and the neat precision suggestive of a military environment. The set further invites the audience to fill in the total environment, leaving both the horror and camaraderie of war in the audience's imagination. Was the staging conceived visually while scripting was in progress? Or were selected autobiographical details and stage business inserted as part of the production process?

GC: Well, firstly, at a purely practical level, the play had to be portable; it had to fit in the back of a *bakkie.* The other thing is that what was there had to be authentic, so it's all proper military equipment. Also whatever's there must be used in performance. But it was pretty much cobbled together during the last two weeks of rehearsal.

DL: In a recent production of Robin Maugham's play *Enemy* at the Courtyard Theatre in Durban, the circumstances were altered from a World War II setting to the South African border. Do you have any reservations about a future reinterpretation by another director?

GC: No, I'd be fascinated, especially to see another culture take it on. They'd have to rewrite bits. I'm sure it would translate very well.

DL: Conscription is a subject with which South African white men can identify. Did an overseas tour elicit similar reactions, particularly from American audiences in light of their Vietnam experience?

GC: *Ja,* there was never any surprise at what had happened. No one ever said: "My God, did that happen in South Africa?" The only surprise was that it was so similar to their own experience. The military animal is pretty much a universal animal, and that's come out quite clearly in the overseas response.

DL: Were white attitudes to conscription culture-based? Did you perceive a difference in the attitudes of English- and Afrikaans-speaking conscripts?

GC: Very much so. I think especially because most of the people I was with were from either Afrikaans- or English-speaking universities, and just traditionally English-speaking universities were more antagonistic towards conscription. I suppose it was rooted in South African English versus Afrikaans culture, but more in that the End Conscription Campaign had a profile at the English-speaking universities that it didn't have at the Afrikaans-speaking universities.

DL: How long was your period of conscription?

GC: It was just over a year.

DL: Where were you stationed?

GC: I started off at Oudtshoorn Infantry School, an army base in the Eastern Cape. I was there for about five months and then I got moved to Natal Command and Mtubatuba [a town in KwaZulu-Natal] up on the north coast [north of Durban], where I had to teach very thick white corporals to speak isiZulu.

DL: Having served in the South African Defence Force, how have your perceptions of nationalist attitudes changed?

GC: I think people seeing themselves as groups is a very dangerous thing. It creates Rwanda. It's what creates Zimbabwe, and it's what creates Kosovo. Yes, national pride is important, but only when it stays away from a sort of mob identity, where the collective intelligence is far lower than the intelligence of any of the individuals involved.

DL: Do you believe that conscription has a place in an independent South Africa?

GC: No! We need a good police force, and we need border control, maybe. That's it.

DL: *White Men with Weapons* conveys a sense of the betrayal that white South Africans—particularly males—have experienced in fighting a "war" that was doomed from the start. The play also portrays the double-edged confusion of whites ensnared in a white betrayal of black aspirations. How important is the balance of these two spheres to the scheme of the material?

GC: It's very important in that in many ways the people in the trenches are the people who've taken the metaphorical knock across the board in South Africa. In my opinion the backbone of black society under apartheid was kept intact by middle-aged black women working as domestic workers, keeping hearth and home together. They're probably at the back of the queue when it comes to receiving rewards in the new South Africa, and it's young yuppies, who've got no real experience of apartheid, who are reaping the benefits. On the other hand, if you look at the Truth and Reconciliation Commission, people like P. W. Botha [former prime minister] and Magnus Malan [former minister of defense] are getting off scot-free. It's the rank-and-file cannon fodder who are getting the rap. Many of them deserve it, the Eugene de Kock's [nicknamed Prime Evil] deserve it, but no more than Magnus Malan deserves to be behind bars. *Ja*, I think there's been a two-way betrayal.

DL: In *White Men with Weapons* you deliver a racially charged subtext through a variety of characters and the play ends with South African independence looming and a far less disciplined attitude. How uncomfortable did these characters' perspectives make you feel, when voicing their fascist viewpoints?

GC: I'm saying this is what happened. These people were there. They're still around. There they are, deal with them.

DL: Does laughter at racially charged moments in the play worry you? Or do you attribute this to a nervous reaction to the irony of the work?

GC: However they respond is their responsibility, not mine.

DL: The title implies ethnic-specific casting. Do you agree with the African-American playwright August Wilson that certain plays demand ethnic-specific casting?

GC: Yes, I think so. Whether you like it or not, your skin has got associations and political implications, as does your accent. Whether you're fat or thin has an effect on your stage presence, and I think skin color and ethnicity is no different.

DL: What cultural group did you see as your target audience?

GC: I wasn't thinking that far ahead. It was my ticket out of teaching. That's all it was. But it has a mainly white audience, there's no doubt about that. That's just more a reflection of the theater-going audience in South Africa, certainly the theater-going audience that will pay, you know, thirty, forty, fifty rand to go to the theater. But I've been very heartened by black responses to the piece. A lot of white people think that black people are going to be offended when they see it, but in fact they tend to laugh more. Firstly, it's no secret to them that there are white racists in South Africa. Secondly, black people—who come to the theater, whose grasp of English is generally good—have a sense of the irony that the characters are actually saying more about themselves than they are about the objects of their racism.

DL: The significance of this work, for South Africans coming to terms with a changing political landscape, lies in the signifier apartheid. How has the play facilitated other racial groups to achieve an understanding of the trials and dilemmas of the "white man"?

GC: One of the first people to come backstage was a member of Umkhonto we Sizwe, an ex-guerrilla. He was one of the first soldiers to say, "This is my story." An ANC soldier would have the same experience as a SADF soldier. With many other black people it's been a case of: "We've always seen those army camps and we've wondered what happened." Also they are astonished that it wasn't fun. They said they imagined that behind the barbed wire, we were having *braais* and just laughing at black people and shooting. So there has been a sort of understanding that takes place that wasn't there before.

DL: Is autobiography for you an exorcism of the ghosts of the past? And was your intention to provide a release for your audience?

GC: I suppose it was an exorcism of ghosts, although it wasn't conscious. Teaching has taught me that conflict can be good, if it's in a controlled environment. I've got the same attitude towards theater. Confront people with things in a controlled environment.

DL: The danger in writing an autobiographical work is the obvious commentary on others that results. Did anyone see the play and recognize themselves in the work?

GC: The only guy I know for sure who has seen it was the guy who also refused to carry a rifle. He loved it. One or two people have recognized characters. But, you know, I don't think most of those real people have ever darkened the hallways of a theater. People have often come up to me and said, "Oh, I know that guy." Because the system produces stereotypes, so many people think they recognize people.

DL: *White Men with Weapons* has been performed in America. How many other countries have you toured?

GC: Eight. South Africa, Namibia, Singapore, Australia, Holland, Belgium, and now the United Kingdom.

DL: Having successfully toured other countries with a bilingual text, are you expecting the reaction from the British audience to be the same as that elicited from a South African audience?

GC: *Ja*, no, it wouldn't be exactly the same. Overseas audiences tend to take the play a bit more seriously. Except in Australia, they laughed as much as everyone else. And when I did it in Singapore, where there are many British ex-pats, they howled with laughter because the Anglican chaplain was a very recognizable type for them.

DL: Many South African actors have seen this play more than once because of the excellent combination of satirical text and the finesse of the performance. Has there been a similar response to other shows that you have performed?

GC: Unfortunately not yet. I'm hoping! But I also think that it's something that's beyond *White Men with Weapons*. I'm proud of the show, but I think it also fills a vacuum in the lives of many South Africans. Americans dealt with Vietnam to death. Apart from *Somewhere on the Border* by Anthony Akerman, this is the only really post-apartheid play dealing with the army experience.

DL: Do you envisage a sequel, a *White Men without Weapons*?

GC: Well, my press release for my later play, *Breasts: A Play about Men*, starts off with something like, "A new platoon of South African males, unarmed and out of uniform." So, there you go!

References Cited

AKERMAN, ANTHONY. "Somewhere on the Border." In *South African Plays*, edited by Stephen Gray. London: Hern, 1994.

Further Reading

ANDERSON, STEPHEN BENNETT. *The End Conscription Campaign in Cape Town, 1983–1989*. Cape Town: University of Cape Town, 1990.

COETZEE, GREIG. *Happy Natives: A Play*. Pietermaritzburg: University of Natal Press, 2003.

COLLINS, B. "A History of the Committee of South African Resistance (COSAWR) 1978–1990." PhD diss., University of Cape Town, 1996.

GRAAF, M., ed. *"Hawks and Doves": The Pro- and Anti-conscription Press in South Africa*. Durban: Contemporary Cultural Studies, 1988.

MOULDER, J. E. "Conscientious Objection and the Concept of Worship." PhD diss., Rhodes University, 1977.

PHILLIPS, M. W. "The End Conscription Campaign 1983–1988: A Study of White Extra-parliamentary Opposition to Apartheid." PhD diss., University of South Africa, 1988.

PRICE, L. "A Documentation of the Experiences of Military Conscripts in the South African Defence Force." PhD diss., University of Natal, 1990.

May 2001

Reflections in a Cracked Mirror

Pieter-Dirk Uys interviewed by Mervyn McMurty

PIETER-DIRK UYS HAS written and, most often, performed in more than fifty-five plays, cabarets, and revues. He has performed to royalty and schoolchildren, in embassies and community halls, in South Africa, the United Kingdom (where he has performed, almost annually, at the Tricycle Theatre in London for more than a decade), the United States of America, Canada, Australia, the Netherlands (in Dutch), Germany (in German), Austria, Switzerland, Denmark, and Slovenia.

Uys was born in Cape Town in 1945; the son of a Jewish Berlin-born mother and an Afrikaner Calvinist father, he quips that he "belongs to both chosen (white) people." After graduating from the University of Cape Town, he studied at the London Film School, where he wrote and performed in his first play, *Faces in the Wall* (1969). After graduating with honors, he returned to South Africa and joined the Space Theatre in 1973.

The Space had opened in 1972 as a non-state-funded theater, the first in the country to openly defy segregation laws and to promote the development of an alternative, oppositional, and local theater. Here Uys wrote, directed, and performed in more than fifty productions in two years. By the end of the 1970s he was considered the *enfant terrible* of South African theater, a reputation based on the iconoclastic intent of the plays and fostered by his many confrontations with the censorship board: in the month of July 1975 alone, on the grounds of indecency, obscenity, blasphemy, and ridicule of a section (Afrikaner) of the population, the script of *Selle Ou Storie* (Same old story) was banned, but not the production, whereas the production of *Karnaval* (Carnival) was banned, but not the script.

Therefore, after 1981 Uys worked largely in a fugitive, nonliterary performance form: the political revue. Under apartheid his revues used to dramatize "headline issues" to serve as daily news reports for a public denied access to information about the turmoil in the country by the restrictions placed on the press during successive States of Emergency in the 1980s. Their titles and linking themes were often derived from speeches by P. W. Botha, then prime minister and later state president: "adapt or die," "total onslaught," and "beyond the Rubicon."

The first of his revues, *Adapt or Dye* (1981), established certain features of his one-person "concerts" (as he calls them). They deal with topical "here today, gone tomorrow" issues that impact on the lives of a spectrum of South Africans (black and white, male and female, young and old, Afrikaners and English, conservative and liberal, oppressors and oppressed). During apartheid the concerns included race classification, conscription, and forced removals; more recently, these have shifted to include violence, crime, corruption, and, in particular, AIDS. He uses three variations of the monologic form: fictional monologues, lampoons of national and international political leaders, and, as himself, a stand-up discourse with the audience that engenders rapport and a sense of conspiratorial collaboration. These "concerts" continue to feature a fictional persona, his alter ego, Evita Bezuidenhout.

Like her namesake, Evita Peron, Evita Bezuidenhout is glamorous, corrupt, and infinitely adaptable, with a desire for self-aggrandizement and celebrity status. Through her, Uys assumes an ironic mask to subversively ridicule those in power; in the 1980s, as the wife of a (fictive) member of Parliament, her apparent naïveté was a means to expose the hypocritical discourse of apartheid without fear of censorship, as she was (and has remained) both too lifelike and too much part of the status quo to be suppressed.

To maintain a sense of her actuality and separate existence, Uys characteristically utilizes various ploys that have made her achieve national celebrity status. She has appeared "in person" at numerous occasions and on her own television talk show with well-known figures who treated her as real, thus reinforcing her actuality in the eyes of the public. She has written to, and received replies from, world leaders (including Margaret Thatcher). When she appeared on television in Australia, viewers telephoned the network to demand her removal from the program because of her "fascist" remarks. Conferences she has called are attended by local and international newspaper and media correspondents.

In the early 1990s, when a change in government appeared inevitable, "Evita Bezuidenhout" resigned from the National Party and prepared to continue her high public and political profile in the new dispensation. She appeared on podiums with Nelson Mandela in African National Congress rallies in 1994 to encourage fair and free elections. She has addressed the South African Parliament twice, in 1999 and 2001. In 2000 she was awarded the Living Legacy 2000 Award in San Diego by the Women's International Center, for her "contribution to the place of women in the last century." (Mother Theresa and Hillary Clinton are past honorees.)

Uys's earlier revues were primarily aimed at "the whites, the lawmakers"; he intended to inform his audiences about what blacks knew from lived experience. Once the apartheid era had ended, and the "honeymoon was over," Uys began to satirize the new "designer democracy" for a South African audience in *You ANC Nothing Yet* (1995) and *Truth Omissions* (1996; the title a play on the Truth Commission): "I have to be careful to offend everybody equally," he says. As a strategy Uys has always based his material on facts: "I hold up a true mirror and leave the comedy to the eye of the beholder." In presenting facts as stage material, characters (and, by association, ideologies) satirize themselves. In the past Uys used to say that the apartheid government wrote his best material; now "the new government has caught up fast." Entertainment has remained the raison d'être of the revues, but this does not negate their satiric qualities: criticism and humor are his means to reflect prevailing political and social conditions, scourge what is ridiculous by using laughter as a weapon, and promote a release of fear through the beneficial power of laughter.

The same applies to his intentions overseas; while his material is founded in the South African context, he adapts the content to the time and place of performance. Racism is an international disease, Uys believes, so he tells audiences elsewhere: "Apartheid was so successful we couldn't kill it: we sold it to Yugoslavia."

In 1999 Jeremy Kingston of *The Times* of London described Uys as a "remarkable performer, whose gifts and intentions are so rare nowadays he may be unique. He is a mimic, he is a comic; in Mrs. Evita Bezuidenhout he has created the most famous white woman in Africa; but above all else, and at the same time underlying it, he is a passionate political and social satirist."

This interview was conducted at the International Convention Centre in Durban in August 2000, prior to his performance as Evita Bezuidenhout before delegates at a medical conference. The occasion was appropriate as, in 2000, Uys had completed a 10,000-kilometer tour of schools in order to promote AIDS awareness, a solo crusade undertaken without private or government sponsorship. In 1999 Uys had decided to retire to his home in Darling, a village an hour's drive from Cape Town. "I felt the moral high ground had been leveled," he told a reporter in the July 23, 2001, edition of *Time*. However, troubled by the "AIDS is from Venus and HIV is from Mars" attitude of the present rulers, he decided to tour the country to educate the youth. His material and experiences were incorporated in shows entitled *For Fact's Sake* (2000). He says: "I'm not a medical expert like President Thabo Mbeki [whom he now lampoons as Dr Thaboo MacBeki]. I'm just a human terrified of dying from love."[1]

MERVYN MCMURTY: As we're going to discuss the ways in which you present yourself and others on the stage, I thought we could begin with how you portray what I'll label the "biographical" Uys. This is a strategy you have employed from your earliest one-person shows: "My name is Pieter-Dirk Uys. I'm over forty. I'm a white South African. I'm an Afrikaner. I'm Jewish." Clearly this mask—that of the Uys persona—was and still is a means to introduce a spectrum of personae, both fictional and nonfictional . . .

PIETER-DIRK UYS: Yes, first I had to create a character called Pieter-Dirk Uys because I didn't have the confidence to be me at all in 1981 in *Adapt or Dye* [revue performed in South Africa, the United Kingdom, Australia, Canada, and the Netherlands satirizing the ideology of apartheid and its advocates]. Then the "me" started coming out in about 1985 when I realized I had to be seen to form opinions and stand up and speak out. Also I had and have to present myself as my first target—I have to be on trial as well, and therefore I established who I am straight away: white, gay, with an Afrikaner father, a Jewish mother, and a colored grandmother called Wilhelmina Opklim. [Reputedly, too, he is related to a seventeenth-century black Cape courtesan]. Once I've got all my dirty linen out of the way, I can introduce the facts of bad politics, and audiences will believe me. Overseas, of course, I had to present my autobiography, I had to tell them who I was, and how to pronounce my name, not "ice" or "arse" but "ace."

And as I've been developing in the 1990s it's become very personal, since 1994, since the alphabet has become free, since I was "freed" from jail by Mandela. And it's become much more difficult, because the targets are much more

---

1. In an article published in the *Washington Post* on September 15, 2003, Mbeki stated that he had no personal knowledge of anyone who had contracted the HIV virus or died of AIDS. Uys responded by sending a letter to all the editors of South African newspapers, calling for the removal of President Mbeki for his "lies" and his "genocidal Mbekivellian policies." His letter was widely published and elicited a response from the president's office. In recent revues Uys refers to Mbeki as "Comrade Undertaker."

confusing and at the same time liberating, because now I have the right to have opinions. I can do a show about the use of taboo words and about my upbringing as a racist—a show like *Dekaffirnated* [1999, subtitled *Calling a Spade a Spade; kaffir* is an actionable insult in South Africa]. I've brought personal reality to the fore. In *For Fact's Sake* I speak about my first sexual experience at the age of fifteen, because if I put myself onstage as number one target, we can share our fears and our experiences.

MM: It is, of course, a satiric device, a means to present certain norms: if the Uys-persona is presented as honest and sane and rational (with the inference that the audience is likewise if they appreciate or share his fears), then the unsympathetic personae appear as deviants from those norms.

P-DU: Absolutely, absolutely, and therefore those characters have got the freedom to exercise all their racist attitudes and their homophobia and their hypocrisy. It's like the reflections in a cracked mirror.

MM: Do you see a difference between that mask and the mask of the playwright who performs the characters?

P-DU: There is a difference. You see, I see myself first and foremost as a stage manager, and a lot of the time I'm really looking at it technically as well. I can be totally involved in a performance and at the same time be thinking about where the next prop is set. So the playwright is the part that is listening for moments when something jumps out that can be used then and there. The Pieter-Dirk Uys performer is very much a structured theatrical character, and it's very important to keep him like that because I've got to speak about him in the third person.

MM: Even in works like *No Space on Long Street* (1997), which tells the story of the Space Theater and your involvement in its early years, the biographical facts are mediated not only by you as the younger Pieter-Dirk Uys, but also by the range of fictional and nonfictional characters who participate in the telling, who comment . . .

P-DU: You know, Penguin commissioned an autobiography, and I finished it, and it stinks. I can't stand it. I can't read paragraph after paragraph of "I . . . me," "I . . . me." Now it's out of my system, it's in a box, and I'm going to start again. Instead, I'm going to write a memoir and illustrate the memoir with characters who will talk about me, in a critical way, giving their perspectives. I loved reading autobiographies in the past, but I'm reading fewer autobiographies now because I know the story before I've read it, whereas I love rereading memoirs.

In writing and performing I need, desperately, my schizo-, no, multi-phrenia, so that I can include a variety of perspectives. I'm frightened of one view, of say, being so modest that it comes across as egocentric, or of trying to go to extremes to protect one's own ego. And I also believe that ego leads to writer's block. The reason I haven't had writer's block is because I don't have time to think of my own ego. Sadly, my face-picture never fits my brain-picture: I think I look like Doris Day when I actually look like Boris Karloff. Actually, Evita [Bezuidenhout] gives me a third aspect, an objective view, a looking-at-oneself, because I let her, I don't interfere . . .

MM: She will no doubt comment on Pieter-Dirk Uys in your memoir.

P-DU: She's already had a very interesting comment: in *A Part Hate a Part Love* [a biography of Evita Bezuidenhout, weaving her fictional life with factual incidents in South African history; the title puns on *apartheid*]. I interview her, and she says: "*Meneer* [Mister] Uys, are you related to that third-rate comedian?" And I quickly reply no, hearing the cock crow three times. That's exactly the sort of deprecating humor a biography needs.

MM: It's an approach that reminds me of Oscar Wilde's quip: "Every man nowadays has his disciples, and it is always Judas who writes the biography."

P-DU: How true, because Judas is more interesting, and his opinion of Jesus is what one would really want to hear. An autobiography is never completely truthful because you're writing what you want people to remember you for. But theatrical characters are true to themselves; the spectator will give them the color he or she wants. In trying to write the commissioned autobiography, even moments of self-discovery didn't work. I thought: I won't have this published, because it was intrusive, it was me commenting on political things without the perspective of a character. But Evita gets away with it. Evita said to the Americans, "Clinton is a liar," whereas when I said that to them they were offended: "Who the hell are you to say that?" And they're right, but Evita has the authority to say it because she doesn't exist. And that brings me back to performance, the theater: I myself have no theatricality, but the characters do, and the interaction with the audience is what is creative. Audiences always see aspects of people that I didn't envisage: a character often spoken about at present is the Jewish countess I created in *Dekaffirnated*, the aging refugee in Hillbrow [who tells her maid: "I come from a holocaust. You just come from a struggle"]. Audiences recognize so many people through her, and I'm amazed at who they've seen. The mirror is clean, but it's partly cracked, and some parts are distorted, mainly for the guilty ones, then and now. Others are strange victims of their own hypocrisy, like Nowell [a pun on Noel, i.e., Christmas; the archetypal pseudo-liberal *kugel,* to whom everything works out "no . . . well . . . fine," recognized in the United States as the Jewish Princess]. But my characters must outlive me on every level. I'm the stage manager, and I see to it that they look right and say things that are honest—for them. I stopped writing the autobiography when I looked at it as a playwright who knew it wouldn't work unless it was restructured as a piece of theater, with characters interacting with each other and me.

MM: Even a character such as Evita is viewed from a variety of biographical perspectives, I think, and therefore you created her family and her history.

P-DU: The extraordinary thing about *A Part Hate a Part Love* was that I knew I needed to explore her prejudices and her opinions and to fit her and myself into an historical time frame. So I did an enormous amount of research. I love research; it's making up for all the time I should have spent in the library while studying at UCT [University of Cape Town]. It took me two years to fill in the actual details that allowed me to explore the absurdity of history. That works for me as a biography because the theatricality is there, there's a texture and a smell, whereas the danger of being truthful about your own life is that it's too boring. Lies are far more fascinating, so I used her biography to create a "virtual" truth.

MM: Evita began as your devil's advocate, the clown who could say things that you, as Pieter-Dirk Uys, could not.

P-DU: She's changed a great deal. Initially, she was a member of the chorus, a way of starting the show (by commenting on topical events). I love drag, the theatricality of it, and the idea of an Afrikaans man as an Afrikaans woman was also the means to begin the show with something that was illegal at the time [in the 1980s, cross-dressing could have been considered—as Uys stated in the guise of a security policeman—"illegal and also against the law in South Africa"]. The disarming reality of her ridiculousness allows her, through her stupidity, to say the things that had to be said. She can still never have a sense of humor, and the danger is that sometimes she becomes witty. She cannot have wit, she cannot have a sense of irony, she must always be deadly serious, and that's how she works as a character. In the old South Africa, because she was so close to the apartheid mindset [through her marriage, and her and her family's supposed association with actual political leaders of the past and present], she could sniff the underpants of the gods on the *Boere*-Olympus, and the audience needed that smell. Now I have to use her in an optimistic way, as a strange sort of Mary Poppins, always positive. She has had to confront the new reality with her prejudice. She's still a liar and a hypocrite and she still doesn't realize it. [Her duplicity and double-speak reflects that of politicians in general, yet "Hypocrisy," she always tells audiences, "is the Vaseline of political intercourse."] She thinks she has been redeemed through her idea of democracy, but she's got to make the audience think, "My god, yes, there are problems, but it's not the end of the world, it's a beginning." After all, she's still here; of all people she should have been the first to be banned, but she's friendly with the new gods, with Nelson Mandela, and everyone loves him. So she's still accepted. Mandela was on her [television] show because he says nobody watches the news: [imitating Mandela] "I have something important to say and I know everybody watches Evita's show." He used me and it was wonderful.

MM: Your work is still based on a commitment to tell the truth . . .

P-DU: Yes, but I have to be so careful—in *For Fact's Sake,* for example—of the danger of moralizing, of wagging the P. W. [Botha] finger. I have to retain my old definition of "49 percent anger and 51 percent entertainment." What has happened to me now is the realization of being fifty-five and feeling both older and younger: older because I've called life's bluff; if I die now I don't mind at all, but I'd like my drawers clear and not to leave bad friends; and yet I feel so rejuvenated by the new generation in this country, those who are not weighed down by the baggage of apartheid, but who are so exciting and aware. And that's why I want to reinvent myself: through the internet book [*Trekking to Teema;* the first South African cybernovel] in daily serial form and the memoir, trying a structure that is new and different. It's been a combination of Evita's optimism, my rediscovery of an energy in Darling that has been a new life for me, with the fact that at my age I no longer have to be polite: the audition is over, I don't have to prove anything, but I must continue to improve. I do corporate work, I do about one function a month, which pays for my life yet leaves me free to do other things. Evita se Perron [the site and name of Uys's theater in Darling; the name is a pun on *perron*—the Afrikaans word for a station platform—and also plays on Evita Peron, one of the inspirations for the character] is now running itself, so I don't have to approach the National Arts Council for money, because I believe that that money is needed elsewhere, and no schools pay to see my AIDS show.

MM: What do you see as your legacy?

P-DU: I never think about it. Never. Survival has been my only trump card. The AIDS show for schools arose instinctively. The election tour of 1999 was such a life-changing experience and filled me with so much excitement about the future.[2] And I realized that the minefield of politics is no longer there, pol-

---

2. In 1999, as Evita Bezuidenhout, Uys conducted a sixty-city voter-education campaign, with free performances, before the general elections.

itics is no longer lethal, it is irritating, it's called democracy, and you're supposed to think, but you're too lazy to do it yourself so you vote others into power to do it for you, and of course they help themselves first. That's democracy.[3] But the minefield has moved into areas like sex. The fact that the innocence of childhood no longer exists has to be addressed, and it's not being addressed enough in schools. So I thought, let me take my entertainment to them—not a *Sarafina III*, because *Sarafina II*[4] caused untold damage, from which we haven't recovered.

MM: Who is your spokesperson in the educational show?

P-DU: For the first performances, in June [2000], I took twenty characters, put them all on the table, and ad-libbed at every performance because every school had a different "alphabet": Grassy Park—no hall so under a tree, Rustenburg—no boys, Herzlia—no foreskins. It was extremely challenging because I was immediately aware it was from my mouth to their ears, and therefore incredibly dangerous. I couldn't make light of something for the sake of a laugh and without being an old NG [Nederduitse Gereformeerde] Kerk *tannie* (auntie).[5] I had to make it because we are now a democracy, I'd take them back to the old South Africa to point out that there is a very simple solution to AIDS: "No sex is the safest sex. Don't do it." But to many of those young people the struggle was about freedom: "You are now free. You have a constitution that protects you. You can say no. Nobody can force you to do anything. But you don't want to be uncool, you want to experiment." And I spoke to them directly, using words they understand, like "cocksucking." The teachers were horrified, not the pupils. But knowledge mustn't be based on fear; we were frightened, and therefore they won in the old South Africa. Young people must know that in five years time there will be 2 million orphaned children with nobody to hold them, touch them, love them.

MM: So you're still dealing with fact—in the early shows you repeatedly

---

3. On the tour Uys, as Evita Bezuidenhout, was challenged, courteously, by a young man: "Madam, we fought for freedom, but all we got was democracy." *The End is Naai* [Afrikaans slang meaning "sexual intercourse"] opened in 2004 as "a celebration of 10 years of democracy in South Africa . . . putting the 'mock' into democracy and finding the 'con' in reconciliation." It was performed in South Africa and the United Kingdom as *Elections and Erections*.

4. Uys is here referring to Mbongeni Ngema's "AIDS musical." It cost R 14.27 million, money granted from the Health Ministry's annual AIDS funding, which was criticized for inaccuracies and blatant misuse of funds.

5. In English, Dutch Reformed Church; Uys is referring to the staunch conservatism of its older members.

stated that you didn't write your material, the government did. Now you're using facts for a different purpose . . .

P-DU: Absolutely, and that's why my most recent show came to be called *For Fact's Sake,* from the experience in the schools. I cancelled my annual London visit this year because I didn't have anything to say there. I was going to do a show called *Foreign Aids,* but I'm not ready to do it yet. It's aimed at their first world, but I'm too busy in my third world. [*Foreign Aids* was presented in London in July 2001; in the performance Uys told audiences: "In the old South Africa we killed people. Now we're just letting them die." After further international tours, in 2004 Uys was awarded an OBIE for the production in New York.]

MM: Where biography is concerned with the past, your plays and revues are concerned with the present, but a present in relation to the past. I remember you saying, "The past is very much the future in this country."

P-DU: Yes, yes, I always think that to ignore the past is to recreate it for the future. Bad politics is so inventive that it now doesn't have names, but numbers. The most powerful nations in the world refer to themselves as G8— that's both Orwellian and Kafkaesque. People don't know what it is now, whereas apartheid was clear-cut.

MM: Since 1994 we South Africans have been writing and rewriting our history . . .

P-DU: It's so important, and I wish more black South Africans could have the opportunity to *tell* their stories; not everyone can write, and that's why I think television must be made available for ten-minute storytellings. We do this in Darling; we have storytelling competitions and record them. Without the texture of individual stories, there is no knowledge. Knowledge isn't the information one gets from the Internet. We have [in Darling] what we've called "Master and Madam classes": *Tant* Siena is too impatient for flowers to grow, so she tells how to make flowers, which she arranges in her ten minutes; *Oom* Jan's master class is "How to *braai* (barbecue) the perfect *wors* (sausage)"; a bricklayer explains to white people how RDP [Reconstruction and Development Programme] houses should be built. Their stories, their language, their words. Their history. This brings the community together. It can happen. The TRC [Truth and Reconciliation Commission] was so important in hearing stories that had to be told before the blood had congealed. It's never happened in that way anywhere else, but it saved our lives. The fact that we did that liberated our country. As Evita says: "We don't need a crystal ball to see what will happen to South Africa tomorrow. The future is certain; it is just the past that is unpredictable."

Further Interest

For a comprehensive account of Pieter-Dirk Uys's achievements and current activities, and his work in Darling in the Western Cape, visit www.evita.co.za.

Uys has donated his original manuscripts, video recordings, reviews, articles, posters, plays, and books to the Drama and Performance Studies program at the University of KwaZulu-Natal (Durban). For information about the Pieter-Dirk Uys collection, see www.ukzn.ac.za/dep/drama.

Publications

Uys has published twenty-five books and plays, in English, Afrikaans, Dutch, and German; the following are selected titles:

No One's Died Laughing. Harmondsworth: Penguin, 1986.
Paradise Is Closing Down, and Other Plays. Harmondsworth: Penguin, 1989.
A Part Hate a Part Love. Johannesburg: Radix, 1990.
Just like Home: South African Plays. Ed. Stephen Gray. London: Nick Hern Books, 1993.
The Essential Evita. Cape Town: David Philip, 1997.
Trekking to Teema. Weltevredenpark: Covos-Day, 2001.
Elections & Erections: A Memoir of Fear and Fun. Cape Town: Zebra, 2003.
Between the Devil & the Deep: A Memoir about Acting and Reacting. Cape Town: Zebra/Struik, 2005.

Films and Videos

Uys has appeared in nearly thirty films and videos, made in South Africa and overseas, many under his own production; the most recent include:

The Funigalore Collection. Ster-Kinekor, 1995.
You ANC Nothing Yet! Channel 4/SABC 3, 1996.
Evita: Live and Dangerous. E-TV, 1999.
Going Down Gorgeous. SABC 3, 2000.
Dekaffirnated. Numetro, 2000.

Compact Disks

Truth Omissions. 3rd Ear Music, 2002.
Foreign Aids. The Listeners' Library, 2003.

Academic Works

BEDFORD, JACOBA WILHELMINA. "The Presence of the Past in Selected Works by Pieter-Dirk Uys." PhD diss., University of Potchefstroom, 1988.

MCMURTRY, MERVYN ERIC. "The Playwright-performer as Scourge and Benefactor: An Examination of Political Satire and Lampoon in South African Theatre, with Particular Reference to Pieter-Dirk Uys." PhD diss., University of Natal, 1993.

August 2000

IX COMMEMORATION, CONFESSION, CONVERSION

These Two Autobiographical Books Are My Identity Document

David Wolpe interviewed by Astrid Starck

IN HIS TWO-VOLUME autobiography, *Ikh un mayn velt* (I and my world), which contains many reproductions of photographs and documents, David Wolpe deals with a century of Jewish history and Jewish life in two different worlds—Europe and South Africa—bound together through Yiddish. Born on September 7, 1908, in Keidan, Lithuania—which at that time belonged to tsarist Russia—Wolpe grew up with six brothers and sisters in a Yiddish-speaking religious family. At the age of fifteen he privately published poems in Hebrew. After joining the *Ha-Shomer ha-Tsair* (Zionist-Socialist Youth), he immigrated to Palestine in 1930, until his expulsion and return to Keidan in 1936 because of his communist activities. Volume one of *Ikh un mayn velt* covers his life until 1951, when he emigrated to South Africa, where he still lives today. It deals with the annihilation of the Jews in Lithuania; his experience in the Lithuanian army; his deportation, first to the Kovner Ghetto, then to the concentration camp in Dachau; and his hospitalization near Munich following liberation by the Americans. The first volume concludes with his participation in the reconstruction of Yiddish culture. This includes his editorship of the journal *Undzer Veg* (Our way) and his activities as the first secretary of a newly founded society for Yiddish authors and journalists who had survived the Holocaust. The second volume of his autobiography deals with his life in South Africa, where he continued his activities as a Yiddish author participating in the Yiddish cultural scene that was flourishing in the years after his arrival. This ranges from his editorship of the journal *Dorem Afrike* (South Africa) (1958–1970) to the many invitations he extended to Yiddish authors and artists to visit South Africa, conferences he organized, and theater productions he was involved in, some of which he wrote and directed. Besides his dozens of articles, essays, and critical appraisals Wolpe likes to single out two of his larger unpublished works. The first is *Ahad Meir: A Drama from Ghetto Life*. Originally composed in Hebrew in the summer of 1945 in Germany, then translated into Yiddish in 1955 in Johannesburg, it was read at the Ghetto Commemoration in Johannesburg in 1996. The second—extracts of which were published in the paper *Die Zukunft* —is *The Cockroach Man*, a fantastic-realistic novel in Yiddish that deals with the rise of dictatorship and terror in the middle of the twentieth century. In 1983 David Wolpe was honored in Tel Aviv with the Itzik Manger Prize, the most prestigious prize for Yiddish literature.

Astrid Starck interviewed David Wolpe by fax. The interview was conducted in Yiddish, after which it was translated into German. Wolpe authorized the English translation based on the German. Where intelligibility and the poetic quality of the language were in conflict, the choice was made mostly in favor of the latter, in the belief that it would give non-Yiddish readers a flavor of the language of Wolpe's writing.

DAVID WOLPE: In order to read and understand my autobiography, one has to put oneself into the complex background and the national and spiritual atmosphere of the writer, his origin, and background, the Yiddish language, *di yidishe heym* and *di yidishe gas*. In other words: I am an original product of the Yiddish people *(folk)* of the twentieth century, who suffered the sad fate to live through a miracle, of finding myself at the door of death and a half-destroyed country and entered into a purportedly liberated world and there built up from afresh a home *(heym)* and have a family. The epic of miracles and sorrow was leveled and mended with my two saved hands and my shattered soul. A beginning of absolute loneliness in a hospital for Holocaust survivors. Where did this powerful will to live come from? Shortly before, in the last days in the camp Dachau-Kaufering, my limbs had capitulated before the annihilation. I cannot answer this question. No one can. In the spirit alone, a last spark of Jewish-genetic survival heroism sprang up to step across from the end into a new beginning. And that is in principle the story of my life, as it is focused on in my autobiography, in all its revelations. It is open like a broad gate, with a deep perspective on that which is near, on the far off, and on the inside. That is the atmosphere in which I exhale reanimated memories: scraps of the holy days and pieces of my parents' home. Youth. *Shtetl* (village) and bloody end. And the further developments till today. In writing I felt how the words lived, how they move themselves and bring together my and my generation's complete and fractured past. Often I felt a type of wonderful feeling as if I had touched the roots of my heart and my parents' home, my perished family and generation.

I have written parts of this long narrative with the warm ink of tears. And in my eyes these pages are the most holy book of commemoration for the generation of the Holocaust.

ASTRID STARCK: Could you relate your autobiographical writing to other Yiddish or Jewish auto/biographies from the region and the diaspora?

DW: My autobiography—two volumes—spans ninety years of my life: 1908–1998. The first volume, which contains the sections "Khurbn Keydan" (The Destruction of Keisan) and *A Yid in der Litvisher Armey* (A Jew in the Lithuanian Army), covers the first forty-three years, filled with activity, delusions and confusions, quests, and problems. Later seductive ideals and false hopes, along with other disappointed friends, drove me into the jaws of the Nazi beast: the ghetto Slabodko, Kovno. Dachau-Kaufering. Liberation, 1945, with the Holocaust survivors. Munich 1951.

The second volume leads the way through the second and last station of my itinerant life: South Africa. My struggle, and the unbelievable difficulties to create a home in a foreign environment, with little help and mostly enmity from the family settled there, is set in Johannesburg. I sensed a powerful impulse to record a complete picture of my life and not to conceal the dark scars of the painful relationship to my brother's family.

In my opinion my autobiography has little in common with others of a similar kind. It stands on a plane of its own and is especially marked by the contents and the facts of my individual life. With the exception, obviously, of the chapters of the Holocaust years, it is related to the Holocaust literature, which cannot be divided according to special categories. My style is different too. I can just add that my autobiography is a type of original style and fluid narration, which can be felt on the tongue with juicy pleasure. Of course, in the broader sense of Yiddish culture, my autobiography stands in the same relationship to all the others.

AS: Could you expand on the relationship between your autobiographical writing and other autobiographies from the southern African region?

DW: In principle I have already looked at my personal I-image, as I see it, in the preceding answer. It is the complete, authorized legitimate documentation of my life to the extent that my memory has mirrored it in the language of my thought and creation. That suffices for me. I do not want to know the relationship to others and also do not seek it either. My autobiography is no experiment for me and I leave the analogies and the relationships to the professional researchers.

AS: How do you see Yiddish and Jewish autobiographical and biographical writing in relationship to southern African writing in general?

DW: They represent very different, peculiar phenomena with deeper specific comparisons. During racist apartheid, every humanist literary work—be it autobiographical, be it literary—was in part a cry of anger and horror on the side of those who were suffering. In this, they correlate to the Nazi-racist genocide of the Jews and other peoples that had taken place earlier. These homicidal violent memories are common to all who are discriminated against on the basis of race, and they are mirrored in the autobiographical memoirs and in the fiction of the affected generation in English, Afrikaans, or other African languages. This element of race is the contact point and connection my autobiography has with the writing on persecution and repressions in South Africa. And I am proud of standing on this frontline.

On the one hand, I have read a few South African autobiographies and a selection of special chapters. On the other hand, I have read dozens of autobiographies, memoirs, and essays that were written after the Second World War by authors who were directly affected by the Holocaust. Among them are well-known Yiddish authors whom I had known personally and about whom I had written. This universal memoir literature, in various genres and in dozens of languages, bears the essentially specific and common sign of this bloody history: the barbaric, wildly chaotic and planned extermination of a people that was carried out by psychopathic dictators and their regimes in the middle of civilized Europe in the twentieth century. A thread of the individual suffering, struggle, and self-rescue runs through all literary creations of note. Just a small percentage remained fortunately alive. The greatest sacrifice of this mass murder, though, was the East European Jews, whose language was Yiddish. And because all generations and families, young and old, perished, no heirs were left to the language. This tragic phenomenon has an effect on the treatment of Yiddish writings every year, in which the question of language comes to the fore time and time again.

AS: Turning to the connections between individual and collective identities, what would you say is the significance of ethnicity in the construction of individual identity in Yiddish and Jewish autobiography, especially in an ethnically minded South Africa?

DW: Of course my autobiography, in Yiddish, is a unique ethnic cultural phenomenon in the multiethnic South Africa. During my arrival, while setting roots in this country, I became a member of the secular ethnic group of Jewish emigrants from eastern Europe who conserved and kept on talking Yiddish, the language of their old home, even here. But for me it has also been the literary language in which I have been creatively active. At that time, a few years before 1951, the prewar immigrant generation had only just founded an ethnic cultural organization. The main goals were: to preserve and nurture our heritage, Yiddish, as a spoken and written national language; and the education of the children too. As a cultural organization, they also had their own journal, a journal for literature, cultural and social problems, of which I was the editor fifteen years long from 1955. A small remainder of this Yiddish ethnic group has, with difficulty, held out till the last decade of the twentieth century and dissolved naturally because there were no young descendants.

Then I completed my autobiography on my ninetieth birthday. The first volume appeared in 1997, the second in 1999. These two autobiographic books are my "identity document," which proves that I belong to this country and its multiethnic society. I spent the largest part of my life here, and here I have also created my work. In this year, 2002, I am publishing a volume of poetry. And, if God wills, I hope also to publish another collection that I composed in the last years. I thank with my whole heart the country and the nation here, which has given preference to me and allowed me to settle and found a family here after I had survived the Holocaust in the Second World War. This is the radiant star of humanism!

AS: Looking at dissemination and reception, who are your readers and how does their dispersal through the diaspora impact on the way you address them in your autobiography?

DW: In the diaspora, readers of Yiddish have shrunk to a minimum over the last decades. The reactions and greetings, personal and from Y. L. Peretz publishers in Tel Aviv, the publisher of my autobiography, show that a Yiddish author cannot be stimulated creatively. The nominal number of copies sold has a negative effect on one. But, fortunately for Yiddish, the genuinely positive creativity is the real force that turns the spiritually dynamic wheel that screeches financially. And still, we do keep on writing in Yiddish! In fact I found enough creative energy in the authentic wonderful *mameloshn* (mother tongue), Yiddish, to write my autobiography. Unconsciously the desire had bubbled without interruption in my soul to eternalize everything, and I have had a mysterious hope that it would in some way reach the eyes and hearts of the readers. And the age of crisis strengthens the will in me to believe in my Yiddish word and its existence. Recently my new volume of poetry appeared; it is largely devoted to the theme of the Holocaust and annihilation. And I am happy if it reaches my few readers. Nowadays every reader is a sunny happy phenomenon, and there aren't any others to whom one can come with our Yiddish melody. They do not exist! Especially now, with the crossing of the double frontier of a century and a millennium, we have begun to harvest diamond Yiddish letters and words and to express ourselves in singing poetic lines. I hold them caught in the net of my soul as a minute treasure for another golden booklet; to be able to breathe, live, exist.

AS: Could you describe in some detail what the effect of writing your autobiography has been on you?

DW: Details are superfluous after I have already indicated certain effects in my earlier replies. And however few the reactions and the number of readers may be, I am happy to know that a score or more of Yiddish readers can look into my lines. How good! This faithful reader is the only right address for our Yiddish melody. Now, just at the crossing of the double frontier of a century and a millennium, I have felt how mourning and drops of celebration have come together: they have begun to fly out of the spirit as Yiddish lines and words and weave themselves together in a net of song. That is a truly minute jewel for a golden booklet of Yiddish poems. And just in this minute (what a joyous day!) a pile of copies of my new book has been brought into my room. And around me everything felt young and fresh again—even my autobiography—*I and My World*—over ninety and alive!

It is difficult for me to sketch the effect that arises from writing about oneself in detail, because it is much more a psychological-intellectual experience which accompanies the events. Each event, or each bundle of events of the same sentiment or nature, has had its unique effective impact. That's why it is impossible to draw specific effects into the light. They are not selective, but true mirror images of the events constituting a life: persecution, hunger, terror, mourning, fear, crime, and so forth. The reader alone can experience and feel with me most of the effects as they affected me during the writing.

The specific autobiographical-memory-literature of the nightmarish experiences of the ghettos, concentration camps, and murder factories came as a violent necessary shock therapy to shatter the phobias and the shock. These sat like *Dibbuke* (evil spirit, compared to being possessed) on the damaged souls of the victims and did not allow them to live. Writing down the texts and the narratives of dread were to be the healing impulse that give the individual person a shove back onto the tracks of a psychologically normal life. Let's formulate it more precisely with the use of a simple Yiddish folk expression: to spill your heart. I have been practicing this spilling of the heart since my liberation, also in my poems and articles. And more than once, after such mental work, have I felt the pleasant rehabilitation and peace which I need—as urgently as air—to live. I am of the opinion that this formula of writing therapy is valid for all types of human creation.

AS: The new constitution of South Africa protects minority languages, but for each language to make an impact on the national culture it must function either as a spoken or written language or both. How is Yiddish to fulfil this function? Has Yiddish a user/reader community in modern South Africa—Jewish or non-Jewish?

DW: These questions are truly interesting and important, but not in view of the limited topic of this interview on autobiography. Yet, I will try as briefly as possible to make a few comments. For certain, Yiddish would have been more radiant and alive if it had not gone through the bloody and tragic process, namely, the severing of its tongue in the biological genocide of millions of Jews. And the saddest is really, for a person who is creative in Yiddish, to reply to all your questions in the negative. The questions are actually rather directed at historians or linguists. But they also touch on a political moment when there is talk of minority languages and constitutional protection. Unfortunately Yiddish does not benefit as a victim of the Holocaust. It is our terrible sin that we did not demand restitution for all these millions of severed tongues. This should have been a special settling of accounts, a physical and a moral one.

More concretely to the questions: Yiddish no longer exists as a spoken and written language in South Africa because (except for a small group of ultra-orthodox religious Jews) there is no longer a Yiddish organization that speaks it. As a result it also does not have the least cultural function. I do not want to leave behind the incorrect impression of a false prophet who sees the total disappearance of his language of creation. We, the rescued generation who speak Yiddish, who create and write in Yiddish, have lived from time immemorial and still live on with the wonderful mystic belief that Yiddish will live eternally. That is belief plus life. And that means a last prescription of the will for us—that the language that burnt with the people and was transformed into a martyr language must go up in a new light and live on. And each Yiddish Holocaust book, each Yiddish autobiography, each Yiddish poem, and each Yiddish tongue are a holy oath on the Yiddish immortality. Yiddish is not yet that which remains when generations are lost, but literally a successor, a step forwards. It is a joy for me to be woven into this Yiddish wonder.

AS: Usually languages live or die to the extent to which they serve a political or commercial purpose (Latin, English, French, Arabic). Or works that are of such great significance are written in this language that outsiders or non-speakers are compelled to read these works in their original language from which they have been translated. How can Yiddish meet this challenge?

DW: Although this, too, is not relevant to the topic of autobiography I would like to remark briefly. Yiddish has been the language of exile and family life of the dispersed Jews for a thousand years. In the last 150 years it elevated itself and reached the height of a classic literature. But in the current situation it is impossible to face a challenge from the outside.

I started my autobiography with a short line and two laconic questions: "I ... how big am I? Who am I?" That means a warning and paying attention to remaining modest and honest in the description of my life. That was the basic element with which I began and finished my two volumes. Naturally I left out and forgot some important events and persons while writing directly from memory and they are now missing. I recalled many missing things only later, but too late. I notice this with vexation. These empty stains, like the black stains in the universe, truly hurt me. Therefore I—rather than the interviewer—want to put to myself the last and really provocative question that I would like to add to the two questions at the beginning of my autobiography, a question that no one will ever answer but which can later stimulate the creative fantasy of a thinker, a poet, a researcher, and author to a new fine work. The question is: *Where am I?*

References Cited

WOLPE, DAVID. *Khurbn Keydan* (The destruction of Keidan). In the Holocaust magazine *Fun letzten Churben* (From the last extermination). Munich, 1948. Reprinted in *Ikh un mayn velt,* Book 1. Tel Aviv: Peretz Publishing House, 1997. English extracts from this text can be found at: http://mywebpages .comcast.net.acassel/keidan/wolpe.html

———. *Ikh un mayn velt.* Book 1. Tel Aviv: Peretz Publishing House, 1997.

———. *Ikh un mayn velt.* Book 2. Tel Aviv: Peretz Publishing House, 1999.

———. *Above My Ways: Poems and Stories.* Johannesburg: Herb-Dav, 2002.

Further Reading

BERNSTEIN, HILDA. *A Life of One's Own.* Johannesburg: Jacana, 2003.
BERNSTEIN, RUSTY. *Memory against Forgetting: Memoirs of a Life in South African Politics 1938–1964.* London: Viking, 1999.
SACHS, ALBIE. *The Jail Diary of Albie Sachs.* London: Grafton, 1990.
———. *The Soft Vengeance of a Freedom Fighter.* London: Grafton, 1991.
SHERMAN, JOSEPH. "South African Literature in Yiddish and Hebrew." *The Mendele Review: Yiddish Literature and Language.* July 31, 1999. http://shakti.trincoll .edu/~mendele/tmr/tmr03012.txt
SHIMONI, GIDEON. *Community and Conscience: The Jews in Apartheid South Africa.* Tauber Institute for the Study of European Jewry Series. Waltham, MA: Brandeis University Press, 2003.

WOLPE, DAVID. "Chaim Grade: Yiddish Poet, Novelist and Lecturer." *Jewish Affairs* 17, 12 (Dec. 1962).
———. "Leivick as I Saw Him. In the DP Camps in 1946." *Jewish Affairs* 18, 3 (Mar. 1963).
———. "Abraham Sutzkever's Tribute for his 50th Birthday." *Jewish Affairs* 19, 3 (Mar. 1964).
———. *A Cloud and a Way: Poems*. Johannesburg: Kayor Publishing House, 1978.
———. "A Home Consumed by Fire: A Memoir by David Wolpe." http://mywebpages.comcast.net/acassel/keidan/wolpe1914.html
———. *A World in Its Time. Essays and Criticism*. Johannesburg: Kayor Publishing House, 1983.
———. *Homes—Dream—Nightmares*. Johannesburg: Kayor Publishing House, 1987.
———. *The Way Back: Poems and Essays*. Includes drawings by the author. Johannesburg: Dov-Tov Publishing House, 1991.
———. "The Cockroach Man" *Die Zukunft* (May–June and September–October 1992, February–March 1994): n.p.
———, with Abraham Sutzekever. *Across His Poetic Landscape*. Johannesburg: Kayor Publishing House, 1985.

September 2003

Philosophical Reflections on Chronicles of Conversion

Wilhelm Verwoerd interviewed by Stephan Meyer

WILHELM VERWOERD'S *Viva Verwoerd? Kronieke van 'n keuse* (translated by the author as *My Winds of Change*) is as representative as it is unique. Its representativeness lies in the fact that it is a conversion narrative that reflects changes among a younger generation of Afrikaners during the early nineties— the period of negotiation leading from the apartheid regime to the Mandela Republic. As a conversion narrative, it is also a confession. The uniqueness of the conversion-confession lies in its extremity and depth. The book narrates four interrelated conversions or rebirths pertaining to religion, ethnicity, family, and gender, which provide the deep grammar to Verwoerd's decision to join the ANC in 1992 and actively participate in its election campaign. The interview, conducted in Afrikaans at his home in Cape Town, drew on Verwoerd's training as a philosopher to address the philosophical aspects of his book. It was translated by Anita Moore.

STEPHAN MEYER: You open the Afrikaans version of your book by stating that it would be pretentious for a young latecomer to the struggle *(agteroskameraad)* to try and write a more conventional autobiography. What do you see as the features of a conventional autobiography that would make it pretentious for you to write one, and how does *Viva Verwoerd?* differ from a conventional autobiography?

WILHELM VERWOERD: Let me start by explaining how the text originated. Initially the idea started as a relatively limited, personal attempt to convince my father that I didn't make the choice to join the ANC in an impulsive and insensitive way, overlooking the possible effects it would have on my family. My idea was to explain to him in a fairly comprehensive letter why I made the choice he had found so totally unacceptable. And when I started considering possible ways of writing the letter, I sifted through my own letters written to Melanie, my wife-to-be, during my sojourn in Holland in 1986. I felt strongly that my basic point of departure in the letter to my father should be honesty and that I shouldn't try to argue my point—after many hours of argumentation I had not accomplished a thing.

When I was in the process of preparing the letter to my father in 1995, I came increasingly into contact with people who asked me about my membership of the ANC. Journalists from abroad were particularly interested in the story behind the story. A few of them encouraged me to write down my experiences and motives for the general public. That is why I didn't regard writing *Viva Verwoerd?* as an attempt to contemplate my life in general.

I've always associated "autobiographies" with texts written by important people, generally at an advanced stage of their life, and have regarded the form of an autobiography as more of a reflection on one's life as a whole. However, in my case the intention was to explain a specific choice I had made. I deliberately tried not to elaborate on my life up to that point in time. I singled out certain key moments, and I did so circumspectly, all the time aware of a little voice asking, "Who are you to think that you could write this book?" Another point of difference is that conventional autobiography is normally written in a relatively cohesive, chronological order—a single story is told. From experience I felt that people exaggerated the whole issue of me being "Verwoerd's grandson." The more I started thinking about my choice, the more I realized that so many other factors—other parts of myself—played a role. That is why *Viva Verwoerd?* was written as four chronicles (the Afrikaans original is *kronieke*). Every story tried to tell, from start to finish, a part of the whole story behind my choice from the perspectives of Christianity, of being an Afrikaner, of being part of the Verwoerd clan, and of fatherhood.

In a nutshell, my motives for writing this autobiography, my limited focus, the structure I chose, probably all constitute the most obvious factors that made my autobiography different from a conventional one.

SM: How did you go about writing and publishing the book?

WV: I was hoping that I could deal—in a single text—with various experiences that started converging: the conflict with my father; attention from the public; the probing questions asked, and requests for guidance sought by other Afrikaners. Ultimately I hoped to write a text that would largely render irrelevant the focus on my membership of the ANC, that a deeper set of questions and personal changes would emanate from my political choice, impacting on a certain group of people. I'm also not sure whether persuasion or guidance could be regarded as a normal motive of an autobiography. To a certain extent, *Viva Verwoerd?* was an apology for the various choices I'd made—not by means of conventional philosophical argument or theorizing, but by telling a story or four as honestly as possible. That is one reason why I decided to include so many extracts from my letters and diaries. Often, as I was reading those letters and diaries from the eighties, I couldn't believe that I had written them—a painful memory indeed. I realized that if I wanted to be honest about this story, those extracts were the best source at my disposal. At a more simplistic level, I also found it particularly difficult to transport myself back to my overly Christian, Afrikaner-Nationalist days—especially after I had taken my first political step. Besides, I was under a fair amount of pressure when I wrote the text. I was driven by a feeling of urgency—I wanted to move on, wanted to end the torment and turmoil, because I had made a specific choice.

SM: I must say, I was surprised by the extent to which you risked exposing yourself in publishing those extracts.

WV: Well, I was guided by the question, "How could I tell this story as honestly as possible?" Another factor was my desensitization from months of intense interviews, appearing on television and in newspapers. Those journalists taught me that most people are not interested in what makes you tick; they want to feel and experience human drama. From a journalistic point of view that makes for an effective story. I think that this experience influenced my selection of the material. I thought that if I wasn't going to reach people at an intellectual level, but wanted to touch them on a more existential level—to use a cliché—then I had to expose myself.

At Melanie's request, I edited parts of the story. Unlike me, she places an extremely high premium on her privacy. That is one of the reasons why her answers to my letters were not included. Besides, I was desensitized from a very early age—I became used to the fact that people were interested in me because of my family relations. At a more theoretical level one may question the typical separation of the personal and the political spheres. But even from a feminist perspective, the right to privacy is vital.

SM: The extracts from entries in your diary take the shape of conversations with the God of your faith. How do you see the effect of this orientation to God on the self-narration and construction of yourself?

WV: The four different chronicles focus on some of the key relationships I had at the time. My relationship with Melanie was a key relationship, as was my relationship with my grandfather and my family; my relationship with the ethnic Afrikaner group and my relationship with God were also significant relationships in terms of which I could understand myself. The text is therefore a reflection of my relational concept of self.

From a fairly young age I experienced my relationship with God as the most significant relationship in my life. I also realized that, in targeting an Afrikaner audience, it was vitally important for me to accentuate the deep dimension of belief, to emphasize that the choice I had made was, in reality, a "leap of faith." Against my background and beliefs, my relationship with God enjoyed priority over and above my loyalty to and love for my family and my "people."

SM: In your opinion, how does self-narration addressed to a god (*My Winds of Change* 61–62, 93)—in the way that Augustine (1961:21) ostensibly used it to shed light on his choices in his *Confessions*—differ from self-narration addressed to a person like your wife, for instance? What is the effect on the perception and development of yourself?

WV: The most obvious difference is evident in the more indirect communication with God. It is much harder to hear; it is more difficult to comprehend in a reliable manner. Thus, by definition, the narration and understanding of oneself in that relationship take on the character of a search, in which one gradually starts seeing everything more clearly, going in a certain direction that feels right on a deep level, maintaining an open mind that one may possibly not have understood correctly—almost like trying to discern a poor reflection in a mirror. Consequently, one experiences fundamental insecurity. Yet there is an undeniable, gentle, persistent nudging in a certain direction, a quiet conviction growing in one's innermost being, in the core of one's existence, telling one that this is what one ought to do. And, in due course, one develops a feeling about whether this could be described as a relatively accurate answer to your quest. This is communication taking place. Sometimes it occurs by means of a text, such as the Bible, other times through other people, or through certain experiences. I really have a hard time living with myself when I ignore that "inner voice." I can't say for sure where it comes from, but it's a voice that I experience as coming from an ultimate presence. The closer one moves to one's own deeper self, the closer one comes into contact with a type of presence we describe with the word "God."

This approach attributes a vital meaning to the relationship with oneself. It is a relationship constituted partly by the network of relationships in which one is embedded—with one's wife, with one's "people," with one's family. But in the center of these relationships stands the relationship with an ultimate caring presence. To me "God" is not a transcendent signifier. Instead it means moving away from a transcendent concept of God to a radical immanence. The theological tradition behind this is the belief in a "divine indwelling," and I feel quite at home in that tradition. My spirituality thus fulfils a fundamental role, but it is not my foundation.

SM: In that regard, would you say that you have moved away from one of the things I picked up in your text, namely, a search for new foundations? And how should one deal with the Cartesian images you use (Descartes, *Discourse* Part two, 1985:116–122), of being stripped of previous delusions right down to the foundation, of shaking your foundations and of searching for new foundations (*My Winds of Change* 146, 159) in the light of postmodern critiques by Nietzsche (1999:11–17) and Derrida (1987:21–36) alike?

WV: At the end of the chapter entitled "From Soldier for Jesus to a Tree in the Wind," I tried to convey the rediscovery of a life-giving spiritual experience after a period of deep uncertainty and confusion. It is a kind of paradoxical "foundation," if one could use that word. I would have liked to attribute a different meaning to the concept of foundation: rather the image of "a tree in the wind"—with invisible roots, mysteriously anchored, quietly choosing its direction. I prefer using the word "centering" in this regard. Hence, it is not a search for a foundation, but a search for a center, an essence; a quest for one's deepest self.

SM: Do you think it is a shift from a god outside who serves as a guarantor for the truth the autobiographical subject produces about himself (as with Augustine), to a god inside as a guarantor of the truth about oneself?

WV: I've become more cautious in using the word "truth." I would say the criterion I would use is, "Where can I find life? What do I experience as a source of positive energy, creativity, light, lightness, laughter?" I think it was St. Irenaus who said, "The glory of God can be found in a human being fully alive." If you were to push me for an answer, I would be inclined to define truth as authenticity, as true humanity, as true humanness—instead of rational justification. I have a strong suspicion that I might want to justify and defend some of my experiences at a later stage. But at this point in time I am satisfied to accept that the more life, the less heaviness, the more playfulness I find in myself and also in my relationships, the closer I come to the "truth."

In other words, I work with a concept of truth that is more existential. To me the greatest criterion at this stage of my life would be the quality of my relationships with others. And this is why I am fascinated by the problems surrounding reconciliation in post-apartheid South Africa (see Verwoerd, 2001). When I look at the work done by the Truth and Reconciliation Commission, I now realize that the language of "truth and reconciliation" can indeed be used as a tool to describe my own road of change: a road on which I was exposed to lies—lies told by the Dutch Reformed Church about what had been happening in our country; lies the church told about God, lies my family, the nation, our fathers told. A painful road of disillusionment, a growing feeling of realization: I had been deceived; they had deceived me; I had deceived myself. In the process I was confronted by the truth about apartheid, in the sense of a narrative truth—in other words, the existential disclosure of people's pain and suffering. This type of truth (and not necessarily the truth I read about in books), as experienced by concrete individuals, presented me with the "aha!" experience of what had been happening in this country. And with this experience of the truth—insight as opposed to the mere collection of information—I had grasped, as if for the first time ever, what was really happening. What seems to matter here is the crucial difference between knowledge and understanding, between analysis and awareness, between facts and truth. It was truth situated in relationships, as told by flesh-and-blood people, that brought insight. And what followed was a difficult process of reconciliation with myself.

Coming to terms with painful truth is one way of thinking about reconciliation. Another way is to say that one is, in fact, restoring a relationship after it had been broken. An alternative would be to start a brand-new relationship. Initially, it amounted especially to a restored relationship with myself—partly coming to terms with my grandfather's ghost, to accept the fact that I am part of the Verwoerd family; partly as a redefinition of my Afrikaner character to afrika-ner; partly confrontation with my deep-set chauvinism, my theoretical feminism—as an essential condition for the sound foundation of my marriage to Melanie.

I am increasingly convinced that this personal road of "truth and reconciliation" made it possible for me to survive as a researcher and even be creative in the Truth and Reconciliation Commission (from July 1996 to December 1997). In that respect, the concept of "truth" plays a key role in my story. And I understand this role so much better owing to my involvement in a commission whose greatest contribution probably relates to "narrative truth," given the prominence of the public witnesses, of the personal experiences that had been related by individual victims. Thus an important part of my story deals with the struggle I had with an ethical concept of right and wrong. However, as in my spirituality, on a philosophical level, I am also more attracted to a negative morality, where the emphasis is not so much on what constitutes a good life, but on the minimum standards of human dignity. The emphasis is therefore on what has been called a "morality of the depths." The question is: what level of living is not too low for people to experience a life of human dignity? I identify with the ancient Greeks, especially Aristotle, who sought the good life, but I think an attempt to defend "the good life" in the heterogeneous, pluralistic world in which we are living would be a much more complex philosophical exercise. I prefer a more humble search for minimum standards.

SM: To what extent did you aim to create continuity between the old and the new selves, a unity, in which the various elements could live together and, in terms of the very image you used, where the old self and the new self could shake hands? (*My Winds of Change* 140) In other words, to what extent are you tied to a residual modern yearning for a unitary/coherent subjectivity?

WV: The term uppermost in my mind is actually "inner integration," healing. This, I think is psychologically justifiable as a condition for functioning "normally," a *psychological* integration without using it to make philosophical claims about the nature of the subject. Perhaps this is what is meant by coming to terms with the truth. It does not mean that suddenly there is no more tension; that there are no more blemishes. I am not talking about a naive harmony or a strong concept of unity or coherence. One moves through a stage in which one feels torn apart. One has problems with oneself and feels discontented, depressed, confused. Then one takes a certain step, makes a difficult choice, and suddenly one seems to feel liberated. And through liberation one starts feeling more comfortable with oneself to a certain extent. I think that my attempts to maintain the different parts of myself as different parts, as reflected in the structure of *Viva Verwoerd?*, was a result of my awareness of continual, unavoidable conflict. Because of my various commitments to citizenship, fatherhood, philosophy, and so forth, the potential for confusion will always be present. But I still find that there is some sort of growth, an increasing ability to keep on juggling all the different balls. That is why I do not acknowledge the monistic concept of the self.

SM: How would you respond to the Foucauldian assertion that all the way from Augustine, through Rousseau, and up to psychoanalysis, the TRC, and the texts coming out of that, we have been living under a "millennial incitement to confession" (1990:17–35)? What are the effects of this incitement to confess and to do so within the prevailing discourses on your presentation of yourself?

WV: Well, I was obviously influenced by Christian tradition according to which one has to witness. But the need to make the text available in English was probably influenced more by the experiences I had during the dramatic 1994 elections. When people repeatedly came to me in tears and embraced me after my speeches, I began to realize how essential it was for those who had suffered under the apartheid regime to hear and understand where someone like me had come from. At the same time I realized how important it was for me to denounce an exclusively white, Christian-Nationalist, Afrikaner political approach. The choice, as explained in the chronicles, is a symbol of this kind of judgment of the past. It symbolizes a confession that apartheid was evil, was a sin against humanity. But at the same time the question mark in the Afrikaans title, *Viva Verwoerd?*, is a sign of self-criticism, a confession that it took me so long to make my choice. In that respect I can identify with elements of the tradition of confession and the fact that it has to take place in public.

In the chronicles I refer to the problem of pure motives in confessing, in particular when it is done in public and especially when many people respond positively. When does public confession become a way of justifying oneself, an ego trip? Because in humbling oneself, especially when confessing, will one be patted on the back, will one be admired: "You're such a good person because you have recognized your own badness." This is a subtle form of hypocrisy. So I was careful not to do the same thing, but then only in a new context. The moment a moral shift takes place, when one tries to take an honest look at oneself, one becomes ashamed of the mixed motives which are such a strong driving force. Because I was so acutely aware of this problem, I put off joining the ANC for a long time.

Another obstacle was that I had to prevent myself from reverting to the role of an activist, a missionary, where one has too much self-confidence and believes that one's insights at that moment are the only way and truth and life. I had to resist the temptation to preach to people, attempting to convert them to my way of thinking. To me the challenge was (and still is) not to be manipulative in addressing moral issues. How, without being morally superior, can I judge my family, the church, Afrikaners? How does one convince people without making them feel bad? How does one respect the freedom of the audience and of those whom you would like to convince, without falling into this age-old trap? One reason why a person confesses in a conventional way is because he or she hopes that this will also have a message for others. But hope has a dark side, too.

SM: Your reference, in an earlier response, to the ongoing power that the discourse of Christianity holds for you brings to mind the question of the freedom at the autobiographer's disposal to step outside of hegemonic discourses. To what extent did you inevitably subject yourself to existing discourses by engaging with them?

WV: I believe that one is able to exercise a certain degree of control. But when communicating with people who are committed to a (Dutch Reformed) Christian frame of reference, and when one's own roots are entrenched therein, one would obviously be deeply influenced by the images, the language, the moral appeal of some of those things, for example a certain concept of God. The last part of my chronicles dealing with the Christian principles that underlie my choice discusses my discovery that Christian discourse is so much richer than the discourse that I was exposed to in the (white, Afrikaner) Dutch Reformed Protestant tradition, that there are theological traditions characterized by a searching, "negative" theology, as well as mystic, catholic, and liturgical traditions in which I could eventually feel at home.

This kind of journey is also evident in the chronicle entitled "From White Afrikaner to Pigment-poor Afrikaner." I tried to move away from an exclusive, egotistical, arrogant, fearful ethnic awareness, but you cannot really communicate with people who regard themselves as Afrikaners without appealing to those things to which "Afrikaners" are committed. And the fact that I was trained from an early age to think of myself as an "Afrikaner," as someone different from the typical English, individualistic South African person, made it impossible for me to avoid the ethnic source of myself. Inevitably the discourse on apartheid and the role H. F. Verwoerd played in it, as well as the significance of the Verwoerd name, were embedded in me. However, I gradually started realizing that by way of the little control I had over my life, I could attribute a positive meaning to a surname like "Verwoerd," which had such a negative connotation for most people (outside the Afrikaner community, at least). I had a choice to talk about my family and my connection to the politics of a prominent member of my family in a certain way, and this had the potential to enrich and to change the existing discourse. That is why I don't feel comfortable with those extreme deterministic postmodern conceptions of a subject dissolved into discourse.

SM: The hermeneutics of suspicion (Ricoeur 1970:25–28) with which you approach your motives (*My Winds of Change* 137–138) places a question mark over your whole project, and represents another postmodern aspect of your text. To what extent were you guided by the modern autobiographical ideal—as depicted by Rousseau (1953:65)—of making motives, passions and even ostensibly rational elements of the self—transparent? And to what extent do you think this ideal is attainable?

WV: I think that at some stage I was definitely guided by the ideal, as is evident from the emphasis I placed on the criterion of honesty. When I wasn't sure whether to leave something in or omit it, I simply repeatedly asked myself, "Will you really be honest with yourself if you omit it?" Initially I thought I would be able to meet this requirement. But during the writing process, I came to a frightening conclusion that more was probably going on than I suspected. I tried to include these experiences in the text, but even then I was aware of the illusion of being really transparent about oneself.

However, I do think that it is possible to grow more, to become better acquainted with oneself, and to develop the ability to convey that knowledge to other people through a long, therapeutic process. But complete transparency is an ideal not easily attained. And even the ideal to communicate (limited) self-knowledge clearly to others could pose a problem, since language is simply too complex, especially in view of the fact that people hear what you say from their own frame of reference. Thus I cannot control how people will receive the text.

With regard to my specific choice, I tried hard to be as transparent as possible. But I also included self-critical references to guard myself against any pretence of complete honesty or bravery.

SM: *Viva Verwoerd?* plays on these two things: a genealogy of a choice accentuating the historical narrative of a process *(chronos)*, on the one hand; and providing the logical foundation or justification of this choice *(logos)*, on the other. To what extent do you attempt to reconcile these two?

WV: I think both objectives hold true. My first attempt at writing included a chapter aimed at my philosophy colleagues, and it tended to be argumentative. However, my publisher advised me to argue less and simply tell the story. Bearing his criticism in mind, I edited the text, but it was difficult to move away completely from my convictions. My own experiences have taught me that a story is more convincing than an argument, that an argument makes people defensive and evokes intellectual counterreactions. It would also be difficult to criticize and argue against the *story* because it was *my story*. Perhaps it is somewhat arrogant to say this, but morally speaking, I believe that people who pragmatically turn their backs on apartheid, or people who still have a concept of being an Afrikaner with a capital A, are wrong. I'm passing a moral judgment on people in this position, and I think that I'd be able to substantiate my point of view philosophically. It's my desire to change these people. Thus, by relating my story, I am making a moral appeal to these people. In this respect I agree with Martha Nussbaum and Charles Taylor, who argue that the only model of pragmatic reasoning that could be justified at a philosophical level does not rest on an appeal to eternal, solid principles but on a laborious, Socratic process of self-explanation. Elements of the latter model could be found in *Viva Verwoerd?* —a story relating one person's process of moral self-explanation: messy, tiresome, zigzag.

SM: You have touched on the relational notions of the subject evident in your book and in contemporary philosophy. There is indeed a large and diverse body of work on relational notions of the self, such as Habermas's (1994: chapter 8) writing on autobiography as an appeal for recognition addressed by the author to the reading public, Maria Pia Lara's (1998) account of women's narratives in the public sphere and on *ubuntu* (Kuzwayo 1990:122 ff), which can be taken as an example of a social practice of intersubjectivity. Could you expand on the significance of this for you?

WV: While writing the chronicles, I didn't have a detailed theory on what place relationships should take within the conceptions of identity and morality. My awareness of the fundamental role of relationships was intensified by my work for the TRC. In *Viva Verwoerd?* I presented the self behind the choice as a self that is embedded in a network of relationships, a self probably created within this network (without reducing myself to the four relationships accentuated in the book). Part of my personal liberation was to discover the wealth of relationships among ethnic groups, races, and within myself.

SM: And to what extent would your whole book be an appeal for recognition—common in relational notions of identity—addressed to your reading community?

WV: That is a vital perspective. As I said, from the outset, one of the objectives was to foster an understanding in order to be accepted again by a key figure in my life, my father. That factor was of crucial importance throughout the book. Another vital factor was a desire to be accepted by all of the many Afrikaans people who responded so critically: family, but also more than family, conservative people who wrote letters to me and who phoned me, accusing me of being a traitor to the nation, telling me that I was no longer a Christian, that I was no longer "part of them." Regarding the Afrikaans edition, it was important to me to engage in discourse with this group of people. My aim wasn't for them to also join the ANC, but that they should accept my decision as a legitimate choice. I was inspired by the democratic ideal that people ought to move away from rejecting the *enemy*, moving instead to a relatively peaceful coexistence with political *opponents*. I hoped to be acknowledged as a political opponent, and not as an enemy.

In the English edition, the appeal for recognition was extended even further. Here I had in mind specifically black South Africans, individuals I had met, various people who gave me many experiences of hopeful recognition. I hoped that it would contribute to reconciliation, by explaining to others where people like me had come from. At the same time it was partly a personal search for acceptance within the black community, with them recognizing and accepting me for what I was—white, Afrikaans, Christian, man. Some of the work I'm currently engaged in also emphasizes how immensely important it is for other people to recognize one's own relationship with oneself, a respectful acknowledgement of one's worth as a human being, of who one is.

Likewise, many of the TRC's activities were not concerned with exposing the historical and empirical facts, but dealt in particular with recognizing people, or victims, as citizens, as being equal to everyone else, as people whose humanity had been denied in the past. What comes to mind is Thomas Nagel's apt comment that a truth commission "is not about knowledge, it is about acknowledgement," and Nancy Fraser's (1997:11–40) emphasis on justice as redistribution *and* justice as recognition. In short, there are a few theoretical ideas I would refer to in support of the social construction of self, and how fragile and vulnerable people are when there is a lack of recognition.

References Cited

AUGUSTINE. *Confessions*. London: Penguin, 1961.

DERRIDA, JACQUES. *Positions*. London: Athlone Press, 1987.

DESCARTES, RENÉ. *The Philosophical Writings of Descartes*. Trans. John Cottingham, et al. Vol. 1. Cambridge: Cambridge University Press, 1985.

FOUCAULT, MICHEL. *The History of Sexuality*. Vol. 1. London: Penguin, 1990.

FRASER, NANCY. "From Redistribution to Recognition?" In *Justice Interruptus: Critical Reflections on the "Postsocialist" Condition*, pp. 11–40. New York: Routledge, 1997.

HABERMAS, JÜRGEN. *Postmetaphysical Thinking: Philosophical Essays*. Cambridge: MA: MIT Press, 1994.

KUZWAYO, ELLEN. *Sit Down and Listen*. London: Feminist Press, 1990.

LARA, MARIA PIA. *Moral Textures*. Cambridge: Polity, 1998.

NIETZSCHE, FRIEDRICH. *Morgenröte*. Munich: de Gruyter, 1999.

RICOEUR, PAUL. *Freud and Philosophy: An Essay on Interpretation*. New Haven: Yale University Press, 1970.

ROUSSEAU, JEAN-JACQUES. *The Confessions*. London: Penguin, 1953.

TAYLOR, CHARLES. *Sources of the Self: The Making of Modern Identity*. Cambridge: Cambridge University Press, 1989.

VERWOERD, WILHELM. *Viva Verwoerd? Kronieke van 'n keuse*. Cape Town: Human and Rousseau, 1996.

———. *My Winds of Change*. Johannesburg: Ravan Press, 1997.

———. "On Our Moral Responsibility for Past Violations." *AlterNation* 8, 1 (2001): 219–242.

Further Reading

DERRIDA, JACQUES. *Cosmopolitanism and Forgiveness.* London: Routledge, 2001.
NAUDÉ, BEYERS. *My land van hoop: Die lewe van Beyers Naude.* Cape Town: Human & Rousseau, 1995.
NIEHAUS, CARL. *Fighting for Hope.* Cape Town: Human & Rousseau, 1994.
VAN WOERDEN, HENK. *The Assassin.* Trans. Dan Jacobson. London: Granta, 2001.
VERWOERD, WILHELM. "Continuing the Discussion: Reflections from within the Truth and Reconciliation Commission." *Current Writing* 8, 2 (1996a): 66–85.
———. "(My) Fatherhood vs. Feminism." *Agenda* 28 (1996b): 83–93.
———, and Charles Vicencio-Villa, eds. *Looking Back, Reaching Forward: Reflections on The Truth and Reconciliation Commission of South Africa.* Cape Town: University of Cape Town Press, 2000.
———, and Mahlubi "Chief" Mabizela, eds. *Truth Dawns in Jest.* Cape Town: David Philip, 2000.

January 2000

X CONFESSING SEXUALITIES

Speaking about Writing about Living a Life

Stephen Gray interviewed by Judith Lütge Coullie

STEPHEN GRAY'S IMPACT on southern African literature and its reception both in South Africa and abroad has been immense. In addition to being a widely published critic, he has compiled anthologies of southern African poetry, prose, and drama and has thus exposed a wealth of material that might otherwise have remained in obscurity. He is himself a poet of international repute, having published many collections of his poems. A successful playwright, he has also written eight novels and highly acclaimed biographies of Beatrice Hastings (2004) and Herman Charles Bosman (2005). A traumatic experience led him to turn his considerable talents to another use—the writing of his autobiography. The interview was conducted at Stephen's home in Mayfair, Johannesburg, on a beautiful sunny day in February 1996. The time lapse notwithstanding, Stephen's insights contribute significantly to the debate on the act of autobiographical composition. Furthermore, *Accident of Birth* has not attracted the critical attention it deserves; it is hoped, therefore, that this interview will do something to stimulate interest in an autobiography that tackles the politics of intimacy and the intricacies of politics with rare candor.

JUDITH LÜTGE COULLIE: Most South African autobiographers whose books came out before yours did in 1993 steer clear of anything that's remotely impinging on their sexuality or their intimate personal relationships. It must have taken a lot of courage to deviate from that tradition of reticence, and I wondered if there was any point at which you thought, "Hold on, this is getting too close to the bone; it shouldn't go into print"?

STEPHEN GRAY: I have to give a bit of a roundabout answer, because I am not sure of the final truth on this issue myself, even if it is the main issue of what became *Accident of Birth*. What are the politics of intimacy, or let's put the question a little bit further back: is there a dividing line between public and private? Well, in all my writing I've expressed the notion that—in South Africa at large—there is a kind of prohibition, a sort of conspiracy of secrecy, about the very nature of privacy. Bit by bit I've been digging away at what for thirty years I've seen as my main theme: that the private is political, that what happens intimately in the household is directly connected to the outer political world. I think as citizens of apartheid we fooled ourselves that we were detached from it, but the very fact that we could have thought that was part of the ignorance that apartheid spread. But now, in this autobiography, I don't think I was particularly revealing as there are still things about my life that I am not going to share with anybody, and that maybe I don't even share with myself. My particular aim was not to come my guts, as it were. But once the narrative is framed, I use the technique of question and answer to the psychiatrist to convince myself of the rightness, or wrongness, of my point of view. The whole first part of the book is meant to be that confession to an analyst. So I made a point of jumbling the public and the private all in there together.

It's also a book about nervous breakdown; it's about collapse, about learning to come to terms with the posttraumatic stress syndrome that I was suffering. I was terribly damaged by that awful experience of having been at the knifepoint of death, unexpectedly and, I thought, undeservedly. That was the accident of the title, and it's a book about the kind of truths that just seep out, no matter how you try to put the cap on things and be all right. You can't, because your unconscious, your sense of the meaningless universe, with all the guilts and privileges of the person you are in the South African situation as it goes into our stressful changes, won't let you. Of course, it's called a middle-age crisis, isn't it?

JC: Yet you are more prepared to take the reader into your confidence than most other South African autobiographers have been.

SG: Maybe, but it's a tactic. I'm really the cold-blooded author who revised that text, let me tell you, about six times. I don't think I've revealed more than I wanted to. But I felt I should use the idea of giving away intimacies as a dramatic tactic in that text. I must say that some of the autobiographies you are referring to I find are formally boring, perhaps because formal innovations are not releasing content in any fresh way. South Africans are great at hearing only our own echoes. But I had to use other methods to deliver a different message. I am talking about writerly problems, like how to break through and talk in real terms about historical problems.

JC: But your very controlled narrator doesn't give a sense of collapse.

SG: Well, if that's the case, I'm sorry because I planned for those small moments that I hoped would be atomically explosive—at the end of the second chapter, after the first episode of confession about childhood, for example. The grabbing for the cigarettes? Little domestic details like that. And that moment comes back, at the end of the book during the trial, when I'm in the witness stand. Fumbling in the pocket for cigarettes . . .

JC: And not remembering how to address the magistrate . . .

SG: And not remembering . . . that's how stress manifests itself. I did not want to belabor the whole thing. I think a little crack in the exterior can suggest something very frightening.

JC: Do you think that in order to tell a pleasing story the emphasis has to shift from telling the *truth* to *telling* the truth? Foucault has argued that "[t]he least glimmer of truth is conditioned by politics." Could you talk about the politics of truth?

SG: I agree with Foucault in this instance. I'm fascinated with seeing how I have changed since the days of my own upbringing, which did rather teach me that politics was out there in the world, was something done by Nationalists in government, and had nothing to do with this little colonial child playing on the beach around Table Bay. My whole life has been a discovery of how false and misleading that is. The very apoliticality that was taught us was just a way of keeping us under control. It's all to do with our heritage. Now, thank goodness, we are stepping out of thought control, of censorship. Look what a diminished literature we were left with and how crimped our natural desires to flourish and be challenging and mature as people became. The apartheid society almost crippled us. My book could be written only as a strategy against that monstrous situation, to try and build a more open, free mind-space, if you want to use a corny phrase like that. I think the key word of our recent times really is "struggle": there was an inner struggle that had to be fought in our heads, perforce, as well. And I am quite angry about the fact that our leaders misled us; that was criminal.

JC: Yes, but for many non–South Africans, white South Africans bemoaning their oppression may come across as self-indulgent whinging. I don't perceive it that way, though, because I understand your anger.

SG: But I'm reminded of Angus Wilson, who had his childhood in Natal and was a wonderful satirist. When he paid a return visit in 1963, he said English South Africans are unique in the world because their only attempt at being political is complaining!

JC: To be able to write a narrative autobiography, you would have to conform to certain conventions to have it accorded the status of a truthful document. How do you see your project of truth-telling in *Accident of Birth*?

SG: As I kept writing, at the top of every page I wrote the word "stocktaking." Stocktaking Chapter 2: Childhood; Stocktaking Chapter 4: Pre-teens, and so on. Even deciding the periods was a huge leap forward in terms of patterning and working out the interrelations. And I realized as I first wrote each chapter I was also, in my stocktaking, writing that thing off. I can't tell you the amount of searching that went on in this house, of old suitcases for photographs and for letters. The book is also hugely quoted from other sources—from things I'd written previously, from things other people have said, and especially from books I've read. In fact, one of my themes there is that I am what I read. At the end it all comes to trial, and the big question that nobody ever has the guts to ask about themselves is forced upon me when I am in the dock, about to condemn others: should I not perhaps condemn myself? That was me facing my deepest truth.

JC: The act of endeavoring to tell the truth in narrative must of necessity be structured around the economy of confession, that is, through a complex relationship of disclosure and concealment. How do you see this at work in *Accident of Birth*?

SG: I agree that that's what it is. But I had this awful continuum of questions, like am I holding the reader? Is the reader going to be interested by this? How can I twist it so that I can keep them all? Or not them, usually a reader is one person.

JC: But that sort of calculated thinking—you know, I'll keep them amused for five pages and then I'll hit them on page 6—that wouldn't have happened as you were writing under such pressure . . . ?

SG: It did. It has to, it controls it all, and it was that control that saved me. Otherwise I couldn't have faced the roiling, muddled, hysterical chaos that I then felt was my collapsing and shapeless life.

JC: So that was there, at the most fundamental level?

SG: Yes, I felt that if I was a writer, I should write my way out of all that, otherwise I was dead. But remember also that in the opening scene I kept thinking of my buddy Richard Rive, who had been stabbed to death in similar circumstances—twenty-eight times! He must have put up a brave fight for his life with those two damned intruders. And I grieved over that—I wrote not one, but two obituaries for Richard. It seemed like an apartheid thing—good people being killed, in Richard's case in his own kitchen. I was tied up in my own living room with this monstrous event that had happened to Richard happening to me. I sat there bound in a yellow rope, freezing to death, with blood coming out of my throat, asking myself, "Richard, what did you do wrong?" I'm not saying Richard replied, but I realized instinctively, at that fighting survival level, that Richard was a very aggressive type who fueled his life with a kind of aggro. So I thought, don't do that, try another way; don't antagonize them; if they want something, just say yes, because I was outnumbered three to one, and they were even better armed than the intruders who visited Richard. And so Richard gave me a little gift of a lesson, which was: "Win by the word, it's worth your life." And as I was still tied up, not knowing the outcome of my own story, I thought: my God, I've got a book, if I live to write it!

JC: The title, *Accident of Birth,* is drawn from the epigraph, which reads: "We shall not let our creed be determined by the mere accident of birth in a particular age or a particular part of the earth's surface," but out of that context, the title implies the opposite. Did you intend this sort of ambivalence?

SG: Not really. I had fallen on the phrase "accident of birth" before I actually found the quote (via Olive Schreiner) from Herbert Spencer. Later I discovered two wonderful points that Spencer made relatedly, that the only two things a human person cannot control are who they are—in other words, who your parents are—and where you are born. The rest of your life you can control. I thought that was the most basic statement of the problem of identity in an autobiographical framework.

JC: But the sentiments expressed in the quotation—that identity and beliefs should not be determined by mere accident of birth—are, in terms of contemporary theoretical orthodoxy, idealistic and impossible. To what extent do you feel that your own life, and the story that you told of it, testify to the validity of Spencer's assertion about individual freedoms?

SG: I think he is countering that mid-to-late Victorian determinism that came from two sources, both still potent in our self-formation. One is the Darwinian scientific natural selection school that puts such stress on character, as in Hardy's notion that character is destiny. The other school is the Marxist revolutionary school of thought that is also deterministic, even mechanistic, in presuming that the individual ego is a social function. I wanted to counter Darwinism and Marxism, the two schools that inform our thinking in the twentieth century, by saying that I feel some things do happen by accident, and that rebirths, transformations, are possible. So I am agreeing with him—not that I am a covert student of Spencer or anything like that. But I must stress that at the time of writing I was not influenced by thoughts like that at all. It's only later that I found them in my own text. I just worked by instinct. I didn't have a title at all until three-quarters of the way through.

JC: To what extent are you and your story the products of a specific historical moment?

SG: Well, hugely. This is what I am interested in, in my writing: catching the texture of each historical moment, not just one, and remembering that you and I and everybody else in our country have been going through such shifting historical moments. I thought I should catch the excitement of their transformation.

JC: For Virginia Woolf, what's worth recording are those very brief—but rare—moments when we are truly alive in between the usual sludge of mere existence. In your autobiography, have you set out to extract those kinds of moments, or are you trying to record an entire chronological pattern?

SG: I think in the end it's you, the critic, who must decide that.

JC: The large-print emphasis of *"Birth"* and 'Gray' on the cover is most striking particularly because the blood-red lettering and the scarlet fetus invoke the physicality of birth. How does the cover design render commentary on the text?

SG: I can't give an authoritative answer because traditionally the cover is not in the realm that an author can control. But this is a COSAW publication, with the Congress of South African Writers agreeing that writers must have an active role in the book-making. So, unusually for me, I was there while Andrew Lord assembled it. But in the end it's his work; that's his view of the text (which he also typeset, by the way), so he was absolutely integral in its packaging.

JC: The representation of you on the cover anchors you to the act of autobiographical testimony and the authorial signature in a way that is quite conventional.

SG: There's another photograph on the back cover as well.

JC: The one on the back announces even more explicitly, "Here I am."

SG: The one on the back is the breezy, genial guy in his workplace, which is right in this room, right at that desk.

JC: How long did it take you to write *Accident of Birth*?

SG: It's all gone into a kind of merciful fog of forgetting. The action actually is dated because in the framing or the hold-up narrative I give the date of the invasion of my house as in October 1990, and it ends with the trial following that New Year, which coincides with the first sensational Winnie Mandela trial. And it's more or less so that I first drafted it between the hold-up and the trial. But that's cheating a bit, as anybody in book-making knows you don't get a big work done in three or four months. In fact, another three years of drafts passed before it was actually finalized.

JC: Did you learn anything about yourself and/or your life as you were writing it?

SG: Hugely, all the things I had been avoiding facing. Autobiographies are very demanding because you have to get the most personal layers and use them, which one does when one's doing other things like poetry or novels but not in the way that's so awkwardly revealing and potentially embarrassing.

JC: On page 10 you say, "This round I will attempt to tell the truth." Do you want this to be read as an unproblematic record of your life or do you want the reader to engage with the fictiveness that necessarily results from the narrativization process and from endeavors to tell about events that are blurred due to the vagaries of memory?

SG: The answer must be the latter because there isn't ever a direct record that accurately records something that is or is not the truth and delivers it unproblematically over to a reader, who says that is true and that is false, finish and *klaar*. That is why I decided to make the last scene the trial, because in a trial that is what is being judged—whether you are lying or telling the truth, whether you are moral or immoral. What the magistrate does is sit there deciding. But I am perforce an ironist, a humorist, and I think the truth is very difficult to touch directly at all.

JC: How do you see this text intersecting with other genres?

SG: You mean of my own?

JC: Of your own.

SG: Well, when I write poetry, I think in a certain way. When I write fiction, I think in another way. If it's theater or criticism, different ways, because that old thing about the medium is the message is halfway true. Certain genres are designed to deliver certain goods. For me it was altogether fresh, stepping into autobiography as a genre.

JC: Do you see this as perhaps one volume of a multivolume autobiography, the other volumes of which are your poetry, your critical work, your novels?

SG: Emphatically no. This is, I'm pretty sure, the only labeled autobiography I will do. I'm not going to produce further volumes—I mean, who is interested, and who the hell am I to think that people would be? Many South Africans just can't stop at one, but I believe in doing extremely economical work; I try to make my texts diamond-hard and as complete as possible. I've done that one now; I won't do it again. I'm not really writing from an inner need, I'm trying to make good books.

JC: What my question was pointing to was how autobiographical is your other work?

SG: Unavoidably there are traces of autobiography there, because no writer —I keep referring to this generalized writer, but it's common sense—no writer would do something that doesn't fascinate them at the moment. So there is a kind of deep desire in everything that a writer writes, stretching from a book review through to the most elaborate poem. But to say that it's all autobiographical is a very big supposition.

JC: Do you see *Accident of Birth* primarily as testimony, confession, or self-portraiture?

SG: Elements of all three. While I was within the text, working it out bit by bit, I did read quite a lot of theory about autobiography and noticed those three categories. I started to read other autobiographies; inevitably one has to. I mean, I went back to Jean-Jacques Rousseau's *Confessions*. I came to realize that there is a link between autobiography and the western concept of the highly developed individual ego. That's one of ten points I began to pick up, but I was burrowing ahead like that mole not quite knowing where I was going—a mighty lot of digging with no real direction, and thinking I can use that, or I can't use that. I thought, okay, it's a bit of a Rousseau-like confession, but I'm not confessing for the same reasons, if you like. That's one little example. It all really started by chance when I got pushed into a corner by the History Workshop here at Wits University a few years before, for whom I did a paper on Peter Abrahams. I came across various autobiographical texts of Peter Abrahams about his life in Vrededorp and Mayfair, my area of Jo'burg, and I found that, because they were written at different times, if you put them together you got three different people. That stuck in my memory, and I learnt that autobiographies are predicated on lies, not on truths, which was interesting.

JC: How much influence did your publisher have on the final version of the text?

SG: None, because I did not have a publisher at the time. In fact, I had a few problems getting this book published at all, I must tell you, as my regular publishers turned it down—for various perfectly good reasons of their own.

JC: Did you have any readers read over it in draft stages?

SG: Yes, many. Normally only an in-house editor would work on a book for stylistic corrections; the content is normally held pretty well sacred, as it's considered the writer's right to write what he or she wants. But in this case I felt it needed refereeing, because I had decided that I was not going to offend anyone. Although I think it's a hugely offensive book, it's even obscene and rawly aggressive and confrontational, that was not going to happen in the area of personalities. So I mailed sections to everybody who gets some attention in the book, asking them to confirm that they would not be miffed by anything. For example, Athol Fugard, Cecil and Thelma Skotnes, Phil du Plessis, and others who play roles in the text. They all came back with, "Oh for God's sake, you are free to say what you like!"

JC: So, there were no revisions as a result of that sort of refereeing?

SG: There were. Even then, if I sensed a bit of fussiness, I took it out.

JC: Whom did you think of as your potential audience? It seems to me that the absence of explanations of certain South African terms indicates an implied audience of local readers.

SG: Yes, it's for my generation here, and I hope the future generation—a community of South African English-speakers who would not have trouble understanding it. Not for export overseas, like much South African literature that is so generalized that people in London, New York can read it without a problem. This is business conducted between me and my extended family, and you know that the readership for a thing like this is actually quite small.

JC: What are your thoughts on the political implications of who reads and who writes in contemporary South Africa?

SG: I do think that reading and writing is still a scandalously elitist activity, and of course I support educationists like yourself who are encouraging wider literacy. However, as one rises in the hierarchy of letters, I know one loses the community of oral culture. But then, beyond all that, I can only agree with Doris Lessing who says that in the end the book is the greatest liberator man's ever thought of.

JC: Looking at the kind of output that is coming out of this country in the late eighties and early nineties, one sees that the autobiographers who were producing in numbers are black South Africans.

SG: That's an utterly appropriate phenomenon of the moment, presumably the biggest selling autobiography of all time produced by a South African being Mandela's. But Doris Lessing's last one is doing well in the bookshops at the same time.

JC: Names in autobiography serve to secure the text's referential status; I wondered, though, whether at any time you might have felt the need or desire to fictionalize names, as Breytenbach did in *The True Confessions of an Albino Terrorist*?

SG: There are just one or two who have false names, simply to avoid libel, but they are not fictionalized as such. But the portrayal of the famous in an autobiography I spotted early on was a fatal trap, ending in a string of gossip cameos. I am afraid I've got people like Nadine Gordimer walking in and out of the book, but I scrupulously avoided—please let's stress this—portraying a situation where "Nadine said to me" and "I said to Nadine." I could have gone on name-dropping forever otherwise.

JC: I just wondered if there might have been times where you felt that it was necessary to talk about somebody without letting a reader know who it was.

SG: There were. But I have a friend called Francis King, the British novelist, who has been everywhere, knows everyone. He once said to me, "I'll never get talked into writing my autobiography because it will just have to be a string of anecdotes about those who have been more successful than me." That stuck with me.

JC: Freud and his followers have placed a premium on the fundamental truth value of disclosures about sexuality. In this respect *Accident of Birth* flies its truth-telling flag quite high. Did you perceive this as a measure of your ability to be honest and truthful?

SG: I have to reply Yes and No. The No in a nutshell is that I think sexuality is not the final measuring stick of truth about a psyche. There is not necessarily an organic relationship within the person between sexuality and performance out there, or the intellect, or the creative potential. I think all sexualities can have all of those results in different combinations. The Yes side is that when you are doing an autobiography, you know that readers are very turned on by revelations of sexuality, and that the bland, evasive South African habit of not talking about it is part of the general cover-up. In doing that stocktaking I've mentioned, I could not leave out my different stages of sexuality—I've talked a lot there about my sexual experiences, particularly bisexual problems. But not a wham, in-your-face thing. It is a big theme generally in my work, though.

JC: But was there also a sense that to reveal those private aspects of your life was for you a way of confronting publicly who you are?

SG: That's the way you see it. The way I saw it was that I could not evade the sexuality issue, just as I could not evade all the other ones—the educational issue, the political issue.

JC: So you will not compartmentalize yourself and say, well, only this is okay?

SG: Quite. But I had a very good analyst, and it was a real course that I was going through. That person Ruth, whom I didn't say very much about, is actually a real analyst called Ruth, who has a very holistic view, to use a post-Freudian, wishy-washy term. But yes, I am looking for a more holistic understanding of identity.

JC: I looked forward to interviewing you enormously because I liked the autobiographical narrator. Did you find that naïve conflation of yourself with the narrator in other critical responses to the text?

SG: When people have responded, I've automatically gone deaf; I just watch their lips, pretending I'm interested, but I don't actually listen . . .

JC: But what about reviews?

SG: There have been precious few, and reading reviews is a habit one gets out of early on in a writing career . . . otherwise you'd slash your wrists every second week, and I've only got two wrists. The work is in the public world and must lead its own life.

JC: Nadine Gordimer said in an interview in 1995 that she would never write an autobiography because "she is much too secretive."

SG: Well, Gordimer has the perfect right to do anything she likes, which many people won't let her have, or won't let me have, for that matter. There are a lot of pressures on the writer in South Africa to perform certain things that are expected of them, and not to do others because they are considered in poor taste or inappropriate, or whatever. And so I'm very interested in how another writer is situated. But having said that, one has to rely on one's ability to do whatever comes up, to challenge oneself—and the contingent is always a factor. I didn't know that those three invaders would force me to take a new direction. I realize now that for quite a long time I'd been taking the preliminary steps. For example, open a letter, something completely unexpected—University of Iowa Writers' Workshop—they want a memoir of my days there. And I produced it with great pleasure and ease over a weekend, sent it off; three years later it comes back in an anthology, and I took strength from that. Then there was a message from my agent to do a "growing up under apartheid" piece for this magazine, quick, quick, for bucks (which, in the end, I didn't get). But subsequently it was reproduced in France, which I had never dreamed of, and reprinted in my *Human Interest* collection. I really cracked the lockjaw that I was suffering when I wrote a number of journalistic reports in which I included myself as a character—well, as the uncharacterized narrator who characterizes everything around him. Remember, I used to be a weekend writer when I was a professional academic, so I did "diary pieces" to fill the jigsaw in a bit more. I found that I'd built up the courage to do the big one without even realizing it.

JC: Were you conscious of a need to withhold details as the composition process went on, or did you feel that the abandonment of the therapy structure in Chapter 10 allowed you to be less detailed?

SG: Yes, but there are eighteen all in all. So Chapter 10 is the transition.

And the first nine, apart from the frame, use a more or less linear chronology, looking at the character in development. But once I got to 1969—and this is true of my real experience—and settled in Johannesburg, my life became very static. So I took the second life as a whole and looked at sections of it and the chapters become more essayistic, much more theoretical. But do you mean you want to know whether I am being forthright about coming out or not?

JC: No, I just wondered whether the therapy structure had in any way made you more forthcoming . . .

SG: Yes.

JC: . . . and whether the abandonment of that had freed you? You know, because the whole question of sexuality is fundamental in analysis, whereas it doesn't have to be fundamental in other kinds of self-exploration.

SG: Agreed, but firstly there was a narrative situation. If I'd kept up with those sessions of psychoanalysis, it would have become so tedious and so self-indulgent that the reader would have stopped reading. I had to vary that. But there is a bigger answer, and that is I wanted to portray the process of healing, and healing involves using something, grabbing it while you need it and rejecting it when it has served its purpose. So there is a larger story, which is of a mental development as I get my life in order. I wanted to dramatize a crisis and look deeply into the healing process. In the second half, bits are coming together, things are getting organized.

JC: One reader remarked that he thought you'd cheated by being quite forthcoming about your sexual exploits in the sixties and then becoming much more reserved later. He said it was almost clichéd for people to be honest about what they did in the sixties.

SG: Quite true, it's a fair point. But there are other things I left out, for obvious reasons. As things became closer to me, inevitably I became more discreet. There are people around who don't want to be told that they were slept with. I left out almost all my professional life, too; I think I mentioned the place where I worked for all of twenty-three years only once, and twenty-three years at that time was half my life.

JC: I wanted to ask you about that. When did you retire from the English Department at the Rand Afrikaans University?

SG: During the process of writing the first draft of the book.

JC: Is there any connection between the book and leaving your job as professor?

SG: Yes, but I omitted all that as I hadn't taken stock of it. I just thought I would open my private study door, but not my office door. The last thing I wanted to do was an English department exposé.

JC: Foucault argues in his *History of Sexuality* that a confessional relationship is a power relationship: while the confessor might feel he's unburdening himself to heal himself, the power actually resides with the one to whom the confession is being given.

SG: Maybe, but I see myself as containing many people and I know that I have a certain kind of power in choosing, on my terms, to manipulate other people's attitudes to sexuality. I could see that it's a power game to play that hurts people and moves people. And I know that using the sexual element can be devastating. I have huge respect for my friend Pieter-Dirk Uys because I think he can catch South Africans on such an awkward nerve that, while trying to evade it by laughing it off, they actually can break through to new ways of seeing. I have a lot of time for gay theory, and I have a lot of time for theatrically subversive strategies. And heavens, when you are in this business you have got to use them all. I can't accept that the reader terrorizes me; I have to try and out-maneuver the reader.

JC: What is your life like after autobiography?

SG: It's more different than I could ever have imagined. Because I feel freer and easier. That stocktaking was very important for me in order for the healing to occur at all. In fact, I just wanted to tell people, look, if you're in a mess you've got to go through it, and you've got to come out changed. And I meant that as a model for everybody's behavior. We are talking about life experiences, and I thought what I could do for my readers was show them that, kicking and screaming, against all the odds, I went through it all and could come out and change. You are free if you make freedom for yourself. It's more an existential view, if you like.

JC: You said that your life post-autobiography had changed . . . ?

SG: Firstly, the whole thing had been shucked off. It's gone. It's now between the covers of this COSAW book. That's it. When I look at it, it does seem like a family album of the past for me.

JC: Coming back to the question of gender and genre now. At times your frank discussion of sexuality raises the issue of gender politics in that the bisexuality transgresses the sex equals gender equation. Do you see any connection, formal or otherwise, between fluid gender roles and fluid generic practices?

SG: Well, I always have kept myself pretty well informed about the feminist debate, and then more recently about gay studies. I've always tried to break the old rigid, hierarchical, heterosexual, racially exclusive casts in which ideology and its literary product has been molded. So in the second half of *Accident,* all sorts of new forms are being invented, which are expressive of the impact of these alternative ways of formulating life.

JC: If we agree that gender is produced through the discourses of self-representation, then how is this particular attempt at variance with other more conventional autobiographies?

SG: Let me refer to the ur-text for me, Joyce's *A Portrait of the Artist as a Young Man,* in which for each rebellion in the different chapters there is a kind of compensatory gain in artistry. I'm not sure others end up presenting themselves as rebel artists.

JC: Feminists like Leigh Gilmore have argued that the political ideology of individualism that defines our understanding of autobiography has been complicit with the oppression of women.

SG: Yes, I agree.

JC: Would you agree that this applies also to gays and bisexuals?

SG: Absolutely.

JC: Then would you describe the textual strategies that you had to adopt?

SG: Well, anything but the linear realist, macho storytelling model, and conducting an experiment with the traps and loopholes of English expression that must be filled in to express something that's always been left missing. It's about stylistics as well as politics.

JC: And to that extent, writing an autobiography as honestly as you could was itself a political act of saying, "I am the subject of my sentence, I am the subject of my utterance and I am the subject of my actions."

SG: Quite.

JC: And that in itself had political resonance. To narrate is to select; did you feel that the necessary selections were reductive?

SG: They were, but I tried to fight against that. While being apparently self-effacing, some autobiographies are actually quite self-aggrandizing; I found that a bit phony and silly.

JC: You remark on page 49 that memories of journeys you had undertaken have now been obscured by your fictional descriptions of them. Is it not equally likely that the self of those times is obscured by the fictions?

SG: It is equally likely, yes. The end result is when you come back to survey what you've done you can't remember what was the work and what was the reality because for you it has become the words of a text.

JC: *Ja,* just as a photograph that you talk about also in your text replaces a visual memory and becomes the memory.

SG: It's pure Roland Barthes.

JC: If an autobiographical narrative can be described as mapping a terrain, what areas are left unnamed, unmapped?

SG: I tried not to leave anything unmapped within the part of the field that is included. But then I suppose one must look for the erasures and absences in the area that is under scrutiny that perhaps should have been presented. But at various ages one feels differently about things, that's all I can say. One's perspective is always changing; it's a biological thing, rather than an intellectual thing. For example, I'm not nearly as self-absorbed as I used to be. It's a change in me and that has to be reflected in the portrayal in the book.

JC: How simple is the inhabiting of the "I" in daily life? Is it easier or more difficult in autobiography?

SG: Autobiography is easier, an easier way to get back into a difficult life. But when you're suffering from posttraumatic stress and trying to cure yourself, remembering is terribly difficult because every time you go back in memory, you remember the knife at your throat. But you have to unblock, and in order to unblock, you have to come to terms with the trauma. Then you can begin to remember in a more orderly fashion.

JC: *Accident of Birth* explores the two facets of confession/testimony: in the first few chapters there is the therapy structure; later, there is the legalistic aspect. Here, the narrator is a witness testifying both to the crime that was perpetrated against him as well as to the truthfulness of his life story. But these two features can be said to be operating at cross purposes to one another because in the therapy scenario, the narrator offers up guilty secrets—both sexual and political—and is on trial, so to speak, while in the testimony given as legally binding, he's an innocent victim. How do these two tendencies seem to you to inform the narrative and is there a tension, productive or otherwise, between them?

SG: Yes, there is a productive tension between them. I agree those are the two dramatizations of confession: section A—therapy, B—on trial. But there is a third factor, the writing of the book as therapy. At one point the writing of the book overtook the therapy. The book was doing the job better and quicker. It was just my way of fixing things.

JC: Can the autobiography be read in part as an attempt to refuse the status of victim?

SG: Oh, absolutely. Here I am and this is me. That's not a victim.

JC: Okay, and the very last question. I referred earlier to the cover design: what does the Stephen figured there look towards? Which is just another way of asking, what next?

SG: If you open the book out, you've got three Stephens there. One sucking his thumb in a bath of blood—prenatal; the other before he had his teeth done—relaxing in his study; and the third one . . . well, Nostradamus looking off the page. And I hope you enjoy all three!

References Cited

BREYTENBACH, BREYTEN. *The True Confessions of an Albino Terrorist*. London: Faber and Faber, 1984.
FOUCAULT, MICHEL. *The History of Sexuality*. Vol. 1: *An Introduction*. Trans. Robert Hurley. New York: Vintage Books, 1978.
GRAY, STEPHEN. *Accident of Birth: An Autobiography*. Johannesburg: COSAW, 1993.
———. *Human Interest and Other Pieces*. Johannesburg: Justified Press, 1993.
JOYCE, JAMES. *A Portrait of the Artist as a Young Man*. London: Heinemann, 1979.
WOOLF, VIRGINIA. *Moments of Being*. Ed. Jeanne Schulkind. New York: Harcourt Brace Jovanovich, 1976.

Further Reading

GRAY, STEPHEN. *Free-lancers and Literary Biography in South Africa*. Amsterdam: Rodopi, 1999.
———. *Beatrice Hastings: A Literary Life*. London: Viking Penguin, 2004.
———. *Life Sentence: A Biography of Herman Charles Bosman*. Cape Town: Human & Rousseau, 2005.

February 1996

Man-bitch: Poetry, Prose, and Prostitution

Johan van Wyk interviewed by Judith Lütge Coullie

IN 2001 JOHAN van Wyk, Afrikaans poet and academic, self-published the sexually explicit confessional narratives of an Afrikaner academic who bears the author's name. Published as an abridged version on CD as *My Name is Angel but I'm Not from Heaven in Any Way* and unabridged in book form as *Man-bitch* (also sometimes now spelled *Man-Bitch* or *ManBitch*), the narrator recounts his relationships with a number of prostitutes. The narrative is relentless in its depiction of inner-city decay—the world of seedy bar flies, sex workers, beggars, and social outcasts. The desperation of the narrator in his quest for love is eclipsed only by the at times defiant desperation of the prostitutes: young black women who live with the consequences of apartheid and with gendered disempowerment. They also live with the threat of AIDS; one of the protagonist's lovers dies of AIDS in circumstances of extreme poverty.

Reaction to these publications has been mixed: a reviewer in the Afrikaans magazine *De Kat* (April 2001: 88) says the CD is narrated in a "heavy, dry funereal voice." It is a "terrible narrative" that conveys the social decay "so realistically that it is painful to listen to" (my translations). The book, referred to by van Wyk himself as a novel and as autobiographical in an interview with Carel Lessing (*Sunday Tribune*, 20 May 2001: 6), has been described as "sensational" but as "profoundly and powerfully philosophical," as "sometimes grammatically incorrect and simple," but also as able to rise at times to "captivating eloquence." In another article, Shanta Reddy proposes *"Man-bitch* is a record of a man's journey through the barriers of convention. It is inspiring and jolting. ... It is absurd that no publisher has yet had the courage to publish this book and sad that the public is missing out on an honestly written and truly remarkable story of a spirit that is at one with conformicide." (*The Independent on Sat-*

urday, 21 April 2001: 12.) This interview was conducted at the University of Durban-Westville in October 2001. The following year van Wyk was severely assaulted in his home and has since been forced by the resultant ill-health to leave the university.

JUDITH LÜTGE COULLIE: Comment on your use of the term "man-bitch" as the title of this text.

JOHAN VAN WYK: Originally the idea was to call the book "Life is a Bitch," then just "Bitch," but while in Europe I saw that some famous feminist had already monopolized the title. The title *Man-bitch* derives from a passage in the book where the narrator is accused by one of his mistresses, Angel, of being a man-bitch, that is, someone who cannot be trusted in love relationships. The title is ambiguous, referring to a man who is a bitch and a man in relationships with women associated with the trade of selling their bodies. But the emphasis is on the former. The narrator is not someone to be trusted. Betrayal is one of the important themes of the book.

JC: How would you classify this text? Is it autobiography, or memoir, or loosely autobiographical? How does the generic classification influence or impact upon the writing process?

JVW: This is a difficult question, and I don't have a ready answer for it. The idea was that the book should be about language, therefore poetry. It had to capture the poetry of Durban as a place, and the poetry of the type of relationship described. Unfortunately I failed miserably, and maybe I will give it a rewrite. The problem was transforming it from what Barthes called *notations* (detailed description to evoke the texture of "reality") to a narrative. Maybe the original diary form worked better (although it included a lot of useless detail and information, which in the end can be interesting in its own right).

Whether autobiographical? Yes and no. In the process of writing the book I've become aware of how slippery life is for someone trying to capture it, how different a text is that is based on notations to one based on memory. You could see the difference in the ending where there is a shift to the use of memory—it moves faster, is more like narrative rather than still life. Nevertheless it is great to indulge in the Romantic mythology by being confused as author with the narrator.

I discovered this Cuban author, Juan Pedro Gutiérrez who wrote *Dirty Havana Trilogy*, during my recent visit to Germany. It is basically the same book as *Man-bitch*, although better written. That discovery was quite a disappointment, as I wanted *Man-bitch* to be a unique book. Gutiérrez, though, does not deal with the sadness of these types of relationships; it's more about sex than love. The tone of *Dirty Havana Trilogy* is different—too much humor—but his (or the translator's) use of language and narrative structure is brilliant.

JC: The narrative is confined to your experiences during a very circumscribed period of about four years at the end of the twentieth century and the beginning of the new millennium. Why was this period especially significant?

JVW: Be careful of phrases like "your experiences"; don't confuse me with the narrator. I *crafted* these experiences into text through a rather painful and slow process of distortion, fantasy, selection, and ability to recall words for things. Yes, it has contact points with my life, but it is not my life. The point is that I wanted to write *the* post-apartheid text. I was a bit tired of the "disgrace" phenomena with all the moaning and groaning about the new South Africa. I wanted to develop a new style to express the beauty of the decay—something that is completely urban, as I'm also really sick and tired of the haunting phantom of the farm novel. The farm novel is just so unreal that it can only function as allegory for infants.

The period of the turn of the century described in *Man-bitch* is significant in that it allowed me to immerse myself in the abundance of decay and joyous tragedy, as Nietzsche would have called it, that marked South Africa at this time.

JC: Do you see yourself writing a more conventional autobiography at some point in the future, one that recounts your childhood and adolescence, your student days, your marriage, and so on?

JVW: Yes, I'm thinking of it. Possibly as ego-text on the web. The beginnings are already there. I've had a very rich and beautiful life, thanks mainly to my parents. I would like to recount my youth in Welkom, in Salisbury [Harare], and Mozambique and the whole social situation of that period. It's difficult though. Apartheid has basically destroyed my ability to remember and to communicate. So the text would have to derive from photographs and interviews.

JC: I'd like to ask more about this: one's experience of the passage of time is seldom as linear and as ordered as narrative usually implies. At any one moment one may drift off, in one's thoughts, into the past or into the future. Yet your account seems to be quite strict in the disallowance of memories of other periods in your life and of people who were significant at other times. Was this a conscious decision? And if so, can you explain your thinking in this regard? Or was it due to the fact, as is implied at times, that the narrative was composed from diary notes?

JVW: As said, I find it difficult to remember. Because of my views during the apartheid period I learned to live with silence. My mind was also pretty messed up by the military experience. I was in DB [detention barracks] as a pacifist, and eventually only managed to escape by being classified a schizophrenic. It was a pretty horrible but interesting period. The problem was that I lost my ability to think coherently or to remember. I can only remember through note-taking. A further problem is that I do not like the narrative structure that comes through memory. It always seems to me to be fake, or wrong. I wish I could use mental tools like memory—then the different characters would have been rounded off.

JC: You say, "Time needs a battery, the battery of the imagination" (2001: 40–41). Can you explain whether this has relevance for your understanding of the imperatives and conventions of autobiographical writing?

JVW: I suppose there are many poststructuralist implications to this remark, one being that memory is imagination. Regarding its imperatives for writing autobiography, it has to do with the tension between what Freud called primary and secondary processes in the production of writing. When the battery is flat, then it is difficult to retrieve information that has already become part of the secondary structure of the mind.

JC: A related question concerns the fact that unlike most South African autobiographers who talk about their careers or their lives in politics, your tale concentrates almost exclusively upon your/the protagonist's private life. While we learn little about your professional life, you divulge intimacies that no other South African autobiographer has ever seen fit to recount before. Can you explain? I am interested in your thoughts about the kind of self that you wished to portray and your reasons for this, what you omitted and why. Also, how do you see this text fitting in with the genre as practiced by South Africans?

JVW: As I said before, my book was intended to be about language. A prominent question in my mind was whether it would not have been more effective if written in the third person. I did not want to portray a hero, I wanted to express the textures (when translated into words) of the area where I (and the narrator) live and the people encountered. I'm not a great reader of autobiographies for the very reason that they usually do not contain in-depth critical reflection on the self or poetry in language. Autobiography has become predictable and boring, unless you start delving into the textual contradictions and unearth the textual unconscious. The sexual to me is poetry—it is where the boundaries between all things living in real life and fantasy life disappear.

Regarding omissions, the original notes would show how much has been omitted. I know I should not distinguish between literature and autobiography. I don't want to deny the literariness of autobiography, it is just that I see it as usually bad literature. I wanted to write a literary text that is subservient mainly to poetry in language. I was not concerned about facts—facts are lies as Aristotle already realized in his *Poetics* when he aligned poetry with philosophy rather than history. Other autobiographies are concerned with facts—facts that are blinding lies.

JC: How does the text compare with autobiographies or memoirs written by other Afrikaners? And have you had any response from Afrikaans readers?

JVW: There are some beautiful autobiographies and memoirs in Afrikaans. I'm thinking of especially M. E. R.'s *My beskeie deel*, but here again it is because of the skillful use of language. I would think the link between my text and others is stronger with Afrikaans literature: authors like R. R. Ryger, Dan Roodt, and Chris Pretorius, who used to be active in theater. The book has not been reviewed by the Afrikaans press. A few cult followers have read it, but outside of Durban little is known about the book. I quite like the slow, ominous way in which it is inserting itself into the South African consciousness. Afrikaners generally blame me for not writing it in Afrikaans.

JC: Most of the women with whom the protagonist has sexual relationships are prostitutes. He attempts to counter arguments that these must be exploitative relationships by arguing that he is not a moral person. Also he argues to himself that the women too are exploitative (2001:38). Could you comment on the gender politics that inform this narrative?

JVW: I don't really use the word prostitute in the text. It belongs to the class of words that became prominent with the emergence of nineteenth-century sociology and criminology and the universal drive then to classify. It is reductive. Sex for money is an act rather than a definitive essence. The narrator loved dearly all the women he was involved with in the text: the money part is a side issue and linked to the general poverty described—he had relationships with them as human beings and not as prostitutes. If there are exploitative facets to these, then it is because that is part of the world described. It is certainly not a utopia. That would have been very boring and pointless to write about.

Yes, the question of morality is important—as said in the text, I consider morality as part of a drive to persecute: moral people usually cannot deal with the contradictions inside themselves and then they look for easy scapegoats by using reductive and simplistic analyses. That is why literature is important—to counter simplistic discourses.

Gender? I believe the narrator is really only interested in the human and the exchanges between human beings, and he himself is only human—prone to betrayal and avoiding his responsibilities, seeking self-satisfaction, but getting tied up in the problems—their legal and financial battles—of people he encounters, falling in love with them. I think that indicates a type of reluctant commitment—better than if he had withdrawn to the suburbs to live a cozy boring life, not knowing the real extent of the tragedy of this "country" and having no story to tell. But maybe I'm lying. He is intensely involved. He is highly moral and he loves women—or then again this might be a play by the unconscious—all these things might mean the opposite.

JC: The narrator wanted Angel to give up "this life of bitching" (2001:18) and says that what he wants is a woman who will stay with him and not demand payment for sex (2001:20). Can you comment on the ambivalence or even paradox that seems to be inherent in the desire motivating the relationships with these women?

JVW: I suppose you are touching on one of those ambivalent moments in the text when the narrator reverts to being this conventional chauvinistic man driven by those crazy human impulses of love and the need to care for someone, as against someone able to live with the diversity and fecundity of life— "the abundance," as a Zulu informant to the nineteenth-century missionary Callaway formulated it in anticipation of Nietzsche. Life is tragic, but good. I don't know.

The question relates to closure. Is there a conclusion to this text? It ends with the letter Z, an abbreviation for a name—pointing to the end of the alphabet. It ends with sex during menstruation, but also with an asexual character. The menstruation and asexuality point to abundance, which is blood and violence—but that is already inscribed in the way God wrote the world. Menstruation signifies that there is more in life than we can cope with, and also points to the absurdity of life. There are lots of things the creator did not think through when creating the world, or he or she certainly did not think in the way humans think.

JC: Are there any other autobiographies or even fictionalized life stories that inspired you?

JVW: No, not really. Literature, yes. The German writer Peter Handke and the clarity of Georges Bataille's style when dealing with the erotic. As I said, I've just discovered Juan Pedro Gutiérrez, which is unfortunately like a mirror text. It just kills me. I worked so hard at this, thinking I'm doing something different, and then I discover this book by accident in a German bookshop, and it is as if I'm reading this thing I wrote myself, except much better.

JC: Can you comment on the choice of prose narrative as the medium, as opposed to poetry or drama?

JVW: The long poem "Staatsgreep" [Coup d'état] that ends my previous volume of poetry, *Oë in 'n Kas,* was a preliminary study for *Man-bitch.* I have been interested in epic poetry since doing classics at Wits [University of the Witwatersrand] as a student. This poem was also inspired by a very interesting nineteenth-century study of multiple personality and the unconscious by Morton Prince, *The Dissociation of a Personality: The Hunt for the Real Miss Beauchamp*. Prince wrote about a memoir written by the unconscious of the patient (when she was in a state of not being "herself"). Now the unconscious is very attentive to detail, things not noted by the conscious. People did not really understand "Staatsgreep" as poetry and its listing of details leading nowhere, and it was bluntly received. So I thought that my next project would need more narrative fleshing out. In *Man-bitch* I did not always succeed in marrying detail to narrative. I have to think this text through again—to make it move faster and to intensify the poetic effects of the prose.

With regard to drama: I was working on a drama about a professor living with this traumatized schizophrenic girl who discovered she has AIDS when it was traced in her three-year-old child. It is the same person that the character Z was based on in *Man-bitch*. While I was away in Europe, Z discovered this drama on the computer and, in anger and not aware that literature is not life, deleted it. A lot of precise detail went missing. It is impossible to recover. I would love to write a drama on these topics.

When in Europe last year, I had to develop a short piece from the *Man-bitch* material to read in Poland and Britain. Back in South Africa I decided to record it on CD and distribute it. The CD is called *My Name is Angel,* and it is still available at Ike's Bookshop. I think it is quite interesting, especially when compared with the full text. The use of voice gives it that extra eerie dimension.

Incidentally Z is in the process of completing her life story, called *Death, the Only Way Out* [subsequently published as *No Way Out*]. It is one of the most disturbing things I've ever read. It should be compulsory reading to all politicians and all South Africans when it appears.

JC: Can you comment on the role of race in your narrative? What is the significance, in terms of your aims in the portrayal of the autobiographical protagonist, of your narrator's whiteness and of his being an Afrikaner? And can you comment on your aims in the depiction of the race of his lovers in this tale?

JVW: Another very complicated question. I grew up in working-class surroundings. My parents were not really religious or political when I was young —or they certainly did not discuss it with us. I remember my father as a very reasonable and fair person. There was this ambiguous thing: treat Africans fairly, but don't mix with them and don't allow them to know that they are your equals. At first, when I was very young, I think South Africans were pretty innocent and really unaware. As the repression increased in the sixties, seventies, and eighties, everything became much more political; it was pushed to consciousness. But by that time it was already embedded in me that human beings are human beings, and this was further endorsed by reading the Sestigers [the Afrikaans literary avant-garde of the sixties, including Ingrid Jonker, Breyten Breytenbach, André Brink, Jan Rabie, and Elsa Joubert], especially Adam Small—one of the most underrated South African authors, by becoming conscious of the struggle against censorship, and reading black-consciousness material.

I'm not sure whether I'm really white anymore. I'm a South African, a person from the Point in Durban. I'm proud of the way people live together there: rich, poor, white, and the full spectrum of black. I tried to keep race out of the text itself and avoid words like "black" and "white." In some places I know race still crept in, as the unconscious always does. Lewis Nkosi recently called me a racist, and I refused to deny it. I am who I am—take it or leave it. I don't go around accusing people of what they are. I just cannot do it because I really don't know and *cannot* know what they are. Close reading of *Man-bitch* would clarify the issue in terms of the narrator and implied author.

Regarding the women, I'm attracted to the blackness of skin, the beauty of the African body—and ironically what I see as the cleanliness, the hygienic and healthy quality of the African body. Am I crazy or obsessed? Basically, I'm also interested in that raw intelligence of African women. But then that is maybe not the narrator of the book. I don't know how the narrator expresses/justifies the obsession. He doesn't as far as I know. It is just something that is. But there is no aversion to white women, as his relationship with a white woman in Poland shows. In the end race is not important.

JC: Would it be possible to depict contemporary South Africa in a fictional work *without* specifying the racial classification of the characters therein? Has democratic South Africa now got beyond such labels and groupings?

JVW: That is what I would have liked to have done, but did not succeed. We should move beyond the labels or just be open about our prejudices, rather than repressing them all the time, the way Gutiérrez has done it. Repressing prejudice means that it will return in a socially destructive way. I think that books by Zazah Khuzwayo *(Never Been at Home)* and Zinhle Mdakane *(No Way Out)* will go a long way in destroying racism. These texts point to the beginning of post-apartheid literature—our birth as human beings; and it is great that they are written by the people of the margins, those struggling to survive, sometimes by selling their bodies.

JC: The tenses shift quite erratically throughout the narrative. Were you trying to achieve a particular effect? And if so, what was it?

JVW: That betrays the process of taking notes, sometimes noting things happening at the moment and sometimes remembering things from a week before. Chapters on particular women are either predominantly in the present tense or past, depending on how final the relationship between the narrator and a particular woman was, although he could not repress any completely, I would imagine. It has to do with wish-fulfillment.

JC: The book is self-published. Tell us about your efforts to get it published and why you decided to publish it yourself.

JVW: I submitted versions of the text to various Afrikaans publishers. I don't think any of them even forwarded it to outside referees. Then 24.com was interested, but they went bankrupt before being established. I sent it to an agent in London by email. She said it had to be successful in South Africa first. I sent a copy to Natal University Press, but never received a reply. Maybe it never reached them. Another email copy went to David Philip. I don't think they opened it. The Afrikaans publishers want it to be in Afrikaans, otherwise they are not interested. The English publishers don't really exist.

I could have been a millionaire today if the book had been published when that scandalous article in the *Sunday Times* appeared. I'm very unlucky as I've missed my chance to become this rich decadent sugar daddy. Well, then I thought why not print a hundred copies and have a little launch around the book? The book is basically known to people in Durban. People from other cities are not aware of its existence.

Interestingly it is translated into Polish and might be published there soon. I will possibly become famous in Poland first. I think there could be a conspiracy. I sent review copies to the *Mail and Guardian*, but they always seem to boycott everything I do. I don't fit the stereotypes they are promoting—it confuses their readers. I get very angry, for instance, when they don't review an important text like Zaza's, possibly due to a prejudice against self-published work. [It is now published also by David Philip.] The same with the other newspapers. Maybe, I'm enemy number one, someone not to be mentioned.

JC: Did you write with a specific reader, or readers, or even type of reader, in mind?

JVW: I love cult followings; young South Africans, young people generally. I find it difficult to accept that I'm getting older. It is nice when the women of the Point actually read the book and identify with it, or students who feel that it describes a world that they know. I never really thought about readers. I'm the main reader myself and am really critical when I feel I have not achieved the poetic effects I wanted to.

JC: To those of us who know you, some of the individuals depicted are recognizable, even if you have given them pseudonyms. Is the identity of many or most of the individuals represented in your narrative obscured by the use of pseudonyms? Of those for whom you did not disguise their extratextual identity, why did you feel empowered not to do so?

JVW: I find it difficult to mess around with the material supplied by the world because it is imbued with so much poetry. The imagination cannot compete. Can "Charity" really be replaced by "Beauty" [as words in the text], or Zaza by Zodwa? Sometimes there were striking changes such as Z for Zinhle. Mbali, I could not change. She was dead already and couldn't object. And the power of the word meaning "flower" in isiZulu and her negative reaction to flowers in the text is so important [textually]. Neither could I change the name of Angel, although she spells it Engel. The women on whom these characters are based really hate being recognizable in texts or being photographed. They are very private. But literature is my religion; it is, at the end of the day what determines my decisions.

JC: Have there been any repercussions regarding the revelations of some very personal details of the lives of some of the people with whom you interacted?

JVW: I suppose so. A cousin threatened to kill me. She has not read the book. People were a bit funny after the newspaper article. At airports and cafés and restaurants I was suddenly greeted by very friendly Africans, while whites tended to be very angry and Indians somewhere in between. This racial divide in the reactions was very interesting. I think the book, or the newspaper article, made professors and workers, white and black, all equal at a deep level. How could a professor destroy the conventional class and race barriers in this way? I suppose that was unconsciously on people's minds. For me it is just a book.

JC: What prompted you to write the book?

JVW: After living with Mbali for about a year, I suddenly realized that this provided important material for a book and I should start taking notes.

JC: The narrator asks whether he "could disappear into the filthy sidewalks" (2001:9), along with the street children, the drunks, the whores, the disabled derelicts. Is this book an attempt to answer in the negative?

JVW: As a form of therapy I suppose yes. But the narrator, who is confused with me, is so much part of that area that he and I will always be associated with it and the people. I love the place intensely. When I was in Europe recently, I really missed the noise of people from the streets and just the life and the buzz.

JC: Was the act of writing, the writing process, therapeutic?

JVW: I don't know. Can I as author ever really be forgiven for the way I treated Mbali or my own family and the other nonsense in my life? Does literature give me the right to do this? These are difficult questions. With people beginning to die around us, these are questions for all white South Africans to answer, and especially those in power and those great financial institutions that are laying off people daily. With the lifting of sanctions, the internal South African market has become expendable for those who govern financially and politically. So why should they care? The anti-apartheid struggle has come to show its real face. It was a struggle by finance to rationalize this society for the benefit of the few who export and those who manage it.

JC: Can you comment on the dedication: "This book is more real than the truth as lies always are." What is "real"?

JVW: Difficult question. Let's leave it to the philosophers, starting with the Socratic view of the "real."

JC: Liz Stanley (1992:96) argues that the critical reader of autobiography is likely "to embrace anti-realist principles but then also slip into quasi-realist readings of autobiographical writings." To what extent, and in what ways, did your extensive knowledge of contemporary theories infuse the way you approached the process of self-representation? Do you find a similar confusion or ambiguity in your own conception of the autobiographical act?

JVW: I did not really think about the theories; their relevance just became apparent as the text unfolded. The "real" would be in the unconscious of the text, and when it becomes conscious, it slips into the unconscious again. This is not a text about reality in the nineteenth-century sense of the term. The texture of things and details and events were co-players in a game, but their reality can never be determined, except in a philosophical sense where ideas become more real than the world.

JC: Why did you write in English, when Afrikaans is your mother tongue?

JVW: I want to enter the international literary arena.

JC: Some reviewers have criticized *Man-bitch* for being poorly edited.

JVW: I have to agree. I hope to make changes. It went through the hands of at least three English-speaking proofreaders. This is important as I'm striving for absolute clarity in style. I did not have the time to do a decent job of it; my attention was divided between work at UDW and completing the text.

JC: Did an awareness of different conceptions of self in non-westernized and westernized cultures, such as the relational self versus individualism, impinge upon characterization in *Man-bitch*?

JVW: I'm not so sure whether it is valid to say that there are differing conceptions of the world by westerners and non-westerners. If there was a difference, it would have to be very carefully formulated. Apart from skin color and money, my experience is that people are very much the same; some are just much harder hit by the tragedy of the world, while others are so affluent and unaware that they are close to nonexistence. I did not seek to depict the narrator in any particular way except that I used the notational approach for gathering material. I must still learn how to create characters with thoughts and internal lives.

JC: If self is a question, not an answer, what questions have you explored in this book? Are there other questions about yourself that you have not raised? And if so, why?

JVW: The question of betrayal is the main one, and the relationship between love and sexuality another. The questions I still have to ask relate to evil. What is evil and to what extent is its source the good intentions of human beings? What is its relationship to language (not literature) and science? What is responsibility and what are the limits of responsibility when it comes to writing literature?

JC: Early in the narrative (2001:9), when you recount Mbali's impending admittance to the hospital, you ask, "Is our country becoming a concentration camp without fences?" Did you intend that your autobiographical story would answer this question?

JVW: The question is the answer.

References Cited

ARISTOTLE. *Poetics*. Oxford: Oxford University Press, 1981.
GUTIÉRREZ, JUAN PEDRO. *Dirty Havana Trilogy*. London: Faber and Faber, 2001.
KHUZWAYO, ZAZAH. *Never Been at Home*. Durban: Self-published, 2001.
——. *Never Been at Home*. Cape Town: David Philip, 2004.
LESSING, CAREL. Review of *Man-bitch*. *Sunday Tribune* May 20, 2001: 6.
MDAKANE, ZINHLE CAROL. *No Way Out*. Durban: University of Durban-Westville, 2001.
M. E. R. [M. E. ROTHMAN]. *My beskeie deel: 'n Autobiografiese vertelling*. Cape Town: Tafelberg, 1972.
PRINCE, MORTON. *The Dissociation of a Personality: The Hunt for the Real Miss Beauchamp*. Bristol: Thoemmes Press, 1998.
REDDY, SHANTA. Review of *Man-Bitch*. *The Independent on Saturday*, Apr. 21, 2001: 12
Review of *My Name is Angel But I'm Not from Heaven*. *De Kat* (Apr. 2001): 88.
STANLEY, LIZ. *The Autobiographical I: The Theory and Practice of Feminist Auto/biography*. Manchester: Manchester University Press, 1992.
VAN WYK, JOHAN. *Oë in 'n kas*. Cape Town: Human & Rousseau, 1996.
——. *Man-bitch*. Durban: Self-published, 2001.

Further Reading

VAN WYK, JOHAN. *Deur die oog van die luiperd*. Cape Town: Human & Rousseau, 1976.

———. *Heldedade kom nie dikwels voor nie*. Johannesburg: Perskor, 1978.

———. *Bome gaan dood om jou*. Cape Town: Human & Rousseau, 1981.

———. Index of works. http://nymphs.udw.ac.za/jvanwyk/Index.htm

October 2001

XI RE-COLLECTING THE NEW NATION

Group Portrait: Self, Family, and Nation on Exhibit

Paul Faber, Rayda Jacobs, and David Goldblatt interviewed by Stephan Meyer

THE EXHIBITION *Group Portrait South Africa: Nine Family Histories,* hosted from October 2002 to September 2003 by the KIT Tropenmuseum in Amsterdam, moved to the National Cultural History Museum in Tshwane (formerly Pretoria) in January 2004. Curated by Paul Faber of the KIT Tropenmuseum, it is a massive multimedia project on which over forty authors (such as Rayda Jacobs), photographers (such as David Goldblatt), artists, and other art professionals, mainly from South Africa, collaborated. Family serves as the organizing principle for the auto/biographical portraits of around fifty individuals from several generations that are collected under the unifying and bounding banner of "South Africa." Auto/biographical representations of each of the nine families are housed in an enclave holding mementos and objects from everyday life that members of the families have chosen as particularly representative of themselves, individual and group portraits from the past and present, and audio/visual recordings. The façade of each enclave, which opens onto a shared common area suggesting a spatial concretization of a joint destiny, is covered with a life-size group photograph of the respective family in front of their home. Accompanying the exhibition is a catalog/book, *Group Portrait South Africa: Nine Family Histories* (2003). It contains nine family narratives, along with pictorial reproductions of some of the objects and images on display and combines, as Faber says in the Introduction, "interesting human stories with a stimulating, strongly visual portrayal" (2003:8). Educational workshops and resources, an Internet website (http://www.kit.nl/tropenmuseum/ tentoonstellingen/zuidafrika/), and updates on the families' present doings, including their contact details, further supplement the display (http://www .see.org.za/group_portrait.htm). As Nelson Mandela notes in his foreword to the catalog, one of the functions of sampling "as many as possible of the countless stories of ordinary folk, their reconstructions of their own past and their memories" is to "arrive at a more intimate understanding of what lies behind the official versions of history" (in Faber 2003:5). Perched, as Faber says, between "the personal dimension" of "little stories" (ibid.:8) and the imagined community of the new South African nation in the making, *Group Portrait* also prompts readers and visitors to explore the ways in which subjects seek to understand and establish their own identities through identification with others. That the exhibit presents the new South African nation is particularly evident from the inclusion of a link to its website in a section of the official South African gateway devoted to auto/biography and national heritage (http://www.southafrica.info/10years/familyholland.htm).

This interview was conducted with three individuals who participated in the project. The electronic interview with the curator, Paul Faber, explores one institutional framework (in this case the museum) within which auto/biographies are produced and consumed. A telephone interview with the author Rayda Jacobs explores issues such as truth and the reliability of auto/biographical projects and their relations to issues of justice. Finally, in the interview conducted electronically with the photographer David Goldblatt, Goldblatt elaborates on the nature of portraiture and its place within the auto/biographical enterprise in present-day South Africa.

STEPHAN MEYER: Since Saartjie Baartman (1789–1815), southern Africans and their life stories have been on exhibition and consumed in Europe (Lindfors 1998). Could you explain how you see this tradition of imperial spectacles as well as the ideas that guided you and the practical steps you took to transform this legacy?

PAUL FABER: The KIT Tropenmuseum was formerly the Colonial Museum, part of the Royal Colonial Institute, founded in 1910, with roots reaching back to 1864. In other words our direct predecessors were involved in presenting the former colonial empire, mainly the Dutch East Indies, to a Dutch audience. It did so by stressing the economic possibilities of the colonial enterprise and underlining the noble mission of pacification and education. The fact that a small nation in western Europe dominated a huge complex of societies and cultures on the other side of the world was never questioned: it was legitimized. The museum was the showcase of private colonial enterprises and of the Ministry of Colonial Affairs.

South Africa did not have a specific place in this Colonial Museum, but the general Dutch sentiment in the early twentieth century was one of solidarity with the repressed Boers, who lost their war against the British. Early South African collections in the museum go back to private donations of Dutchmen working on Boer government projects like the construction of the railways in the late nineteenth century. The later donations, as the one made in the 1950s on the occasion of the Jan van Riebeeck commemorative festivities, represent typical examples of decorative art, such as beadwork, while the black population itself stayed largely invisible.

This image changed drastically in the 1960s and 1970s, both outside and inside the museum. In the 1970s the Tropenmuseum (the new name being given in 1950) changed its orientation again. Directly connected to the new Ministry of Development Cooperation, it transformed itself into a center for conveying knowledge and awareness about the daily life of ordinary people in what was then called the Third World. Outside the museum, a strong anti-apartheid movement was formed in the Netherlands, with Amsterdam as the center. Inside the museum, photographs of Eli Weinberg were shown. [Weinberg was a trade unionist and photographer who lived in South Africa from 1929 to 1976. The photo exhibition was "1908 Libau—1981 Dar es Salaam."] These were the struggle years—in South Africa as well as in the terrain of museums and exhibitions around the world. The Tropenmuseum was one of the pioneers.

Around 2000, when the *Familieverhalen uit Zuid-Afrika* exhibition (Family stories from South Africa) was developed, the museum found itself in a new situation, trying to reinvent itself again, now as a center for global culture and history based on equality and respect. South Africa, too, found itself in a new situation after the first democratic elections in 1994. The *Familieverhalen* exhibition was an attempt to construct an exhibition on South Africa that did justice to the main movements of its twentieth-century history, to the current situation of the Republic, and to a large variety of personal emotions connected to the birth and being of a new democratic society. A seemingly impossible task.

In an early stage of the preparation we were thinking through the concept of "identity" as the central focal point. South Africa seemed to us a battleground of identities, identities that were changing, forced upon, demanded, created, invented, dictated, used, and abused. I discussed this idea with the well-known Dutch sociologist Jan Nederveen Pieterse, who played an important role in an earlier successful exhibition in the KIT Tropenmuseum, "White on Black" (1991), on the image of black people in western popular culture.

However, this time our ideas on identity got stuck on the conceptual level, and it seemed impossible to translate them into a visually inviting spectacle, which is a necessity for any large long-standing exhibition.

The two breakthroughs to tackle this problem were to choose in favor of microstories to tell a macrohistory and to concentrate on concrete individual experiences. One of the most decisive factors that brought me this insight was a personal one: at eighty-six, my father published a book of short stories dealing with his childhood in a poor family in the north of Holland. I realized he wrote about a period that I had learned about at school through boring texts on governments, laws, and statistics. In my father's book the image was humane and direct, still reflecting general conditions of life, but mixed with personal joy and hardship. We realized we could use family history—as perceived by family members themselves transforming family histories into family stories—as an instrument to evoke the complex South African social tapestry in a simple and concrete way, thereby making it accessible to our visitors. We would try to develop an exhibition built on family stories carried by family members in different generations, reflecting different periods but also stressing the different perspectives on the same events. In that sense the idea of history as a narrative that would be (re)created was already there.

At the same time we were well aware that this would lead to many practical problems (apart from the fact that we started an exhibition concept without a collection!): how to identify the families, how to manage the reconstruction of the past, what to show, what to tell, and would it appeal to our visitors? We decided from the outset that our families should certainly not be typical "representative" families (representing set categories such as linguistic, cultural, or ethnic groups), but "real life" families, with internal contradictions, individual complexities, and multiple identities. The aim of the exhibition would be to confuse our visitors, to unsettle them, instead of giving them a simplified picture.

The practical problems were tackled step by step. With the assistance of Dutch advisers and connections we had to South Africa, we managed to create an informal but effective local network of helpers, guides, and friends who explained what I was after. Many suggestions were given to me for families that had interesting stories to tell. Simultaneously I built up a network of photographers, artists, and writers who could contribute in recreating history in close connection with the members of the families. At this stage the South African artist Penny Siopis was an important guide and broker.

Around every family a team was built. Many choices were made during the process, such as selecting one family member to focus on in each generation.

And also that every family line should "end" with a teenager, in the process creating a group of teenagers that together would evoke an image of the future Republic of South Africa. It seemed impossible to run the whole organization from Amsterdam directly. Instead three coordinators were appointed, one in Johannesburg, one in Cape Town, one in Durban. Identification of the families was, in the end, unavoidably an arbitrary affair. We used criteria such as availability of documentation (ego-documents, especially for the early generations), internal contradictions and complexities, variation in economic, geographical, and cultural backgrounds. But mainly the choices were made on the grounds that it would make a good compelling story. We included some individuals who were well known (in South Africa that is!), but mainly for the fact that it was easier to reconstruct their lives. In the final round, of course, we had to make choices to create a group in balance, that would somehow, somewhere evoke the major aspects of national history.

SM: How did the location and reception of such an exhibition in the European and the South African public spheres compare?

PF: From the start we intended that this should be an exhibition that needed to be shown in the Netherlands as well as in South Africa itself. How it would be perceived in these two different locations we could not guess, although we expected that the impact in South Africa would be much greater. That expectation was fed during the production. Many people I worked with were very enthusiastic about the approach and insisted the show should come to South Africa. I realized the importance also when looking at the South African museum scene. Many museums were searching, unsure how to act in the newly defined society. Many elements of the *Familieverhalen* exhibition seemed to connect to the active search to deal with the past and construct new narratives that would make sense to this new society-under-construction—narratives that would bring people together. In that sense the exhibition in the Netherlands did not have such a profound impact and meaning. It was seen here in a period when South Africa was no longer the center of interest. Besides that, it was shown in a museum-rich society with many cultural presentations to offer: in that competition the *Familieverhalen* exhibition was a "difficult" exhibition that required time and attention from the visitors. If the visitors were hooked, they would give the time needed. If no connections were made, they would lose interest. In South Africa all visitors can directly link themselves to at least one of the stories. In Holland this was less the case. We requested a more abstract empathy from visitors—more difficult but not impossible. Many visitors could link themselves with the human condition of our protagonists.

SM: *Group Portrait* is a heterogeneous and wide-ranging exhibition that must at times have been unwieldy and required some managing. While you yourself refrain from offering a unifying metanarrative in your introduction to the catalog accompanying the exhibition, you rely on implicit devices to achieve some sense of cohesion. Could we explore some of these, starting with the variety of media employed and their relation to auto/biography: how would you characterize the distinctive contributions of each of the different media—for example, the written narratives in the book, the photographs, and the material objects—to drawing auto/biographical profiles of the protagonists? Could you elaborate on how they interact and relate to each other in creating auto/biographical accounts?

PF: In creating the exhibition we tried to make some radical choices. We wanted to retreat as museum/author and give space to the families as the authors of their own stories. The use of *text* was one of the strongest agents. In the final choice we (the museum) wrote only one text for each family, namely, a short overview of the overall history of the family in the twentieth century (the chosen time span of the project). All texts that could be found inside the family presentations were texts spoken by family members. Instead of traditional captions for objects and photographs (for instance: "golden earrings, Indian style, early twentieth century"), we used quotations that made sense in a personal way ("these earrings were bought by my grandmother for my father's bride to be," etc.). These caption-like texts were partly derived from direct source material (for example, a response to a question such as, "Janey, could you tell me what is so important about these earrings?") or were taken from the long texts that were made for the catalog.

The texts in the book were an important contribution to the project. The exhibition was essentially an attempt to construct a visual auto/biography, as an exhibition should primarily be a visual experience. But as there was so much to say and tell about and by these families, the book was an essential companion. In the book we had the time and space to sit down, as it were, and really talk and reconstruct. I asked all the authors to talk seriously with the chosen representatives of the different generations, to bring out their own life history, and the events that marked it. Usually the representatives of the oldest generation(s) were no longer alive, and the authors had to go back to written documents or memories of their descendants. The texts were meant to be based heavily on quotations, taken verbatim from the spokespersons. The texts were meant to comment on major national or regional events that affected their lives, but also important personal experiences. Thanks to the length of the texts, there was space for meaningful details that colored and gave life to the outline of the individual life stories and the intergenerational relations.

Regarding the *photographs:* we used two basically different photographic sources. The first source was the "family album": photographs owned by the family members, private snapshots, made at the usual family occasions, marked by intimacy, familiar contexts. Sometimes there were more formal ones, pictures taken by photo studios, or official ones owned by families that played important roles. The family pictures enable us visually to go back in time: for example, to show Lily Louw's wedding portrait in 1946 besides photographs of her taken by her grandson Cedric Nunn in the 1990s. The personal pictures fill in interesting and touching details, showing Tumi Plaatje, for instance, as a young nurse, but also participating in a Miss Hot Pants contest. Such family-album pictures present counterimages in respect to official photographs of the time, with other objectives (government propaganda or struggle solidarity), creating images of a different humane life. One finds pictures of moments of importance to individual lives: marriage, presenting a new child, getting a school diploma. Amazing finds occurred, also, where we did not expect them. That was, of course, an important aspect we were aware of: the great difference in the quantity and age of photographs. Some families had hundreds, spanning 150 years (the Steyns); others had only a handful, taken only in recent times (the Galadas). But also in the latter case, images were a rich source, giving a compelling view of the early years of Cynthia and Elliot Galada's life in their hostel room, poor but dignified.

The second category was formed by the photographs we commissioned, taken by professional photographers. Contrary to the family-album pictures, these professional photographs taken between 2001 and 2002 were all fixed in the same time. The aim was to capture people and their lives in the present. Still, contemporary lives testify to history too. Many photographs in this category show the protagonists in meaningful situations: at the family house; with a grave of an ancestor; with objects referring to the past. The ways the people have been represented by the various photographers vary a lot. Each photographer had a distinctive way of looking at "their" protagonists. Where David Goldblatt, for instance, focused on posed portraits, Paul Grendon made narrative series of activities of members of the Le Fleur family. The view of one specific outsider (that is, the photographer) thus added to these contributions, offering another metastory that formed part of a web of other stories woven in each family unit.

The most outspoken contrast between the two categories of photographs mentioned above was in the exhibition in the Mthethwa unit. Dominantly present was a beautiful series of black-and-white photographs taken by Paul Weinberg, focusing on the Mthethwas' life in their house in Inanda Newtown, and on the ceremonial life in the homestead of the patriarch Zizwezonke Mthethwa during the yearly *isikhumbuzo* festival. Next to that we presented a facsimile of the photo album of one of Zizwezonke's grandsons. This gave a completely different view of the same family: all the boys in neat trousers, white shirts and ties, images of bouncing babies, dancing lessons, the new car, and all, of course, in color, machine-printed snapshots. Representation versus self-presentation. The difference in images was intensified by our presentation: a gallery-like presentation of Weinberg's framed photographs and the album as an album, lying on a small bench in a corner. In the Mthethwa case we broke our own rule when we added a few historical photographs that were not directly related to the family members. But in this case neither Weinberg's pictures nor the family pictures allowed us to portray the past. We felt the need to present some images that would stir the imagination of the visitor/reader.

Apart from these two main categories of photographs that formed part of each unit, some incidental variations were added. In the Galada family story we asked Cynthia Galada to use some disposable cameras to capture the Christmas holiday (2000) the family celebrated back home in Barkley East. The result was great. Cynthia and the others who joined her obviously enjoyed doing so, and the photographs breathe a relaxed and intimate atmosphere. In the Rathebe story we showed some of the glamorous photographs Jürgen Schadeberg had taken of Dolly Rathebe in the 1950s for *Drum Magazine*. They are magnificent pictures of a beautiful and talented woman, but value was added when we could contrast these images with some private photographs owned by Dolly that no one knew about, like a studio portrait made in Sophiatown just before she became famous and an intimate and endearing portrait of Dolly showing her first-born, Zola.

Apart from still pictures, in one case—namely, the Juggernaths—we used family videos taken over the last fifteen years. They show not only the intimacy and joy connected to important moments of family life, but also the changes in fashion, relations, and the peoples themselves, in images as well as in sound! That fascination is also to be found in the family photographs: you see the people you come to know a bit grow old. Very simple but very touching. You grow along with them.

As for *objects* I had a strong conviction of using only objects that had direct and personal, emotional value for the people presented. The idea was to show objects that did not necessarily have a great visual or artistic importance, but were meaningful only on the more personal level. This idea was based on the principle of creating historical narratives in different media, but was also meant to counteract usual museum practice that removes objects from the personal relevance to their former owners. As with the family photographs, the objects may tell little and grand stories, but often they signify only abstract feelings or moods. What these objects convey is quite different from what written stories can transfer. In many cases I found the objects on the first glimpse trivial, but on second thoughts fascinating, touching, and always meaningful: An old simple stool owned by Lily Nunn, for instance, weathered and rounded by time, immediately evoked a long life in simple circumstances, as do the small artifacts kept by Cynthia Galada's father, Petelele Sobayi, representing his long career as a farm laborer. Or Janey Juggernath preserving the spectacles of her father who passed away; Ebrahim Manuel with his small souvenirs of his life as a seaman; or Kobera Manuel's scarf she made in Mecca during her pilgrimage, etc. These family artifacts were juxtaposed with new artworks made on commission by artists such as Langa Magwa, Willie Bester, and Robert Lungupi, much in the way the family snapshots were juxtaposed with the newly made photographs. The artworks formed an outsider's interpretation of relevant moments or immaterial aspects of life that could not be trapped visually in another way.

SM: How did you use the ways in which you managed the contributions to create some cohesion? Did you give a brief to the many contributors to ensure some consistency and unity? And how did you ensure that contributors kept within the parameters you had in mind? In particular, could you explain your brief and your working relationship with the author Rayda Jacobs and the photographer David Goldblatt?

PF: The structure behind the project was quite free in the sense that I was well aware that I worked with different teams of creative individuals who would also need their artistic freedom to build up their contribution. On the other hand, complete freedom would result in chaos. The structure that was conceived for the exhibition was passed on in writing to all contributors, but I did not make a standard briefing for each individual participant. These instructions were always given and discussed in bilateral meetings, followed by e-mails, and shared by the coordinators. In other words the work that was carried out by all of us was more based on direct personal relations and discussions than on documents or guidelines. Without e-mail this project would not have been possible.

For the writers the structure was based on writing a story of a family, focusing on one representative of each of the four or five generations, spanning more or less one century. In the case of the Manuel family, we decided on Kobera Manuel, Ebrahim Manuel, and Gavin Mauritz, with Kobera's father Bakaar representing the first generation. He passed away in 1983, but left a compelling personal testimony in a diary he had kept of the trip to Mecca he made with his wife in 1904! Documents like these formed an important criterion in selecting our families.

For David Goldblatt we had a double request. We approached him to do nine "family portraits" and individual portraits of each teenager. David Goldblatt shot them quite directly in front of their houses. The idea was to photograph them in such a manner that they would appear life-size in the exhibition and eye to eye with the visitor. The nine teenager portraits were grouped together, directly linked with an interactive video program in which the nine teenagers would give their answers to three basic questions about their future expectations. For picturing the Steyn family, Goldblatt acted in the same way as the other family photographers. There too the main protagonists had already been identified. It was up to Goldblatt to portray the family in a way that would characterize their lives in the present-day timeframe. He decided to capture the stories in the faces and locations of the frontal static portraits he eventually opted to take.

SM: Two further ways in which cohesion is achieved is through the organizing principle of the family and the boundary of the South Africa nation. Shall we start with the family? By situating selves within the larger context of families, you cover the middle ground between conventional auto/biography, which zooms in on the life of an individual, and traditional history, which narrates the life of the nation. Could you elaborate on the specific advantages and disadvantages of using the family as organizing principle for auto/biographical representation? On the mediating position of family between the individual and the nation? And on the metonymical proximity of family and nation, as in the reference to Winnie Madikizela-Mandela as the mother of the nation?

PF: The family in this case gave me an instrument to cover a longer historical period (a century) broken down into several perspectives, but still connected to each other in a meaningful way. It links individual lives in a way that everyone can relate to. It also marks changes with each generation that everyone can relate to, as we all have parents (and all are—and some have—children), and we all experience shifts and changes as well as continuation going through the generations. The family translates the history of abstract entities (like nation) into a framework with which we can readily identify. By comparing different generations we can see how specific generations are also burdened by certain events, and that young generations can, to a certain extent, make fresh starts.

The complexities were also marked by the family system, as families are dynamic social structures with hierarchies, containing problems people do not want to bring out into the open. Already in the selection phase we left out a specific family because so many painful things were brought up in the preliminary research that the family simply could not handle going on with it. In the Rathebe story, the history was dominated by one person, Dolly Rathebe. We could not easily access other family members, as Dolly was protective of the image of her family in the outside world.

The idea of the family as metonymy of the nation was never a leading idea to us. On the contrary, we realized that the concept of family was in the end a very culturally defined concept as such. What is a family really? Who is part of it and who not? Is it a permanent institution or something that constructs itself on certain moments or occasions? Is it a given thing, a cherished institution, a façade, or a trap? In fact, the nine families represent nine different ideas of what a family is as much as they represent nine different views of what history is and how it is perceived and used. Finally, the nine family stories also led to nine different ways of recreating history in exhibition terms. For us, these insights were surprising and enlightening.

SM: Tracing family genealogies and thus stretching auto/biographical accounts beyond the timeframe of one individual's existence has decisive effects for our notion of the self. Could you comment on this in view of *Group Portrait*?

PF: That is very true. In different cases one finds, as I said before, different ways of looking at history. There are, for instance, different ways of identifying with ancestors, or more precisely, of identifying oneself in respect to predecessors. Zizwezonke Mthethwa is a strong case. He distances himself from his father, Focela, who was converted, married one wife, and had a job as a servant to Europeans. His grandfather, on the other hand, opposed British rule and defended Zulu traditions. Zizwezonke modeled himself after his grandfather. Likewise Zizwezonke's eldest son, Mfanawezulu, constructed his life consciously in a different way from his father, while his son Qondokuhle respects his grandfather strongly. Similar patterns are to be seen in other families, like Theuns Steyn (the strong tradition of naming children after ancestors is an interesting point), who, as eldest son, breaks a family law and leaves the family land. In contrast, Theuns's nephew Klein Colin is so tied to the past that he can hardly accept his grandfather's death several years ago. And then there is Tumi Plaatje, who is very active in keeping the image of her great-uncle Sol Plaatje alive. Many other examples testify that, certainly in South Africa, family members are strong models for identification and self-definition, in affirmative or negative ways. The strong dedication of many family members to reconstruct their family histories testifies to their desire to link their individual existence to a larger network of social relations that are important to them.

SM: Whereas family constitutes the internal organizing principle, South Africa constitutes an outer boundary that serves to hold the stories together. Could you comment on the significance of place for auto/biographical narratives, a connection foregrounded in Niyi Osundare's assertion—which serves as a motto to the introduction of this volume—namely, that "[t]he autobiography of an African is the autobiography of a place"?

PF: One of the reasons that the catalog and exhibition had such an impact was due to the accumulation of these extremely different stories. When delving into these detailed family stories, the reader or visitor forgets that all these extreme and unlikely events, which sometimes seem to have taken place in different continents, all share one thing: the South African nation. The second insight was that you could not only set these nine stories against the backdrop of the South African national history, but that one realized that it was stories like these that actually made up that history.

The nine stories had different relations to geographical locations. In the nine units in the exhibition and in the chapters of the book they were ordered along geographical lines. For instance, the Nunns are besides the Mthethwas, as the early Nunn generations lived maybe fifty kilometers apart from the Mthethwas. The younger Nunn generations moved toward Johannesburg, as did the Rathebes, who had common roots with the early Plaatjes. Sol Plaatje wrote a diary during the Mafeking siege when Martinus Steyn fought on the other side. The Steyns moved towards Oranjevrijstaat at the time the early Le Fleurs were pushed out, and so on. Through mapping the family lines onto the country one could describe a complete circle, of course, with many connections to routes that started outside South Africa. In several ways you could almost claim that "the autobiography of a South African is the autobiography of a displacement." The histories of these individuals and families are, however, linked with the locations in a deep way. The family stories are stories firmly rooted in the Highveld or the sea, the gold- and diamond-fields, the cattle pastures or the sugar-cane plantations, the deserts or the cities.

SM: South Africa is, of course, not only a circumscribed space but also a contested symbolic entity. How do you see the role of projects such as *Group Portrait* in creating imagined communities of belonging for individuals in the South African nation?

PF: It was said before that we did not offer a grand narrative in this project. Still, the choice of family stories definitely had an underlying ambition to connect people and bring them together. By breaking down stereotypes, by showing many contrasts within a family, between generations, inside one generation, we also tried to demonstrate that one should not view families, let alone groups of people, as uniform blocks, but as individual human beings with hopes, ambitions, joys, and sorrow. We all try to make our lives acceptable for ourselves and our loved ones, and we should respect each other. That was the main reason to choose the family angle. We offered a model that anybody can identify with, irrespective of color, religion, wealth, political opinions; a model that would transcend previous conflicts. The historical angle ensured that people realized that they all created this nation and this society, that they could not be understood without the country, nor the country without them.

But we did not stress this ambition: I would see that as an immodest ambition for a project started by an outsider. But the wish was there, and the fact that the project was created by so many South Africans in a certain way proved the possibility. The fact that the exhibition was taken to South Africa and that it formed the starting point of a large and effective educational project made it even more real.

The ultimate experience for me, however, took place on the opening day of the exhibition in Pretoria on March 30, 2004. Representatives of all nine families were there and met each other for the first time. They were walking around proudly and were photographed together. This was for me an incredibly moving moment. It was a visible statement that it was possible to create a humane society together in spite of all these hardships and conflicts in the past. I was proud that I had come to know all these people, and that I had had the opportunity to work together with so many creative South Africans to bring this project together. In that sense the process of making this project was as important as the product itself.

SM: In the portraits of Dolly Rathebe and the portrait of the Manuel family, there are hints regarding the role of media technology (such as print journalism in the 1950s and now the Internet) and economic forces in generating an interest in personalities and auto/biographies as commodities. What trends have you observed in this regard? Could you relate these observations to *Group Portrait*?

PF: The question for me relates specifically to the difference between the private and the public. Interestingly, we had two examples in *Group Portrait* of life stories presented in popular printed media: several articles on Dolly Rathebe in *Drum Magazine* and two articles in illustrated magazines about the Steyns, one covering the society wedding of Theuns and Elize Steyn in the *Sarie*. In both families the awareness of a public image besides an internal way of dealing with family history was clearly present. In recent times this was the case with more families who now also played a part in creating this public image. The Juggernath family published a printed brochure on their family history. Photographer Cedric Nunn consciously documented the life of his family since the 1980s. Zizwezonke Mthethwa showed me a popular book on the Zulu in which he was presented (Derwent 1998:141, 148, 154) in a way he did not appreciate. Ebrahim Manuel focused on his early family history and was dedicated to making it public. In that sense the *Group Portrait* exhibition was also a vehicle for his own ambitions, although the exhibition stressed the twentieth-century family history rather than the eighteenth-century roots that were important to him. Later on, Ebrahim's version of this early history was contested by another family. Ebrahim's undertaking is not dissimilar to the activities of Tumi Plaatje with regards to the legacy of Sol Plaatje, the activities of the Le Fleurs in supporting Khoisan heritage and Le Fleur monuments and sites. The feeling of having been neglected, misrepresented, or even eradicated from public history is in my eyes a strong motivation for many family actions in playing a part in writing that history. The possibilities in different media enable these strategies.

This feeling of historical justice may sometimes have an economic background as well, as many have also suffered economically by events during the apartheid years. Dolly Rathebe, for example, lost her position as star in the fifties through repression. The recognition of the part she played then in the nineties made it possible, not only to regain a part of her self-esteem but also to come back successfully on stage. As a star, she was also much more aware of the problematic issues relating to the public image than members of the other families. A few months after the launch of *Familieverhalen* in Amsterdam, a plot of former family land in Simon's Town was returned officially to Kobera Manuels. Besides these considerations, the interviews in *Group Portrait* are influenced much more by the wish for justice or for getting a rightful place in history than by economic considerations.

STEPHAN MEYER: How did you get involved in writing the portrait "Near the Mountain, Near the Sea" about the members of the Manuel family for the *Group Portrait* project?

RAYDA JACOBS: It is quite uncanny how that happened. Usually I do not write nonfiction. But stories come to me often through people, and this story came to me. I got a call from Ebrahim Manuel one day, telling me a little about himself, that he had read *The Slave Book* (Jacobs 1998), and that he had a story to tell me. So he told me this story about a graveyard and a sultan—some ancestor who dwelled in a cave—and offered to take me up to Simon's Town to see the *kramat* (holy place) of the son and grandson. It sounded a bit far-fetched, and I did not do anything. Not many months after that Paul Faber came to Cape Town and said he was thinking of putting together this book. Then the story came up again, and I thought maybe I should research it a bit. This time I asked Ebrahim Manuel to give me a more thorough version of his story. The story grew larger as the months passed, and I wrote it, but told Paul Faber that I was not entirely convinced.

I had by now met Juleiga Anthony, who had the *real* story. Juleiga claimed that the sultan was *her* ancestor and that he had been captured by the Dutch, locked up in a jail in Simon's Town, from where he escaped to a cave called Antonie's Gat, where his spirit still dwelled today. I made a documentary film —*The Tuan of Antonie's Gat*—about her story, which is a far different one. It is true, though, that Ebrahim Manuel did a lot of hard work: he did go to Indonesia, he did find dates, and he did have people give him the family tree. But you know, sometimes when you have worked so hard at something, and get so close, you make things fit. In the end it became a sad affair. "Near the Mountain, Near the Sea" had already been written before I had Juleiga Anthony's story. Having said all of that, however, the story of Ebrahim Manuel and his family is still a delightful one. Auntie Koebie Manuel is a very likable and believable character. I am not sorry that I did the portrait because I believe it is a lovely story about Auntie Koebie and her father and Ebrahim Manuel's genuine quest to research his roots.

SM: Of course these are characteristic developments in the life of biographies. Once the auto/biographical account has been published, new things happen, and as it circulates in the public sphere, people keep adding more sides to it.

RJ: Yes. And people do not only ask if this is the *whole* story but also if it is the *real* story. It was getting to the bottom of the real story that drove me to subsequently make the film.

SM: So was the filming of the Anthony family's story a way of washing your hands of the previous account, which you had increasingly come to doubt?

RJ: The film was an attempt to finish what I had started for the Anthony family. They have the *kitab* (sacred book/paper) to prove their story. It has been looked at and verified by a lot of people from overseas. Juleiga Anthony told me that the sultan, deceased in the 1700s, had come to her in a vision and asked that I be the person to tell their story. If you are not familiar with the metaphysical aspects of the *kramat*s in the Cape, you will not understand this. This is the culture of the people and they believe it. I was skeptical, but decided to make the film, because I was dissatisfied with the version of the story I had thus far.

SM: Although you are a fiction writer, you are not new to life writing: your first collection of short stories, *The Middle Children* (1994), is described as semi-autobiographical. Could you explain what you see as the particular significance of auto/biography to literature in South Africa at the moment?

RJ: When you are writing nonfiction, you have to stick to the facts. With fiction you create and kill off the characters. You play God. Not that you cannot be creative with nonfiction; there is definitely a creative thread in my portrait of the Manuel family. But I still tell the story as it has been reported to me, so it is just putting it into a reader-friendly or entertaining form. Actually, I am not really that interested in writing other people's stories. Maybe it is selfish, or maybe I do not get enough of a fix. Still, as I was walking this morning, the opening line came to me for my new book: *The thing I remember most about my childhood is the dappled light . . .* And then I realized that what I am actually thinking of writing is the opening of a future autobiography.

To be honest, I do not read biographies. I have such limited time. Maybe South African biographies are important to South Africans so that they can know about their own people. For myself, I would like to know more about J. M. Coetzee because he is such an elusive character. And Nelson Mandela—but to be honest I have not read their autobiographies yet.

SM: Can we digress for a moment to another publication of yours, namely, *The Mecca Diaries* (2005), in which you write about your recent hadj? How did it come about that you wrote and published a journal of that experience?

RJ: Two weeks before my departure to Mecca, my publisher took me to lunch and asked when they could get another book from me. I answered that I have too much other stuff to do and that it would be more than two years. When I mentioned that I would be journaling while on the pilgrimage—because I want to take some notes for myself—they asked me to write a book. I said I could only write it if it's in the moment; I can't come back and write it. That's why it takes the diary format. When you're reading it, it's as if you're performing hadj yourself. As I'm seeing it for the first time, so are you. If I hadn't been asked, I wouldn't have written about it, because I didn't want to make money out of my experience. I thought that if my book would help other Muslims, then I must write it, because it's beholden to me as a writer to do so. God didn't give me this gift for nothing. And if my book would enlighten others about Islam, that would be a good thing too.

SM: Is this the first time you've kept a journal, or have you done it before in your life, for private purposes?

RJ: I started as a child, keeping journals and notes, like girls do. Especially if you have a lonely kind of childhood—your mother has to work to support the family because there is no dad and no one to spend a lot of time listening to you—you seek solace. So I always journaled; I suppose it was a coping mechanism.

SM: Do you still keep a journal?

RJ: No, because I write every day, so I work out all my *angst* on the page, I guess. The reason I was going to do it for Mecca was because Mecca was going to be very intense. *The Mecca Diaries* is different from my other books because it's nonfiction. It is also a memoir, my daily journal about what was happening. But it is also about what was happening to me as a person. And I also write bits of history, for example of the layout of the Prophet's burial chamber and the ritual pilgrims perform, running between the hills of Safa and Marwah, where Hajar ran to and fro for water for her infant son Ishmael.

SM: Are you aware of any other journals by women on the hadj?

RJ: Nobody has ever done one as far as I know.

SM: Would you say that your perspective in *The Mecca Diaries* differs from those of journals kept by men, such as the journal Bakaar Manuel kept of his 1903–1904 hadj that you integrated into your portrait of the Manuels in "Near the Mountain, Near the Sea"?

RJ: My book is different from Bakaar Manuel's, because his deals with things on the surface—what you *do* in Mecca—whereas I give insight into my own personal responses. There are many things women can't do there, like not being able to stand in front of the Holy Prophet's *kab-r* (grave). That's one of the things I was upset about, because I love the Prophet. I can't say how I'm different from other writers, because I don't know about others' experiences. In Mecca, whether you're a prince or a pauper, you all wear the same clothing. But everyone has their own unique experience; I was reminded constantly of my mortality.

SM: What kinds of responses did you seek to evoke in your readers?

RJ: I did not set out to evoke any particular response. I did not think of the reader. But the book has only had a very positive response, selling well in a Muslim bakery and a Muslim boutique. People are buying it as gifts for pilgrims who are going to Mecca. And people who have been to Mecca are buying it for all the photographs and the memories. People who have called me, especially the women, have been very emotional about the book.

SM: Looking at your journal afterwards, what is its effect on you?

RJ: Mecca had a profound effect on me. Looking at the galleys of the book, three months after I returned, I was a little ashamed. When I was in Mecca I had made three promises to God. By the time I read the galleys I had broken one promise already and one was hanging by a thread. I immediately restored the one promise. The other one I can do nothing about. In Mecca I felt very close to God. When I came home I realized Mecca doesn't change you. I was already good when I went and I'm still good. I'm sometimes a little naughty. But God created me and I have my prayer mat. The Koran is my guide, the *Diaries* a wonderful reminder of where I've been.

SM: Turning to the social dimension of auto/biography: how do you view the role of auto/biographical narratives as people's appeals for recognition for their particular individual or collective identity?

RJ: I think that is part of it, but it is not the whole reason for telling your story. I think telling a story is like hearing yourself read something out loud. You have to hear it in your own ear, come to your own understanding. It is a coping mechanism. I also think in telling your story you are putting it out there and you are getting feedback from other people. And in a way you learn about yourself.

SM: And what about economic justice: what role do you see testimony playing in struggles over distribution and redistribution, for example, in reclaiming land that had been appropriated or restitution claims for human rights violations?

RJ: I would say it depends very much on the people. The Anthony family told me outright that they were not interested in receiving money for their story. They did not want any glory. They just wanted the truth to be told, that *they* are the family. It was their intention to take the film to the Indonesian and the Dutch governments and say to the Dutch: "You captured this man who was a sultan in Indonesia. This is our family. Here is the film made about him. People on the island suffered because he and his son were taken away. You have to help the people on that island." That is what they are doing it for. But they themselves want nothing in return. There are people in Cape Town who do family trees and go back to find, not only their ancestors, but also the ancestors of other people, for absolutely no money. They do it because the stories must be told, they must be in the history books. And this is why I did this, to set the record straight.

SM: Certainly there is a long-standing tradition related to so-called high art that it is an insult when one brings money into the equation, as if literature and writing about the self are sullied or distorted thereby. On the contrary, I believe that there are different legitimate ways in which people express, for example, their property rights. What I am interested in knowing is to what extent the stories people tell about their lives could also sometimes be veiled claims for economic justice.

RJ: Yes, there are people who need the money, everybody does. But there are people who are pursuing land restitution because the property meant something to them. Maybe in your eyes it is not a bad thing to do these things for money. As far as I am concerned, this is the first year in my life that I am making money from writing.

SM: You use a mixture of multiple, fractured, and reverse chronologies to construct the narrative of the lives of the Manuel family. How do you view time as a means for individuals to order events in their life and thereby derive meaning from it?

RJ: Well, if you read *Confessions of a Gambler* (2003) and *Sachs Street* (2001) you will see that I write in two time frames: the present and the past. I do not really sit and think about time the way you have asked the question. I do it because it works. For me it is a technique I started to use after *The Slave Book* (1998). It is purely for entertainment value, to take you in and out of a situation, a clever way to do things that adds a bit of mystery to the writing. In my piece "Near the Mountain, Near the Sea" in *Group Portrait South Africa* I think it worked nicely because I take you into two different landscapes. It makes it interesting for me as a writer too. If I am not entertained doing this, I am not going to be entertaining you. For me, telling a story in a straight line would be boring. This is true of my earlier work, and I do not think I will go back to telling a story in a straight line.

SM: You have just mentioned taking the reader into two different landscapes, and your profile of the Manuel family deals very specifically with different landscapes and with issues of location and dislocation. The importance of location and dislocation is evident in the title "Near the Mountain, Near the Sea" and in your portrayal of Koebie Manuel's loss of home due to the forced removals of 1968. Could you say something about the importance of being able to situate oneself geographically for defining one's identity?

RJ: It is very important. I cannot speak for Auntie Koebie, but I would say that for people when there has been a loss and recovery of identity, their stories are all the same. And in that sense my story is the same as Auntie Koebie's: forced out of the country, away for twenty-seven years, longing to come back, and writing about this country while I am living in another country [Canada]. It is all a means of trying to hang on, to retain something, to come to the place that you know. Maybe I can answer it for you like this: I walk every morning to the house where I was born and the mosque in Diep River where I went as a seven-year-old girl. On my first walk there, on my return, I walked down the street from that house with my eyes closed trying to recapture that walk as a child. I also walked to the mosque, saw where I had gone all those afternoons after school, and cried. Why do I go there? I am trying to connect with that little girl, to understand some things about myself as a child. It is the same as with Auntie Koebie wanting to go back to Simon's Town. It is your identity. You identify with a place, with a sensibility, with a culture. If you take somebody out of that, you disturb their balance.

SM: *Group Portrait* seeks to locate individuals in families, and families within the bounds of the new South African nation. Your portrait of the Manuel family, however, pulls in two other directions too: it stretches to genealogical-geographical communities beyond the borders of the South African nation state, in this case Indonesia and Mecca. And it extends the scope to the religious community of Islam, which is a world religion. Could you explain why you saw it as important to locate the individuals in these additional contexts, which exceed the collective identity of South Africa?

RJ: That is just part of their story. It is not that I intended to take them outside of South Africa.

SM: But even if it is part of their story, you as a writer still face the matter of selection. Which facets of a life do you represent and which do you forego?

RJ: I could not leave out something as important as Bakaar Manuel's journal of his pilgrimage to Mecca. Also, interspersing extracts from his journal throughout the stories of the other members of the family is a device that makes for interesting reading. As a writer I do not look at why I take characters outside the country; I look at what works for the story. In all my writing my area of interest is culture, identity, and religion. I do not limit myself to South Africa and I do not write just for the local reader. I write about the humanness of people.

STEPHAN MEYER: I am interested in your view on the relationship between photographic portraiture (which offers a present moment frozen in the photograph) on the one hand, and life narratives (which seek to portray the subject as she or he presently is in the light of her or his past). To what extent do you see the photographer as dealing with the subject's past life beyond the moment in which the portrait is taken?

DAVID GOLDBLATT: What is the purpose of the photography? Is it for the use of a client, an editor, an institution, etc.? Or does it evolve from some personal interest or project? These questions are fundamental in determining my approach. In this case the imperatives were clearly those of the KIT Tropenmuseum and its historical project, and I tried to bear these in mind throughout the months it took to complete the assignment. The approach was discussed in some detail with Paul Faber, who directed the project. I was commissioned to do three parts of the project: a detailed essay on the Steyn family; a group family portrait of each of the nine families; and a portrait of a "key" teenager in each family. For each of these, a somewhat different approach was dictated by the needs of the project.

Regarding the detailed essay on the Steyn family, I needed to immerse myself to some degree in the life histories of the family members and the dynamics of their interrelationships. However, I like to rely on my gut responses to people and generally try to avoid too detailed a knowledge of them. Portraits of the kind that I sought among the Steyns would ideally convey a sense of their values, the past that had produced these people, a sense of what was immanent or potential in their lives, and a sense of their presence—high and unattainable ideals for which nevertheless I strived.

The group portraits of the nine families needed to have a common treatment. I photographed each family in front of their home. This had the advantage of instantly enabling the viewer to place the family in a socioeconomic context and the disadvantage of having to fit them into a formula that was not always photographically the most effective solution. The enlarged figures in the final display needed to be rendered to more or less the same scale. Since the homes and the spaces in front of them differed widely, it was sometimes difficult and inhibiting to follow the formula. I must record that a design fault in some of the family group portraits is due to an oversight on my part—Paul Faber had told me that I needed to provide space at the left of each such portrait for a text panel. This I failed to do and as a result there is a certain "discomfort" in some of the pictures—especially that of the Steyns who are too far to the left of their frame.

Finally, the teenage portraits were intended to be enlarged to life size and to be concentrated on the person rather than his or her context. Again, the formulaic approach was somewhat inhibiting. In retrospect I thought that these photographs could have been stronger had I spent more time with the subjects and if there had not been the need to render them to the same scale. However, having now seen the exhibition in Pretoria, I think that the treatment of the teenagers was, on the whole, appropriate for the purpose.

SM: What sources did you draw on in familiarizing yourself with the past and present lives of the subjects?

DG: I made a preliminary visit to the Steyn family farm outside Bloemfontein with the writer Sonya Loots and Paul Faber. We looked at family pictures, met a couple of family members, and got a sense of the place and its history. Later I dined with the Cape Town Steyns and got to know them better as I began to photograph.

SM: During these visits to the Steyns, what were some of the specific clues from their past and present that guided you in the way you chose to portray them?

DG: It soon became clear that Colin Steyn was not simply interested in the family history and that of the Afrikaner *volk*. He was obsessed to the point where his behavior was bizarre. He needed to reenact the Anglo-Boer war [see portrait in *Group Portrait*, p. 123]. He was also obsessed by the need to relive his experiences as an officer in the South African army in the Angolan campaign against the ANC and SWAPO. Yet withal, he seemed not an aggressive man; nor did he profess right-wing political sympathies. He more or less dragged Klein Colin, his son, along in these Afrikaner fantasies. But the boy had his own mania [see portrait in *Group Portrait*, p. 125]. Klein Colin believed that his grandfather, who had claimed him at birth and taken him into his bed, and who had died some three years prior, was still alive. He operated the model railway that his grandfather had built on the basis that certain rolling stock was not to be used because his grandfather had forbidden it. While running the railway, he listened to tapes of his grandfather telling stories with a strong undertone of violence and even of racism. Whether he was psychotic or not I do not know, but there was an uncomfortable air of possession about him.

Theuns Steyn and his family were moderate, sophisticated urbanites, accomplished professionals and students. Theuns was outspoken in his criticism of his brother's dalliance with the past and with hobbies rather than a proper engagement with the present and the need to run the farm. He resented strongly that, notwithstanding his distance from the farm, its management was left largely to him. I thought that a photograph of him in his professional capacity was appropriate. Paul Faber thought rather that he should be photographed at the family farm Onze Rust. Paul was right. I think that in the published photograph there is a nice tension between Theuns in his carefully casual country self, but obviously not a farmer, and his place as the eldest in front of the family homestead [see portrait in *Group Portrait*, p. 124].

The ways in which Elize and Martine Steyn expressed themselves on the family history and their respective priorities in life left me in little doubt about the kind of photographs I sought of them. Isabella, the sister, had her own obsession, graphically expressed in a bust of her father that she had sculpted; I found her a sophisticated and self-confident, perhaps even domineering, woman, yet with a quality of vulnerability. Somewhat to my surprise I found

Yvonne, the mother, to be less matriarchal than I had anticipated [see portrait in *Group Portrait*, p. 125]. She seemed less than even-handed in her treatment of her children, with Theuns coming in for considerable criticism.

SM: Could you elaborate on the scope you gave people to represent themselves—for example, through their choice of clothing, the seating arrangements and pose—and how you represented them by arranging the image?

DG: While portraits of others might tell much about the photographers who took them, this is not something to which I give much thought. My concern is with the subject and in particular where the imperatives are those of a client, I am concerned with meeting those needs. Representing myself is therefore not in my mind, though it might be an unintended subtext. Regarding the relationship between self-representation and being represented, to me the strongest and most rewarding portraits are those in which the subject portrays him or herself with as little interference from me as possible. In general, I prefer to allow the subjects to choose their clothing and to arrange themselves. Relationships, affections, power are often made manifest by how people dispose themselves for a photograph, and I try to be sensitive to these. For this project, however, I needed to make coherent and visually strong photographs and if the "spontaneous" arrangements were confused or could be made more photographically coherent, I did not hesitate to change things. Except in the case of the teenage photographs, I do not recall making any changes to clothing choices.

On the matter of creating coherence: as far as I can recall, in the Mthethwa family photograph the men and women did not group themselves easily around the old man. Possibly there were questions of hierarchy at stake, of which I was not aware. But I needed to bring some kind of structure to the group, so I placed a few and others then disposed themselves accordingly.

With the Plaatje family picture there was a distinct lack of intimacy between the three subjects. It later became apparent why this was so—Tumi Plaatje-Molefe and Popo Molefe were divorced not long after. At the time, however, I did not know of these tensions and in order to give the photograph a semblance of familial intimacy I asked them to move closer to each other. Popo then put his arm—rather awkwardly—over his daughter's shoulders and drew her to him while the mother held her hand.

The Manuel family did not compose themselves "naturally," and I think I had to place each person. The outcome was not satisfactory—Ebrahim Manuel is awkwardly supporting the wall. I should have given him something to sit on or helped him to find a comfortable way of standing. Some people are not at ease with their own bodies and find it difficult to dispose their limbs in front of the camera. It is then the job of the photographer to help them. I think I failed Mr. Manuel.

SM: What were some of the telling responses of the subjects to the process of being photographed and to seeing their portraits?

DG: Most people are glad to be "noticed," and these were no exception. I received willing cooperation and cannot recall any negative responses other than the usual disclaimer "I'm not photogenic." Except for Theuns and Elize Steyn, who seemed delighted, I was not present when any of the subjects saw their portraits.

SM: How do you view the relationship between your portraits and the other media used in the exhibition and the catalog, such as the Internet website, the objects displayed, and the biographical narratives as ways of telling people's lives?

DG: I have to confess that I have had no contact with the other media employed in this project. In my opinion—this important qualification will not be mentioned again, but it stands before everything that follows—this project was excellent in conception but overly ambitious and poor in parts of the execution of its presentation. I feared for its outcome when I was told at an early stage that the interior of each family's "home" on the exhibition floor would be designed by a different person, and that this design was largely in place before material had been collected and photographs taken. To me that put carts before horses. If photography was to form an essential element of the family story, it seemed to me that one needed to design the presentation around the photographs after they were done rather than trying to fit them into a preconceived plan. I wondered about the wisdom of the plan to commission works of art. How were the very different methods and intentions of documentary photographers and artists to be brought together? There was a potentially interesting outcome, but a strong potential for confusion and thus a dilution of the intended result.

I shall not go into a detailed critique of what I have seen in Pretoria, except to say that the feared confusion is manifest in many aspects of the exhibition. A few examples must suffice. Paul Weinberg took a magnificent photograph of Zizwezonke Mthethwa dancing with a live snake. It has been presented as a green print on a canvas-like paper. Why? To give it the status of "art"? What an appalling confusion of values and indeed, lack of respect for the subject, the photograph and the photographer! The designer of this family exhibit is seemingly quite out of touch with modern thinking about photography. The exhibition generally suffers from a lack of understanding that while photography is not inherently a good medium for storytelling, it can be turned to very good account when, combined with words, they are used with careful calculation of connections between pictures and the "psychic" values inherent in them. The results can then be both coherent and effective in telling stories. Instead photographs have in many instances been "slapped" on walls or in panels with little concern for their interconnections, often unsupported by captions or text.

The commissioned "artworks" are a puzzling aspect. A huge piece by Willie Bester stands in a cramped space with neither title nor any indication of who had made it. If I did not know his work, I would have had no clue that he was the artist. But that aside, it is simply too big and complex a sculpture for that space. Indeed, as far as I can recall, all of the commissioned artworks are without titles or attribution. The effect is to make the artworks seem like curiosities without any apparent place in the show.

The two family stories that work best do so because they have been designed in a straightforward way with careful thought to coherence. These are Le Fleur and Steyn. I don't know who designed these spaces, but in the first case panels by Conrad Botes of his comic book tales have been placed simply and connectedly on the wall. In the second my portraits of the individual Steyns have been similarly treated and supplemented by clear captions. Similar treatment has been given to family and archive photographs so that the whole Steyn story has a well integrated coherence.

SM: What role do you see portraits in general playing in the ways in which people in contemporary South Africa come to interpret or understand themselves and others?

DG: An editor with whom I worked used to say, "People are interested in people." I think this is true and is generally exemplified by their warm responses to portraits. However, to what extent this interest indicates their ability to interpret and/or understand themselves or others, I do not really know. In my opinion the bombardment of images in various media to which we are now subjected tends to raise the level of sensitivity to photographs while at the same time tending to desensitize responsiveness to their content.

SM: How do you see the role of portraits in general, and in particular portraits such as those in the *Group Portrait* project, in creating an imagined community of belonging in the South African nation?

DG: My impression is that portraits of this kind or any other have very little practical effect in creating such an imagined community of belonging. My answers are highly speculative—there is need for systematic research if your questions are to be more authoritatively answered—but in my view there is little likelihood that viewers will link themselves to a bigger South African family through these portraits. What is more likely is that some of the photographs and their stories will be retained in memory and gradually, along with other images and experiences, bring about shifts in awareness or consciousness. I think this is a subtle process, more comparable to percolation or osmosis than to clearly definable changes of attitude or association. At best I think that this project could lead to a greater awareness that other families also have histories, different from one's own yet in some respects similar, and thus perhaps to greater consciousness and respect for others.

References Cited

DERWENT, SUE. *Zulu*. London: New Holland, 1998.
FABER, PAUL, comp. and ed., and ANNARI VAN DER MERWE, ed. *Group Portrait South Africa: Nine Family Histories*. Cape Town: Kwela, 2003.
GOLDBLATT, DAVID. Various portraits. In *Group Portrait South Africa: Nine Family Histories*, edited by Paul Faber and Annari van der Merwe. Cape Town: Kwela, 2003.
JACOBS, RAYDA. *The Middle Children*. Toronto: Second Story, 1994
———. *The Slave Book*. Cape Town: Kwela, 1998.
———. *Sachs Street*. Cape Town: Kwela, 2001.
———. *Confessions of a Gambler*. Cape Town: Kwela, 2003.
———. "The Manuel Family: Near the Mountain, Near the Sea." In *Group Portrait South Africa: Nine Family Histories*, edited by Paul Faber and Annari van der Merwe, pp. 156–170. Cape Town: Kwela, 2003.
———. *The Mecca Diaries*. Cape Town: Double Storey, 2005.
———. *The Tuan of Antonie's Gat*. Documentary film. N.d.
LINDFORS, BERNTH, ed. *Africans on Stage: Studies in Ethnological Show Business*. Bloomington: Indiana University Press, 1998.
MANDELA, NELSON. "Can We Learn from History?" In *Group Portrait South Africa: Nine Family Histories*, edited by Paul Faber and Annari van der Merwe, pp. 4–5. Cape Town: Kwela, 2003.

Further Reading

AMOATENG, ACHEAMPONG YAW. "The South African Family: Continuity or Change?" Paper presented at the Human Sciences Research Council Ten Years of Democracy series, August 5, 2004. http://www.hsrc.ac.za/media/2004/8/20040805Paper2.pdf
AMOATENG, ACHEAMPONG YAW, and L. RICHTER. "The State of Families in South Africa." In *State of the Nation: South Africa 2003–2004*, edited by J. Daniel, A. Habib, and R. Southall, pp. 242–267. Cape Town: HSRC Press, 2003.

BRINK, ANDRÉ P. "Want ons ís stories." Review of *Group Portrait South Africa* 2003. http://www.boekwurm.co.za/blad_boeke_efgh/faber_paul.html
"Familieverhalen uit Zuid-Afrika." *De Kat* (Summer 2003): 61–67.
GOLDBLATT, DAVID. *South Africa: The Structure of Things Then*. Cape Town: Oxford University Press, 1998.
———. *Fifty One Years*. Barcelona: Museu d'Art Contemporani, 2002.
GOLDBLATT, DAVID, with NADINE GORDIMER. *On the Mines*. Cape Town: Struik, 1973.
JACOBS, RAYDA. *Postcards from South Africa*. Cape Town: Juta, 2004.
MAART, BRENTON. Review of *Family Stories of South Africa: Nine Family Histories*. *Art South Africa* 4 (Winter 2004): 70–71.

September 2004, August 2005

Resituating Ourselves: Homelessness and Collective Testimony as Narrative Therapy

Valentine Cascarino and Jonathan Morgan interviewed by Sam Raditlhalo

READERS HAVE PRAISED the celebration of the human spirit in the text by William Kennedy (1984) dealing with homelessness and its circumstances. In South Africa, texts by South African authors such as Zakes Mda (1995) and Sello K. Duiker (2000) treat the same theme. While this is easily achievable in fiction, it is the factual nature of being homeless, the edgy reasons of displacement, loss, and alienation that lift *Finding Mr Madini* (1999) above the fictive. In narrating themselves (with the assistance of social psychologist Jonathan Morgan), in an attempt to evaluate themselves, the GASP (Great African Spider Project)[1] writers open a wide range of specific, assigned vignettes or "windows"[2] into their lives by discussing their a) origins, b) becoming homeless, c) hitting the road, d) homeless living, and e) signing off as a tapestry of human existence. And in the process of telling and sharing their stories with one another the eponymous Mr Madini literally disappears, so that, within the interstices of life writing is also the mystery of his absence. The history of political upheaval, dispossession, displacement, and life as a refugee, with Johannesburg as the magnet for possible salvation, form the backdrop to these life narratives. The book is fascinating in that it allows the reader to see homelessness not as a form of delinquency but as a structural political problem of modern society, with all the concomitant problems. It is a very powerful read of

---

1. In referring to the participants as spider writers, Jonathan Morgan highlights the fact that all of their lives and story lines (beginning in Ethiopia, Lithuania, Eastern Cape, Kimberley, Cameroon, etc.) converged in Gauteng in 1999, much like the legs of a spider.
2. In the context of the book, "windows" refer to glimpsed bits—short but detailed and richly voiced and textured accounts of fragments of their lives—that might otherwise (if not for the writing workshops) have been forgotten and left devalued.

self-discovery and self-validation within a group structure. In the words of Rian Malan, writer and critic, it is "brilliant and timely."

SAM RADITLHALO: In writing about yourselves through the various stages of the windows exercise, which window in particular was difficult, and why?

VALENTINE CASCARINO: The window dealing with my struggle to find a foothold (sociofinancial) on the streets of Johannesburg. It was particularly difficult because of where I was coming from. After living in Canada in a relatively sound financial environment, I just thought people would think me insane leaving everything behind and coming to South Africa of all places. Also, I was wondering what my friends and family members back home in the Cameroon are going to think of me. My family (from my grandfather's side) is middle class. I could easily have gone back to the Cameroon or to France and lived in comfort; after all there's no place like home.

JONATHAN MISHA MORGAN: I would have to say the one in which I come out as someone who did time in a psychiatric hospital. This experience was perhaps the best training I received for my present occupation as a clinical psychologist. Putting it out there via this window was a bit like putting this on my curriculum vitae and reframing it for myself within a "wounded healer" kind of framework. The experience of being hospitalized, diagnosed, medicated, and psychoanalyzed without any positive effect has remained with me as a memory and as a personal symbol of the extreme arrogance and impotence of the mental health profession. Had I been admitted or committed to a similar kind of place earlier in the century, I would no doubt have been lobotomized. ECT (electric shock therapy) was offered to me as an option.

Nevertheless, to speak so openly of this at the time of *Finding Mr Madini* (1999), when it was not quite yet a "worked through" trauma (whatever "worked through" means), was both healing as well as a stretch, but one I now believe to be an important stretch. To speak out in this way to an audience, some of whom I knew and would read the book, others—the vast majority—whom I knew I would never meet, was quite a leap. I had been conditioned to feel shame around this experience of hospitalization, and I remember one particular version of my actual curriculum vitae in which I attempted to disguise/create an alibi around this black hole in my life, a great depression that lasted several years. Including that time of my life with all the details in *FMM* was a protest of sorts against internalizing a whole lot of shame and stigma, and as I have said, at the same time difficult and liberating.

SR: Would you attribute the difficulty in writing this particular window to being afraid of (over) self-revelation with regard to the others?

VC: I'm not quite sure whether I understand this question well. Anyway, I think it is part of human nature to hide that which would taint one's image. That's why people keep secrets. Those who choose to reveal secrets or certain things about their past are very cautious because such information could later be used against one. Politicians can attest to this.

JM: I may answer this with reference to *Long Life*, a more recent book and project about HIV-positive lives prolonged via access to antiretrovirals. Stories were told via body maps, life-sized tracings of the body, and how the body remembers and records via scars, wounds, laugh lines, birth marks, beauty marks, etc. I was amazed how people told and revealed stories and images around what I consider to be intensely personal, details about sex, inclusion of the genitals, speaking candidly about invasions, rapes, vulnerability, etc. I had a taste of having my own body map on display, and I felt very exposed. Both in *FMM* and *Long Life* I take my hat off to those who shared their stories so openly.

But to answer your question more directly, high levels of self-disclosure by the therapist are frowned upon in most schools of psychotherapy, but in autobiography it is considered necessary, powerful, an honest assessment, etc. In narrative therapy, it is akin to leveling the playing field and to be symbolic of the two-way nature of therapy, an acknowledgement that the therapeutic conversation has the potential to create change both for the therapist and the client. It is kind of reassuring to me that if as a client I am expected to share deeply, the therapist is also willing to give me a glimpse of what he or she is feeling and thinking, as well as trading parts of her story for mine. The opposite would be for him or her to just say "mmmm," to stroke his or her beard [sic], and to make theory-driven interpretations. In *FMM* it helped a lot in the whole mood and politics of the project when I began to offer glimpses of myself via the windows and stopped acting so much like *Herr* Director/*baas*. With regard to disclosure, *FMM* and projects like it in some ways challenge the notion that therapy and healing need to take place in "private practice," "behind closed doors," where "patient-client confidentiality" is an inviolable dictum. By having control of the case notes, by turning these records into patient-held files, and, going beyond this, by valuing them as a story in the making, and as writing with some literary value, all that goes towards shifting some of the blame and self-held shame that goes along with secrecy and telling one's story only to the person one pays to listen.

SR: In going through the various windows stages, did you feel the need to censor yourselves? Was it possible to be able to explain everything in your past, or did you feel certain aspects of your lives inexplicable?

VC: Well, no biography or autobiography is ever complete. It would take a lifetime to read. Those who are paranoid about censorship should know that everything is censored—even the food you eat. Why the body accepts and rejects portions is any man's guess. However, in writing the book, we had windows to follow that would guide us in writing only the very important things in our lives that would make people aware of the seriousness of homelessness. Why these particular windows? Well, censorship-mongers should feast here.

JM: By its very nature, this windows exercise demands that we select only six out of countless possible choices/memories of lived experience and offer these up as a narrative representing one version of our life story. The next day or to another audience you might want to repeat the exercise and tell other, entirely different stories, or you might want to substitute one window that might give a whole new slant to the pack of six as they stand together, that is, the plot might change. The process, just like any self-representation or pick-up line, censors more than it reveals, but there is a huge amount of choice and creativity on line. I have always held that madness is the inability to get your lived experiences into a coherent form, into a story. I am so often (most of the time) overwhelmed by my senses, and it is only once I have "explained" these experiences to myself and to others in story form that I become less crazy.

SR: In the book, none of the participants place any significant detail on a "cultural" identity. Do you feel that such an identity is inhibiting or unnecessary?

VC: There's never been a need for cultural identity in the world before the times we're living in now. Especially with the speedy Hollywood takeover. Like June 16th or 9/11, cultural identity helps us reassert ourselves. However, just as we have different cultures, we have different opinions about cultures. Personally, I try and avoid any culture that enslaves people.

SR: In writing about your*selves,* what do you feel is being recognized? Your humanity? Or the specific achievement of actually writing about yourselves and revealing your particular identities?

VC: We represent the struggle of the homeless worldwide. What the homeless in South Africa are experiencing is similar to what the homeless are experiencing in Glasgow. More often than not, their plights are not heard. Penning down stories of ourselves in a certain sense takes this fight to another level, the human and not the political level. In the process of doing so, we reveal our identities. This gives the readers the opportunity to know who they are dealing with and at the same time making them aware that the homeless have needs like anybody else. With this in mind, the readers come to realize that the homeless did not find themselves on the fringes of society by accident.

JM: I'm not sure what you mean with this question, but I'd say for me it's all about just taking the time to recover, reclaim, and richly describe for yourself and others, that is, the minutia or details of your own unique life and weird thoughts about things. In your language ("resituating yourselves") I suppose this means the Great African Spider Project gave us a chance to locate our own insecurities and problems within a pool or range of shared, common, similar ones, that is, it gave us an opportunity to normalize our *selves* if we were feeling too weird, and to get creative about reinventing our *selves* using the powerful written word, each other, and Jo'burg as our props and sounding boards—tools that would not have been otherwise available. By rearranging these memory fragments, which are often almost forgotten and devalued (unremembered, unfussed-over experiences) and by remembering them in words and paragraphs, etc., and by a witnessing ritual of sorts, by sharing them in the group, and having them acknowledged in this way, and then in the book itself, the performance/broadcast/conversation went wider and the opportunities for ever more refracted and shifting perspectives multiplied. It was also in the overlapping and juxtaposed stories and histories that a greater picture of humanity emerged.

SR: The common thread that bound the group was "homelessness," and you respond to it in various ways (Virginia—one of the writers participating—feels that it is emasculating). Would you say it is the sort of experience that robs people of their selves? Do we attach the self to possessions/houses/cars, or do these justify our*selves*?

VC: Homelessness is relative. Those serious about their religion would say we're all homeless on earth and that our true home is in Heaven. Anthropologists see homelessness differently. So do politicians. In order to find out what homelessness meant for us, a debate would have to be stirred concerning one's conduct towards homelessness. Can one be homeless—without material property, like St. Francis of Assisi—and still be happy? If yes, then homelessness here would mean the satisfaction we get from the knowledge that people know we exist, even if it doesn't translate to wealth. A sense of belonging, so to speak. On the flip side of the argument, another question comes up: Can one have material possessions, including a decent roof above one's head, and still feel homeless? I'll leave this for you guys to deliberate on.

JM: Well, people like the Shakyamuni Buddha and other mythical and historical characters have forsaken home and things to free themselves of attachment and materialism. This is different from people who are dispossessed by political upheavals, colonization, forced removals, etc. Having said this, street or on-the-edge living seems to bring with it hard-won lessons about what is important and perhaps transcendental, aspects of being alive that are not bound up with things and identity around what you wear and what you have. Resourcefulness, compassion, a sense of humor, and irony in the face of difficulty stand out as important human attributes. But this would be a seriously flawed romanticization of homelessness. Homelessness and poverty also bring out the worst in people. This tension was apparent in many of the windows. As a footnote I'd add that Mr. Sipho Madini—whose name and disappearance became the title and if you like overarching symbol or metaphor for all of our stories—still stands out for me as a kind of street poet/philosopher who embraces homelessness in a poignantly philosophical way, with traces of the gypsy, the hermit, the Beat poets, and Rimbaud.

SR: The South African Constitution foregrounds "the right to dignity." Through your varied experiences, would you say the state bears the principal burden of responsibility in ensuring that "homelessness" is not dehumanizing? What would you have the state do? What are your thoughts of past experiences and how do you feel the state ought to intervene? Certainly well-off countries, such as the Netherlands with its freezing winters, have innovative ways in which "homelessness" is tackled; it is not left entirely to NGOs.

VC: It is the duty of every government to look after those who cannot look after themselves for one reason or another. No one can argue that the government of South Africa has been sleeping in the fight against homelessness. Nevertheless, if there's anything we've done with the book, it is that we strengthened the awareness that a lot still has to be done to curtail homelessness. Whether that's the duty of the government or the society as a whole or both, I'm not quite sure.

JM: I'm not sure about this either. But I am drawn to the notion of the state creating job opportunities in an emergency Marshall Plan kind of way so that people without jobs can add value to the world we share, and also get their hands on some dignity, cash, choices, homes, etc. If the state doesn't address this, no one else is going to; the free market doesn't give a damn, when you feel you are on a winning streak, it's easy to find oneself, exercising one's own privilege in quite insensitive selfish ways, and not seeing the direct relationship between our own reluctance and refusal to share with, for instance, the homeless man at the traffic light who is seen as a pest/leper/affront. In fact, there is more than enough to go around.

I also really like the idea of mixed income suburbs or town planning, whereby we can see less segregation along class/race/cultural lines, less fences, high walls, booms, and barricades, and more Sophiatown, more District Six-like places: vibey neighborhoods where neighbors with different stories might know or come to know each other and hang out together in some public spaces like streets, parks, town squares, street markets, sports fields, etc. This idea seems like a great challenge.

SR: In writing about the *self*, in what ways does each person feel disempowered as an (South) African? That is, to what extent do nationalities shape identities?

VC: One's nationality is one's inherited identity. This fact cannot be changed. Does it shape one's identity? It does, of course. Can any South African trust a Nigerian unconditionally? I don't think so. Can an Iraqi trust an American? But are all Nigerians crack dealers or are all Yanks gun-wielding? The fact that one comes from a particular country automatically gives one an identity tag that is very difficult to shake off. And if one is from one of those notorious regions, one's identity is nothing but a terrible omen.

SR: A crucial part of ten years of democratization of South African society was to "liberate" the oppressed. Your contributions—except for June 16, 1976—are depoliticized. Was this a conscious decision? Do we need a *political* identity or does homelessness render such an identity superficial?

VC: June 16th, to a South African, is like 9/11 to a Yank. Throughout history, dates such as these are always used as reference points for one thing or another. In our case (and I sincerely think it had nothing to do with politics) June 16th came up as a matter of historical consciousness. Sort of to make people aware that some of the homeless know what's been happening in the country. About political identity in general: the Democratic Alliance Party (DA) would tell you political identity is crucial a few weeks before people go to the polls. Otherwise I can't think of a homeless person who hasn't got some kind of a party membership card, but unfortunately—depending on what homelessness is to them—it's not done their homelessness any good.

SR: What do you feel is the reason why the political process of democratization does not feature in any of the participants' contributions? Is the political process unreal, or is it not felt at all? Where were you on April 27, 1994, and what were your feelings then?

VC: April 1994 I was either in France or the Cameroon—I can't remember. Well, I heard on the radio that South Africans are going to the polls. It meant nothing to me. Politics has never ever interested me, and I've never voted for any political party in my life and never will. It's got nothing to do with homelessness. I've read and watched politics and politicians since Napoleon, and I find both in bad taste. With the book, I just wanted to tell my story. If some of the windows end up politically inclined, it was by accident.

JM: Does one have to reference political events (rallies, riots, freedom days, etc.) for writing to qualify as political writing or expression or protest, etc? Is the story about Virginia—having to watch Boetie on her granny's back while Virginia, a Muvenda child, lives out her life in the backyard of this white family as an illegal—not political? In Stephen's stories about the strip searches on the mines—who was stealing what from whom? What of Robbie's stories about young "colored" men killing each other as a result of engineered structural inequalities, etc? These all struck me as overtly political stories.

SR: Self-writing is said to be therapeutic. Would you agree that the very act of writing about your*selves* made you face up to challenges ahead in your lives? That is, prior to writing about your *selves* and after, what kind of person emerged? Is it the same person that you wrote about (the autographed self) or a different person (the historical self)?

JM: We *are* the stories we and other people hold about us. For me the act of entering into *FMM* was powerfully life-changing. Before *FMM*, the story I lived by was one about a depressed, powerless, mother-blaming—in the Freudian sense—white man living out a legacy of post-pogrom and post-Holocaust neurosis. This was my lineage and my story line, the obvious place to go walkabout. The story I had to beat was *Once Were Warriors*.

Through *FMM* I entered into a previously unexplored narrative about myself as a writer, adventurer, group person, quirky, fun, and happy person, someone who could find buried treasure in myself and in others. I identified and backdated this story about myself, I found myself thanking my parents for giving birth to me and for raising me, instead of blaming them for making me neurotic. I engaged more deeply with Jo'burg and with life itself in the year of *FMM* than I thought myself capable of. And I promised myself that this was to be my last fling with that city, calling the project my goodbye present to myself and to Jo'burg, and I rode that rocket right out of there to Cape Town, where I reinvented myself as a surfer. While my surfing is nothing to write home about, I love the waves, the huge unpredictable swells, the danger, and the calm behind. I also like to believe we are all capable of great change—and the journey I am most interested in is one involving an inward journey to the land of great wondrous breaths, stillness, appreciation, and control over one's own emotions and actions. I'm tired of being out of breath, out of energy, and out of control. This is the new story I plan to write and perform. Exactly and just what and who I am not. Total fiction. This is the power of storytelling, creative writing. GASP was the creation of a new forum for mutual witnessing and definitional ceremony, history-taking, history-making, retelling, spin-doctoring, and making things up.

VC: Narrative therapy is therapeutic. Jonathan is right. When writing the book, one was relieved to find out that one was not the only one going through what one went through. Grief is shared and experiences as well. I'm not quite sure whether much has changed in me personality-wise. If there is any change, it is that I've become more sympathetic to the plights of others. I think before I didn't care that much.

SR: Has being part of the GASP collective changed your life in any other ways?

VC: Besides making me more humanitarian, I think being a member of the GASP also helped put my name on the writing platform, paving my eventual entry into the world of newspapers.

JM: When I think about who and what I am, I see a red book with my name and the words *Great African Spider Writers* on the cover, and this makes me feel good in ways that few things do. *FMM* helped me to define myself as a different kind of person who has perhaps less of his own very private personal issues and more shared human and public issues to deal with in community with others. See the opening line in *FMM:* "The last time I stood with ten other people was in long socks . . ." Now the last time was not even in *FMM*, it keeps on happening.

SR: How has living in South Africa impacted on you as a person? Are you happier or sadder for the experience? Does being African in an African country carry any resonance for you, given the attempts to form a pan-African front, given the reality of the African Parliament? Or do you feel exiled from Cameroon or Canada?

VC: I've got to know more about Africa in South Africa. Jo'burg being one hell of a melting pot, one meets all kinds of people from all over the world, and from them one learns different things. I have mixed feelings about living in South Africa. With all sorts of policies by the government to secure jobs and resources for a privileged few, it looks more as if this isn't a country for immigrants anymore. About the Pan African Parliament or a pan-African front: I've never believed or supported anything that embraced a select minority. I don't consider myself part of anything that's exclusively European, African, American, black, white, or whatnot. I believe in a body or structure that's there to serve humanity. The world has always been an oyster to me. I'm at home anywhere in the world.

SR: In what ways do you feel your narrative from Cameroon to Canada to Zimbabwe to South Africa "truthful," be it in terms of a semantic, pragmatic, or verificationist theory of truth? Is biography necessarily fictitious?

VC: What is fiction? In essence: it never really happened, or to put it short —it's a lie. Well, some may think it's a lie that the Yanks have Saddam Hussein. Others that Armstrong ever landed on the moon. Many more believe Jesus was never resurrected. To me, the most important thing about reading is whether I have learnt something new. The truth as we all know is relative.

SR: When writing about your*self,* are there episodes that really stand out for you that you wish you could have elaborated on further?

VC: It's always the case with writing, isn't it? Freelancers would readily agree. I think my childhood memories are some of the best memories I have left. I would have loved to have continued writing about growing up in the Cameroon.

SR: Do you still contribute to *Homeless Talk* or *The Big Issue?*

VC: I still work with *Homeless Talk*. It's been years since I contributed to *The Big Issue* because I'm more committed with many mainstream publications.

SR: Do you feel the childhood experiences that you describe—the "hopper section"—have made you a better person?

VC: What we leave behind after death is usually used to judge us. Whether I'm a better or worse person since describing the "hopper section" I cannot tell. What I do know for certain is that I try to avoid that kind of pitfall.

SR: As a proponent of narrative therapy, you placed a great deal of faith in the power of such narratives to heal others. Did it work equally for you, and in what ways?

JM: I am aware that it might be easier for someone who feels that they already have some degree of power over their problems—in a personal as well as political sense—to begin to *further lever* stories to resituate themselves in relation to these problems. The other thing is that it is the backdrop of hardship and challenge that defines the starting point to any hero story. I would add that in order to begin to explore and enact the counterplot to the victim one, it needs someone or a group who can act as outsider witnesses to acknowledge the story and the struggle in fresh ways. As GASPers, we performed this function for each other.

SR: The need to go to Israel is not so well articulated in the text. Did you, being Jewish, feel ancestry, a need to reconnect with the motherland at a cultural or political level? Was it an identity asserting exercise or experience?

JM: I have a great-grandfather who used to walk the streets of Jerusalem asking Jews from the Diaspora—Turkey, Yemen, Ethiopia, Eastern Europe, China, the former Soviet Union—to sing him their songs and tunes. These he recorded in an anthology of Jewish liturgy. I don't have a scrap of musical talent, but the spirit of Avram Zvi as harvester and recorder of stories lives on in me. Whatever Jewish identity I have now has very little to do with Israel. I just applied for and received Lithuanian passports for myself, and my children, Masego and Taiji, based on the fact that my father was born there. These little books, and the stories they will come to tell in the vocabulary of stamps thumped by officials at borders, these new passports feel like important identity documents, ones that make all three of us, with all the Tswana, Japanese, and Jewish blood mixing, somehow members of the EU/Litvaks/world citizens. National or any kind of identity seems to me to be much more about the stories and adventures we are able to make up; they seem to me not to be rooted in any place, but rather the place is merely the landscape we move across in our life stories, which are, I suppose, road movies, or journeys of some sort. The place can be the launching pad as in motherland, birthplace, or it can be a destination. Of course there are less modern stories in which generations remain in one place, and in these stories, identity and place are deemed to be much more fused.

SR: Your home environment seems to engender harmony. Was it at any stage a source of friction? (Valentine narrates how through his *faux pas,* you felt it was necessary to defend your marriage to Kyoko.) Has your decision alienated you from others—family/friends/acquaintances?

JM: No and yes. My parents are very open-minded and open-hearted, but the Jewish community is not, and I received feedback that I am considered a turncoat and a disappointment. I don't consider my kids to be *halfoos* (Japanese for half-caste), but *doubloos;* they have double the stock of ancestral culture, diversity, and richness to draw on.

SR: Did the decision to write the collaborative text lead directly to your interest in the memory boxes project? Would you elaborate on how successful this project is with regard to the *Madini* one?

JM: *FMM* exploded in a very condensed timeframe and somehow the energy, commitment, and creativity came easily to all of us—there was no funding, and we felt like we were on a roll, meeting in downtown Jo'burg Saturday morning after Saturday morning for a few months. The next phase involved more sweat, more editing, and as you may imagine, quite lonely work.

Soon after that, when I heard about memory boxes, I was very drawn to the notion of lots of people writing and editing and publishing their own stories, with me holding less power and less responsibility. I was all storied out, having absorbed so many powerful and difficult stories as part of *FMM* and as a therapist. Memory boxes seemed to offer another possibility. I could be a facilitator, but needn't edit, direct, coauthor, or even listen to or hear the stories—so much the better if they were in languages I can't understand—of which there are many. This is being borne out to some extent in the ten million memory project, in which people all over Africa are doing memory work and making hero books—too many for me to possibly read.

SR: In *Finding Mr Madini* you write correctly of your feeling jaded at times as well as feeling that the group was not representative, thus the need for Robbie. Did you feel equally that, say, an Indian homeless person would have made a difference? Were there any Indian homeless then in Johannesburg?

JM: The book was a slice of Jo'burg and didn't try to be totally rainbow or representative. Jo'burg has so many homeless characters from so many backgrounds, more than one could represent in any book.

SR: At some point Virginia writes of how you became a *baas*. Did you resent this as a (white) South African? Does the matter of whiteness make you uneasy or question your motives when working collaboratively with others?

JM: Not at all, I am full of self-irony about this and seem to remember that I raised the issue before Virginia did. I believe it is important for me to constantly locate my voice and my position as a white male. I really cringe when I hear white people—settlers like myself—introduce themselves as Africans. I find this to be dismissive and insensitive to what has gone before, to the very loaded privilege they have enjoyed without rightfully earning it, that by its design dispossessed and denied so many other people access to the privileges they had. Race as a category and social construction is horribly huge in South Africa and doesn't easily go away. In *FMM* my stories and I owning this position was deliberately used as a counterpoint against which to juxtapose the other stories and present them in relief to this obviously other kind of story from the other side of the railway tracks. Both in *FMM* and in real life, as my son would say, by acknowledging this difference of position up front, it is perhaps easier to begin breaking down barriers, mistrust, prejudice, etc.

I nearly always feel white in this country, in ways that don't feel good and that constantly remind me of how the rat race began. There are too many reminders that the start was not fair; some runners had their legs tied. I hate to admit it, but I mostly feel my whiteness in the form of white guilt and racism —racism in the sense that if I encounter a new black person I have never met before, the first thing I register about them is that they are black and this comes with a whole lot of other associations. Had I gone to a school that was not a whites-only school and had I had black friends as a child, I believe I wouldn't be carrying this horrible baggage.

SR: At some point you write about how the narratives did not necessarily have to do with "truthfulness" as defined. Does the "constructedness" of a life make it more interesting than a record of "simple verifiable facts"?

JM: For me it does, I am prone to exaggeration and to retelling as an art form pushing the limits of artistic license to make it more memorable and true in spirit, rendering it closer to an icon or symbol of the complex set of realities you are trying to get across. Once I have constructed it in this way, this is the way I remember it as having happened—which is often a little different from the "simple verifiable facts."

SR: At the end of the text, as you are interviewing or are interviewed by Valentine, you reply how the experience "makes you feel a part of Africa." Could you elaborate on this aspect?

JM: Through *FMM* I engaged deeply with people and places that are African that I might well have not otherwise engaged with. While I have lots of resistance around calling myself African, there is this. As you know the majority of Jews and lots and lots of other whites left this country in the years just before and after apartheid ended. Many left deep in the dark days of apartheid because they hated being a part of it, and I have no truck, that is, I have no issue/criticism with those. I once however read an in-flight magazine article about a club or support groups for failed emigrants—people who had left and who couldn't hack it in Sydney or LA or wherever they landed up and had decided to return. Things hadn't turned out so well for them there, and they had been surprised to see that the economy hadn't collapsed here, the rand hadn't lost all its value but had strengthened, there had been no Mau Mau, etc. Some woman who had also left, but not quite left, had seen a commercial angle in this and had started some kind of exclusive club to help them get back and settle in. Their mantra was "Actually, we know this now because we left and realized only once we had gone, that SA is the best country in the world." When I read this, I reached for my vomit bag, I felt ashamed to be white, but I also felt proud that I'd stayed as a white South African and African in a way that was not only tinged with guilt but also with other horrible mixed feelings. I actually thought, "Fuck you, hope you have to buy your mansions back at top dollar and at unfavorable exchange rates, that you can't find jobs not because of affirmative action but because there are better qualified and positioned people to do those jobs," and lots of hugely ungenerous thoughts like those. Maybe then I felt kind of a post-independent African South African—a memory I would like to hang on to.

References Cited

DUIKER, SELLO K. *Thirteen Cents*. Claremont: Ink, 2000.
KENNEDY, WILLIAM. *Ironweed*. New York: Penguin, 1984.
MDA, ZAKES. *Ways of Dying*. Oxford: Oxford University Press, 1995.

MORGAN, JONATHAN, and the GREAT AFRICAN SPIDER WRITERS. *Finding Mr Madini*. Claremont: Ink, 1999.
MORGAN, JONATHAN, and the BAMBANANI WOMEN'S GROUP. *Long Life: Positive HIV Stories*. Cape Town: Double Storey Press, 2003.
TAMAHORI, LEE. *Once Were Warriors*. New Line Studios, 1996.

Further Reading

BURMAN, SANDRA, and PAMELA REYNOLDS, eds. *Growing Up in a Divided Society: The Contexts of Childhood in South Africa*. Johannesburg: Ravan Press, 1986.
GUNNER, LIZ. "Writing the City: Four Post-apartheid texts." Paper delivered at Advanced Research Seminar, Wits Institute for Social and Economic Research, University of the Witwatersrand, February 24, 2003. http://wiserweb.wits.ac.za/PDF%20Files/wirs%20-%20gunner.PDF
"Johannesburg: The Elusive Metropolis." Sarah Nuttall and Achille Mbembe, guest eds. *Public Culture* Special Issue. 16, 3 (Fall 2004).
MATSHIKIZA, JOHN. "Finding Ourselves in the Tapestry." Review of *Finding Mr Madini*. *Mail & Guardian*. October 1, 1999.
MORGAN, JONATHAN. "Malunda: Someone Who Sleeps Just Anywhere." *Dulwich Centre Journal*. 3 (1999): 55–74.
———. "The Ten Millions Memory Project." *AIDS Bulletin* 13, 22 (June 2004). http://www.mrc.ac.za/aids/june2004/millions.html
———. "Publishing Your Life." AIDS and Society Research Unit working paper, *Stories from the Pandemic* 3. Cape Town: University of Cape Town Press, 2002.
MOTSEMME, N. "Gendered Experiences of Blackness in Post-apartheid South Africa." *Social Identities* 8, 4 (2002): 647–673.
MPE, PHASWANE. *Welcome to Our Hillbrow*. Pietermaritzburg: University of Natal Press, 2001.

November 2004

GLOSSARY

abakwetha (var. *bakwetha*)   a Xhosa initiate to manhood, ritually circumcised and isolated from other people for a prescribed period (isiXhosa).

agteroskameraad   a comrade who joined the struggle late, like an ox following at the back (Afrikaans).

ANC   African National Congress. National organization and political party that opposed the apartheid government in South Africa. Banned from April 1960 to February 1990, it became the majority party in the Government of National Unity in 1994 and has been South Africa's ruling party since 1994, having won the elections of 1994, 1999, and 2004 with large majorities.

ALA   African Literature Association.

assegai   a wooden spear with a metal tip for throwing or stabbing.

assimilados   Mozambicans who had "passed tests" to become Portuguese citizens (Portuguese).

Azanian People's Liberation Army (APLA) military wing of the Pan Africanist Congress.

baas   boss (Afrikaans).

BAB   Basler Afrika Bibliographien.

bakkie   a light truck, a pick-up, a one-ton truck (Afrikaans).

bakwetha (see *abakwetha*)

Battle/War of the Axe   frontier war between Xhosa and British (1846–1847).

Black Sash   protest campaign by the Women's Defence of the Constitution League in South Africa. Organized in opposition to the disenfranchisement of "colored" voters. Their work these days is mainly "the protection and advancement of civil liberties" through research and a network of advice offices.

Bondelswartz   the Nama people living in Namibia and Namaqualand.

bonga (see *ukubonga*)

braai/s   barbecue/s. Food grilled over an open fire. Usually carries sense of an informal outdoor gathering (Afrikaans).

Cato Manor   residential area near Durban, site of racial conflict in 1949 and forced removals in 1960s.

colored   a person classified as of mixed ethnic origin.

conscientize (conscientise)   to raise awareness about an injustice; e.g., to conscientize people about their political or health rights.

COSAW   Congress of South African Writers.

di yidishe gas   the Jewish street (Yiddish).

di yidishe heym   the Jewish home (Yiddish).

Diwali (var. *Deepavali*)   the Festival of Lights. Major religious festival of the Hindu year (Tamil).

finish and klaar   "finished and done"/"over" (Afrikaans).

frikkadel   rissole, ball, or cake of meat or fish, minced and then cooked (Afrikaans).

Great African Spider Project   group of ten writers who participated in a writing workshop that eventually led to *Finding Mr Madini* (Morgan, et al. 1999).

Grupo Dinaminazador   enforcement arm of Samora Machel's Republica Popular de Mozambique.

hadj   pilgrimage to Mecca (Arabic).

hona joale   right now (seSotho).

ibeshu   animal-hide "skirt" traditionally worn by a married Zulu man.

iimbongi (see *imbongi*)

ilobola (see *lobola*)

imbongi (var. *imbonga*, pl. *iimbongi, izimbonga*)   a Xhosa or Zulu praise poet.

Institute for Black Research   research institute at the University of KwaZulu-Natal.

inyanga (pl. *izinyanga*)   traditional African healer, doctor, herbalist, diviner (isiZulu).

isicathamiya (var. *iscathamiya*)   music, named after Zulu words describing singers' movements, which combine "stalking," "walking stealthily," and "standing on tiptoe."

izangoma (see *sangoma*)

izibongo (var. *isibongo*, pl. *izimbongo*)   a Xhosa or Zulu praise poem (isiXhosa/isiZulu).

izibongo mbaliso   a historical praise poem (see also *izibongo*) (isiXhosa).

izibonono   a mourning poem (see also *izibongo*).

izimbongo (see *izibongo*)

izinyanga (see *inyanga*)

kab-r   grave of the Prophet Mohamed (Arabic).

kitab   sacred book, in particular the Koran (Arabic).

klaar   see *"finish and klaar."*

knobkierrie   short stick with knobbed head used as a weapon (Afrikaans).

knuppel   a baton (Afrikaans).

kramat   holy place. In Cape Malay community, an Islamic shrine/tomb of a holy man (Malay).

kronieke   chronicles (Afrikaans).

kugel   derogatory term for wealthy (Jewish) woman who is preoccupied with materialism and frivolities (slang, South African English, derives from Yiddish).

kwaito   a South African style of popular music blending elements of hip-hop, House, and a variety of earlier South African popular music styles, with lyrics, usually in one of South Africa's indigenous languages, mostly addressing day-to-day concerns of young South Africans (neologism probably derived from Afrikaans *kwaai*, angry/cool, or from 1950s *Amakwaitos*-Gang from Soweto).

lithoko   a praise poem (seSotho).

lobola   custom among many southern African peoples of giving cattle, goods, or money to the parents of a girl or woman to secure her hand in marriage (isiXhosa/isiZulu).

mameloshn   the (Yiddish) mother tongue (Yiddish).

Mandela Republic   the period in which Nelson Mandela was the president of the Republic of South Africa (term coined probably by Lewis Nkosi).

maskanda   Zulu traditional music played on western instruments.

matric (short form for matriculation)   a school-leaving examination also used as a criterion for university entrance.

mbaliso   narrative praise poem (see also *izibongo*) (isiXhosa).

miffed   annoyed, irritated.

mohlolo   miracle (seSotho).

muti   medicine (isiZulu).

oom   uncle (Afrikaans).

PAC   Pan African Congress.

P. E.   Port Elizabeth.

perron   railway platform (Afrikaans).

PIDE   Policia Internacional de Defesa de Estado. Portuguese secret police (Portuguese).

pieperig   weak, sickly.

RedRibbon   foundation which funds research into and raises awareness about AIDS.

Republica Popular de Mozambique   Republic of Mozambique.

SADF   South African Defence Force.

sangoma (pl. *izangoma*)   traditional healer or diviner.

Sestigers   a group of Afrikaans authors and poets of the 1960s who were innovative in theme and technique, and were especially influenced by French literature (Afrikaans).

skoffelpik   a hoe (Afrikaans).

Spoornet   South African railway company.

tant (var. *tannie*)   aunt (Afrikaans).

toktokkie (var. *tok-tokkie*)   name given to several tapping beetles (Afrikaans).

toyi-toyi a quasi-military dance step often performed at protest marches and gatherings (probably derived from Ndebele and Shona).

ubuntu humanity, goodness, the spirit of community (isiXhosa/isiZulu).

UCT University of Cape Town.

UDW University of Durban-Westville.

ukubonga (var. *bonga*) to chant poetry, to perform praise poetry (isiXhosa/isiZulu).

Umkhonto we Sizwe Spear of the Nation. The armed wing of the African National Congress.

umutsha waist band worn by a Zulu man.

undenza umuntu "you are making me a person" (isiXhosa).

veld open, undeveloped countryside.

verkrampt(e) extremely conservative (Afrikaans).

volk people, a nation, Afrikaners.

whinging whining, complaining.

Wits (University) University of the Witwatersrand Johannesburg.

wodge a bulky mass, a chunk or lump; a wad of paper.

wonky lop-sided, nonfunctional.

wors sausage, especially a traditional sausage made of a mixture of ground beef and pork seasoned with spices.

WTO World Trade Organization.

The editors would like to thank Leela Pienaar, Associate Editor, Dictionary Unit for South African English, Rhodes University, Grahamstown, and Colin Muller, coeditor, *Dictionary of South African English on Historical Principles,* for their assistance in compiling this glossary. This glossary is based on material in the *Dictionary of South African English on Historical Principles.* New York: Oxford University Press, 1996.

CONTRIBUTORS

DAVID ATTWELL is a professor of English at the University of the Witwatersrand. He is the editor of J. M. Coetzee, *Doubling the Point: Essays and Interviews* (1992) and numerous journal articles and chapters in books on Coetzee and postcolonial writing. His books include *J. M. Coetzee: South Africa and the Politics of Writing* (1993) and *Rewriting Modernity: Studies in Black South African Literary History* (2005).

BREYTEN BREYTENBACH, poet, writer, painter, and activist, was born in Bonnievale, Western Cape. The recipient of numerous awards, he currently divides his time between Europe, Africa, and the United States. The work of Breytenbach includes many volumes of poetry, novels, and essays, many of which are in Afrikaans. He is also known for his art works and has exhibited in numerous cities around the world including Johannesburg, Hong Kong, Stockholm, and New York.

DUNCAN BROWN is professor in the Programme of English Studies, University of KwaZulu-Natal, Pietermaritzburg. He has published widely on South African literary and cultural studies, in particular oral literature and performance. His books include *Voicing the Text* (1998) and *Oral Literature and Performance in Southern Africa* (1999).

DENNIS BRUTUS, poet and activist, has taught, lectured, and campaigned for justice and equality of opportunity worldwide. He is currently professor emeritus in the Department of Africana Studies at the University of Pittsburgh, and has held visiting professorships at Worcester State College, Worcester, Massachusetts, and the University of Durban-Westville, now KwaZulu-Natal.

DUNCAN CARTWRIGHT is a clinical psychologist. He is currently a senior lecturer in the School of Psychology, University of KwaZulu-Natal, Durban.

VALENTINE CASCARINO was born of a French father and a Cameroonian mother. After a stint as one of the Great African Spider Writers who collaborated on the collective auto/biography *Finding Mr Madini,* he now works as a freelance journalist for the *Sunday Times* and *Homeless Talk* and as a presenter for Radio Veritas.

VANITHA CHETTY is a senior lecturer in Criminology at the University of KwaZulu-Natal. She is the daughter of Dr. Goonam, one of the first Indian South African women to become a medical practitioner and author of the autobiography *Coolie Doctor.*

WILFRED CIBANE is the coauthor of *Man of Two Worlds,* in which he describes his ascent from a rural boyhood to a successful business partnership and lifelong friendship with Robert Scott.

GREIG COETZEE is an actor, director, and playwright whose autobiographical play entitled *White Men with Weapons* has won several local and international prizes. He has also won an FNB Vita award for Best Director for the production of his play *Seeing Red* and awards from both the BBC (in 2004) and the Sony Radio Academy (in 2005) for the radio drama *Banana Republic.* Other plays by him include *Solomon's Pride* (written with Bheki Mkhwane), *Black Mamba* (written with John van der Ruit and Ben Voss) and *Johnny Boskak Is Feeling Funny.*

J. M. COETZEE is a research fellow at the University of Adelaide. He is the author of ten novels, numerous critical essays, and two memoirs, namely, *Boyhood: Scenes from Provincial Life* and *Youth.* He is the recipient of a host of awards, including the Nobel Prize and the Booker Prize (twice).

JUDITH LÜTGE COULLIE is a professor in English Studies at the University of KwaZulu-Natal. She has coedited the CD-Rom on Roy Campbell and a volume of critical essays on Breyten Breytenbach. Her collection of South African women's life writing, *The Closest of Strangers: A Century of South African Women's Life Writing,* was published by Wits University Press in 2004.

MARGARET DAYMOND is a professor in English Studies at the University of KwaZulu-Natal. She has published widely on South African writing, is the editor of *South African Feminisms,* and coeditor of the southern African volume in the *Women Writing Africa* (2002) series.

PAUL FABER is an art historian and exhibition maker. Since 1997 he has been the Africa curator of the KIT Tropenmuseum, Amsterdam. His major projects have included: Modern Art in Africa (Amsterdam, 1980); Art from Another World (Rotterdam, 1988); Sranan, Culture in Suriname (Rotterdam, 1992); Ethiopia, Heritage of an Empire (1999); Family Stories from South Africa (2002); All about Evil (2004).

VANESSA FARR is Project Manager on the gendered aspects of disarmament, demobilization, and reintegration at the United Nations Institute for Disarmament Research. She has published widely on women's innovative participation in peacebuilding and reconciliation in South Africa and elsewhere in Africa.

DAVID GOLDBLATT was born in Randfontein in 1930 of Lithuanian Jewish parents. He was the founder of the Market Photography Workshop in Johannesburg, which teaches visual literacy and photographic skills to young people, with particular emphasis on those disadvantaged by apartheid. In addition to professional work for magazines, corporations, and institutions, his personal interest consists of critical explorations of South African society, a number of which have been exhibited and published in book form.

STEPHEN GRAY is a poet of international repute, a successful playwright, and the author of eight novels and of the highly acclaimed biographies of Beatrice Hastings and Herman Charles Bosman. In addition to being a widely published critic, he has compiled anthologies of southern African poetry, prose, and drama, and has exposed a wealth of material that might otherwise have remained in obscurity. A traumatic experience led him to turn his considerable talents to another use— the writing of his autobiography, *Accident of Birth*. Recently he has published *My Serial Killer and Other Stories*.

DORIAN HAARHOFF is both a wordsmith and story "wright." Since childhood, he has explored the subterranean forges of fiction and memory, to which he is increasingly alert and attuned. In the last decade, Haarhoff has discovered another rare gift—that of sharing with others the deeper, endogenous springs connecting individuals to communities. His published work, often influenced by the climate and topography of Namibia where he was a professor of English Literature, includes poetry, drama, work for children, compilations of student work, and academic research. He is the author of the influential *The Writer's Voice: A Workbook for Writers in Africa*. Haarhoff now travels widely in the southern African region and internationally, facilitating and participating in workshops in writing and storytelling.

RAYDA JACOBS grew up in Cape Town, spent twenty-seven years in Canada in exile, and returned to Cape Town in 1994, where she now lives and writes. She has published six books of fiction, including *Confessions of a Gambler*, for which she won the Sunday Times Fiction Award and the Herman Charles Bosman Award in 2004. In addition to regular contributions to the press, she has also made six documentaries and published her account of her pilgrimage, *The Mecca Diaries* (2005).

MARGARETTA JOLLY is a lecturer at the School of English, University of Exeter. She is the editor of *The Encyclopedia of Life Writing* (2001) and *Dear Laughing Motorbyke: Letters from Women Welders of the Second World War* (1997). Her forthcoming book is *Burning Letters: Women Writing to Women since 1970*.

ELSA JOUBERT is the author of several novels written in Afrikaans. Most popular of these is *Die Swerfjare van Poppie Nongena* (The long journey of Poppie Nongena), in which a Xhosa woman narrates her life under apartheid. "Poppie's" auto/biography, which is listed as one of Africa's hundred best books, has been translated into thirteen languages and has won many local and international prizes. In 2005 President Thabo Mbeki awarded her the Order of Ikhamanga for her literary work and the Department of Arts and Culture crowned *Die Swerfjare van Poppie Nongena* as the best prose in Afrikaans.

K. LIMAKATSO KENDALL is the editor of Mpho Nthunya's autobiography, *Singing Away the Hunger* (1996). Kendall also edited *Basali! Stories by and about Women in Lesotho* (1995) and is the author of *A Passionate Guest: Two Years in Southern Africa* (2005). Kendall was a Fulbright Scholar at the National University of Lesotho and taught Performance Studies at the University of Natal in Pietermaritzburg (now University of KwaZulu-Natal). She lives in southern Texas.

SUSAN NALUGWA KIGULI is a lecturer in the Department of Literature, Makerere University. She is currently a doctoral student in the School of English, University of Leeds. She has researched and published on oral poetry and performance, with particular focus on Uganda. She is also one of Uganda's widely recognized poets.

ESTER LEE, born and bred in Mozambique, is the author of *I Was Born in Africa* (1999), a biographical account of her mother's courage and pain in living through the chaotic revolutionary changes that swept through Mozambique in 1974. The book is also, however, about the author's own personal pain in having to endure her mother's decision to stay committed to Mozambique, whether under Portuguese or postcolonial rule. Ester Lee resides in Durban, South Africa.

SIMON LEWIS teaches African literature at the College of Charleston and edits the literary magazine *Illuminations*.

DORIS LESSING was born in Kermanshah Persia, now Iran, and grew up in what was then called Southern Rhodesia, now Zimbabwe. In 1949 she moved to Britain, where she still resides. Besides her many influential novels, such as the *Children of Violence* sequence and *The Golden Notebook*, Lessing has also published two autobiographies, *Under My Skin: My Autobiography to 1949*, and *Walking in the Shade: My Autobiography, 1949–1962*.

DEBBIE LÜTGE is head of the Department of Drama Studies at the Durban Institute of Technology. She is a Durban Theatre Awards judge and also a playwright, actor, director, and academic.

SINDIWE MAGONA is the author of two volumes of autobiography, *To My Children's Children* (1990), published in Xhosa as *Kubantwana babantwana bam* (1995), and *Forced to Grow* (1992). She has published two collections of short stories, *Living, Loving, and Lying Awake at Night* (1991) and *Push-push* (1996), and a biographical novel, *Mother to Mother* (1998). After serving at the United Nations in New York, she has returned to South Africa, where she is currently working on a poem cycle of her parents' lives.

N. CHABANI MANGANYI is a clinical psychologist and vice-principal at the University of Pretoria. His publications include three biographies, *Exiles and Homecomings: A Biography of Es'kia Mphahlele* (1984), *A Black Man Called Sekoto* (1996), and *Gerard Sekoto: "I Am an African"* (2004). He has published collections of essays including, among others, *Looking through the Keyhole: Dissenting Essays on the Black Experience* (1981), *Treachery and Innocence: Psychology and Racial Difference in South Africa* (1991), and essays on auto/biography.

MARGARET MCCORD was born and raised in South Africa. She authored *The Calling of Katie Makanya: A South African Memoir*, which won the Alan Paton–Sunday Times Prize in 1995. Katie's auto/biography is based on oral recordings McCord conducted with Makanya, who was a family friend and the sister of Charlotte Maxeke, founder of the precursor to the ANC Women's Movement. The book is a unique record of an African woman's rural youth, her 1891 trip to Britain as a member of the African Choir, and her life as a nursing pioneer in Natal at the turn of the twentieth century.

MERVYN MCMURTRY, a professor and program director of the Drama and Performance Studies program, University of KwaZulu-Natal, Durban, has published twenty-six articles and directed and designed more than fifty productions.

STEPHAN MEYER is a lecturer at the Language Centre of the University of Basel. He has taught Philosophy, English, and Gender Studies at the University of Durban-Westville (now KwaZulu-Natal), the University of Zurich, and the University of Basel. His research interests and publications focus on collaborative auto/biography, South African writing, and critical theory.

CHERYL-ANN MICHAEL is a lecturer in the Department of English at the University of the Western Cape, South Africa. Her fields of interest are nineteenth- and twentieth-century literature, including children's literature, and the history and philosophy of language. She is coeditor of *Senses of Culture: South African Culture Studies* (2000).

ZOLANI MKIVA was born in Idutywa in the Eastern Cape. He has performed as an *imbongi* for several prominent figures, including Nelson Mandela, Walter Sisulu, and Thabo Mbeki. He is a graduate of the University of the Western Cape, and has produced a number of CDs, including *Halala South Africa* (1997), *Qadaffi* (2000), and *Mazenethole* (2002). He is reigning chief executive officer of the Xhosa Royal Council.

JONATHAN MORGAN is a not-very-clinical psychologist in public practice. He is currently working for REPSSI (Regional Psychosocial Support Initiative) on the Ten Million Memory Project, which is aimed at scaling up life story and memory work as a form of psychosocial support to children facing difficult circumstances across Africa. His preferred way of working combines elements of narrative therapy, art therapy, and participatory action research.

ES'KIA MPHAHLELE, professor emeritus of African Literature at the University of the Witwatersrand, is one of the founders of contemporary South African writing. His *Down Second Avenue* is a standard work in southern African autobiography. Mphahlele is the author of numerous novels and critical works that expound on the notion of African humanism and on African literature. His two most recent collections of essays are titled *Es'kia* (2002) and *Es'kia Continued* (2004).

THENGANI H. NGWENYA is an associate professor in the Faculty of Education at the University of KwaZulu-Natal. His research and publications focus on South African autobiography and biography. He is the editor of a special issue of Alter*nation* (2002) on South African auto/biography.

ROB NIXON is the Rachel Carson Professor of English at the University of Wisconsin, Madison. His most recent books are *Homelands, Harlem and Hollywood*, and *Dreambirds: The Natural History of a Fantasy*.

MPHO NTHUNYA is the oral narrator and author of *Singing Away the Hunger*. In this book she tells of her experiences as a woman growing up and living under the extremely harsh conditions of Lesotho and apartheid South Africa. Nthunya returned to post-apartheid South Africa and lived there with K. Limakatso Kendall from 1995–1999 and in 2000 spent six months living in the USA with Kendall. Nthunya now lives with her extended family in the Roma Valley of Lesotho.

SARAH NUTTALL is an associate professor of Literary and Cultural Studies at the Wits Institute for Social and Economic Research (WISER) in Johannesburg. She is the coeditor, among others, of *Negotiating the Past: The Making of Memory in South Africa* (1998) and of *Senses of Culture: South African Culture Studies* (2000), editor of *Beautiful-Ugly: African and Diaspora Aesthetics* (2005), and author of *Literary Cultures and Life Worlds* (forthcoming).

THOMAS OLVER is an editor and teacher in South Africa. He has coedited anthologies of South African short stories and poetry and a special issue of the *Journal of Literary Studies* on *Alternative Modernities in African Literatures and Cultures*. He has also collaborated on research projects and taught literature at universities in South Africa and Switzerland. His research focuses on gender and post-colonial writing.

JEFF OPLAND was born in Cape Town in 1943. He taught at the University of Cape Town, the University of Durban-Westville (now KwaZulu-Natal), the University of Toronto, Rhodes University, Yale University, Vassar College, and the University of Leipzig, and is currently retired from full-time teaching. He is the author of a number of books that present poems and contain further information on David

Yali-Manisi, such as *Xhosa Oral Poetry: Aspects of a Black South African Tradition* (1983), *Words that Circle Words: A Choice of South African Oral Poetry* (1992), *Izwi labantu* (edited with P. T. Mtuze, 1994), *Xhosa Poets and Poetry* (1998), and *The Dassie and the Hunter: A South African Meeting* (2005).

SAM RADITLHALO teaches at the University of Cape Town, specializing in African literary studies and South African life writings. He holds a PhD from Rijksuniversiteit Groningen, for which he read about the construction of identities in twentieth-century South African life writings, with interest in cultural studies.

ROBERT SCOTT has been the life-long friend and business partner of Wilfred Cibane, whom he assisted in writing his autobiography, *Man of Two Worlds*.

MARILET SIENAERT completed an MA in French Literature and a PhD in South African Literary Studies. She worked at the universities of Natal (Durban) and Durban-Westville as a lecturer and in later years as a professor in Language and Literature Studies (1979–1999). Currently she holds the position of director of research at the University of Cape Town, but she still maintains a keen interest in the art and writing of contemporary South Africans.

GILLIAN SLOVO was born in South Africa in 1952, the daughter of anti-apartheid campaigners Joe Slovo and Ruth First, and came to England in 1964. She has worked as a writer, journalist, and film producer. In addition to her family memoir *Every Secret Thing*, she is the author of ten novels, including *Red Dust* (2000)— which deals with the Truth and Reconciliation Commission and has been made into a film starring Hilary Swank and Chiwetel Ejiofor—and the Orange Prize shortlisted *Ice Road*. With Victoria Brittain, she has written the play *Guantanamo– Honor Bound to Defend Freedom*. She lives in London with her partner and daughter.

ASTRID STARCK studied German at the University of Strasbourg and Yiddish at the Oxford Centre for Postgraduate Hebrew Studies. She is a professor of German and Yiddish at the Universities of Haute Alsace (Mulhouse) and Basel. Her most recent publications include a translation of the seventeenth-century collection of Yiddish stories *Eyn shön Mayse bukh* into French (2004) and contributions to contemporary German and Yiddish literature.

ALEX J. THEMBELA was a professor of Education with a long-standing interest in traditional music. He studied music at the Trinity College of Music in London and published books and journal articles on a variety of educational topics, including a biography of Joseph Shabalala, the leader of the famous group Ladysmith Black Mambazo, *The Life and Works of Joseph Shabalala* (1993).

PIETER-DIRK UYS, a leading playwright and performer in South African theater since the early 1970s, has written and acted in almost fifty original productions, produced twenty-five films/videos, and has twenty-four books and plays published. He is the recipient of honorary doctorates from Rhodes University, the University of Cape Town, and the University of the Western Cape. In 2001 he received the Truth and Reconciliation Award. He is both South Africa's leading satirist and a philanthropist of note.

JOHAN VAN WYK was born in 1956 in Welkom, in the Orange Free State. He is one of the founders of the (now defunct) Centre for the Study of Southern African Literatures and Language (CSSALL) and at the time of the interview he was acting director of the School of Languages and Literature at the University of Durban-Westville (now KwaZulu-Natal). His academic work includes the multilingual anthology *South Africa in Poetry*, a study of Afrikaans worker writing as well as several contributions to Alter*Nation*, the journal of CSSALL. He has published five volumes of poetry in Afrikaans and also *Man-bitch*, a post-apartheid narrative based on his experiences.

WILHELM VERWOERD is attached to The Glencree Centre for Reconciliation in Ireland. He studied Theology and Philosophy in South Africa and at Oxford and served as a researcher on the Truth and Reconciliation Commission. He has lectured at Stellenbosch University and various universities in Ireland, Europe, and the United States. His wide range of publications includes articles on reconciliation and restorative justice and co-edited books: *Looking Back, Reaching Forward: Reflections on The Truth and Reconciliation Commission of South Africa* (2000) and *Truths Drawn in Jest* (2000). In his autobiographical account *Viva Verwoerd? Kronieke van 'n keuse* (1996), translated as *My Winds of Change* (1997), he explores his multiple conversions pertaining to religion, race, family, and gender.

DAVID WOLPE was born on September 7, 1908, in Keidan. After the Second World War he immigrated to South Africa where he continued his activities as a Yiddish author. His two-volume autobiography, published in Yiddish, *Ikh un mayn velt* (I and my world), covers his life in Europe (including his experiences in Palestine, his service in the Lithuanian army, his incarceration in Dachau, and the annihilation of the Lithuanian Jews) and in South Africa (where he served as editor of the journal *Dorem Afrike*). In 1983 he was honored in Tel Aviv with the Itzik Manger Prize, the most prestigious prize for Yiddish literature.

D. L. P. YALI-MANISI, acclaimed Thembu oral poet, was the author of five published volumes of Xhosa poetry, among them *Izibongi zeenkosi zama-Xhosa* (1952) and *Imfazwe kaMlanjeni* (1983). The most complete collection of his poetry, both oral and written, can be found in English translation in Jeff Opland's biographical account, *The Dassie and the Hunter: A South African Meeting* (2005). He was born on September 17, 1926, in the Khundulu valley near Queenstown, where he died on September 18, 1999.

TERENCE ZEEMAN has edited several anthologies of Namibian dramas, including Dorian Haarhoff's Independence trilogy, *Goats, Oranges and Skeletons*, and *New Namibia Plays*, Volume I. Formerly the executive director of the National Theatre of Namibia, he now regularly participates in exchanges with Namibian drama practitioners with whom he has published the drama manual *Action!* He has lectured at the University of Namibia, Baylor University, Texas, and the University of Ulster.

ABOUT THE EDITORS

JUDITH LÜTGE COULLIE is professor in English Studies at the University of KwaZulu-Natal. She has co-edited the CD-Rom on the poet and writer Roy Campbell, entitled *Campbell in Context* (Killie Campbell Africana Library Series, 2004), and a volume of critical essays on Breyten Breytenbach entitled *a.k.a. Breyten Breytenbach: Critical Approaches to His Writings and Paintings* (Rodopi, 2004). Her collection of South African women's life writing, *The Closest of Strangers: A Century of South African Women's Life Writing*, was published by Wits University Press in 2004.

STEPHAN MEYER is a lecturer at the Zentrum Gender Studies and at the Language Centre of the University of Basel. He has taught philosophy and English at universities in South Africa and Switzerland and has co-edited a special issue of the *Journal of Literary Studies* on *Alternative Modernities in African Literatures and Cultures* and of *Current Writing* on *Black Atlantic Interlocutions*. His research interests and publications focus on collaborative auto/biography, South African writing, and critical theory.

THENGANI NGWENYA is senior lecturer in the School of Education at the University of KwaZulu-Natal. His research and publications focus on South African auto-biography and biography. He is the editor of a special issue of Alter*Nation* on South African auto/biography.

THOMAS OLVER is attached to the English Department of Zurich University. He has co-edited anthologies of South African short stories and poetry and a special issue of the *Journal of Literary Studies* entitled *Alternative Modernities in African Literatures and Cultures*. His research focuses on gender and post-colonial writing.

INDEX

Abrahams, Peter: auto/biography, 15, 23, 25, 76n. 66; cosmopolitan identity, 43; and Mphahlele, 247, 250–251; paper on, 386; travel accounts, 17. Works: *The Black Experience in the Twentieth Century*, 17; *Dark Testament*, 250; *Mine Boy*, 250; *Return to Goli*, 17, 20; *Tell Freedom*, 21
abuses: alcohol, 37; drug, 37; gender, 49, 294–295; human rights, 42; marital, 229; perpetrators of, 4, 5, 19, 24, 37, 42, 322, 323, 393; physical, 38, 260, 261, 262; rape, 38, 332, 338; of apartheid victims, 5, 19, 24, 26, 27, 44
activists: of all races, 25; anti-apartheid, 22, 32, 154, 157, 229, 291, 296–298, 301, 315, 373; biographies of, 32; Black Consciousness, 33; burnout, 34; cultural, 62, 133; feminist, 187–188, 205; HIV/AIDS, 38; human rights, 269; *izibongo*, 132; PAC, 33; political, 32, 187; who achieved fame, 23; who witnessed brutalities, 35. *See also* specific names
African-American literature, 250–251
African humanism. *See ubuntu*
African National Congress, 32, 34, 38, 291, 315, 342, 366–367, 430
African Renaissance, 7, 134, 140, 143
Africa's Hundred Best Books Award, 59, 243
Afrikaans language, 13, 21, 23, 28, 29, 174, 175, 177
Akerman, Anthony, *Somewhere On the Border*, 343
Alan Paton–Sunday Times Award for Nonfiction, 59, 192, 205, 207
amnesty, 36, 321. *See also* Truth and Reconciliation Commission
ANC. *See* African National Congress
Angola, 34, 145, 430

anonymity: in auto/biography, 25, 26, 226, 233–234; of racism, 75n. 52. *See also* identities: protection of
anthology, of interviews: and interviewee, 65–67; limitations of, 10, 63, 65; objectives of, 10, 62; requirements of, 63–64; as research tool, 64; scope, 10, 62–63; themes, 64, 67
Anthony, Juleiga, story of, 423, 426
apartheid, 325, 360, 366; abuses, 24, 42; anti-apartheid themes, 32, 49; auto/biography, 10, 15, 16, 19–38, 40, 41–43, 49, 52; brutalities, 24, 27, 35; chemical and biological warfare program, 34; conscription, 34; distinction between private and public lives, 51, 52; endorsement of, 28; and expatriates, 30, 36; individual experience under, 26, 29–31, 33; living conditions under, 21, 24; and memory, 44, 396–398; military memoirs, 34, 397–398; National Intelligence Service, 34; opposition to, 21, 27; press freedom, curtailment of, 32; prison memoirs, 22; publicizing iniquities of, 21, 22, 74n. 40; and publishers, 16, 21, 27, 28, 46; and race, 22, 26, 28–29; racist legislation under, 20–21, 31; stories of oppressed, 21, 24–27, 33; texts condemning, 20–22, 24, 27, 28, 29, 33, 187; texts supporting, 28, 34; and university autonomy, 32; victims of, 5, 19, 24, 26, 27, 30, 261; white apathy, 326; white perceptions of, 28. *See also* auto/biography; banned works in South Africa; *izibongo*; racism; racist legislation; specific authors; testimonial works
Appiah, Kwame Anthony, 5, 40
aquifer metaphor, 258, 259
Arizona, and Karoo, 285–287

army. *See* military experience
authorship: individualism and, 45; monological notions of, 45; western conceptions of, 13
auto/biographers: banned, 22; black men, 17, 23, 29; black women, 17, 24, 25, 53, 219, 224; Christian intellectuals, 38; mission-educated, 25; professional, 25; white men, 27, 28, 29, 30, 33, 34, 35, 36, 60, 73n. 35; white women, 23, 28, 24, 36, 315. *See also* specific names
auto/biography, 35, 37–39, 40–43, 44, 324; aesthetic concerns in, 50, 51, 148; Afrikaans, 13, 21, 23–24, 29, 174, 175, 177, 178, 182, 269, 340–341, 352, 353, 360, 366–367, 373, 376, 399; apolitical accounts, 31; as art, 244. *See* banned works; by black South Africans, 17, 21–33, 46, 53, 74n. 43, 387; with black subjects, 19, 20, 22, 24, 25, 32, 181, 205–211; characteristics of, 38, 39, 58, 71n. 19; and civil liberty, 41, 42; as collage, 256, 329; and collectivist cultures, 39; and community, 25, 410, 428, 434, 444, 446–447; conditions conducive to, 8, 38, 41, 44–45; contemporary context, 1, 11, 17, 20; contestation of, 2–4, 12, 22; definitions of, 1–3, 8, 39, 44, 45, 47, 52, 53; dialogical approach in, 3, 5, 66; dissemination of, 57–59; ethical concerns in, 51–52; as genre, 4, 16, 17, 38, 51, 52, 53, 54, 57, 59, 62, 63, 67, 213–215, 217, 231; and growing up, 48; historical evolution of, 9; and HIV/AIDS, 19, 37, 38, 348, 438; impact of, 8, 22, 38, 39, 51, 57, 59, 62; and incarceration, 43; and inclusion, 25, 27, 50–51, 62; and individualism, 39–40, 45, 67; intimacy in, 9, 50; and language, 2, 6, 8, 12, 13, 14, 62, 358; mediation in, 46; of ordinary people, 16, 25, 226, 278, 280, 282–283, 318, 410; output by race, 13, 21, 23, 29, 30; and paratext, 47–48; parental, 315–318, 320–321; and place, 43, 75n. 64; portraits, 409, 428; post-apartheid, 35–38, 43, 397; post-colonial, 217; post-production of, 57–59; practices, 3, 6, 8–12, 17, 38, 39, 57, 62; privacy and, 52; production of, 13, 23, 30, 38–39, 44–47, 173; racial spread, during apartheid, 23; readership of, 15, 21, 26, 27, 58; relations to others, 48; as stocktaking, 382, 388, 390–391; structure of, 55, 150, 164–167, 175, 181, 220, 260, 316, 324–325, 338, 349, 352, 368, 382, 390, 391, 393, 397–398, 418–419, 431; themes of, 38, 47–50; transformation in, 16, 135, 145, 184, 257, 269, 271–274, 282, 285, 303, 329, 383–384, 396, 411, 412; and the visual, 47, 48, 414; which escaped banning, 23, 24; which recover history or experience, 31; with white subjects, 16, 17, 19, 23, 25, 27–31, 34, 35, 36, 60, 73n. 35; by white South Africans, 28, 31; of workers, 46. *See also* biography; diaries; *izibongo*; letters; life narrative; memoirs; reminiscences; specific writers; testimonial works
autre-biography, 1, 216
awards. *See* drama awards; literary awards

Baartman, Saartjie (Sara), 14, 410
banned persons: auto/biographies, 21, 22; house arrest of, 22, 75n. 49; memoirs of, 22, 23; prison accounts of, 31; South Africa's black writers, 21, 153, 156. *See also* specific names
banned works in South Africa: of anti-apartheid activists, 21, 32, 187; auto/biographies, 20, 21, 22, 23, 31–32, 34, 74n. 40, 291, 345; biographers, 22, 24; prison accounts, 22, 23, 31; works that escaped banning, 23, 24
Barnard, Lady Anne, 13; 72n. 21
Barrett, Jane, *Vukani Makhosikazi: South African Women Speak*, 25, 27, 46
Barter, Catherine, 14
Barthes, Roland, 392, 396
Basler Afrika Bibliographien, 256
Benhabib, Seyla, on identity, 3, 5, 42, 44, 61, 69n. 2, 70n. 6
Bester, Willie, 417, 433
betrayal, as theme, 396, 399, 406
Bezuidenhout, Evita, 55, 346–347, 350–352
Biehl, Amy, 220–221, 223, 228
The Big Issue, 445
Biko, Steve: biography of (Woods), 21; as hero, 186; as political activist, 32, 33
biography: and apartheid, 21, 34, 49; and auto/biography, concepts of, 9, 69n. 1; award-winning, 30; dissemination of, 57;

INDEX

dramas, western style, 26; effect on subject of, 61; and HIV/AIDS, 19, 38; impact of, 59–61; of indigenous people, 14, 35; and individualism, 39; of Nkwenkwe, 20; postcolonial, 305, 307; prison accounts, 32. See also auto/biography; banned works; diaries; izibongo; letters; life narrative; memoirs; reminiscences; specific names; testimonial works
Black Consciousness, 33, 140
Black Renaissance, 200. See also African Renaissance
Bond, Kathy, 26
Botha, P. W.: homage to, 28; satire, 352
Botswana, 71n. 11
Bozzoli, Belinda: and social sciences and auto/biography, 18; Women of Phokeng, 18, 25
breakdown. See identity: crises of
Breytenbach, Breyten: as activist, 269; brother Jan, 34; cult of "strong man," 16, 272–273; drama, 270; exile, 269; identities, 5, 17, 29, 35, 36, 43, 269–275; imagination, 271; imprisonment, 269; memoir, travel, 17, 269; memory, role of, 269, 271, 273–275; "Middle World," 270; mirror as metaphor, 270, 274; oppression, 272; painting, 269, 272; prison accounts, 269; private and public self, 275; racism in writing, 29, 270, 272; trauma in work, 269; victimhood, 271; writing as social commentary, 270–273; Zen and poetry, 272. Works: Dog Heart: A Travel Memoir, 36, 269; Return to Paradise, 269; 'n Seisoen in die Paradys, 269; Die Toneelstuk, 270–271; The True Confessions of an Albino Terrorist, 23, 27, 269, 387
Breytenbach, Jan: The Buffalo Soldiers: The Story of South Africa's 32 Battalion, 34; Eden's Exiles: One Soldier's Fight for Paradise, 34
brutalities, under apartheid, 10, 20, 24, 27, 35, 306–307
Brutus, Dennis: as activist, 40, 154, 157; and apartheid victims, 156; as banned person, 153, 156; censorship, 153, 156; contrasted with political memoirs, 154; exile, 153, 155, 156; global apartheid, views on, 157; identity, 40, 154–155; impact of political life on, 153; imprisonment of, 43, 153, 155; inspiration for work, 156; interview process, 153; on liberation struggle, 156; poetry as auto/biography, 153, 154; and racism, 153, 157; relationships, family, 154; self in work, 153–155; trauma in work, 117, 155–157; as voice of community, 154. Works: "Bury the Great Duke," 154; Letters to Martha, 155; "My Father, That Distant Man," 154; A Simple Lust, 153, 154; Stubborn Hope, 153; "What Am I in Her Eyes," 154

Cachalia, Amina, 291
Campbell, Joseph, 265
capitalism, 12, 13, 202
Carl Schlettwein Foundation, 256
Cascarino, Valentine, 7, 436, 444–445. See also Finding Mr Madini
caste system, 294–295
censorship, 28, 153, 156, 179, 254, 264, 345, 381, 402, 438, 439. See also banned works in South Africa
Central News Agency Award, 59
characterization, in auto/biography, 53, 245, 332, 334, 337–338, 343, 350, 396, 400–402, 404–406
childhood, 4, 11, 32, 48, 213, 243, 246, 247, 255, 261, 277, 282, 287–288, 315, 324, 353, 381, 445. See also specific names
Churchwomen Concerned, 229
Cibane, Wilfred: auto/biography, 30, 203; Black Renaissance, 200; as exile, 202; inspiration for story, 201; Man of Two Worlds: An Autobiography, 30, 35, 200, 201–202, 203; publication of book, 201; reconciling African and European worlds, 35, 58, 201–202; relationships, personal, 30, 46, 201–203; Scott, Robert, 30, 200; self-revelation, 203; and sexual identity, 203; traditions, 201
classification, racial. See racial classification
Coetzee, Greig: African National Congress, 342; Anderson, Garth, 339; audience, 61, 342; auto/biography as exorcism, 44, 343; auto/biography and performance, 47; awards, 59, 330, 331n. 1; characters, 332, 334, 337–338, 343; collage, 329; conscription, 34, 329, 339–341; de Kock, Eugene,

341; drama, 329–344; End Conscription Campaign, 341; Grotovski, 336; identity, 339–341; Malan, Magnus, 341; method acting, 336–338; military experience, 331–333, 335, 339–343; murder, 332; Natal Command, 341; National Arts Festival, 331, 333, 334, 336; one-man show, 339; Phillips, James, 335; racism, 332–333, 342; rape, 332, 338; recording of work, 331; self-representation, 45, 329, 332–333, 336–337, 339; *Slaughterhouse 5* (Vonnegut), 333; *Somewhere on the Border* (Akerman), 343; South African civil war, 329, 341; South African Defence Force, 329, 341–342; structure of work, 338; as teacher, 333–335, 343; theatre, 320; title, 331; trauma in work, 44, 335; Truth and Reconciliation Commission, 341; Umkhonto we Sizwe, 342; van der Spuy, Milton, 335; Vietnam, 343; views on truth, 50, 56, 331, 338; voice, 333; writing, motivation for, 334. Works: *Breasts: A Play about Men*, 344; *Men Only*, 331, 333; *White Men with Weapons*, 329, 330, 331, 335, 337, 342, 343

Coetzee, J. M: *autre*-biography, 1, 216; childhood memoirs, 213; confessional writing, 213, 216; émigré years, 213; feminist auto/biography, 217; and genre, 57, 213–214, 215, 217; identity politics, 217; impact of work, 59; and interview process, 65–67; Nobel prize, 31, 213; post-colonial auto/biography, 217; Rousseau, Jean-Jacques, 217; and self, 59, 213, 215; stories, 282; truth, 57, 215; writing as autobiography, 52–53, 214, 221, 222; Wordsworth, William, 214–215. Works: *Boyhood: Scenes from Provincial Life*, 31, 213, 216; *Disgrace*, 213; *Doubling the Point*, 65, 213–215; *Giving Offense*, 213; *Life and Times of Michael K*. 213; *Stranger Shores*, 213; *Waiting for the Barbarians*, 213; *White Writing*, 213; *Youth*, 31, 213, 215–216

collaborative auto/biography, 446; black southern African scribes, 46; black women subjects, written by whites, 25, 45, 49, 173–184, 186–187; and construction of self, 9, 178, 181; definition, 4, 9; of families, 409; Goonam, Kasavel, 291–292; HIV/AIDS stories, 438; by men, 200; of ordinary lives, 48–49; testimonial, by apartheid victims, 27; types of, 46. *See also* auto/biography; life narrative; specific names; testimonial works

colonial works: auto/biography, 12–15, 43, 73n. 35, 80n. 99; oral indigenous vs. writing practices, 12. *See also* travel accounts

color bar. *See* racial discrimination; prejudice; racial; racism

communism, 235, 238–241

concentration camps, 40, 358, 362, 406

confession, in auto/biography. *See* writing: as confession

Congress of South African Writers, 384, 391

conscription, 34, 329, 339–341, 346. *See also* military experience

COSAW. *See* Congress of South African Writers

crime, violent: 29, 31, 332, 345, 380. *See also* violence in South Africa

cross-dressing, 351

Daily Dispatch, 146

death, 311, 382

de Klerk, F. W.: dismantling of apartheid, 36; and forced removals, 31; as hero, 48, 186; *The Last Trek*, 4, 48

de Kock, Eugene: amnesty application, 36; human rights violations, 19, 22, 29; *A Long Night's Damage*, 4; Prime Evil (nickname), 341; psychobiography of, 19, 37; social struggles, 5. *See also* Gobodo-Madikizela, Pumla

democracy. *See* South Africa

Democratic Alliance, 442

Department of Arts and Culture Award, 173

deserts, 255, 258, 259

detective genre, 315, 324

determinism, 383

diaries, 25, 37, 46, 72n. 21, 234, 295, 308, 310, 424

dictionaries, biographical, 16

discrimination. *See* racial discrimination; gender

District Six, memoirs of, 32

domestics. *See* workers

Dona Ermelinda. *See* Lee, Ester

dowry system, 295

drag, 351

INDEX

drama, auto/biographical, 8, 26, 31, 45, 173, 180, 182, 219, 269, 270, 329–344, 345–355
drama awards, 330, 331n. 1, 354. *See also* literary awards; specific awards
Drum Magazine, 243, 245, 250–251, 416, 421
Dutch Reformed Church. *See Nederduitse Gereformeerde Kerk*

End Conscription Campaign, 341
ethics, 51, 48, 271, 315, 399–400
exhibition, group family. See *Group Portrait South Africa: Nine Family Histories*; specific names of families
exile. *See* identities: and exile. *See also* specific writers
exorcism, in auto/biography, 44, 343
expatriates, 30, 202

Faber, Paul, 7, 48, 409–410, 423, 429–430. See also *Group Portrait South Africa: Nine Family Histories*
family: father-son relationships, 281, 285; memoirs, 6, 61, 281, 287, 289, 315–317; mother-daughter relationships, 9, 236, 299, 303–306, 308–311, 319–321; parental auto/biography, 33, 53, 211, 222–225, 234, 409–436; personal relationships, 6, 24, 236–238, 280, 282, 296, 298–300, 309–311, 316–319, 359, 397, 401, 419, 444, 446
fantasy, 284, 286
feasts. *See* traditions
feminism, 5, 19, 27, 46, 51, 187–188, 205, 210, 217, 229, 300, 301, 391–392
fiction: and auto/biography, 9, 17, 24, 47, 51–54, 56, 79n. 89, 169, 220, 229, 232–235, 238–240, 245–247, 254, 262, 316–317, 323, 392, 395, 424, 444; and memory, 54–56; and truth, 261
Finding Mr Madini: auto/biography and fiction, 444; auto/biography and truth, 445, 447; *The Big Issue*, 445; Buddha, Shakyamuni, 440; Cascarino, Valentine, 436, 444–445; censorship, 438, 439; childhood, 445; collaborative auto/biography, 47, 446; Democratic Alliance, 442; democratic elections, 442; Duiker, Sello K., 436; forced removals, 440, 441; Great African Spider Project, 444; HIV/AIDS, 438; holocaust, 443; homelessness, 37, 436, 439, 440, 441–442; *Homeless Talk*, 445; identity, 439, 441, 442, 445, 446, 447–448; Johannesburg, 436–437, 447; journey, inner, 443; Kennedy, William, 436; life narrative, 436; loneliness, 446; *Long Life: Positive HIV Stories*, 438; Malan, Rian, 437; Mda, Zakes, 436; memory boxes project, 446; memory in narrative, 437, 439, 445; mental health, 437; migrancy, 437, 444, 448; Morgan, Jonathan, 436–443, 445; Pan African Parliament, 444; racism, 447; refugees, 436; relationships, family, 446; and self, 436, 437–439, 440, 443; South African Constitution, 441; space, 446; St. Francis of Assisi, 440; testimonial works, collective, 436–449; trauma, 437; white guilt, 447; windows exercise, 437–439; writing as liberation, 437; writing as protest, 443; writing as therapy, 437–438, 443, 445; Zvi, Avram, 445
First, Ruth, 315, 320–324; as hero, 48; *117 Days*, 22; political activist, 32; prison memoirs, 23
flashback, in writing, 220, 315
Fleur du Cap Award, 330
forced removals, 31, 346, 440–441
foundry workers. *See* workers
freedom: of expression, 30, 32, 35, 39, 41, 42, 45, 46, 66, 117, 127, 143, 156, 254, 259, 271, 319, 348, 350, 353, 373, 381, 387, 391, 417, 442–443; of movement, 21, 30, 39, 42–43, 45, 155–156, 200, 203, 250, 319, 341. *See also* liberation movement
Freedom Charter, 319
freedom struggle. *See* liberation movement
Fugard, Athol, in Gray, 387, 391. Works: *The Captain's Tiger: A Memoir for the Stage*, 31; *Cousins*, 6; *"Master Harold" . . . and the Boys*, 26

Galada family, 415–417
GASP. *See* Great African Spider Project
gender: abuse, 49, 294–295; diversity during apartheid, 23; equality, 19, 183, 187; in Goonam, 39, 78n. 83, 300; and identity, 5, 45, 366–368, 371, 377, 391; in Indian com-

munities, 39; in interviews, 8, 65; in life stories, 23; neutrality to racism, 26; politics, 399; as theme, 8, 48

genealogy, 419

ghettos, 362

ghostwriting, 79n. 84, 280–281. *See also* collaborative auto/biography

Gobodo-Madikizela, Pumla: changes in auto/biographical practice, 46; experience of trauma, 44; *A Human Being Died That Night*, 4–5; psychobiography of Eugene de Kock, 19, 37; social struggle, 4; travel accounts, 17

Goldblatt, David: coherence in work, 431; *Group Portrait South Africa: Nine Family Histories*, 409, 410, 428–434; motivation for work, 428; photographer, 48, 409, 410, 428–434; process of portraiture, 429–431; representation of self and others, 431; views on exhibition, 432–434. See also *Group Portrait South Africa: Nine Family Histories*

Goonam, Kasavel, Dr.: abuse, gender, 294–295; activist, anti-apartheid, 291, 296–298, 301; African National Congress, 291, 300; auto/biography, collaborative, 291; Black Sash, 300; Cachalia, Amina, 291; caste system, 294–295; color bar, 291; *Coolie Doctor*, 20, 29, 291–295, 296–299; democracy, 301; diaries, 295; dowry system, 295; exile, 291–292; family relationships, 296, 298–299; feminism, 300; gender issues, 39, 78n. 83, 300; imprisonment, 291, 296; Institute for Black Research, 291–294; liberation movement, 300–301; marriage, 297, 299; Meer, Fatima, 291, 292–293, 300; mentors, 298; migrancy, 296–297; mother-daughter relationships, 299; Naidoo, Phyllis, 300; her name, 294–295; personal relationships, 296–298; Peters, Beryl, 290; pioneer role as doctor and writer, 291, 300; prison accounts, 293, 300; *Prison Diary* (Meer), 300; publication of book, 291–293; racism, 20, 291, 300; representation of self, 299; Second World War, 293; sexism, 300; social life, 298; *Summer Moonbeams on the Lake* (Singh), 300; traditions, 299, 300; trauma in work, 293, 297,

299; woman as victim, 294, 295, 300; on women and careers, 294, 296, 298, 300

Gordimer, Nadine, 279, 280, 284, 387–389

Gray, Stephen: Abrahams, Peter, paper on, 386; aesthetic in auto/biography, 50; apartheid, 381; autobiography, black authors of, 387; autobiography, as stocktaking, 382, 388, 390, 391; autobiography and truth, 381, 382, 385, 386, 388; Barthes, Roland, 392; book cover, significance of, 384, 393; Breytenbach, Breyten, 387; censorship, 381; character, 383; childhood, 381; confession, writing as, 380, 381, 382, 386, 391, 393; Congress of South African Writers, 384, 391; as critic, 379; determinism, 383; du Plessis, Phil, 387; ethics in auto/biography, 51; feminism, 391, 392; fiction and auto/biography, 392; Foucault, Michel, 381; freedom of individual, 383; Fugard, Athol, 387, 391; Gordimer, Nadine, 387–389; identity, 379, 380, 381, 382, 388, 390–392; individualism, 39, 392; Joyce, James, 392; King, Francis, 388; language and reality, 392; Lessing, Doris, 387; liberation, of reading, 387; literacy, in South Africa, 387; Lord, Andrew, 384; Mandela, Winnie, trial of, 384; Marxism, 383; memoirs, personal, 389; memory and autobiography, 385, 392, 393; nervous breakdown, 380; oppression, 381; politics of intimacy, 50, 379; post-traumatic stress syndrome, 380, 393; private and public, 48, 52, 380, 388; Rive, Richard, murder of, 382; Schreiner, Olive, 26, 383; and self, 380, 382, 385, 386, 388, 390–391, 392; sexuality, 379; Skotnes, Cecil and Thelma, 387; testimony, work as, 386, 393; title of work, origin of, 383; trauma, 379–380, 382, 390, 393; University of Iowa Writers' Workshop, 389; Uys, Pieter-Dirk, 391; victim, status of, 380, 393; Wilson, Angus, 381; writing, aspects of, 45, 380, 382, 384, 387, 389–390, 391, 393. Works: *Accident of Birth*, 29, 50, 379, 382, 383, 384, 386, 388, 391, 393; *Beatrice Hastings: A Literary Life*, 379; *Human Interest and Other Pieces*, 389; *Life Sentence: A Biography of Herman Charles Bosman*, 379

Great African Spider Project, 436, 440, 444

Group Portrait South Africa: Nine Family Histories, 41, 409–436; African National Congress, 430; aims of, 414; Anthony, Juleiga, story of, 423, 426; as auto/biography, 409, 414, 424, 428; Baartman, Saartjie (Sara), 410; Bester, Willie, 417, 433; choice of families, 412; *Drum Magazine*, 416, 421; Dutch East Indies, 410; exhibition, group family, 409; *Familieverhalen uit Zuid-Afrika* exhibition, 411–422; family narratives, 409–436; Galada family, 415–417; genealogy, 419; Grendon, Paul, 415; historical justice, 422; identity, 410, 411, 412, 418, 419, 426, 427, 420; Juggernath family, 416–417, 422; KIT Tropenmuseum, Amsterdam, 409–411; launch of exhibition, 421; Le Fleur family, 415, 420, 422–433; life narrative, family, 409, 411–412, 428; location of exhibition, 413; Lungupi, Robert, 417; Magwa, Langa, 417; Mandela, Winnie Madikizela, 418; Manuel, Ebrahim, 423; Manuel family, 417, 421–423, 425, 428, 431; memory, 409; modus operandi, 414; motivation of, 420, 421; Mthethwa family, 415–416, 419–420, 422, 431–432; multimedia project, 48, 409; National Cultural History Museum, Tshwane, 409; Nunn family, 415, 417, 420, 422; objects, 416–417; photographs, 415–418, 428–434; Pieterse, Jan Nederveen, 411; Plaatje family, 415, 419–420, 422, 431; Rathebe family, 416, 419, 421; Siopis, Penny, 412; South African Defence Force, 430; Steyn family, 418–421, 429–431, 433; stories, 422–428; structure, 417, 431; traditions, 419; Van Riebeeck, Jan, 411; videos, 416; website, national heritage, 410, 432; Weinberg, Eli, 411, 415, 416, 432. *See also* Faber, Paul; Goldblatt, David; Jacobs, Rayda
Gutiérrez, Juan Pedro, 396, 400

Haarhoff, Dorian: abuse, physical, 260, 262; apartheid, 254, 256, 262; aquifer metaphor in, 258, 259; Basler Afrika Bibliographien, 256; *Breaking the Silence*, 262; Campbell, Joseph, 265; Carl Schlettwein Foundation, 256; censorship, 254, 264; childhood, 261; construction of self, 255; deserts, 258, 259; exile, 257; fiction, 54, 254, 262; Frankl, Victor, 261; identity, 41, 42, 45, 257, 263; individual, 256; inner travel, 257, 258, 259; Jung, Carl, 265; language and reality, 263; Lorca, Garcia, 265; memory, 255, 256, 260, 261; metaphor in writing, 265; mythology, 254, 255, 265, 266; Naipaul, V. S., 263; Namibia, censorship in, 254; origin of work, 255; ostriches, 254; poetry, 255, 266; private and public, 257; "right brain, left brain" theory, 261, 263, 264; self, 255, 257, 262, 263; teaching writing, 259, 261, 262, 264, 265; tortoise stories, 257, 258, 266; trauma in work, 45, 254–255, 260–262; "trickster" in work, 54, 255, 265; truth and fiction, 56, 261; voice, 254, 255, 263; Williams, William Carlos, 266; writer's block, 264; writing and imagination, 55, 256, 257, 260, 261, 262; writing as therapy, 254–255, 261; writing workshops, 255–256, 260. Works: *Big, Red and Dangerous*, 255; *The Colour of Water*, 259; *Desert December*, 255, 258; *Goats, Oranges and Skeletons*, 265; *Grandfather Enoch's Pipe*, 255; *Guano Girl*, 255; *The Inner Eye: Namibian Poetry in Progress*, 257; *Legs, Bones and Eyes*, 255; *The Missing Namibian*, 258; *Personal Memories: Namibian Texts in Progress*, 261, 262; *Skeleton*, 259; *Space Racer*, 255; *Water from the Rock*, 255; *The Writer's Voice*, 258, 259

Harare, 397. *See also* Zimbabwe
Harlem Renaissance, 250–251
Hermer, Carol, *The Diary of Maria Tholo*, 25, 46
heroic, and auto/biography, 16, 21, 25, 26, 34, 48–49, 79n. 85, 186, 245, 315–316, 318–322, 326, 358, 398
historical justice, 422
history of South Africa. *See* South Africa
HIV/AIDS: auto/biography and, 19, 20, 38, 395, 401; and education, 352; and gender equality, 19; *izibongo*, 141; and memory boxes, 38; raising awareness of, 38, 346–348, 352 353; stories of, 37, 74n. 46, 438
Holocaust, 350, 357–361, 363, 443
homages: to H. F. Verwoerd, 28; to P. W. Botha, 28

Homeless Talk, 445
homelessness, 37, 436, 439, 440, 441; solutions to, 441–442; state's role, 441; as structural problem, 436
homophobia, 49, 349
Hope, Christopher, *White Boy Running*, 27, 29
house arrest. *See* banned persons
human rights: abuses, 42; activists, 269; in different countries, 81; protection of, 30; violations of, 19, 22, 29

identities, 382; abstract, 418; African, 15, 17, 19, 20, 29, 35, 46, 67, 72, 74n. 47, 125, 134, 139, 140, 143, 160, 180, 201–203, 205, 227, 266, 402, 443, 444, 447, 448; Afrikaner, 29, 37, 348, 401; aging, 403; alternative, 10, 18; Appiah's views on, 5, 40; auto/biographical, 9, 69n. 2; Benhabib on, 3, 5, 42, 70n. 6; collective, 1, 2, 5–7, 9, 11, 19, 39, 40–41, 70n. 4, 410, 428; colored, 31; and community, 5–7, 11; construction of, 277; cosmopolitan, 43, 285, 360; crises of, 8, 36, 43, 380, 390; cultural, 5, 40, 439; diasporic, 289; English, 34, 144, 297, 315, 340–341, 347, 374, 381; ethnicity, 35, 37, 366, 368–369, 371, 373–377, 401, 420; and exile, 43, 163–164, 202, 243, 247–248, 257, 269, 277, 291, 315, 363; and family, 366–374, 376, 411; fictive, 346; gay, 348; and gender, 5, 45, 366–368, 371, 377, 391; geographical, 427, 428; group, 22, 410; Indian, 31; individual, 2, 3, 5–7, 11, 14, 18–19, 36, 40–41, 42, 360, 410, 428; Jewish, 348, 445–446; and language, 5, 29, 40, 41, 70n. 4; as mask, 275, 346, 348–349, 404; metaphors of, 270; military, 340; mob, 341; multiethnic, 361; multiple, 270, 412; narrative, 1, 5, 7, 17–19, 40; national, 6, 32, 35–36, 263, 271, 341, 358, 420, 442, 446; of outsider, 269; performance of, 9, 47, 59; and politics, 7, 8, 19, 7In. 15, 217, 442; as process, 274; protection of, 176, 226, 233–234, 317, 419; psychological, 398; racialized, 31, 35, 36; recognition of, 2, 61; and religion, 366–371, 373–374, 376–377; scapegoat, 272–273; self, 1, 3, 5–9, 35, 36, 40, 59, 61, 167–168, 263, 274–275; sexual, 19, 7In. 15, 203, 339, 379, 388, 390–392, 395, 398;

shaping of, 5, 69n. 2, 442; shared, 271, 273; social settings of, 3; South African, 227, 228; and space, 43, 146, 238–239, 364, 437, 446; and trauma, 8, 29, 44, 45; and the visual, 47; white African, 17, 35; white South African, 289–290, 341, 348, 383, 447–448; Xhosa, 24, 25, 29, 120, 125, 174–175, 219; Zulu, 200–202
imagination in writing, 55, 256, 257, 260, 261, 262, 271, 398
imbongi/iimbongi: as adjudicator, 136; as community mouthpiece, 138; as critique singer, 136, 141; as cultural activist, 62; as healer, 137; as historian, 133, 136; importance of knowledge for, 136–137; initiation of, 134; as leader, 136; and liberation movement, 133; and performance, 47; social role of, 40, 61, 132–133, 135; traditions of, 134, 141. *See also izibongo;* names of specific *iimbongi*
imprisonment, 153, 156, 269, 291, 296
inclusion, 25, 27, 50–52, 62
indigenous languages. *See* seSotho; isiXhosa; isiZulu
indigenous people: as authors, 15; and auto/biography, 13, 14; and biography, 14; as colonial subjects, 14, 15, 19; impact of European settlement on, 13; influence of missionary policies on, 14; and *izibongo*, 10; oral auto/biographical practices of, 12; and racism, 20; scientific interest in narratives, 14; tradition of praising in southern Africa, 13; traditions of, 10, 12, 35; and travel accounts, 14; writings of, 15, 21
individual freedom, 383
individualism: and authorship, 45, 300; and auto/biography, 39–40, 45, 67, 75n. 58, 383, 392; and collectivism, 40, 256; enabling conditions of, 40, 45; westernized, 67, 405
Institute for Black Research, 291–294
interview process: with Brutus, 153; with Coetzee, 65–67; with Magona, 223–224; with Manganyi, 166; with Thembela, 149. *See also* anthology of interviews; self; self-representation
intimacy. *See* identity, sexual; politics of intimacy
isicathamiya, 149, 151

isiXhosa: *izibongo* in, 10, 121, 122, 124, 125, 133, 143, 147; publication and, 21; Magona's work in, 219, 223
isiZulu: *izibongo* in, 10, 11, 25; publication and, 21; Thembela's biography of Joseph Shabalala in, 148, 150, 151
Itzik Manger Prize, 358
izibongo: activists, 132; and community 11; compared with auto/biography, 137; composition, 10–11; defined, 10–11, 71n. 13, 137; dynamics of, 133; forms and function of, 132; as gift from ancestors, 135; history of, 73n. 29; and identity, 11, 47; issues in, 141; and language medium, 144; for leaders, 132; *lithoko*, SeSotho, 10; motivation for, 144; of national heroes, 26; as opposition voice, 21; oral modes of, 141; of ordinary people, 25; and performance, 21, 47; personal, 132; as recorded medium, 142, 144, 146; responses to, 61, 138, 139; sources of inspiration for, 47, 136, 138, 142, 145; structure of *Call Me Woman*, 41; subjects of, 11; target audience, 144; techniques, 142, 143; of whites, 25; for women, 41; written modes of, 141; of Xhosas, 119, 121; of Zulus, 11, 25, 26. See also *imbongi/iimbongi*; names of specific *imbongi/iimbongi*
izihasho. See *izibongo*

Jabavu, Noni, 24; background, 25; and racial oppression, 15; travel accounts, 17. Works: *Drawn in Colour: African Contrasts*, 17, 24; *The Ochre People*, 17, 24, 62
Jacobs, Rayda, 48, 409, 410, 422–428; Anthony family, 423, 426; Coetzee, J. M., 424; diaries, 424, 425, 428; identity, 426; loneliness, 425; Manuel family, 423, 425, 428; Mecca, 424; responses to work, 425; structure of work, 427; writing, motivation for, 424. Works: *Confessions of a Gambler*, 427; *The Mecca Diaries*, 424; *The Middle Children*, 424; "Near the Mountain, Near the Sea," 427; *The Slave Book*, 422; *The Tuan of Antonie's Gat*, 423. See also *Group Portrait South Africa: Nine Family Histories*
James Tait Black Prize, 231
Jenkin, Tim: *Escape from Pretoria*, 22; *Inside Out: Escape from Pretoria*, 31

Jews: in Nixon, 357; in Lessing, 238; and Morgan's identity, 445–446, 448; and Uys' identity, 345, 348, 350; in Wolpe, 357–360, 363–364
Johannesburg, 436–437, 447
Joseph, Helen, 6, 32. Works: *If This Be Treason*, 23; *Side by Side*, 6, 22; *Tomorrow's Sun: A Smuggled Journal from South Africa*, 23
Joubert, Elsa: *Africa's Hundred Best Books*, 59; Afrikaans in *Poppie*, 174, 175, 177; Blignaut on *Poppie*, 183; censorship in *Poppie*, 179; credibility of *Poppie*, 176; Degenaar on *Poppie*, 183; identity of "Poppie," 176; influence on readers, 61; interviews in *Poppie*, 177; literary awards, 61, 173; memory, 54; origin of *Poppie*, 61, 174–175, 180, 182–183; problems of understanding others, 60, 178–179; profits from *Poppie*, 182; racist legislation in *Poppie*, 174, 176, 179–180; relationship between Joubert and "Poppie," 47, 175–178; religion in *Poppie*, 178, 180; representation of other, 178, 180; responses to work, 61, 173, 180, 182; role of writer in *Poppie*, 46, 47, 181–183; structure of work, 55; and truth, 53–55. Works: "Agterplaas," 178; *The Long Journey of Poppie Nongena* (English translation), 173; *Missionaris*, 178–179; *Poppie: die drama*, 173, 180, 182; *Die Swerfjare van Poppie Nongena*, 24, 46, 55, 59, 61, 173; *'n Wonderlike geweld*, 174
Juggernath family, 416–417, 422

Karoo, and Arizona, 285–287
Kendall, K. Limakatso: as editor/facilitator of Mpho Nthunya's story, 30, 188–197; structuring of work, 55. Works: *Basali*, 191; *Singing Away the Hunger*, 30, 46, 55, 58, 61, 188–192; *When Spirits Call Me Home: Spiritualities in Southern Africa*, 188. See also Nthunya, Mpho
Kerfoot, Caroline, *We Came to Town*, 25–26, 46. See also literacy: classes
KIT Tropenmuseum, Amsterdam, 409, 410, 411
Krog, Antjie, 321–323; Afrikaner identity, 37; *Country of My Skull*, 37, 45, 62, 321; racialized identities, 35; trauma in work, 45, 322; travel accounts, 17; on "Truth,"

54. See also Truth and Reconciliation Commission
Kuzwayo, Ellen, 319; *Call Me Woman*, 25, 27, 41, 59, 62, 319; essays on, 12; trauma in work, 41, 319; and *ubuntu*, 5, 376
kwaito, 151

labor class. See workers
Ladysmith Black Mambazo. See Thembela, Alex J.
language: and auto/biography, 2, 6, 8, 12–14, 32, 43, 62–63, 358, 395; and identity, 5, 29, 40, 41, 70n. 4; indigenous, 16; of liberation, 21; as medium of auto/biography, 148, 194, 223, 405; and reality, 168, 263, 313, 392; and truth, 54, 214–215
Lee, Ester: on aging, 310; biography, post-colonial, 305, 307; death, 311; diaries, 308, 310; *Double Life of Dona Ermelinda* (film), 310; Ermelinda, Dona, 303, 304, 305, 306, 307, 308; family relationship, 310–311; *I Was Born in Africa*, 303, 304, 306; language and reality, 313; loneliness, 311–312; Machel, Samora, 305–307; Marxism, 305, 307; memory, 312–313; migrancy, 307; mother-daughter relationship, 303–306, 308–311; motivation for writing, 45, 304; Mozambican writers, 312; Mozambique, 45, 303–308, 310–311; Mucavele, 303, 305, 308–312; religion and auto/biography, 305; self, 304, 306, 310, 313; sexual identity, 309; trauma, 45, 305–309; and truth, 60, 303, 311, 312, 313; writing as therapy, 45, 60, 303, 306
Le Fleur family, 415, 420, 422–433
Lesotho, 14, 61, 189, 190, 191, 194
Lessing, Doris: all writing as autobiography, 221; anonymity, 233–234; autobiographies, 278, 284; autobiography as discovery, 235, 241; autobiography and fiction, 52, 53, 232–235, 238–240; autobiography and truth, 235; children, 237–238; Coetzee, J. M., 240; communism, 235, 238–241; *Darkness at Noon* (Koestler), 235; diary, 234; family, 4, 236–238; identity, 231; impact of writing, 59; Klein, Carole, 4, 234; literary awards, 231; memory, 231–234, 236; mother-daughter relationships, 236; motivation for writing, 234; racism, 237; self and others, 234, 241; space for writing, 238–239; war, 235–236; women and careers, 237, 241; Zimbabwe, 236, 239, 241. Works: *African Laughter: Four Visits to Zimbabwe*, 237; *Children of Violence*, 236; *The Fifth Child*, 234; *Landlocked*, 239; *Martha Quest*, 236, 237; *A Proper Marriage*, 236; *The Sweetest Dream*, 239–240; *Under My Skin, Volume I of My Autobiography, to 1949*, 4, 231, 233; *Walking in the Shade, Volume II of My Autobiography, 1949–1962*, 231, 233
letters, 8, 22, 24, 29, 32, 72n. 21, 165, 319, 366–367. See also auto/biography; biography; diaries; *izibongo*; memoirs; specific writers; testimonial works
Levinson, Daniel, 166. See also Manganyi, N. Chabani
Lewin, Hugh: *Bandiet: Seven Years in a South African Prison*, 22; *Bandiet: Out of Jail*, 31
liberation movement: and auto/biographical writing, 6, 15, 16, 21–22, 30, 33–34, 40, 42, 49, 57, 60, 71n. 15, 80, 128, 134, 153, 161, 170, 173, 186, 188, 246, 300–301, 315, 318, 319, 350, 411; and English language, 21; *imbongi/iimbongi*, 133; and reading, 387. See also freedom; Freedom Charter; specific writers
life narrative, 10, 12–13, 15, 28; and apartheid, 15, 22, 26, 27, 35; about blacks, by whites, 24, 32; about black women, by white women, 24–25, 173–184, 186–187; by blacks, 27, 39, 43; black readership, 26; book awards, 59; in Bozzoli, 18; collaborative, 27, 186–187, 436; collections, 23, 25, 32; conversion, 37, 366; definition, 8; dissemination of, 57; family, 409–436; fictional elements in, 53; and gender, 23, 49; heroic, 186; historical accuracy, 22, 262, 354; of homeless, 37; and identity, 3, 5, 7, 19; of indigenous South Africans, 15; individual, 3, 28, 414, 428; interpretive framework, 55; of ordinary persons, 48–49; in letters, 8, 22, 24, 29, 33; and liberation struggle, 15–16, 22, 186; mediation and, 46; in new South Africa, 33, 35; Ngwenya on, 55; post-apartheid, 35–36; and racism, 15, 20–21; reconciliation of African and

European worlds, 35; refugees, 37; repetition in, 27, 40; and social science, 18; and truth, 46, 55; of workers, 24–26, 38, 146. *See also* auto/biography; banned works; banned persons; diaries; feminism; *izibongo;* letters; memoirs; reminiscences; specific writers; testimonial works
life-history method, 18
literacy: black readership and, 26, 27; classes, 26, 46; lack of, in auto/biography, 46; orality and, 12; in South Africa, 387
literary awards, 27, 30, 31, 34, 49, 59, 80n. 97, 173, 205, 207, 213, 219, 231, 243, 358. *See also* drama awards; specific awards
lithoko. See seSotho; *izibongo*
Living Legacy 2000 Award, 347
lobola. See dowry system
location. *See* identities: and space
London Film School, 345
loneliness, 311–312, 358, 446
Los Angeles Times Book Prize, 231
Luthuli, Albert: biography of (Benson), 21–22; *Let My People Go,* 6, 21, 74n. 40; Nobel Peace Prize, 21

McCord, James, *My Patients Were Zulus,* 206
McCord, Margaret: African Native Choir, 205; Alan Paton–Sunday Times Award, 205, 207; background, 205; Bantu Women's League, 205; *The Calling of Katie Makanya,* 30, 49, 181, 205–211; *The Seed is Mine* (van Onselen), 206
Machel, Samora, 305–307
Madiba. *See* Mandela, Nelson
Magona, Sindiwe: activist, 229; apartheid, 229; as auto/biographer, 219, 224; Biehl, Amy, 220–221, 223, 228; as biographer, 222, 224; confessional writing, 226; as domestic, 219; empathy, 228; fiction and auto/biography, 51, 52, 53, 220, 229; interview process, 223–224; and language, 223, 227; and marriage, 221–223, 225–226, 229; memory, 59, 62, 225, 226; motivation for writing, 227; nomination for M-Net Prize, 219; ordinary life, 48, 226; poverty, 225; protecting identity, 51, 226; racism, 29; role of work, 62; self and writing, 50, 222, 225, 229–230; South African identity, 227, 228; structure of work, 220; as teacher, 219; traditional wisdom, 224; trauma in work, 45, 221, 223, 225, 227–228; violence, 219, 221, 228; writer as narrator, 47, 220; writing as therapy, 45, 223, 225, 226, 228, 229, 230. Works: *Anatomy of Infidelity,* 219–222, 229; *Forced to Grow,* 29, 219–221; "Imida," 219; *Kubantwana babantwana bam,* 219; "Lilian and Penrose," 222, 224; *Living, Loving, and Lying Awake at Night,* 219, 221; *Mother to Mother,* 219–221, 223, 227, 228; *Push-push,* 219; *To My Children's Children,* 29, 219–221; *Vukani!* (Wake up!), 219
Makanya, Katie: auto/biography, with Margaret McCord, 205; conflict in belief systems, 209–210; conflicting views of biography, 205; history of patients, 206, 210; as leading black feminist, 205; personal relationships, 30, 46, 207; privacy issues, 207; relationship with James McCord, 49, 210–211; relationship with sister, Charlotte Maxeke, 205–206
Malan, Rian: literary award, 27; review of *Finding Mr Madini,* 437; *My Traitor's Heart,* 27, 29
Malawi, 76n. 74
Mandela, Nelson, 291, 347, 348, 352; biographies of, 21, 33; as hero, 16, 186; *izibongo* about, 26, 138, 146; *Long Walk to Freedom,* 33, 48, 59, 62; use of "we" in auto/biography, 279
Mandela, Winnie Madikizela: autobiographical text from tapes (Benjamin and Benson), 24; mother of nation, 418; *Part of My Soul Went with Him,* 22; trial of, 384; *Winnie Mandela: A Life* (du Preez Bezdrob), 48
Manganyi, N. Chabani: background, 160–161; as biographer, 161, 163–164; choice of subjects, 161; civil rights movement, U.S., 161; collaborative auto/biography, 165; as exile, 43, 163–164; on fiction and auto/biography, 52, 53; as hero, 169; on identity, 168; influences on, 161; interest in life history, 161; interview method, 166, 169; Levinson, Daniel, 165–167; private and public, 161, 167; psychobiography, 19, 40, 160; Sekoto, Gerard, 19, 169; self and biography, 44, 161, 164, 168; structure of works, 164–165; as

therapist, 44, 163–166; titles of works, 163; trauma in work, 163, 164, 170; voice in biography, 165, 169. Works: *A Black Man Called Sekoto*, 160, 163, 165, 166, 168, 169, 170; *Exiles and homecomings: A Biography of Es'kia Mphahlele*, 19, 40, 160, 163–165, 167, 169, 170, 243; *Gerard Sekoto: "I Am an African,"* 160

Manuel, Ebrahim, 423

Manuel family, 417, 421–423, 425, 428, 431

marriage and auto/biography, 221–223, 225–226, 229, 297, 299, 368–371

Marxism, 305, 307, 383

masculinity: in auto/biography, 19, 288–289; effects of racism on, 29; and identity, 29

mask, identity as, 275

Matanzima, Kaizer: *Independence My Way*, 28; oral poem about, 117

Mathabane, Mark, *Kaffir Boy*, 27, 29

Matshikiza, Todd: auto/biography, 247, 251; *Chocolates for My Wife*, 17, 26

mediated testimony. *See* collaborative auto/biography; testimonial works

Meer, Fatima: *Coolie Doctor* (Goonam), 292–293; *Prison Diary*, 300

memoirs: in Afrikaans, 399; by black women, 25; celebrity, 278–289; childhood, 213, 277, 282, 287–288; collaborative, 4; comparison of, in South Africa and U.S., 278–280; of District Six residents, 32; in exile, 291–292; family, 6, 281, 289, 315–317; of liberation struggle, 33; of Mandela, Nelson, 33; military, 34; of ordinary lives, 48–49; personal, 31, 278–280, 289, 349–350, 389; of political movements, 6; prison, 22, 23, 25, 269, 284; rationale for, 287; suffering and recovery, 281; travel, 36, 269; of TRC commissioners, 37; by white men, 36; by white South Africans, 28, 36; by white women, 23. *See also* auto/biography; diaries; *izibongo*; letters; life narrative; reminiscences; testimonial works

memory: and agency, 78n. 83, 437, 438, 445; and apartheid, 44; and auto/biography, 59, 207, 225, 226, 231–234, 255–256, 260–261, 269, 271, 273–275, 287, 312–313, 319, 323, 325, 364, 385, 392–393, 396–398, 409; fiction and, 54–56, 245–246, 283; and identity, 231–234, 359; memory boxes project, 38, 446; personal, 6, 48, 349–350; as weapon in liberation struggle, 30

mental health, 437

metaphor: function of, 265; of identity, 270; of mirror, 270–274, 345, 347, 349–350, 369; of self, 244

method acting, 336–338

"Middle World," 270

migrancy, 127, 151, 152, 257, 277, 285–289, 296–297, 307, 311, 357, 360, 437, 444, 447–448

military experience, 331–333, 335, 339–343, 397–398

Mkiva, Zolani: Africanness, 46; African Renaissance, 134, 140, 143; beginnings, 133; Black Consciousness, 140; as communications specialist, 144; and community, 133; as cultural activist, 133; as educator, 143, 145–146; genealogy, 139, 146; as graduate, 140, 141; impact of poetry, 61, 62; inspiration, 42, 134; as leader, 143; and liberation movement, 133; and Mqhayi, S. E. K., 143; as performer, 47; philosophy of, 135; "poet of Africa," 143; and recordings, 142, 144, 146; roles and allegiances, 40, 46, 47, 144–145; sources, 47; space, 43; trauma in work, 145; work at *Daily Dispatch*, 146. Works: *Mazenethole*, 146; *Qadaffi*, 146; *Railway Poetry*, 145, 146. *See also imbongi*

M-Net Prize, 219

Modisane, Bloke: auto/biography, 247, 251; *Blame Me on History*, 3, 21, 29; exile, 20; and liberation movement, 15; Nkosi's reviews of, 3

Mokgatle, Naboth, *The Autobiography of an Unknown South African*, 20, 22

montage in writing, 220

morality. *See* ethics

Morgan, Jonathan, 7, 37, 41, 47, 436–443, 445. *See also Finding Mr Madini*

Mozambique: First, Ruth, 324; Lee, Ester, 303–308, 310–311; political changes, 303–308, 311; van Wyk, Johan, 397; writers, 312

Mphahlele, Es'kia (Ezekiel): Abrahams, 247, 250–251; African-American literature, 250–251; Africa's Hundred Best Books

INDEX

Award, 59, 243; Auden, W. H., 249; autobiography, 15, 56, 60, 244, 246; bigamy, 248; biography of, 243; character in, 245; childhood, 243, 246, 247; criticism of work, 3, 246–249; Dhlomo, 250–251; *Drum Magazine*, 243, 245, 250–251; Eliot, T. S., 245; escapism, 252; exile, 243, 247–248; fiction and autobiography, 52–53, 56, 245, 247; Harlem Renaissance, 250–251; Head, Bessie, 251; as hero, 245; and identity, 5, 40, 43; and inclusion, 50; Kerr, Martin Jarrett, 248; La Guma, Alex, 251; Maimane, Arthur, 251; Matshikiza, Todd, 247, 251; Matthews, James, 251; memory in, 245–246; metaphors of self, 244, 245; mission-educated, 25; Modisane, 247, 251; Plaatje family, 250; poetry, teaching of, 249; psychobiography of, 19, 40, 160, 163–165, 167, 169, 170; racism in, 29; Rive, Richard, 251; Themba, Can, 251; trauma in work, 246–247, 251; travel accounts, 17; ubuntu, 5; *Uncle Tom's Children* (Wright), 251; voices, 246; writing and therapy, 60. Works: *The African Image*, 244; *Afrika My Music*, 17, 243, 250; *Bury Me at the Marketplace*, 165, 243; *Chirundu*, 244, 248, 250; *Corner B: Essays*, 244; *Down Second Avenue*, 3, 22–23, 29, 59, 62, 165, 243–245, 247–249; *Father Come Home*, 249–250; *Man Must Live*, 251; *Voices in the Whirlwind*, 244; *The Wanderers*, 244, 248–249

Mqhayi, S. E. K., 123–126, 143. See also Mkiva, Zolani; Yali-Manisi, D. L. P.

Mthethwa family, 415–416, 419–420, 422, 431–432

multimedia, 47–48, 409; CD of Mkiva's work, 142, 144, 146; interactive video, 418; Juggernath family video, 416. See also *Group Portrait South Africa: Nine Family Histories*

murder, 36, 153, 315, 322, 332, 380, 382

mythology, 254–255, 265–266

Naipaul, V. S., 263, 277, 285

Namibia, 34, 42, 254, 256–265, 344

narcissism, 3, 281

National Arts Festival, Grahamstown, 331, 333, 334, 336

National Cultural History Museum, Tshwane, 409

Nationalist Party, 20, 346

National Vita Award, 59, 330

Nederduitse Gereformeerde Kerk, 353, 371, 374

Nietzsche, Friedrich, 52, 370, 397, 400

Nixon, Rob: Arizona, and Karoo, 285, 286, 287; Coetzee, J. M., 282; democracy, South African, 16, 277; Drakulic, Slavenka, 279; exile, 36, 277; fantasy, 284, 286; Ghosh, Amitav, 283; ghostwriting, 280–281; Gilroy, 286; Gordimer, Nadine, 279, 280, 284; Hornby, Nick, 286; identity, 277, 285, 289–290; inner journey, 286; Jackson, Albert, 284; Julian, Isaac, 286; Kafka, Franz, 285; Lessing, Doris, 278, 284; life narrative of ordinary persons, 48–49, 278, 280, 282–283; Mandela, Nelson, 279; masculinity, 288, 289; memoirs and auto/biography, 277, 278–280, 281, 282, 287, 288, 289; memory, and fiction, 283; memory and autobiography, 55, 287; migrancy, 277, 285, 287, 288, 289; motivation for writing, 278; Naipaul, V. S., 277, 285; narcissism, 281; ostriches, 278, 282, 283, 285, 288, 289; prison accounts, 284; rationale for memoirs, 287; relationships, father-son, 281, 285; Sartre, Jean-Paul, 286; Schalkwyk, David, 284; Sebald, W. G., 283; self, 278, 279, 281; trauma in work, 278, 282, 287; travel, 285; U.S. ties with South Africa, 277–280, 281–283, 285; Verwoerd, Hendrik, 280; voice, 280, 288; writing as healing, 288; zeitgeist, 281. Works: *Dreambirds*, 277, 280, 281–284, 286, 288, 289; *Homelands, Harlem and Hollywood: South African Culture and the World Beyond*, 277; *London Calling: V. S. Naipaul, Postcolonial Mandarin*, 277

Nobel Prize: Coetzee, J. M., 31, 213; Luthuli, Albert, 21

Noma Award, 49, 59, 79n. 85

Nthunya, Mpho: *Child of the Dark* (de Jesus), 192; feminist movement, 187–188; heroic life writing, 186; inspiration for work, 189, 197; language in work, 194, 195; liberation movement, 186; nomination for Alan Paton Prize, 192; Nthunya's responses to book,

190–191, 197; personal relationships, 30; production process, 189–191, 195–196; *Singing Away the Hunger,* 30, 46, 55, 58, 61, 188–192; writing and healing, 60. *See also* Kendall, K. Limakatso
Nunn family, 415, 417, 420, 422

OBIE Award, 354
official history, 410. *See also* historical justice
one-man shows, 329, 339, 346
oppression stories, under apartheid, 15, 21, 24–25, 27, 48, 156, 272, 380, 381. *See also* apartheid
oral modes: auto/biography, 4, 6, 8, 9, 12, 18, 20, 46, 47, 55; dissemination of, 57; indigenous practices, 12; ordinary people, 25; performance, 16; poetry, 26, 124, 143; relationship with literacy, 12; TRC testimony, 44; vernacular, 21; of victims of racism, 30
oral poetry. *See izibongo*
Order of Ikhamanga, 173
orientation, sexual. *See* identity: sexual
ostriches, 254, 278, 282, 283, 285, 288, 289
outsider, identity as, 269

painting, 269, 272
PAC. *See* Pan African Congress
Pan African Congress, 33
Pan African Parliament, 444
passbook system. *See* racist legislation
performance. *See* drama, auto/biographical
Plaatje family, 415, 419–420, 422, 431
poetry: and auto/biography, 55–56, 153, 224, 395–396, 399–400; in childhood, 255; process of, 266; teaching, 249; women's, 262; and Zen, 272
political repression, 48
politics of intimacy, 9, 50, 379
post-apartheid: auto/biography, 35–38; literature, 402; and reconciliation, 370
poverty, 25, 141, 225, 279, 395
praise poetry. *See izibongo*
praise poets. *See imbongi/iimbongi*
prejudice, racial. *See* racism; racial discrimination
press freedom, curtailment of, 32
Prime Evil. *See* de Kock, Eugene

Pringle, Thomas: "Bechuana Boy," 46; "Makanna's Gathering," 46; travel accounts, 14
prison accounts, 22–23, 25, 31–32, 153, 269, 284, 291, 296, 320. *See also* imprisonment; memoirs: prison
privacy: in auto/biography: 48, 51, 52, 60, 179, 207, 317–318, 380, 388; right to, 51, 60, 368
private and public, 2, 12, 18, 48–52, 60, 161–162, 167, 226, 257, 275, 312, 317, 319–320, 367, 373, 380, 388
prizes. *See* name of prize. *See also* drama awards; literary awards
prostitutes. *See* sex workers
psychobiography, 6, 19. *See also* de Kock, Eugene; Gobodo-Madikizela, Pumla; Manganyi, N. Chabanyi; Mphahlele, Es'kia
publishers: government, 42; international, 58; local South African, 58; opposed to apartheid, 27; preference for English material, 21; self-publication, 58, 395, 403

Qabula, Temba, 25

racial classification, 345; and auto/biographical writing, 30; as determining experience, 22, 26, 27, 29, 174, 176, 180, 402; effect on Tsafendas' life, 32
racial discrimination: effect of legislation, 28, 49, 52, 154, 174, 176, 180, 360; effect on auto/biographical writing, 10. *See also* racial classification; racism; racist legislation
racism, 291, 300, 332–333, 342, 347, 349; anonymity of, 75n. 52; and black writing, 31–33; as experienced by black South Africans, 31; and gender neutrality, 26; and identity, 2; in Israel, 270; and masculinity, 29; and other injustices, 49; prior to apartheid, 20; questioning of identities, 35, 154; and self-esteem, 29; testimony of victims, 30; white auto/biographers' attitudes, 29; whites, awareness of, 42, 237, 402, 447. *See also* racial classification; racial discrimination; racist legislation
racist legislation, 20–21, 31, 52, 154, 174, 176, 179–180, 345. *See also* racial classification; racial discrimination
Radebe, E. P. M. *See* Thembela, Alex J.

Rathebe family, 416, 419, 421
Reconstruction and Development Program, 354
refugees, 436
Regional Vita Award, 330
relationships: auto/biography and space, 43; family, 6, 236–238, 296, 298–299, 311, 316–319, 359, 446; father-son, 281, 285; in interviews, 65; mother-daughter, 9, 236, 299, 303, 308–311, 319–321; personal, 46, 248, 296–298, 303, 305, 308–312, 395–396, 400–402, 404, 406; with self, 57, 369–370, 375, 377; sexual, 20, 395, 399–400, 406. See also identities; self
religion, 5, 178, 180, 208
research process, 49, 149–151, 163–165, 175, 179, 207–208, 223, 316, 320, 351
resistance movement. See liberation movement
resistance writing, 10, 19, 20, 42, 48–49, 187
reviews, of auto/biography, 318, 395
"right brain-left brain" theory, 261, 263–264
rituals. See traditions
Rive, Richard: African-American influence, 251; on auto/biography and change, 61; on dislocation, 43; on inclusion, 50; on individualism, 39; murder of, 382; on social change and auto/biography, 61; *Writing Black*, 27
Rousseau, Jean-Jacques, 39, 50, 217, 372, 374, 386

Sachs, Albie: *Island in Chains*, 32; *Jail Diary*, 21, 22
Sachs, Wulf, *Black Hamlet*, 4, 15, 19
satire, 347–348
scapegoat identity, 272–273
Scotsman Fringe First Award, 331n. 1
Scott, Robert. See Cibane, Wilfred
Second World War. See war
self: aging, 310; analysis of, 2, 19, 27, 36, 39, 43–45, 57, 154, 203, 229, 234, 367, 375, 385, 398, 436; Benhabib's views of, 3, 5, 44, 61, 69n. 2; Christian conceptions of, 13; constructionist view of, 57, 255, 262, 368, 372, 377; discovery of, 241, 350, 436; exploration, 155, 240, 244, 269, 280, 289, 390, 412; and identity, 255, 257, 274–275; and interview format, 65–67; mediated, 349; metaphors of, 53, 244, 245, 369; narrative, 1, 5; in new South Africa, 33, 35, 440; notions of, 1–9, 12–13, 36, 41, 59; private and public, 18, 52, 161–162, 167, 226, 241, 275; and reconciliation of African and European worlds, 35; reinventing, 164, 167, 168, 179, 217, 244, 255, 262, 265, 271, 273, 352, 360, 368, 377, 410–411, 413, 415, 419, 427, 440, 443, 447, 448; representation of, 178, 180, 392, 405, 409, 419; rescue, 360; revelation of, 203, 204, 227, 229, 282, 289, 317, 358, 368, 380, 385, 388, 389–391, 402, 437–439; as theme of collection, 48, 64; and therapy, 60; transformation of, 306; transparency of, 39, 44, 45, 46, 60, 374–375; and travel, 263; validating, 436. See also identities; self-representation
self-portraiture, 213, 269, 337, 348, 386, 393, 398–399, 401, 410, 419, 428, 431–433
self-publication, 58, 395, 403
self-reconciliation, 37
self-representation: in auto/biography, 1, 4, 7, 9, 57, 222, 225, 229–231, 234, 299, 304, 306, 329, 332–333, 336–337, 339, 398, 405; contemporary notions, 9; contemporary practices, 12; and emotions, 337; and indigenous people, 10, 25; and interviews, 65, 67; in new South Africa, 36; oral texts, 25; of others, 7, 9, 234, 313; in theatre, 45. See also identity; self
servants. See workers
seSotho: *lithoko* in, 10; in Nthunya's stories, 195; publications in, 21, 194
sexism, 2, 49, 300. See also feminism; gender; identity; masculinity
sex workers, 37, 49, 395–396, 399–400
Shabalala, Joseph. See Thembela, Alex J.
Shostak, Marjorie, *Nisa: The Life and Words of a !Kung Woman*, 4, 15, 46
Siopis, Penny, 412
Sisulu, Elinor: biography of Walter and Albertina Sisulu, 6, 16, 49; Noma Award, 59
Slovo, Gillian: abuses, 322–323; activist, anti-apartheid, 315; African National Congress, 315; amnesty, 321; apartheid, 325, 326; *Call Me Woman* (Kuzwayo), 319; childhood, 315,

321, 324; confessional writing, 316; *Country of My Skull* (Krog), 321; Diski, Jenny, 316; domestic workers, 320; ethics, 317; exile, 315; family relationships, 316–319; fiction and auto/biography, 316, 317, 323; First, Ruth, 32, 315, 320–324; flashback in writing, 315; Freedom Charter, 319; heroic, 315, 316, 318–322, 326; Krog, Antjie, 321–323; Kuzwayo, Ellen, 319; letters, 319; liberation movement, 315, 318; memoirs, family, 6, 315–317; memory, 48, 59, 319, 323, 325; Morrison, Blake, 316; mother-daughter relationships, 319–321; motivation for work, 316, 324; Mozambique, 324; murder, 315, 322; *117 Days* (First), 320; parental auto/biography, 315–318, 320–321; political auto/biography, 43, 324; prison accounts, 320; private and public, 51, 60, 317, 319–320; research process, 316, 320; responses to work, 326; reviews of, 318; rewriting history, 322; Schoon, Jeanette, 322; Simon, Barney, 316; Slovo, Joe, 48, 315, 321; Slovo, Shawn, 323; structure of work, 315–316, 324–325; suicide attempt, 320–321; trauma in work, 315, 319–323; thrillers, 315, 324; truth, 317–318; Truth and Reconciliation Commission, 321–323, 325; *The Unfinished Autobiography* (Joe Slovo), 33, 321; Unterhalter, Elaine, 319; war crimes, 322; Williamson, Craig, 322, 325; women and careers, 319–320; Women's March on Pretoria, 319; *A World Apart* (Shawn Slovo), 72n. 22, 323; writing of ordinary people, 318. Works: *Every Secret Thing*, 6, 33, 315, 316, 323, 324; *Red Dust*, 323
Slovo, Joe, 48, 315, 321
Sotho. *See* seSotho
South Africa, 19, 33, 37, 301; democratic elections, 277, 347, 353, 372, 442; historical accuracy, 22, 254, 256, 262, 322, 354 422; official national Internet website, 410, 432; States of Emergency in, 346; on travel accounts, 17. *See also* historical justice; specific topics
South African Constitution, 37, 363, 441
South African Defence Force, 329, 341–342, 430
Space Theatre, 345, 349

Steyn family, 418–421, 429–431, 433
Sunday Times, 403–404
Swaziland, 78n. 79

teaching, 333–335, 343, 348, 352–353
testimonial works: of apartheid victims, 4, 6, 12, 19, 23–27, 30, 32; as auto/biography, 6, 386, 393; about black South Africans, mediated by whites, 4, 24, 32; by black writers, 23; collective, 436–449; definition, 4; in literacy classes, 26, 46; oral, 30; personal, 12; by those with HIV/AIDS, 19, 38; and TRC, 4, 56; by women, 25. *See also* auto/biography; diaries; *izibongo*; letters; life narrative; memoirs
theatre. *See* drama
Thembela, Alex J., 48, 53, 54; collaborator with Radebe, E. P. M., 148, 150; contemporary popular culture in, 151; ethnographic dimension of work, 149; interview process, 149; *isicathamiya*, 149, 151; *kwaito*, 151; Ladysmith Black Mambazo, 148–152; language in, 148, 150; origin of work, 148; Shabalala, Joseph, 148–151; traditional music, 149; views on contemporary popular culture, 151; writing process, 55, 149, 150. Works: *The Life and Works of Joseph Shabalala and the Ladysmith Black Mambazo*
therapy. *See* writing: as therapy
Third World, 411
tortoises: 257, 258, 266
trade unions: *izibongo* of, 11; oral poetry, 26; Qabula's work, 25, Weinberg, Eli, 411
traditions, 201, 295, 299, 300, 419; of *imbongi/iimbongi*, 134, 141; of indigenous people, 10, 12, 35; in music, 149; wisdom of, 224
trauma, 61; as catalyst in auto/biography, 44–45, 254, 437; in Breytenbach, 269; in Brutus, 117, 155–157; in Gillian Slovo, 315, 319–323; in Goonam, 293, 297, 299; in Gray, 379, 380, 390, 393; in Greig Coetzee, 44, 335; in Haarhoff, 45, 254–255, 260–262; identity and, 8, 29, 44–45; in Krog, 45, 322; in Kuzwayo, 41, 319; in Lee, 45, 305–309; in Magona, 45, 221, 223, 225, 227–228; in Manganyi, 163, 164, 170; in Mkiva, 145; in Morgan, 437; in Mphahlele, 246–247,

251; in Nixon, 278, 282, 287; and post-traumatic stress syndrome, 380, 393; in van Wyk, 395, 397–398, 401; in Wolpe, 40, 43, 358–360, 362; in Yali-Manisi, 127
travel accounts: colonial, 13–15, 43; contemporary, 17, 20; first by black woman, 17; and identity, 17, 36; indigenous subjects in, 15; inner, 257–259, 285–286, 443; memory of, 392; by missionaries, 14; perception of indigenous people in, 15; post-apartheid, 36; and self, 263
trickster, 255, 265
TRC. *See* Truth and Reconciliation Commission
Truth and Reconciliation Commission, 321–323, 325, 341, 354; apartheid stories, 34; and Afrikaner nationalism, 37; de Kock's amnesty application, 36; memoirs, 37; testimonies from, 4, 27, 56; and truth, 56, 370–372, 376–377
truth in auto/biography, 53–56, 235, 303, 311–313, 317–318, 331, 350, 368, 370–371, 381, 385–386, 399, 405, 445, 447
truth-telling, 352, 382, 388, 390

ubuntu, 5, 41, 46, 376
Umkhonto we Sizwe, 342. *See also* African National Congress
United States: ties with South Africa, 277–280, 281–283, 285
uprisings. *See* violence in South Africa: political
Uys, Pieter-Dirk: African National Congress, 347; apartheid and performance, 347, 351; auto/biography as performance, 345–355; banned works, 345; Bezuidenhout, Evita, 55, 346–347, 350–352; Botha, P. W., 352; characters, 350; childhood, 353; conscription, 346; crime, 345; cross-dressing, 351; democratic elections, 347, 353; forced removals, 346; HIV/AIDS, 346–348, 352–353; Holocaust, 350; homophobia, 349; identity, 346, 348–349; liberation movement, 38, 47, 49, 350; Living Legacy 2000 Award, 347; London Film School, 345; Mandela, Nelson, 347, 348, 352; Mbeki, Thabo, 348; mediated self, 349; mirror metaphor, 345, 347, 349, 350; motivation for writing, 347; National Arts Council, 352; National Party, 346; *Nederduitse Gereformeerde Kerk,* 353; OBIE Award, 354; one-man shows, 346; personal memoir, 31, 349, 350; racism, 345, 347, 349; Reconstruction and Development Program, 354; research process, 351; rewriting history, 354; satire, 347, 348; self-discovery, 350, 352; Space Theatre, 345, 349; State of Emergency, 346; as teacher, 348, 352–353; truth and auto/biography, 350, 351, 352; Truth and Reconciliation Commission, 354; violence, 346; Wilde, Oscar, 350; Women's International Center, 347; writer's block, 350. Works: *Adapt or Dye,* 346, 348; *Calling a Spade a Spade,* 349; *Dekaffirnated,* 349, 350; *Faces in the Wall,* 345; *For Fact's Sake,* 348, 349, 352, 354; *Foreign Aids,* 354; *Karnaval,* 345; *No Space on Long Street,* 349; *A Part Hate a Part Love,* 350, 351; *Selle ou Stories,* 345; *Trekking to Teema,* 352; *Truth Omissions,* 347; *You ANC Nothing Yet,* 347

van Onselen, Charles, *The Seed Is Mine: The Life of Kas Maine, a South African Sharecropper,* 30, 206
van Riebeeck, Jan, 13, 411
van Wyk, Johan: Angel, 396, 400, 404; audience, 403; auto/biography and truth, 399, 405; Barthes, Roland, 396; Bataille, Georges, 400; betrayal, 396, 399, 406; Breytenbach, Breyten, 402; Brink, André, 402; censorship, 402; characters, 396, 400–402, 404–406; concentration camps, 406; fiction and auto/biography, 56, 395; Freud, Sigmund, 398; gender politics, 399; Gutiérrez, Juan Pedro, 396, 400; Handke, Peter, 400; Harare, 397; HIV/AIDS, 395, 401; identity, 396, 398, 401, 403, 404; imagination, 398; individualism, 405; Jonker, Ingrid, 402; Joubert, Elsa, 402; Khuzwayo, Zazah, 402; language, 398, 405; Mdakane, Zinhle Carol, 402; memoirs, Afrikaans, 399; memory, 44, 67, 396–398; M. E. R., 399; military experience, 397–398; morality, 399–400; Mozambique, 397; Nietzsche, Friedrich, 397, 400; Nkosi, Lewis, 402; poetry, 395–396, 399–400; post-apartheid

auto/biography, 37, 397; post-apartheid literature, 402; poverty, 395; Pretorius, Chris, 399; Prince, Morton, 401; racial classification, 402; racism, 402; relationships, 395–396, 399–400, 400–402, 404, 406; representation of self, 398, 405; reviews, 395; Roodt, Dan, 399; Ryger, R. R., 399; self, 398; self-publication, 58, 395, 403; sexuality, 50, 395, 398; sex workers, 37, 395–396, 399–400; Small, Adam, 402; *Sunday Times*, 403–404; title of work, 395–396; trauma in work, 395, 397–398, 401; voice, 401; Welkom, 397; writer as narrator, 395–406; writing, aspects of, 395, 397–398, 404. Works: *Man-Bitch*, 50, 395–397, 400–402; *My Name Is Angel but I'm Not from Heaven in Any Way*, 395, 401; *Oë in 'n Kas*, 400

Verwoerd, H. F., 280; assassin of, 32; homage to, 28; role in apartheid, 374

Verwoerd, Wilhelm: activist, 373; African National Congress, 366, 367; apartheid, 366; Aristotle, 372; Augustine, 372; auto/biography and truth, 54, 56, 368, 370; confession in auto/biography, 60, 372, 373; conversion narrative, 366; democratic elections, South Africa, 372; Derrida, Jacques, 370; Dutch Reformed Church, 371, 374; Fraser, Nancy, 377; Habermas, Jürgen, 376; identity, ethnicity, 35, 37, 366, 368–369, 371, 373–377; identity, family, 366–374, 376; identity, gender, 366–368, 371, 377; identity, religious, 366–371, 373–374, 376–377; Kuzwayo and *ubuntu*, 376; Lara, Maria Pia, 376; letters, 366–367; marriage, 368–371; mirror metaphor, 369; Nagel, Thomas, 377; Nietzsche, Friedrich, 370; Nussbaum, Martha, 375; post-apartheid, 370; privacy, 51, 60, 368; Rousseau, Jean-Jacques, 372, 374; self, analysis, 60 366, 367, 369, 375; self, construction of, 368, 372, 377; self, relationship with, 369–370, 375, 377; self, revelation of, 368; self, transparency, 374–375; St. Irenaus, 370; structure of work, 367, 372; Taylor, Charles, 375; as TRC researcher, 37; truth, narrative, 371; Truth and Reconciliation Commission, 370–372, 376–377; *ubuntu*, 41, 376; Verwoerd; H. F., 374; *Viva Verwoerd? Kronieke van 'n keuse* (Winds of change), 366, 370, 372, 374–376; writing, motivation for, 366–367, 376; writing, as therapy, 366, 372, 375

victimhood, 271

victims: of abuse, 5, 19, 24, 26, 27, 44, 261; of apartheid, 5; of crime, 29, 31; of Holocaust, 363; narrators as, 188; oral testimony of, 30; and racial classification, 26, 27; reconciliation, 5, 44; status of, 380, 393; testimony of, 27; women as, 294–295, 300; writers as, 156

violations, human rights, 19, 22, 29

violence in South Africa: political, 32, 173–174, 219, 221, 228, 346; structural, 173–174, 183; student uprisings, 32. *See also* abuses; crime, violent; victims

"virtual truth," 351

VITA Prize, 59

voice in writing, 188, 246, 254–255, 262, 280, 288, 333, 401

war: Cold War, 235; crimes, 322; of Liberation, Zimbabwe, 236; Second World War, 236, 293, 357–361; South African civil, 329, 341

websites: International Auto/Biography Association, 81n. 99; national heritage of South Africa, 410, 432

Weekly Mail, 403

Weinberg, Eli, 411, 415, 416, 432

white guilt, 447

Williamson, Craig, 322, 325

window exercise, 437–439

Wolpe, David: apartheid, 360; auto/biography and language, 358; concentration camps, 40, 43, 358, 362; ethical concerns, 51; exile, 43, 363; family relationship, 359; ghettos, 362; as hero, 358; Holocaust, 357–361, 363; identity, 40, 43, 358, 360, 361; Itzik Manger Prize, 358; Jewish life and history, 357; language and auto/biography, 358; literary awards, 358; loneliness, 358; memory, 359, 364; migrancy, 40, 357, 360; persecution, 360; racial discrimination, 360; Second World War, 357–361; self, rescue, 360;

South African Constitution, 363; space, 364; trauma in work, 40, 43, 358–360, 363; writing, as therapy, 60, 363; Yiddish culture, 357, 358, 359, 360, 361, 363; Zionist-Socialist Youth, 357. Works: *Ahad Meir: A Drama from Ghetto Life*, 358; *Dorem Afrike*, 357; *Ikh un mayn velt* (I and my world), 357
women: and careers, 237, 241, 294, 296, 298, 300, 319; and mother-daughter relationships, 9, 236, 299, 303–306, 308–311, 319–321; and praise poetry, 41. *See also* feminism
Women's International Center, 347
Women's March on Pretoria, 319
Women's Peace Movement, 229
Wordsworth, William, 214–215
workers: under apartheid, 25, 26, 31, 33, 38, 46, 219; domestic, 320. *See also* auto/biography; life narrative; sex workers; trade unions
writer: as facilitator, 24, 58, 188; as narrator, 4, 41, 43, 46, 181–183, 187, 208–211, 220, 395–406
writer's block, 255, 264, 350
writing: as confession, 6, 9, 50, 51, 60, 61, 203, 213, 215–216, 226, 272, 316, 372–373, 380–382, 386–387, 389, 391, 394–395; and imagination, 256, 257, 260, 261, 262, 271; as liberation, 437; motivation for, 144, 145, 201, 234, 239, 245, 316, 324, 334, 347, 366–367, 368, 374, 376, 380, 384, 404, 422, 447; origin of, 316, 366; as protest, 4, 19, 443; responses to, 326; "right brain, left brain" theory, 261, 263, 264; and self, 263; as social commentary, 26, 270–273; structure in, 41, 55, 56, 150, 164–166, 175, 181, 220, 261, 315–316, 324–325, 338, 350–352,

367, 372, 382, 389–390, 393, 397–398, 417; teaching, 259, 261, 262, 264, 265; as therapy, 5–7, 9, 10, 14, 38–62, 223, 225, 226, 228, 229, 230, 254, 255, 261, 263, 288, 303, 306, 362, 363, 366, 372, 375, 380, 389, 390, 391, 393, 404, 437–439, 443, 445–446; workshops, 255–256, 260, 389. *See also* memoirs
writing, prison. *See* imprisonment; memoirs: prison; prison accounts
writing, travel. *See* travel accounts

Xhosa. *See* isiXhosa; identities: Xhosa

Yali-Manisi, D. L. P.: background, 118; becoming an *imbongi*, 123–124; discussion of Mqhayi's poems, 123–126; dissemination of work, 57; involvement in politics, 127–129; *Izibongo zeenkosi zama-Xhosa*, 121; *izimbongo*, 47, 117, 120, 121, 122–127, 125, 130; missionaries, 129; Mqhayi as inspiration, 125; participation in ANC, 129; source of knowledge, 127; source of talent, 126; trauma in, 127; views on homelands, 129; Xhosa *imbongi*, 117–118, 122
Yiddish culture and language, 357, 358, 359, 360, 361, 363
Yiddish poetry, 357, 361, 363

Zambia, 163, 249
Zeitgeist, 281
Zen, and poetry, 272
Zimbabwe, 231, 236, 237, 239, 241, 293, 341, 444; Liberation War, 236; writers, 60, 78n. 81
Zionist-Socialist Youth, 357
Zulu. *See* isiZulu

HAWAI

Production Notes for
COULLIE / SELVES IN QUESTION:
INTERVIEWS ON SOUTHERN AFRICAN AUTO/BIOGRAPHY

Cover and interior designed by Leslie Fitch
in Scala with display type in Akzidenze Grotesk

Composition by Josie Herr

Printing and binding by The Maple-Vail Book
Manufacturing Group.

Printed on 60# Sebago Eggshell, 420 ppi